The Transformation of Athens

Martin Classical Lectures

The Martin Classical Lectures are delivered annually at Oberlin College through a foundation established by his many friends in honor of Charles Beebe Martin, for forty-five years a teacher of classical literature and classical art at Oberlin.

John Peradotto, *Man in the Middle Voice: Name and Narration in the* Odyssey

Martha C. Nussbaum, *The Therapy of Desire: Theory and Practice in Hellenistic Ethics*

Josiah Ober, *Political Dissent in Democratic Athens: Intellectual Critics of Popular Rule*

Anne Carson, *Economy of the Unlost: (Reading Simonides of Keos with Paul Celan)*

Helene P. Foley, *Female Acts in Greek Tragedy*

Mark W. Edwards, *Sound, Sense, and Rhythm: Listening to Greek and Latin Poetry*

Michael C. J. Putnam, *Poetic Interplay: Catullus and Horace*

Julia Haig Gaisser, *The Fortunes of Apuleius and the* Golden Ass*: A Study in Transmission and Reception*

Kenneth J. Reckford, *Recognizing Persius*

Leslie Kurke, *Aesopic Conversations: Popular Tradition, Cultural Dialogue, and the Invention of Greek Prose*

Erich Gruen, *Rethinking the Other in Antiquity*

Simon Goldhill, *Victorian Culture and Classical Antiquity: Art, Opera, Fiction, and the Proclamation of Modernity*

Victoria Wohl, *Euripides and the Politics of Form*

David Frankfurter, *Christianizing Egypt: Syncretism and Local Worlds in Late Antiquity*

Robin Osborne, *The Transformation of Athens: Painted Pottery and the Creation of Classical Greece*

The Transformation of Athens

PAINTED POTTERY AND
THE CREATION OF
CLASSICAL GREECE

Robin Osborne

PRINCETON UNIVERSITY PRESS
PRINCETON AND OXFORD

Copyright © 2018 by Trustees of Oberlin College

Published by Princeton University Press, 41 William Street, Princeton, New Jersey 08540
In the United Kingdom: Princeton University Press, 6 Oxford Street, Woodstock, Oxfordshire OX20 1TR

press.princeton.edu

Exterior of a red-figure cup attributed to Makron, ca. 480. Toledo Museum of Art, Toledo, Ohio, purchased with the funds from the Libbey Endowment, Gift of Edward Drummond Libbey, 1972.55.

All Rights Reserved

ISBN 978-0-691-17767-0
Library of Congress Control Number: 2017957816

British Library Cataloging-in-Publication Data is available

This book has been composed in Garamond Premier Pro and Trajan Pro

Printed on acid-free paper. ∞

Printed in the United States of America

10 9 8 7 6 5 4 3 2 1

Contents

LIST OF FIGURES   vii
LIST OF PLATES   xiii
ABBREVIATIONS   xv
PREFACE   xvii

I

1   The Art of Transformation   3
2   Athenian Pottery and Athenian Culture   26

II

3   Changing in the Gymnasium   53
4   Changing the Guard   87
5   Courting Change   122
6   Sacrificing Change   151
7   Drinking to and Reveling in Change   168
8   The Changing City of Satyrs   188

III

9   Morality, Politics, and Aesthetics   207
10   The Road Not Taken   228
11   The Transformation of Art   249

BIBLIOGRAPHY   259

INDEX   277

Figures

1.1 Red-figure type A amphora, attributed to Phintias, ca. 510–500. — 4
1.2 Red-figure calyx krater, attributed to Euphronios, ca. 510–500. — 4
1.3–4 Exterior of red-figure cup, attributed to the Nikosthenes Painter, ca. 510–500. — 8
1.5–6 Exterior of red-figure cup, name vase of the Painter of Cambridge 72 (close to the Codrus Painter), ca. 430. — 8
1.7 Late Geometric II pitcher, attributed to the Workshop of the Painter of Athens 897. — 11
1.8 Proto-Attic "Burgon Lebes," early seventh century BC. — 11
1.9 Black-figure dinos and stand, signed by Sophilos as painter, ca. 580. — 12
1.10 Red-figure oinochoe, attributed to the Goluchow Painter, from Athens, ca. 520. — 14
1.11 *Kore* of Nikandre, from Delos, ca. 650. — 16
1.12 *Kore* of Phrasikleia, from Merenda, Attica, ca. 540. — 16
1.13 *Kouros* of uncertain origin, ca. 560. — 17
1.14 *Kouros*, height 1.01 m, said to be from Anaphe, sometimes known as the Strangford Apollo, ca. 490. — 17
1.15 Kritios Boy. — 21
1.16 One side of a base for a *kouros*, found in the Themistoklean Wall. — 21
2.1 Interior of red-figure cup, with signature by the potter Pamphaios, found at Cervetri, ca. 500. — 27
2.2 Red-figure pelike, attributed to the Chicago Painter, found at Vulci, ca. 450. — 29
2.3–4 Exterior of red-figure cup, attributed to Makron, from Vulci, ca. 490. — 37
2.5 Reverse of red-figure Nolan amphora, attributed to the Phiale Painter, from Nola, ca. 440. — 38
2.6 Reverse of red-figure Nolan amphora, attributed to the Phiale Painter from south Italy, ca. 440. — 38
2.7 Red-figure cup, signed by Hieron as potter and attributed to Makron as painter, from Vulci, ca. 480. — 39

2.8 Red-figure volute krater, name vase of the Pronomos Painter, from Ruvo, ca. 400. 44
2.9 Red-figure cup, attributed to the Dokimasia Painter, from Vulci. 47
3.1 Panathenaic amphora, late sixth century. 54
3.2 Grave stele, of Eupheros, shown as a young athlete, from the Athenian Kerameikos cemetery, ca. 420. 59
3.3–4 Red-figure type A amphora, signed by Andokides as potter, found at Vulci, ca. 520. 62–63
3.5 Red-figure type A amphora, attributed to Phintias, found at Vulci, ca. 510. 65
3.6 Red-figure calyx krater, attributed to Euphronios, found at Capua, ca. 510. 65
3.7–8 Red-figure psykter, attributed to Oltos, found at Campagnano, ca. 500. 67
3.9 Red-figure hydria, attributed to the Pezzino Group, found at Vulci, ca. 500. 70
3.10 Red-figure cup signed by Douris, provenance unknown, ca. 480. 71
3.11–13 Interior and exterior of cup, attributed to the Euergides Painter, ca. 500. 73
3.14–16 Interior and exterior of red-figure cup, attributed to the Villa Giulia Painter, found at Tarquinia, ca. 460–450. 76
3.17–18 Exterior of a red-figure cup, attributed to the Penthesileia Painter, provenance unknown, ca. 460–450. 77
3.19 Exterior of red-figure cup, attributed to the Briseis Painter, found at Vulci, ca. 460. 79
3.20–22 Red-figure cup, attributed to the Carpenter Painter, provenance unknown, ca. 500. 80–81
3.23–25 Red-figure cup attributed to the Akestorides Painter, found at Orvieto, ca. 450. 82–83
3.26 Interior of red-figure cup, attributed to Onesimos, found at Orvieto, ca. 500. 85
3.27 Exterior of red-figure cup, attributed to the Eretria Painter, ca. 435. 85
3.28 Marble copy of the Diadoumenos of Polykleitos of Argos, from the Roman theater at Vaison; made in the second century AD. 86
4.1–2 Black-figure amphora, provenance unknown, 525–500. 96
4.3–4 Black-figure amphora, attributed to the group of Bologna 16, from Vulci, 525–500. 96
4.5 Interior of red-figure cup, signed by Pheidippos as painter and Hischylos as potter, from Vulci, ca. 510. 99
4.6 One side of red-figure column krater, attributed to the Painter of the Louvre Centauromachy, from Nola, ca. 440. 99
4.7 Red-figure calyx krater, signed by Euphronios as painter and Euxitheos as potter. 101

4.8 Black-figure interior of red-figure cup, attributed to Oltos. Found at Vulci.	102
4.9–11 Interior and exterior of red-figure cup, signed by Epiktetos as painter and Pamphaios as potter, from Vulci, ca. 510.	103
4.12 Exterior of red-figure cup, attributed to the wider circle of the Nikosthenes Painter, ca. 500.	104
4.13 Interior of red-figure cup attributed to the Epidromos Painter/Apollodoros (the interior bears the inscription "Epidromos *kalos*"), from Chiusi, ca. 500.	105
4.14 Exterior of red-figure cup, attributed to the Epeleios Painter. Provenance unknown.	105
4.15 Exterior of red-figure cup, signed by Brygos as potter and attributed to the Painter of the Oxford Brygos, from Cervetri, ca. 480.	107
4.16 Red-figure oinochoe, attributed to the Chicago Painter, found at Gela, ca. 460.	108
4.17–18 Exterior of red-figure cup attributed to the Brygos Painter, found at Vulci, ca. 480.	111
4.19 Red-figure lekythos, attributed to the Phiale Painter, found in Sicily, ca. 430.	112
4.20–21 Exterior of red-figure cup, signed by the potter Pamphaios, found at Cervetri, ca. 500.	114
4.22 Red-figure pelike, attributed to the Chicago Painter, found at Vulci, ca. 450.	115
4.23 Red-figure pelike, attributed to the Achilles Painter, ca. 440.	119
5.1–2 Black-figure cup, attributed to the Amasis Painter, from Kamiros, ca. 540.	125
5.3–4 Black-figure amphora, attributed to the Painter of Berlin 1686, from Vulci, ca. 540.	127
5.5–6 Exterior of red-figure cup, signed by Peithinos as painter, from Vulci, ca. 500.	129
5.7–8 Exterior of red-figure cup, attributed to Makron, ca. 480.	132
5.9 Exterior of red-figure cup, attributed to the Foundry Painter, ca. 490.	135
5.10 Exterior of red-figure cup, attributed to the Briseis Painter, from Cervetri, ca. 490.	135
5.11 Exterior of red-figure cup, attributed to the wider circle of the Nikosthenes Painter.	136
5.12 Red-figure pelike, attributed to the Hasselmann Painter, from Nola, ca. 440.	139
5.13 Red-figure bell-krater, attributed to the Dinos Painter, from Capua, ca. 420.	139
5.14 Red-figure oinochoe, attributed to the Shuvalov Painter, from Locri, ca. 430.	140

5.15–17 Red-figure cup, attributed to the Wedding Painter, acquired in Florence.	142–43
5.18–20 Red-figure cup, attributed to the Calliope Painter, said to be from Magna Graecia.	144–45
5.21 Red-figure nuptial lebes, attributed to the Painter of London 1923, from Greece, ca. 440–430.	145
6.1 Red-figure Nolan amphora, attributed to the Phiale Painter, ca. 440.	153
6.2 Interior of red-figure cup, attributed to Makron, ca. 480.	154
6.3 Interior of red-figure cup, attributed to Oltos, ca. 500.	157
6.4 Interior of red-figure cup, attributed to the Winchester Painter, ca. 500.	157
6.5–7 Red-figure oinochoe, attributed to the Thomson Painter, ca. 440.	158
6.8 Red-figure lekythos, attributed to the Berlin Painter.	160
6.9 Interior of red-figure cup, in the manner of the Akestorides Painter, ca. 470.	160
6.10 Interior of red-figure cup, attributed to the Triptolemos Painter, ca. 480.	162
6.11 Exterior of bell-krater from Spina, ca. 410.	163
6.12 Red-figure hydria, attributed to the Pioneer Group, ca. 510.	164
6.13 Red-figure hydria, unattributed, from Athens, ca. 430.	165
7.1–2 Interior and one exterior side of red-figure cup, attributed to the wider circle of the Nikosthenes Painter, ca. 500.	169
7.3 Red-figure amphora, signed by Euthymides son of Polios, from Vulci, ca. 510.	172
7.4–6 Red-figure cup, attributed to the Epeleios Painter, from Vulci, ca. 500.	173
7.7–8 Red-figure stamnos, attributed to the Kleophon Painter, ca. 440.	174
7.9–10 Red-figure amphora, attributed to the Flying Angel Painter, ca. 490.	176
7.11–12 Exterior of red-figure cup, attributed to the Briseis Painter, ca. 480.	177
7.13 Interior of red-figure cup, attributed to the Nikosthenes Painter, ca. 510–500.	180
7.14–15 Exterior of red-figure cup, attributed to the Triptolemos Painter, ca. 480.	180
7.16–17 Exterior of red-figure cup, attributed to the Brygos Painter, ca. 480.	182
7.18 Exterior of column krater, attributed to the Florence Painter, ca. 450.	183
7.19 Exterior of bell-krater, attributed to the Lykaon Painter, ca. 450.	184

7.20–22 Exterior and interior of a red-figure cup, attributed to the Foundry Painter, ca. 480.   185–86
8.1 Exterior of a red-figure cup, attributed to Douris, from Vulci, ca. 480.   190
8.2 Exterior of a red-figure pelike, attributed to the Kleophon Painter, from Gela, ca. 440.   191
8.3–4 Interior and exterior of a red-figure cup, attributed to the Brygos Painter, ca. 480.   192
8.5 Exterior of red-figure bell-krater, attributed to the Lykaon Painter, ca. 440 (reverse of 8.15).   193
8.6–7 Exterior of red-figure cup, attributed to Makron, ca. 490.   195
8.8 Red-figure oinochoe, unattributed, from Athens, ca. 420.   197
8.9 Exterior of red-figure cup, attributed to the Chelis Painter, from Vulci, ca. 500.   197
8.10 Red-figure oinochoe, attributed to the Clephan Painter, ca. 440.   198
8.11 Red-figure cup, attributed to Epiktetos, from Vulci, ca. 500.   200
8.12–13 Red-figure cup, attributed to the Eretria Painter, ca. 430.   200
8.14 Red-figure oinochoe, unattributed, ca. 430.   201
8.15 Exterior of red-figure bell-krater, attributed to the Lykaon Painter, ca. 440 (reverse of 8.6).   202
8.16 Red-figure calyx krater, attributed to the Niobid Painter, from Altamura, ca. 450.   203
9.1 Interior of red-figure cup, signed by Hieron as potter and attributed to Makron as painter, from Vulci, ca. 490.   210
9.2 Interior of red-figure cup, attributed to the Calliope Painter, from Nola, ca. 430.   210
9.3 One side of a base for a *kouros*, found in the Themistoklean wall.   219
9.4–5 Red-figure stamnos, signed by Smikros as painter, ca. 510.   222
9.6 Red-figure stamnos, attributed to the Kleophon Painter, from Vulci, ca. 440.   223
9.7 Red-figure Nolan amphora, attributed to the Phiale Painter, from Nola, ca. 450.   225
10.1 The Westmacott athlete.   229
10.2 The Tyrannicides.   230
10.3 Red-figure stamnos, attributed to Syriskos/the Copenhagen Painter.   232
10.4–5 Red-figure amphora, attributed to Syriskos/the Copenhagen Painter.   232
10.6 Red-figure lekythos, attributed to Oionokles Painter, ca. 480–470.   234

10.7 Red-figure bell-krater, attributed to the Pan Painter (name vase), from Cumae, ca. 460.	234
10.8 Apollo from the west pediment of the temple of Zeus at Olympia, ca. 460.	236
10.9 Centaur and lapith from the west pediment of the temple of Zeus at Olympia, ca. 460.	236
10.10 Metope from west frieze of temple of Zeus at Olympia: Athena receives the Stymphalian birds from Herakles.	236
10.11–13 Front and sides of the so-called Ludovisi Throne, maximum height 0.9 m.	238
10.14 Bronze statue of Zeus recovered from the sea off Cape Artemision.	239
10.15 Bronze statue of a warrior, "Warrior A," recovered from the sea off Riace Marina.	241
10.16 Bronze statue of a warrior, "Warrior B," recovered from the sea off Riace Marina.	241
10.17 Frieze of the Parthenon, Athens; North XXXVIII.	241
10.18 Grave stele, from Athens.	243
10.19 Stele of Dexileos.	245
10.20 The seer from the west pediment at Olympia.	247
11.1 Hippolyte Flandrin, *Study (Young Male Nude Seated beside the Sea)* 1835–36.	255
11.2 Interior of red-figure cup, name vase of the Painter of Cambridge 72, ca. 430.	255

❧ Plates

1 Exterior of red-figure cup, diameter 0.34 m, attributed to the Nikosthenes Painter, ca. 510–500.
2 Exterior of red-figure cup, diameter 0.215 m, name vase of the Painter of Cambridge 72 (close to the Codrus Painter), ca. 430.
3 Exterior of red-figure cup, diameter 0.287 m, attributed to Makron, from Vulci, ca. 490.
4 Exterior of red-figure cup, diameter 0.287 m, attributed to Makron, from Vulci, ca. 490.
5 Red-figure calyx krater, height 0.348 m, attributed to Euphronios, found at Capua, ca. 510.
6 Red-figure psykter, height 0.346 m, attributed to Oltos, found at Campagnano, ca. 500.
7 Interior and exterior of red-figure cup, diameter 0.23 m, attributed to the Villa Giulia Painter, found at Tarquinia, ca. 460–450.
8 Exterior of red-figure cup, diameter 0.238 m, attributed to the Penthesileia Painter, provenance unknown, ca. 460–450.
9 Red-figure cup, diameter 0.305 m, attributed to the Carpenter Painter, provenance unknown, ca. 500.
10 Red-figure cup attributed to the Akestorides Painter, found at Orvieto, ca. 450.
11 Interior of red-figure cup, diameter 0.225 m, attributed to Onesimos, found at Orvieto, ca. 500.
12 Exterior of red-figure cup, diameter 0.26 m, attributed to the Eretria Painter, ca. 435.
13 Black-figure amphora, provenance unknown, 525–500.
14 Black-figure amphora, height 0.44 m, attributed to the group of Bologna 16, from Vulci, 525–500.
15 Red-figure calyx krater, height 0.458 m, signed by Euphronios as painter and Euxitheos as potter. Provenance unknown.
16 Exterior of red-figure cup, diameter 0.273 m, attributed to the wider circle of the Nikosthenes Painter, ca. 500.
17 Interior of red-figure cup, diameter 0.198 m, attributed to the Epidromos Painter/Apollodoros (the interior bears the inscription "Epidromos kalos"), from Chiusi, ca. 500.

18 Red-figure lekythos, height 0.343 m, attributed to the Phiale Painter, found in Sicily, ca. 430.
19 Red-figure pelike, height 0.425 m, attributed to the Chicago Painter, found at Vulci, ca. 450.
20 Black-figure amphora, height 0.345 m, attributed to the Painter of Berlin 1686, from Vulci, ca. 540.
21 Exterior of red-figure cup, diameter 0.34 m, signed by Peithinos as painter, from Vulci. ca. 500.
22 Exterior of red-figure cup, diameter 0.287 m, attributed to Makron, ca. 480.
23 Exterior of red-figure cup, diameter 0.237 m, attributed to the Briseis Painter, from Cervetri, ca. 490.
24 Red-figure cup, diameter 0.227 m, attributed to the Calliope Painter, said to be from Magna Graecia.
25 Interior of red-figure cup, diameter 0.287 m, attributed to Makron, ca. 480.
26 Interior of red-figure cup, diameter 0.19 m, in the manner of the Akestorides Painter (grouped by Beazley with the "Followers of Douris"), ca. 470.
27 A and B. Red-figure hydria, height 0.40 m, unattributed, from Athens, ca. 430.
28 Interior and one exterior side of red-figure cup, diameter 0.273 m, attributed to the wider circle of the Nikosthenes Painter, ca. 500.
29 Red-figure cup, diameter 0.335 m, attributed to the Epeleios Painter, from Vulci, ca. 500.
30 Red-figure stamnos, height 0.402 m, attributed to the Kleophon Painter, ca. 440.
31 Exterior of red-figure cup, diameter 0.315 m, attributed to the Triptolemos Painter, ca. 480.
32 Exterior of red-figure cup, diameter 0.237 m, attributed to the Brygos Painter, ca. 480.
33 Exterior and interior of a red-figure cup, diameter 0.285 m, attributed to the Foundry Painter, ca. 480.
34 Exterior of a red-figure cup, attributed to the Brygos Painter, ca. 480.
35 Red-figure amphora, attributed to Syriskos/the Copenhagen Painter.

Abbreviations

ABL Haspels, C.H.E. 1936. *Attic Black-Figured Lekythoi*. Paris.
ABV Beazley, J. D. 1956. *Attic Black-Figure Vase-Painters*. Oxford.
ARV Beazley, J. D. 1963. *Attic Red-Figure Vase-Painters*. 2nd ed. Oxford.
Beazley Addenda Carpenter, T. H., T. Mannack, and M. Mendonça. 1989. *Beazley Addenda: Additional References to* ABV, ARV² *and* Paralipomena. Oxford.
CEG Hansen, P. A., ed. 1983, 1989. *Carmina Epigraphica Graeca*. 2 vols. Berlin.
CVA *Corpus Vasorum Antiquorum.*
DAA Raubitschek, A. 1947. *Dedications from the Athenian Acropolis: A Catalogue of the Inscriptions of the Sixth and Fifth Centuries B.C.* Cambridge, MA.
IG *Inscriptiones Graecae*
LIMC *Lexicon Iconographicum Mythologiae Classicae*. Zurich.
ML Meiggs, R., and D. M. Lewis. 1969. *A Selection of Greek Historical Inscriptions to the End of the Peloponnesian War*. Rev. ed., 1988. Oxford.
OR Osborne, R., and P. J. Rhodes. 2017. *Greek Historical Inscriptions, 478–404 B.C.* Oxford.
Para. Beazley, J. D. 1971. *Paralipomena: Additions to Attic Black-Figure Vase-Painters and to Attic Red-Figure Vase-Painters (2nd ed.)*. Oxford.
RO Rhodes, P. J., and R. Osborne. 2003. *Greek Historical Inscriptions, 404–323 B.C.* Oxford.

Preface

The pots painted in Athens in the middle of the fifth century BC depict different scenes from those painted at the end of the sixth century and depict them in a different way. This fact is so well known to scholars that it is taken for granted. In this book, I look more closely at what changes, and in particular at the changes in the scenes depicted, and I argue that rather than taking the changes for granted we should see them as the best evidence we have for the moral, political, and aesthetic preferences that constituted and distinguished classical Greek culture. Athenian pottery, I shall claim, not only offers us an unparalleled window through which to view the transformation from archaic to classical Greece, but also an insight into why that transformation took place.

This book aspires to rewrite the history of classical Greek art by showing that the history of art—that is, the history of art of any period—needs to be a history that pays attention not only to an artist's style but also to an artist's choice of what to depict. It devotes its first chapter to establishing why, as a matter of theory, this is necessary and to showing what is problematic about the way in which the history of Greek art has been written until now.

More particularly, this book aspires to rewrite the history of Athenian red-figure pottery in the years between the invention of the red-figure technique circa 520 BC and the middle of the fifth century. As chapter 2 argues, red-figure pottery offers unique possibilities for the sort of rewriting of art history that I am advocating because of the quantities in which it survives and because of the range of subject it represents. Past scholarship has often concentrated on the artists, at the expense of the subject matter of their art, or, when analyzing subject matter, has ignored the fact that the choice of scene changes over time; by contrast this study takes diachronic change as its central problem.

Most ambitiously, this book aims to change the way in which we write Greek history. In a way that both complements and reinforces the arguments that I made in *The History Written on the Classical Greek Body* (Osborne 2011), I argue that the changing representation of the world by painters of pottery offers a history of classical Athens that has the advantage of being quite independent of the categories, in particular the status categories, established and policed by literary texts.

In chapters 3–7 I look in turn at five subjects that attracted the attention of painters of red-figure pottery: athletics, warfare, sexual relations, relations with the gods, and the drinking party and its aftermath. My primary question in these chapters is how the choice of scenes relating to soldiers, athletes, courtship and sex, sacrifice and libation, the symposium and the *komos* changed over time. But to assess the significance of these changes I run them against what we know from other sources of the history of these activities in Athens. I demonstrate that the changes in the scenes represented correlate most strongly not with changes in those particular activities in life but with the changes that occur in the representation of all scenes of "everyday life." That is, the history of images of warfare or of athletics or of sexual relations or of relations with the gods or of the symposium and *komos* is not determined by changes to fighting or what happened in the gymnasium, or to changes in how men and women or humans and gods related, or to changes in what happened in and after drinking parties, but rather by a changed view of the world that encompassed all of these activities. I then test this observation by looking at the representation of the imagined life of satyrs and show that the changes that occur in the way that satyrs are represented follow precisely the same pattern as the changes in representation of areas of human life.

In the three concluding chapters I discuss how we might understand the historical significance of the pattern that I have discerned. I note that the pattern is exactly paralleled in sculpture that is produced throughout the Greek world. I explore the moral and political implications of the changes in the selection of scenes represented and make the case for the impact of aesthetic factors on how people saw the world and considered their own relation to it. I then discuss in some detail the ways in which the history of sculpture does and does not parallel the history represented in painted pottery and argue that the history of sculpture enables us to see an alternative view of the world being briefly espoused and then rejected. In a concluding discussion, I urge the historical importance of the impact of considerations of beauty.

It will not be hard, I hope, for a reader to perceive why this book aspires to change the way the history of art is written. What artists choose to represent was long neglected, as if style existed separate from content. But what of the revolution that I hope to effect in the writing of (Greek) history? The texts that we study were almost all written not simply at a definitive moment but for a definitive purpose; this makes it hard to recognize from texts when the way they present the world is instrumental, a means to an end, and when the way they see the world reflects a view generally shared across the society in which the particular text was written. Pots were painted at a definitive moment but rarely for a definitive purpose beyond "to sell." Painters wanted to attract buyers' attention, and might do that by being thought provoking, but they did not seek to teach. Insofar as the market for pottery was a discriminating one, it was certainly not narrow in its discrimination. The patterns of choice of scene to depict on pottery therefore have a strong chance of reproducing the way in which painters saw the world, unconstrained by any need to persuade others or conform to others' views. Pots therefore offer us a much better glimpse of the way Athenians, and I maintain Greeks more generally, viewed the world than any text can do. Images offer us virtually no help with *histoire événementielle* (but see 10.2–3), but it is with images that we should start in any discussion that concerns popular morality—and that means, among other things, every history of literature or history of philosophy. This is not simply because painted pottery offers a differently distorted and less distorting mirror, but because popular morality is so strongly shaped by how the world is seen, and how the world is seen is never not a matter of aesthetics.

This book originated in a project funded by a British Academy Readership in 1999–2001 to examine the changing iconography of Athenian pottery in the first half century or so of Athenian red-figure pottery production. The core research was carried out in those years in the Beazley Archive at Oxford, and without the hospitality and assistance of Donna Kurtz, Thomas Mannach, and the Beazley Archive team this work would not have been possible. I am grateful to the British Academy and to Oxford University and Corpus Christi College Oxford who allowed me relief from teaching and administrative duties to enjoy the Readership.

My original plan had been to execute the core research in 1999–2001, return to teaching in 2001–2, and then complete this project during sabbatical leave in 2002–3. However, instead I succumbed to an invitation to return to Cambridge, forfeited my sabbatical leave, and landed a grant from the Arts and Humanities Research Board for a research project on cultural change at Athens at the other end of the fifth century—a project that led to *Rethinking Revolutions through Classical Greece* (Cambridge, 2006) and *Debating the Athenian Cultural Revolution* (Cambridge, 2007). An invitation from John Robb led to my involvement in a Leverhulme-funded project, *Changing Beliefs of the Human Body*, and to my *History Written on the Classical Greek Body* (Cambridge, 2011; see also J. Robb and O. Harris, *The Body in History: Europe from the Palaeolithic to the Future* [Cambridge, 2013]). This further enriched my understanding of many issues discussed here, but further delayed this book.

I am very grateful to the Classics Department at Oberlin College for the invitation to give the Martin Classical Lectures in 2007, from which this book directly descends. I enjoyed a most stimulating week in Oberlin and warmly thank all the members of the department and of cognate departments (Elizabeth Colantoni, Todd Ganson, Susan Kane, Ben Lee, Tom van Nortwick, Kirk Ormand, Drew Wilburn) along with Jenifer Neils and the rest of the lively audience, for their hospitality and their engagement with my work.

I have tried out the ideas in chapters 3 and 4, in particular, on a wide variety of audiences, whose reactions have shaped the form in which I present those arguments here. I am particularly grateful to the University of Aberdeen for the invitation to be Geddes-Harrower Visiting Professor of Classical Archaeology in the autumn of 2008, which gave me an opportunity to develop the arguments further, and in particular to situate these arguments in classical art history. I explored versions of the story told here in giving the Dabis Lecture at Royal Holloway, University of London, and the Stubbs Lecture, University of Toronto, in 2015 and in lectures at the Universities of Colorado, Boulder; Cardiff; Durham; and Exeter. I am grateful to all who discussed the lectures with me on those occasions.

Jaś Elsner kindly read drafts of most of the chapters and offered invaluable comments and encouragement, as did the two readers for Princeton University Press; I am most grateful to them. For reading and improving successive drafts of the whole book I am indebted to my wife, Caroline Vout, who has transformed this work, and my life, more than even she realizes.

I

1. The Art of Transformation

1. Art and Society

We all expect that is it possible to recognize the age to which a work of art belongs. We expect those who know anything about painting to be able to tell the difference between a seventeenth-century portrait and an eighteenth-century portrait, between Victorian painting and painting executed in the 1920s. We expect them to do this not on the basis of the fashions worn by any people who are depicted, or of other items of period material culture, but because of something intrinsic to the painting. So we also expect them to be able to recognize the place of origin or of the work of an artist, to be able to distinguish the French postimpressionist work of Vuillard from the English postimpressionist work of Sickert.

If we ask what are the differences between one portrait and another, or one landscape painting and another, the answer normally given is about the way they are painted. Different painters use a different range of colors, different strokes with different brushes. They also have different compositional preferences. We might even acknowledge that people brought up in one country see the world in different ways from those brought up in another, and that different things catch the eye of different painters.

When it comes to the study of the painted pottery produced in Athens in the sixth and fifth centuries BC, the difference between the painted pottery of one generation and that of the succeeding generation has been accounted for almost entirely in terms of the graphic practices and preferences of different painters (**1.1**, **1.2**), associating these graphic practices either with those on other pots signed by a painter—as here with pots signed by Phintias and Euphronios—or on other pots after which a particular artist's hand has been named. That was the way in which Sir John Beazley told his classic tale of *The Development of Attic Black-Figure* (1951), and it has remained the way the story of both black-figure and red-figure pottery has been told (see chapter 2, section 1).

This way of describing differences between art of different periods is not limited to painting. The same is true of sculpture. It was by close attention to the ways in which the same parts of the body were differently presented that Gisela Richter sought to distinguish from one another archaic *kouroi* (naked youths; 1.13–1.14) and *korai* (maidens; 1.11 and 1.12). The fullest modern study of the whole history of Greek sculpture organizes itself in

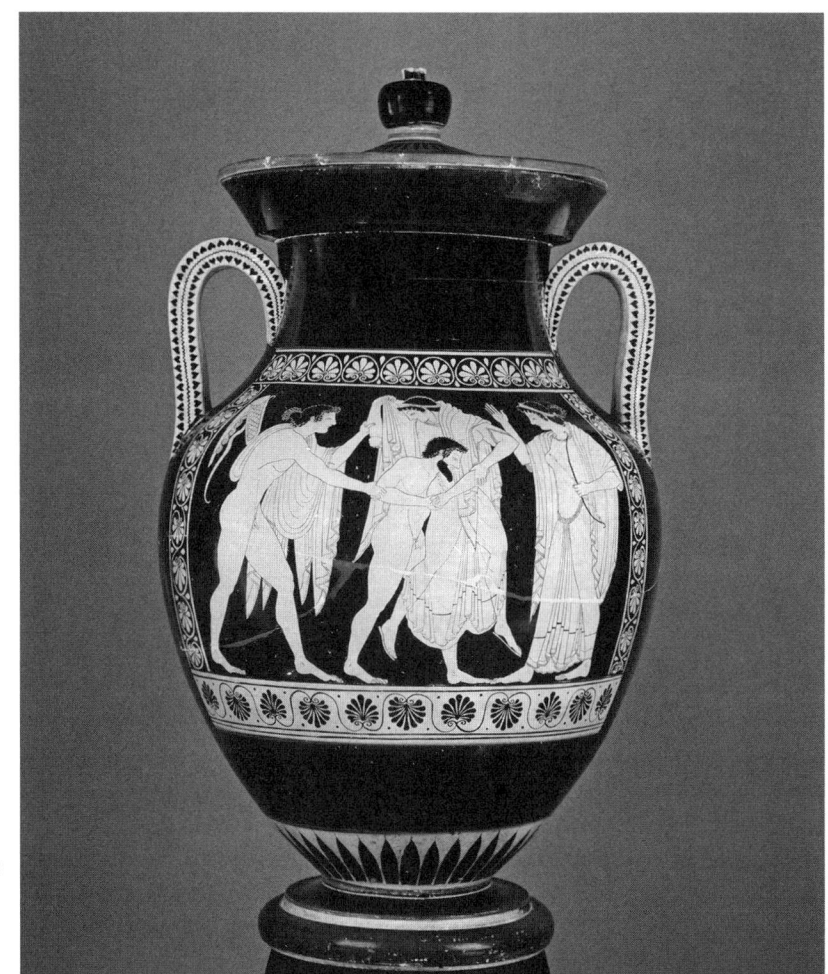

Figure 1.1. Red-figure type A amphora, height 0.60 m without lid, attributed to Phintias, ca. 510–500 (for the reverse see 3.5). Found at Vulci. *ARV* 23.1. Louvre G42. Photo © RMN-Grand Palais (musée du Louvre) / Les frères Chuzeville.

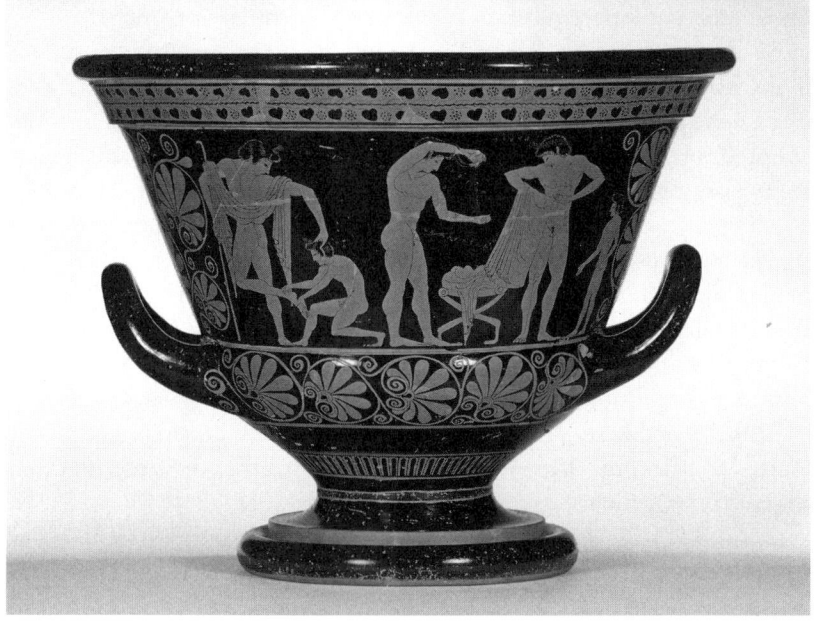

Figure 1.2. Red-figure calyx krater, height 0.348 m, attributed to Euphronios, ca. 510–500 (for the reverse see 3.6). Found at Capua. *ARV* 13.1. Berlin 2180. © bpk / Antikensammlung, Staatliche Museen zu Berlin / Johannes Laurentius.

successive volumes dealing with *The Archaic Style, The Severe Style, Fifth-Century Styles*, and so forth.[1] More importantly, it is in terms of stylistic change that the "Greek revolution" in sculpture has been described, the revolution that saw the formal and frontal *kouros*, who holds his body to attention, disappear from the sculptor's repertoire after 150 years to be replaced by supple bodies that refuse frontality and engage in definitive action, or at least gesture toward it.

There are good reasons why the story of change has been told in this way. Virtually no extant Greek sculptures and only a small percentage of Greek pots bear an artist's signature (see 1.9, 2.1, 2.7, 3.3–4, 3.10, 4.5, 4.7 and plate 15, 4.9–11, 4.15, 4.20–21, 5.5–6 and plate 21, 9.1, 9.4–5); it is only through differences in the detailed presentation of the body, and in the case of pottery differences in graphic technique, that the works of different workshops in sculpture and even different individuals, in the case of painted pottery, can be distinguished with any confidence.[2]

But describing how the painting and sculpture of one period differs from that of a preceding or following period in this way should not be mistaken for offering an account of the change that has occurred. Not only do such descriptions not explain what makes the art of one period or place different from the art of another place or period or reveal why art changes over time, such descriptions frequently fail even to make the observations most relevant to an explanation.

When Michael Baxandall, writing in 1972 about the Italian Renaissance, coined the term "period eye," he analyzed its workings in terms of, among other things, "the body and its language," "figure patterns," "the value of colours," "volumes," "intervals and proportions," and "the moral eye."[3] Baxandall was concerned in his essay "to show how the *style* of pictures is proper material of social history." For Baxandall, "Social facts . . . lead to the development of distinctive visual skills and habits: and these visual skills and habits become identifiable elements in the painter's style," or, as he put it in the conclusion to the work, "the forms and styles of painting respond to social circumstances."[4] But in that conclusion, he insisted also that "the forms and styles of painting may sharpen our perception of the society."[5]

---

[1] Richter (1970; 1968); Ridgway (1970; 1977; 1981; 1997). The same organization according to stylistic change underlies even works that claim to take an innovative approach, including Osborne (1998a), Tanner (2006).

[2] For technical aspects of sculpture, see Adam (1966); for technical aspects of painted pottery, see Noble (1966), Cohen (2006); on artists' signatures, see Viviers (2006), Osborne (2010b), Hurwit (2015). In terms of the relative status of pots and sculpture it is somewhat paradoxical that it should be pottery that lends itself to discussion in terms of artists, while sculpture does not.

[3] Baxandall (1972), vii: these are some of the subheadings of chapter 2, "The Period Eye." Baxandall's "period eye" is heavily influenced by Riegl's notion of "Kunstwollen" or "cultural drive." "Kunstwollen" is an idea that, through Panofsky's *Gothic Architecture and Scholasticism*, which he translated, adding a "postface" (Bourdieu [1967]), lies behind Bourdieu's widely influential concept of "habitus." Bourdieu translated Baxandall's "Period Eye" chapter for *Actes de la recherché en sciences sociales* (Baxandall [1981]) prefacing it with an essay, written with Yvette Desault, "Pour un sociologie de la perception" (Bourdieu and Desault [1981]). See further Langdale (1999).

[4] Baxandall (1972), v, 151.

[5] "For the discipline to elaborate some method and language for analyzing the historical signifi-

Baxandall effectively insists that art and experience are not separate things but intimately linked, but the mutual relationship between a society and its paintings that he conjures up has the initiative firmly with the society. Paintings may do things to us, "sharpen our perception of the society," but they seem not to do anything to society. Somehow, we can learn to see from looking at paintings, but contemporary viewers learned nothing from them.

T. J. Clark, writing in 1985, made the case for painting playing a very much more active role.[6] Certainly for Clark painting is "a way of discovering what the values and excitements of the world amount to, by finding in practice what it takes to make a painting of them—what kind of play between flatness and depth, what kind of stress on the picture's limits, what sorts of insistence, ellipsis, showmanship, restraint."[7] But Clark saw that painting was more than that, insisting that "when a painting recasts or restructures its own procedures—of visualizing, resemblance, address to the viewer, scale, touch, good drawing and modeling, articulate composition— . . . it puts pressure on not just social detail but social structure."[8]

If we acknowledge, with Baxandall, that how members of a culture see, indeed how members of a particular society see, is determined by many different factors, and that this visual experience affects what images those who draw or paint or sculpt in that culture or society will make, our description of those images, and of how those images change over time, needs to reflect this. In particular, the "period eye" affects choice of subject matter, choice of material, choice of color as well as affecting what features of the human body will be shown and in what ways. There will, of course, be particular generic constraints, but our histories of sculpture and of painting, including of painted pottery, need at least to attend to changes to the subject matter of images, not simply to changes to their form.

We need to do this because, unless we do, our account of the history of art, narrowly conceived, will be impoverished, disaggregating form and color from content when these different aspects of an image are in fact closely bound up with each other in visual experience. We also need to do this because unless we do we will never understand the relationship between a culture or society and the work of creative visual artists in that culture or society on which Clark rightly insists. But, equally, if we pay attention to only some aspects of images we will form a very partial view of the culture or society in which those images were created. We will never properly know "the values and excitements" of the world in which the artist lived unless we pay attention to every aspect of the image.

---

cance of different visual stylings and effects" is reckoned by Bert Smith to be "an important future challenge for the discipline" (of classical archaeology): Smith (2002), 100.

[6] For Clark's criticisms of Baxandall's "period eye," see Langdale (1999).

[7] Clark (1999), xxi (preface to the revised ed.).

[8] Clark (1999), xxiv (preface to the revised ed.). I have recast Clark's statement, which he gives in the form "it is only when . . . that it puts." Clark has been drawn to the study of art at precisely moments of political revolution (e.g., Clark [1973a; 1973b; 2013]). Some modern commentators would take contemporary art to be too heavily implicated in the art market to be able to put independent pressure on society (cf. Stallabrass [2004]).

More is at stake here than simply properly exploiting a potentially rich source of knowledge about a past society. Images are never a transcript of the world, they do not merely reflect the visual experience of the artist, providing some mirror image of the world in which the artist lived. What artists do is to offer ways of organizing (visual) experiences, and in an important sense it is their (re)organization of visual experiences that makes the world.[9] The images created by artists, using the term at its broadest, are themselves part of the visual experience of those living in that world. And not a trivial part. The images that artists create play an active role in shaping experience, and not merely a passive role in reflecting it. Drawings, paintings, and sculpture may be conservative or subversive; they can never be neutral, never stand apart from politics and economics, or from other aspects of culture. We must always ask not merely about the role of social, economic, and political changes in changing visual experience, and hence changing what artists do, but about the role of what artists do in social, political, and economic changes. As Clark indicates, there are ways in which art can put pressure on social structure. And not just social structure.

This book is concerned with the way in which artists working in Athens changed their representational choices over a period of just under a century (**1.3–4** and plate 1, **1.5–6** and plate 2). It is concerned to give an account of those changes, not merely in the sense of describing them but of explaining why they may have taken place and how they helped other major social changes to take place. I take only a very limited selection of all the images produced in Athens at this time, focusing on a subset of scenes that relate more or less directly to activities that might be observed in Athens or by Athenians and look at how what is represented changes between around 520 and around 440. My question is: what is the relation to Athenian life of the choice of depicting—particularly but not exclusively on pots—this selection of scenes of athletes (or people having sexual relations, or soldiers, or whoever) rather than some other selection of scenes of athletes? How do these changes relate to what we know of the history of athletes (or soldiers or whoever) from historical documents? How do they relate to each other? What has changed in Athenian visual experience to account for the changes in the images? What I am trying to understand is the implications of representing actions of one sort, rather than another, in one way, rather than another, for how people expected to relate to one another in real life.

The thought that art and experience were closely related in classical Greece is not a new one. J. J. Pollitt's *Art and Experience in Classical Greece* was published in the same year as Baxandall's *Painting and Experience in Fifteenth-Century Italy*. But the approach to understanding change in the visual arts adopted here is not one that has been previously taken by those studying ancient Greek art or by those studying ancient Greek history.[10]

---

[9] Cf. Spivey (2005) and the BBC series of the same name, *How Art Made the World*.
[10] A partial exception to this claim is the work of Jan Bažant, who hid a discussion of the histori-

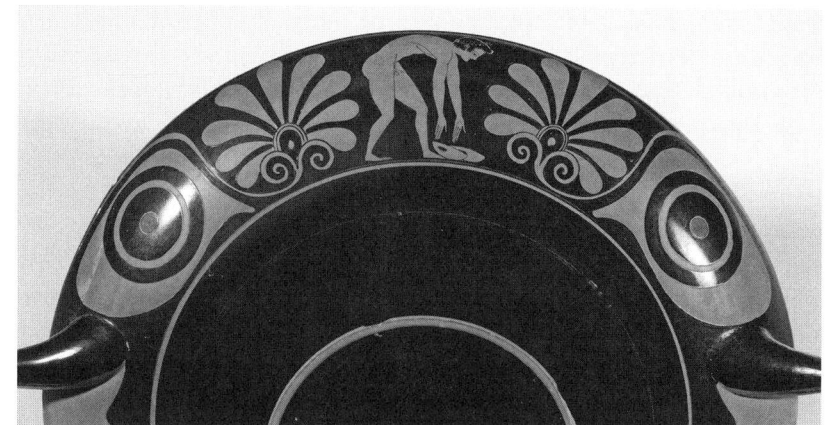

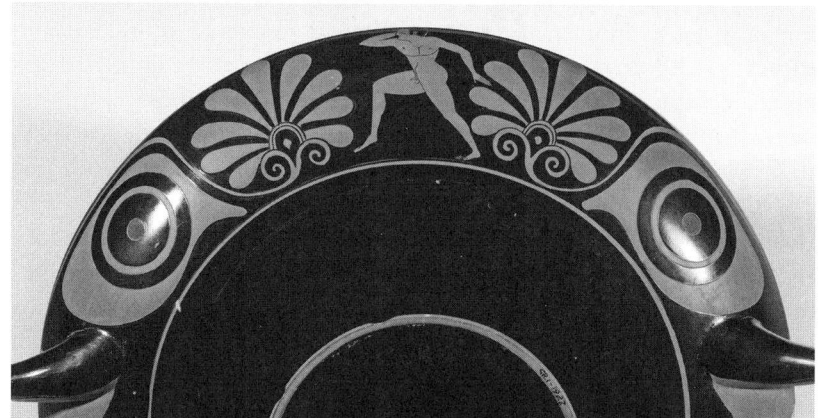

Figure 1.3–4. Exterior of red-figure cup, diameter 0.34 m, attributed to the Nikosthenes Painter, ca. 510–500 (for the interior see 7.13). *ARV* 124.3 Cambridge Fitzwilliam Museum GR.1.1927. © The Fitzwilliam Museum, Cambridge.

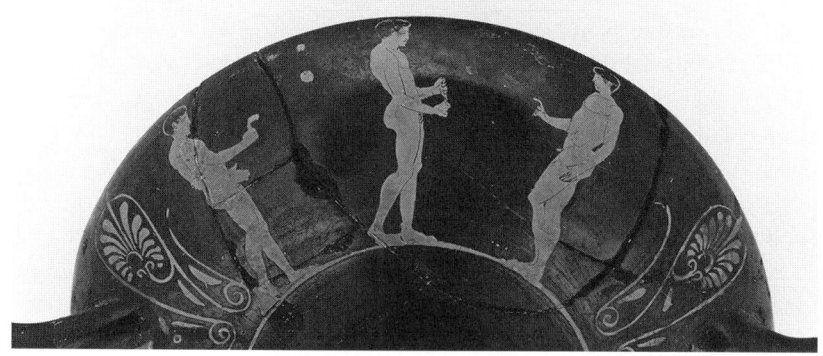

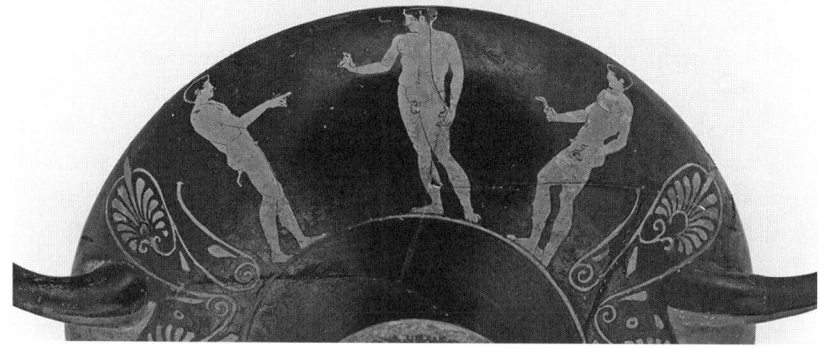

Figure 1.5–6. Exterior of red-figure cup, diameter 0.215 m, name vase of the Painter of Cambridge 72 (close to the Codrus Painter), ca. 430 (for the interior see 11.2). *ARV* 1273.2. Cambridge Fitzwilliam Museum G72 = GR 50.1864. © The Fitzwilliam Museum, Cambridge.

In the next chapter I shall explain why the study of Athenian pottery has shown so little interest in how scenes, other than scenes of mythology, change over time. But in this chapter I place my own work in the context of past histories of Greek art by looking at the models of artistic change that they have offered.

2. Were They Pushed or Did They Jump?

Histories of Greek art variously invoke two factors to drive their story. On the one hand, individual artists themselves experiment as they come to terms with the world around them. On the other they become enchanted by others' technology, learning from visual artists who are outside their culture or their society or from the creative endeavors of those in their own society who compose not images but texts, or overwhelmed by current events that totally change their view of the world. These factors have been invoked both in the history of sculpture and in the history of painted pottery, but they have played out in different ways. I start with the history of painted pottery.

Supply and Demand

When human figures begin once more to be represented on painted pottery after the relentless geometric decoration of the so-called Dark Age, they are "perfectly integrated with their geometric habitat" (**1.7**).[11] Their torsos are triangular, their arms at sharp angles, and artists display a preference for scenes in which many figures adopt the same posture. Yet scholars have insisted that "the development of a Geometric figure style was not internally generated."[12] The favored iconography is dominated by "the battlefield, the chariot file, the heroic death and its funerary celebration,"[13] but scholars have debated whether these reflect what the artists saw happening around them, or express "a mythic consciousness in which they lived and which impelled them to decorate objects at all."[14] They have asked whether "there is a willing separation from the direct experience of reality," suggesting that 'it is a medium for rejecting the world of direct sense and experience in favor of the constructed, the imagined, the interpreted."[15] The imagination invoked by scholars has traditionally been not the imagination of the artist, but of outsiders, of artists elsewhere or of poets—particular figure groups are held to have been borrowed from (for

---

cal interpretation of changing imagery on Athenian pottery in his short book (Bažant [1985]) and a summary article (Bažant [1987]).
 [11] Langdon (2008), 1.
 [12] Boardman (1998), 23.
 [13] Langdon (2008), 3.
 [14] Langdon (2008), 293, cites this as part of a question she attributes to Benson (1988), but which does not seem to appear in that paper.
 [15] Langdon (2008), 1, 3.

example) the art of North Syria, and heroic scenes to have been inspired either by Homeric epic or by folktales.[16] Only in the most recent work has the possibility that geometric artists worked with and on the visual experience of the world in which they lived begun to be explored, as Susan Langdon has insisted "on the utility of Geometric art for ordering and unifying communities."[17]

Around 700 BC there was a revolution in painted pottery (**1.8**). Geometric patterns vanish and are replaced by curvilinear decoration that alludes strongly to the natural world. In Athenian art, human figures are portrayed on a larger scale and in a much greater variety of actions. Above all, incidents and monsters that feature in myth can be identified for the first time, as can representations of the Greek gods. What caused this revolution? The favored explanation has been exogenous: "a tide of Eastern imagery swept away the Geometric style in this period, and Eastern motifs and customs pervaded Greek society at every level," writes Richard Neer.[18]

That many of the motifs that dominate painted pottery in this period were learned from objects made in the Near East there is no doubt. But far from being overwhelmed by the arrival at the end of the eighth century of Eastern artifacts, Greeks had by 700 been long familiar with these exotic objects: "Oriental art was widely available and discreetly imitated throughout much of the Geometric period."[19] We are dealing with active and selective borrowing, not star-struck imitation. But even those who acknowledge this concentrate on form: "eastern forms are for the most part reinterpreted," "the Greek vase painter almost never copied an eastern metal vessel or its decoration directly, and the new forms were introduced piecemeal, assimilated, and rapidly adjusted to serve their new functions."[20] The question of why these forms were found attractive has hardly been asked, let alone answered.[21]

At the end of the seventh century, Athenian pottery underwent another revolution, adopting incision to replace outline drawing and soft-edged figures with silhouettes with sharp outlines and intricate internal detail (**1.9**). The story scholars tell is once more about technique and imagery being carried in from outside, both in terms of medium and in terms of place: "probably under the influence of imported eastern ivories and metal work with incised decoration," "acceptance of the black figure technique in Athens seemed to carry with it some of Corinth's obsession with" animal

---

[16] Cf. Langdon (2008), 4, 5, describing views to which she does not subscribe.

[17] Langdon (2008), 296.

[18] Neer (2012), 94; cf. Sparkes (1996), 10, "the potters and painters at Athens were dazzled for a few generations by the ferment of new ideas created by the influence from the east"; Hall (2007), 260, "one of the features that defines what we call Greek culture in the Archaic period is its tendency to borrow techniques and styles from the east."

[19] Langdon (2008), 9; cf. her reference on the same page to "the now untenable view that Geometric art flourished in cultural isolation, before Eastern naturalism began to seduce Greek tastes and artistic ambitions." See more generally Gunter (2009).

[20] Boardman (1998), 84.

[21] Osborne (1998a), 43, offers an answer in part in the chapter title, "Reflections in an Eastern Mirror."

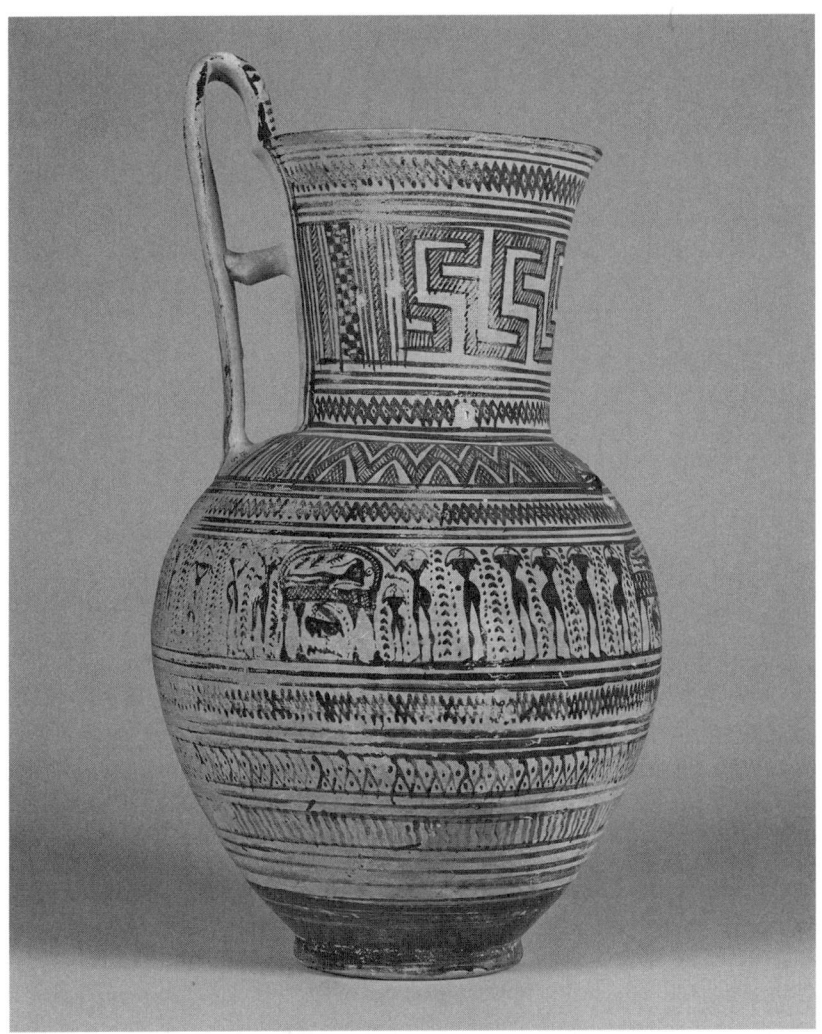

Figure 1.7. Late Geometric II pitcher, height 0.4318 m, attributed to the Workshop of the Painter of Athens 897. British Museum 1912,0522.1. © The Trustees of the British Museum.

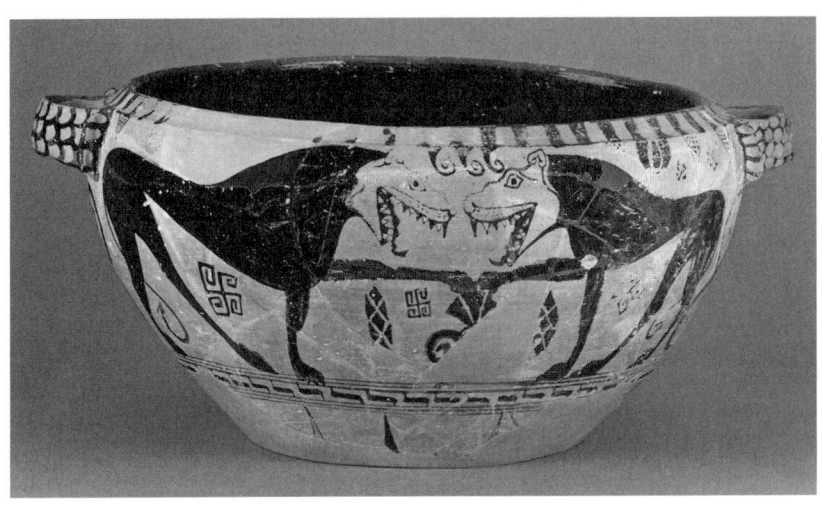

Figure 1.8. Proto-Attic "Burgon Lebes," height 0.25 m, early seventh century BC, from Athens. British Museum 1842,0728.827. © The Trustees of the British Museum.

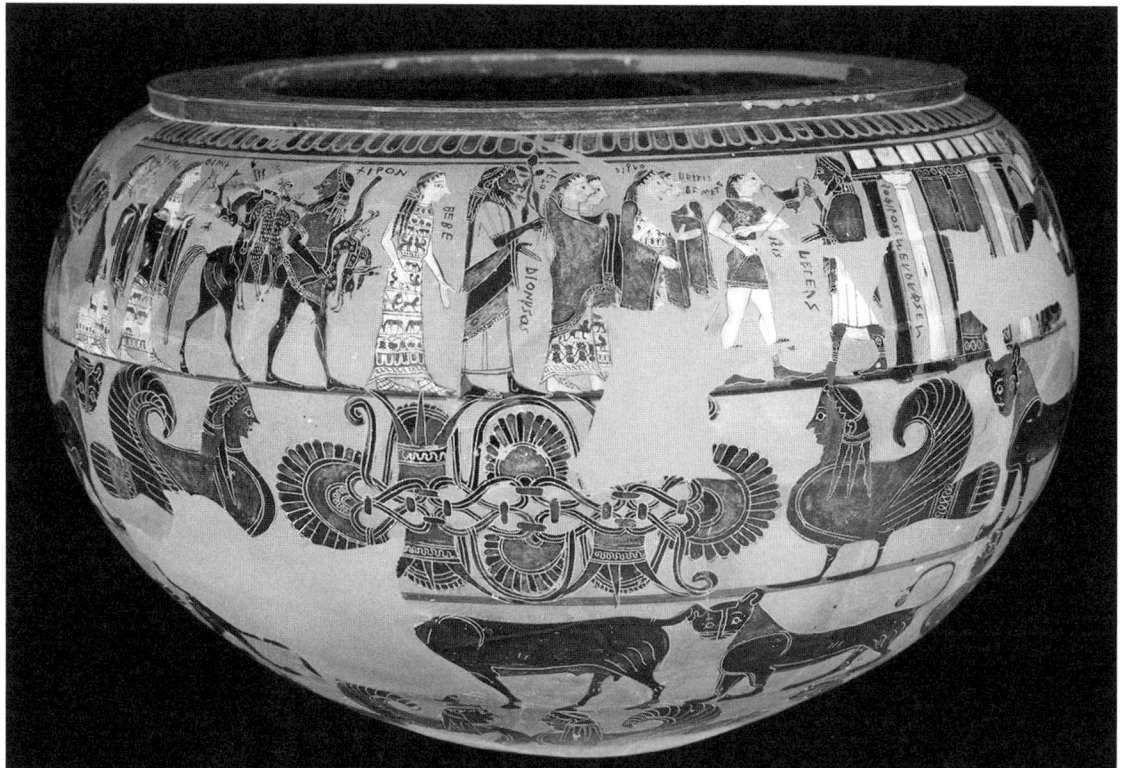

Figure 1.9. Black-figure dinos and stand, height 0.71 m, signed by Sophilos as painter, ca. 580. British Museum 1971,1101.1. © The Trustees of the British Museum.

friezes, writes Boardman.[22] Neer converts this description in abstract terms into a claim about people. He writes that "Corinthian immigrants, perhaps invited by the statesman Solon, gave the industry a powerful boost."[23]

The most influential of all students of Greek pottery, J. D. Beazley, put the emphasis differently. For him the marked change in Attic vase painting at the end of the seventh century is not so much the adoption of a particular technique as the adoption of a particular way of seeing: "the typical and traditional element, indeed, now becomes very strong and remains so throughout the history of black-figure. . . . The elusive multiplicity of the visible world has been condensed into a few well-pondered, crystalline forms, which are adequate to express the main activities and attitudes of man and beast."[24] Beazley too notes that "Athens did not take the lead; a greater part was played by seventh-century Corinth," but for him the model is derivation, not influence: motifs "are derived from Corinthian originals."[25]

Despite calling his Sather Lectures *The Development of Attic Black-Figure*, Beazley devotes very little attention to *why* black-figure vase paint-

---

[22] Boardman (1974), 9, 14. A more elaborate view of influence from metalwork has been argued by Vickers and Gill (1994), 137–41.

[23] Neer (2012), 141. Needless to say, there is no evidence for Solon's involvement, and talk of "the industry" at this time is anachronistic.

[24] Beazley (1951), 13.

[25] Ibid., 13.

ing developed as it did. The reason for this becomes apparent from his justification of his subject matter at the start of his book:

> Greek vases are important to us, not only because they are often beautiful, and because they shed all manner of light on the beliefs and customs of the Greeks in the springtime and summer of their civilisation, but also because, in an incomparable series, they enable us to trace the steps whereby a simpler and even primitive kind of drawing gradually became freer, bolder, and more subtle—the rise, one might say of Western drawing.[26]

While Beazley was prepared to believe that the scenes painted on pots had some relationship with "the beliefs and customs of the Greeks," he attributes to drawing a life course of its own—it simply "became" subtler. His account is designed to enable the reader to see the increasing freedom, boldness, and subtlety, but he is not concerned to account for it. Nor has anyone since tried to do so.[27] Although there have been some pioneering investigations of the ways in which iconographic preferences changed over time, these have focused on narrow periods or a narrow range of subject.[28]

Not surprisingly, when, in the last quarter of the sixth century, there is a further major revolution in the technique of Athenian pottery, and the black-figure technique is replaced by red-figure (**1.10**), one story that scholars have told is internalist. Red-figure is seen as one of a number of experimental techniques for which late sixth-century pots provide evidence, and is distinguished from those other experiments primarily by the fact that it comes to prevail. Here too, however, some scholars have looked for outside influence—whether from relief sculpture or from gold appliqué figures on silver vessels or from textiles.[29]

What scholars have not done is take any serious interest in the significant change in subject matter that accompanies the change from black-figure to red-figure. One reason for this is the way in which several early exponents of the red-figure technique paint "bilingual" pots on which the same subject is explored on one side through the red-figure and on the other through the black-figure technique. But the fact that artists were interested in the way in which the new technique transformed the representation of old themes does not mean that their interest in the new technique was not inspired by the possibility of showing new themes. Martin Robertson emphasized the severe limitations imposed by the black-figure

---

[26] Ibid., 2.
[27] Boardman (1974) is equally without any narrative of development and equally organized on a painter-by-painter basis. Accounts of particular painters treat their development in ways similarly focused on graphic style—cf. von Bothmer (1985), 39–40, on the Amasis Painter: "From the Heidelberg Painter he took little more than the love of stately processions and elegant garments with fringes, as well as some conventions for the anatomical incisions."
[28] Two examples are Shapiro (1990) and Schnapp (1997), chap. 6.
[29] Boardman (1974), 14–15 (promoting relief sculpture); Williams (1991), 104–6 (himself preferring an internalist account, for which cf. Robertson [1992], 8–9); Vickers and Gill (1994), 129–36 (gold on silver).

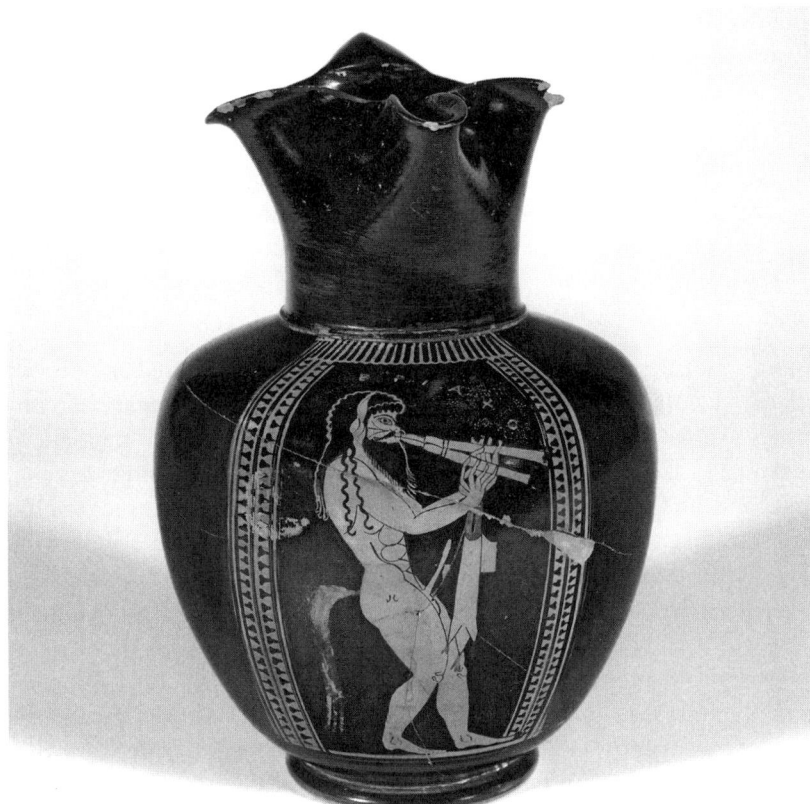

Figure 1.10. Red-figure oinochoe, height 0.205 m, attributed to the Goluchow Painter, from Athens, ca.520. *ARV* 10.3. Cambridge Fitzwilliam Museum G163 = GR 126.1864. © The Fitzwilliam Museum, Cambridge.

technique, and there is good reason to think that that technique both encouraged some sorts of scenes—in particular the spectator scenes studied by Stansbury-O'Donnell—and ruled out other scenes.[30] Because of the close connection between technique and imagery, I consider in detail in this book only changes in imagery in red-figure pottery, but from time to time I shall remark on comparisons and contrasts with the imagery of black-figure.

The Lure of Naturalism

The history of Greek sculpture has also been told with an emphasis on outside influence early in the story, but whether this influence was merely the catalyst of a then seamless evolution or whether outside factors, and indeed world history, continued to impact on the history of sculpture has been subject to dispute.[31]

The earliest Greek sculpture after the "Dark Ages" takes the form of statuettes of bronze, largely recovered from the sanctuaries in which they were dedicated. Bronze statuettes survive in very large numbers from the

---

[30] Robertson (1992), 7; Stansbury-O'Donnell (2006). Because of the importance of the change of technique, I am skeptical about Stansbury-O'Donnell's attempt to link the disappearance of spectators to Athenian political history (2006), 232–33.

[31] For the reason why this is so, see Donohue (2005).

eighth century, but more frequently represent animals (horses, sheep, cows, birds) than humans. Animal statuettes are normally isolated individuals, although there are some groups of mother and offspring. Some human figures, even if represented alone, are represented as engaged in some sort of action—the playing of a musical instrument, engaging in battle—and one salient feature of these representations is the concentration on how human limbs shape themselves for action. Regional styles can be distinguished, and there is reason to posit competition between the craftsmen producing these small bronzes, but as far as scholars can detect they respond largely to each other, and no doubt to customer reaction, rather than to outside influences. For what comes next, however, scholars have been adamant that "real headway . . . lay not in softening up the Geometric but in declaring open house to influence from quite another quarter: the Near East."[32]

From the end of the eighth century, and again from temples and sanctuaries, freestanding statues survive on a larger scale. Three hammered-bronze figures from the temple of Apollo at Dreros may be cult statues, representing Apollo himself, Artemis, and Leto. From around the middle of the seventh century near-life-sized stone figures and much smaller scale freestanding human figures, including the earliest *korai* (**1.11**), share a distinctive style, which has become known as "Daedalic," with triangular, flat-topped, head and wig-style hair.[33] Exogenous factors in the form of the technology of mold-made figurines, which Cretans learned from Syria, have been held to account for both the style and its spread.[34] Use of molds enabled rapid production of identical figures, and their place in cult may have increased their prestige and influence. The magnification of these figures into stone figures, some of which were close to life size, has been widely held to have been inspired by experience of large-scale stone sculpture in Egypt,[35] although a more detailed debt of large stone sculpture to the east, and particularly to Egypt, claimed even by Greek sources (Diodoros 1.98.5–9), cannot be substantiated.[36] Iconographically, Eastern influence has also been suspected in the naked or part-naked female figurines from Crete—an iconography that notably is not adopted elsewhere in Greece.[37]

Kouroi and *korai* appear first in sanctuaries, in particular on the sacred island of Delos; subsequently, but rather selectively, they appear in cemeteries.[38] Both *kouroi* and *korai* take heavily standardized forms. Both are shown standing and isolated, not engaged with other figures. *Korai* are clothed, have feet together, one arm by the side and the other either

---

[32] Stewart (1990), 104.
[33] The classic study is Jenkyns (1936). See also Morris (1994), chap. 9.
[34] Boardman (1978), 13–14.
[35] Cf., e.g., Carpenter (1960), 5–19.
[36] Boardman (1978), 15. For a demonstration that no *kouros* accords with the second Egyptian Canon, see Carter and Steinberg (2010).
[37] Boardman (1978), 13, 14.
[38] The classic catalogs are provided by Richter (1968; 1970); for *korai* an up-to-date list is provided by Karakasi (2000). See also Fehr (1996). For tendentious studies, see Keesling (2003), Stieber (2004).

Figure 1.11. *Kore* of Nikandre, height 1.75 m, from Delos, ca. 650. Athens National Museum 1. National Archaeological Museum, Athens, Photographic Archives (Photographer: V. von Eickstedt). © Hellenic Ministry of Culture and Sports / Archaeological Receipts Fund.

Figure 1.12. *Kore* of Phrasikleia, height 2.11 m, from Merenda, Attica, ca. 540. Athens National Museum 4889. National Archaeological Museum, Athens, Photographic Archives (Photographer: V. von Eickstedt). © Hellenic Ministry of Culture and Sports / Archaeological Receipts Fund.

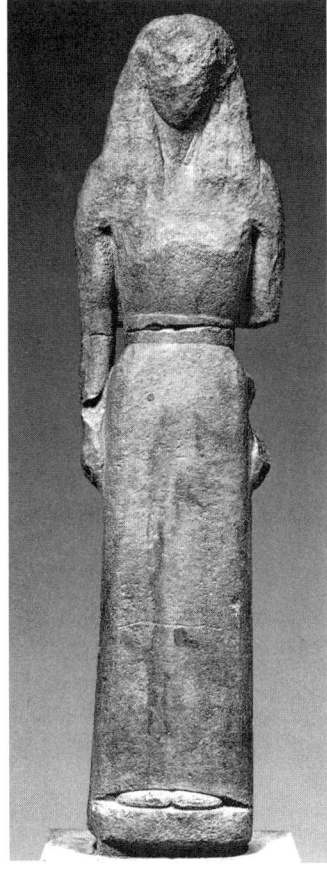
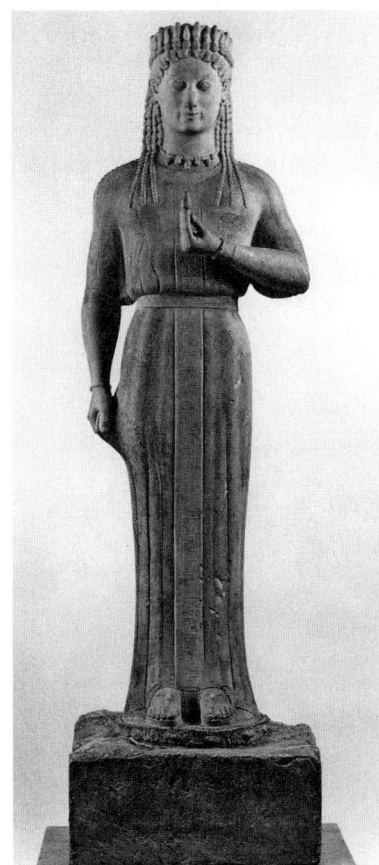

extended forward or folded across the breast. The hand of the extended or folded arm always contains some object, normally a flower, fruit, or bird.

The earliest *kore* bears an inscription naming not only the maiden herself but also her father, brother, and new ("now") husband (*CEG* 403). Nubility is fundamental to the *kore*, and clearly confirmed in the inscription accompanying a *kore* sited on a grave in Attica that declares itself to be the marker of Phrasikleia (**1.12**), who obtained the name *kore* "from the gods instead of marriage."[39] Being on the verge of manhood is equally important for *kouroi*, although that was not the age at which men married. *Kouroi* are normally naked; they put one foot forward, but both feet remain flat on the ground; they force their clenched hands down by their sides. Like *korai*, *kouroi* stare straight ahead.

Although the basic forms of freestanding male and female statues remained unchanging for a century and a half, the detailed execution varied considerably from region to region and from one statue to another. Very few statues have been recovered in an archaeological context that supplies a precise date, and the changes in style have become the basis on which surviving *kouroi* and *korai* are placed into a chronological sequence. Dis-

[39] *IG* i³ 1261; on Phrasikleia's inscription, see Svenbro (1988).

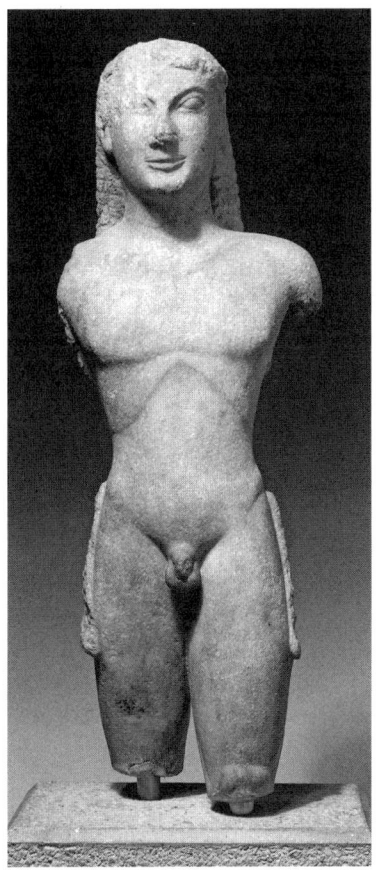 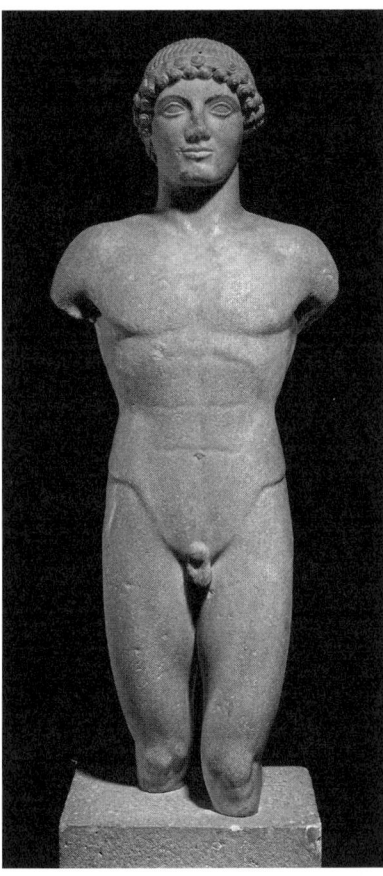

Figure 1.13. *Kouros*, height 0.77 m, of uncertain origin, perhaps from Boiotia, but links with north Ionia have also been suspected; ca. 560. British Museum 1878,0120.1 (B 474). © The Trustees of the British Museum.

Figure 1.14. *Kouros*, height 1.01 m, said to be from Anaphe, sometimes known as the Strangford Apollo, ca. 490. British Museum 1864,0220.1 (B 475). © The Trustees of the British Museum.

cussion of why the style changes has primarily concerned *kouroi* (**1.13**, **1.14**), where the absence of clothing reduces the number of variables in play. Most helpful have been sites with large numbers of *kouroi*, such as, in particular, the sanctuary of Apollo Ptoieus at Akraiphnion in Boiotia, where remains of more than a hundred different *kouroi* have been recovered.[40] Scholars concentrate on hairstyle (which moves over time from long to short), facial features (including the so-called archaic smile), and the presentation of anatomy. Scholars have created a sequence from schematic depictions of anatomy through careful representation of the display of the underlying bone structure on the body surface to presentation of bodies that give the impression of a particular age.

In broad terms, there is little doubt that the evolutionary sequence offered by scholars is correct. Comparison with architectural sculpture, where there is much better contextual (and in the case of the Siphnian Treasury at Delphi textual) evidence for dating, offers a more or less independent confirmation. But should we take the fact that the latest *kouroi* make more detailed reference to the forms of living men than the earlier to demonstrate that artistic change was motivated by striving after naturalism?

[40] Ducat (1971).

The most influential theorization of the development of Greek sculpture is that of the art historian Ernst Gombrich, published in a book subtitled "a study in the psychology of pictorial representation."[41] Gombrich believed that the "Greek revolution," the changes in Greek art that accompany the disappearance of the *kouros* type, marked the point at which a fundamentally conceptual art was replaced by one in which observation played the central role. He suggested that universally, "making came before matching," that is, that making objects that stood for other objects came before making objects that attempted to match the form of other objects. In his view, progress from making to matching was marked by "schema and correction"; that is, attempts to match were compared to the object matched, found wanting, and better matches were devised.[42] For Gombrich what happens in Greek art is that this process continues until a breakthrough is achieved, when the match between the body observed and the body depicted was sufficient to allow narrative. "The conquest of appearances, sufficiently convincing to allow the imaginative reconstruction of mythological or historical events, was the end of classical art in more than one meaning of the word."[43]

As is often the case, conceptual division, as here between making and matching, is sufficiently attractive in itself for its arbitrariness to be overlooked. There can be no matching that does not involve also making, no representation that does not select what it is that it represents because of what it wants to convey about the object represented. And there can be no making that does not also involve matching: even the most symbolic of representations must nevertheless do some matching to ensure successful allusion.

Gombrich's implication that appearances have to be conquered to a particular degree before mythological or historical events can be imaginatively reconstructed is revealed as nonsense by the very history of Greek art. There can be no doubt that viewers of the scenes of the laying out of the corpse on Athenian geometric pots were able on that basis imaginatively to reconstruct the historical event; likewise, even the earliest of *korai* enabled worshippers in sanctuaries to see the real-life exchange of women in marriage that was figured by these nubile maidens holding out their offerings. There was no magic point at which narrative became possible—different sorts of narratives became possible at different stages.

Gombrich's talk of imaginative reconstruction, is, however, extremely helpful. Imaginative reconstruction is what every viewer does with any object that they know or assume to be representational. But what can be imaginatively reconstructed—a person, a person of a particular sex, a person engaged in a particular action, a person of a particular age, a person of a particular sexual orientation, a particular identifiable individual—will depend on what reference the representational object makes to objects outside itself, whether persons or other representations, as well as to the

---

[41] Gombrich (1960).
[42] Ibid., 99. For a critique of the theoretical basis of Gombrich's view, see Bryson (1983).
[43] Gombrich (1960), 123

force of cultural symbols. The earliest *korai* allow imaginative reconstruction of a woman, perhaps of a young woman, and of an action, the action of offering, but they allow little else. Subsequent *korai*, precisely because belonging to a series of similar representations, direct imaginative reconstruction toward women dressed in particular, elaborate ways, and so more strongly toward ceremonial offering and the displaying alike of personal charms and family wealth and status.

That imaginative reconstruction depends on the fundamental link between form and context is clear from the rest of Attica.[44] The series of Acropolis *korai* certainly explore a wide range of ways in which the nubile woman might be presented, but they are all more like each other than they are like the two complete *korai* from the countryside of Attica, which we know or are reasonably confident marked graves—the so-called Berlin Standing Goddess and Phrasikleia. Not only do the *korai* grave markers hold their different offerings differently, they share carved neck jewelry (Acropolis *korai* have jewelry painted or added in metal) and both also wear something (crown, *polos*) on their head, as the Acropolis *korai* mostly do not. Although we are not in a position to reconstruct in any detail what a sixth-century visitor to the cemetery might have imaginatively constructed on viewing these two *korai*, he or she was being offered a distinct set of prompts.

Concentration on what makes one *kore* or one *kouros* different from another obscures what they share. What they share is the frontal gaze. As Jaś Elsner has stressed in his "Reflections on the 'Greek Revolution' in Art," the frontal gaze constitutes a direct address to the viewer, a direct challenge to the viewer to assess the sculpted figure, and indeed in some respect or another to compare the sculpted viewer to himself and to other figures whom he might address.[45] The striking change that comes about when the *kouros* and the *kore* types are given up in 480 is the abandonment of that direct address to the viewer (**1.15**). The viewer ceases to be the second party in an exchange and becomes the third party, an observer rather than a participant. Whatever we make of any particular evolutionary model, no evolutionary model of change is going satisfactorily to explain this revolution.

Elsner himself is reticent about causation. He draws attention to the parallel between what happens in art and what happens in the theater, where the arrival of the second actor changes what happens from direct address to the audience to the playing out of a drama in front of an audience. He further notes other parallels that can be observed in other areas of Athenian culture and that "these changes had a politics and were interrelated."[46] But he insists that "politics and social life seem to follow the forms of aesthetic representation rather than cause them."[47] But while

---

[44] On Attic funerary *korai*, see also D'Onofrio (1982).

[45] Elsner (2006), building on Osborne (1988). For the theological implications of this in the context of temple sculpture, see Osborne (2009), and cf. Marconi (2007), 214–22.

[46] Elsner (2006), 91.

[47] Contrast Zanker (1988), 335: "Only the great ages of transition at the end of the Greek Archaic

Elsner suggests that we need to think in terms of a situation where artists conditioned by viewers' expectations precipitate particular forms of viewer response, he does not offer any clear account of what, historically speaking, is the crucial question: why artists and viewers should have mutually encouraged each other in this direction at this moment.[48]

It is a weakness of both Gombrich's and Elsner's stories that by hardly extending their gaze beyond the *kouros* and the *kore* they ignore the fact that these are far from comprising the totality of archaic sculpture.[49] While *kouroi* may not tell stories, the reliefs of archaic architectural sculpture certainly do. Metopes present episodes of hostile encounter easily identifiable with particular myths (for example, Herakles and the Kerkopes); friezes present moments of decision or complex engagements—Achilles's fate weighed against Memnon's on one face of the Siphnian treasury at Delphi, the battle of gods and giants on another face. And while archaic architectural sculpture makes more use of the frontal face than later sculptures, there is no doubt at all that in these scenes we are spectators. And so we are too in the reliefs on the bases of stelai and *kouroi* found in Athens that show playing ball games (**1.16**), gymnastic activities (see 9.3), or setting cocks to fight. Taking a wider view of Greek sculpture does not invalidate Gombrich's and Elsner's interpretations, but it certainly qualifies them—their revolutions turn out to be effectively restricted to freestanding sculpture.

A quite different aspect of the stylistic changes that saw the end of the *kouros* and *kore* has been emphasized by Andrew Stewart in recent work. Stewart comes at change from the other end—starting from the features of the new "classical" style. For him the change takes place suddenly, and the crucial characteristics of the successors of the *kouroi* are "simplicity, strength, vigor, rationality and intelligence."[50] Stewart suggests that the circumstances of the change also reveal the cause: the Persian Wars. "Sternly repudiating both their elitist archaic past and the defeated and humbled 'barbarian' world . . . the Greeks simply reinvented themselves." Although he sees this as the culmination of certain trends visible in earlier art, for Stewart this is a revolution with leaders—Kritios, Nesiotes, and Pythagoras of Rhegion.[51]

Age and in the Early Hellenistic are comparable in the scale and depth of change [to the revolution of the *saeculum augustum*]. In these two earlier periods as well, new forms of artistic and visual expression had arisen in the wake of political change."

[48] There is a like reticence in Neer's similarly framed treatment of the invention of classical sculpture, though Neer wants to weight his account much more strongly toward evolution (n.b., "emergence" in his title) and toward an internalist account: "the history of fifth-century sculpture is . . . an ongoing adjustment of the relation between image and beholder, and an ongoing elaboration of that dialectic of presence and absence, which characterizes Greek statuary from earliest times" (2010), 102.

[49] Cf. Vout (2014). Elsner (2006), 77–79, extends his discussion to pedimental sculpture, but by doing so concentrates on the form of non-freestanding sculpture most inclined to privilege frontality; cf. Osborne (2009).

[50] Stewart (2008a), 60; cf. (2008b), 601–2.

[51] Stewart (2008a), 63, (2008b), 605–10, which is even more emphatic about the role of Kritios and Nesiotes. The emphasis on the importance of the Persian wars is shared with Pollitt (1972), for which Stewart (2008a) was conceived as a replacement.

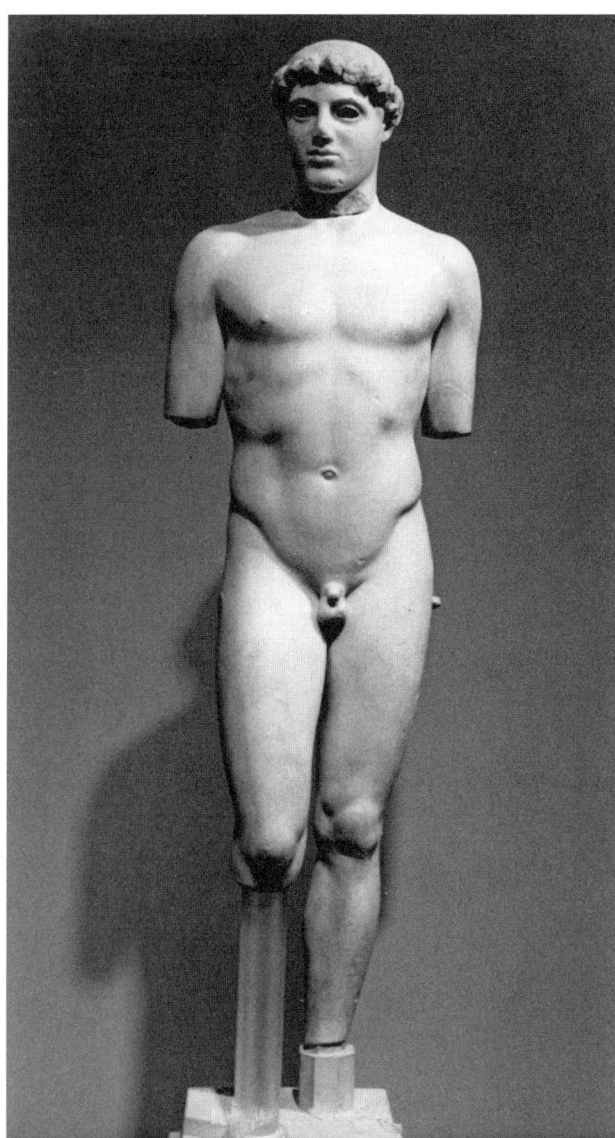

Figure 1.15. Kritios Boy, height 1.167 m. Athens Acropolis Museum 698. Photo by Jeffery Hurwit. © Jeffery Hurwit.

Figure 1.16. One side of a base for a *kouros* (for another side see 9.3), found in the Themistoklean Wall. Athens National Archaeological Museum 3476. © Hirmer Fotoarchiv Munich.

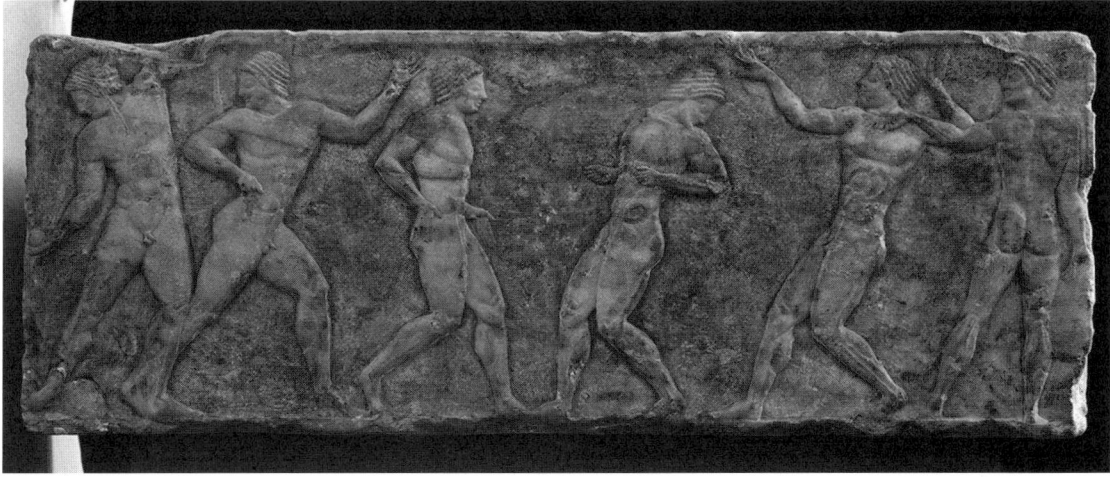

Whether they paint pictures of internal evolution, of a revolution in narrative or visuality, or claim a new mentality resulting from success in the Persian wars, what all these explanations share with one another, and with the explanations of change in painted pottery, is an exclusive concentration on form and style.[52] For all that in some cases they seek corroborating evidence from other areas of Greek culture, their explanations are not merely inappropriately monocausal, as if historical actors existed in merely one dimension, they systematically ignore a significant part of the visual evidence. It is the look of the sculpture or painting, the style of carving or drawing, that plays the central role in these arguments, not what sculptors or painters choose to represent. The subject represented is treated as just so much noise, to be eliminated so that the work of art can be seen more clearly.

There are indeed good reasons for eliminating subject matter from consideration. A list of all the subjects represented on sculpture and in painted pottery would be extremely long, and relatively few particular scenes are repeated. Indeed, as we will see, it is a feature of sculpture and pot painting, despite the repetitiousness of *kouroi* and *korai*, that there is very little precise duplication of scenes. But this does not mean that there are no patterns to what sort of scenes get shown when. It is the contention of this book that paying attention to those patterns will rewrite the history of art. It is also the contention of this book that paying attention to those patterns will rewrite history.

3. The Argument of This Book

The story of making and matching is a story that might be told of many societies. Indeed, for Gombrich the attraction of the model was precisely its potentially wide application: what happened in Greece illustrated a bigger truth about the psychology of art. Gombrich was concerned with why what he termed the "Greek revolution" took place in Greece and not in Egypt, but the explanation he gave looked only to storytelling, and within storytelling to the possible magic of Homer: the *kouros* was turned into the Kritios Boy by the drive to narrative. Not every society has a widely diffused tradition of epic tales, but storytelling was certainly not limited to the Greeks.[53]

Equally generalizable are the stories told of how one pot painter learns from and builds on the work of another. The particular tradition described may be peculiar to archaic Athens, but the pattern of craft apprenticeship, artistic education, and competition within the potters' quarter, fueled by the need to win and keep customers, is one that could potentially apply in

---

[52]This is equally true of discussions that focus on "naturalism as a cultural *system*," as does Tanner (2006), 39, in an account that concentrates on the representation of gods and accounts for the changes with reference to Kleisthenic democracy (92–96).

[53]Cf. Beard (1985). Gombrich's belief that maybe Homer was different is born of a conviction that there was a divide between Greek and Near Eastern cultures.

any culture. Nor is Elsner's revolution in visuality one that can only happen once in history—the choice of whether to make the figures address the viewer or whether to have the viewer spectate a scene in which he or she is not involved is one that has to be made by every maker of figurative images.

That factors that can be found to operate across cultures play a part in the history of art in a particular culture is not in itself a problem—indeed it would be extraordinary if such factors were absent. But it is a problem if those factors are held to act on their own. Art does not develop simply in accordance with the improving observational and motor skills of artists; the history of art is not simply an image of the development of the artistic skills of an individual from childhood to maturity.

But it is equally questionable whether explanations that have art's history shaped by outside "influence' or peculiar historical factors are any more plausible. Historical events and cultural influence shape art history only if they shape the way in which artists see the world, the world that artists see, or the world that their patrons want to have represented. Sculpture or painting on pottery are the means by which artists do things within the world, and when the sculptures or the paintings change, that is because what the artists want to do changes, or because to do the same things in a different world means doing them differently. But sculptures and pots do not do things in the world simply by the way they are painted or the style in which they are sculpted, they do things in the world because of what they represent, and what they represent is a matter of subject matter as well as of style.

The Athenian desire in the eighth century BC to have monumental grave markers created a demand met by outsize pots with figurative decoration. But the decision to show figurative scenes of burial on large pots was not a decision required by the use of pots as grave markers; rather, pots used as grave markers created an opportunity that artists exploited by showing scenes of the laying out of the body. In doing so, and perhaps even more in surrounding the scenes of the laying out of men's bodies with scenes of warriors, chariots, and ships, the artists fed back into the cemetery ideas that will themselves have influenced how Athenians viewed burial and regarded the dead. When, a hundred years later, an Athenian had the Nessos Painter produce an amphora in the black-figure technique showing Herakles attacking the centaur Nessos to stand on a grave, he was making a different sort of intervention in the cemetery—invoking not the idealized community on display at the funeral but the exotic world of myth with its monsters and hybrids. In doing so he presented those who visited the cemetery with an image of death not as a social fact but as something coming from elsewhere that individuals fought with on their own. The different style of the later pot, and the greater proportion of its surface occupied by the scene, play a part in this story—but only a part. The changing subject matter cannot be ignored.

In this book, my concern is primarily with Athenian painted pottery of the later sixth and fifth centuries BC. Although substantial amounts of architectural sculpture survive from classical Greece, providing us with monuments whose temporal and physical context is unusually well secured, we are far less well supplied with freestanding sculpture. Large numbers of dedicatory statues have been recovered in excavations from archaic Greek sanctuaries, but the loss of classical freestanding statues to the melting pot once bronze became the usual material for such statues in the classical period means that even the architectural sculpture that we have cannot be properly contextualized.[54]

By contrast several tens of thousands of the pots painted in Athens in the sixth and fifth centuries BC survive. And while a pot survives in only one of the many contexts in which it was used during its ancient life (most frequently its use in an Etruscan grave; sometimes simply its disuse in rubbish discard), their shapes and to some extent their own figurative decoration enable us to be reasonably confident about at least one other of their earlier contexts of use. What is more, although individual pots can be securely dated only in rare cases, when deposited in association with graves or buildings or episodes of destruction for which we have a firm date, the whole sequence of Athenian painted pottery has been studied in such detail that, despite some recent challenges to accepted chronology, we can be more or less confident of the broad date (plus or minus ten years) of any pot.[55]

The combination of a very large sample, firm dating, and good contextual information means that in the case of pottery, by contrast to that of sculpture, we have a good chance of coming to understand what those who painted, bought, and deployed a pot were trying to do when they chose one scene rather than another. The figurative decoration on these pots is extremely various, but the scenes fall into a relatively small number of broad classes (representing myths and mythical figures, war, athletics, sex, cult acts, the symposium and reveling, and such). In this book, I shall look at a substantial subsection of those pots and at some of those broad classes of scene. The patterns I am interested in are patterns of change in scenes representing, more or less directly, actions in which ordinary men and women engaged on a regular basis.[56] I ask whether the marked changes that occur in the way scenes of athletic, military, sexual, sacrificial, sympotic, and satyric activity are represented on the red-figure pots painted between circa

[54] The best we can do to compare archaic and classical statuary is to resort to Pausanias's account of what he saw on the Athenian Acropolis in the second century AD. See Osborne (forthcoming).

[55] For the challenge and responses, see Williams (1996), 240n50, 245–50.

[56] The question of whether it makes sense to divide the scenes on Athenian pots between "myth" and "genre" has been pointedly raised in recent years by Ferrari (2002), esp. 17–25, (2003), and Topper (2012). I remain convinced that for Athenians the mythical world was continuous with, rather than removed from, the present (hence the dress and equipment of mythical figures is homeostatic and Achilles and Co. wear contemporary armor, etc., cf. Boardman [2002], 158, Topper [2012], 69), and that addition of mythological names adds piquancy to scenes rather than removes those scenes from contemporary relevance (cf. Beard [1991], 21). Satyrs are, in my view, simply at one end of the mythical spectrum, not a quite different phenomenon—hence the possibility of talking of *La cité des satyres* (Lissarrague 2013). So while I have largely excluded scenes where the iconography is determined by a particular myth, the discovery of inscriptions giving mythological identities to figures on the pots I discuss would not alter the arguments here.

520 and circa 440 BC can be accounted for by social, cultural, and political developments. In answering this question, I will try to show why history needs art history, but also why art history needs history.[57] For, on the one hand, attention to changing representations of activities related to everyday life in art can offer us a guide to transformations of social expectations and values more sensitive than that offered by any textual sources. On the other, only when we can understand the implications of the artists' choices of what they represent and how they represent it, can we understand why those were the choices they made.

The chapters of this book fall into three sections. In chapter 2, I provide an account of the nature of Athenian painted pottery, to bring out the features of Athenian pots that make a study such as this possible. In chapters 3 and 4 I use the cases of scenes of athletes and of soldiers to establish the nature of the change in imagery that needs to be explained. In chapters 5 to 8, I examine how the change affects four other bodies of imagery that between them account for a great proportion of Athenian painted pottery—scenes of courtship and sex, of sacrifice, of the symposium, and of satyrs. In chapters 9 and 10 I explore how we can account for the change, and place the change in relation to the observations of both historians and art historians. In a brief conclusion, I then reflect back on what we have learned about classical Athens and what we have learned about the history of classical art.

[57] Cf. Bažant (1985), 44–45: "Ainsi pour interpréter les représentations de la vie sociale il faut trouver le point de vue d'où les peintres ont regardé et représenté la vie. Il convient de tenir compte non seulement du système d'ensemble iconographique et de ses connexions littéraires, sociales, religieuses, etc., mais aussi de la position du peintre face à la réalité qu'il essaie de représenter."

2 ❧ Athenian Pottery and Athenian Culture

1. The Study of Athenian Painted Pottery

In the late eighteenth and early nineteenth century, study of Athenian painted pottery was dominated by the question of where the pots were made. Recovered in large numbers from Italian graves, the black- and red-figure pots like 2.1 and 2.2, that we now identify as Athenian, did not straightforwardly reveal their origins. A popular claim was that they were Etruscan. Given the findspots, and the fact that there are indeed vases in similar techniques that were made in Etruria, this was not a crazy suggestion.[1] But once it became clear from the Greek writing on them, and from parallel finds in Greece, that the pots were in fact Greek, their study got taken up with a range of questions that ignored what had happened to the pot after it had left the potter's workshop and concentrated instead on the potting and the painting themselves.

There is no doubt that how they are potted and how they are painted are vital topics for understanding the history of painted pottery. If the very variety of images on pots and of pot shapes encourages us to focus on individual acts of creation, rather than on manufacturing processes, the presence of statements on pots in the form "Pamphaios made this" (**2.1,** 4.20–21; cf. also 2.7, 3.3–4. 4.5, 4.7 and plate 15, 4.9–11, 4.15, 9.1) or "Smikros drew this" (9.4–5, cf. 1.9, 2.7, 3.10, 4.5, 4.7 and plate 15, 4.9–11, 5.5–6 and plate 21) further encourages an interest in the personalities of the painters and potters involved.

Work on the individual traits of *potters* has in fact never got terribly far.[2] There has been plenty of work done, including important experimental archaeology, on the techniques of painting pottery, and we are now finally close to understanding the processes by which pots were made and decorated.[3] But although some very revealing work of careful measurement has illuminated the sensitivity of cup makers, in particular, to issues of shape and proportion, this work has tended to be generalizing rather than par-

---

[1] For a history of the study of Greek pottery, see Sparkes (1996).
[2] It is revealing that Scheibler's promisingly titled *Griechische Töpferkunst* (1983) should be subtitled *Herstellung, Handel und Gebrauch der antiken Tongefäße*.
[3] Noble (1965), Schreiber (1999).

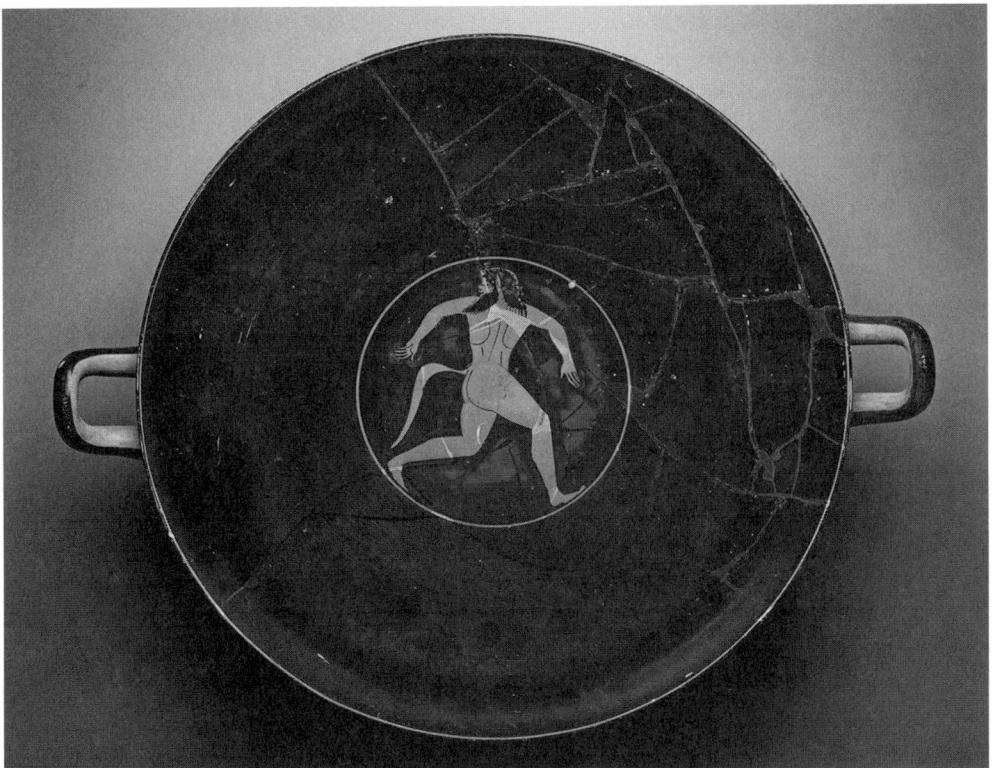

Figure 2.1. Interior of red-figure cup, diameter 0.414 m, with signature by the potter Pamphaios (*epoiesen* can be read running around clockwise from the head of the satyr; only the final letter of Pamphaios's name survives, but can be restored from the exterior of the pot where it is found complete), found at Cervetri, ca. 500 (for the exterior see 4.20–21). *ARV* 128.19. Boston Museum of Fine Arts 95.32. Photograph © 2017 Museum of Fine Arts, Boston.

ticularizing.[4] Shape analysis has primarily been deployed to provide chronological discrimination rather than to examine the ways in which shapes determined, for example, the experience of the drinker, at least beyond discussion of "trick vases" designed to enable liquid to be hidden in and released from secret chambers to the embarrassment of the drinker.[5] Only very recently have some scholars begun to draw attention to how extremely varied the resources available to potters were.[6]

By contrast, during the last quarter of the nineteenth and the first three quarters of the twentieth century studies of the personalities of painters dominated the study of painted pottery. Almost the only monographs on painted pottery beyond general histories were devoted to the study of an individual artist's work.[7] Dominant has been the influence of Sir John

---

[4] Seki (1985); but see also Bloesch (1940).
[5] Noble (1968), Vickers (1975; 1980), Lissarrague (1987/1990), 47–52. See also Turnure (1981) for doubts over the purposes of these special cups.
[6] Cohen (2006). So too studies of the physical remains of Athenian pottery workshops and kilns remain in their infancy; see Monaco (2000) for a summary of the evidence, and Eschbach (2014) for a study of a dump of kiln wasters.
[7] Note, for example, the series *Bilder Griechischer Vasen* edited by Beazley and Jacobsthal and published in Berlin between 1930 and 1939.

Beazley, a man who deployed his outstanding visual memory to sort a high proportion of black- and red-figure pottery—though by no means all—into artists and groups of artists.[8] While others had already observed common stylistic traits in the pots signed by a single painter, Beazley proceeded to observe common stylistic traits in groups of pots that bore no signature, coining names for the artist involved on the basis of the subject or subject predilections or modern location of one or more or the pots in question. Thus we end up with the "Chicago Painter" (**2.2**) named for a stamnos in Chicago, the "Pan Painter" named for the striking subject matter on one bell-krater (see 10.7), the "Foundry Painter" named after an unusual representation of a bronze foundry on one of his pots (cf. 5.9), and so on. Beazley published long, unillustrated, lists of pots that he attributed to these reconstructed artists or to artists who signed some, but in his view not all, of their work (such as Oltos, below 3.7–8 and plate 6, 4.8, 6.3), or Makron, below 2.3–4, 2.7, 5.7–8 and plate 22, 8.6–7, 9.1), offering at most only brief verbal characterizations of their style. He noted also pots that were somewhat like those he attributed to a particular hand, but not identical, although himself wary of presuming any particular explanation (workshop, pupil, and such) for the similarities.[9] In cases where the corpus of pots attributed to a single painter was large, Beazley sometimes suggested that one could plot earlier and later products of the same painter.[10] Others picked up on the issues of links between artists, arguing who might have been the teacher of whom.[11]

The differences of graphic style between different pots painted in the same technique at more or less the same time (insofar as the contexts in which they are found allow independent evidence of date) are clear. Beazley's attributions of a set of pots to a single artist are often highly convincing. Particular graphic habits, such as the way in which the painter renders those features he is unlikely to have thought about while drawing—ears, ankles, collarbone, and so on—can often be seen to go together with particular compositional preferences and preferences for, or avoidance of, certain subjects.[12] In these cases we seem to be dealing with a distinct artistic personality. In many cases, other scholars have been able to attribute, with a high degree of confidence, pots that have become known since Beazley's death to artists defined by Beazley.

[8] On Beazley, see Kurtz (1983), Neer (1997), Whitley (1997), Rouet (2001).
[9] Robertson (1982). There is something of a methodological contradiction involved in thinking that one can identify artists in the Morellian way by their unconscious or subconscious drawing habits and then identifying pupils because they share those habits or something close to them.
[10] Beazley's work is distilled into *ABV*, *ARV*, and *Paralipomena* (*Para.*). For many artists, Beazley provided no full articulation of his case for grouping pots, but for some he offered extensive justification (see, e.g., Beazley [1911; 1922; 1989]). Beazley's methods are explored in Kurtz (1983; 1985), Elsner (1990), Whitley (1997), Neer (1997; 2009).
[11] E.g., Robertson (1950), Sourvinou-Inwood (1975); cf. Smith (2006).
[12] The particular method Beazley employed—looking at the part of the painting the painter drew more or less unconsciously—derived from that devised by Morelli for studying Renaissance painting, see Morelli (1892–93), Elsner (1990), but Beazley was also heavily influenced by Pater, see Kurtz (1985), Neer (2009), 40–46.

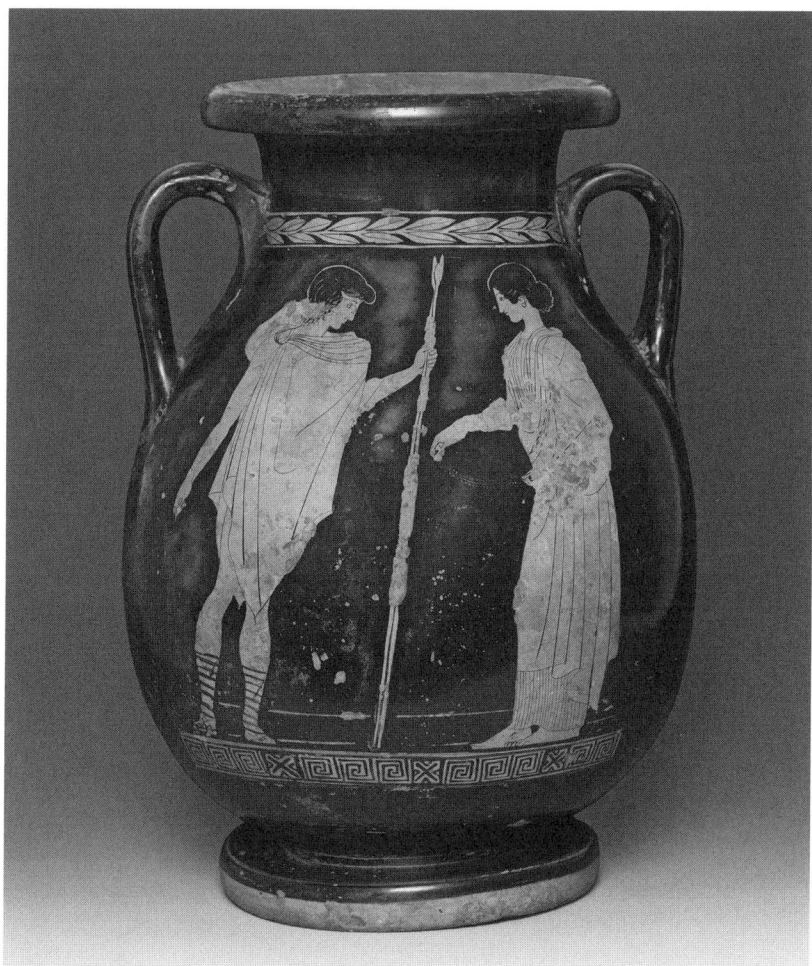

Figure 2.2. Red-figure pelike, height 0.425 m, attributed to the Chicago Painter, found at Vulci, ca. 450 (for the reverse see 4.22). *ARV* 630.26. Paris, Cabinet de Médailles 394. © Bibliothèque nationale de France.

Inevitably, however, along with attributions that seem unquestionable there are more difficult cases, where the links between pots put together by Beazley seem tenuous, or where a particular pot attributed to one hand by Beazley has seemed to others out of place among the other works by that artist and better attributed to another hand.[13] The further we move away from simply grouping vases that look alike in detail, to attributing vases that look somewhat alike to youthful or aged phases of the same artist or to pupils, the more uncertain the inferences become. In a world where one artist learned from another, and where artists worked together in the same workshop, or were rivals in neighboring workshops, close similarities between pots painted by different hands are not surprising.[14] Modern scholars are never going to be in a position to resolve finally the question

---

[13] See, for instance, the debate about which cups should and which should not be attributed to Douris, Buitron-Oliver (1995), 6–7.
[14] On workshops, see Kunze-Götte (2002).

of where the limits of one artist come and where another artist begins.[15] There is plenty of evidence for painters of pots having a sense of humor,[16] and we should not exclude the possibility of one painter deliberately mimicking the style of another. Whether the identity of the artist who painted a pot matters depends upon the question that is being asked. Works that are hard to distinguish in graphic style are unlikely to be far removed from one another in time, even if not from the same hand; only if the artistic personality of a given painter is at issue does the attribution to a particular named individual carry much significance.[17]

Attributionism has come under attack not simply from those skeptical about the theoretical basis for some of the claims, but because of the way in which it suggests that Greek pot painters were like the painters of canvases in the post-Renaissance world, and ultimately because of the commercial uses to which it has been put.[18] Because the methods Beazley used are closely parallel to the methods Renaissance art historians used, the parallel creation of artists' oeuvres leads to a presumption that Athenian pot painting and Italian Renaissance painting were essentially similar enterprises, and has served in both cases to shape the market in the objects in question. Just as the value of a Renaissance painting has come to depend closely on the attribution of works to identified artists, so too pots that can be attributed to particular artists, and particularly to artists known to have painted other very fine pots, have a premium at auction. Renaissance paintings were expensive and valued items when they were created, and particular Renaissance artists, as well as particular materials employed in paintings, did indeed command higher prices.[19] But Athenian pots were never, as far as we know, such highly valued items, and most of them seem to have been extremely inexpensive.[20]

For some classical archaeologists, the distortion of everyday objects into objets d'art is distasteful. The gap between the cheapness of ancient pots, created as functional objects not as "art," and the sums they can fetch by being treated as "art" on the modern market, marks out how historically misleading and idealized the view of classical Greece perpetrated by art markets, collectors, and museums can be.[21] A history of Greek pot painting that constructs itself as a history of individual pot painters is so far from the history that any contemporary Greek could have told that to promote it as *the* story of painted pottery unarguably distorts our understanding of classical archaeology and the classical world.[22] Groups of pots by the same

---

[15] Beazley himself acknowledged this with his terminology (see Robertson [1982]), to the frustration of Neer (2009), 45. See also Sapirstein (2013; 2014) for arguments that Beazley subdivided artists too readily.

[16] Mitchell (2009).

[17] Scholars have recognized this by extending discussion in works ostensibly devoted to a single painter to the wider circle of related pots; see, e.g., Lezzi-Hafter (1976; 1988), Matheson (1996).

[18] Whitley (1997).

[19] Welch (1997).

[20] For a recent discussion, see Chankowski (2013).

[21] Vickers and Gill (1994).

[22] For what classical archaeology looks like if one looks at the Greek and Roman world in the broad terms in which the Greeks and Romans looked at it, see Alcock and Osborne (2007).

painter found in the same tomb or sanctuary may suggest that some who purchased pots had an eye to the products of particular hands—though they may simply reflect the fact that any particular shipment of pots was likely to contain several pots from the same workshop, or a group commissioned for their iconography rather than the artist involved.[23] But we have no evidence that works by particular painters fetched any premium, except insofar as some markets seem to have shown no interest in particularly low-grade works.[24] The assemblages we discover suggest strongly that it was function and shape, together with type of scene represented, not a particular painter's hand, for which customers went out looking. That shape and scene were indeed in customers' minds is, however, easy to demonstrate from the high degree of coherence with regard to shape, or scene, or both, sometimes manifested by pots found together.[25]

Beazley's influence—through his catalogs, through the focus of his own papers, through the organization of the archive of his photographs formed at Oxford after his death and available online, and through the fact that his work offers a chronological framework for objects that have no archaeological provenance—has ensured that the most widely used guides to Athenian vase painting are still works that are primarily organized around a history of individual painters and their work.[26] John Boardman's handbooks (*Athenian Black Figure Vases* of 1974, *Athenian Red Figure Vases: The Archaic Period* of 1975, *Athenian Red Figure Vases: The Classical Period* of 1989) have become more coy over time about displaying in the titles and subtitles of chapters how painter-centered they are, but their basic organization has remained painter-centered from beginning to end. Martin Robertson's magisterial *The Art of Vase Painting in Classical Athens* (1992), produced toward the end of a lifetime of work on Athenian pottery, parades painters' names in the subtitles of virtually every chapter.[27]

The reaction against such an approach had many sources. In other areas of the history of art too, even where the life of the artist can be externally attested, the catalogue raisonné of an artist's work has ceased to be regarded as the peak of scholarship. Attention has shifted to the examination of paintings and sculptures in their historical context of production—sometimes indeed to such an extent that discussion of works of art themselves is reduced to little more than their titles and dates. In other areas of classics there was a marked move to analyzing the Greek and Roman worlds in their own terms. Historians came to prefer to litter their texts, and even their titles, with transliterated, but untranslated, Greek words

---

[23] For batch-buying, see Langridge-Noti (2013); for commissioning, see Burn (1985), Lezzi-Hafter (1997), and more generally Webster (1972), Williams (2013).

[24] Note, for instance, the absence of work by the Pithos Painter from Italy.

[25] The same is even true of sculpture, where literary evidence shows us Roman collectors looking out for works on a particular subject, not works by a particular sculptor; see Cicero *Letters to Atticus* 1.7, 1.8.2, 1.9.2, 1.10.3.

[26] The Beazley Archive can be found at http://www.beazley.ox.ac.uk/archive/default.htm.

[27] The tradition lives on not only through continuing production of monographs on a single painter but also through, e.g., the *Athenian Potters and Painters* volumes (Oakley, Coulson, and Palagia [1997], Oakley and Palagia [2009], Oakley [2014]).

rather than impose upon the Greeks modern concepts (so *miasma* rather than pollution, *aidos* rather than shame, *hybris* rather than violence, and so on).[28] When artists were so far suppressed in the Greek evidence, and even in the evidence of the pottery itself, that Beazley had to invent names for them ("The Fat Boy Painter," "The Woman Painter"), it is hardly surprising that some scholars came to be wary of giving them center stage in the accounts that were trying to understand these works in their original context.[29]

But if not a history of artists, what sort of history of pottery could be written? A history of potters suffers even more disadvantages than a history of painters. Not only are there fewer potters' names preserved than painters' names, but potters' names, for all the interest in some art-collecting circles in the works of such modern "greats" as Bernard Leach, lack the salability even in the modern world that is attached to painters' names. A history of pot shapes has rather more archaeological and scholarly advantages. The link of shape to function guarantees that ancient consumers paid some attention to shape, and the connection between shape and use is indeed highlighted in Aesop's *Fables*.[30] The nonrandom distribution of shapes confirms active local shape preferences, whereas evidence for local preferences for particular painters—rather than just lumpy supply chains—is rather harder to find. A number of scholars have indeed pursued the study of particular shapes of pot, but the oddity, already mentioned, that many shapes were employed variously in completely different contexts guarantees that any history of shape that gets interested in the life of the pot after production is going to be extremely complicated.[31] And, of course, not the least problem is that the *precise* shape of a pot is not its most salient characteristic; indeed, for those handling pots the size, weight, and balance make more impression than do the precise shape, even though these are impossible to convey in textual descriptions or photographs.[32] Even when the whole of a black-figure or red-figure pot is preserved and is visible, it is the painting that primarily attracts attention, not—except in the case of some elaborate "plastic vases"—the pot shape.[33]

It is hardly surprising, therefore, that those who rejected a history of Athenian painted pottery by artist turned instead to a history of Athenian painted pottery by scene. The iconography of Athenian pots had attracted attention from the time that Athenian pots were first excavated in quantity, and indeed early publications of Greek vases, like those by d'Hancarville

[28] Parker (1983), Fisher (1992), Cairns (1993); contrast Williams (1993).
[29] For artists' names as very much to the fore in some early red-figure pottery, see Neer (2002), chap. 3.
[30] In the fable of the crane (or stork) and the fox, Plutarch *Moralia* 614e (Perry [1952], no. 426).
[31] Cf. Puritani (2009); most discussions of particular shapes of pot limit themselves to production and deal with provenance rather minimally, e.g., Bloesch (1940), Philippaki (1967), Brijder (1983; 1991; 2000).
[32] Interest in the weight of pots has been remarkably slow to develop, but see Bentz and Böhr (2002).
[33] On "plastic vases," see True (2006). For early examples, see Williams (2008), for later examples Trümpf-Lyritzaki (1969). The greatest of all the producers of "plastic vases" (e.g., drinking horns in the form of crocodiles devouring blacks) was the potter Sotades, on whom see Hoffmann (1997).

of the pots in Sir William Hamilton's collection, concentrate on explaining their iconography.[34] Beazley himself, although devoting his attention primarily to artists' hands, repeatedly paid close attention to working out the nature of a scene. Many scholars, whose initial training, like Beazley's, was in classical languages and literature, were primarily interested in scenes that could be related to literary texts, and so in identifying Greek myths, and there is a long tradition of scholarship on the relationship between literary texts and painted pottery in the representation of myth.[35] Others, however, realized the potential of pots for also illuminating other aspects of Greek life.

As long ago as 1931, Paul Cloché published a collection of vase scenes relating to Athenian economic life.[36] Most importantly, in 1972, T.B.L. Webster, a scholar trained both in classical literature and in the analysis of painters' hands (he contributed a monograph on the Niobid Painter to Beazley and Jacobsthal's *Bilder griechischer Vasen* series[37]), collected in his *Potter and Patron in Classical Athens* long lists of pots, ordered by subject matter—though the general absence of illustrations from his work made his lists of scenes of little use other than to those already knowledgeable. Webster's book was highly successful at restoring to the scholarly agenda the long-suppressed question of how Athenian pots came to be in Italy. Noting that the Athenian reference of some of the iconography seemed to accord ill with the Etruscan findspot of the pots, he argued that there must have been a market in secondhand Athenian pots. Webster's inclination to identify the scenes on Athenian pots with particular Athenian events on the basis of the presence of historical Athenian names made his invention of a large secondhand pot market essential. Other scholars have seen the Athenian names as much more playful and not requiring us to believe that the pots on which they appeared were commissions, and as a result Webster's secondhand market thesis quickly became notorious and much ridiculed. But the more general problem that the Etruscans acquired pots that represented activities and appearances that cannot have been familiar in Etruria itself has not gone away, and it was Webster's goal to ensure that it did not. He was much less successful in redirecting scholars' attention from artists and representation of myth to the iconography related to everyday life.

It was only with the publication in 1984, and even more the translation in 1989, of a book written by a group of Francophone scholars to accompany an unusual exhibition of photographs of Athenian black-figure and red-figure pottery organized as a joint project of the University of Lausanne and Centre National de la Recherche Scientifique in Paris, that the

---

[34] On d'Hancarville, see Vickers (1987), Haskell (1987), 30–45.

[35] The classic discussion is Robert (1881). See, among many others, Henle (1973), Hedreen (2001), Woodford (2003), Giuliani (2003), and, for links of scenes on pots to tragic and comic drama, Trendall and Webster (1971), Taplin (1992; 2007). Older collections of vase scenes by myth are now superseded by *LIMC*.

[36] Cloché (1931); cf. Ziomecki (1975).

[37] Webster (1935).

possibilities raised by the study of the scenes on Athenian pottery became widely appreciated.[38] This book, *La Cité des images / A City of Images*, offered a series of essays on scenes of particular sorts—"The world of the warrior," "Sacrificial slaughter and initiatory hunt," "Eros the hunter," "The order of women," "Festivals and Mysteries," "Wine: human and divine," "Satyric revels." Although far from exhaustive in covering the range of imagery on Athenian pottery, *La Cité des images* opened up a way of looking at that imagery as a coherent and connected whole, as a "world." Indeed, to such an extent was internal coherence stressed that some contributors to the book seemed to suggest, in a manner that reveals their background in French structuralism, that the imagery had a momentum of its own, independent of the artist (the term *artist*, and Beazley's artists' names, being equally resisted in this book).[39]

Because it banishes the painters, at the same time that *La Cité des images* reveals the possibility of relating the images on Greek painted pottery to the history of the Athenian city-state, it effectively suppresses the history of Athenian painted pottery.[40] The history of painted pottery depends upon Beazley's work because so small a percentage of Athenian pottery can be dated on the basis of excavated contexts. Because it dispenses with data about artists, *La Cité des images* gives a sense neither of the diachronic story of Athenian social life that the changing images on pots reveal nor of the story of how the pots themselves show different things at different times. So, with the exception of Alain Schnapp writing about hunting, none of the contributors shows much interest in chronological sequence or change over time in the images they reproduce.[41] The Greek city is turned into a timeless institution, the life of which was so unchanging that the explorations of social and religious life engaged in by the painters could not be expected to show any patterns over time.[42] The world of imagery is presented as if somehow born fully formed and as if artists simply played with its possibilities as the fancy took them against the background of a culture that was unchanging.

There were good reasons why *La Cité des images* took this approach. When earlier scholars had attempted to relate Greek vases to Greek history, they had attempted to relate them to particular episodes in Greek political history. They did so by looking for precise reflections of historical events in pot painting, and by suggesting that painted pottery served as a form of political propaganda. Pots were used not as historical evidence but

---

[38] Bérard (1984/1988).

[39] For a critique of the book, see Osborne (1991); for the intellectual background, see Osborne (2012).

[40] For the English translation, painter's names were added by Robert Guy to the list of plates.

[41] Schnapp's historical approach is even more apparent in his monograph on hunting scenes (1997). Almost contemporaneously with *La cite des images*, the Czech scholar Jan Bažant was taking a much more historical approach to the interpretation of the images on Athenian pottery and insisting (Bažant [1985], 76) that "on peut montrer que les images du 6ᵉ et du 5ᵉ siècle se referent à deux niveaux très différents de cette réalité. Le contraste qui existe entre ces niveaux rend impossible toutes les généralisations sur 'la vie sociale' illustrée par les vases athéniens de ces deux siècles"; but Bažant's work has been little noted.

[42] This is always a danger with books organized by iconography. Compare van Straten (1995).

as confirmation of what was otherwise known from texts. One particularly prominent example of this is John Boardman's attempt to link the popularity of scenes of Herakles on Athenian black-figure vase painting to the Peisistratid tyranny in Athens. Herodotos and later authors tell us that Peisistratos's second, short-lived, attempt to seize control in Athens was achieved by having a woman dressed up as Athena lead him to the Acropolis; Boardman suggested that when sixth-century pot painters showed scenes of Athena leading Herakles before the gods on Olympus as he joins the Olympian deities they were gesturing toward Peisistratos's entry to Athens.[43]

There are indeed times when it is hard to resist the idea that Athenians looking at a particular pot might recall a particular historical circumstance. When a late sixth-century plate showing a cavalryman in Scythian costume has "Miltiades is *kalos*" written upon it, association with the Athenian Miltiades, who ruled in the Thracian Chersonese and was involved in the Persian king Dareios's expedition against Scythia, looks inviting.[44] Similarly, can the painter who shows a sculptor at work carving a herm, writing "Hiparchos is *kalos*" around it, not have had in mind that Hipparchos son of Peisistratos had been the man behind the erection of herms halfway between Athens and each of the villages in the countryside of Attica?[45]

Such particular allusions are, however, historically rather trivial. They show us that one painter at one moment was persuaded, whether by his own sense of what would attract or amuse purchasers or by a particular invitation, to create an image that would assert its timeliness by responding to a particular event. But they show us little else. There may have been some coded political message in such individual scenes, but if decoding them was the preserve of a particular patron or a small circle, their historical significance remains minor. It may be possible, where we have information about how a pot was used and the sort of assemblage in which it was found, to construct something a bit more substantial in the way of a political history around a particular pot. One promising case involved the finding of a pot showing the statues of the tyrannicides (see 10.2) in the grave surmounted by the memorial to one Dexileos (10.19), killed in war in the first decade of the fourth century BC. In this case, the peculiarities of the epitaph, which alone of all epitaphs from classical Athens records the date of birth of the deceased, already suggested that his death with the cavalry in 394/393 was celebrated in politically charged way; Athenians who read the inscription and contemplated the monument were being subtly informed that the Athenian cavalry who were losing their lives in the Corinthian War were not men who had previously sided with the Thirty Tyrants but were young men of unimpeachable democratic credentials.[46] The presence of tyrannicide imagery on the pottery further stresses those creden-

---

[43] Boardman (1972; 1975b). For various critiques, see Osborne (1983), Cook (1987b).
[44] *ARV* 163.8; Ashmolean Museum AN1879.175.
[45] *ARV* 75.59; Copenhagen NM 119; see further Osborne (1985).
[46] See RO 7, Azoulay (2014), 109, 142–46; cf. Osborne (1998a), 13–16, Ober (2003), Osborne (2010d).

tials. But such cases are rare, and it is notable that in this case the history comes not from the image on the painted pot alone, but from the context in which that pot is found.

Over the past two decades, scholars have attempted to reestablish the importance of the artist, by going beyond simply seeing artists as a collection of particular graphic habits, and have tried to establish better ways of relating pots to history. They have done so, however, primarily by choosing particular case studies and exploring them in depth. Thus the most interesting work on artists has focused on the so-called pioneers of red-figure vase painting, attempting to capture something of their interactions with each other and with the Athens of their time as well as understanding better their graphic habits.[47] Similarly, the most ambitious attempt to read Athenian attitudes out of the scenes on pots concentrates its attention on the bystanders often included, particularly by black-figure painters, as spectators of the central scene—an approach whose value for diachronic discussion is severely limited by the relationship between technique and composition.[48] For all that these works have pioneered new methodologies and enriched our understanding of Athenian pot painting, they have ended up keeping style and subject matter apart. My concentration in this book on what happened "generally and for the most part" inevitably means that I largely pass over the distinctive contributions of individual painters, but I do so in an attempt to bring back together the story of what is painted and the story of the style in which it is painted.

2. The Peculiarity of Athenian Painted Pottery

In the chapters that follow I explore the history that is centrally the history painted on Athenian pottery. I focus not on individual pots in individual contexts but on the way in which the general trend of imagery changes over time. In doing so I exploit three features that make archaic and classical Athenian painted pottery stand out when compared to either more recent ceramics or other ancient ceramics: their individuality, their distribution, and their contexts of use.

First, although these pots were inexpensive and made in large quantities, very few of the images painted on them are found in multiple copies.[49] There are plenty of pots showing the same theme, or showing the same basic composition, and indeed it is a notable fact that most themes appear on a wide range of shapes of pot.[50] But no artist seems to have sat down

---

[47] See Neer (2002), Hedreen (2016).
[48] Stansbury-O'Donnell (2006).
[49] The question of just how cheap has been much debated: Vickers and Gill (1994), Pritchard (1999), Neer (2002), Bresson (2015), 374. As Lissarrague (2013), 21, points out, the same absence of repetition marks out Athenian drama, where every play was put on just once.
[50] Neatly shown in two pie charts for late archaic scenes of women bathing and classical scenes of a kneeling bather by Sutton (2009a), 274.

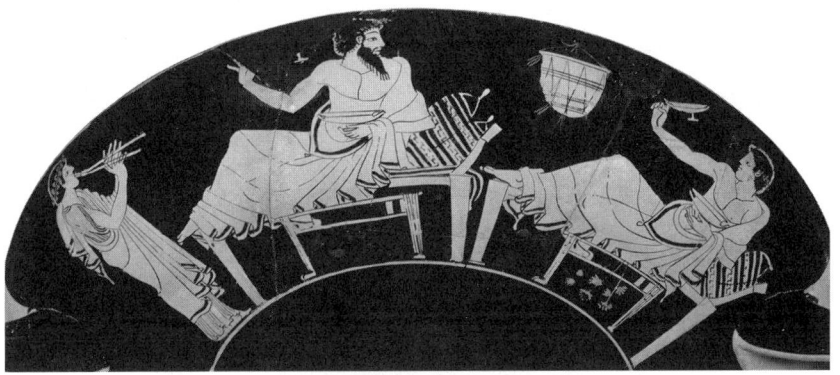

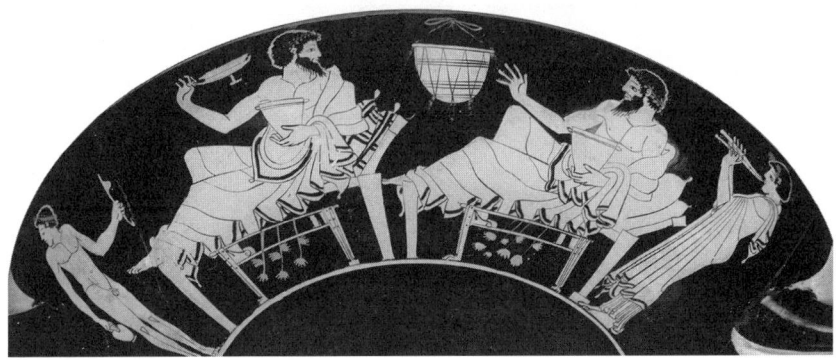

Figure 2.3–4. Exterior of red-figure cup, diameter 0.287 m, attributed to Makron, from Vulci, ca. 490. *ARV* 467.126. Munich Staatliche Antikensammlung en 2643. © Staatliche Antikensammlung en und Glyptothek München. Photograph by Renate Kühling.

and painted a dozen of the same thing in a morning.[51] Not a dozen, not, with a few exceptions, even two. Most commonly even artists who repeat essentially the same scene from one side of a pot to another or from one pot to another, tease the viewer into a game of "spot the difference," changing the details even while they retain the same basic subject and composition (**2.3–4** and plates 3 and 4). Only when using the one or more (regularly three) standing figures as space fillers on the "back" sides of pots do some artists come close to repeating themselves (**2.5–6**).

We know of only one workshop where any degree of specialization seems to have been practiced, the so-called Penthesileia workshop.[52] Here one artist painted insides, another outsides; one artist tended to paint only particular sorts of figures, and so on. But even this workshop did not produce multiple identical products. Nothing about the products of that workshop suggest that the way they organized their painting gave them any competitive advantage over other workshops, and no other workshop copied this pattern of work. Instead, in every workshop each pot was differently decorated. There might be pairs of pots, and iconographic discus-

---

[51] Steiner (2007) discusses what she calls repetition in Athenian vases, but she chooses to treat as the same images that are actually different.
[52] Osborne (2004c); note the unusual concentration of works from the Penthesileia workshop at Cerveteri, La Genière (2009), 344.

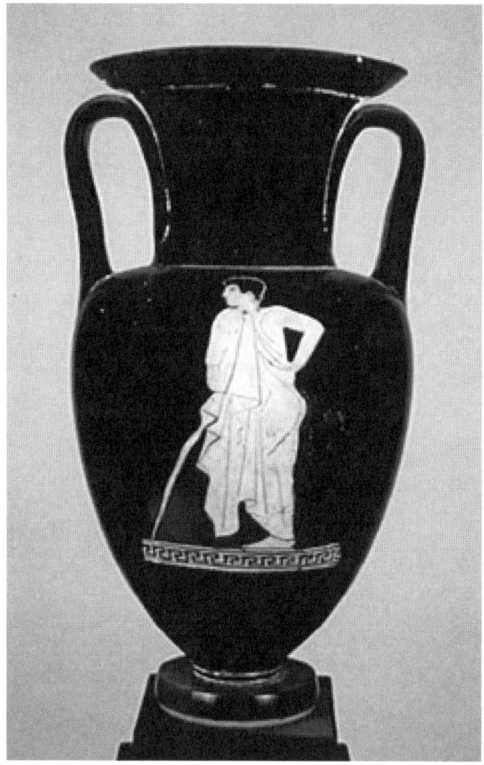 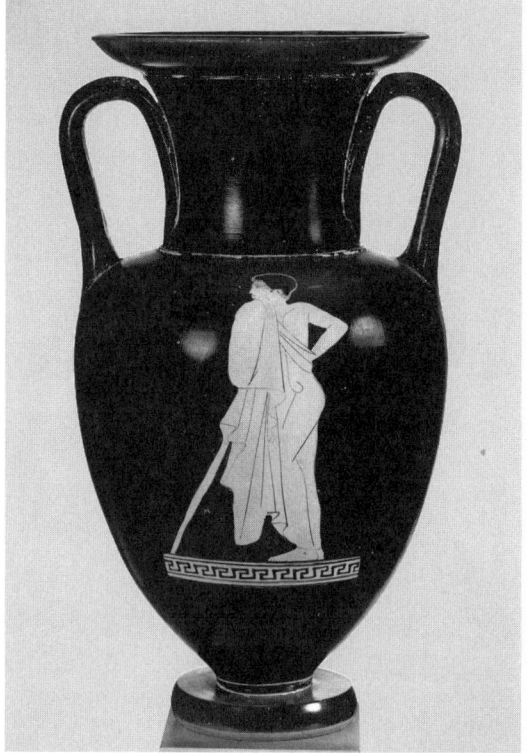

Figure 2.5. Reverse of red-figure Nolan amphora, height 0.34 m, attributed to the Phiale Painter, from Nola, ca. 440. *ARV* 1014.1. Louvre G436. Photo © RMN-Grand Palais (musée du Louvre) / Hervé Lewandowski.

Figure 2.6. Reverse of red-figure Nolan amphora, height 0.325 m, attributed to the Phiale Painter from south Italy, ca. 440. *ARV* 1014.2. Munich Staatliche Antikensammlung en 2330. © Staatliche Antikensammlung en und Glyptothek München. Photograph by Renate Kühling.

sions need to be aware of this possibility, but there were no sets of identical images.[53] If anyone set out to buy a "*symposion* service," it was coordinated imagery that they acquired, not identical imagery. They might even have difficulty acquiring identical shapes.[54] Particular potters certainly seem to have specialized in particular shapes: some (for example, Kleophrades) seem generally to have made large vessels (amphoras, kraters, hydriai); some (for example, Hieron (**2.7**, 9.1) or Python) seem generally to have made cups—and to have done so for several painters. Some (notably Sotades) seem to have been endlessly inventive.[55] But to judge general prac-

[53] One example where the existence of a "pair" should affect interpretation is when Makron paints two cup interiors showing maenads aiming a blow at a satyr with a thyrsus (Munich 2654, *ARV* 462.47, Kunisch [1997], no. 340; N.Y. Met. 06.1152, *ARV* 493.52, Kunisch [1997], no. 151), two where relations seem equivocal (Florence 3943, *ARV* 478.311, Kunisch [1997], no. 188; private collection, Kunisch [1997], no. 189) and a fifth in which a maenad has her arm around a satyr (Louvre G 144, *ARV* 462. 43, Kunisch [1997], no. 98). Four of the five cups are comparable in size, and three of the four are signed by Hieron as potter. See McNally (1978), 125; Kunisch (1997), 79.

[54] Cf. Lynch (2015), 236–56, for the constantly changing shape preferences displayed in sympotic assemblages at Athens.

[55] Hoffmann (1997).

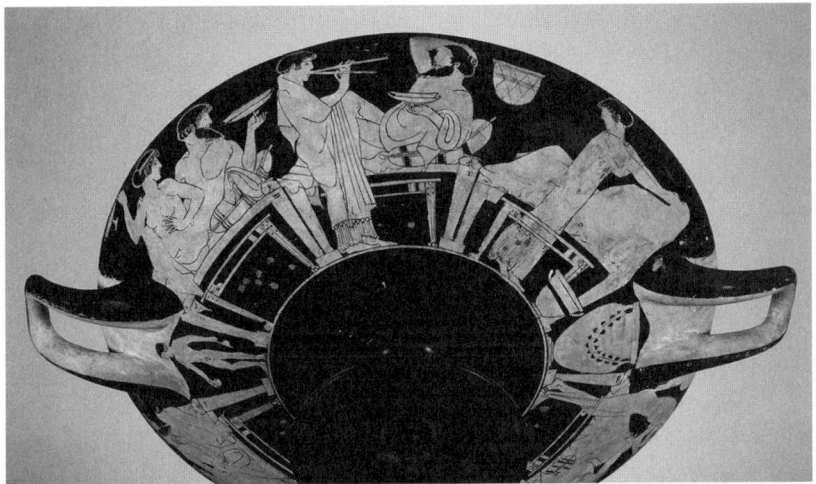

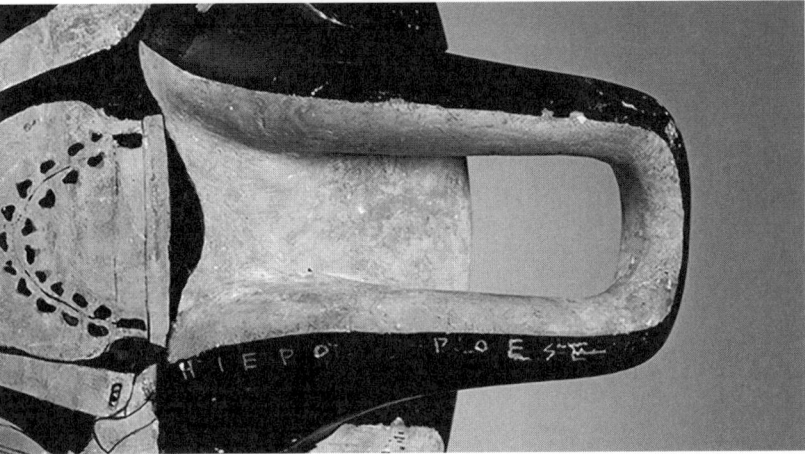

Figure 2.7. Red-figure cup, diameter 0.415 m, signed by Hieron as potter on the handle and attributed to Makron as painter, from Vulci, ca. 480. *ARV* 467.118. New York Metropolitan Museum of Art, 20.246. www.metmuseum.org.

tice by the practice of those who sign their pots, potters seem to have been no more inclined than painters to set up a production line and churn out large numbers of close-to-identical products.

How can I be sure about this when we have certainly lost the vast majority of what was potted and painted? Robert Cook reckoned that we have about a quarter of 1 percent of all pots ever made.[56] He made this calculation on the basis of calculating the total number of the distinctive "Panathenaic" amphoras full of oil given out as prizes at the athletic and musical festival of the Panathenaia and comparing to this the number that survive.[57] There are all sorts of questions about this calculation and about whether survival rate for prize amphoras, which seem to have become "collectors' pieces," is likely to be the same as for other vessels, but this figure is

[56] Cook (1959).
[57] See chapter 3.

probably more or less of the right order of magnitude.[58] But if only one in four hundred vases survive, then in theory for every unique pot we know 399 identical pots might have perished. That may be a theoretical possibility, but the chances of the (say) twelve million pots once made containing tens of thousands of duplicates, when the upwards of 30,000 or so pots that survive contain perhaps a couple of dozen duplicates, are more or less nil. Whatever biases have affected the survival of painted pottery there is no reason to think that those biases have systematically discriminated against the survival of multiple copies of the same shape and scene. The fraction of pots once painted that survives may be small, but there is no reason to doubt that it constitutes a valid sample.

The question of sample is relevant to the second and third oddities about archaic and classical Athenian pottery. The specimens of Greek pottery that dominate the museums of western Europe and North America were found primarily outside Athens, outside Attica, the territory in which Athenians lived, and indeed outside mainland or Aegean Greece. As I noted at the start of this chapter, most of the best-known and best-preserved Athenian pots, including most of the pots I discuss in this book, have been found not in Greece but in Italy, and primarily in Etruria or areas of Italy that were under Etruscan control.[59]

The third feature that sets Athenian painted pottery apart is the wide range of contexts in which it was used. Painted pots were certainly employed in domestic contexts. Fragments of painted pottery occur in houses that have been excavated and in rubbish deposits dumped in the bottom of wells both in Athens/Attica and elsewhere, and this makes it clear that some shapes of painted pottery were to be found in at least limited quantities in many Greek households and used more or less day to day, alongside plain black pottery.[60] Painted pots were also an important type of offering in sanctuaries to gods and goddesses. Once more, this did not apply to all shapes of pot, nor did every sanctuary attract pottery in the same quantity or pots of the same shape, but there is reason to believe that at least some pots were painted specifically for dedication. Finally, pots were deposited in graves in Athens as well as in Etruria, but the practices of burial were different in the two places, and this affected the quantity, the form, and (not least since form and imagery were linked) the imagery of the pots deposited in the graves.

In Athens in the fifth century what was put into the grave seems to have been largely limited to vessels used in the course of the funerary ritual.[61]

---

[58] There are certainly reasons for thinking that in some cases, at least, we have a slightly higher proportion surviving than this, see Bresson and de Callataÿ (2013), 21n4; Sapirstein (2013), 494; Sapirstein (2014), but we would be talking about up to 1 percent, not a completely different order of magnitude.

[59] Spivey (1991), Reusser (2002). For the question of whether Athenian potters painted a particular selection of scenes specifically for the Etruscan market, see further below.

[60] For one particularly fine household collection of sympotic pottery, see Lynch (2011). For a reiteration of the evidence for use of pottery (as opposed to metalware) in households, see Neer (2002), 206–15.

[61] Kurtz and Boardman (1971), 100–105.

Scenes on some lekythoi (oil flasks) themselves show lekythoi being used to adorn the outside of the grave, and it is lekythoi that are particularly deposited in Athenian graves, along with some cups, bowls, and jugs. By contrast, lekythoi are more or less absent from Etruscan burials, where the graves often take the form of rooms cut into the soft rock, rooms that receive decoration and objects as if they were places for living. The Etruscan grave assemblage tends to be dominated by pot shapes associated with drinking parties: we find the amphoras (for example, 1.1) that are wine containers, the hydriai (for example, 3.9) that contained the water to mix with the wine, the kraters (for example, 1.2/3.6 and plate 5) in which wine and water were mixed, and both shallow and deep cups (kylikes [for example, 4.9] and skyphoi), from which the wine was drunk. At some Etruscan sites, there seems to have been a "set" of shapes that were standardly deposited in a grave (for example, krater plus drinking vessel in fifth-century Spina) but such "sets" neither come from the same workshop nor share the same iconography.[62]

What is important is not simply that Athenian painted pots are to be found in the three distinct contexts of domestic use, religious dedication, and commemoration of the dead, but that pots of the same shape, and showing essentially the same scenes, may be found in any of those three contexts. There are very few exceptions to this, of which the white-ground lekythos, found only in funerary contexts and only in Athens and rather few sites elsewhere (notably Eretria and Gela), is the most important.[63]

The absence of repetition among Athenian pots, the finding of these pots predominantly outside Attica, and the absence of any exclusive association between pots bearing particular scenes and any particular context of deposition are features upon which my analysis in this book depends. The individuality of Athenian pots, that is, the close-to-uniqueness of virtually every single pot, makes it both possible and plausible to imagine that each pot tells its own story, and means that particular care needs to be taken in drawing generalizations from any individual image. In the case of mass-produced pottery, one can generally be confident that if one pot of a particular kind or bearing a particular image was made, then tens, hundreds, or thousands were made, and one can be equally sure that no pot of that sort would be made unless the manufacturer anticipated that there would be a more or less general demand for it. By contrast, in the case of Athenian pottery, where almost every pot is unique, there is nothing to prevent a pot being a one-off idea or a particular commission. It is always possible that the picture painted on a pot was painted for a customer or agent who came into the workshop and dictated what he wanted shown.[64] But equally, there is no need to invoke unique patrons in order to explain unique scenes, since painters had little reason to constrain their subject matter to subjects they knew from past experience would sell, given that

---

[62] Cf. Langridge-Noti (2013), 68–69 with n. 36.

[63] On white-ground lekythoi, see Oakley (2004).

[64] The clearest example of this involves mythical scenes and a grave context: see Burn (1985), Hoffmann (1997). See further note 22 above.

the downside risk of painting on a single pot a scene that no one liked was too small to cause concern. That *every* pot tells its own story only renders speculation over specific patrons' demands vain, and makes all the more striking the coordinated changes that occur across the whole corpus of individual pots.

Just like the unconscious artistic habits that enabled Beazley to identify coherent artists, common trends across individual pots promise to reveal an underlying coherence of attitudes. In principle, these might be attitudes shared by patrons and imposed by them on painters, or might be shared by the painters themselves. The very variety of scenes painted, however, strongly suggests that the market imposed only light constraints upon painters as to what they should paint. We should therefore take the fact that individual decisions by painters display the same tendencies to indicate that it is the painters' own common ways of thinking, indeed their underlying collective ideology, that is on display. The worldview suggested by painted pottery is bottom-up rather than top-down.

The use of the pots of similar shapes and bearing similar images in very different contexts similarly enhances the confidence that we can have that the range of imagery displayed on pots was not primarily determined by the circumstances in which the pot was finally removed from use. Specialist shapes apart, such as, most importantly, the fifth-century black-figure and white-ground lekythoi made very largely for the single purpose of being put into graves in Athens and in relatively few other places, Athenian pottery seems to have been adapted neither in shape nor imagery either for dedication or for deposit in the grave.[65] This implies that outside Athens, Athenian pots were not in general acquired specially for deposit in graves, and there is little evidence in the fifth century for the Athenian pots put into graves outside Athens having been specially selected for that purpose on the basis of their imagery.[66] The quality of pots found on the Athenian Acropolis suggests that some care was taken in the selection of material for dedication there, but the range of shapes and of imagery (including the presence of sexually explicit imagery), suggests that the fact of dedication imposed only loose constraints on what material was regarded as suitable.[67]

If the individuality of Athenian painted pottery and its multifarious use can be seen more or less straightforwardly to guarantee that the imagery that appears on surviving pottery is not systematically biased as a result of the contexts in which it has been preserved, the fact that most of the best-preserved pots were found in Etruria might seem, on the surface, to skew the sample in a problematic way. Ironically, one effective way of showing that this is not the case is to examine a pot that is one of the small number

---

[65] It is notable that even the very large "parade cups" that are plausibly explained as made for dedication in sanctuaries, have turned up more frequently in Etruscan graves than on the Athenian acropolis: see Tsingarida (2009).

[66] For suggestions of careful selection of pots for a grave in Sicily, see Marconi (2004) (with comments by Osborne [2004c]).

[67] For the pottery from the Acropolis, see Graef and Langlotz (1925–33), Wagner (1999; 2001).

that have seemed highly likely to have been painted in response to a particular commission. In looking closely at an unusually specific image, we get to see how its uniqueness conspires with issues of use and distribution to encourage the view that the history painted on Athenian pottery is fundamentally an Athenian history.

The example I take is the famous, and puzzling, late fifth-century volute krater in Naples known as the Pronomos Vase (**2.8**). This pot gets its name from the seated figure depicted and named at the center of one side: the Theban pipe-player Pronomos.[68] Pronomos, a figure about whom we are informed by surviving texts, is shown surrounded by the actors of a play for which he was, presumably, the musician, and which, given the victory tripods, was presumably successful. The individual members of the cast, together with the figures of playwright and director who are on either side of Pronomos, are, like Pronomos himself, named. There seems to be such a high degree of particularity to this vase that the temptation is strong to regard it as commissioned to celebrate the victory of the play in question, and as showing the cast of an actual performance.[69] Even here, however, it is worth pausing to note that scholars' confidence in this hypothesis is partly drawn from what they know of other pots. That is, the absence of comparable pots is one of the things that has encouraged scholars to think that this is not simply a scene that a theater lover might collect in order to have a souvenir of a recent dramatic victory, but was exceptionally commissioned. Although there are different kinds and degrees of uniqueness, the singularity of *all* Athenian pots should lead us to pause before attributing too much force to this argument.

The findspot of this pot complicates the picture. For the Pronomos Vase was found not in Athens but in Italy, not among household remains or dedicated in a sanctuary, but in a grave. How could a pot made specially to celebrate a victory in the Dionysiac festival at Athens end up in a tomb at Ruvo in Italy? The multiple contexts in which painted pottery was used stand in the way of offering a simple answer to this. This particular shape, a volute krater, might be used in the context of a symposium, it might be offered as a dedication, or it might be deposited in a tomb, if not in Attica then certainly in Italy. The fact that this is a pot, or even that this is a particular shape of pot, does little to restrict the theoretical options on its use. And the very popularity of Athenian pottery of all types in Italian tombs, and of volute kraters in Italian tombs of late fifth- and fourth-century date, makes it possible that the imagery on the pot has rather little to do with the decision to deposit it in this tomb. There are grounds then, even in this case, for hesitating before we construct an exceptional story to account for the presence of this pot bearing this scene in this tomb.

It is worth reviewing the range of possible stories we might tell in order to account for the presence of the Pronomos Vase in this Ruvo tomb. We might present a series of alternatives. Either the satyr play for which

---

[68] For the latest discussions of this pot, see Taplin and Wyles (2010).

[69] I offer some arguments on the basis of onomastics against the latter assumption in Osborne (2010e); cf. also Juncker (2003).

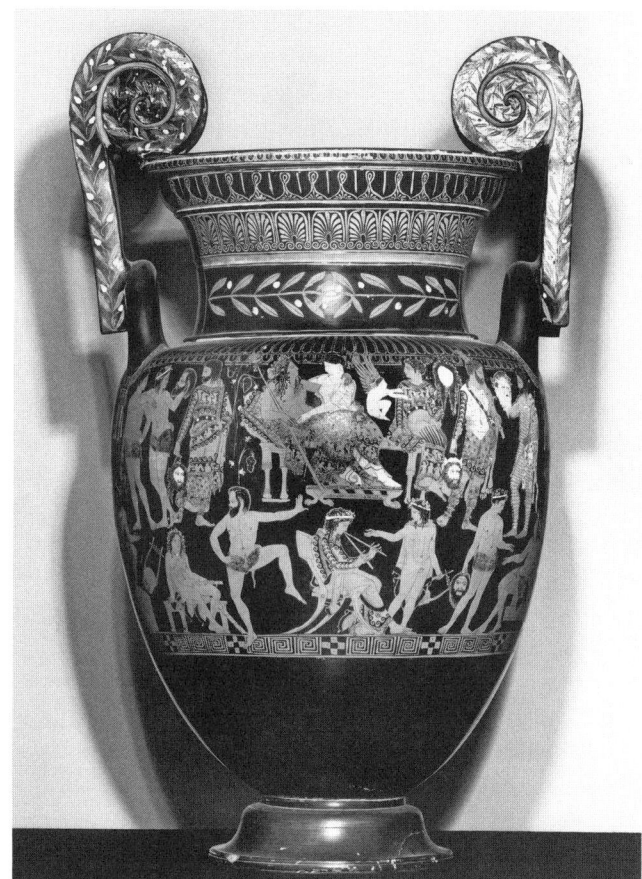

Figure 2.8. Red-figure volute krater, height 0.75 m, showing cast of and scene from a satyr play, for which the aulos player Pronomos is shown playing the double aulos, name vase of the Pronomos Painter, from Ruvo, ca. 400. *ARV* 1336.1. Naples 3240. © Hirmer Fotoarchiv Munich.

Pronomos played is historical or it isn't. If historical, either it happened in Athens or it did not. The vase was either commissioned or not. If it was commissioned, it was either commissioned by a resident of Athens or not. Either the vase was deposited in the grave at Ruvo when new, or not. It was either acquired legitimately or not. If it was acquired legitimately, it was presumably either purchased or received as a gift. We can form these various possibilities into more or less complex stories. But there is no unproblematically simple story. Even if we believe in satyr drama being performed with a Boiotian aulos player in Ruvo, perhaps the least likely of all hypotheses, it is not clear why anyone would commission from an Athenian workshop a pot commemorating such a play, only then immediately to use it in a grave. But if we opt for the vase commemorating an actual performance in Athens of a satyr play, so that the play's victory might be celebrated at a party at which the vase was used (perhaps at some revival of the play in a deme theater, so as to allow time for the krater to be potted and painted after the victory?), then we may be able to tell a simple story from production to use, but we are left with a very uncertain story of how the vase gets from Athenian party to Ruvo grave.

If we want a simple story about the Pronomos krater we have, in fact, to downplay the historicity of the performance, and hence the reference of the names to real people, and stress the pot as an exploration of appearance and reality. Rather than taking this to be a pot painted to a specific order and for a specific occasion, we must contemplate the possibility that it was painted to attract a buyer who would see in that issue of appearance and reality an appropriate image of his or her own uncertainties about the reality of the afterlife. There is plenty in this vase that does indeed play on appearance and reality, and not least the juxtaposition of actors turned into satyrs by their satyr breeches to the "real" satyrs of myth. There are, in fact, plenty of Athenian pots that apply the names of real people to painted figures, so why should this not be simply one of those—a generic dramatic scene where the painter has chosen to use a "real" aulos player's name to the aulos player?[70]

It is important to emphasize the consequences of adopting this simple story, or indeed adopting any view that rejects as not historical a satyr play for which Pronomos was the aulos player and Demetrios the poet.[71] The pot ceases to be evidence for any historical event and becomes at best only indirect and distant evidence for Athenian dramatic history. If we go for the simple story, which makes this pot like the great majority of Athenian pots, a pot painted with a scene thought likely to attract a buyer and on which the painter amused himself by adding, for those who might appreciate it, a contemporary allusion, like the contemporary allusions made by *kalos* names, we jettison precisely the historical occasion that has seemed, on the basis of the specific writing on the pot, so clear, and that encouraged the view that this was a pot that had been specially ordered.

What is true of the Pronomos krater is true also of the vast bulk of Athenian pottery found in Italy: the context in which the pottery is found has no direct or specific connection with the particular imagery shown. This strongly suggests that at least a significant part of the consuming public for Athenian pottery read even the most highly specific images either in a generalizing way or in a way not conceived of by the Athenian producers. Ironically, the more confident we are that a particular historical event triggered the production of this pot, the more we must accept that the purchasers of Athenian pots in Italy were voracious in their appetite for attractive pottery, whether or not the scene meant anything to them. It is this voracity that underpins this book.

The tension between the three features of Athenian painted pottery that I have signaled as odd in the history of pottery, applies not simply to the Pronomos krater but generally. The pots are highly individualized, not standardized, yet very few of them end up in contexts that obviously

---

[70] Webster (1972), chap. 2, collects instances of pots with real names, which he takes in all cases to indicate special commissions; contrast Neer (2002), chap. 3, on the use of real names by the Pioneers. Where we know the findspots of pots on which the Pioneers name themselves or each other, those findspots are in Italy.

[71] We know, in fact, of no Athenian poet of satyr-plays by the name Demetrios, see Osborne (2010e), 149.

explain their peculiarity. Pots were used in unusually various contexts, but correlating context of find to nature of imagery is, with the exception of some limited classes of pot, more often than not far from straightforward. Whereas one would expect the flexibility of Athenian potters and painters with regard to shape and image to mean that they matched image and shape to market, both in the sense of geographical market and in the sense of context of use, those correlations are rare rather than common.[72]

The manifest imitation of Etruscan bucchero shapes by the prolific late sixth-century Athenian workshop associated with the potter Nikosthenes is one of the things that marks that workshop out as uniquely concentrating on the Italian market,[73] or, rather, it marks out the fact that other workshops do not so concentrate. That particular Nikosthenic shapes were popular in particular towns of Etruria further stresses the *possibility* of significant market discrimination that extended to the sorts of scenes shown and makes it particularly marked that no other workshop followed suit.[74] Scholars have sought to explain some classes of imagery on Athenian pottery by reckoning them to have been made specifically for the Etruscan market, but, as with the Nikosthenic shapes, it is easier to find cases where Athenian artists assume that the Etruscans will want a different sort of imagery than to find cases where clear selection processes were at work. Thus there is not much doubt that the curious group of stamnoi and one-handled kantharoi from the so-called Perizoma group, on which athletes are clad in loincloths, were potted and painted in that way for the Etruscans, a culture that did not practice athletics naked, unlike the Greeks—though some Etruscan tombs happily display naked athletes.[75] But claims that the particular group of Dionysiac scenes on stamnoi known as "Lenaians" or that sexually explicit scenes (**2.9**) were made especially for the Etruscans are much more dubious.[76]

The broad overlap in imagery between pots found in Italy and those found elsewhere makes clear that Athenian potters and painters in general did not feel the need to create new iconographies in order to satisfy these specific markets. That some Athenian workshops occasionally thought to

---

[72] Cf. Stissi (2009), 34: "My stress on special patterns and differentiation should not let us overlook that (a) any Siana cup (by any painter, with any kind of image) could go anywhere, to any context and (b) most kinds of images and almost all painters were not focused on specific areas or functional contexts, and can be found in any find spot of Siana cups."

[73] For Nikosthenic pottery and its market, see Tosto (1999), Lyons (2009). Note also Malagardis (1997) on mastoids, Bundrick (2015) on eye-cups.

[74] Cf. Lyons (2009), who notes that at Orvieto and Chiusi there is a preference for having Nikosthenic pyxides in matching pairs and that "discriminating choices were made in accordance with local ceremonial needs, for which the imagery of heroic apotheosis, dancing, processions, horse-races, and mock-combats were *a propos*," and that whereas "pyxides from Etruscan contexts are oriented towards a masculine sphere of heroic *agones*, athletic contests, and battles" "subjects that appeal to feminine sensibilities—marriage, childbirth, and religious processions—are predominant in Greek and eastern Mediterranean religious precincts" (2009), 171. For an overview of peculiar Etruscan acquisition patterns, see La Genière (2006), 11–14. For Nikosthenes and the East, see Williams (2013), 48; Tsingarida (2008).

[75] Shapiro (2000), 318–29; Lesky (2007).

[76] I discuss this claim about the Lenaians, made by La Genière (1987), in Osborne (1997a); for the claim of sexually explicit scenes (La Genière [2009]), see chapter 7.

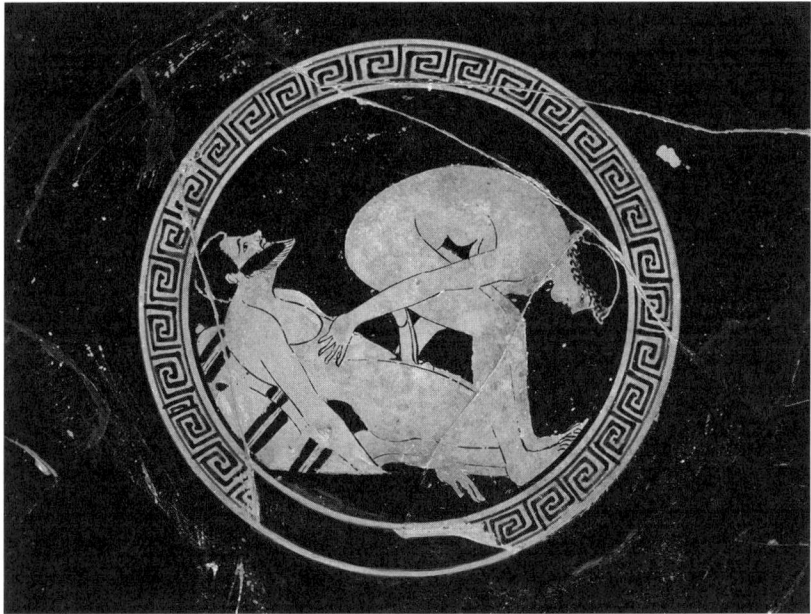

Figure 2.9. Red-figure cup, diameter 0.226 m, attributed to the Dokimasia Painter, from Vulci. *ARV* 412.10. London, British Museum 1836,0224.173 (E 818). © The Trustees of the British Museum.

cater especially to the Etruscan eye shows that Athenian painters expected the Etruscans to be interested in what was shown (that is, they did not think of their pots as merely "salable ballast"), but the Etruscans, it seems, although they bought Athenian pottery for itself and not for its contents (unlike, for example, those who purchased Corinthian perfume containers), bought Athenian pottery whether or not what was painted upon it observed their particular local preferences or reflected a world with which they were familiar.[77]

The generally weak correlation between image and market has advantages and disadvantages. The disadvantage is that writing the history of an individual painted pot turns out to be far from straightforward: we cannot read off a unique circumstance of use from a unique scene. The advantage, however, is that, since the chances of an image being created for and matched to a particular market or purchaser are slim, we do not have to know the individual circumstances of use of a pot in order to appreciate the burden that it carried for contemporary viewers and users. Our unique pots will, after all, allow certain kinds of generalization—indeed they demand it.

If the distribution of scenes does not correlate closely with geographical distribution, what does it correlate with? The broad patterns of icono-

---

[77] For salable ballast, see Gill (1991). For the general contention, cf. Lissarrague (1987), 261 (abstract of his article): "It seems that people exported vases, rather than images," 268, "En raisonnant sur les choix iconographiques, on oublie que les images ne sont pas immatérielles. Véhiculées par des vases . . . elles sont secondaires par rapport au vase lui même."

graphic change that I shall discuss in the remainder of this book are themselves the evidence here. What would we have to believe about the Etruscans in order to believe that Athenian pots had their iconography determined by the Etruscan market, not simply occasionally and in specific cases—as has sometimes been thought, with regard to scenes of Aineias for instance[78]—but systematically and in the vast majority of cases? The coherent patterns that we shall find to the changing iconographic choices of Athenian painters show that we would have to reckon that the widely scattered towns constituting "the Etruscan market" changed their iconographic demands in some coordinated way. This is a highly implausible suggestion a priori; it is even more implausible in the light of what the distribution of Nikosthenic pots shows about the different demands of different Etruscan towns. It is a much more economical and plausible hypothesis that pot painters working in Athens painted for those whom they knew and whose tastes and prejudices they could predict—for their fellow Athenians. There is no difficulty in believing that a single political unit, and in particular one that put as much stress as did democratic Athens on internal unity, should display coordinated changes in preferences and taste. What this requires us to believe about the Etruscan market is simply that it was, at least when treated as a whole, omnivorous, that is, that Athenian pottery as such was sufficiently attractive for the imagery it bore to have little effect on its finding a buyer somewhere in Etruria.[79]

Revealing the coordinated trends in Athenian imagery is the concern of this book. In concentrating on trends, I shall bypass the individual concerns of particular painters and purchasers of pots to gain access to the preference and prejudices of the pot-producing and pot-purchasing population more generally. I take as my examples very largely pots painted in the red-figure technique, from its origins around 520 BC to the middle of the fifth century. There are all sorts of problems with the absolute dating of Athenian pots. There are very few well-dated archaeological contexts—the tomb of the Athenians who died at Marathon in 490 is one, the deposits (pits on the Acropolis, wells in the Agora) in which debris from the Persian sack of Athens was buried are the most important—and dates for the inception of red-figure and its subsequent development turn on them. After a lot of recent debate, most scholars would accept that red-figure began *after* rather than *before* 520.[80] Dating individual pots still in general rests on views about the relationship of one painter to another, or of that pot to the rest of the painter's body of work. Fortunately for the purposes of my discussion it is sufficient to situate images into a relatively broad chronological range. Although I will in some cases try to tell a story of development, my main concern is with how the choice of scene painted on pots in the middle of the fifth century compared with the choice of scene

---

[78] See the remarks of Canciani in *LIMC* I.1 395.
[79] I argued the case for the voracity of the Etruscan market in more detail in Osborne (2001); compare also Reusser (2002). I make the case for the iconography of Athenian pots being broadly understandable in Osborne (2012).
[80] See Rotroff (2009), T. L. Shear (1993); Williams (1996), 245–50; Neer (2002), 186–205.

painted on pots around 500. It is important to me that the world of around 500 BC is indeed a pre-Persian-Wars world, and that the world of the middle of the fifth century is both post-Persian Wars and pre-Peloponnesian War, but it is not important to me to be able to give precise dates to individual pots. Not only does precise dating pretend to a knowledge that we do not have, it is in danger of creating a false impression of the rapidity with which knowledge is transmitted in the ancient Greek world.

I have limited myself to red-figure pottery and to a broad-brush picture for two reasons: on the one hand, I wish to eliminate such changes in imagery as may be occasioned by technical changes in how the images were drawn, such as the change from the black-figure to the red-figure technique; on the other, I wish to reveal the city that painters shared, not the idiosyncratic city of the individual artist. There is no doubt that the invention of the red-figure technique was seized upon by artists as an opportunity to explore types of scene that, for one reason or another, they had previously regarded as unsuitable for depiction on black-figure pottery, and in particular as an opportunity to explore scenes that relate to life rather than to myth. There is equally no doubt that individual artists were attracted to different aspects of the world they saw, and of the world they imagined, and different painters produce significantly contrasting ranges of imagery, even when painting very much the same shapes for very much the same market. The contrasts between the scenes painted by Exekias and by the Amasis Painter have often been observed, and so too those between the scenes painted by the Kleophrades and the Berlin Painters.[81] But as far as I am concerned in this study such differences are mere noise, since I am not here primarily interested in individual painters. I shall take advantage of Beazley's work for establishing a chronological framework, but I shall focus not upon the iconographic choices of individual hands identified by Beazley, but upon iconographic trends that cut across artists and workshops. My interest is in revealing how the scenes on Athenian pottery that relate not to myth but to life changed over time, and in accounting for the changes.

Since I will frequently make claims about whether a scene or a combination of scenes is common or rare, I must make the basis of this clear. This work is largely based on the pots classified by Beazley in *ARV*, initially inspected through the photographs in the Beazley archive. I have not based myself on Beazley's descriptions of what is shown, nor on the descriptions that appear in the database of the Beazley Archive, but classified the scenes myself, assisted by detailed published descriptions where these are available. On the whole I have refrained from giving precise quantification, both because I have no doubt that there are pots that have escaped my notice and because the vagaries of any classification mean that precise numbers have little meaning, but I will from time to time indicate the sorts of numbers that are involved when I make claims about increasing or decreas-

---

[81] The most famous pithy comparisons of the Berlin and Kleophrades Painters occur in Beazley (1918), 35–44, esp. 35 and 40–41.

ing popularity of a scene. My interest is in overall patterns of imagery, and although the sample of pots on which my claims are based is no doubt subject to various sorts of bias, I am confident that the patterns I describe would be replicated in any representative sample.[82]

---

[82] For the surviving pots forming a representative sample of what was produced, cf. Sapirstein (2013; 2014), whose work on the productivity of specialist painters and of painter-potters both relies on and supports this assumption.

II

3 ❧ Changing in the Gymnasium

Greek history begins, traditionally, with athletics. The date calculated in antiquity for the first Olympic games, 776 BC, has been held to divide prehistory from history.[1] The earliest Greek literature, too, dating from the late eighth or early seventh century, has Greeks competing in games. Book twenty-three of the *Iliad* tells of a chariot race, boxing, wrestling, running, armed fighting, throwing a lump of iron, archery, and javelin throwing at the funeral games of Patroklos; book eight of the *Odyssey* has the Phaiakians holding games involving running, wrestling, jumping, discus throwing, and boxing; Hesiod's *Works and Days* tells of poetic competition at the funeral games of Amphidamas. By the end of the sixth century there was an established festival circuit, involving games at Olympia, Delphi, Nemea, and Isthmia (the "Crown games" as they came to be called) that were open to all Greeks. When Kleisthenes of Sikyon wanted a suitable husband for his daughter Agariste, the woman who would become the mother of the Athenian constitutional reformer Kleisthenes, Herodotos tells that he advertised at the Olympic games and then tested the suitors by prolonged athletic competition.[2]

1. Athletics at Athens: The Civic Investment

At Athens, athletic activity had been part of formal civic life at least from the second quarter of the sixth century, when the festival of the Great Panathenaia was reorganized.[3] Part of this reorganization involved rewarding victors and runners-up in athletic events with olive oil in distinctive "Panathenaic" amphoras.[4] These amphoras were decorated with an image of Athena on one side and an athletic scene on the other (**3.1**).[5] The earliest show scenes of running, of three events of the pentathlon (discus, javelin, jumping), and of equestrian competitions. Boxing and running in hoplite armor appear in the third quarter of the century, and by 480 the full range

---

[1] For how this date relates to what was going on at Olympia at that time, see Morgan (1990).
[2] Hdt. 6.126–31.
[3] Kyle (1987).
[4] Neils (1992b).
[5] Bentz (1998), Bentz and Eschbach (2001).

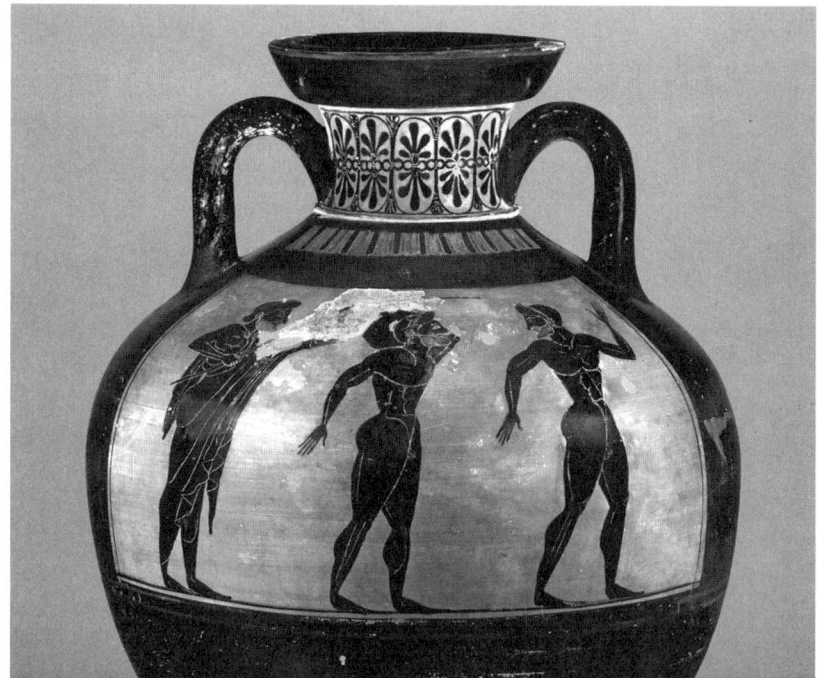

Figure 3.1. Panathenaic amphora, height 0.635 m, late sixth century. British Museum 1852,0707.1 (B 136). © The Trustees of the British Museum.

of athletic activity is shown. Victors seem most probably to have received amphoras that showed a selection of events, rather than simply the event in which the prize was won, and so these variations may indicate which images were popular (either with painters or with consumers), rather than which events were part of the program.[6] Indeed, after circa 470, equestrian events disappear from the amphoras for about a century, even though there is much evidence that they continued to be held. Panathenaic amphoras continued to be produced in the black-figure style long after that style had ceased to be used for most other pots, a rare material manifestation of institutionalized cultic archaism.

By the early fourth century, the Athenians were awarding as many as 140 amphoras of oil to the winner of just one event, the two-horse chariot race, and a total in excess of 2,000 amphoras seem to have been given as prizes in the year (circa 370) from which part of an inscribed record survives.[7] This at a time when an amphora of oil was worth at least twelve drachmas. By the same date cash and other prizes were being awarded in the musical competitions and sacrificial cows in the team events (armed

---

[6] Hamilton (1996), 137–62. Hamilton notes that pictures of events for which the prize was not oil do not occur on Panathenaic amphoras, though they do occur on other pots.

[7] In the surviving portion of *IG* ii² 2311, 819 amphoras are listed, but an additional 628 can confidently be added for the men's events, and around 600 for the hippic competitions for which the record is not preserved on the inscriptions; see Shear (2003b), 102, and cf. Johnston (1987). The 102 Panathenaic amphoras sold off together among the property confiscated from those found guilty of mutilating the herms and/or profaning the Mysteries (i3 422.41–60, cf. 21) are likely to have come from a victory in an equestrian event, though recreating a Panathenaic chariot race victory for Alkibiades in 418 on the basis of them is highly speculative (Neils 1992b, 50).

dancing, torch race, boat race).[8] In the late fifth century the total state expense on the Great Panathenaia certainly exceeded five talents and may have been well in excess of nine talents.[9]

The individual competitions at the Panathenaia were not restricted to Athenians. Athletes were attracted from all over the Greek world, and the distribution of the findspots of Panathenaic amphoras has reasonably been taken broadly to reflect this, although there is some evidence that suggests that there were collectors of Panathenaic amphoras.[10] But the team events at the Panathenaia were restricted to Athenian citizens. We do not know at what date the team events were first included, but in the classical period the Kleisthenic tribes were the basis for team membership (except for the armed dancers [*pyrrhikhistai*][11]), so these events must have been reorganized, or indeed created, after the Kleisthenic reforms of 507. At least one of these events, the pyrrhic dance, seems to have featured at the Lesser (that is, annual) as well as the Great (that is, quadrennial) Panathenaia, and the same may be true of the torch race.[12]

No other Athenian festival seems to have had athletic events for individuals, but team competitions were quite common. The addition of competitive team events to existing festivals, and the creation of new festivals including competitive events, is particularly a mark of the years immediately after the introduction of democracy.[13] Eventually team torch races, for example, were a feature of the Aiantea, Anthesteria, Apatouria, Epitaphia, Hephaestea, Promethea, Thesea, festival of Pan, and festival of Bendis as well as of the Panathenaia (although in several cases the earliest attestation of the race is late in the Hellenistic period), but only in the Panathenaia were pots given as prizes.[14]

The Athenians also awarded top-up prizes to Athenian athletes who won at Olympia and the other pan-Hellenic festivals. These awards were held by the Athenians to have been instituted by Solon, and there can be no doubt that they go back at least to the sixth century, but they were reiterated in the late fifth century.[15] In offering victorious athletes civic hospitality at the prytaneion, the Athenians treated them as major public benefactors. This was in line with the widespread practice of according victors in pan-Hellenic competitions a special place in warfare.[16]

---

[8] See also [Aristotle] *Constitution of the Athenians* 60.3.

[9] ML 77. 66–68, 84. 5–8 (OR 170. 66–68, 180. 5–8); Golden (1998), 164–65. This compares with an estimate of almost eighteen talents for the total expense of *choregoi* on the Great Dionysia: see Wilson (2000), 95.

[10] Hamilton (1996), 142–43.

[11] Whether or not the *pyrrhikhe* was tribal is much debated. See in general Ceccarelli (1998), and on this particular issue Wilson (2000), 324n137. I discuss representations of the *pyrrhikhe* not in this chapter but in chapter 7.

[12] Lysias 21.2, 4.

[13] Osborne (1993), Fisher (2011).

[14] Rhodes (1981), 638.

[15] Plutarch *Solon* 23.3, Diogenes Laertios 1.55; *IG* i³ 131.11–18; Demosthenes 20.141; Kyle (1984).

[16] Plutarch *Lykourgos* 22.4, Diodoros 12.9.5–6; Kurke (1993). A late fifth-century list of war dead from Thespiai records when the deceased was a victor at the Crown games: *IT* 485.

2. Athletics at Athens: The Ideology

Recognition by the city was the formal counterpart to popular support. That support is manifest in the way that individual men may be identified in both historical and oratorical texts as "the wrestler" or "the runner of the stadion."[17] And it had political consequences, both in the archaic and in the classical period. The stories of Kylon's attempted political coup in the late seventh century lay stress on his having been an Olympic victor.[18] Herodotos's story of the relations between Peisistratos and his sons and Kimon son of Stesagoras emphasizes Kimon's repeated chariot-racing victories at Olympia: even ascribing his victories to the tyrant does not buy Kimon off; appropriately when he is assassinated it is with his horses that he is buried.[19] More remarkably, Thucydides has Alkibiades, more than a century later, parade before the democratic assembly his unprecedented Olympic success in 416, when chariots he financed achieved first, second, and fourth places, as grounds for the Athenians supporting him in his views about the invasion of Sicily.[20] In the fourth century, too, athletes could be chosen as ambassadors or political leaders: the Arkadians sent Antiokhos the pankratiast as their representative to negotiations to renew the King's Peace in 367, and the author of [Demosthenes] 17 claims that Alexander had set up a wrestler, Khairon, as tyrant in Pellene.[21]

But the Athenians notoriously figure rather seldom in epinician poetry—just two odes of Pindar and one fragmentary ode of Bacchylides—and commentators have wondered whether "the disadvantages of prestige display of an overtly individualistic kind were especially felt in democratic Athens."[22] Outside Alkibiades's speech, athletic prowess, and even the contribution to a victory in a tribal or team event, is not something that we find boasted about in surviving speeches, whether speeches in the assembly or speeches in the Athenian law courts—though the presence of one Isthmionikos (Mr. Isthmian Victor) among the signatories to both the Peace of Nikias and the Athenian alliance with Sparta (Thuc. 5.19.2, 5.24.1) suggests that some Athenian families were not backward in advertising their athletic achievements.[23] More generalized expectations are displayed when Xenophon has Socrates get Charmides to agree that, for someone who is able to win honor and glory for his city by victory in one of the Crown games, not to compete would be to show himself "soft and cowardly."[24]

---

[17] For identification of individuals by athletic epithets, see Xenophon, *Anab.* 5.8.23, Demosthenes 21.71, 59.121, 124; Aiskhines 1.156; Hypereides *Lykophron* 5.
[18] Herodotos 5.71; Thucydides 1.126
[19] Herodotos 6.103
[20] Thucydides 6.16; Plutarch *Alkibiades* 11 quotes Euripides's victory ode for the occasion, which has Alkibiades achieve first, second, and third places. Note also that Alcibiades's victory in a horse race at Nemea is said to have been celebrated in a painting in the *pinakotheke* in the Propylaia on the Acropolis, Pausanias 1.22.6. For the politics of the Olympic victory, see Papakonstantinou (2003).
[21] [Demosthenes] 17.11.
[22] Carey (2007), 206n29.
[23] Hornblower (2004), 261.
[24] Xenophon *Memorabilia* 3.7.1.

What does get mentioned by Athenians keen to make a good impression is the sponsoring of athletic events.[25] Litigants in court told the jurors not only about their generous funding of the navy as a trierarch or of the Dionysia, Lenaia, or Thargelia, with their tragedies, comedies, and dithyrambs, as a *khoregos*, but also about the athletic events they had sponsored. Financial support was required for various team events—pyrrhic dancing, the torch race, the boat race to Sounion. The famously generous defendant of Lysias 21 had financed all of these events; elsewhere we find Andokides mentioning that he was gymnasiarch at the Hephaistia, Demosthenes that he was responsible for a chorus (either dithyrambic or pyrrhic) at the Panathenaia, and the speaker of Isaios 5 that he was responsible for a pyrrhic chorus.[26] It remains notable that the torch and boat race make so little impact, and given the way that the liturgy system worked it seems quite likely that those who knew they would have to spend money in liturgies preferred to sponsor drama, dithyramb, or dancing, rather than races. The only sculptural celebration of such liturgical activity that we know, the so-called Atarbos base, celebrates a victory with *pyrrhikhistai*.[27]

Alkibiades's willingness to boast of his equestrian successes causes surprise not simply because there would seem to be no logical connection between the ability to pay for the best horses, trainer, and drivers for chariot racing, and wisdom in determining Athenian foreign policy. It is also surprising because there is much less archaeological evidence for the public prominence of athletic victors in Athens after 480 than before. A number of dedications made on the Athenian Acropolis in the sixth and fifth centuries can be more or less securely associated with athletic success. Three of these are dedications apparently by boards of *hieropoioi* responsible for the earliest Panathenaic festivals, all of them probably dating to before 550.[28] Of eighteen other dedications that make explicit reference to victory, or originally included a tripod, or where we otherwise know about the athletic activities of the person or people named, five are sixth century in date, ten are datable to the first quarter of the fifth century, and just three date to later in the fifth century, none of these being later than circa 440.[29] Among the monuments on the Acropolis mentioned by Pausanias are statues of Epicharinos running in armor by Kritios, of Hermolykos the pankratiast, and of Kylon (whose presence, given his failed coup, worries Pausanias, who explains it in terms of his beauty and athletic success). Here again none of these figures is classical.[30] This distribution of surviving athletic dedications broadly reflects the distribution of inscribed monuments from the Acropolis more generally, and the absence of athletic dedications

---

[25] Wilson (2000), 89–93; Davies (1971), xxi–xxiv.
[26] Lysias 21.1-4 with *APF* D7; Andokides 1.132; Demosthenes 21.156; Isaios 5.36.
[27] Acropolis 1338, *IG* ii² 3025, *APF* 2679, Wilson (2000) 39-40, 305, Shear (2003a).
[28] *DAA* nos. 326–28 (*IG* i³ 507–9).
[29] *DAA* nos. 59, 61, 317, 318, and 319 are the sixth-century candidates, 21, 76, 111, 120, 154, 156, 171, 320, 321, and 322 date to ca. 500–ca. 475, and 139, 163, and 174 to later in the fifth century.
[30] Pausanias 1.22–28; for Hermolykos, see Herodotos 9.105.

after 475 BC suggests that athletes did not buck the trend to greater reticence in advertising individual achievements, however lauded those were by the public.

The continued respect given to athletes is apparent in classical Attic grave reliefs. Identification of individuals by their occupations is relatively uncommon on grave monuments, and athletes and soldiers are the only two occupational groups explicitly represented with any frequency on both in archaic and in classical Athenian reliefs. From the archaic period, we have stelai showing young men with aryballoi or holding a discus and figures identified by their bound hands and their beaten ears as boxers.[31] We have no Athenian sculpted grave monuments from between circa 480 and circa 430, but athletes are represented on some of the earliest reliefs when they reappear (**3.2**). In his standard catalog of *Classical Attic Tombstones*, Clairmont lists sixty-eight athletes not engaged in any activity, most of them holding strigil and aryballos; most of these are represented alone, but some appear in two-, three-, or four-person groups. He lists a further fifteen as "Athletes engaged in activity," but eight of these are either scraping themselves with a strigil or anointing themselves. One is certainly and one possibly crowning himself, one a boxer, one a pankratiast, one has a hoop, and one is a boy with, perhaps, a ball. Only the possible image of an athlete crowning himself refers directly to athletic victory, and we have no reason to think that we are seeing here some boasting of peculiar success, but we are certainly seeing an expression of pride in athletic prowess, and an expectation that others too will admire the athletic body. In total, some fifty-eight of the 101 stelai representing just one adult male recorded by Clairmont represent that person as an athlete.

The most powerful evidence for the continued high profile of athletes comes arguably from the repeated criticisms made of them. Already in the seventh century Tyrtaios had insisted that endurance in battle, not excellence in running or wrestling, was real *arete*, and Solon is said to have maintained a similar position.[32] Around 500 Xenophanes of Kolophon objected that an athlete won public respect, front seats at contests, and free meals, even though the qualities he had to display to win did not help the city to better laws or bring the city prosperity. Much better, he asserted, was the wisdom of an intellectual like himself.[33] Athenaios, who quotes this tirade in his section on gluttony, quotes also an attack on athletes from Euripides's satyr play *Autolykos*.[34] In this passage, the speaker and context of which is quite unknown, athletes are attacked as the worst of the myriad of evils Hellas suffers, since their skills are both useless to their cities and ruinous to those who practice them, and they end up bitter in old age, slaves of their bellies and unable to live without great riches. The attack in Euripides's play seems to have been paralleled in a comedy by Eupolis,

---

[31] Richter (1961) nos. 25, 26, 28, 31, 32, 37, 48, 52; Frel (1984).

[32] Tyrtaios 12.1–14, Diogenes Laertios 1.55. For the image of the athlete in literary texts from Homer to Euripides, see Visa-Ondarçuhu (1999).

[33] Athenaios 413f–414c, Xenophanes frg.2 Diels-Kranz.

[34] Euripides frg. 282, Athenaios 413c–f.

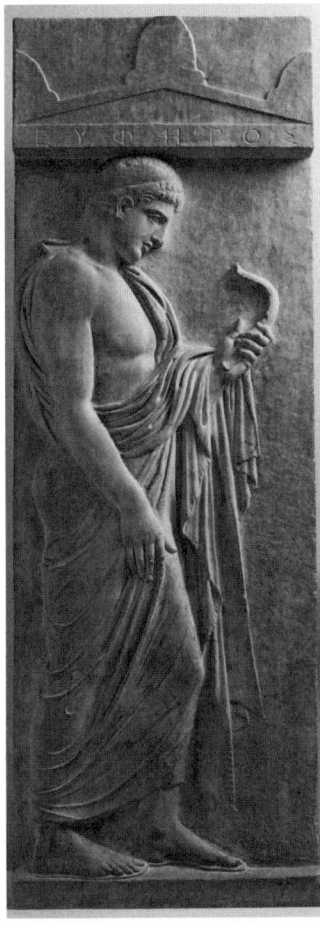

Figure 3.2. Grave stele, height 1.47 m, of Eupheros, shown as a young athlete, from the Athenian Kerameikos cemetery, ca. 420. Kerameikos Museum P 1169, I 417. Photograph Michael Krumme, Deutsches Archäologisches Institut Athen, Neg. No. D-DAI-ATH-2006/1081F. All rights reserved.

where it was wryly observed that athletes got rewarded with bowls when useful citizens did not.[35]

Public interest in and enthusiasm for athletic events in fifth-century Athens seems indisputable. Athens's pride in its civic festivals and the way in which it had made them available to all citizens is clear from the place they play in the argument about the way in which democracy reinforced itself, which is given in the late fifth-century pamphlet preserved among the works of Xenophon.[36] The author notes that Athens has more festivals than any other city, and that festivals and sacrifices are enjoyed by the people.[37] He claims that the people both undermine the practice of athletics and *mousike* by the rich and have insisted on the rich funding them in such activities and on the provision of *palaistrai* at public expense for themselves.[38] Stories of slow runners in torch races being jostled and chivvied

---

[35] Athenaios 408d, Eupolis 129 K-A, where, however, Eupolis seems to undercut the criticism by referring to the *lebetes* awarded to athletes in some competitions as *kheironiptra*, "hand-basins."

[36] The author is often referred to as the "Old Oligarch," but this is misleading, and I refer to him here simply as [Xenophon]. For this work see Osborne (2004b), Marr and Rhodes (2008).

[37] [Xenophon], *Constitution of the Athenians* 2.9, 3.2.

[38] [Xenophon], *Constitution of the Athenians* 1.13, 2.10.

by spectators further confirm the intense public involvement in the competitions.³⁹ The contrast drawn by Stronger Argument in Aristophanes's *Clouds* between those who follow the old education, and spend their time in gymnasia acquiring gleaming bodies, and those who follow the new education, and spend their time in the agora so that they end up pale and physically underdeveloped, does not paint its contrasts between old and new in class terms. But both the prominence of the gymnasium and *palaistra* as a place to meet for the set of rich young men who feature centrally in Plato's *Dialogues*, and the way in which Aischines mentions that his father had been an athlete as a way of countering allegations that he was of low birth, suggest that taking part in athletics continued in practice to mark out the more prosperous.⁴⁰

3. The Image of the Athlete on Athenian Red-Figure Pottery

Athletes of one description or another appear on more than a thousand red-figure pots painted between the beginning of the technique in the last quarter of the sixth century and the period of the Peloponnesian War a century later.⁴¹ Groups of athletes practice their skills, sometimes to the accompaniment of an *auletes*, or stand around in the gymnasium; individual athletes throw the discus or javelin, run (sometimes in armor) and jump; victorious athletes are garlanded with ribbons; pairs of athletes box or wrestle. They are shown doing these things on amphoras, on kraters of various shapes, on oinochoai, on psykters, but above all they are shown on cups, both inside in the tondo and outside between the handles (and in many cases both inside and outside). Except for a small number of athletic scenes on lekythoi or alabastra, it is predominantly upon vessels made for use at the symposium that athletes are depicted in red-figure.⁴²

Athletes had appeared on black-figure pots before red-figure was invented. They had appeared upon the Panathenaic prize amphoras from their inception, but they had also subsequently appeared on other pots. They come to appear on black-figure (non-Panathenaic) amphoras more than twice as frequently as they appear on black-figure cups, and they gain

---

³⁹ Aristophanes *Frogs*, 1089–98, and the saying "Keramic blows" (Hesychius k2263).

⁴⁰ Aristophanes *Clouds*, 1002–19 (cf. 973–74, Aischines 2.147). For the long-running dispute over the status of athletes at Athens, see in particular Pritchard (2003; 2013), Fisher (2011). The evidence is insufficient to show who participated (Pritchard's argument about inaccessibility of trainers for the less wealthy depends on an apparent belief that everyone called a *paidotribes* was a professional and that all the young men with branches in their hands who are apparently giving instructions to athletes on pots represent professional trainers) but sufficient to show that athletics retained elite associations.

⁴¹ The changing imagery of the athlete on Athenian pottery was briefly described by Bažant (1985), 12–16; (1987), 34. Webster (1972), 196–215 variously classifies and lists more than 1,500 athletic scenes (almost 1,400 of them red-figure), offering tables of their distribution by shape and provenance.

⁴² For distribution across shapes, see the table in Webster (1972), 214.

a significant popularity on black-figure lekythoi.[43] Although boxing and wrestling appear earlier, general gymnasium scenes, jumpers, and javelin throwers all appear for the first time after the middle of the sixth century.[44] There is, indeed, a marked gap between the great expansion of competitive athletics marked by the foundation of the Pythian games at Delphi, the Isthmian games and the Nemean games, in the '80s and '70s of the sixth century, and of the Panathenaic competitions themselves in the '60s, and the appearance of athletes in Athenian iconography.[45]

With the adoption of the red-figure technique, athletes become very much more common on pots. Part of the explanation for this surely lies in the new possibilities afforded by the technique. In place of the flat silhouettes of black-figure, the lighter figures against a black background offered new possibilities for modeling that might be expected to be particularly attractive when it came to showing off the athletic body. But this can hardly be the whole explanation. Black-figure had very frequently shown the male body naked, and had done so in circumstances that make it clear that the naked body as such had a positive value. This is especially true of showing warriors naked, where the nudity does not reflect the realities of warfare (compare below chapter 4) but must be adopted for its symbolic value. The decision to draw scenes of athletes is part of a major change in direction in the iconography of Athenian painted pottery that accompanies the change of technique: scenes relating to the life of the city become much more prominent, and scenes of mythology less pervasive. Arguably the new technique both responded to and encouraged an increased desire to reflect upon and interact with the world of the city itself through meditation upon scenes related to the activities that could be regularly observed.

In what follows I trace first the emergence and changing nature of the gymnasium as a subject in red-figure painting in the last quarter of the sixth century and the first quarter of the fifth. I then turn to the solo athlete and trace his story through into the middle of the fifth century.

Pioneering Views of the Gymnasium

Athletes appear on some of the earliest red-figure pottery, paired with black-figure scenes. Both these bilingual pots and some other early red-figure athletic scenes sometimes combine the athlete or athletes with a

[43] So Webster (1972), 214, based on Beazley's *ABV* and Haspels's *ABL*.

[44] Webster (1972), 197, 201, 206. Miller's claim (1997), 284, with reference to Hollein (1988), 71–85, that "—with the obvious and explicable exception of the Panathenaic amphora—Attic vase painting abruptly adds nude athletes to its standard repertoire of depictions in the period between 520 and 510 BC" exaggerates the lateness and suddenness of athletes' arrival on pots. Miller appears to mistake Hollein's discussion of red-figure material for a discussion of all vase images, and even as a characterization of red-figure the claim for the "abrupt" addition of athletes misrepresents the rather gradual adoption of these scenes displayed in Hollein's graph on p. 85.

[45] Chariot races, by contrast, do appear in quite large numbers from the second quarter of the sixth century on, see Webster (1972), 189–94.

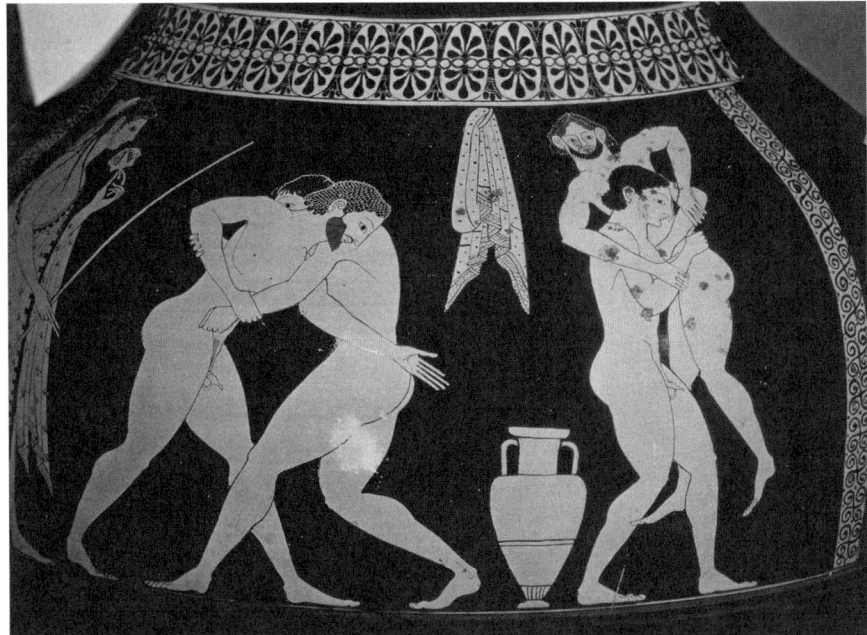

Figure 3.3–4. Red-figure type A amphora, height with lid 0.582 m, signed by Andokides as potter, found at Vulci, ca. 520. *ARV* 3.1. Berlin 2159. © bpk / Antikensammlung, Staatliche Museen zu Berlin / Ingrid Geske (3.3), Isolde Luckert (3.4).

scene from mythology or a picture of a satyr. Such combinations had been found occasionally on black-figure pottery, but later (after circa 500), although satyrs appear occasionally on the same pot as athletes, combinations of athletics with myth become extremely unusual. The iconographic world of black-figure athletes had been one of vigor: even scenes on non-Panathenaic amphoras tend to contain athletes who are engaging in running, boxing, wrestling, throwing, or whatever, with as much energy as is displayed in the celebration of the Panathenaic competition. The iconographic world of even the earliest red-figure athletes is more relaxed, and rapidly the scenes acquire new elements.[46]

To understand this change we need to look more closely at the early red-figure scenes. I take two examples that juxtapose gymnasium scenes with episodes from mythology and then compare these to what is shown on pots where scenes from the gymnasium are totally dominant.

A red-figure amphora (**3.3–4**), found at Vulci, signed by Andokides as potter, and among the earliest of all known red-figure pots, shows on one side two pairs of men wrestling, watched by a richly dressed youth with the "wand" that is the mark of the trainer or umpire. Each of the pairs has one bearded and one beardless figure, and the "trainer" is smelling a flower. On the other side, the beardless Apollo, in a highly ornate short garment and carrying his bow, takes hold of one leg of the tripod that the bearded Herakles is attempting to make away with; the god and the hero are flanked by

---

[46] Myth scenes are never subsequently popular companions to gymnasium scenes, except insofar as various artists in the second quarter of the fifth century, those to whom the collective title "Mannerists" is often given (as in *ARV* chapter 34) and some of their near-contemporaries, sometimes combine gymnasia scenes with myth, particularly Dionysiac myth, when painting kraters.

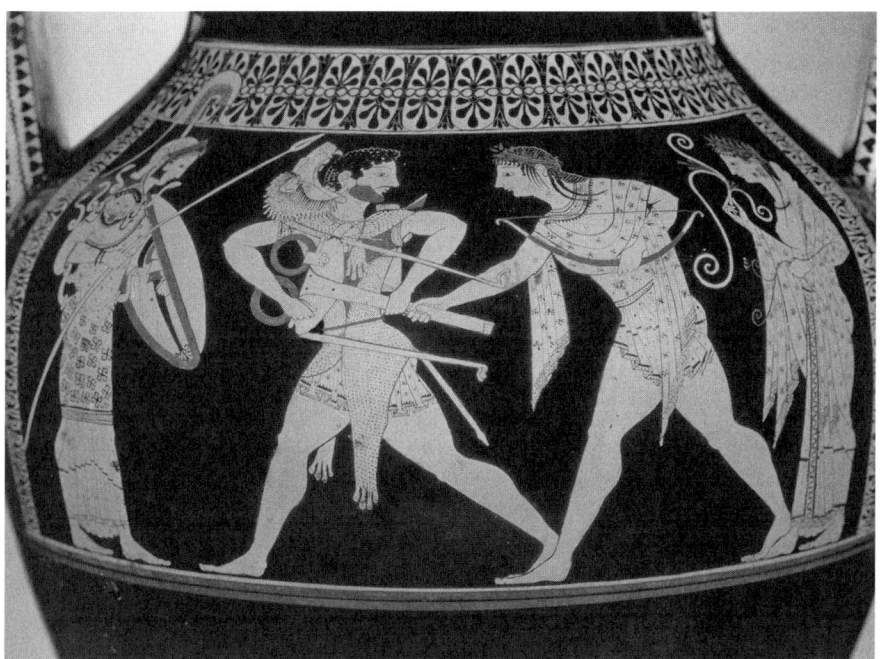

a fully armed Athena and by Artemis who holds an elaborate plant in her hand.

The two sides of this amphora echo each other; in particular, there is a very close correspondence between the pose of Artemis and that of the "trainer" and between that of Apollo and that of the left-most of the wrestlers. But the two scenes also have clear differences; the decision to include two pairs of wrestlers emphasizes that we are not being shown a particular combat in the *palaistra*. It is wrestling in general that we are asked to compare with the struggle for the tripod, not a particular wrestling bout. We are encouraged to contemplate not the particular holds shown, but the narrative of wrestling that leads from one position to the other. In the nudity of the athletes and the presence of an amphora, which we are to assume contains water to keep the dust down as the men wrestle, the scene makes some concessions to athletic life as observed, but this is no casual observation.

By giving the young man a flower, emphasis is moved from his potentially active role of policing the activity he observes to a passive role of appreciation—and appreciation of the sensory experience of wrestling, not just the feel of flesh and of tightening muscles but the smell of sweat and of skin burned under the sun. This scene encourages the viewer to see wrestling in the *palaistra* as an activity that can stand in the same relationship to the observer's life as can the stories of myth, as something that is enjoyable to perceive and that offers a template against which to read everyday activities. The quotidian activity of wrestling in the *palaistra* is turned into a potential allegory, where the struggles of the wrestlers in front of spectators can stand for the most serious struggles of life.

Something very similar can be observed on another very early red-figure amphora, attributed to Phintias and also found at Vulci (1.1, **3.5**).[47] On one side, Apollo, naked but for his cloak draped over his left shoulder and arm, and with his bow and quiver hanging behind him, reaches forward to take hold of the elbow of Tityos and the forearm of his mother Leto, whom Tityos has lifted off the ground and is trying to run off with; an animated Artemis, her bow in her left hand and her right arm raised, watches and frames the composition. On the other side, a bearded man in a himation and with a stick watches as one youth raises his discus to the level of his head, preparatory to throwing it; another youth tightens the thong wound round his javelin as he prepares to throw it; a naked bearded man holding a javelin and observing the youths intently frames the scene. The scene is scattered across with writing: we have four names, Sosi[a]s, Chares, Sotinon, and Demostratos (or Demostrate), an acclamation "Chaire" ("Fare well" in both its senses, and perhaps to be taken with Demostrate—"Fare well Demostratos"), and a *kalos* name, "Sostratos is fair." Neither side has the elaboration of costume or the suggestion of sensuousness offered by the Andokides Painter's scenes. The urgency of Apollo's action to restrain the athletic Tityos from his violence against Artemis is paralleled by the intensity of the scrutiny afforded by the older men to the youths' exploits with javelin and discus. Just as Apollo's claim to manhood (and godhood) depends upon his ability to restrain Tityos, so the claims to manhood of these youths now sprouting downy hair on their cheeks depend upon their ability to display not only a well-toned musculature but also skill with the tools of the gymnasium.

To these pots, I juxtapose another "Pioneer" pot, a calyx krater attributed to Euphronios and found in Capua (1.2, **3.6**, and plate 5).[48] In the center of one side is a naked youth, against whom the name Antiphon is written. He is beginning the arm swing preparatory to throwing the discus and appears to be under instruction from another youth ("Hipp[ar]chos"). Hipparchos is draped in a himation, holds a trainer's wand, and points firmly with a long right arm, as if to reinforce a spoken point. This pair is flanked to the right by a youth ("Polyllos"), who folds his himation and is about to give it to an implausibly tiny boy, and to the left by another equally small boy ("*ho pais*" 'the boy"). This small boy has some item of clothing over his shoulder and extends his arm as if to urge care on the youth with a thong who prepares to secure, or more probably has just untied, his penis. Beside this youth is written "Leagros [k]alos" "Leagros is fair." The stature of the boys is plausibly meant as an indicator of their slave status. In the equivalent position on the left of the other side of the pot, a naked boy, "Tra[ni]on," a name not otherwise attested at Athens, examines the foot of a naked youth ("Hippomedon"), seen from the back. Hippomedon has his himation draped round his shoulders and supports himself on a knobbly stick and by putting a hand on the boy's head. In the center a naked

---

[47] *ARV* 23.1, Louvre G42; Pasquier and Denoyelle (1990), no. 62.
[48] *ARV* 13.1., Berlin 2180; Pasquier and Denoyelle (1990), no. 1.

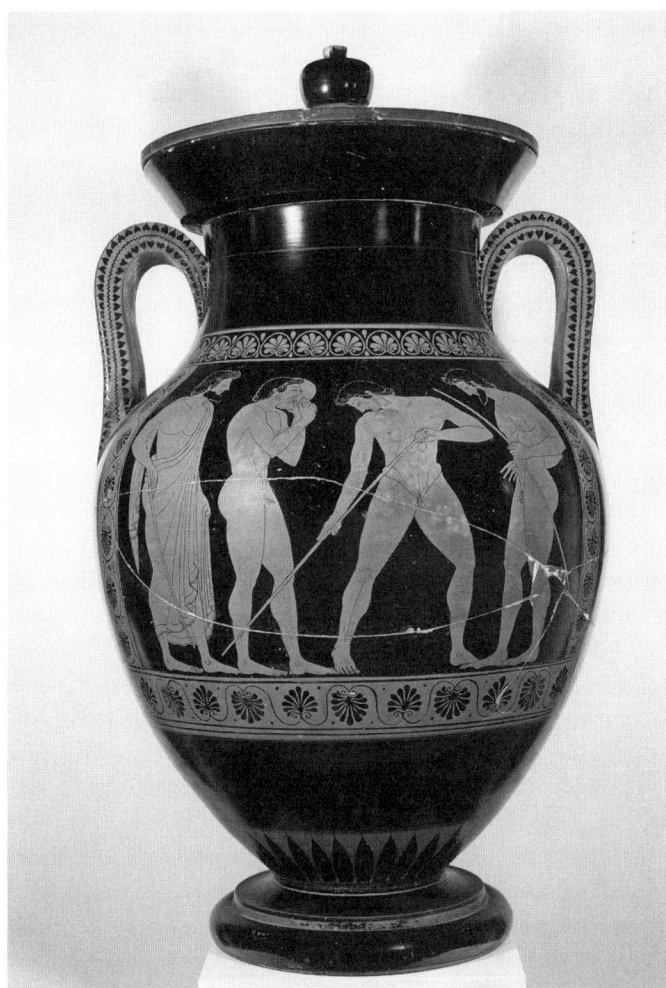

Figure 3.5. Red-figure type A amphora, height 0.60 m without lid, attributed to Phintias, found at Vulci, ca. 510 (for the reverse see 1.1). *ARV* 23.1. Louvre G42. Photo © RMN-Grand Palais (musée du Louvre) / Hervé Lewandowski.

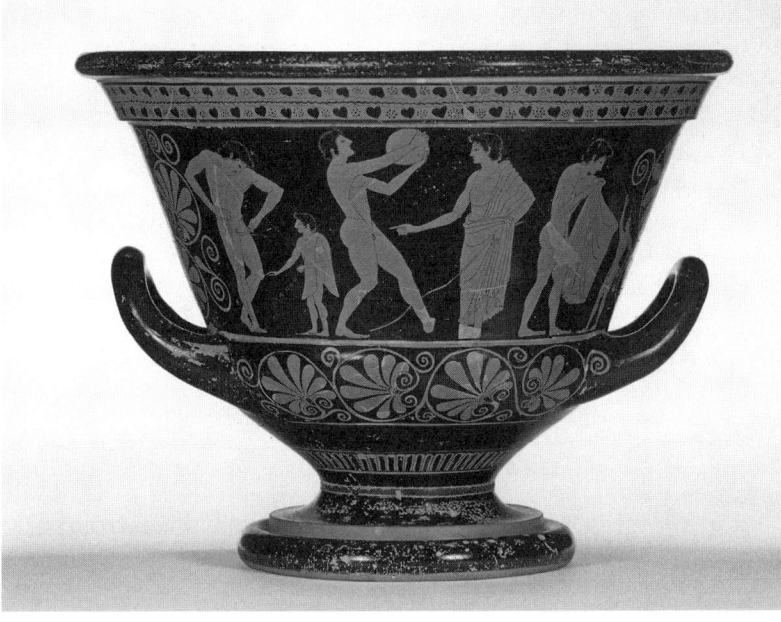

Figure 3.6. Red-figure calyx krater, height 0.348 m, attributed to Euphronios, found at Capua, ca. 510 (for the reverse see 1.2). *ARV* 13.1. Berlin 2180. © bpk / Antikensammlung, Staatliche Museen zu Berlin / Johannes Laurentius.

youth ("Hegesias") pours oil into his left hand from an aryballos on a thong around his right wrist. Below his hand "Leagros kalos" is written again. To the right, beside a stool on which garments are folded, a youth ("Lykos") folds a himation and a small boy waits with hand ready to take whatever is passed his way. All the figures on this side are garlanded.

The absence of any other world against which the activities of the gymnasium are measured, and the studied variety of gymnasial activities that are shown, mean that this pot presents athletes and athletics in a quite different way. The scenes by the Andokides Painter and by Phintias on their amphoras had challenged the viewer to compare and contrast the templates of myth with the templates of the gymnasium, and so encouraged a focus on the narrative of athletic activity. This calyx krater offers the gymnasium as a world of its own, encouraging comparison only with the world of the symposium in which the vessel is used and observed. And the world of the gymnasium in this view is not a world in which physical challenges are faced and met, but a world where what matters is grooming.

It is the care taken to maintain and display the body in the gymnasium, rather than the athletic exercise that might be held to produce it, that is here offered for our observation and note. These scenes are all about touch—the touch of garment on flesh, oil on body, hand on hair of slave, slave touching foot, athlete touching his own penis, and so on. This gymnasium is a both a social and a sensual world, a world in which young men display themselves for admiration—and display themselves as sexually desirable. Two aspects are notable here. The first is the choice to represent one athlete as having just untied (or less plausibly as about to tie) his genitals, and to direct attention at them. Other pots that show solo athletes with their genitals clearly ligatured make it clear that restraining the genitals with a thong was a practical measure that some athletes took to prevent their genitals swinging uncomfortably.[49] But although the frequent ligaturing of men in the gymnasium, including those only playing the aulos, might be understood in such practical terms, the presence of ligaturing among bearded men in the *komos*, and above all among the satyrs on Douris's psykter, now in the British Museum, showing wild drinking games, makes clear that the ligatured penis was also a sign of sexual control that drew attention to the potential for sexual excitement.[50]

The second aspect to note is that it is next to this figure untying his penis and next to the figure pouring oil into his hand on the other side of the krater that "Leagros kalos" is written. That is, male beauty is evoked, through the name of the most acclaimed beauty of the period, precisely in connection with one figure whose sexual potential is signaled and another

---

[49] Cf. notably the amphoras by the Kleophrades Painter (Leningrad 609, *ARV* 184.19) and the Triptolemos Painter (Munich 2314, *ARV* 362.14), both showing javelin throwers, and compare also the Terme Boxer, Museo Nazionale Romano, Palazzo Massimo alle Terme, inv. 1055. The realism of ligaturing contrasts with the unreal depiction of the genitals themselves: had the genitals of Greek men been as small as they are depicted, there would have been no need of ligaturing; cf. Dover (1978), 124–35, McNiven (1995).

[50] London, British Museum E768, *ARV* 446.262. For the history of this psykter, see Vout (2013), 231–33.

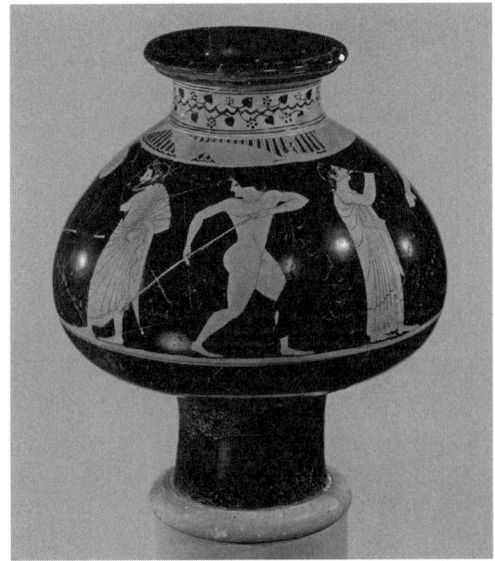 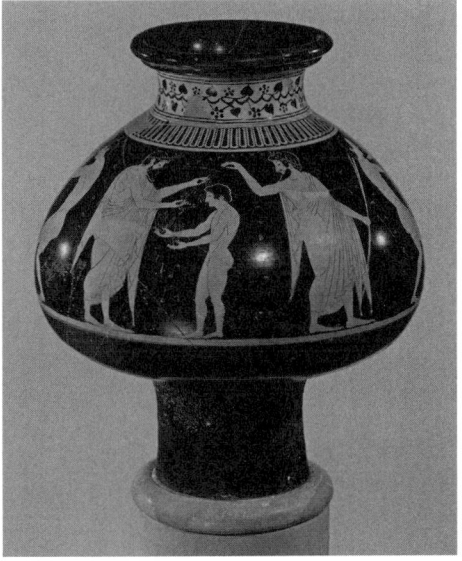

Figure 3.7–8. Red-figure psykter, height 0.346 m, attributed to Oltos, found at Campagnano, ca. 500. *ARV* 54.7. New York Metropolitan Museum 10.210.18. www.metmuseum.org.

who is marked as about to pass his hand over his body. Although the naming practice of the Andokides Painter's and of Phintias's scenes is essentially closely parallel, and accords with the practice more generally observed by the so-called Pioneers, its effect is quite different in the two cases. For whereas the juxtaposition of gymnasium and myth on Phintias's amphora urged the viewer to see those named athletes as having an exemplary role, like that of nameable mythological figures, the naming of figures on this krater emphasizes the quotidian nature of the scene: here are a selection of those Athenians who frequent the gymnasium—a selection into which the company of an outstanding male beauty may be appropriately invoked.[51]

Exceptional in its preservation, and unusual among the earliest red-figure gymnasium or *palaistra* scenes in its emphasis on the grooming that accompanied athletic activity, Euphronios's krater, rather than Phintias's amphora, sets the model for gymnasium scenes on subsequent early red-figure pots. To Phintias himself is attributed a wine-cooling vessel (psykter, a novelty invented in the last third of the sixth century and the ultimate refinement at the symposium) with some thirteen named figures in a gymnasium context.[52] Similar scenes with many figures in a gymnasium are also to be found on psykters attributed to the Pezzino group and to Oltos (**3.7–8**).[53] But on those psykters two new elements appear that serve to alter the tone of the images: the aulos player and the boy victor.

[51] For the naming practices of the "Pioneers," increasingly recognized to be playful in a wide range of different ways, see Neer (2002), chap. 3, and esp. 93–96; Topper (2012), 142–55; and Hedreen (2016). For Leagros, see Shapiro (2004). M. J. Osborne and Byrne (1994) included names from pots as Athenian names.

[52] Phintias's psykter is *ARV* 24.11. For the history of the psykter, see Isler-Kerenyi (1987).

[53] *ARV* 32.3bis (1621) now in the University of Zurich Archaeological Museum, L 250; *ARV* 54.7 (N.Y. Met. 10.210.18.).

Aulos Players and Youthful Victors in the Gymnasium

Although a black-figure Panathenaic amphora from the middle of the sixth century shows a costumed youth wearing the *phorbeion* lip band (as seen in 1.10) and playing the aulos for an acrobatic display involving an armed dancer with two shields and a kind of pole vaulting, *auletai* appear in black-figure athletic scenes only in the last quarter of the sixth century, contemporary with the earliest red-figure scenes of athletes and *auletai*.[54] Euphronios himself painted an aulos player as part of gymnasium scenes on a now-fragmentary calyx krater (which also features Herakles and Kyknos) and on a stamnos (which also features Peleus and Thetis).[55] The psykter ascribed to the Pezzino group has twelve figures, including one pair of wrestlers, one pair of pankratiasts, and two separate boxers binding their hands. The bearded *auletes* is one of three mature men (the others are a man in a himation and the man festooning a boy victor with ribbons), and appears between the youth squatting and binding his hands ready to box and the pair of pankratiasts. Although there is writing between the figures, it seems all to be nonsensical. The *auletes* on the psykter by Oltos is a youth and appears, as one of eight figures, between a youth tightening the thong on a javelin before throwing it and a youth swinging jumping weights. Next to the jumper is a man festooning a youthful victor, and beyond him a trainer, a discus thrower, and a further trainer. Here the abundant writing not only names each figure but also includes instructions for the viewer ("He's about to leap!" of the jumper, named Dorotheos, "Drink me" and "I open my mouth wide" between the trainer, named Antimenes, and the javelin thrower, named Batrakhos ["Mr. Frog"]).[56] This commentary only further encourages the viewer to see these athletes as performing for the spectator.

The scenes on pots frequently associate playing the aulos with throwing the javelin, and with jumping, and indeed a javelin thrower appears two figures away from the *auletes* on the Pezzino group psykter. While it is hard to see much role for music in boxing, wrestling, or indeed running, the timing and coordination of movement required for ancient weight-assisted long jump, and for throwing the javelin, could be materially assisted by rhythmic tunes from the aulos (which was also used to keep heavy-armed soldiers in time). The *auletes* on these pots, whether a youth or a man, regularly wears the more or less elaborate costume that we associate with official occasions. In one image from the last third of the fifth century a costumed

---

[54] The Panathenaic amphora is Paris, Bibliothèque Nationale 243. For armed dancers, see below. Other *auletai* appear in *ABV* 345.2, 365.65, 169, 118, 371.40, 383.8, 384.19, 386.6, 9, 401.1. Although *auletai* continue occasionally to be shown in gymnasium scenes on Athenian red-figure pots down to the end of the fifth century, they appear with particular frequency in the earliest red-figure. On the uses of the aulos at Athens, see Wilson (1999).

[55] Stamnos, *ARV* 16.6 (Leipzig, Antikenmuseum T 523); fragmentary calyx krater: Leon Levy and Shelby White Collection, New York.

[56] The name Batrakhos not only recurs on another more or less contemporary pot (*ARV* 316.4) but is also recorded by Osborne and Byrne (1994) as the name of an Athenian citizen in some five different demes during the fifth to third centuries BC.

auletes and a figure of Nike bringing a ribbon to adorn an athlete with a discus appear in the same image, and in this case, we must surely think in terms of the *auletes* playing for the competition.[57] At least when the *auletes* is shown in costume he would seem to import the idea of competition alongside that of discipline and training.

If the presence of the *auletes* points to the training and skill required in the gymnasium, as well as to competition, the competitive element is highlighted on the two psykters by the presence of the boy victor being garlanded by a man. Black-figure artists had alluded to athletic victory by showing men carrying tripods, sometimes themselves with a garland in hand, and sometimes in the company of others who hold branches, garlands, or ribbons. Some of these scenes have a processional element, particularly where multiple tripod bearers appear, and an aulos player may be part of the group. But fully crowned athletes festooned with ribbons appear in black-figure only at the end of the sixth century, at the same time as these red-figure psykters were painted.[58] Red-figure painters from the beginning choose to show beribboned or otherwise festooned youth and boy victors, both on their own and in groups. The solo youthful or boy victor is a particularly frequent iconographic choice in the works ascribed to Oltos, but continues to be in the repertoire until around the end of the first quarter of the fifth century.[59] Where the beribboned victor appears in a group, one of the most notable features is the consistent youthfulness of the victor. So, on a late sixth-century hydria ascribed to the Pezzino group (**3.9**), we see a youth raising a discus at the beginning of his preparations for a throw, a youth running vigorously, a man wrapped in a mantle, his head back, about either to sing or to make an announcement, and a man ribboning a boy who holds a leafy branch in his hand—apparently an allusion to the *phyllobolia* or pelting with leaves, which one ancient source attests to have been the fate of victors.[60] This scene looks like a survey of the types of event for which there were festival competitions, but it is for the boy that the glory of victory is reserved.[61]

This concentration on the boy victor can be understood in the context of the concern with the gymnasium as a place of training that we saw manifested in the introduction of the *auletes* into the picture. Boys are encouraged by the glory of victory to undertake the rigorous training that is marked by the *auletes*' rhythms, and, when they win, it is not their houses that are enriched by the award of a tripod but their bodies that are adorned with ribbons to mark them out for the immediate admiration of those around. We might think that the advantage of serious training in athletics

---

[57] For the *auletes* plus Nike, see *ARV* 1186.24.

[58] The development of victor iconography is well reviewed by Kephalidou (1996), esp. 146.

[59] Kephalidou (1996), 148–49.

[60] Why a palm branch is given to victors is debated at Plutarch *Moralia* 724A–F (cf. Plutarch *Theseus* 21.3).

[61] The iconographic treatment of victors in horse races is rather different, with Nike making an earlier appearance, but the exclusively youthful nature of the victors is a shared feature (Kephalidou [1996], 152–53). Only in scenes of victory in chariot races is a bearded victor to be found (Kephalidou [1996], 153–54).

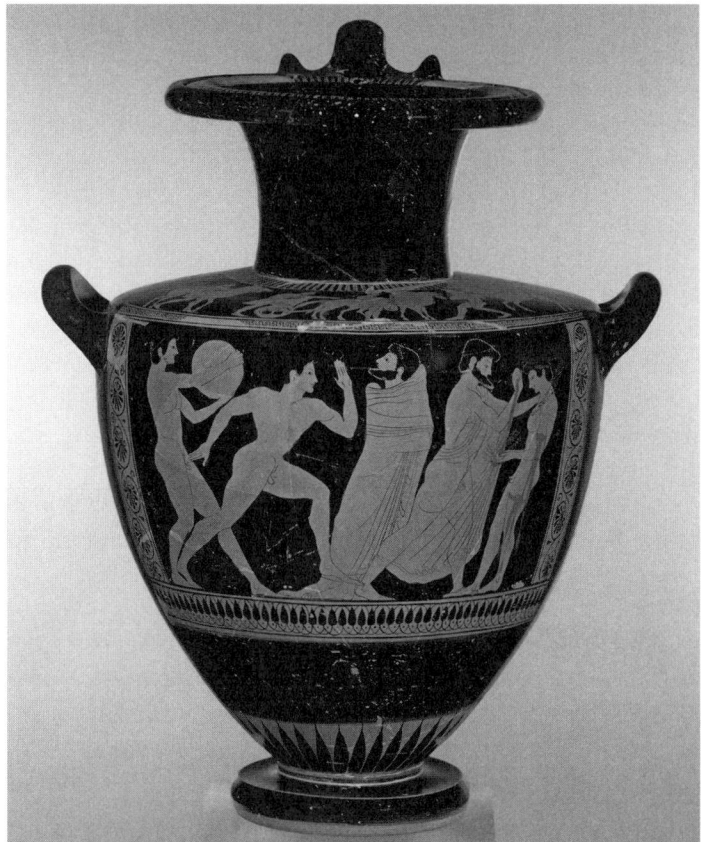

Figure 3.9. Red-figure hydria, height 0.54 m, attributed to the Pezzino Group, found at Vulci, ca. 500. *ARV* 32.3. Munich Staatliche Antikensammlung en 2420 (J.377). © Staatliche Antikensammlung en und Glyptothek München. Photograph by Renate Kühling.

was that it gave the citizen the body to fight with and be proud of, but the physical strength of the victorious athlete is not what is marked in these victors.

The concentration on the boy victor needs to be understood in the context of sexual desire. This is seen most clearly in an image on a lost cup from the first quarter of the fifth century signed by Douris (**3.10**). Here, on one side of a cup, we see a youth with leafy branches in his hands (the *phyllobolia* motif) and wearing a peculiar cap with a long ribbon at the end. Such a cap features, with some variations, on one other victor depicted by Douris and on four or five more victors shown by painters who are his near contemporaries.[62] On the lost cup the figure is flanked by two bearded men wearing himatia and carrying sticks.[63] The one behind the victor holds a flower, the one in front extends one hand toward the youth's thigh; these gestures recall courtship motifs, and courtship is confirmed when a further youth wearing a himation is shown about to receive a hare

[62] Kephalidou (1996), 131–36.
[63] On this pose, see Hollein (1988), Wees (1998), 359–60.

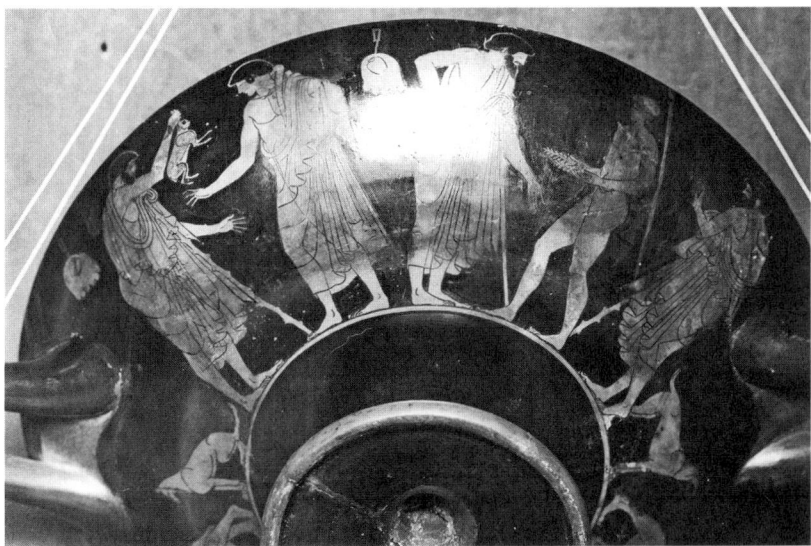

Figure 3.10. Red-figure cup signed by Douris, provenance unknown, ca. 480. *ARV* 430.33. Formerly Dresden, Staatliche Kunstsammlungen; now lost. (BA 205077). © Staatliche Kunstsammlungen, Dresden.

or rabbit extended toward him by a bearded man with a stick. On the other side of the cup two further youths, one of them closely mantled, are offered hares by bearded men. On the inside tondo of the cup a man in a himation and with a stick holds out a small bag;[64] behind him is a stool or the end of a couch, above which hangs the athlete's kit of aryballos and sponge.

This cup makes the viewer think about the feting of victors in the context of exchanges of other sorts between males. Different sorts of exchange are being juxtaposed, as they are on a number of cups of this period.[65] To the love gift of a hare, accepted in two cases, spurned in the third, is compared the offering of a small bag (with no recipient in view but with "Khairestratos *kalos*" written around the outstretched hand)—and the rewarding of a victorious youth. The man holding the flower, a motif we have already met on the Andokides Painter's amphora and that is found in conjunction with the ribboning of a victor on another cup also ascribed to Douris, draws attention to the sensuality of the scene, and the gesture of the other man resembles the moves made in many overt "courtship" scenes.[66] Given the company it keeps, the bestowing of leafy branches upon a victorious youth becomes both a recognition of the erotic attractions of the successful young athlete and the first move in courtship.[67]

[64] On the motif of the (money) bag, see chapter 5, section 2.
[65] Villa Giulia 12 B 16 fr. (Reden [1995], fig. 2, makes a particularly apt comparison).
[66] The other cup ascribed to Douris is London British Museum E52, *ARV* 432.59; for the courtship motif see Dover (1978), 94–96, and Shapiro (1981), Lear and Cantarella (2008), 38–52, and the discussion in chapter 5.
[67] This applies whether or not the ribbons, wreaths, and branches are taken, with Neils (1994), 154–59, to denote victory in the Euandria ("manly goodness") competition. Given that the *euan-*

The Case of the Solo Athlete, from Earliest Red-Figure to the Classical Period

From earliest red-figure, athletes appeared on pots on their own, as well as in gymnasium scenes. The solo athlete was a particularly favored motif on cups, both between the eyes on the outside of an "eye-cup" (1.3–4 and plate 1) and in the interior tondo. Athletes engaged in various activities were figured in this way; we find jumpers (particularly favored on the tondos of cups), javelin and discus throwers, hoplite runners, and athletes running or preparing to run, using picks, or oiling or scraping themselves. Garlanded or beribboned athletic victors also appear on their own. Over time, the popularity of particular solo athletic activities changes, and the company that the images keep, that is, the other images on the same pot, change too.

As with groups of athletes in the gymnasium, so also individual athletes sometimes appear on early red-figure pots along with scenes of myth. A cup attributed to Oltos shows a jumper in its tondo and scenes of Herakles and Geryon and Achilles with a chariot on the outside; a little later a cup ascribed to the Euergides Painter combines a jumper with scenes of a *komos* and scenes of Theseus and the Minotaur and Herakles and the lion (**3.11–13**).[68] Another cup, signed by Euergides as potter and also ascribed to the Euergides Painter combines an athlete picking up a discus with scenes of Herakles and the lion and with a scene of two maenads with a satyr.[69] Never frequent, such combinations of scene quickly become extremely rare.[70]

Scenes of a solo athlete, like gymnasium scenes, are frequently accompanied by other scenes that show further athletics, young men with horses, hoplites, or *komastic* activity. The relative popularity of these accompanying scenes varies over time. Hoplites are among the earliest company of red-figure athletes, even appearing on "bilingual" cups (see 4.8).[71] They continue to appear occasionally, in particular with jumpers, down to the end of the sixth century; after that they are to be found with boxers for a little longer, but otherwise they become very rare; only hoplite runners are to be found with any frequency, and even they are not shown juxtaposed

---

dria was a tribal, not an individual, competition, this suggestion seems to me unlikely to be true (see Kephalidou [1996], 134–35).

[68] *ARV* 62.84, 89.21.

[69] *ARV* 89.23.

[70] The latest gymnasium scene paired with a mythical scene is perhaps *ARV* 227.9, ascribed to the Eucharides Painter, where Apollo and Artemis appear on the other side, until the "Mannerists" use such pairings briefly (e.g., *ARV* 562.1, 563.5, 569.45, 584.20, 593.41, 594.52, 618.5, 618.6, 619.16, 620.23; cf. also 534.5) before they disappear from the repertoire again. An isolated late occurrence of a solo athlete (using a pick) juxtaposed to Herakles and Theseus is *ARV* 454.3, attributed to the Ashby Painter.

[71] Fig. 4.8, *ARV* 56.27, ascribed to Oltos, has an athlete between the eyes and a black-figure hoplite on the tondo; *ARV* 71.12 ascribed to Epiktetos, has a garlanded red-figure jumper between the eyes and a black-figure hoplite on the tondo. Note also *ARV* 55.13, ascribed to Oltos, which has a discus thrower between the eyes on one side, a javelin thrower between the eyes on the other, and a black-figure archer in the tondo.

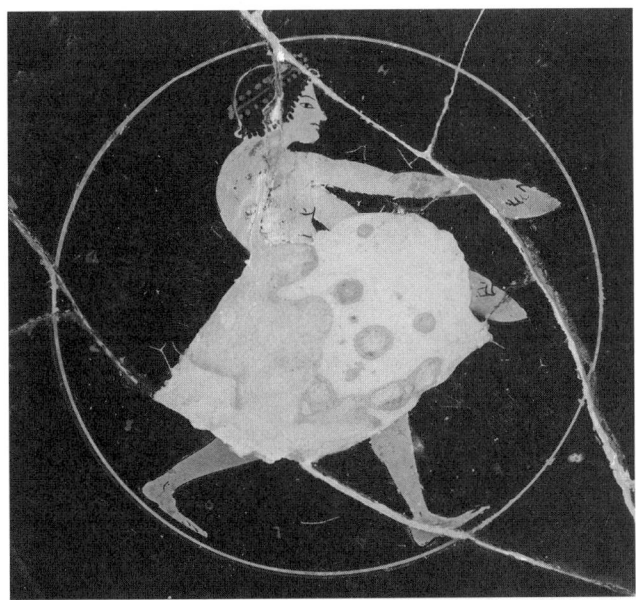

Figure 3.11–13. Interior and exterior of cup, diameter 0.316 m, attributed to the Euergides Painter, ca. 500. *ARV* 89.21. Paris, Musée du Louvre G71. Photo © RMN-Grand Palais (musée du Louvre) / Hervé Lewandowski.

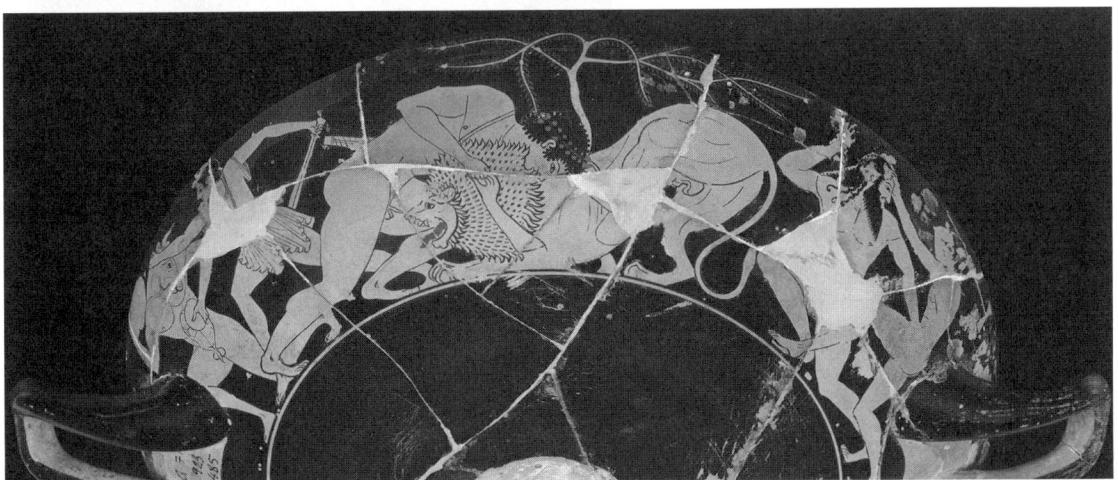

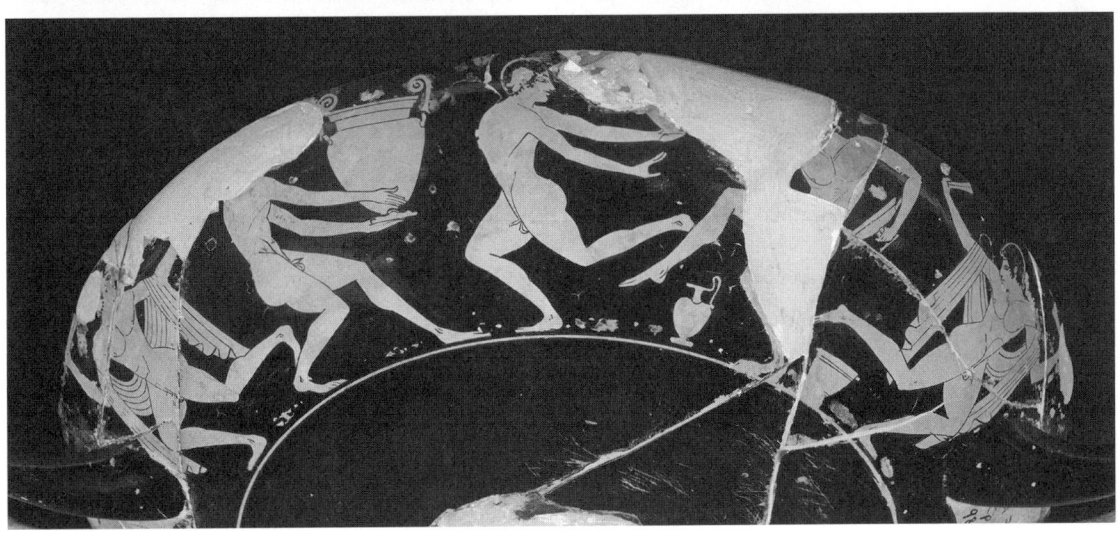

to other hoplite scenes on pots painted after circa 500.[72] In fact athletes increasingly inhabit a world of their own, where one scene showing an athlete is most frequently accompanied by other scenes showing athletes or else by scenes of youths engaged in no particular activity. Even the *komos* is not frequently shown with solo athletes in scenes painted after 500.

The changing company of the solo athlete situates him increasingly in a world removed from the heroic competitions of mythology and from the citizen's duty in warfare. It is a world separate even from the world of the symposium and from reveling—despite the fact that the cups on which the scenes were painted were bought for and used at symposia. It is as if the solo athlete ceased to be good to think with in relation to other men of action, and good only for contemplation in his own right or as a way of introducing further thought about young men in the gymnasium. The athlete is a cue to think about the young naked male body. Such a conclusion derives some support from his subsequent fate.

While athletes continue to attract painters' attention, scenes of actual athletics cease to be a subject of major interest to artists after the first quarter of the fifth century. Whatever particular activity is taken, the story is the same. Discus throwers, javelin throwers, jumpers, hoplite runners, athletic victors, athletes oiling themselves, all of these become subjects of only occasional interest from painters whether they are painting cups or larger pots. The same is true of boxing. I count, for instance, some sixty scenes in which a discus thrower is the subject by the artists included in Beazley Books 1–4 (early and late archaic cup and pot painters), ten in the remainder of *ARV*; the equivalent number for scenes of boxers is forty-four and fourteen, for javelin throwers fifty-six and twenty-one. The only solo athletes who continue to be depicted with any frequency, indeed are depicted with slightly greater frequency, are those not actually engaged in any definite activity, but standing around by an altar or by the boundary stone that marks out the gymnasium—itself more prominent now that the activities do not themselves reveal the identity of the space—holding a javelin or scraping themselves with a strigil (**3.14**). I count twenty-two scenes of individual athletes scraping themselves down to the end of "late archaic," thirty-five subsequently.

The Classical Gymnasium

General gymnasium scenes continue to attract pot painters and their customers through the classical period (I count 170 down to the end of late archaic, 225 subsequently), but their nature too changes. While the late sixth-century scenes reviewed above show a variety of athletes in action or preparing for action, from the second quarter of the fifth century onward most gymnasium scenes largely or entirely lack action.

---

[72] For one of the rare exceptions see *ARV* 427.4, signed by Douris and bearing a Khairestratos *kalos* inscription (cf. *ARV* 430.33 discussed above). This combines a discus thrower on the interior with scenes of hoplite duel and mixed warfare on the exterior.

Two examples will illustrate the sorts of scenes that dominate in the middle of the century. The first is a cup attributed to the Villa Giulia Painter (**3.14–16** and plate 7). In the tondo of this cup we see a youthful athlete standing next to a substantial pillar marking the edge of the gymnasium or *palaistra* with a square block on the other side. He looks away to his right and holds out a strigil in his right hand. On both exterior sides, we see the boundary pillar again, in each case accompanied by three figures. On one side, we have a seated youth with a stick, a naked youth holding out a strigil, very like the youth on the interior, and another naked youth with a javelin. On the other, a youth in a long himation and with a javelin observes two naked youths boxing, one seems to bear the mark of a cut below the eye although currently the youths are at arm's length from each other.

The second is the exterior of a cup attributed to the Penthesileia Painter, and painted in the second quarter of the fifth century well illustrates the sort of gymnasium scene current then (**3.17–18** and plate 8).[73] To the left of one side a youth in himation, holding the trainer's forked stick, stands next to a pillar that identifies a gymnasium; in the center is a naked youth carrying a discus in a sling and two javelins; to the right a naked youth carries a pick off right, looking back. On the other side, from left to right, we find a pillar, a naked youth bent over at right angles—Gardiner thought him in starting position for a race, but he is not like other starting runners we know and the actions of the others in the scene do not suggest this is a race—two empty slings hanging, a youth in himation holding a forked stick, a discus hanging in a sling, and a naked youth, facing left, holding two jumping weights in one hand and with the other hand pointing vaguely in the direction of the other athlete.[74] The interior of this cup shows two youths, one seated wrapped in a mantle, the other wearing a himation and gesticulating in an animated way. Just as this is a scene of conversation, so the exterior scenes are more conversational than of athletic action, their topic the gymnasium rather than the activity of athletics. On other cups, we find the naked athletes standing in pairs as if conversing with each other (compare 1.5–6 and plate 2).[75]

The world of the gymnasium as shown in these later vases is not primarily a place of competition or training, but where youths go to talk to each other. It is a space very largely peopled by the young. The bearded men who figure as spectators and trainers in the earliest red-figure vases are more or less banished from the gymnasium. Trainers continue to appear, but they are beardless youths like the athletes themselves. For all that the world of real-life athletic competitions attracted competitors who continued active for two or more decades, the painted world of the gymnasium becomes a world of young men, not only in its competitors but even in its spectators and judges.

---

[73] Caskey and Beazley (1954), 63–64.
[74] Gardiner (1930), 135 and fig. 88.
[75] *ARV* 942.45 is a good example of such a scene.

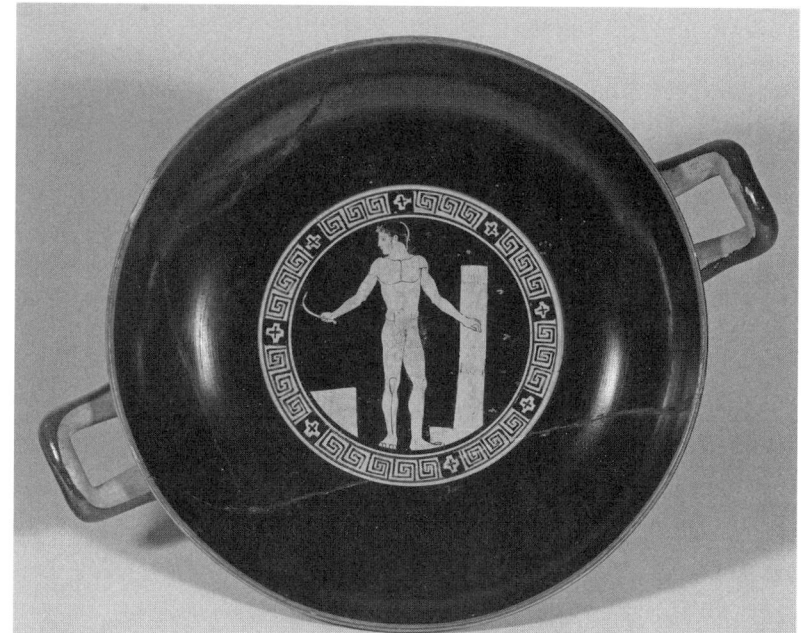
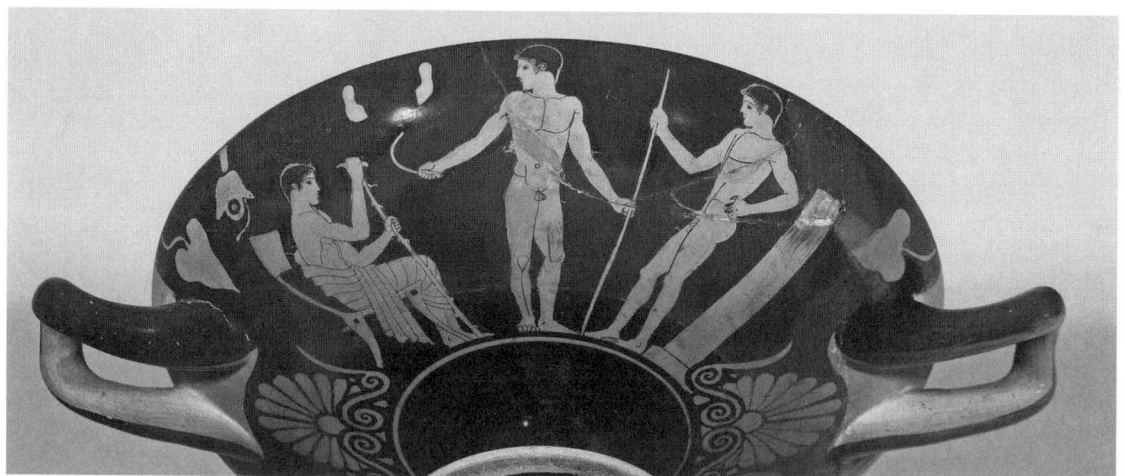
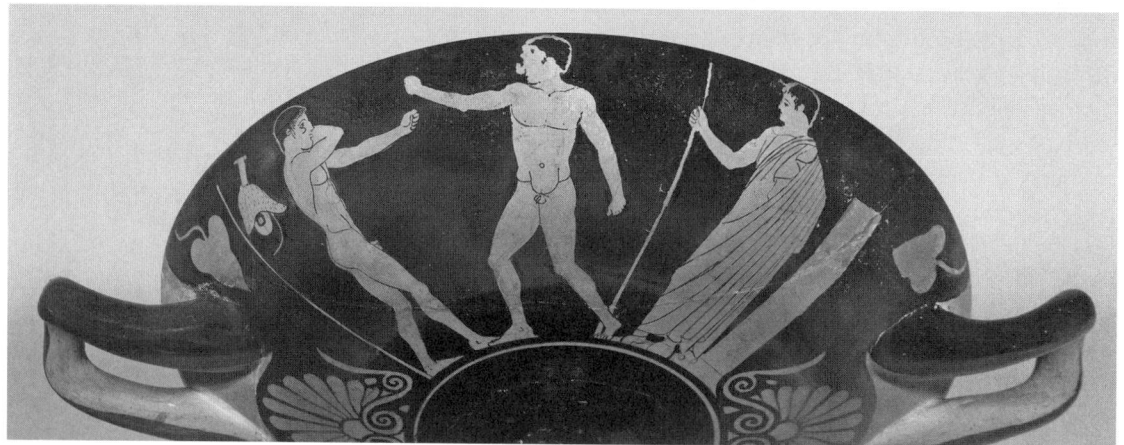

Figure 3.14–16. Interior and exterior of red-figure cup, diameter 0.23 m, attributed to the Villa Giulia Painter, found at Tarquinia, ca. 460–450. *ARV* 625.101. Berlin 2522. © bpk / Antikensammlung, Staatliche Museen zu Berlin / Ingrid Geske.

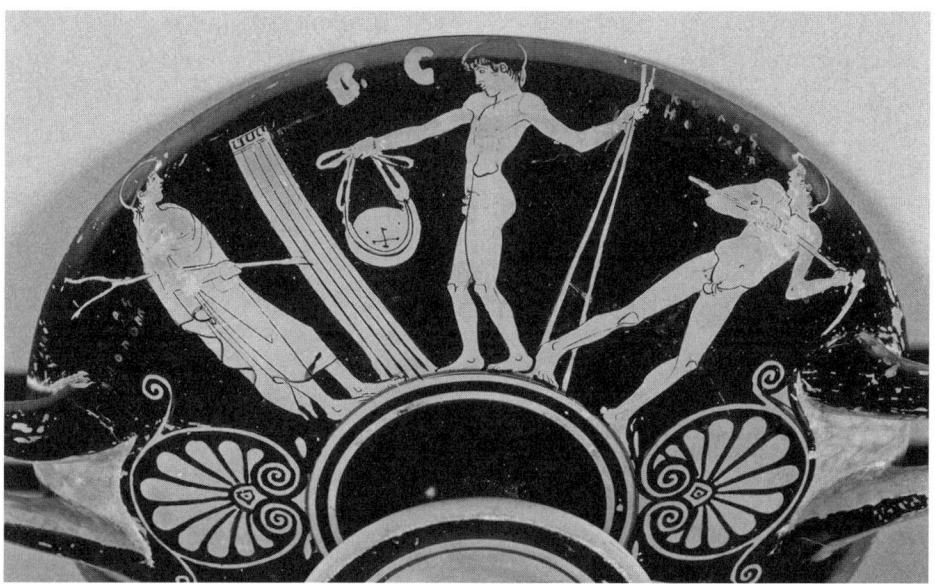

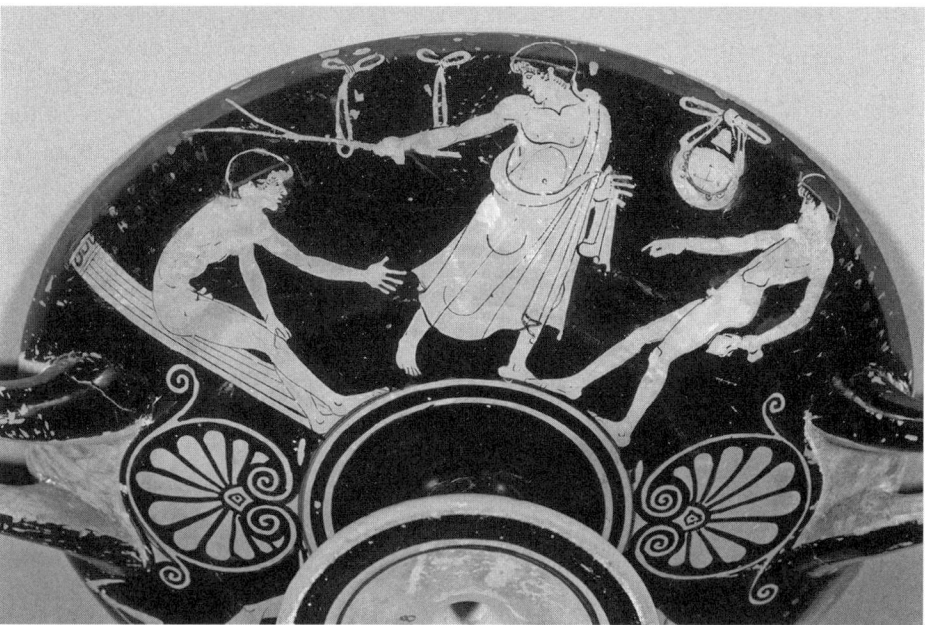

Figure 3.17–18. Exterior of a red-figure cup, diameter 0.238 m, attributed to the Penthesileia Painter, provenance unknown, ca. 460–450. *ARV* 882.36. Boston Museum of Fine Arts 28.48. Photograph © 2017 Museum of Fine Arts, Boston.

The increasing removal of the gymnasium from the rest of the world can be seen too in the changing way in which victory is signaled and celebrated. Representations of men or fellow youths festooning youthful athletes with ribbons and leafy branches become distinctly less numerous after the first quarter of the fifth century, and in their place come representations of the goddess Nike (Victory) bringing ribbons to the victor, which I have already had occasion to mention. Representations of Nike are quite absent from early red-figure and seem to have been introduced by one particular artist: the Berlin Painter.[76] To the Berlin Painter are ascribed more than twenty-five representations of Nike, most of them showing her on her own, but often with a candidate for victor on the other side of the pot. In several cases the putative victor is a kitharode, but in one case we are shown an athlete running, apparently originally carrying a lamp.[77] On one oinochoe Nike presents a wreath to a youth in a himation who holds a javelin.[78] The outward vestiges of athletic victory are present only in some of the representations of Nike, but the important point in this context is that it is in scenes with Nike that figures with ribbons, leafy branches, and other signs of victory (in one case a tripod) are now to be found, and it is Nike who becomes the standard agent awarding victory, not some man or youth (**3.19**).[79]

The gymnasium of early red-figure representations was put on show as a place where young men learned athletic skills and where winning competitions was recognized and rewarded by older men and by youthful contemporaries. From the early fifth century, victory becomes increasingly a metaphysical attribute, not something that exists because other people recognize it but something that happened to an athlete, as it were of its own accord and also as something fleeting.[80] At the same time the gymnasium is increasingly marked out as a space of its own, signaled by pillars and bounded by *horoi*. It is a space where young men are to be found with the accoutrements of athletics, with javelins, with the discus for which they have a special sling, with the sponge and aryballos kit, with the pick, but above all with the strigil. The mature bearded man has increasingly little place in this gymnasium, and neither such activities of the citizen as fighting wars nor even such allegorical thought about broader issues as is carried by myth, are associated with this space. From highlighting the gymnasium as a place where whole dramas are played out, whether in terms of the athletic competition itself or in terms of the personal conquests that athletic display facilitates, the gymnasium becomes the place where the individual athletic young man can be contemplated. Any dramatic encounter between older men and youthful athletes now comes not on the cup or krater, but between the mature male drinker and figures on the pots he uses.

[76] The one early red-figure pot that shows a winged female figure identified as Nike, *ARV* 85.21 ascribed to Skythes, is a bilingual cup and shows Nike in black-figure. Nike is not common in black-figure: *LIMC* VI 582–83 lists just eleven black-figure examples. On representation of Nike more generally in archaic and classical art, see *LIMC* VI s.v. Nike, Isler-Kerenyi (1969), Gulaki (1981), Goulaki-Voutira (1994).

[77] *ARV* 202.89. For Nike and a kitharode on opposite sides of the same pot, see *ARV* 203.100 and 203.104; in both these cases Nike herself carries a lyre, as she does also on 202.74 where a youth is found on the other side of the pot.

[78] *ARV* 210.184bis (*Para.* 345).

[79] Kephalidou (1996), 150–52, and catalog 204–16; cf. also *ARV* 1186.24 discussed above. Note however that the interior of the Briseis Painter's cup shows a youth being embraced by an older man: the hints of the social and erotic rewards of victory have not disappeared, despite the role of Nike on the exterior.

[80] On the fleetingness of victory, compare Osborne (1996a), 68–69.

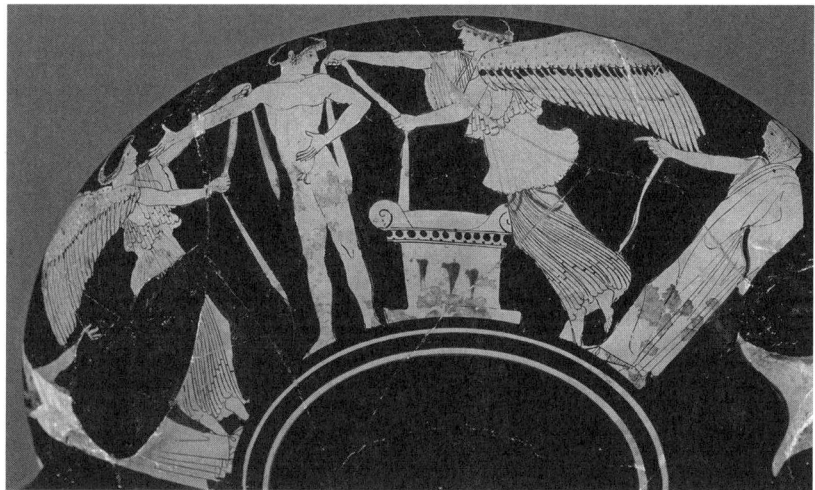

Figure 3.19. Exterior of red-figure cup, diameter 0.263 m, attributed to the Briseis Painter, found at Vulci, ca. 460. *ARV* 407.16. Paris, Louvre G278. Photo © RMN-Grand Palais (musée du Louvre) / Hervé Lewandowski.

4. The Changing Gymnasium

What happens to images of athletics can be neatly summed up by looking at two cups. A cup attributed to the Carpenter Painter, painted circa 500, shows on its exterior two scenes of athletics (**3.20–21** and plate 9).[81] On one side we see five garlanded and bearded athletes. Four of them are shown in successive stages of throwing the javelin; it is, indeed as if we are seeing four frames from a motion picture of throwing the javelin. The fifth figure comes in from the right, past an altar, running toward the left but looking back and holding up in one hand a discus with an owl motif upon it. On the other side of the cup are four garlanded youthful athletes, a youth with a pick, and a youthful *auletes*. From left to right we are shown a discus thrower beginning his swing, a jumper running with his weights in one hand and looking back toward the *auletes*, who is equipped with *phorbeion* and long robe, two pairs of javelins, tied together to form an X standing on their own, a discus thrower running to the left, a runner proceeding to the right, and a youth, his himation tied around his waist, wielding a pick.

The two sides present quite a contrast. The bearded athletes with the javelins are in serious action, providing us with our best textbook illustrations of the art of throwing the javelin.[82] The youths on the other side, by contrast, run around the gymnasium but hardly engage in actual athletic activity at all. Despite the *auletes*, equipped to adorn a festal competition, these youths mill around quite without any sense of the rhythmic motion so clearly conveyed by the bearded javelin throwers on the other side of

---

[81] Von Bothmer (1986). For works ascribed to the Carpenter Painter by Beazley, see *ARV* 179. Von Bothmer identifies him with the H. P. Painter, for whom see *ARV* 454.

[82] Waddell (1991), 103–4.

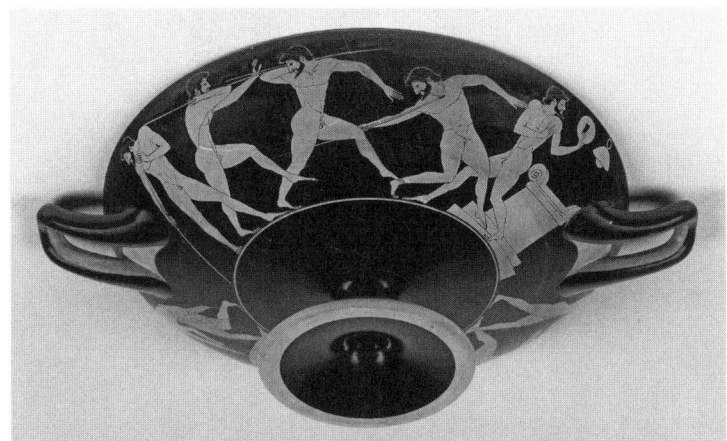

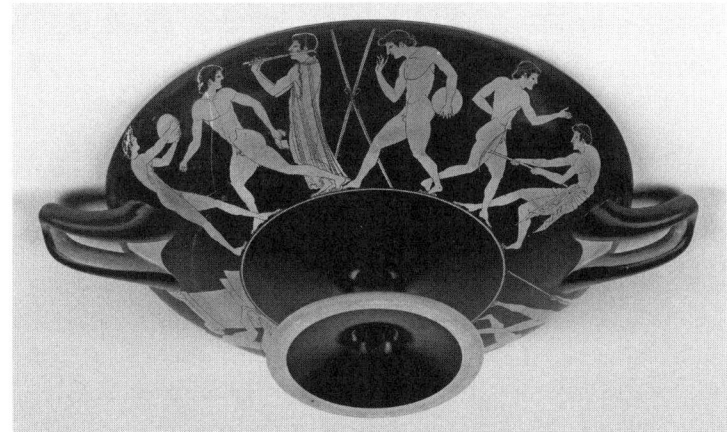

Figure 3.20–22. Red-figure cup, diameter 0.305 m, attributed to the Carpenter Painter, provenance unknown, ca. 500. J. Paul Getty Museum, Malibu 85.AE.25. Digital image courtesy of the Getty's Open Content Program.

the cup. Even without looking at the interior scene on this cup, the viewer must be struck by the difference between the two sides, and by the exclusively bearded participants on the one side, the exclusively youthful on the other.

On the interior of the cup the viewer finds another bearded man and another youth, but they are not engaged in athletics (**3.22**). A garlanded youth, draped from the waist, sits on a block. He reaches up, puts his hands round the back of the head of a garlanded bearded man dressed in a very short cloak, who is bent over toward him, and pulls him down to kiss him. The two sides of the gymnasium here come together in an erotic relationship. The men who are serious athletes turn out to be showing off their paces not simply to the viewer but to the young men for whom jumping weights and the discus are as much symbols as tools, and for whom prowess with regard to the javelin is displayed as much from getting it to balance against another javelin as from throwing it. The older men parade their skill, the younger parade their bodies, all as part of the preliminaries to serious courtship. As the drinker lifts the cup he offers the others at the symposium a choice of images of himself, in the guise of either the older or the younger man in the gymnasium. What he himself sees in the bottom of

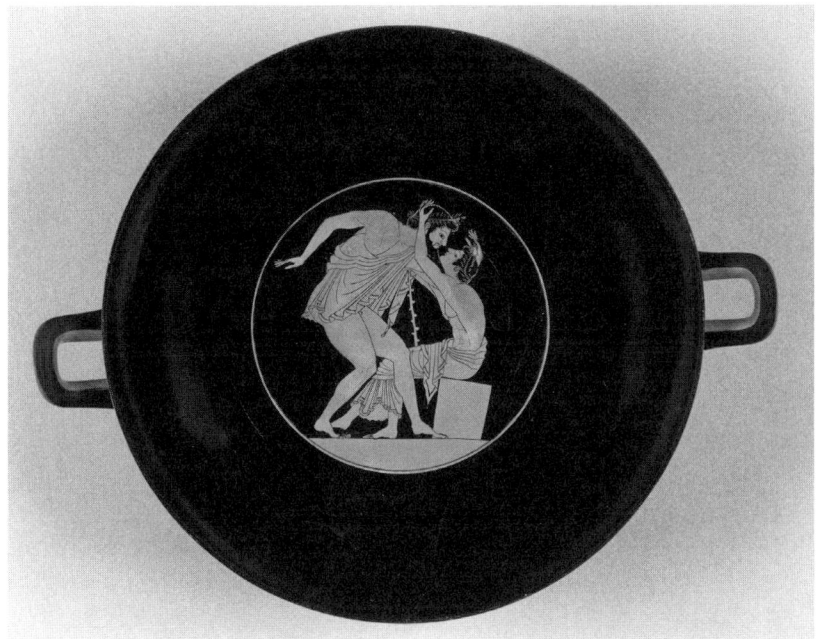

the cup is why offering an image is important: how you are seen to perform in the gymnasium has pulling power.

Some forty years later a painter known as the Akestorides Painter also painted both a youth and a bearded man on the interior of a cup (**3.23**). Here the man, wearing a himation and carrying a straight stick, faces a naked youth, identified as an athlete by the two jumping weights that he holds. On the outside of the cup are two further scenes involving men and youths (**3.24–25** and plate 10). On one side a youth, draped from the waist down, sits on a block reading from a scroll on which words are written that can be identified as part of an epic hexameter.[83] A youth in a himation and holding a lyre faces him, stretching an arm in his direction. To the right, and facing right but looking back, is a man in a himation and with a stick who has one hand on his hip and the other arm slightly extended. On the other side a man in a very similar pose but looking forward observes a youth wearing a himation and carrying a writing case. Another youth, well-draped in a himation, stands facing to the right but looking left.

Precise identification of figures as *paidagogoi* or teachers is not possible, but it is clear that this cup is about education, *paideia*. On the outside, we see the schooling of the mind, schooling in the reading of epic poetry, the playing of the lyre, and in basic literacy skills. On the inside, we see the training of the body, in the form of what is purely theoretical instruction in the complicated techniques of the long jump.

School scenes begin in red-figure around or shortly after 500 BC and are often combined with scenes showing youths or men and youths. A number

---

[83] Beazley (1948), 338–39, giving the text as ὡς δή μοι καὶ μᾶλ<λ>ον ἐπέσ[συτο θυμὸς ἀγήνωρ] comparing *Iliad* 9.399 and 13.638. The words that can be read would be sufficient to establish that the text is a hexameter without offering any definitive content.

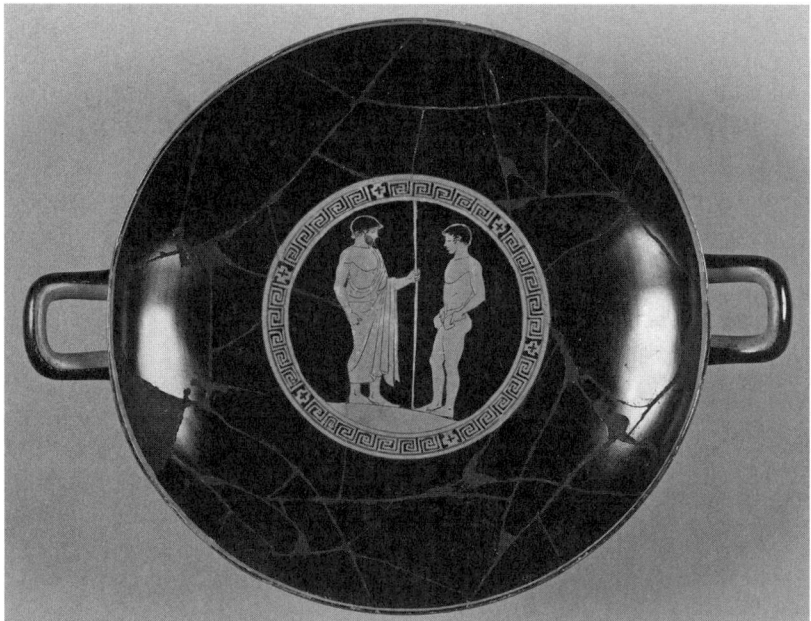

Figure 3.23–25. Red-figure cup attributed to the Akestorides Painter, found at Orvieto, ca. 450. *ARV* 781.4. Washington 136373. © Department of Anthropology, Smithsonian Institution.

of pots show the reading of texts on which words are indicated clearly enough to enable us to read them, and most commonly these are epic texts. One further such scene is in fact also attributed to the Akestorides Painter.[84] Combining such a scene with an athletic scene is not common,[85] but such a combination is entirely consistent with the changed world of the gymnasium. The gymnasium pictured in the late sixth century was a place of competitive social interaction, a place of games in which older and younger men struck poses and offered themselves and their bodies for admiration. The gymnasium of the middle of the fifth century was a place of education, a place in which the young man acquired a fit body. Young men wealthy enough to do so went to the gymnasium, as they went to school, because that was what wealthy young men did. As at school they acquired a competence in music and literacy sufficient to enable them to cope with the political and social demands of the life of the leisured citizen, so in the gymnasium they acquired the ability to talk with knowledge and experience about athletics and to instruct the next generation in skills requiring bodily coordination as well as those involving the application of the mind.[86]

The scenes of the gymnasium painted in the last quarter of the sixth century are primarily interested in the individual incidents that occur there, both the individual episodes of athletic endeavor and the incidental episodes of human interaction. They move from seeing these incidents in the grand terms suggested by mythological parallels to emphasizing the particularity of the activities and encounters by offering names for the protagonists. The gymnasium of these early red-figure pots is an exciting place

---

[84] *ARV* 781.4bis (1670).
[85] For a rather later example, see *ARV* 1254.80, but the school scene there is a mythological one.
[86] For gymnasium talk, cf. Aristophanes *Wasps* 1190–95.

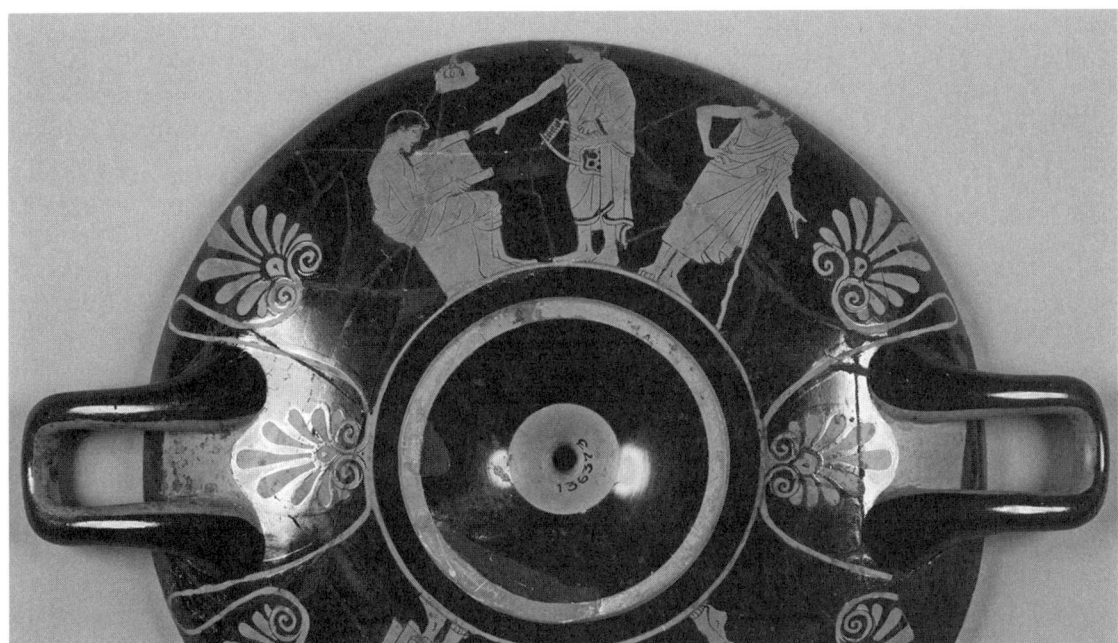

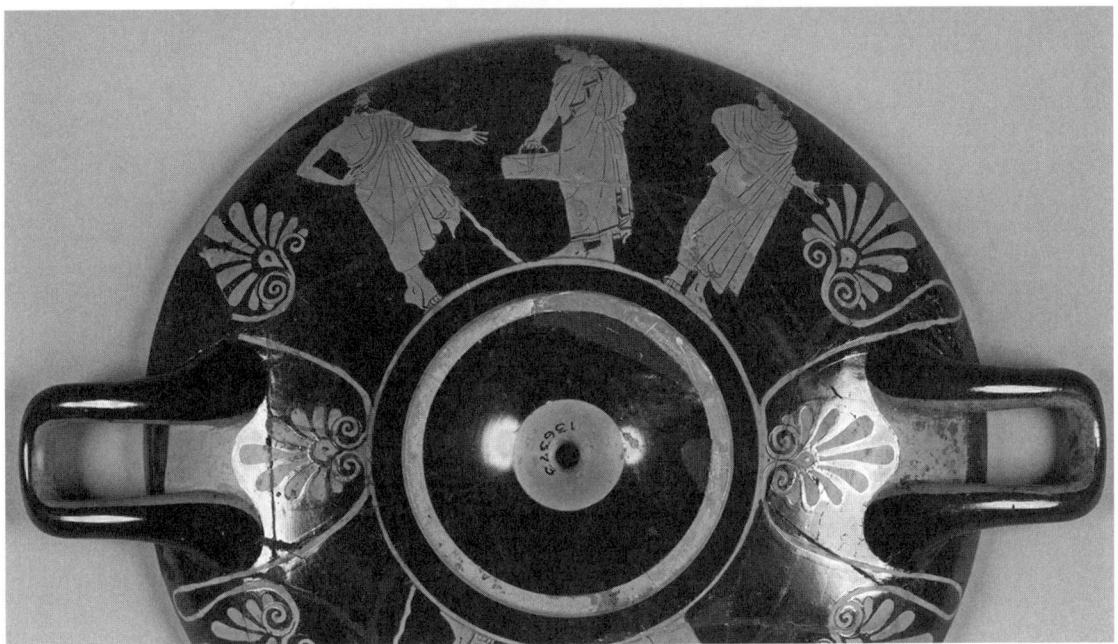

in which things are going on—things that do meet the eye and things that do not. There is an intensity to the human relations here, an intensity that has a more or less manifest sexual charge.

The scenes of the gymnasium painted after the Persian Wars increasingly lack such an intensity. Victory flies in to reward those who win, replacing the admiring assessment carried in the gaze of the older man as he offers the ribbons or other tokens of victory. Youths pass the time of day in the gymnasium, and they acquire there what is needed to pass as an athlete,

CHANGING IN THE GYMNASIUM   83

but no longer do the scenes on the pots focus on their particular gymnastic activities. Wielding the strigil has become as important as wielding the discus. If a well-trained body continues to be something every citizen should be able to sport, competitive pulling power over older men is no longer advertised.

How does the changing representation of the gymnasium and of athletic activity relate to the history of athletics and the gymnasium in Athens? As we saw, we have good reason to believe that athletic activities remained central to, and indeed became more important in, Athenian festival life. Athenians reaffirmed their desire to give athletes civic rewards and continued to want the money of the rich to go on the liturgies that provided for athletic festivals, and even to tolerate rich men who claimed political influence on the basis of securing athletic success. The Athenians as a whole certainly did not lose interest in athletic competition.

But if the relationship between representation and life is not straightforward, the possibility that there should be no connection between images of the gymnasium figured on pots used and talked about at symposia and athletic activity in real life is essentially nil. To judge from the good evidence given by the Platonic dialogues, precisely the same people frequented gymnasia and symposia. What has happened is that the features of athletics most salient in visual discourse have altered. Athenian painters have come to see the gymnasium differently and to present a different gymnasium to those who bought and used the pots they painted. Whatever social, political, or art-historical factors we think may have played into the changes, there has been, in a very basic sense, a change in perception—in the literal sense of the word, a change in aesthetics.

At the same time that the nature of athletic scenes has changed, so has the way in which the scenes are drawn. The style in which athletes are represented in the middle of the fifth century is different from the style deployed by artists of the late sixth century. The change from vigorous to inactive male bodies is a change from extravagant gestures to relaxed postures, from hard bodies, adapted for action, putting themselves and their musculature on show, and drawing attention to body parts through elaborate depiction and use of relief lines, to soft bodies, with rare use of the relief line, evoking fragility and tenderness, displaying and encouraging contemplation and self-absorption. This stylistic change is by no means limited to painters of pots. The contrast between the athletes of the Andokides Painter (3.3) and the athletes of the Akestorides Painter (3.23), or between Onesimos (**3.26** and plate 11) and the Eretria Painter (**3.27** and plate 12), is closely paralleled by the contrast between the ball players on the stele base from late archaic Athens (1.16) and Polykleitos's *Diadoumenos* (athlete binding himself with a fillet) now known only from later copies (**3.28**). The focus of interest has shifted in similar ways in the two cases. The athletes' bodies are in each case both made and matched, but what is matched is different and what is made is different: the different emphases produced by the changed style of depiction result in quite different takes on what is proper to the athlete. If we are seeing here a changed

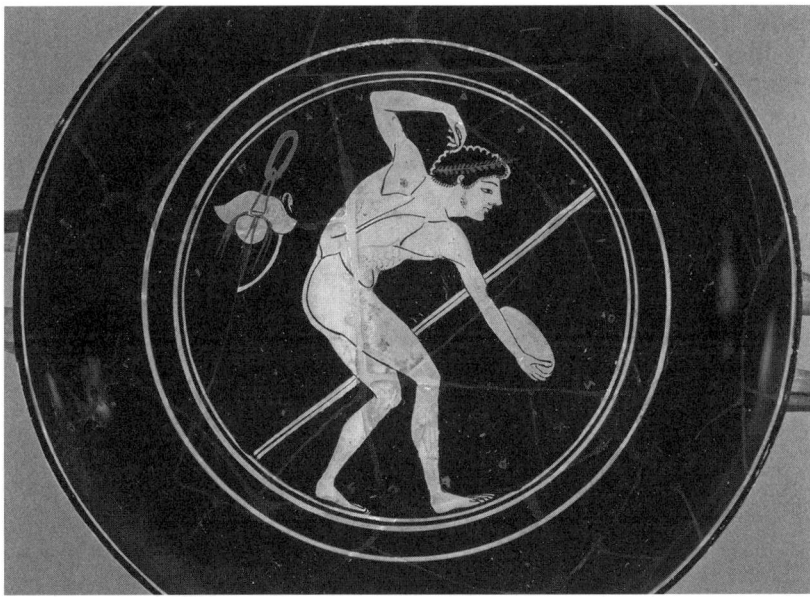

Figure 3.26. Interior of red-figure cup, diameter 0.225 m, attributed to Onesimos, found at Orvieto, ca. 500. *ARV* 321.22. Boston Museum of Fine Arts 01.8020. Photograph © 2017 Museum of Fine Arts, Boston.

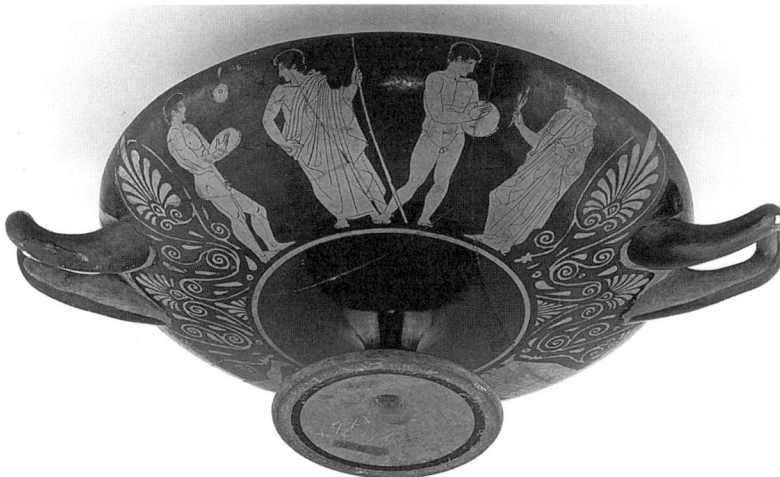

Figure 3.27. Exterior of red-figure cup, diameter 0.26 m, attributed to the Eretria Painter, ca. 435. *ARV* 1254.73. Blanton Museum, Austin 1980.38. © Blanton Museum of Art, the University of Texas at Austin, Archer M. Huntington Museum Fund and the James R. Dougherty, Jr. Foundation 1980.

aesthetic we are also seeing what is at stake in a changed aesthetic: real people's relations in real life.

The changes that we observe in the representation of athletics on pots (and in sculpture) involve changes in the representation of how individuals behave toward one another. If these changes are not divorced entirely from life then our story of aesthetic change will also be a story of changing views

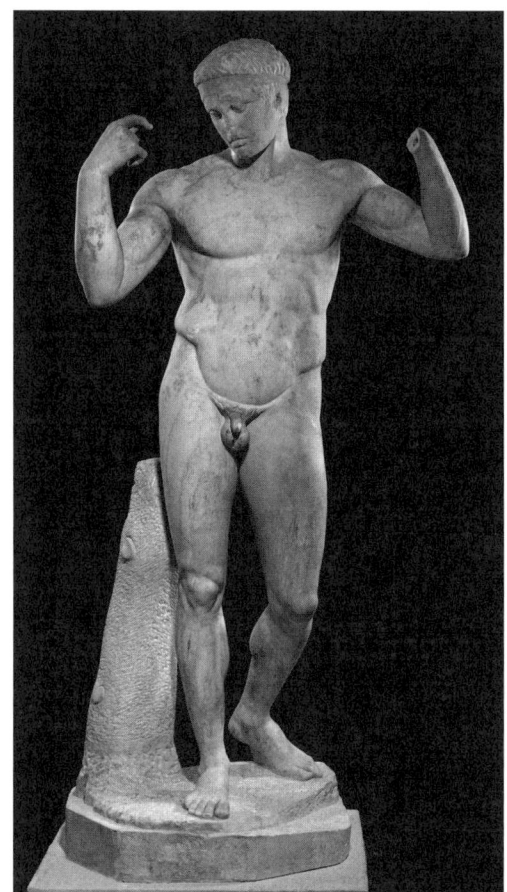

Figure 3.28. Marble copy, height 1.89 m, of the Diadoumenos of Polykleitos of Argos, from the Roman theater at Vaison; made in the second century AD. London, British Museum 1870,0712.1. © The Trustees of the British Museum.

of interpersonal relations within Athenian life and (given the currency of Polykleitos) Greek life more generally. But is what we are looking at here a matter of changing relations in the gymnasium, or are we in fact dealing with a more widespread transformation? To answer that question, I extend my scrutiny from the gymnasium to the battlefield in order to observe whether and in what ways Athenian pot painters came over time to represent soldiers differently.

4 ❧ Changing the Guard

> "One of the sergeants looks after their socks," says Alice.
> —A. A. Milne.

Kleisthenes's reforms to Athens's political organization also transformed Athenians' experience of warfare. Athenian tradition told of a number of military engagements during the sixth century, but we know very little about the sixth-century Athenian army. Peisistratos was famous for using non-Athenian troops, including mercenaries, to help him achieve power in Athens, and the Aristotelian *Constitution of the Athenians* claims that he completely disarmed the Athenians—something that his son Hippias may actually have done.[1] But already by the time that Herodotos was writing, the constitutional reforms of Kleisthenes were associated with a marked change in Athenian military performance, and there is no doubt that the last decade of the sixth century saw a radical reorganization of the Athenian army based on citizen soldiers divided into units according to the ten new Kleisthenic tribes.[2]

Further changes to the army command structure followed in the second decade of the fifth century, when the ten elected generals took overall command of the army out of the hands of the polemarch, who was now chosen by lot.[3] The same years saw the beginning of the massive expansion of the Athenian fleet that significantly altered the social balance of the Athenian military force.[4] Neither Athenian army nor Athenian navy ever became a "standing" force, each was always newly recruited and constituted for particular campaigns or campaigning seasons, but from the time of the great war against Persia onward those campaigns came thick and fast. The Athenian armed forces were involved in almost continuous action, and only the physically incapable among the Athenian citizenry could expect to avoid frequent call-up.

Athenian painted pottery shows a continuous interest in the soldier. Already in black-figure pottery military scenes were frequent. Some of

---

[1] Hdt. 1.61.4, cf. 64.1, [Aristotle] *Constitution of the Athenians* 15.2, 17.4, 19.4, for use of non-Athenian troops by Peisistratos. [Aristotle] *Constitution of the Athenians* 15.3–5, for Peisistratos disarming the Athenians. Thuc. 6.58 for Hippias disarming the Athenians. See Wees (2013), 71–72.

[2] Hdt. 5.78; Wees (2004), 99, 204.

[3] [Aristotle] *Constitution of the Athenians* 22.2, Hdt. 6.109–11.

[4] Wees (2004), 207–9.

them are explicitly connected with myths, but others are not. Red-figure continues this interest, but although the heavily armed soldier attracted almost continuous attention, the ways and the contexts in which the soldier was portrayed did not remain unchanged, and the range of scenes in which soldiers were shown in the early fifth century was very different from the range in the late sixth century, and different again by the middle of the fifth century.

Whereas our literary evidence for Athenian athletic activity is thin, military activity is one of the few areas of Athenian life during these years where both rich contemporary or near-contemporary literary evidence and abundant contemporary images are available. This chapter attempts to assess the changing place of military activity in the life of the Athenian state, to chart its changing representation, and to explore the possible relationship between the changing experience of military life and its changing representation.

1. The Development of the Athenian Armed Forces

Although the development of new heavy armor in the seventh century has often been held to herald a revolution not only in warfare but also in the social and political structure of the Greek cities, traces of a hoplite army are hard to find in archaic Athens.[5] Rather than tell of a string of large-scale battles by which Athenian territory was defended or enlarged, the traditions of archaic Athenian military activity concern what appear to be small-scale skirmishes over the island of Salamis and the Megarian town of Nisaia, or battles that are really part of a civil war (the battle of Pallene at which the tyrant Peisistratos established himself in power in the middle of the sixth century; the battle at Leipsydrion at which an unsuccessful attempt was made to unseat Peisistratos's sons from power in 514).[6] Some of these incidents are of dubious historicity, and how far any of them involved a regimented army, as opposed to ad hoc recruitment for a specific end, is unclear.

Whether there was such a thing as a regimented army in Athens depends largely upon the interpretation of the property classes into which Solon divided the Athenians. Of the four classes, the names of the highest (*pentakosiomedimnoi*, 500-bushel men) and lowest (*thetes*) certainly make no military allusion, but the names of the two middle groups, *zeugitai* and *hippeis*, have been thought to allude to hoplites and to cavalry respectively. The other evidence we have for cavalry (Pollux 8.108) claims that each of the forty-eight naukraries provided two cavalrymen.[7] Such an organization

---

[5] On the "hoplite revolution," see Osborne (1996b/2009), 170–76/161–66, with references at 369/350; Wees (2004), chap. 12.

[6] Herodotos 1.59, 62–63; 5.62. For a list of archaic Athenian battles, see Frost (1984), Singor (2000); on the Athenians and Salamis the evidence is collected and discussed by Taylor (1997); see also Osborne (1994).

[7] On naukraries, see Wees (2013), 44–56.

is incompatible with a purely wealth-based criterion for membership of the cavalry, which would require numbers to be flexible, and in any case some military service is surely to be expected from the *pentakosiomedimnoi* also, and this can only have been as cavalry. As for the *zeugitai*, debate continues as to whether the name derived from ownership of a pair of draft animals or from the metaphorical yoking together of men in the hoplite line, but the likelihood that the *hippeis* are not classified by their military role strengthens the case for the *zeugitai* having, rather than being, a yoked pair.[8] The term *telos*, which gets translated as "census-class," is a term that refers to the payment of tax, and Solon's classes should be seen as primarily tax classes—as Pollux puts it, "the *zeugesion* is a tax that those who keep a pair of oxen pay."[9] That those who had horses tended to end up in the cavalry, those who had only yokes of oxen among the hoplites, is very likely, but "hoplite" was a military role, not a status, and "the hoplites" were those who were serving as hoplites at any one time.

Scholars have often speculated that Peisistratos deliberately avoided engaging citizen troops in military campaigns, for fear that to arm them would be to arm a force that might overthrow him. As Connor has pointed out, early Greek land warfare was an elaborate system, functioned as a ritual, and offered a representation of social reality, making visible the different contributions different groups made within the city and so offering roles to which citizens could aspire.[10] Warfare created leaders as well as followers and offered means for the fighting body and its commanders to win (and lose) prestige before the body of older and younger men and of women who waited in the city and observed the fortunes of war. As with athletic success, where the Peisistratids' discomfort with the repeated successes of Kimon led to his murder (Hdt. 6.103), so too with success in warfare, autocratic rulers needed to control access; in the case of warfare they were in a position to do so, at least until such time as civil war broke out.

As well as claiming that Peisistratos disarmed the people, [Aristotle] claims that it was only under democracy that the custom of carrying arms at the Panathenaia began, explicitly denying the opposite story, which is represented in Thucydides.[11] Although the claim that the Athenians were unarmed at the Panathenaia has been seen as intended to exculpate them for not coming to the aid of the "tyrannicides," Harmodios and Aristogeiton, it is equally possible that it was emulation of the tyrannicides that caused Athenians to take up arms at the Panathenaia. At stake here is the

---

[8] On the Solonian census classes, see Foxhall (1997); Wees (2013), 85–91. On cavalry, see Bugh (1988), 4–7, 20–34. Whitehead (1981) attempted to demonstrate once for all that zeugitai were hoplites (cf. de Ste. Croix (2004), 14–28), but recent opinion has weighed in the other direction (Foxhall [1997] ,131, and n. 109; Rauflaub [1997], 55 and n. 31; and esp. Wees [2006] [2013], 85–91). Despite the claims of both de Ste. Croix and Wees, who stand on different sides in this debate, I see no reason why the classification of the super-rich by bushels demands that other classes were defined by bushels rather than by ownership of a horse or of a pair of oxen.

[9] Pollux 8.132 καὶ ζευγήσιόν τι τέλος οἱ ζευγοτροφοῦντες ἐτέλουν.

[10] Connor (1988).

[11] *Ath. Pol.* 18.4; Thucydides 6.58.

Athenian self-image: did Athenians present themselves at their major festival as an army or not?

Herodotos tells us that when the Spartans attacked Athens to expel Hippias in 510 it was one thousand Thessalian cavalry, summoned through an alliance with the Peisistratids, who saw off the initial seaborne invasion led by Anchimolios and then bore the brunt of the attack and of the losses (more than forty men) when king Kleomenes led a successful land invasion.[12] Four years later, after the Boiotians and Khalkidians had taken advantage of a further Spartan invasion of Attica, which was then called off, in order to raid Athenian territory, the Athenians launched an attack on the Khalkidians. The Boiotians joined in the war and were defeated, with much loss of life and seven hundred men captured alive; the Athenians proceeded to defeat the Khalkidians too and sent four thousand settlers to occupy their land. From the ransom money raised from the prisoners, the Athenians set up on the Acropolis a monument to the victory.[13]

The story of these events of 506 indicates how marked a change had occurred in Athens in the intervening period. In 510 there is little sign of an Athenian army (when the Thessalians are defeated, the war proceeds by siege); by 506 Athens can muster an army that is capable not only of defeating its neighbors but also of doing so on a massive scale. And on achieving that victory the Athenians marked the revolution by placing on the acropolis, where all recent monuments were personal dedications and where it was victories in games, not war, that were dominant, a magnificent monument that almost certainly greeted visitors as they first passed through the gateway. That monument was such a sufficient source of pride that the Athenians had a new version created and erected after the Persians had destroyed the original.[14]

Athenian military success in 506 might be simply a product of uniting an unusually large population behind a campaign that satisfied a widespread desire for revenge upon neighbors who had been seeking to exploit Athenian domestic troubles. Herodotos's own verdict on the success, which I cited above, might be held to link the success more to morale than to army structure. Kleisthenes's reforms did bring a change of army structure, however, and that change is as likely to have occurred sooner as later.[15] What we know for certain is that in or subsequent to the archonship of Hermokreon and twelve years before the battle of Marathon, generals were for the first time elected one from each tribe.[16] The year/s 501/500 (assum-

---

[12] Hdt. 5.63–65.

[13] Hdt. 5.74–77

[14] Fragments of both the original and the replacement monument survive: ML 15 (*DAA* 168, 173, *IG* i³ 501A and B). The siting of the monument is controversial since Herodotos (5.77.4) has been understood to indicate a different location from that given by Pausanias (1.28.2) and the findspot of 168, but it is likely that the original monument was just inside the Propylaia.

[15] A "long chronology" for Kleisthenes reforms was championed by Badian (2000), who implied that the war with the Boiotians and Khalkidians was a factor slowing down the introduction of the constitutional changes, but did not consider whether the successful fighting of that war required basic reforms already to have been carried out.

[16] [Aristotle] *Ath. Pol.* 22.2 with Rhodes ad loc.

ing inclusive counting) is therefore a firm *terminus ante quem* for an army organized according to the ten new Kleisthenic tribes. It is not, however, inevitable that the new tribal army was invented at the same moment as the new tribal generals. Some formalization of military obligations is already implied by the inscription recording the conditions upon which settlers are sent to Salamis, for they are obliged to pay taxes to Athens and to fight for the Athenians, providing their own armor to the value of 30 drachmas.[17] The precise date of this inscription is not known, but the chances that this, the first extant Athenian decree, dates to the end of the era of the tyrants seem slim, and the most attractive context is in the immediate aftermath of the Kleisthenic reforms.[18]

The case for a tribal army being at the heart of Kleisthenes's reforms rests in part upon the difficulty of finding other practical, as opposed to abstract, roles for the Kleisthenic tribes and more particularly for Kleisthenic *trittyes*. These "thirds" of tribes are remarkably shadowy institutions, rarely mentioned in either the literature or the epigraphy of the fifth and fourth centuries. [Aristotle] tells us that *trittys* was the name given to the group of demes assigned to a single tribe from a particular region (city, inland, coast), and that the purpose of the *trittyes* was to ensure that every tribe should include demes from each region.[19] But a mixture would have been much better assured by ascribing demes to tribes at random, rather than by combining three groups of (normally) contiguous demes. No other role performed by tribes seems to depend upon or be assisted by the existence of *trittyes*. But both the call-up and the subsequent deployment of tribal army contingents will plausibly have been assisted by *trittyes*: their geographical compactness will have facilitated call-up, and they offered a subdivision of the rather large tribal unit of a more or less consistent and militarily useful size (deme units would be too small and might, to judge by the different number of councilors different demes were expected to provide, vary in size by a factor of forty-four). Evidence for *trittys* units may exist in the form of stones, inscribed to be muster points for members of *trittyes*, which have been found both in Athens (on the Pnyx and in the Agora) and at the Peiraieus.[20] Although these might be mustering *trittys* members for political purposes, the discovery of examples in the Peiraieus points toward a military role.

Whatever the precise timing and details of the army reform, there can be no doubt that the decade 510–500 saw an army revolution in Athens. By 500 the Athenians had a hoplite army organized in ten tribal units, each with their own tribal officers appointed annually. The following two decades saw a comparable naval revolution.

Archaic Athens does seem to have had a fleet, though we never see it in use for any more than transporting a few troops to Salamis. The same pas-

---

[17] ML 14, *IG* i³ 1.
[18] This is the orthodox position, argued for, against the earlier dating by Luria, at ML p. 27.
[19] [Aristotle] *Ath. Pol.* 21.4.
[20] Traill (1986), 93–115; Siewert (1982). See also Effenterre (1976).

sage of Pollux that attests that each *naukraria* provided two horsemen to form a cavalry force of ninety-six in Athens also attests that each *naukraria* provided a ship.[21] In 499 the Athenians sent twenty ships to assist the Ionians in revolting against their Persian overlords; by the end of the 490s they are said to have had fifty ships and acquired twenty more from Corinth for their war against Aigina; after Marathon Miltiades was able to call on seventy ships for his attack on Paros.[22] Massive expansion of the fleet followed in the 480s, on Themistokles's initiative, so that by the time of the battle of Salamis the Athenians could field two hundred ships.[23] The nature of the Athenian ships in 499 is not known (Herodotos seems to draw a distinction between the Athenian "ships" and the Eretrian "triremes"[24]), but even were they all triremes, the tenfold expansion of the fleet would have increased the number of sailors required from something over three thousand in 499 to something over thirty thousand in 480 (compare the eight thousand Athenian hoplites who fought at Plataia in 479[25]).

As will already be clear, neither the army nor the fleet was a paper exercise. Involvement with the Ionian revolt, the long-running war with Aigina, Miltiades's activities on Paros, and conflict with the Persians in 490 and 480–79 meant that both fleet and army were well-practiced in the first two decades of the fifth century. From 478 onward, as the Athenians took over command of the continuing campaigns against Persia and the liberation of Asia Minor, both navy and army were annually engaged in campaigns. The experience of being a young man in Athens in the early fifth century was quite different from the experience of being a young man in Athens under the Peisistratids. And those young men's experiences, and deaths, were impressed upon the rest of the population too.

After the victory over Boiotians and Khalkidians in 506, the commemorative monument had taken the form of a chariot, and the inscription accompanying it celebrated the achievement of the "sons of the Athenians." This became the first of a series of monuments to Athenian military success, erected in Athens or elsewhere. After Marathon, there may have been a dedication made in the name of the (dead) polemarch Kallimakhos in the form of a figure of Iris or Nike on a column. After both Marathon and Plataia the Athenians made victory dedications at Delphi. After Salamis a monument, possibly bearing herms, was erected at an unknown location in Athens.[26] Some years later the battle of Marathon was represented in the Painted Stoa in the Athenian Agora.[27] The Athenians went on to approve

[21] Pollux 8.108; compare *Lex Segueriana* I.283.20 and the discussion by Wees (2013), 44–68.
[22] Hdt. 5.97.3, 5.99.1; 6.89; 6.132.
[23] Hdt. 7.144.1–2, [Aristotle] *Ath. Pol.* 22.7 with Rhodes (1981) ad loc.; Wallinga (1993), 148–57.
[24] Wallinga (1993), 133, but see Wees (2013), 64–65.
[25] Hdt. 9.28.6; compare the figures of 10,000 and 9,000 given for Marathon by Justin 11.9 and Nepos *Miltiades* 5.1 respectively. On whether there were any Athenian cavalry at this time, see Bugh (1988), 7–13.
[26] For these monuments, see ML 18, 19, 25, 26.
[27] Pausanias 1.15.1–3, 5.11.6.

the monumental commemoration of Kimon's victory at Eion, although strict controls were put on its form.[28]

But victory monuments were not the only way in which their military success was impressed upon the Athenians themselves and upon other Greeks. Diodoros says that the Athenians instituted games in celebration of those who had died in war and the oration in praise of them in 479.[29] Pausanias says that public burial of the war dead in Athens began after the Athenian defeat at Drabeskos in 465, although Thucydides implies that it went back further.[30] From at least the 460s, the names of the dead in war were listed annually by tribe on inscribed stone monuments.[31] One way and another, warfare and its successes were laid before the Athenians as they had never been before.

How did Athenians react to these massive changes? What were the responses to the demands made by increasingly frequent warfare on an increasingly large scale and, with the development of the fleet, involving an increasingly greater social range? The absence of any Athenian literature surviving from the period 550–480 means that literary sources give us little help in answering such questions. Our best chance of an answer comes from looking at what happens to the imagery of war on Athenian pots.

2. The Hoplite in Sixth-Century Iconography

Soldiers of all sorts appeared regularly, and warships occasionally, on Athenian black-figure pots painted between circa 550 and circa 510.[32] We find hoplites, arming and departing (sometimes with chariots), dueling (often between spectators), and dicing (in scenes modeled on Exekias's scene of Achilles and Aias dicing, but most often without either warrior being named), engaging with archers or cavalry, fighting over the bodies of the fallen, and carrying the dead from the battlefield; we find cavalry parting and in procession, galloping and in combat; we find lightly armed troops on horseback and on foot, fighting and lying in wait.[33] Hoplites, and the archers associated with them, are sometimes identified with mythological

---

[28] Plutarch *Kimon* 7.4–6, Aiskhines 3.183–85, with discussion in Osborne (1985).

[29] Diodoros 11.33.3; Osborne (1993), 23.

[30] Pausanias 1.29.4 supported by Jacoby (1944). For discussion, see Gomme (1956) on Thucydides 2.34.1 and OR 109.

[31] *IG* i³ 1144 is the earliest certain list of war dead, and is apparently part of a stele recording the dead of a single tribe. For other fifth-century lists, see *IG* i³ 1145–47bis, 1149–1193bis. See also Clairmont (1983), Arrington (2014).

[32] For representation of warships, the starting point remains the catalog of Morrison and Williams (1968), chap. 4.

[33] For scenes with archers, cavalry, and light troops, see Lissarrague (1989). What follows is much indebted to Lissarrague's account, and to some extent in dialogue with it. Many images of fighting are analyzed by Muth (2008), but her focus on violence alone, despite her recognition that "violence" was not a meaningful category for the Athenians, removes these scenes from the context in which they need to be understood. The chronological changes in military images were briefly described by Bažant (1985), 7–12.

figures by labeling or iconography, or shown to be heroes by the equipment they carry, but lightly armed troops and cavalry are not so identified.[34]

The tone of these sixth-century black-figure images is frequently dark. The mere choice of labeling a warrior who is arming "Achilles," as the Amasis Painter does on a neck amphora found at Orvieto, brings a tragic overtone.[35] It is the corpse of Achilles, carried by Aias, which provides the model for one soldier being carried from the battlefield dead over the shoulder of another.[36] Death is rarely far away in these scenes, and some painters seem particularly to dwell on it. So Exekias can paint the carrying back of the corpse of a dead warrior on both sides of an amphora and make fighting over a fallen body the subject on both sides of the outside of his only extant cup.[37] It is a reasonable guess that the scene of Achilles playing dice with Aias, whose power comes from the foreshadowing thrown by what is to happen to these two heroic warriors, was invented by Exekias.[38]

What should we take to be the relationship between these scenes and the warfare with which Athenians living under the tyrants were familiar? The scenes on the pots have sometimes been taken to demonstrate the existence of Athenian cavalry in the sixth century.[39] The ease with which scenes are rendered "heroic" by the addition of names or (for example) Boeotian shields, and the ease with which Amazons are introduced into scenes whose iconography is otherwise identical to that in scenes that might be taken as illustrations of contemporary warfare, should warn us against seeing representations of contemporary warfare on these pots.[40] Lissarrague has well shown how images of light-armed troops, cavalrymen, and particularly archers painted in the sixth century serve to define by contrast the role of the hoplite.[41] Such an exploration clearly depends upon the appearance, equipment, and actions of the archer, peltast, or cavalryman being credible in the eyes of the viewer, but just as the ability of the artist to show Amazons at war does not rely upon sixth-century Athenians having met Amazons in battle, so the presence of those who fight with bow or light shield or on horseback does not depend upon the Athenians them-

---

[34] Lissarrague (1989), 78, for the Boeotian shield of dead warriors carried from the battlefield.

[35] Boston, Museum of Fine Arts 01.8027, *ABV* 152.27 (from Orvieto). The reverse shows Herakles and Apollo struggling for the tripod.

[36] This scene, known from ivory and metalwork since ca. 700 BC, appears first on Attic black-figure vases on the François vase, with Aias and Achilles named: Florence, Mus. Arch. 4209, *ABV* 76.1 (from Chiusi); *LIMC* I s.v. Achilleus pp. 185–93, nos. 860–96.

[37] Amphora: Munich Museum Antiker Kleinkunst 1470, *ABV* 144.6; cup: Munich, Museum Antiker Kleinkunst 2044, *ABV* 146.21 (from Vulci).

[38] Vatican Museums 344, *ABV* 145.13 for Exekias's amphora (from Vulci). *LIMC* I s.v. Achilleus, pp. 96–103, nos. 391–427.

[39] Lissarrague (1989), 234; Spence (1993), 10; Greenhalgh (1973), 75–77 and 111–36 (all discussing the views of Helbig). For a similar argument applied to Scythian archers, see Vos (1963), chap. 4, esp. p. 66.

[40] So Brussels R300, *ABV* 288.9 (an amphora thought to be from Cervetri attributed to the Group of Würzburg 199 and showing Herakles and Kerberos on the reverse) or London, British Museum B 323, *ABV* 362.33 (a hydria from Vulci attributed to the Leagros group with an arming scene on the shoulder).

[41] Lissarrague (1989).

selves, or the customers who purchased these pots, possessing and deploying such forces.[42]

Analysis of two images will reveal something of what is at issue in these black-figure images.[43] A black-figure amphora painted early in the last quarter of the sixth century (**4.1–2** and plate 13) shows on one side two heavily armed soldiers with Boiotian shields in combat; they make overarm thrusts with their spears over the fallen body of another heavily armed soldier who sprawls on the ground, his shield raised above him for protection.[44] On the other side it shows a similarly armed hoplite in the process of collapsing, a curiously bent spear in hand, between two mounted figures. The mounted figure on the left is beardless, wears a Scythian helmet, and levels a spear in each hand. His counterpart on the right is beardless and bareheaded; he holds the reins in one hand and two spears in the other. The two sides of the amphora frame hoplite combat. They set it apart from Athenian warfare by the Boiotian shields and by the adoption of combinations of armor and poses that are highly unlikely to be those of any historical hoplites and cavalry. But they indicate the centrality of the heavily armed infantryman to all conflict: whoever fights, the death of the heavily armed soldier is the prize.

Another amphora, now in Munich, can be seen to emphasize the same centrality of the heavily armed soldier in a different way (**4.3–4** and plate 14).[45] On one side we see a scene of a soldier's departure for battle. On the left stands an old man, saying farewell. He says farewell to a hoplite, standing there in his armor, but also to an archer, who stands directly behind the hoplite, his Scythian helmet showing, but not much else. A dog stands by their legs. Behind this pair are a woman and another Scythian. Both the Scythian archer and the heavily armed infantryman are here put into the domestic frame, but it is the infantryman who is in the foreground. The archers draw attention to, but do not divert attention from, the central scene of a hoplite parting from his family. Nevertheless, the close association of the archer as the "double" of the hoplite here cannot but draw attention to the dangers that archers also face.

That point is made again in the scene on the reverse of this pot. Here two pairs of horses face each other over not one but two fallen bodies. On the left we see a mounted soldier in hoplite helmet and breastplate, with two spears in his right hand. Beside him is a riderless horse. Facing him are, in the foreground, a horseman in Scythian helmet, pulling on the reins of his horse with his left hand and holding two spears in his right. Just visible behind is a second horseman, this time again wearing hoplite helmet. Fallen centrally below is a hoplite, his spear still gripped in his hand but his eyes already closed in death. To the left the second fallen figure wears a Scythian helmet and his quiver stands up next to the horse's legs. Hoplite

---

[42] On the hoplite in Etruria, see D'Agostino (1990).
[43] Compare Lissarrague (1989), 193–95.
[44] Lissarrague (1989), C20, giving a date of 520 (provenance unknown). The date of 500 given by Greifenhagen (1935), 443 (no. 17) seems to me implausibly late.
[45] Lissarrague (1989), A 165/466, *ABV* 285.1, from Vulci. Munich 1509.

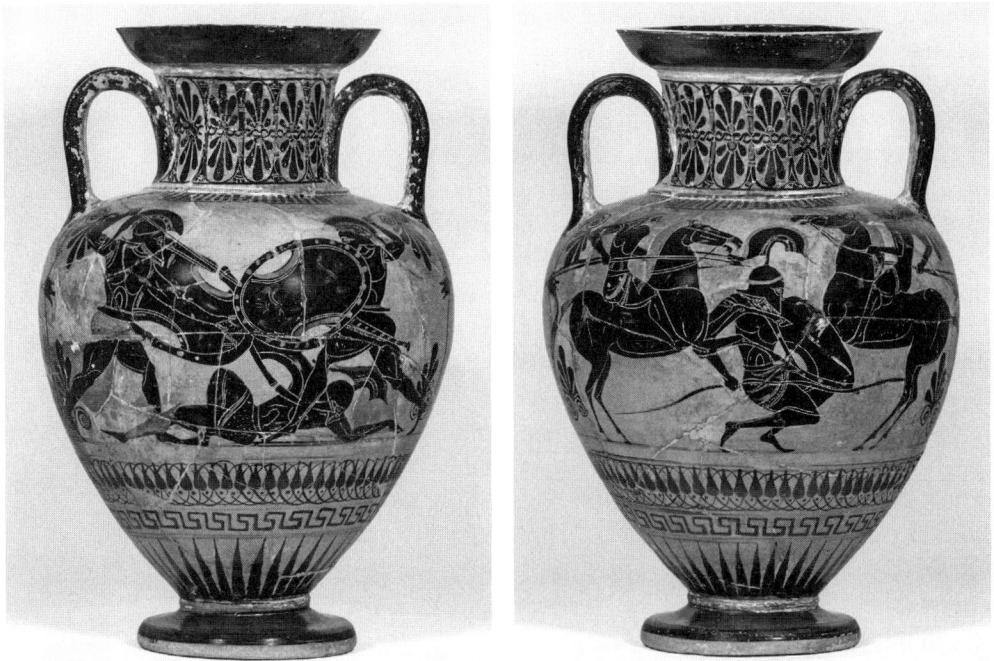

Figure 4.1–2. Black-figure amphora, provenance unknown, 525–500. © Bonn Akademisches Kunstmuseum (Fontana collection, no. 40).

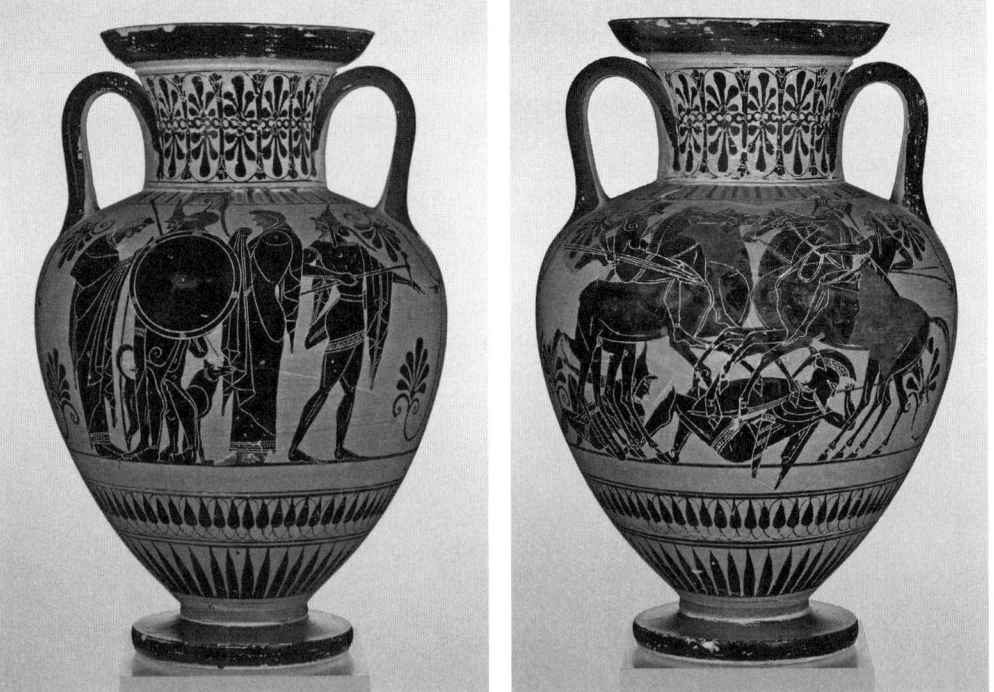

Figure 4.3–4. Black-figure amphora, height 0.44 m, attributed to the group of Bologna 16, from Vulci, 525–500. *ABV* 285.1, Munich Staatliche Antikensammlung en 1509. © Staatliche Antikensammlung en und Glyptothek München. Photograph by Renate Kühling.

and archer are equally victims of war here, of a war to which we are invited to think that they rode together as the Scythian and hoplite ride side by side above. All manner of fighting mixes here in a way that is tactically highly improbable. We do not have the image of a battle, and it is useless to debate whether the mounted figures are cavalry properly speaking or simply soldiers who use their horses for transport. Fallen horses do not figure on these sixth-century pots; the pity of war invoked here is not the pity for the collateral damage done, it is pity at the death of the central actor, the hoplite and of the other warriors who die in his train.

These later sixth-century black-figure images constitute an exploration of the status of the heavily armed warrior that is independent of the particular realities of contemporary warfare, either in Athens or in Greece generally. The use of mythological names and anachronistic, or at least non-Athenian, arms and armor shows this up particularly clearly. Modern arguments as to whether or not one can call a particular figure a hoplite (or a cavalryman) are irrelevant; the status of the heavily armed soldier is an issue whose exploration goes on regardless of the details of any depiction. The presence of lightly armed soldiers, archers, and cavalry, of Scythian hats or black squires, does not imply or depend upon their presence and familiarity in any Athenian army; the heavily armed soldier is not being distinguished from actual light-armed or mounted comrades in arms.[46] Rather, the experience of the heavily armed soldier is being constructed as what the experience of war was for those who viewed the pot, something that we may indeed consider to be enabled, rather than obstructed, by the probable absence of any permanent corps of Athenian peltasts or archers, and perhaps even of cavalry, within Peisistratid Athens.[47]

3. New Model Army Imagery

Whatever branch of military activity one looks at, the view offered by pots painted in the first quarter of the fifth century is quite different from that offered by those painted in the last quarter of the sixth. In the case of naval imagery, what happens is that with red-figure it vanishes.[48] There had never been much interest, and what there had been was sometimes evoked by the desire to treat the wine inside a container as if it were the wine-dark sea, which did not really work when the background color of the pot was dark not light.[49] In other branches of the armed forces we are dealing not with total disappearance but with transformation.

---

[46] For Memnon and his squires, see Lissarrague (1989), 21–29.

[47] I discuss the question of the rise and fall of the Scythian archer on Athenian pottery in more detail in Osborne (2004a). See also Ivanchik (2005).

[48] The sole context in which an oared ship appears in red-figure is that of Odysseus sailing past the sirens, tied to the mast: see the red-figure name vase of the Siren Painter, *ARV* 289.1, London, British Museum E440, from Vulci.

[49] Lissarrague (1987/1990), 112–14. Note that Nikoxenos provides the latest examples of the trope, executed in black-figure, perhaps in the first decade of the fifth century (*ARV* 225.1 and 2), is

The most dramatic change involves archers. Archers in Scythian helmets practically vanish from all scenes involving heavily armed troops: we can ascribe a date later than 500 only to two of twenty-six scenes in which such archers are present in scenes of arming, to none of the twenty scenes of hieroscopy (examining the liver of a sacrificial victim prior to battle), to two of twenty-eight scenes of the return of the dead from the battlefield, to four of the 130 scenes of departure for war, to two of 134 scenes with chariots, and to six of seventy-one scenes of combat.[50] Solo archers in Scythian dress also more or less disappear (nineteen up to 500 (**4.5**), one after), but solo archers not dressed as Scythians remain more or less as popular as ever (twenty-eight up to 500, eighteen after), as do naked archers in combat scenes (eight up to 500, eight after). Archers not dressed as Scythians appear just once before 500 in arming scenes, four times after 500, and hoplites with a bow appear only twice before 500, seven times afterward.

The rejection of the Scythian can be seen, if less dramatically, among light-armed peltasts and cavalry. Sixteen of the twenty cases of peltasts with Scythian helmet date to before 500, by contrast to just three of the eleven peltasts of Thracian type. But in this case seventeen of the twenty-two images of peltasts identified as neither Scythian nor Thracian are also before 500 in date. In the case of cavalry, twenty-four of twenty-seven cavalry with Scythian helmet are dated up to 500, in contrast to thirty-two out of seventy-two cavalry in Thracian costume.[51]

More is at issue here, however, than fashions for Scythian helmets or for Thracian cloaks and boots, let alone than real Scythians departing from Athens.[52] Along with those Scythian helmets go out satyrs dressed as peltasts (nineteen of twenty-four date up to 500) and peltast cavalrymen (twelve of fourteen up to 500). Of the forty cavalry with elements of Thracian costume painted after 500, twenty-eight are on foot (**4.6**), twelve mounted (the figure for up to 500 is seven on foot, twenty-five mounted).[53] Of scenes that involve archers and horses, none of the eighteen scenes in which the archer is mounted on horseback, or between rearing horses, is after 500 in date, whereas four of the sixteen scenes of archers on foot leading horses are after 500.

What is rejected with the Scythian helmet is a whole way of thinking about service in war. The hoplite is no longer placed alongside Scythian archers and cavalry and defined by contrast. Archers and peltasts are no

---

described by Boardman (1975a), 111, as "an adequate black figure painter of the Leagros Group who misguidedly took to red figure."

[50] All these figures, as those later in this and the next paragraph, derive from the catalogs of Lissarrague (1989). See further Osborne (2004a).

[51] These figures from Lissarrague (1989) Catalogue C do not include cases where an archer also appears.

[52] Contrast Vos (1963), 61: "All this suggests that between 500 and 490 B.C. the Scythians left Athens, so that the vase-painters had no examples before their eyes and had to rely on their memory." We must be grateful that Athens continued to abound with centaurs, satyrs, and amazons for painters to copy. Even Lissarrague (1989), 234, seems curiously reluctant to reject explanations of this sort.

[53] Even among Scythians it is worth noting that of the six Scythian cavalry shown on foot leading a horse, two are after 500.

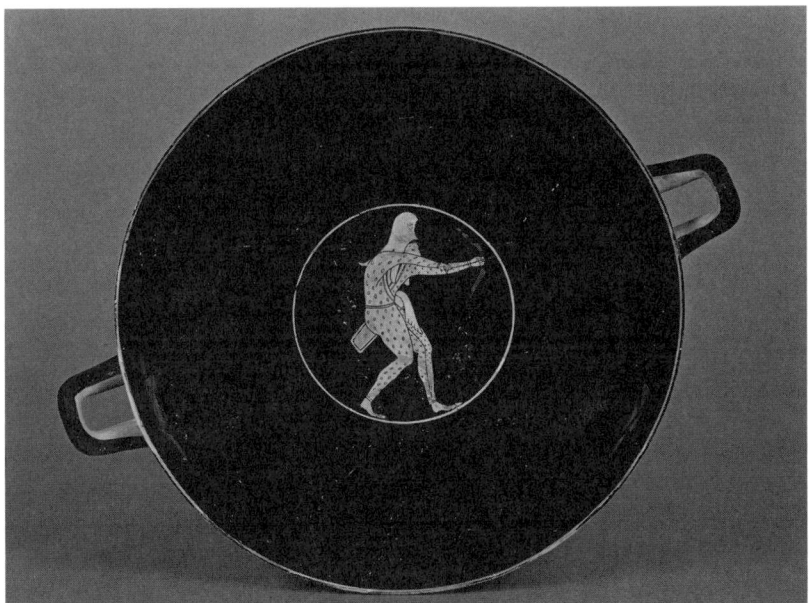

Figure 4.5. Interior of red-figure cup, diameter 0.335 m, signed by Pheidippos as painter and Hischylos as potter, from Vulci, ca. 510. *ARV* 166.11, British Museum 1846,0512.2 (E6). © The Trustees of the British Museum.

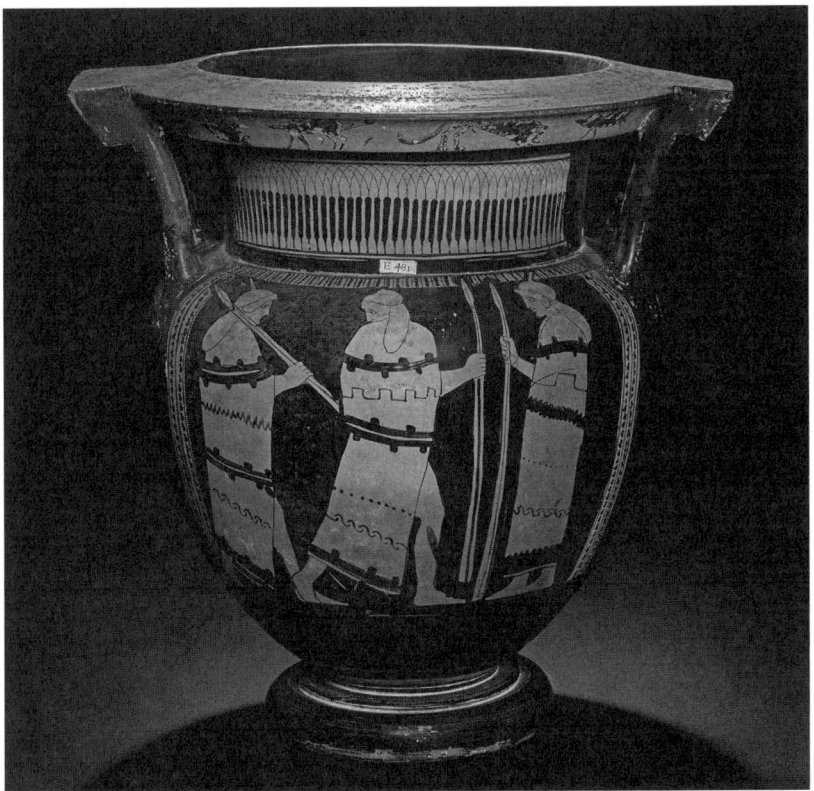

Figure 4.6. One side of red-figure column krater, height 0.3556 m, attributed to the Painter of the Louvre Centauromachy, from Nola, ca. 440. *ARV* 1090.33, British Museum 1836,0224.227 (E 481). © The Trustees of the British Museum.

longer other, they too represent possible identities for the viewer. Archers continue to be of interest, but now in their own right. The peltast, in a similar way, continues to attract the attention of the painter, but not as an exotic other; the much-reduced interest in the satyr peltast is relevant here. Most revealing of all is the change in the representation of cavalry; images of cavalry continue to abound, but of cavalry outside the context of warfare.

The crucial thing about Scythians was that in the sixth century they were like satyrs; the Athenians had no experience of them and they knew about them almost entirely on the basis of stories.[54] Thracians they had some experience of, partly through Miltiades's activities in the Thracian Chersonesos, but not of Scythians. Just as in Herodotos, the Scythians famously act as a "mirror" of Greek warfare, above all in the context of defeating the Persian king Dareios, so too on sixth-century pots Scythians are the mirror that reflects back glory onto the heavily armed warfare that was strongly associated with the heroes of epic.[55] The Scythian in the sixth century was to all intents and purposes as fictional as the Amazon, to whom indeed he is visually related. Sixth-century Athenian artists devised a variety of schemata that meant "war," in which the fantastic and the mythical had a starring role. But once the Athenians were themselves active on the field of war, it was experience, and not just fable, that they brought to the symposium: after 500 war gets broken down into different elements—elements that arguably relate rather more directly, if very selectively, to the Athenians own experience of warfare. Once Scythians were known, they could not be other in the same way. Their disappearance from the imagery goes together with their presence in Athens: from perhaps somewhere in the second quarter of the fifth century the Athenians maintained a force of Scythian archers as a sort of riot police, a group of outsiders made responsible for ensuring civic order.[56]

4. Hoplites, Persians, and the Demise of the Hoplite Battle

Soldiers were not a very popular subject with the so-called Pioneers of red-figure painting. Euphronios was indeed capable of showing a very close interest in details of armor and weapons in scenes of myth (so his scene of Herakles, Athena, and Kyknos on a calyx krater), but only one nonmythological scene of hoplites can be ascribed to him, a scene on a calyx krater of five hoplites arming (**4.7** and plate 15); even this is in close contact with mythology, with Sleep, Death, and Sarpedon shown on the other side of

---

[54] "The archers in Scythian dress on Attic late sixth-century vases belong, as regards their nature, entirely to the epic legends," Pinney (1983), 139.

[55] For Herodotos's "mirror," see Hartog (1980).

[56] Exactly when the Athenians began using Scythian archers as a police force is uncertain. Andokides 3.5, which would put the date at 446, cannot be trusted. Their first comic appearance is in Aristophanes *Acharnians* 54. Cf. Suda σ771. See Bäbler (1998), 166.

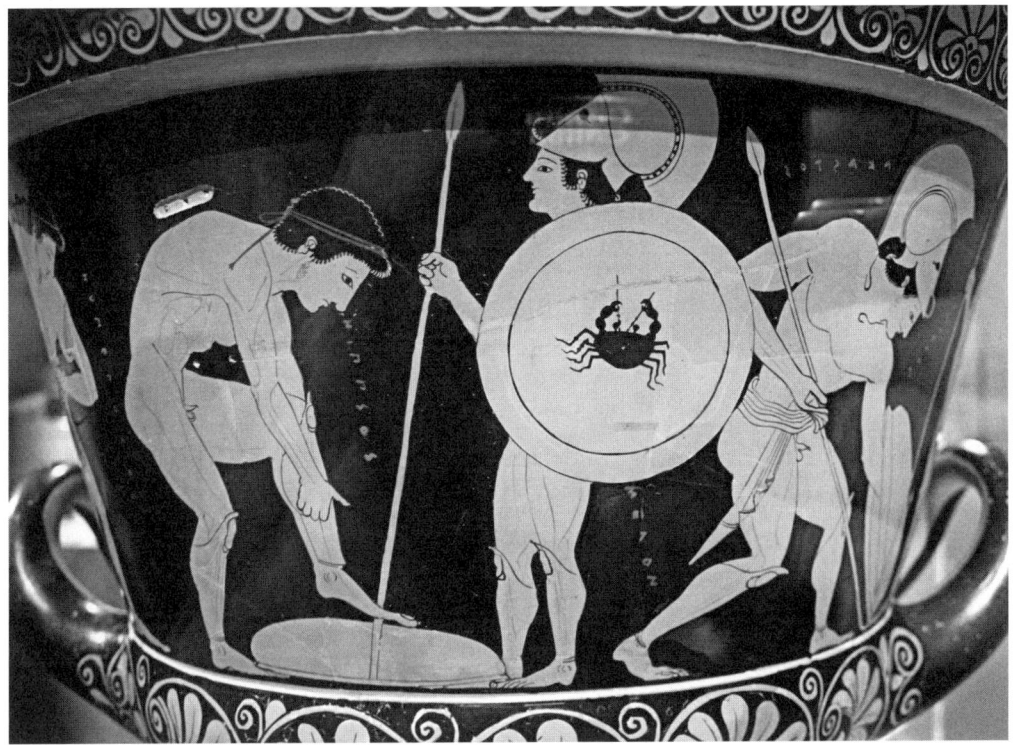

Figure 4.7. Red-figure calyx krater, height 0.458 m, signed by Euphronios as painter and Euxitheos as potter. *Beazley Addenda* 404. Cerveteri, Museo Archaeologico. (ex N.Y. Met. 1972.11.10) CC BY-SA 3.0 Rolfmueller at the English language Wikipedia.

the same pot.[57] Euthymides also depicts one arming scene, and he explicitly names the warrior arming "Hektor."[58] The absence of archers from both these arming scene divides them from the norm in black-figure, but their mythological links place them firmly with the run of sixth-century warrior scenes.[59] Viewers are encouraged to see warfare not as a matter of specific soldiers fighting in a specific way at a specific time and place, but as something that has strongly generalized features involving costly preparation, painful encounter, and the threat of annihilation.

The soldiers who were popular, by contrast, with early red-figure cup painters were most strongly particularized. Hoplites feature on both the cups signed by, and on a particularly high proportion of the cups attributed to, Oltos, usually ascribed to the decade 510 to 500. A single hoplite occurs on the interior of more than a dozen cups painted by him (**4.8**),

---

[57] The five hoplites are named but with names neither found together in any known myth nor known to be in use in late sixth-century Athens: Axippos, Akastos, Medon, Hippsos, and Hypeirochos; see von Bothmer (1976), 486, 494. Herakles and Kyknos is in the Shelby White and Leon Levy collection, Osborne (1998a), fig. 74.

[58] *ARV* 26.1 from Vulci, Munich 2307. On the reverse (7.3) is the famous *komos* scene in which Euthymides invites comparison with Euphronios.

[59] The only other "Pioneer" arming scene is on a fragmentary amphora ascribed to the Dikaios Painter, who combines it with a scene of Apollo, Artemis, and Leto: *ARV* 30.1 from Orvieto, Vienna Univ. 631b.

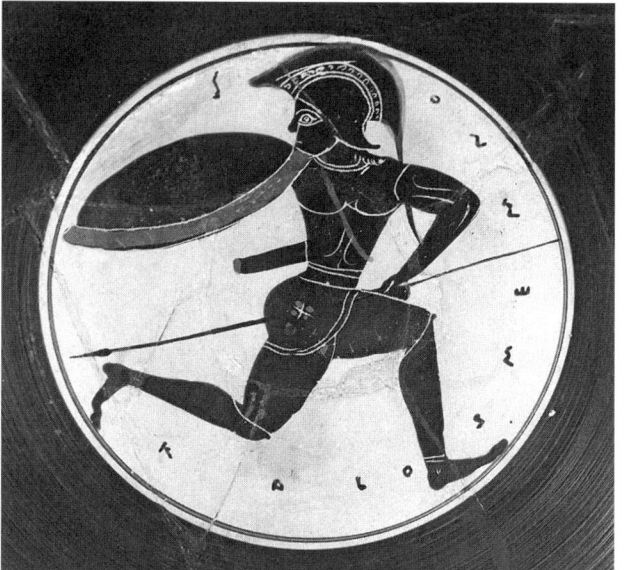

Figure 4.8. Black-figure interior of red-figure cup, diameter 0.325 m, attributed to Oltos. Found at Vulci. ARV 56.27. Oxford Ashmolean Museum 515 = AN1896-1908 G.265. Image © Ashmolean Museum, University of Oxford.

single archers and peltasts on the interiors of others, and hoplite duels on the exterior of still others. The hoplites, some in black-figure on bilingual pots, stand, run, crouch, or play the trumpet. They combine with images on the outside of the cup of further soldiers, of athletics, of women dancing or, in two cases of satyrs and maenads with Dionysos. Such a Dionysiac company for the warrior seems to be a peculiarity of this artist and is not found in other late sixth-century red-figure cups featuring solo hoplites: they prefer direct allusion to the sympotic context through scenes of the symposium itself or the *komos* (**4.9–11**), or combine solo hoplites with further scenes of hoplites in action, or youths and horses (but not the world of the gymnasium).[60] These individual hoplites do not excite mythological comparanda on the exterior, but some cups showing hoplite duels both identify the protagonists in the duels as figures from myth and juxtapose them to the exploits of Herakles (against Kyknos, the Nemean lion, or centaurs).[61]

The hoplites in these scenes nevertheless come in a very limited range of types. Most are fully equipped with greaves, cuirass over short chiton (though sometimes this appears virtually as a single sleeveless and legless bodysuit), round shield (with a great variety of shield devices), helmet, and single spear.

The main, and most radical, variant is that the hoplite sometimes appears naked. When three hoplites are shown, with the central figure either fallen and fought-over or attacked from both sides, the central hoplite is frequently naked, apart from helmet and, often, greaves (**4.12** and plate

---

[60] A cup potted by Pamphaios with a solo figure with pelta but hoplite helmet does have satyrs, maenads, and Dionysos on the exterior, *ARV* 129.22.

[61] *ARV* 60.64 (cf. perhaps 60.67, 61.68) for mythological names given; 74.35, 79.6, 90.36 for juxtaposition to Herakles. Herakles is juxtaposed to solo archers on *ARV* 96 (137, Maplewood, also showing Theseus), 138.1 (anc cf. 173.4).

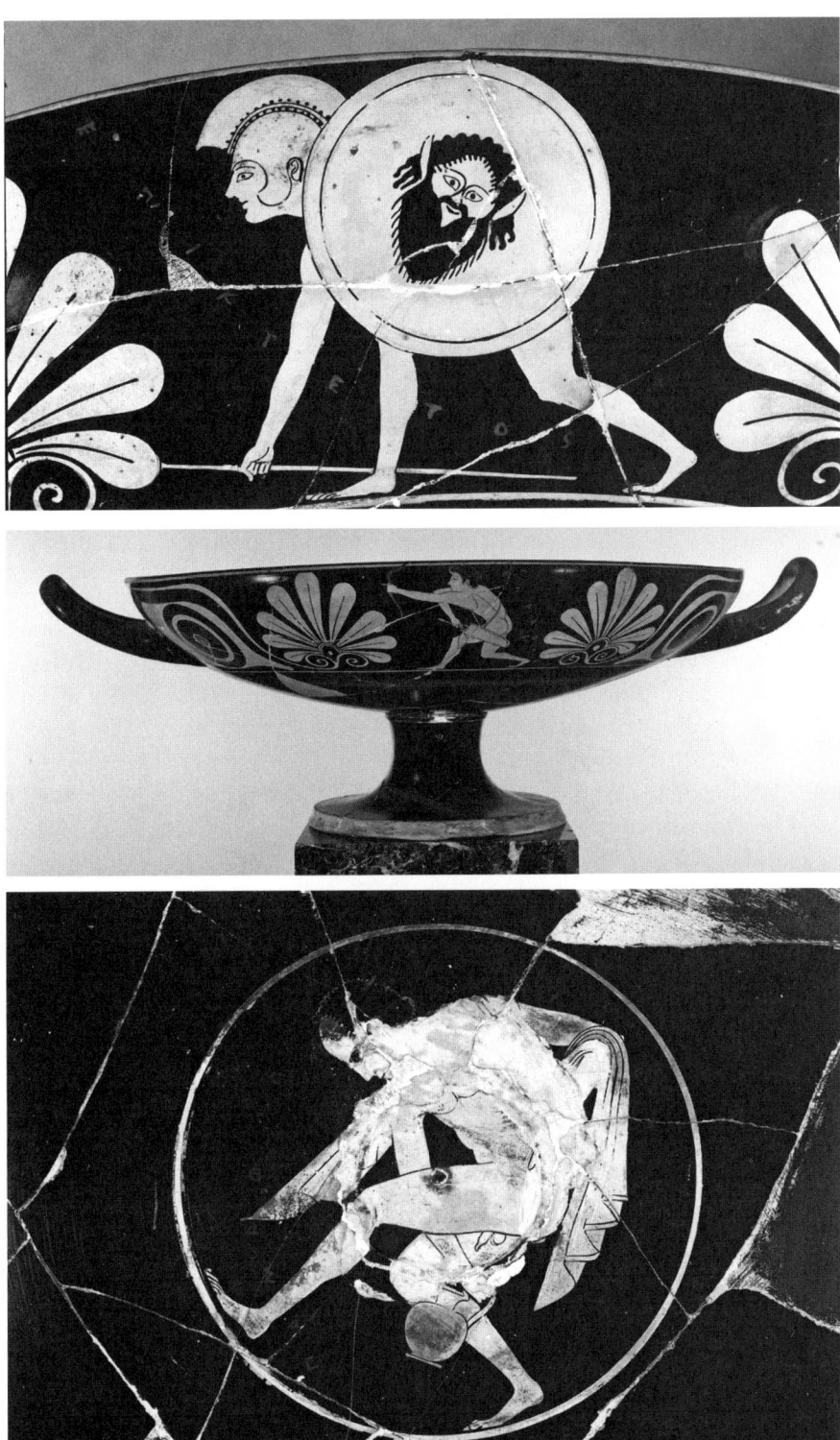

Figure 4.9–11. Interior and exterior of red-figure cup, diameter 0.32 m, signed by Epiktetos as painter and Pamphaios as potter, from Vulci, ca. 510. *ARV* 71.14, Louvre G5. Photo © RMN-Grand Palais (musée du Louvre)/Les frères Chuzeville.

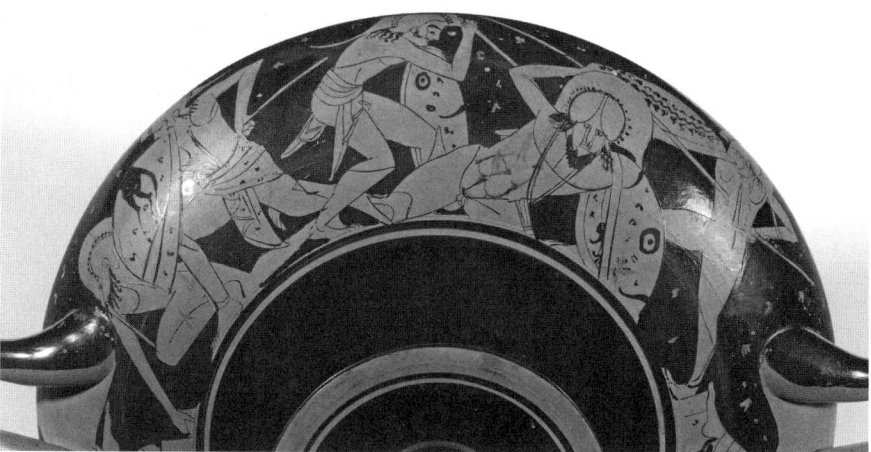

Figure 4.12. Exterior of red-figure cup, diameter 0.273 m, attributed to the wider circle of the Nikosthenes Painter, ca. 500 (for the interior and other side see 7.1–2). *ARV* 135.13, Cambridge, Fitzwilliam Museum GR 19.1937. © The Fitzwilliam Museum, Cambridge.

16).[62] If this practice began because the nakedness was suitably expressive of weakness, it seems soon to have been subverted. Two cups attributed to the Euergides Painter show three hoplites engaged in fighting, one shows them all fully armed, the other shows them all naked.[63] A cup attributed to the Epidromos Painter shows a naked beardless hoplite in helmet and greaves dispatching a bearded fully armed figure with his sword (**4.13** and plate 17). The solo hoplite on his own similarly appears naked as well as fully armed. To some extent this seems to be a matter of the preference of individual artists: some seem generally to have depicted the solo hoplite in full armor (so Oltos), others depicted him generally naked (so the Euergides Painter).

The second, and much less common, variation concerns animal pelts. A number of hoplites are shown wearing an animal pelt over, or occasionally instead of, their chiton, or carrying an animal pelt behind, or instead of, their shield.[64] In some of these cases the pelt seems intended to convey an unusual ferocity in the warrior; one cup, attributed to Oltos, gives a warrior wearing a pelt of a lion as his shield device, and on another cup, attributed to Epiktetos, the hoplite with the pelt has a shield bearing a frontal satyr head.[65] On a cup attributed to the Epeleios Painter (**4.14**) it is an otherwise naked hoplite, with shield, helmet, and greaves, who has the pelt; since he faces a fully armed hoplite, the combination of nudity and animal skin serve to suggest a degree of bestiality (though to the right a second naked hoplite, without a pelt, flees, and his nudity suggests vulnerability).[66]

It has an important bearing on the interpretation of the whole set of these images that the major variations in the representation of the hoplite

---

[62] *ARV* 54.6bis, 60.64, 60.67, 61.68.
[63] *ARV* 90.36, 91.50.
[64] *ARV* 56.24, 60.66, 70.2, 76.73, 147.25.
[65] *ARV* 60.66, 76.73.
[66] The presence of women makes this something other than a scene of normal warfare, though Mingazzini (1971), 17–18, who ascribes this cup to Oltos, argues that the pelt is insufficient to identify this scene as the duel between Herakles and Ares.

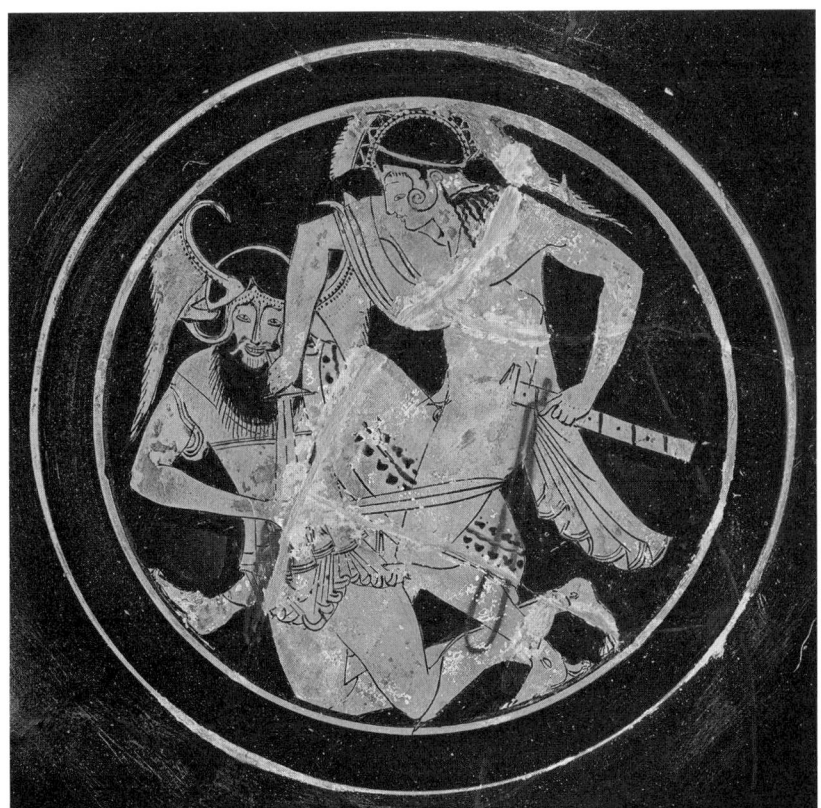

Figure 4.13. Interior of red-figure cup, diameter 0.198 m, attributed to the Epidromos Painter / Apollodoros (the interior bears the inscription "Epidromos *kalos*"), from Chiusi, ca. 500. *ARV* 118.13, British Museum 1892,0718.6 (E43). © The Trustees of the British Museum.

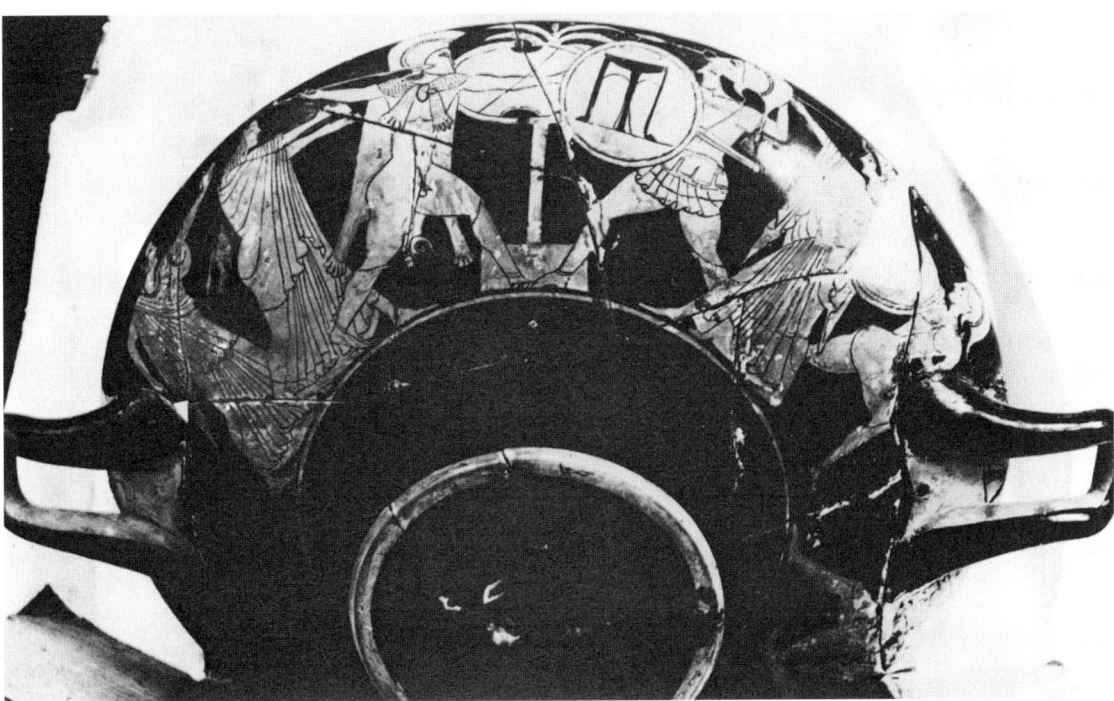

Figure 4.14. Exterior of red-figure cup, diameter 0.323 m, attributed to the Epeleios Painter. Provenance unknown. *ARV* 147.25. Villa Giulia 50393. Image after Mingazzini (1971) Tav. CIV 1/639.

concern nudity and the carrying of animal skins. These are not images that derive their power from the observed details of actual warfare. Neither nudity, nor the use of animal skins, can have been a feature of any actual hoplite battle during this period. Just as we have seen black-figure artists at the end of the sixth century framing the hoplite with Scythians and archers, so these red-figure images of hoplites from those same years explore what it is to be a hoplite not against the background of the realities of war, but against a symbolic background in which the culture of the city is juxtaposed to signs of the wild, and to the ambiguous and ambivalent sign of the naked male body.

The popularity of the hoplite duel declines rapidly in the early fifth century. Much reduced is the frequency of portrayal of single pairs of hoplites fighting, perhaps over a fallen or falling body, and of larger groups of hoplites, paired or lined up. Almost two-thirds of all such Attic red-figure scenes date to before circa 500, and a very large proportion of the rest were painted before 480. In as far as any nonmythological battle scenes continue to be popular after 480 it is scenes that involve hoplites fighting not against other hoplites but against those who are differently armed. These opponents vary from cavalry to figures who are not regular soldiers at all (such as the man with slashing sword and rustic hat on a lekythos attributed to the Syracuse Painter[67]). Prominent among these differently armed opponents is a new figure: the Persian.

Images of Persians appeared first on Attic pottery circa 490, and never became frequent.[68] Greeks had come across Persians, both in and out of military contexts, long before this date, but, despite the colorful presence their clothing offered, they had not excited any interest among painters of pottery. There is little doubt that the arrival of Persians in Athenian imagery relates directly to the Persian invasions of 490 and 480 (**4.15**). But these images remain very far from being "history pictures": they do indeed always show Greeks victorious over Persians, but the only case in which a specific victory may be alluded to is the famous oinochoe of circa 460, which shows a rather different scene in which the Persian is labeled "Eurymedon," the name of the river at which the Athenians and their allies defeated the Persians in a naval engagement in the 460s, and where, on any interpretation, the defeat is being satirized.[69] In other examples no details link the images with any particular historical episode.[70]

Yet Persians do not initially play the same role in the imagery of painted pottery as Scythians have played. It is true that when, on the tondo of a cup ascribed to Douris, a hoplite and an archer in Scythian dress are shown running side by side, the hoplite's shield device is a lion head of a form that

[67] *ARV* 521.52.
[68] Bovon (1963), counts fifteen scenes of Persian warriors; Hölscher (1973) counts eighteen, thirteen of them also showing Greeks; Raeck (1981) has sixty-five examples of Persians on pots in his catalog (pp. 326–29), but this includes Persians in other contexts than war.
[69] Schauenberg (1975). The precise interpretation is disputed, see Pinney (1984); Davidson (1997), 170–71, 180–82; Smith (1999); Miller (2010).
[70] Hölscher (1973), 44–48. The wicker shields of the Oxford Brygos cup (4.13 and plate 17) seem to me insufficient to identify the scene as the Battle of Plataea, despite Barrett and Vickers (1978).

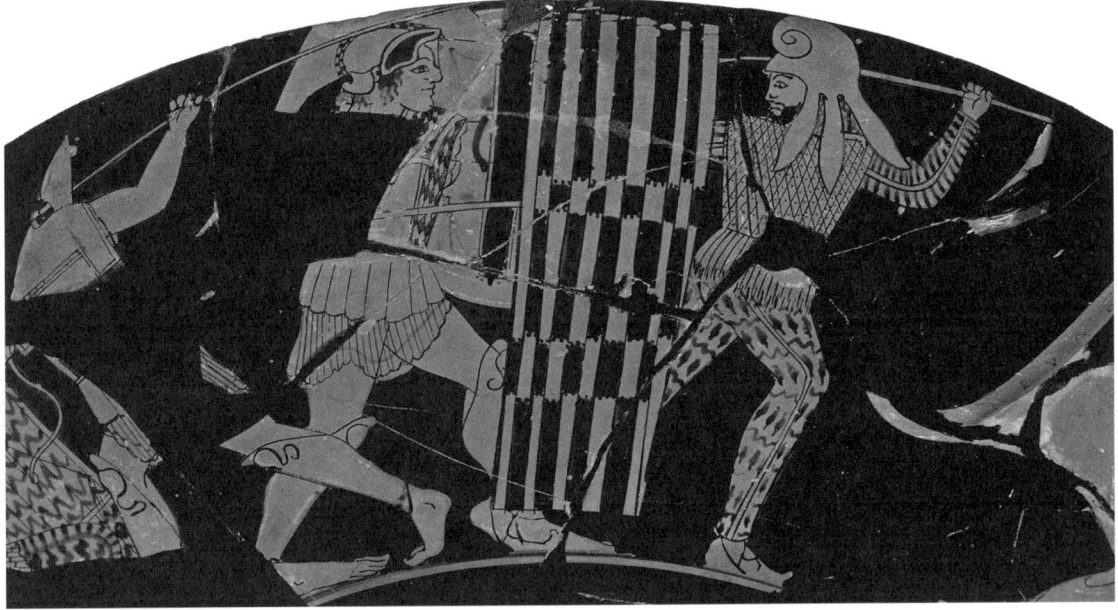

Figure 4.15. Exterior of red-figure cup, diameter 0.33 m, attributed to the Painter of the Oxford Brygos (signed by Brygos as potter but not painted by the Brygos Painter), from Cervetri, ca. 480. *ARV* 399. Oxford Ashmolean Museum AN 1911.615. Image © Ashmolean Museum, University of Oxford.

echoes Persian gold lion-head bracteates.[71] Here the allusion to Persia seems to function just as the Scythian costume does: the Greekness of the hoplite is emphasized by his juxtaposition to the otherness of the archer and the shield device. But once Persians had become not just other but the real and exemplary enemy, they cease, despite the great overlaps between their iconographies, to be possible substitutes for the Scythians. Persian archers appear mounted on horses, as Scythian archers do not, a reflection perhaps of the reality of Persian warfare. If Persians are substitutes for anything in earlier Athenian iconography it is rather for Amazons, since it is Amazons that share with them the attributes of being other and of never fighting on the same side. It is hardly by chance that Amazons come at this period for the first time to be portrayed in Persian costume, whereas previously they had been shown as female hoplites (as indeed they continue sometimes to be shown later, including on the Parthenon west metopes).[72]

If Amazons become Persians, Persians are not simply male Amazons. Amazons, their femininity shown by differential skin color, had traditionally been shown adopting Greek styles of warfare; when Penthesileia faces Achilles, she is armed as he is armed. Persians can never adapt, for if they did it would not be possible to distinguish them from Greeks. Persians

---

[71] *ARV* 442.215; Miller (1997), 59. Whether the hoplite and archer are Amazons is debated: denied by von Bothmer, it is affirmed by *LIMC* s.v. Amazones.

[72] *LIMC* s.v. Amazones. Note that Amazons also become mounted only in the fifth century. There is, however, only one possible example of a mounted Amazon with a bow known to me, and that may in fact show two Persians not two Amazons: *LIMC* Amazones no. 721 dated to ca. 450. For a discussion of violence in Amazonmachies, see Muth (2008), 329–412.

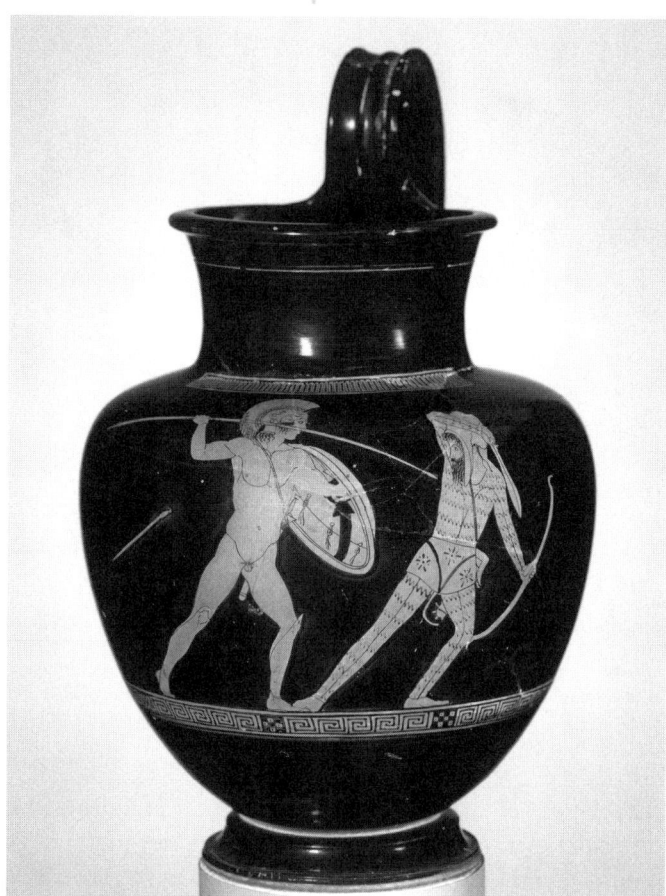

Figure 4.16. Red-figure oinochoe, height 0.193 m, attributed to the Chicago Painter, found at Gela, ca. 460. *ARV* 631.38. Boston Museum of Fine Arts 13.196. Photograph © 2017 Museum of Fine Arts, Boston.

carry a variety of weapons, but the one that they are most regularly shown using is the short and slightly curved slashing sword (**4.16**),[73] which was not in the hoplite's armory and not previously in that of the Amazon either. A short sword known as the *akinakes* is indeed very prominent in literary accounts of the Persians. It was part of regular military equipment, a prized personal possession and sometimes gilded or with gold handles. It is the standard royal gift in Herodotos and the Athenians dedicated captured gilt *akinakai* on the Acropolis.[74] It is absurd, however, to think that the *akinakes* was the primary Persian weapon in actual battle. The prominent use of the short slashing sword, along with the bow, on pots marks out the Persian as not just a foreign enemy, but a particular foreign enemy.

If Persians begin by making an impact on Attic iconography because they were the actual enemy of the day, scenes involving Greeks and Persians quickly become subsumed into the wider body of mythological wars. The clearest evidence for this concerns nakedness. Persians are never shown

---

[73] Compare the Eurymedon oinochoe (Hamburg 1981.173) of similar date.
[74] Herodotos 7.54.2, 8.120 (and, for its slashing use, 3.118); *IG* i3 343.8, 349.54. Miller (1997), 46–48.

naked.[75] Their Greek opponents, however, having been represented fully armed in the earliest examples, appear naked in some later examples (as in 4.14). The Greeks no more fought the Persians naked than the Persians fought only with the *akinakes*: the realities of warfare are not what is at issue here.

Mythological wars continued to be popular in fifth-century Athenian iconography. Centauromachies were the least frequently represented, amazonomachies the most frequently. Gigantomachies were more often depicted in the fifth century than they had been in the sixth. Fighting as such continued, therefore, to be quite a popular subject for pot painters. But the anonymous combat between hoplites, which was a popular theme on the earliest red-figure pots, particularly cups, was quite out of fashion by the time of the Persian wars. The introduction of scenes of Greeks fighting Persians did little to arrest this decline, but it does reveal a desire among the painters, comparable to the desire evinced by Aeschylus's *Persai*, to turn this real encounter too into a mythical one, merely using the accoutrements of reality to produce a new variety of heroic encounter.

Scholars who are inclined to interpret every representation of Amazons, centaurs, and giants painted after the Persian wars as a commemoration of those wars have got the picture reversed.[76] Amazons come to be shown, on occasions, like Persians not because the Persian conflict is the model, but because the Persian conflict has been incorporated into the mythical scheme of conflict, to offer new resources of costume to the traditional subjects portrayed in that scheme. Rather little of the real-life fighting that the Athenians undertook after 480, and particularly after 470, consisted of land battles against Persians. The real-life fighting that took place on land was against other Greeks. But such conflicts generated no direct response from painters of pottery; hoplite battles were good to think with only if they could be subsumed into the mythical model of conflict, and the Persians alone were good for that.

5. Arming and Parting

The reduction in the number of hoplite duels is quite closely matched by a reduction in the number of hoplites shown on their own. Again, something between a half and two-thirds of such solo-hoplites painted in the first century of red-figure occur on pots painted down to 500, and more than three-quarters are on pots painted before 480. Similar, or even more extreme, patterns of decline are found in other particular scenes of hoplites; so almost all cases of a hoplite with a horse antedate 500. But this does not mean that the hoplite disappears from the pot-painter's repertoire. Two scenes involving hoplites remain popular, scenes of arming and scenes of departure, and these two scenes also become more closely assimi-

---

[75] Raeck (1981), 108–9.
[76] For more extensive discussion, see Veness (2002).

lated to each other.[77] In the case of scenes of arming, representations antedating the Persian wars do outnumber those from the second and third quarters of the fifth century, but in the case of scenes of departure, scenes from before 480 account for less than a third of the total number of scenes known from circa 525 to circa 425.

Arming provides one of the stock scenes in the *Iliad*,[78] and scenes of a hoplite arming, sometimes explicitly identified as the arming of heroes, had long been popular in Greek imagery. They are found on shield bands and in Corinthian pottery and had been popular in black-figure pot painting, particularly on amphoras. Down to the end of the sixth century arming remained predominantly a black-figure subject on closed shapes, although in early red-figure it was cup painters, rather than painters of amphoras, who occasionally painted an arming scene.[79] When, from about 500, arming scenes do become popular on all shapes of red-figure pot, some elements of the black-figure iconography, above all the motif of the hoplite putting on greaves, continue to be frequently found. But other elements disappear, and in particular, as discussed above, the Scythian archer is no longer to be found in the scene.[80]

Although a warrior lifting his leg to strap on a greave is the single most commonly repeated item in the iconography of arming in early red-figure, a wide range of stages in the donning of heavy arms and armor is portrayed, sometimes, as in Euphronios's krater (4.7 and plate 15), in a single scene: warriors strap on a cuirass, put on their sword, pick up their shield, or receive a proffered helmet or spear (**4.17–18**). Columns or the like situate some scenes explicitly indoors; dogs may give a domestic tone or chariots a heroic tone; some scenes involve only hoplites, others surround the warrior with old men, women, or youths; some warriors are beardless, some bearded; some add greaves, a helmet, and a shield to a naked body, others wear full armor. Even motifs found only occasionally, such as the motif of the warrior taking his shield out of its wrapper, tend not to be exclusive to a single period.[81] But the dominant scene does change over time. From shortly before the middle of the fifth century, putting on greaves ceases to be the constant element in these scenes, and the focus moves from the greaves to the helmet. This is one manifestation of the way in which the scenes become generally much less active and more stable. The taking of the helmet, previously only one motif among several, becomes the most frequently repeated element (**4.19** and plate 18, 4.22 and plate 19, cf. 4.17,

---

[77] The division between arming and parting is to some extent arbitrary, since the handing over of arms or armor to the departing warrior is often implicit, if not explicit, in scenes where the focus is on the pouring of a libation (cf. *ARV* 370.13, 499.11), and the pouring of a libation may be implied in a scene where armor is being put on (so *ARV* 274.45, 518.3). I talk here of scenes of departure although it is not always possible to be confident that departure rather than return is at issue.

[78] Armstrong (1958).

[79] But note Hector putting on a cuirass on an amphora by Euthymides (*ARV* 26.1) and a fragmentary amphora attributed to the Dikaios Painter (*ARV* 30.1).

[80] On scenes including Scythians, see Lissarrague (1989), 36–42.

[81] Cf. e.g., *ARV* 167.12, 168.14, 185.37, 373.48, 619.8; Beverly Hills, Summa 18/9/81: 9; London Sotheby 5/7/82: 351 (attributed to Bowdoin Eye Painter).

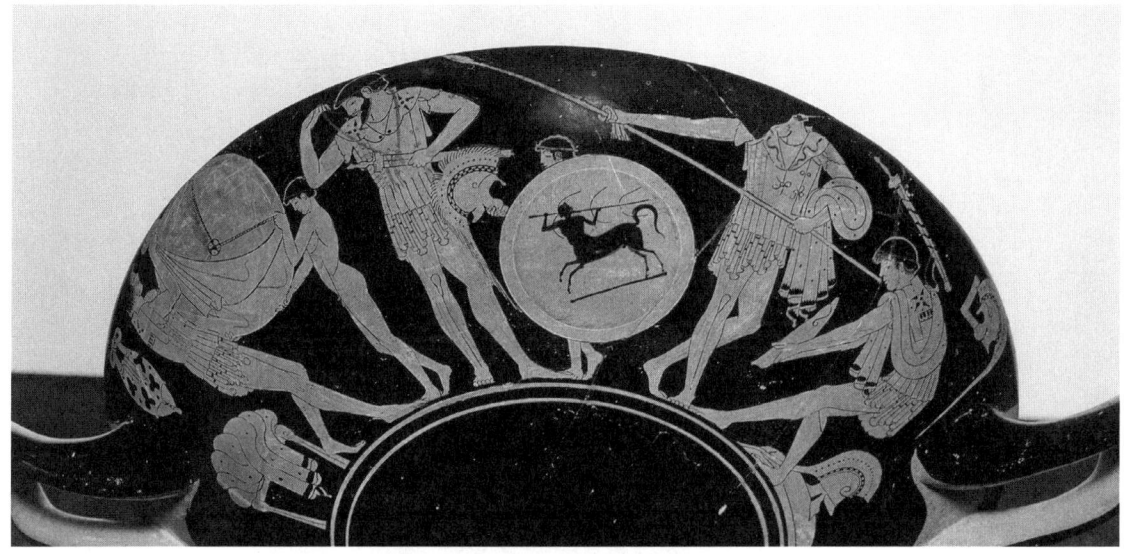

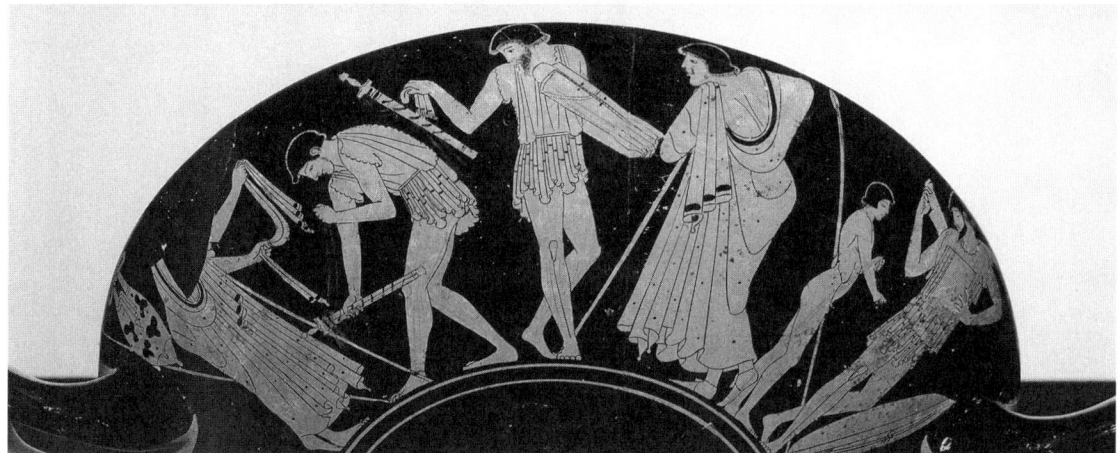

Figure 4.17–18. Exterior of red-figure cup attributed to the Brygos Painter, found at Vulci, ca. 480. *ARV* 373.48, Vatican 16583. Photo © Vatican Museums. All rights reserved.

4.20). Along with this goes an almost exclusive concentration on the youthful hoplite. Earlier arming scenes do indeed frequently show youths, but bearded men also appear. From the early fifth century, the bearded hoplite becomes a rare sight, and in the second quarter of the century if a bearded man is shown arming there is usually an explicit excuse (as in the skyphos, which is the name vase of the Euaichme Painter, where the man who is arming is named "Nestor" after the great epic hero).[82]

One of the effects of arming scenes becoming less active is that they become very much more like departure scenes, so that the classification becomes almost arbitrary. Departure scenes are a familiar element of black-figure iconography, but are not popular in the red-figure until after circa

---

[82] *ARV* 785.2 for the Euichme Painter (but note 1170.8 for a man without explicit excuse). Bearded men arming are last regular in the circle of Douris: *ARV* 427.3, 434.75, 444.234, 449.7.

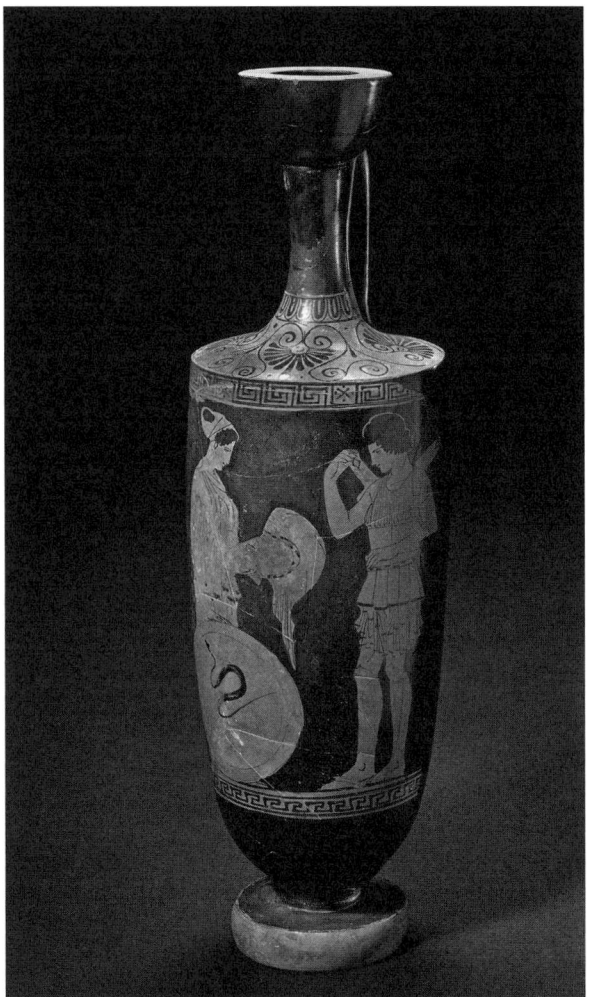

Figure 4.19. Red-figure lekythos, height 0.343 m, attributed to the Phiale Painter, found in Sicily, ca. 430. *ARV* 1021.116. British Museum 1863,0728.440 (E 596). © The Trustees of the British Museum.

500.[83] One particular black-figure departure scene, the scene in which the departing warrior consults the liver of the sacrificial victim before setting out, hardly makes it into red-figure.[84] As we have already seen, black-figure departure scenes are one of the types of scene in which archers are regularly involved, but when departure scenes begin to be popular in red-figure it is without the archers. The regular red-figure iconography involves a hoplite with a woman, an old man, or both; further spectator figures, usually male, may also be involved.[85] The hoplite may hold a phiale and the woman a jug,

---

[83] Spiess (1992); the transformation in the iconography of the hoplite departure was signaled by Bažant (1985), 10; (1987), 33–34.

[84] This may be a special case in that the Etruscans were well known for their skill in hepatoscopy and all examples of the scene with known provenance come from Etruria, but this does not itself explain why the scene appears in red-figure only in three cases, *ARV* 60.64bis (1623) (where the warrior is identified as Antilochos by the naming of the old man as Nestor), 181.1, 220.3 (see Spiess [1992], 261, who, however, misidentifies the cup by Oltos as *ARV* 61.75). Eighteen black-figure examples are known; see Lissarrague (1989), chap. 3.

[85] Departure scenes on fifth-century red-figure vases are analyzed by Matheson (2005; 2009).

or the woman may hold both; the libation may be shown in the act of being poured, either into the phiale, or from the phiale onto the ground or onto an altar. Libation had rarely been part of the iconography of warrior departure in black-figure,[86] but in red-figure the scene gets progressively more popular decade by decade, with half or more of the known red-figure departure scenes painted between circa 520 and circa 420 painted after 460. Iconographically there are few innovations. One of the few is the appearance of Nike. Nike appears rarely in an arming scene, but appears in several departure scenes, making these scenes anticipate, if they do not depict, victorious return.[87]

As the scenes themselves change, so does the company they keep. This is to some extent a consequence of the declining interest in hoplites fighting, which we have already observed. Hoplites fight on a relatively small number of pots that also show arming down to around the time of the Persian wars, but not thereafter. Even in the years when hoplite battles were themselves a popular subject with pot painters, they do not appear on pots that show canonical departure scenes.[88] More generally, down to circa 480 hoplites arming appear with myth scenes, particularly scenes involving Herakles, with satyrs (and maenads), and occasionally with athletic scenes. Subsequently, combination with mythological scenes becomes quite rare, combination with satyrs and maenads vanishes, and the dominant combination is with scenes of youths or men (or both), or libation, with an occasional combination with hoplite departure scenes. Departing hoplites, who also appeared with mythological scenes (rarely Herakles) and scenes involving satyrs and maenads, show the same tendency to combine primarily with more or less anonymous scenes of youths, men and youths, girls and youths, from as early as circa 500, with only the most occasional appearance of satyrs, although combinations with mythological scenes do still appear relatively often.

The changes in emphasis on pots bearing these scenes of arming and parting can be highlighted by comparing two pots. A late sixth-century cup (**4.20–21**) signed, inside and out, by the potter Pamphaios, presents a particularly well-populated, but otherwise quite typical, example of an early red-figure arming scene; a pelike painted shortly before the middle of the century, and attributed to the Chicago Painter, shows an equally typical classical red-figure hoplite departure scene (**4.22** and plate 19). The contrast between the active setting of the former, in which warfare and facing up to the other is emphasized, and the much more personal and domestic feel of the latter, effectively encapsulates the change that had taken place in the representation of the world of war.

On one side of Pamphaios's cup a naked youth raises his left shin to put on a greave (he already has a greave on his right shin). Facing him, a woman

---

[86] Spiess (1992), 83 and 252 (catalog).
[87] Nike in arming scene *ARV* 1043.1; in departure/return scenes *ARV* 990.50, 1038.1, 1039.11, 1044.3, 1054.54, 1124.1, 1251.40, 1257.1.
[88] Later departure scenes occasionally appear with Amazonomachies. So *ARV* 830.1, 1041.5, 1241.40.

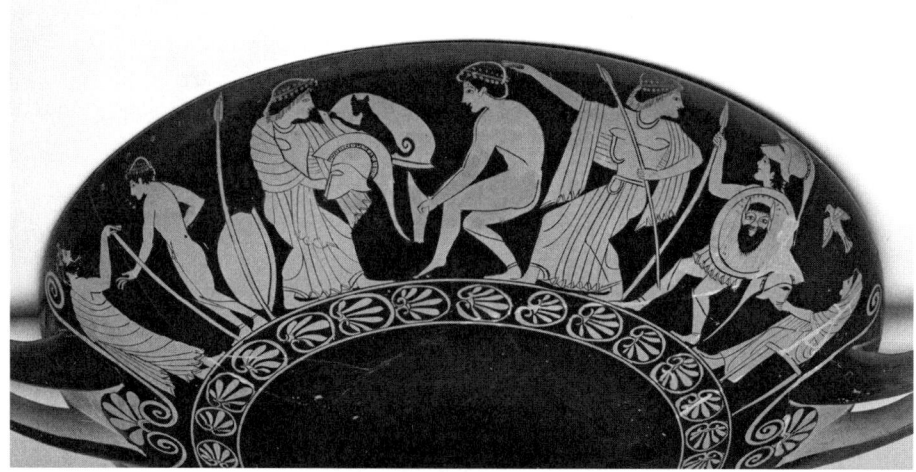

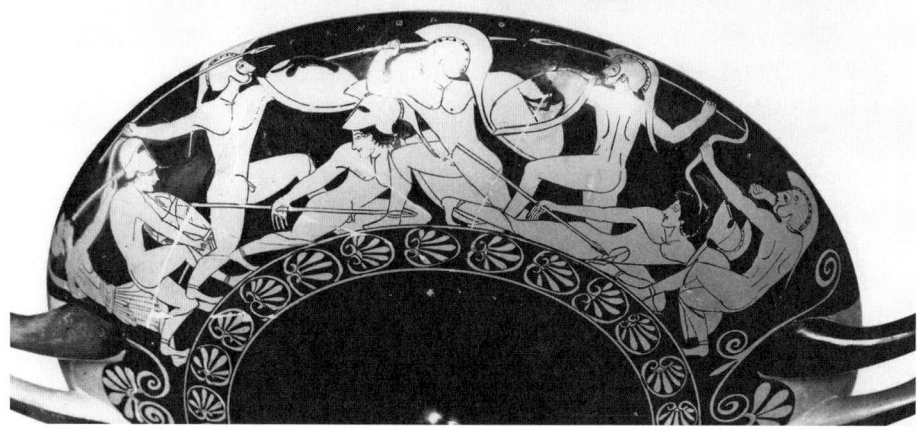

Figure 4.20–21. Exterior of red-figure cup, diameter 0.414 m, signed by the potter Pamphaios, found at Cervetri, ca. 500 (for the interior see 2.1). *ARV* 128.19. Boston Museum of Fine Arts 95.32. Photograph © 2017 Museum of Fine Arts, Boston.

in chiton and himation holds a helmet in one hand and shield in the other. This pair is flanked, on the left, by a bearded man, a naked youth in a garland, and a spear stuck into the ground beside a shield, and, on the right, by a woman carrying a spear, who moves toward the central pair but looks back, a hoplite in full armor carrying a shield bearing a frontal satyr head as its device, and a seated woman holding a helmet. On the other side of the cup a trumpeter and an archer, both in hoplite helmets, flank a scene in which one naked hoplite runs to the right, his spear held out ahead in attack, and it met by two similar naked hoplites, one seen from the front and one from the back, running to the left; below them lie two collapsing hoplites, heads to right, one with his helmet falling off. Inside, on the tondo of the cup (2.1), we see a rather roughly drawn naked satyr running to the right, his face turned back to the left and his torso seen in back view.

The pelike attributed to the Chicago Painter bears on each side one male and one female figure. On one side a naked youth, his cloak over his left

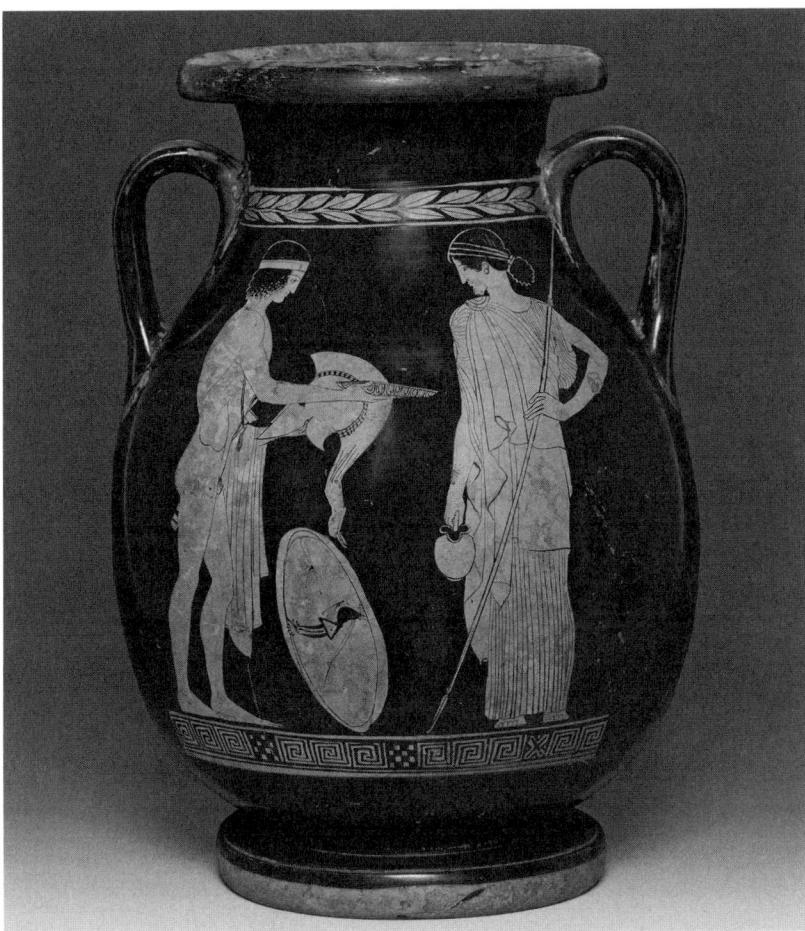

Figure 4.22. Red-figure pelike, height 0.425 m, attributed to the Chicago Painter, found at Vulci, ca. 450 (for the reverse see 2.2). *ARV* 630.26. Paris, Cabinet de Médailles 394. © Bibliothèque nationale de France.

arm, his helmet in his left hand and a phiale in his right hand, faces a young woman, in chiton and himation, who has a jug in one hand and spear in the other. On the other side (2.2) a youth stands somewhat awkwardly, his body is shown frontal and he is holding two spears in his left hand, but he is looking to the right, to a woman who faces him holding a branch of myrtle in her hands. Although this latter scene has no explicit indication of parting, it belongs to a wider class of scene in which a young man in himation and petasos, with two spears, takes leave of a woman, often with the pouring of a libation. Scenes of that sort first appear around the time of the Persian Wars, and from that point on becomes quite popular.[89] The iconography of these scenes is generally distinct from that of parting warriors, with no armor in sight, but scenes of warriors and of these young men do sometimes appear together on the same pot, and on occasion the ico-

---

[89] *ARV* 485.30, 554.84, 603.35, 604.36, 609.14, 610.24, 616.2 for early examples.

nography is combined.[90] The young man in himation or chlamys, with his petasos on or behind his head and carrying two spears, had first appeared earlier in scenes of active hunting,[91] and although scenes of active hunting continue to be painted only occasionally, a strong association with hunting hangs over these scenes of young men parting.[92]

Pamphaios's cup situates the arming warrior in a context where the group is preparing for war and the group is engaged in war. We see not the lone individual preparing for an unknown fate but the group that will fight donning their armor together and, when we turn the cup, we see the fighting. These are not scenes that are interested in verisimilitude; the painter offers little detail and chooses to present the fighting warriors naked. But these are scenes in which the focus is on action, in which we see both the warriors and the women with them doing things. They are not, however, unreflective scenes. The fallen warriors in the scene of fighting, the frontal satyr head on the shield as the warriors arm, the satyr who runs across the tondo, all of these keep visible the reality of warfare as encounter, encounter with the enemy but also encounter with death.

The classical pelike, by contrast, offers no scenes of action and does not raise the specter of the other. Parting for war is not a matter of the group getting ready but of an individual parting from the domestic unit and from a person with whom he has strong affective bonds, whether we think of that person as mother, sister, or wife. For a young man to go to war is here treated as but another experience, like a young man's going hunting: it is a moment worth a formal farewell, a moment of family pride not without a certain apprehension, but it is a routine moment, such as every family regularly experiences. Everything is understated, everything left for the viewer's own construction. We are offered no glimpse of the future, either in literal or in allegorical terms, there is no battle and no satyr. Just as any young man can put on a cloak and traveling hat, pick up two spears, and go off to hunt, so any young man can take a hoplite helmet when one is offered to him and join the call-up. There is no young soldier, indeed no young man, to whom this image is inapplicable: whether or not this act of parting is the prelude to full-scale hoplite battle, the picture fits.[93]

---

[90] *ARV* 603.35 for the iconographies combined (cf. 610.25), 487.57, 604.56, 604.60, 616.5, 616.9, 928.68, 930.102 for examples of both scenes on a single pot. Note the appearance of Nike even in scenes where no arms or armor are present, as in *ARV* 579.1, 580.1.

[91] Earlier red-figure hunting scenes tend to have naked youths (sometimes with a cloak over the arm), as *ARV* 57.42, 74.35, 179.3. The youth hunting wearing the chlamys and petasos and carrying two spears appears from ca. 480, often in contexts of the boar hunt (*ARV* 336.16, 577.52, *CVA* GB 15 [Castle Ashby] plate 37 for boar hunt, 600.17 for similar configuration in a deer hunt). For the boar hunt, see Schnapp (1997), 366–90.

[92] For rare examples of overtly hunting scenes in which the youths are so presented from the second half of the fifth century, see *ARV* 1134.18, 1269.5. Hunting scenes in general are rare in the middle and later part of the fifth century, and when shown the hunters often do not wear the petasos, cf. *ARV* 1067.2bis, 1294 (Louvre G 623).

[93] For those worried that not all could fight as hoplites at Athens, one should note Thucydides's explicit mention of thetes as marines in the Sicilian expedition, 6.43.

6. The Axis of Reflection

The textual evidence available to us indicates that there were very marked changes in the organization, nature, and frequency of Athenian military activity in the century from Peisistratos's coup in the middle of the sixth century to the Thirty Years' Peace agreed between Athens and the Peloponnesian League in the middle of the fifth. The changes in military activity Athenians experienced saw them turned from at best occasional soldiers to men who regularly knew their place in a highly organized and regimented army, from men who rarely witnessed death in military action to men who became used to recognizing the names of friends in the annual list written up on stone to commemorate the war dead. What is more, these became men for whom military service repeatedly meant going to sea—even for those serving hoplite soldiers (transported by ship and playing an important role in naval battles as marines)—and repeatedly meant fighting against fellow Greeks, more or less indistinguishable from themselves.

Examination of the imagery on black- and red-figure pottery has shown that there were equally marked changes in the way military activity was represented in images painted on Athenian pots. The changing representations of soldiers increasingly separate hoplites from other forms of military activity, take the soldier out of the allegorical and heroic battleground, become ever more reluctant to represent battle, and concentrate more and more exclusively on the moment at which the hoplite leaves the domestic context that is itself increasingly reduced to the single figure of the wife or mother.

So described, the changing agenda of representation of soldiers and warfare seems to connect at virtually no point with the changed experience in life of soldiers and warfare. That there should be a disconnect between image and reality is not in itself a puzzle, the puzzle is that the changing imagery on pottery should apparently correlate neither with real life experience of military engagement nor with any change in the selection of stories about warfare that are told—episodes such as the battle of the Seven against Thebes remain good to think with for tragedians throughout the fifth century. So not only the real but also the imagined experience of warfare fails to manifest the marked changes we can see in the imagery.

Should we think that there was indeed no connection between the changing representation on pottery (and, as we shall see, at least to some extent in art more generally) and the changing experience of those who produced and in part consumed that pottery?[94] Can this have been a society in which the soldiers whom pot painters drew were quite unconnected with the soldier whom pot painters knew (or were) and saw on stage? A society, perhaps, where the formative influence of stories of past

---

[94] This is what Muth suggests in the case of scenes of violence, where she argues that variation from time to time between more and less drastic depictions of violence has nothing directly to do with the Athenians experience of violence (2008), 618–27 (English summary 643–44).

heroes was so strong that the vision conjured up by "soldier" or "war" was a vision not of contemporary reality but of the world of the oral or written text? Did the men who came back from campaign to relax at the symposium reflect, on seeing heavily armed soldiers on the pottery in front of them, only on the stories they had been told and never on the military life they had led? Merely to spell out the possibility is to spell out its grossly improbable nature.[95] What we observe in the representations of soldiers on pots is not that they are stuck and fixed, but on the contrary that they change, and in ways that are not trivial but quite fundamental. Any attempt to explain this by suggesting that these are images of stories told informally has to assume that the stories told are changing. In effect this simply moves the problem from a medium that is preserved, the images on pots, to a medium that is not preserved, the oral stories told by and to Athenians. Instead of needing to explain why the images change in ways that do not directly reflect changing historical experience of warfare in Athens, an explanation that sees the imagery as reflecting stories needs to explain why the stories told about warfare change in ways that neither directly reflect that experience nor are themselves reflected in the formal stories explored in tragedy.

There is one respect in which this fantasy that transfers the representation in visual art to representation in verbal stories is helpful. For it is not at all difficult to contemplate a rich fund of stories lying behind the images of early red-figure; no problem here picking up a cup or contemplating a krater in the symposium and spinning a story starting or ending with the scene shown. But, by contrast, the quite undramatic and largely unindividualized scenes of hoplites parting of the middle of the fifth century offer little or no inspiration for any particular story; the only story they offer is the generic story of young men going to war; another young man responds to call-up and leaves his loved ones to join the war effort. The most that we get is a hint that Victory is already part of the story even at the moment of departure (**4.23**). Scenes of war draw attention to the fact that one of the things that the red-figure imagery has dropped in the middle of the fifth century is the invitation to spin a particular story—and that is true of scenes relating to athletics as much as to scenes relating to war. The invitation instead is to tell of what (young) men, if they are worthy to be part of this society, are going to do, or ought to be going to do.

But if the story changes, is that because the old stories had ceased to be wanted by those who used the pots on which the images were painted? Had the symposium ceased to be a place where particular stories were told? I will explore more of the history of the symposium and of its representation in a later chapter, but it is sufficient to note here that although the decline of the particular story is manifest across a number of areas of representation, there remain plenty of pots still being painted that engage with

---

[95] Cf. Muth (2008), 619: "So falsch es ist, die Darstellung der Gewalt als direkten Spiegel für die Einstellungen der Athener zur Gewalt zu interpretieren, so falsch ware es nun gleichermaßen, ihnen jede historische Aussagekraft abzusprechen."

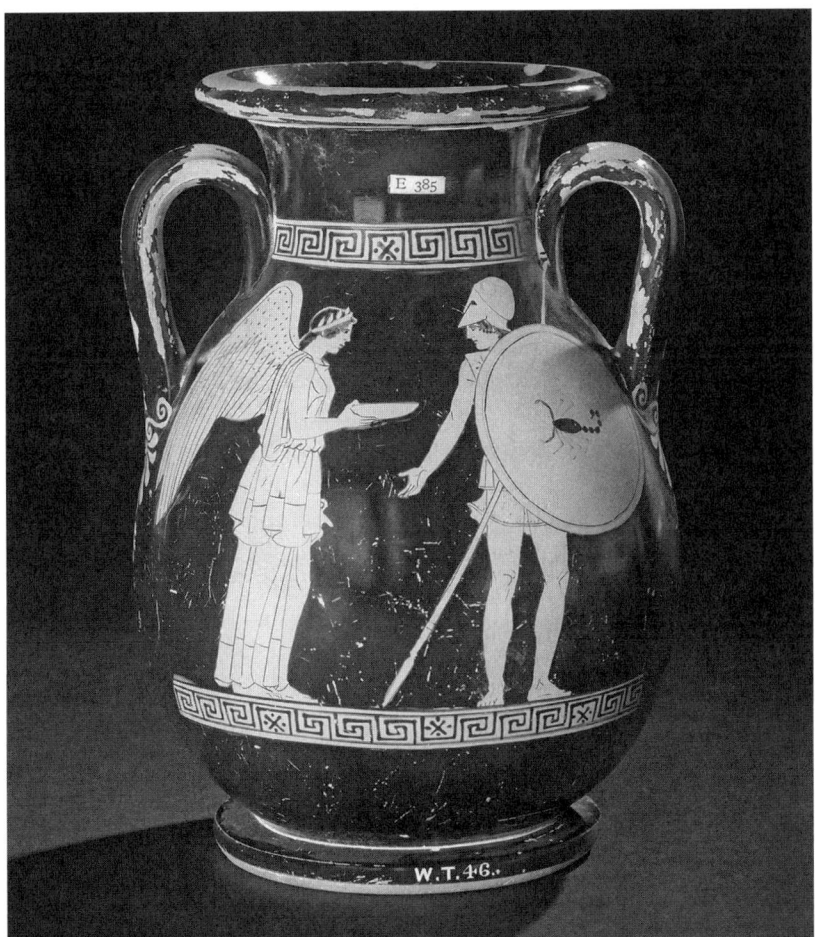

Figure 4.23. Red-figure pelike, height 0.254 m, attributed to the Achilles Painter, ca. 440. *ARV* 990.50, British Museum 1856,1226.46 (E 385). © The Trustees of the British Museum.

identifiable stories, in particular with mythological stories. The decline of the particular story seems not to be a feature of the symposium (though we might note that it is not a feature of Plato's *Symposium*), but a feature of attitudes to certain sorts of activities.

There might be a temptation to think that the Athenians had particular reasons for not wanting to tell particular stories of real wars and for wanting to keep stories of wars to stories of mythical wars. Casualties in Athenian wars had certainly been heavy in some years in the 450s; what exactly Thucydides's comment with regard to the Egyptian expedition that "out of many, few returned" is meant to mean (he will say the same of the Sicilian expedition) is hard to tell, but the loss of large numbers of lives is not in doubt.[96] When fighting was as frequent an experience as it was for Athenians in these years of endless anti-Persian and anti-Greek activity, it is easy to imagine that talking more about the details of war might not be what

[96] Thuc. 1.110.1, 7.87.6 (cf. 3.112.8). See Hornblower (1991), 176–77.

Athenians wanted to do over their cups. But even were this plausible—and we have no other reason to believe the Athenians so traumatized by battle, and some reason from old comedy to think that narratives of war exploits were regularly the stuff of conversation—it cannot be the whole explanation. For the parallel decline in interest in the particular athlete and in showing athletic competition can hardly be similarly motivated; there is no other sign of the Athenians being gymnasium weary.

Whatever explanation we embrace for the changes in the imagery of warfare must plausibly also account for the parallel changes in the imagery of athletics.[97] For the abandonment of the hoplite actively engaging in the activities of war is closely parallel to the abandonment of the athlete actively engaging with the pursuits of the gymnasium.[98] The young men who stand about in the gymnasium with vertical javelins or dangling strigils are close relatives of the young men who stand while a libation is poured or while they are proferred a helmet. Yet Athenian foreign policy gave Athenian soldiers as little time for contemplation as did the competitions of Athenian festivals.

It is also as true of these scenes of soldiers as it was of those of athletes, that the changes we observe concern how the figures shown relate to one another. Here the scenes of soldiers offer us, as those of athletes did not, the opportunity to compare and contrast scenes that superficially appear to show exactly the same thing: soldiers arming. And on the face of it, the difference between a soldier putting on a greave observed by other members of the household and a soldier receiving his helmet from a female member of the household might seem minimal. But the absence of other soldiers, particularly of the contrasting Scythian archer, and increasingly the absence of other items of the hoplite panoply, significantly alters the relationships. The black-figure images gave the hoplite soldier pride of place among a varied army; the greaves symbolized, still more powerfully than helmet or shield, what made the heavily armed warrior different. To put on greaves was to join the ranks not of any soldiers but of the soldiers celebrated in epic. For a young man to take his helmet, however, particularly when not in other respects yet prepared in any other way for war, is to accept the duty to leave civilian pursuits and leave the private role in the household to take on the public role in the city. We expect the soldiers arming on black-figure pottery to become champions; we expect these young men to play their part alongside everyone else in the ranks. The relationship is no longer competitive, and ironically the isolation of the single figure, because it removes the opportunity to compare and contrast, takes the emphasis away from the individual, seen competitively, while

---

[97] Muth's discussion of changing scenes of violence seems to me to be undermined by her attempt to understand changing scenes of violence only in relation to changes relating to violence; see esp. Muth (2008), 626–27, for her explanation of the changes in her data set parallel to the changes I have discussed in this chapter. But note Muth's own comments at (2008), 627.

[98] And although I have not traced the changes in detail, very closely parallel also to the translation of the active young hunter into the young hunter departing for the hunt.

raising the issue of individualism and what the individual must and must not do.

The young men who swapped the household for the army, private life for civic duty, will certainly have seen active service. So too, the young men who stood waiting with their javelin would not leave the gymnasium without throwing it, those who scraped themselves down with strigils had worked up a sweat through the running, jumping, and other activities they had practiced. But the scenes that artists choose to represent are not those of action, their interactions with others not those of competition, their self-presentation not one designed to attract any particular set of eyes. The discussions for which the mid-fifth-century scenes cue the symposiast are not discussions of who was, or how to be, most successful in battle or the gymnasium, they are discussions of the place that the gymnasium enjoys in civic life, of the importance of army service for the strength of the city.

We cannot deduce from these changing scenes anything about what was actually happening in the armed forces or in the gymnasium. But from the fact that the scenes representing two different areas of Athenian life change in a coordinated way we can, I think, deduce that something was happening to the way that those who produced and consumed the pottery bearing these images saw the world—not simply to the way they thought and talked about fighting or about athletics but to the way they thought about and their attitudes to behavior more generally and to the question of how the individual should react to and relate to the group of which he was part. These changing scenes correlate in one way or another with changes in the expectations about how the individual will take part in group activities. While the discourse of the late sixth century expected the individual to engage competitively, to show that he can do better, win prizes, come out on top, the discourse of the mid-fifth century expected the individual to participate without regard to achieving particular personal distinction.

If these changes signal changing relationships, then they should show up in scenes that focus on relationships. In examining scenes involving soldiers we have already had cause to consider images in which soldiers relate to women and in which they are involved in the religious ritual of libation. It makes sense therefore to consider these images against the background of other scenes in which men and women interact and other scenes of religious ritual. It is to such scenes that the next two chapters are devoted.

5 ❧ Courting Change

In the two previous chapters of this book I showed how the choice of scenes of athletes and warriors painted on Athenian pots changed markedly between what might broadly be called "archaic" and "classical" red-figure pot painting, between what was painted prior to the Persian War period and what was painted in the middle of the fifth century. In this and the next two chapters I ask how this changed way of seeing the world impacted how sexual relations, relations with the gods, and relations in the symposium were represented. My aim is to reinforce my argument for an all-encompassing change in how the world is represented and to enrich my characterization of the changed worldview.

In examining changes in the representation of relations between women and men on painted pottery we face very particular source issues. Warfare was something about which Greeks in general worried in every form of literary expression—epic, elegy, tragedy, comedy, oratory, history, and public and private documents. Although the genre of the literary material clearly affects the sorts of issues concerning warfare that get discussed, we have some relevant literary material available from more or less all periods. That was not true of athletics, where the interest taken by tragedians, comic playwrights, historians, and orators is at best sporadic and where the disappearance of epinician poetry massively changes our source base. It is similarly not true of relations between men and women. Epic, lyric, and iambic poetry, tragedy, and comedy all in their different ways make relations between men and women one of their central concerns, but historians and orators are far less consistently interested in such issues, and gender roles impinge only on certain types of public document.

It has long been a fundamental question in the study of Athenian society how one reads the evidence of tragedy.[1] Nor is the evidence of comedy any more straightforward, for all the prominence of women and women's issues in Aristophanes.[2] Scholars often maintain that the need to persuade jurors who knew what Athenian life was like constrained orators in the courts, but the capacity of people to imagine that others behave very differently from themselves should not be underestimated, and in any case

---

[1] The classic debate is to be found in Gomme (1925), reprinted in Gomme (1937), 89–115; and Kitto (1951), 219–36.

[2] For a general discussion see Robson (2009), 82–91; more radical are the challenges explored by Zeitlin (1981) and Ruffell (2011), esp. 393–96.

occasionally lurid spotlights, such as those cast by Lysias discussing Euphiletos and his wife in the speech *Against Eratosthenes* (1), or by Apollodoros discussing Neaira (in [Demosthenes] 59 *Against Neaira*) hardly allow for the writing of a continuous history of changing or unchanging behavior, expectations, or attitudes.

Because the textual source material for writing a diachronic history of relations between men and women, or indeed a diachronic history of women, is problematic, scholars have paid attention to the visual evidence on this question far more than they have in the case of warfare, or even of athletics. But what to make of changing iconography over time has been far from clear to those who have discussed the issue.[3] By examining the changes in imagery involving women and men in the context of changing iconography more generally, I hope to establish more firmly the ways in which the scenes painted on pots do and do not enable us to write a history of gender relations at Athens. I group together here scenes that have in the past been treated by scholars separately. We have no idea how an Athenian would have grouped scenes, and I certainly make no claim that an Athenian would have grouped them as I do, but the more the changes to which I draw attention override the boundaries of any ancient classification the clearer it is that a general, and not a subject-specific, explanation of the changes is needed.

1. The Archaic Background

Relations between men and women are explored from the earliest Greek figurative art, just as they are in the earliest preserved Greek literature. The figures painted on Athenian pottery in the eighth century offer rather little to distinguish them one from the other, but they do distinguish gender. Women are regularly skirted and sometimes breasts are indicated; men are regularly shown naked. Already on some eighth-century pots it seems to be the relationship between men and women that is explored.[4] The proto-Attic pottery of seventh-century Athens had used figurative decoration to explore stories from mythology, and these included stories to which relations between men and women were central, most notably the attempt of the centaur Nessos to rape Deianeira and Herakles's response.[5] Among the scenes early black-figure painters favored was the marriage of Peleus and Thetis (1.9).[6]

---

[3] See Lewis (2002), 134, 170–71, 212; Lewis is inclined (esp. 129, 134, 212) to give a major role to the declining export market for Athenian pots to their changing imagery, which she sees as coming to conform more closely to Athenian society. Against this see chapter 2, section 2.

[4] Scholars have speculated that a particular myth may lie behind the representation of a man and woman on a large scale side by side beside a ship on a louterion/krater in London (British Museum 1899.2–19.1), but whether we are to think of myth or not, we are certainly to think of gender relations (see Langdon [2008], 19–22, 50, 54, 224).

[5] New York, Metropolitan Museum 11.210.1.

[6] Shapiro (1990), 132.

Mythology remained the primary medium by which relations between men and women were explored throughout the history of black-figure painting, although the increasing interest in satyrs and in their relations to nymphs or maenads offered scope for exploring heterosexual relations that was not tied to a particular mythological narrative. Outside the context of mythology, such exploration of male-female relations is largely restricted to depictions of sexual intercourse.

Explicit representation of heterosexual intercourse on Athenian pottery begins in the second quarter of the sixth century with so-called Tyrrhenian amphoras and Little Master cups. Tyrrhenian amphoras are a type of vessel that seems, on the basis of the findspots, to have been made with the Etruscan market in mind.[7] The sexually explicit scenes on these amphoras are both homosexual and heterosexual; they show pairs of men and women, with the men sexually excited and about to penetrate or in the act of penetrating the naked women from the rear and the women turning their heads to kiss the men, and men and youths in various states of sexual excitement and sexual activity, which include the sodomy of bearded men by youths.[8]

Heterosexual intercourse between couples who are standing, with the man behind the woman, is the most common form of sexual intercourse shown on Little Master cups, although various other forms of sexual intercourse and sexual activity also appear on these. Little Master cups and related cups with sexually explicit scenes have a wider geographical distribution than Tyrrhenian amphoras; of the forty-two cups and cup fragments Sutton cataloged, just two come from Vulci, five come from elsewhere in Etruria, four come from elsewhere in Italy or Sicily, seven come from Athens (five from the Acropolis, two from the Agora), one from Aigina, three from Rhodes, two from Naukratis, and one each from Thera, Smyrna, and Cyprus. Other amphora and cup shapes also have sexually explicit imagery, heterosexual and sometimes homosexual, as do skyphoi, hydrias, an oinochoe, a plate, a stemmed dish, a stand, and three lekythoi of early fifth-century date, one from an Athenian child grave, but, with the exception of one hydria, the homosexual images do not include sodomy.[9]

Exceptional among black-figure pots is a cup-skyphos by the Amasis Painter that explores not sexual intercourse but courtship (**5.1–2**).[10] A bearded and naked man is shown presenting a cock to a naked woman, who herself holds a flower. This unique scene can be understood, however, only in the context of the rest of the scene on this cup. The Amasis Painter

---

[7] Kluiver (1992); shapes other than amphoras produced by the Tyrrhenian group are found more widely distributed, see Tuna-Nörling (1997).

[8] Sutton (2009b), 85–86, lists thirteen Tyrrhenian amphoras with sexually explicit scenes, of which four have known provenance, three coming from Vulci and one from Tharros, Sardinia; *ABV* 102.95–102, *Para*. 35, 36, 41 (Dover [1978], B51–53). The scenes of men and youths are discussed in detail by Lear and Cantarella (2008), 123–28.

[9] Data from Sutton (2009b), 86–88; for the lekythos, see Parlama and Stampolidis (2000), 198–99 no. 289; La Genière (2009), 343–44; for the hydria showing sodomy (not in Sutton [2009b], see Lear and Cantarella [2008], 115–16, fig. 3.8, appendix 2.100; Parker [2015,] 44–45, 121).

[10] Von Bothmer (1985), 200–203.

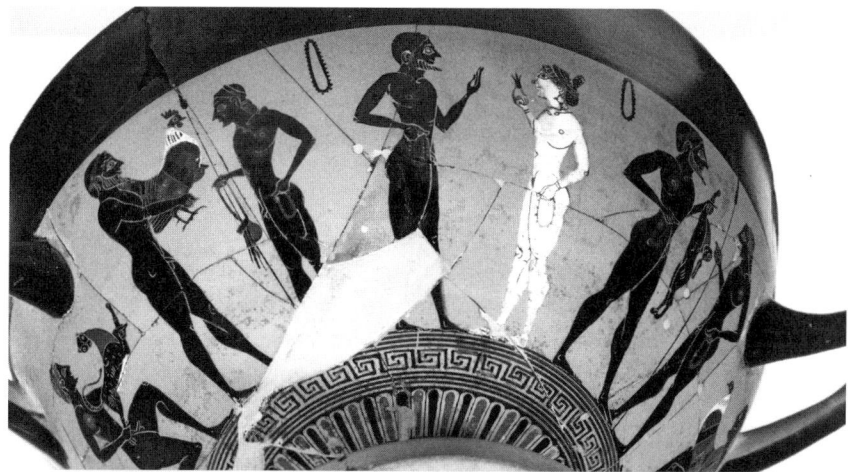

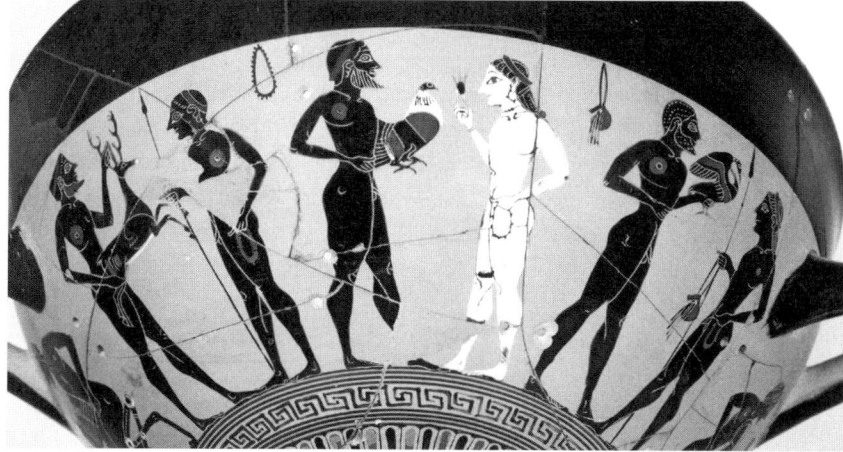

Figure 5.1–2. Black-figure cup, diameter 0.179 m, attributed to the Amasis Painter, from Kamiros, ca. 540. *ARV* 156.80, Paris, Louvre A 479. Photo © RMN-Grand Palais (musée du Louvre)/ Les Frères Chuzeville.

sets his scene of heterosexual courtship in the middle of scenes of homosexual courtship. All round the cup naked bearded men offer a variety of animals and birds, including a hare or rabbit and a miniature stag as love gifts to beardless naked youths. The youths are shown equipped with javelins or spears or with the aryballos that marks the athlete. Under one handle we see an older man holding a colorful bird yet to be given, under the other a youth holding a feline animal already received. The older men are to be thought of as displaying the results of their own success in hunting to attract those whose athletic prowess has caught their eye. Such scenes of courtship of youths by men can be widely paralleled in other black-figure pots.[11] The importance of the Amasis Painter's cup, however, is that, by the exotic variety of animals shown and by introducing a naked woman into what might otherwise be taken to be a scene that reproduced real-life courtship rituals, the painter invites the viewer not to contemplate a reflection of life but to reflect on the nature of the exchanges that courtship gifts establish.

[11] Cf. *ABV* 314.6; Schnapp (1997), 251, no.182 (A, B); and Lear and Cantarella (2008), appendix section 2.

The offering of gifts is not, however, the most frequent mode of courtship by which older men seek on black-figure pots to establish sexual interest among youths.[12] Most common is the representation of the older man, who may or may not exhibit his own sexual excitement, attempting to establish physical contact with the younger man by fondling the chin and the genitals. Various sixth- and fifth-century texts dwell on the attractions of the downy hair of the youth blossoming into manhood—something thought to have occurred up to four years later than it does today—and of pubic hair.[13] Painters most often show the young man as of more or less the same stature as the older man, but in some images the younger man is very much smaller. The younger man is not normally shown experiencing sexual excitement at being touched up—and Xenophon will maintain that youths experience no sexual excitement in their relations with older men—but younger men sometimes convey in other ways their enthusiasm for the relationship.[14]

Some pots show a third mode in which older men engage with younger men. In this the older man is shown in a state of sexual excitement, touching his erect penis against the younger man's body. The action in these scenes is often referred to as "intercrural intercourse," but it is not clear that the penis is in fact inserted between the thighs—often the penis is shown too high for that, although the motif frequently shows the older man bending his knees to get to the right level for what he wants to do.[15] Whatever range of actual physical contact is being signaled in these images, there is little doubt that the older man obtains a sexual thrill from pressing his own body against that of the youth.

The various ways of representing the courtship by men of younger men are all shown together on an amphora in the British Museum (**5.3**).[16] Here a figure in a himation, open at the front, runs or dances across the scene, his head turned around to look behind him. Behind him are two couples and in front of him a third couple. The couple on the left consist of a sexually excited bearded man and a beardless youth; the youth carries in his arms a small stag with fine antlers and looks back at the older man from whom he seems about to walk away. The couple to the right, in front of the runner/dancer, consists of an older man, displaying sexual excitement, reaching for the almost invisible genitals of a younger and slightly taller man, with whom he practically touches noses. The younger man has a garland in his right hand, the older man cradles a cock in his left; behind them,

---

[12] For the classification of modes of homosexual courtship on Athenian black-figure pottery, see Beazley (1947); cf. Shapiro (1981), Cantarella and Lear (2008), Parker (2015), Osborne (2018).

[13] Davidson (2007), 80–81, on "the great puberty shift."

[14] Xenophon *Symposium* 8.21; Boston 08.292, Dover (1978) B598, has two scenes of courtship that invite a sequential reading in which the courting activity causes the rather small boy to leap with excitement in response to the attention that he receives.

[15] Osborne (2018); Parker (2015), 39, acknowledges both that pottery does not offer representations of actual sexual acts and that literature has no descriptions of what he calls "interfemoral" sex, but continues nevertheless to think that intercourse by means of rubbing the penis between the partner's thighs is being shown here.

[16] Dover (1978), B250; Schnapp (1997), 252 no. 184.

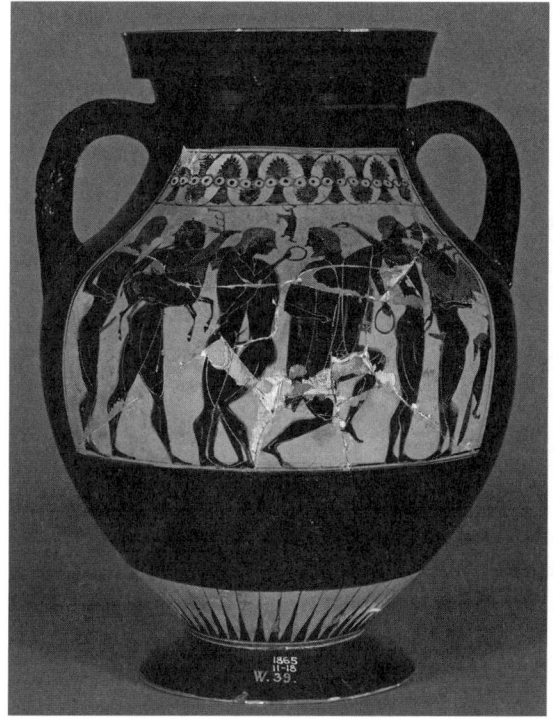 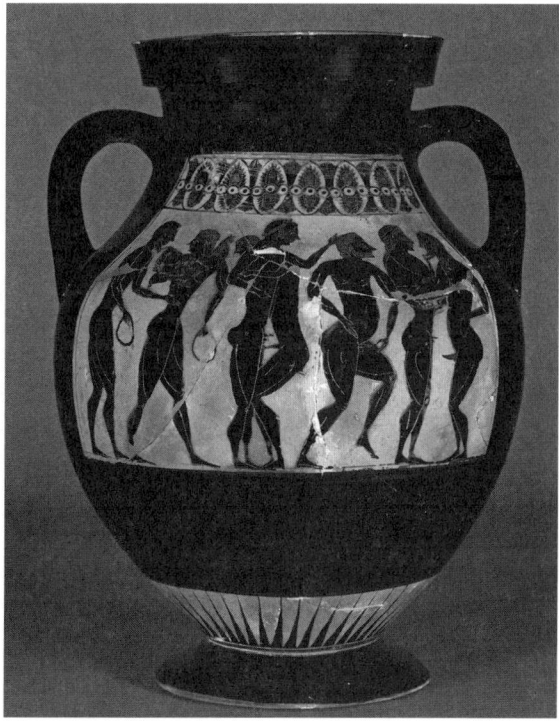

Figure 5.3–4. Black-figure amphora, height 0.345 m, attributed to the Painter of Berlin 1686, from Vulci, ca. 540. *ARV* 297.16, British Museum 1865,1118.39 (W39). © The Trustees of the British Museum.

as if strung up against the border of the picture, is a dead fox. Immediately behind the runner/dancer, and perhaps to be thought of as the cause of his gazing backward, are an older man embracing a younger man, his head bent over the young man's left shoulder. Both men display sexual excitement, and the older man bends his knees as he apparently presses his penis into the younger man's genitals.[17] The younger man once more carries a (rather small in this case) garland in his right hand, above which a dead rabbit or hare hangs from the picture frame.

The other side of this amphora (**5.4** and plate 20) similarly shows three couples consisting each of an older and a younger man. Once more there is one exchange of love gifts, as a young man turns his body from an older man, carrying off a colorful bird but looking back to the putative giver of the gift. Once more there is a scene of fondling, this time of the chin. And once more there is a scene in which an older man and younger man embrace, and the older man, his knees bent and his head over the young man's left shoulder, thrusts his penis into or just below the young man's genitals. Once more on this side there is one single older man. Again he moves to the right, but this time in a less energetic fashion. He is naked here and puts his hands to his own genitals.

[17] The sexual excitement of the young man here is exceptional, and the attempt to deny it by Dover (1978), 96–97, is unconvincing: this painter knows how to make the merest hint at the presence of genitals when that is what he wishes to do. Here we must take him to want to show something of the range of possible relationships and reciprocation.

COURTING CHANGE 127

There can be little doubt that the painter of this amphora wished to explore the different modes in which older men might engage in sexual relations with younger men. Not only does each side offer images of each of the modes of courtship that modern scholars have isolated, it also reminds the viewers of the more solitary sexual pleasures of voyeurism and masturbation. It is clear from later texts, and above all from Plato's and Xenophon's dialogues titled *Symposium*, that the nature of erotic relations was a constant topic of conversation, and in Xenophon's writings more generally there is repeated exploration of the interrelationship of the attractions of beauty and sex and of the link between sex and the formation of affective bonds.[18] While we should not foist the views of Plato, Xenophon, or the characters in their works back onto the sixth century, the topics of the sympotic poetry of Theognis, Anakreon, and others encourage us to believe that sixth-century drinking parties also discussed these issues. Those who drank and conversed with older or younger companions at a symposium at which wine decanted into this amphora was drunk had the choice of how to pursue a relationship with a younger/older man displayed before them, both suggesting a topic for conversation and exposing, for any choice they chose to take, the alternative choices not taken.

2. The Sexual World of Archaic Red-Figure Pottery

Faced with the iconographic alternatives developed by painters working in the black-figure technique, red-figure artists themselves exercised choice. All three of the modes of courtship represented in earlier black-figure pottery are shown on red-figure pots, but not at all in the same proportions. In addition, from earliest red-figure on there is a new interest in scenes of sexual pursuit, whether involving bodily contact between the pursuer and the pursued, or, more normally, involving no contact.

Scenes of men courting boys and youths courting boys figure among the scenes painted by the Pioneers of red-figure painting. Scenes in which some sorts of fondling occur dominate the earliest red-figure, with a particular interest being shown in fondling of boys by beardless youths. Several such scenes appear not on sympotic vessels but on a group of alabastra that have become known as the "Paidikos alabastra."[19] These vessels for perfumed oil to be spread about the body carry images in which older hands, of bearded men or beardless youths, are passed over youthful bodies.

The most famous of all courtship scenes on early red-figure, however, occurs on a cup (**5.5–6** and plate 21). This shows, on the interior, an image of Peleus, who, as usual, is beardless, struggling with Thetis, and, on the exterior, scenes of youths courting boys and youths courting women.[20] The

---

[18] Hindley (1999).

[19] *ARV* 100.20, 101.2 (provenance unknown), Athens Kerameikos 2713 (*Para.* 331).

[20] Of the four pots or fragments attributed to Peithinos, one other also shows a courtship scene, but this time a scene involving the giving of a hare by a draped figure to a beardless youth: *ARV* 116,

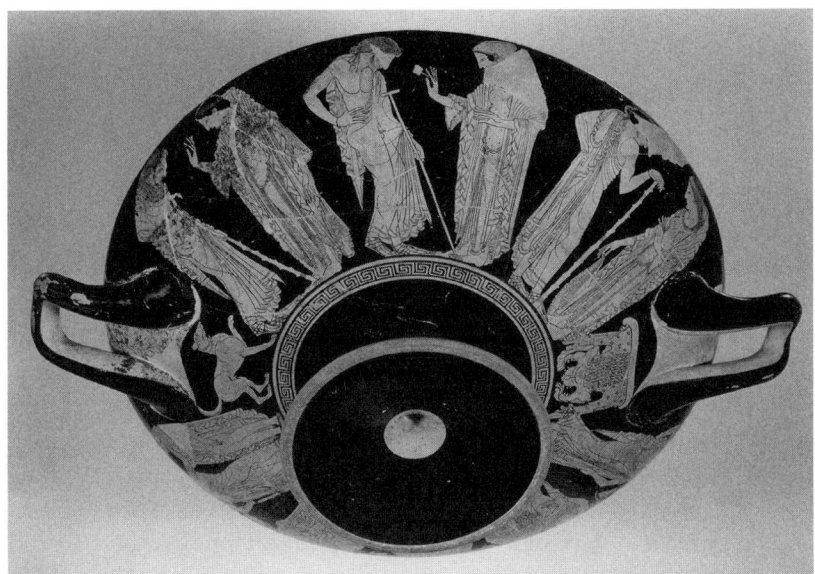

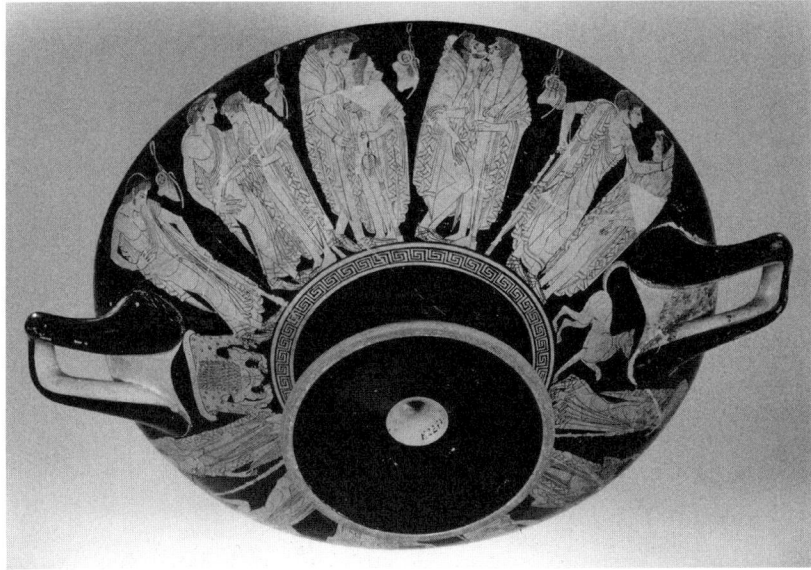

Figure 5.5–6. Exterior of red-figure cup, diameter 0.34 m, signed by Peithinos as painter, from Vulci, ca. 500. *ARV* 115.2, Berlin Antikensammlung, Staatliche Museen F. 2279. © bpk / Antikensammlung, Staatliche Museen zu Berlin / Johannes Laurentius.

artist signs himself "Peithinos," but very few other images can be ascribed to him other than this cup, found at Vulci. Since the name "Peithinos" might be translated as "Seducer," this artist seems to have named himself for the painting of just such a scene as this. The youths on both sides are quite precisely depicted, for although beardless they have elaborately shaped sideburns, indicating the spreading of hair to the cheeks, if not yet to the chin. On one side, they engage the boys closely—putting an arm behind a semicloaked head or reaching for the boys' genitals and bringing their mouths close to the boys' own lips. In all cases the boys exercise some

---

Athens, Acropolis 248. On Peithinos see further Hedreen (2016), 280–93, who suggests that Peithinos is a pseudonym for Euphronios, chosen to suit the subject of the cup.

control over the youths' movements, placing a hand on the lower or upper arm to limit the freedom of the youths' hands. One of the boys carries an aryballos, and there are sponge-bag gym kits suspended in the background. On the other side their engagement with the women is more distant, with no physical contact. On both sides the conversations are carried out, at least in part, in the language of clothes. The three boys all partly cover their heads with their cloaks but leave their naked bodies on display, as do two of the three youths. The youth who limits himself to fondling the back of the boy's head keeps himself draped with his himation. In the exchanges with the women, one of the youths keeps himself fully covered up with his himation, his arms and hands concealed within it. The other two youths wear their himation in the conventional fashion, leaving their right arms and part of the right side of the chest exposed. All three youths use sticks, two knobbly, one smooth. The women all wear copious himatia, cascading in regular folds, over chitons, which are shown with decorative patterns and revealing the shape of the breasts. One of the women wears the head scarf that scholars term a sakkos. She also holds a flower, while one of her companions lifts the edge of her chiton, as if to draw attention to its fineness and to her legs beneath. All the women have bare feet, but the men wear elaborate sandals.

The modes of courtship privileged on Peithinos's cup prove not to be the modes subsequent pot painters would favor. Genital fondling remains occasionally shown, but only a very small number of subsequent pots show either a youth or a bearded man fondling a boy, with neither scene surviving in the iconography beyond 480.[21] Nor were red-figure artists any more persistently concerned to show men rubbing their penis against the body of a boy. A small number of red-figure representations of this sort exist, but they too do not continue beyond 480.[22] Red-figure painters do show some youths and men embracing boys, but these scenes too remain relatively infrequent and disappear early in the fifth century.[23]

What dominates the scenes of men courting boys, youths courting boys, and men courting women (to cite the different combinations in order of declining frequency of representation) is the offering of some form of love gift. Different painters seem to favor different gifts, but men are shown variously offering hares or rabbits, cocks, lyres, sashes, joints of meat, money(?) bags, and balls to youths or boys; youths offer hares, cocks, a garland, and fruit to boys. These scenes go on being painted after 480, with scenes of men offering gifts to boys remaining the most frequent. But scenes showing youths (only) courting women are different. Here the most frequent motif, appearing just occasionally even after 480, is the embrace,

---

[21] Youths fondling boys: *ARV* 157.85bis, 292.32, Malibu 82 AE 53. Men fondling boys: *ARV* 378.137, 410.65, 478.306.

[22] *ARV* 362.21, 443.224, Dover (1978), R502, R573; also Dover (1978), R371 (attributed to the Eucharides Painter, not in Beazley); I include here only relations between mortal—the one context in which later artists show such relationships is between figures marked as not belonging to the human world, cf. Shapiro (1992). See further Osborne (2018).

[23] Malibu 85 AE 25 (above fig. 3.14–16), *ARV* 318, 322.37bis, 407.16, 443.224; cf. 348.4.

and only on pots painted toward the middle of the fifth century do gifts regularly appear—hares and joints of meat.[24]

We have already seen some of the iconography of courtship through the giving of gifts in the discussion in chapter 3 of scenes of older men presenting younger men with the tokens of athletic victory. That assimilation between awarding the prize for victory and giving a love gift is itself typical of the way in which in these scenes what counts as courtship is always itself under scrutiny. The way in which youths face up to women on Peithinos's cup is read as having an agenda of sexual attraction largely because of the manifest sexual interest taken by the youths in the boys on the other side of the cup and because of the presence of Peleus and Thetis in the tondo. Any scene involving male and female, or younger and older male figures, is potentially a scene of courtship, and painters encourage viewers to explore the dynamics of interpersonal relations through the inferences they make on the basis of actions and objects.

The most debated object in courtship scenes is the small bag seen dangling from the hands of men and youths in their relations with women and with youths. A good example is afforded by a cup by Makron, an artist with whom scenes of courtship are particularly frequent (**5.7–8** and plate 22).[25] On one side of a cup we see a man and a youth in similar poses, each dressed in the standard himation, draped over the left shoulder and leaving the right arm and right part of torso free, each holding out a bag containing some sort of small objects—scholars suppose either coins or knucklebones.[26] In front of the youth is a seated woman, wearing a sakkos, the top part of her himation wrapped around her waist leaving her short-sleeved chiton on display and with it the form of her breasts. Although her right hand, holding a flower, trails in the direction of the youth, she looks away toward the encounter between the older man and the woman who stands facing him and holds up another flower above the back of her chair. The standing woman is bare-headed and dressed with her himation largely concealing her chiton, which in any case falls in pleated folds rather than gripping the body. She holds a wreath in her right hand. In the background hangs the athlete's sponge bag with a net of marbles and, behind the standing woman, an aulos case.

On the other side of this cup we again find two men and two women, with one woman seated and one standing. On the right is a bearded man wearing his himation in the standard way and with a stick in his left hand. He holds up a small branch in his right hand. Facing him is a seated woman in a sakkos and wearing earrings, her himation dropped to around her waist and her hands held out extending a wreath toward the man. Between them hangs the athlete's sponge bag. Behind the woman is another bearded man,

---

[24] Youths and women embracing: *ARV* 86 (6), 101 (1), 118.14, 177.1, 177.2, 179 (4), 180.1, 468.144, 468.146, 572.88. Gifts: 892.8, 895.78.

[25] Kunisch (1997), no. 179.

[26] Meyer (1988); Lewis (2002), 194–99; Ferrari (2002), 14–16; note also Kilmer (1993), 84n11. For cases where only money can be in question, see *ARV* 24.14, 256.1 (10.5), 285.1, 285.2, 445.252, 540.4, 596.1.

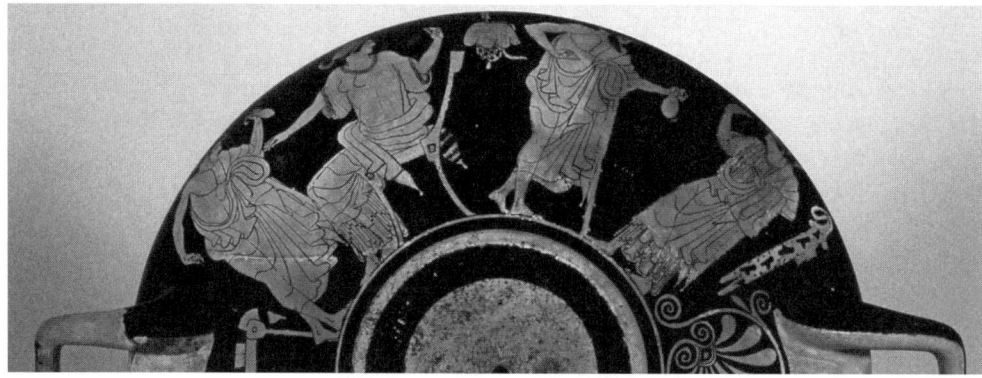

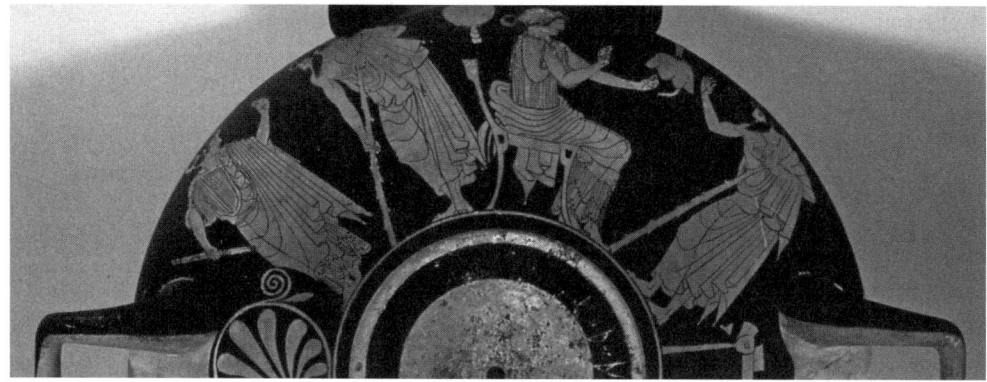

Figure 5.7–8. Exterior of red-figure cup, diameter 0.287 m, attributed to Makron, ca. 480 (for the interior see 6.2 and plate 25). Toledo Museum of Art, Toledo, Ohio, purchased with the funds from the Libbey Endowment, gift of Edward Drummond Libbey, 1972.55.

much like the other except that he has both his hands on his stick. Facing him is a woman in chiton and himation who is turning to the left but looks back at the man and holds up a flower in her left hand. In her right, she holds a double aulos. In the background hang a mirror and the athlete's sponge bag.

What are we to make of these encounters? Some scholars have no doubt that the women here (though not on the interior of the cup that shows (6.2 and plate 25) a woman pouring a libation on an altar) are prostitutes.[27] What with the mirror, the aulos and aulos case and the sponge bags, sensual attractions and athletic prowess are certainly being paraded, but rather more is going on here than merely exchanging money for sex. This scene has to be understood in the context of other scenes in which the person to whom the bag is extended is not a woman but a youth. In some such scenes the money bag is one of a number of different possible gifts, as on another cup ascribed to Makron, the exterior of which shows six pairs consisting of a man and a youth, where two men offer hares, one offers a money(?) bag, and one youth takes a cock.[28] The bags, whatever we think they contain, stand for something that the men have to exchange, but in the context

[27] So Kunisch (1997), 179; Beard (1991), 28–29.
[28] *ARV* 471.198; Kunisch (1997), no. 396.

of a wide range of exchanges, for the flowers and wreaths are exchange items too, as indeed is the provision of the music of the aulos.

Rather than showing snapshots of ancient curb crawling, these pots focus on the difficulty of dividing the exchanges that lead to sexual relations between courtship on the one hand and purchasing sex on the other.[29] Different scenes emphasize different sorts of exchange and different relations between the parties involved. In some cases, the story is more or less explicitly about sex, as in the case of a further cup ascribed to Makron where the dangling of a money bag before a youth in the tondo is juxtaposed to an exterior with six pairs consisting of a man and a youth, in two of which the man displays his sexual excitement.[30] But this does not mean that every story is about sex, or every woman shown in a scene where a youth or man offers a bag should be identified as a prostitute. We have hints of a wide range of possible stories in these scenes with bags being offered. In the case of the cup in Toledo the hints are of stories about musical evenings, removing the himation, putting on wreaths, and so on, but there is no single narrative, and the question of the status of the men and women involved is left to the storyteller to impose. As in Xenophon's story of Theodote in *Memorabilia* 3.11,[31] there is much that teases on the Toledo cup, but there is nothing in view that is not respectable, yet we know from other versions of the scene that we are on the edge of respectability.

In all the ways already emphasized, late archaic and early classic red-figure courting imagery tends to be less sexually explicit than that on black-figure pots, and to put less stress on the physical aspects of sexual attraction. But that is not true of the representation of sexual intercourse between men and women. In black-figure, as we have seen, scenes of standing love making appeared on Tyrrhenian amphoras; Little Master cups and other cups and skyphoi showed a wide range of sexual positions, often in miniature, but penetration from the rear continued to dominate.[32] Multiple couples were often shown on the same pot, or a scene of sexual intercourse might be flanked by figures masturbating. Some of the earliest red-figure cup painters occasionally paint scenes of heterosexual intercourse,[33] but such images are most popular with painters of the second generation, Beazley's "late archaic period," at the beginning of the fifth century, in particular the Triptolemos Painter, the Brygos Painter, the Dokimasia Painter (2.9), the Foundry Painter (5.9), the Briseis Painter (5.10 and plate 23), and Douris.[34] The choice of sexually explicit scene they show, however, is quite different from that chosen by black-figure painters.

[29] The best evidence for those difficulties in real life is provided by Apollodoros's speech prosecuting Neaira ([Dem.] 59), where Neaira's life story, even when presented by a man who wants to claim that she was always a prostitute, reveals the ease of movement between categories that ancient law and modern scholarship wants to keep apart.
[30] *ARV* 472.206bis (1654); Kunisch (1997), no. 227.
[31] Goldhill (1998).
[32] Sutton (2009b), see above.
[33] E.g., Epiktetos, *ARV* 1705.79bis.
[34] *ARV* 367.93, 94; 377.101, 403.33bis, 406.5, 408.36, 408.37, 444.241. Given his liking of

More or less gone from the imagery are scenes of masturbation (with few exceptions only satyrs do it, and then infrequently[35]), and scenes of multiple couples having intercourse. There are three "orgy" scenes painted by painters in the first generation of red-figure, but subsequently, with two exceptions, insofar as there are more than two people in a scene of sexual intercourse the others are spectators.[36] It is in the context of such "orgy" scenes that oral sex, absent from black-figure, is now occasionally shown. What is new in red-figure is that scenes of sexual intercourse have acquired a context. Black-figure sex scenes tend either to have no sort of background or to have minimal indication that the context is indoors or outdoors. While that remains true of many red-figure examples, there are also numerous indications of a setting in the form of the cushions of a symposium, with or without the sympotic couch itself. We are not simply being shown sex, we are being shown sex in a fantasy sympotic context.

There is little doubt that scenes explicitly showing sexual penetration were from the beginning intended at least to titillate, if not to shock. Black-figure scenes had appeared on amphoras or mostly on the exterior of cups and skyphoi. Red-figure continues to show sex scenes on the outside of cups, but increasingly the more explicit scenes appear on cup interiors—and often, as in 5.9 and 5.10 (also plate 23), on cups that are plain on the exterior. The decision to paint a scene on the interior of a cup is a decision to paint these scenes where they will be revealed only to the drinker and only slowly in the course of the symposium, as the wine is drained. Some images exploit the fact that the first sight of the image will not be clear. So the cloak of the balding man penetrating a woman inside a cup attributed to the Triptolemos Painter and found at Tarquinia is hung up in such a position that at first sight it looks like the tail of a satyr, just as his balding head at first sight appears satyric too.[37]

Most commonly, however, the effect of gradual revelation is used to uncover details of the presentation that encourage the viewer to construct a context for the action and to deduce something about the status of the actors. So the Foundry Painter (**5.9**) has the naked young man retain the skullcap that seems to mark the athlete while having the bent-over woman, who has a ribbon tied round her hair, rest her head and breasts on a full wineskin, parts of which resemble the shape of female breasts. The riddling oracle to Aigeus, quoted in Euripides's *Medea* 679, warning him not to "loose the neck of the wineskin," comes to mind. In two cups by the Briseis Painter, it is not headgear that the copulating man retains but his sandals or slippers (**5.10** and plate 23).[38] Douris has the woman use her arms like

---

courtship scenes, it is notable that Makron does not paint such scenes. On sex scenes in red-figure, see Kilmer (1993).

[35] Male masturbation: *ARV* 24.12bis, 76.70, 97.10, 113.7.

[36] Three "first generation" scenes: *ARV* 86.α (Pedieus Painter), 113.7 (Thalia Painter), 132 (Boston 95.61, Nikosthenes Painter). The exceptional later scenes are by the Brygos Painter (*ARV* 372.31) and the Pan Painter (*ARV* 552.28, fragmentary).

[37] *ARV* 367.94.

[38] *ARV* 408.36, 37.

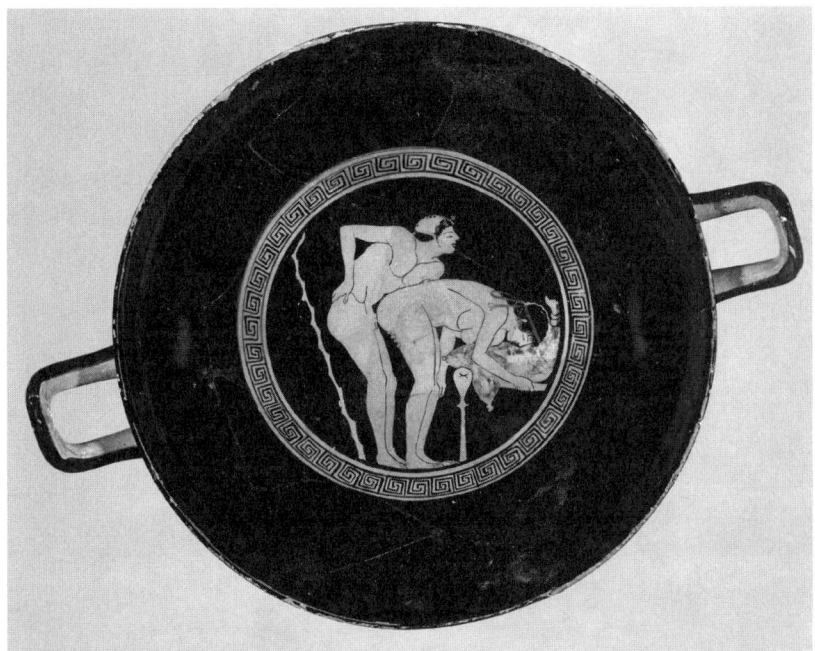

Figure 5.9. Exterior of red-figure cup, diameter 0.235 m, attributed to the Foundry Painter, ca. 490. *Para*. 370.33bis, J. Paul Getty, Malibu 86 AE 294. Digital image courtesy of the Getty's Open Content Program.

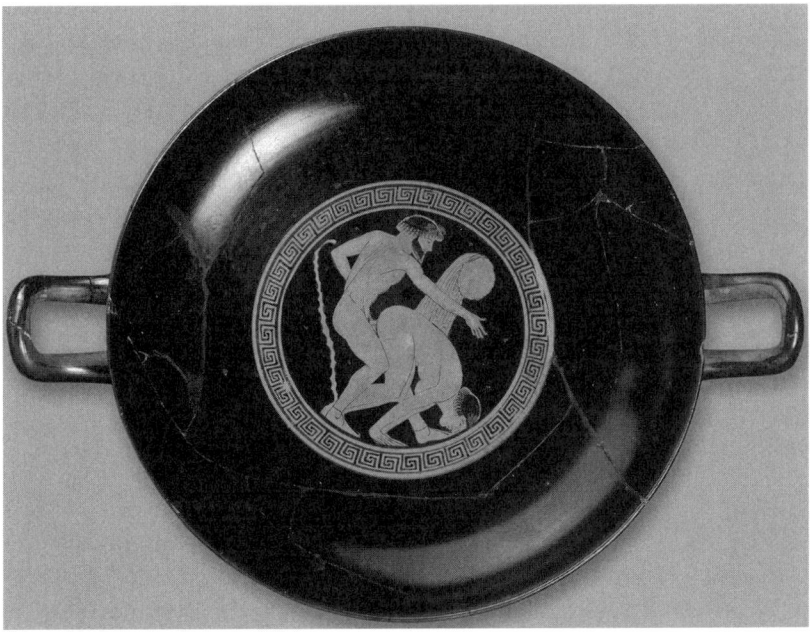

Figure 5.10. Exterior of red-figure cup, diameter 0.237 m, attributed to the Briseis Painter, from Cervetri, ca. 490. *ARV* 408.37, Oxford Ashmolean Museum AN1967.305. Image © Ashmolean Museum, University of Oxford.

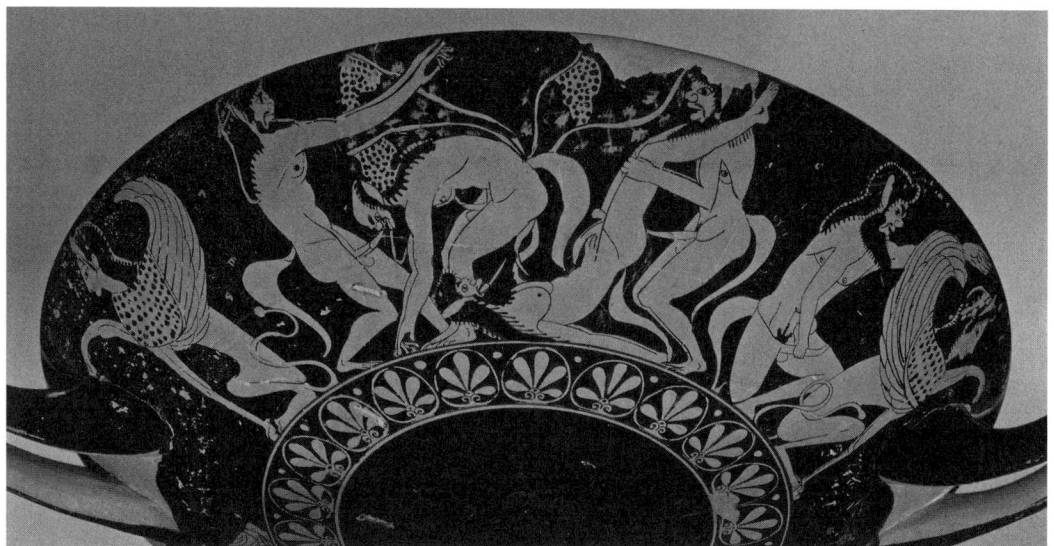

Figure 5.11. Exterior of red-figure cup, diameter 0.326 m, attributed to the wider circle of the Nikosthenes Painter. *ARV* p. 1700, *Para*. 334, Berlin 1964.4. © bpk / Antikensammlung, Staatliche Museen zu Berlin / Johannes Laurentius.

the front legs of an animal—and has her place them on a lion-foot stool, as if to raise the question of how like an animal she, and this form of human behavior, is.[39]

Red-figure painters seem in general to have taken rather more interest in women's sexuality than had black-figure artists. There are a small number of images in which women appear to be masturbated by another woman or a man, and a greater number in which women are shown with smaller or larger model phalluses, in some cases being used as dildos.[40] All these scenes date from before circa 480.

The limits of what humans can properly be represented as doing on pots intended for the symposium are indicated by the use that is made of satyrs.[41] Satyrs engage from earliest red-figure in a form of courtship not practiced by men: they creep up on sleeping maenads and variously attempt to grope or rape them.[42] These scenes sometimes have a spectating as well as an active satyr, and in one fragment that satyr is shown not simply masturbating but ejaculating.[43] When satyrs are shown in multiple and complex sexual activity, that activity is all homosexual, and this is the only context in which homosexual oral sex and sodomy is shown (**5.11**).[44] Although the motif of the satyr approaching the sleeping mae-

[39] *ARV* 444.241.

[40] *ARV* 120.9bis, 326.87(?) for female masturbation, but also, exceptionally, later, 1029.16; 75.60, 76.77, 125.15, 134 (14), 238.5, 242.67, 279.2 for dildos.

[41] For the use of satyrs more generally, see chapter 8.

[42] Osborne (1996a).

[43] Cf. fragment ascribed to the Kleophrades Painter, J. Paul Getty Museum, Malibu, 85 AE 188, and more generally Lissarrague (2013), 73–96; Vout (2013), 181–92.

[44] Beazley describes this cup as showing "satyrs misbehaving"; the interior shows Ares, and the other side Herakles and Apollo struggling for the tripod.

nad continues to attract red-figure artists down to and beyond the middle of the fifth century (8.6–10), these more explicit scenes of sexual activity involving satyrs, are, like those involving humans, very largely limited to the years before circa 480.

3. Pursuing Sex in the Middle of the Fifth Century

Interest in exploring sexual relations between men and between men and women continued after circa 480, but to the ongoing scrutiny of courtship and gift exchange was added an interest in scenes of sexual pursuit. Red-figure artists from the beginning had taken an interest in those myths that related how heroes and gods variously wooed and pursued the objects of their sexual desire. The earliest scenes—other than those in which satyrs pursue maenads—are of Menelaos and Helen and Theseus and either Helen or Antiope, and are shown on cups.[45] From the beginning of the fifth century, and particularly the work of the Berlin Painter, it is the loves of the gods that figure most prominently, and it is on either closed vessels or kraters that they are mainly shown.[46] In some of these scenes the pursuer lays hands upon the pursued; more commonly, there is no bodily contact.

Often the figure pursued in these scenes cannot be definitively identified, either because the painter gives no name or distinguishing attributes and literary texts do not tell any appropriate story, or because the particular pursuer is recorded in texts as chasing a number of different young men or women. It is partly the anonymity of the figure of the pursued in many of these scenes that makes it clear that, despite the divine protagonist, the interest of the scene is not with engaging with a particular story, far less with a particular text, but with erotic pursuit more generally. This is why, even in a study that is primarily interested in scenes involving "ordinary" men and women, these scenes of the gods cannot be ignored.

Showing gods engaged in sexual pursuits, like showing satyrs engaged in sexual pursuits, liberates artists to explore some aspects of sexual desire otherwise rarely brought to the viewer's attention. One aspect of this is female sexual desire: the active pursuit of men by women. Although scholars have suggested, with greater or less plausibility, that the expressions and gestures of some women in scenes on Athenian pottery are meant to suggest that those women are eager for intimacy with the man or men in the scene, sexual pursuit offers the only certain context in which women's sexual desire is explored.

From the very first scenes of sexual pursuit involving gods, painters explore female sexual pursuit through the figure of Eos, the dawn.[47] Scenes of Eos in pursuit continue to be painted down to about 420. This contrasts

---

[45] Menelaos and Helen: *ARV* 53.1, 67.137, 119.3; Theseus: *ARV* 27.4, 62.77.
[46] Kaempf-Dimitriadou (1979).
[47] See the catalog in Kaempf-Dimitriadou (1979), 81–93; and discussion in Osborne (1996a); Stansbury-O'Donnell (2009), 362–72.

markedly with scenes of the gods in homosexual pursuit, where scenes of Zeus and Ganymede are frequently represented down to the middle of the fifth century but die out sharply at that point, and where the only two scenes of gods pursuing youths are found after circa 460, both of Hermes pursuing a boy.[48] The chronological pattern found in the case of Eos pursuing Tithonos or Kephalos is more closely paralleled by the pattern of gods pursuing women, but even in those cases it is often the case, except with Boreas and Oreithyia, that after 440 pursuit is replaced by peaceful encounters.[49]

The disappearance of divine homosexual pursuit can be paralleled in what happens to the representation of sexual relations between men and youths more generally. Through the middle of the fifth century, scenes of men offering gifts to youths, or youths offering gifts to other youths or boys, continue to be painted, particularly with Eros as the gift giver, and Eros also appears pursuing youths (**5.12**); men no longer, however, try to stroke the chin or grope the genitals of youths, and scenes in which they press their erect penis into a youth also disappear. The sole candidate for an explicit homosexual scene is an image with no precedents, found on a bell-krater in London attributed to the Dinos Painter (**5.13**); here a crowned, naked youth climbs onto the lap of a seated, crowned, naked youth, watched by a bearded man from within a colonnade and a woman behind a half door. Scholars have suggested that this should be interpreted as taking place at the festival of the Anthesteria. The erect penis of the seated youth guarantees that this is a scene of sexual encounter, but the nature of the intended encounter is quite unclear.[50]

In a similar way, the mellowing of scenes of divine heterosexual pursuit can be paralleled with what happens in the case of the explicit representation of sexual relations between men and women. There is just one scene of sexual activity involving more than one man and one woman—a stamnos attributed to Polygnotos that shows on one side two naked beardless men lowering onto the erect penis of one of them a naked woman who masturbates the other man, while a youth in himation playing the barbitos watches from the right; on the other side is a naked woman with an aulos between two sexually excited bearded men, one of whom threatens her with a sandal.[51] This pot is notable for its isolation, both in terms of the work of Polygnotos, whose scenes otherwise, even when representing the symposium and the *komos*, are not at all sexually explicit, and whose satyrs do not display sexual excitement, and in terms of contemporary imagery.

[48] Kaempf-Dimitriadou's catalog of scenes of Zeus and Ganymede is significantly enlarged by Lear and Cantarella (2008), appendix; for Hermes, see Lear and Cantarella (2008), appendix 5.89 (= Kaempf-Dimitriadou [1979], catalog no. 46), 5.147.

[49] Kaempf-Dimitriadou (1979), catalog pp. 93–109.

[50] Kilmer (1993), 23–25; Lear and Cantarella (2008), 175–77; Vout (2013), 29–31, 210. For the suggestion about the Anthesteria, see von Blanckenhagen (1976), for criticism of this view, see Parker (2015), 66.

[51] Paris Louvre C 9682 from Etruria; *ARV* 1029.16; Matheson (1995), 57–58 and P17; Kilmer (1993), 55–57, 109–10, 168–69 (R898). Kilmer thinks the barbitos player female.

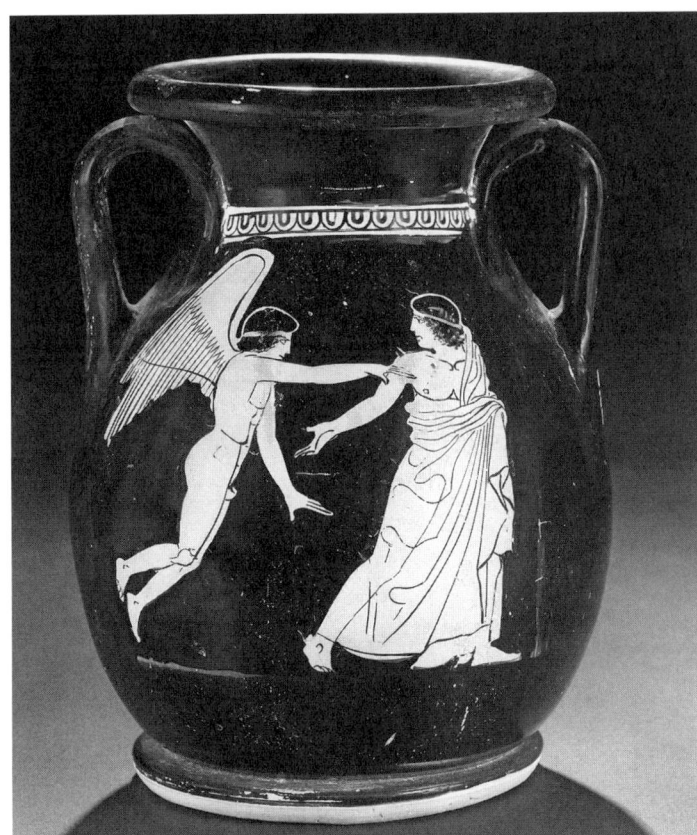

Figure 5.12. Red-figure pelike, height 0.2095 m, attributed to the Hasselmann Painter, from Nola, ca. 440. *ARV* 1136.1, British Museum 1836,0224.83 (E 397). © The Trustees of the British Museum.

Figure 5.13. Red-figure bell-krater, height 0.28 m, attributed to the Dinos Painter, from Capua, ca. 420. *ARV* 1154.35, British Museum 1772,0320.154 (F65). © The Trustees of the British Museum.

COURTING CHANGE 139

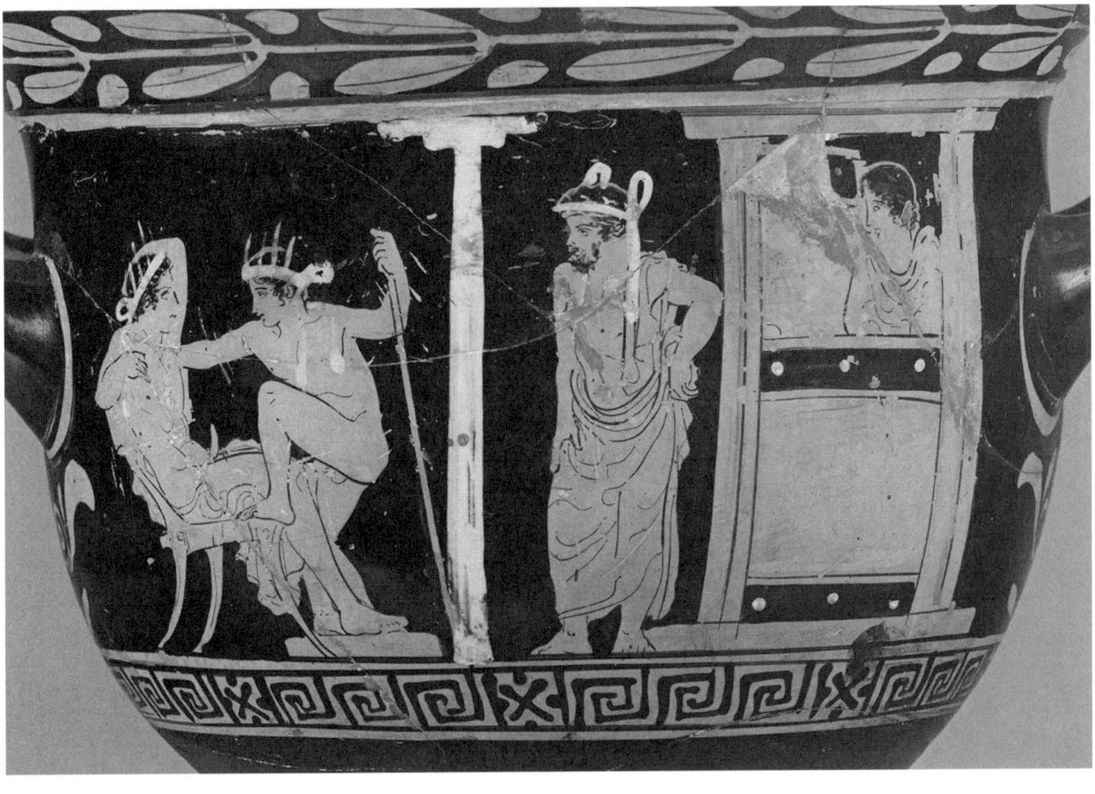

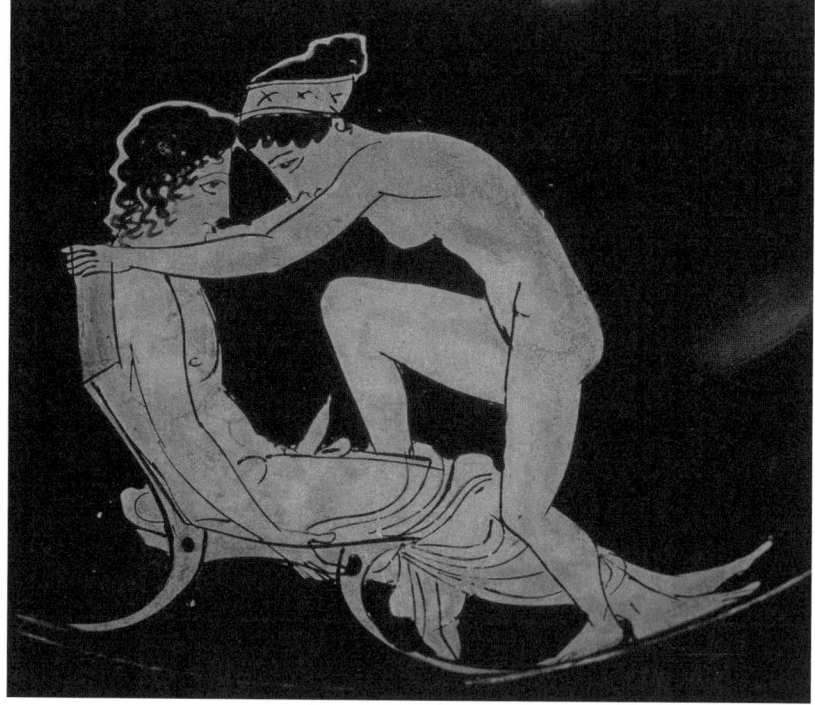

Figure 5.14. Red-figure oinochoe, height 0.155 m without handle, attributed to the Shuvalov Painter, from Locri, ca. 430. *ARV* 1208.41, Berlin F2414. © bpk / Antikensammlung, Staatliche Museen zu Berlin / Johannes Laurentius.

Even scenes of couples making love are rare by the middle of the century. In the quarter century before 450 scenes of sexual intercourse were painted occasionally on the tondos of cups, all involving beardless youths rather than bearded men, with scenes appearing for the first time in which the woman sits on the lap of the youth, either facing him or facing the same way as he does.[52] An askos, found in the Athenian Kerameikos, with two scenes of sexual intercourse, also probably belongs to this period.[53] After 450 just one scene is known, on an oinochoe found in Locri attributed to the Shuvalov Painter and to be dated perhaps to the 430s (**5.14**). This scene presents a close parallel, indeed is perhaps the model, for the Dinos Painter's bell-krater that shows incipient sexual relations between two youths: the oinochoe shows a naked young woman climbing onto the lap of a naked youth who is seated on a chair. The two look into each other's eyes.[54]

Once more, this is an exceptional image, not only in being the Shuvalov Painter's only scene of (incipient) sexual intercourse but also in being the only oinochoe of this shape, which is in any case rare in pottery, to have

---

[52] *ARV* 869.63bis and Malibu 83.AE.321 (Kilmer [1993], R814, R824) for sitting on the lap; otherwise *ARV* 923.29 (Kilmer [1993] R864).

[53] Athens Kerameikos 1063; Kilmer (1993), R1184; Hoffmann (1977), 5.5–6; Paleothodoros (2012), 28–30; Parker (2015), 103–5.

[54] Lezzi-Hafter (1976), S47; Kilmer (1993), R970.

figured imagery.⁵⁵ The scene, which is placed very high up on the oinochoe, so that it is best seen when the vessel is tipped up to pour wine into a cup, also has, exceptionally in the Shuvalov Painter's oeuvre, no framing decoration—the couple are the only decoration on the whole pot.⁵⁶ But there are other ways in which this scene is fully consonant with the rest of the painter's work. The seated youth shares the long hair, downturned head, and upturned eyes of several other young males that he painted, including Eros, two lyre players, Polyneikes (in a scene with Eriphyle), a youth holding a spit, a youth beside an incense burner, and two youths flanking Eros.⁵⁷ The young woman's head with hair-band is paralleled by a seated woman facing Eros, a woman with a basket facing a woman with an alabastron, and a woman pursued by Apollo, and she shares the pose of two young men shown with one leg resting on a block.⁵⁸ More importantly, the theme of young people's relationship with each other, signaled so strongly by the exchange of glances, is one repeatedly found in the Shuvalov Painter's work.⁵⁹ This context within the imagery that the painter employs not only casts doubt on too-ready identification as a snapshot of life in which the woman should be considered to be a prostitute but also suggests that we should see this image as part of the wider exploration by the painter of how young people relate to each other, and the role played in these relationships by sex, music, participation in games and in ritual, and so on.⁶⁰

More surprising than the disappearance of sexually explicit scenes is the near disappearance of scenes of courtship. Whether we look at courtship by men of boys or youths, the courtship by youths of boys or other youths, or the courtship of women whether by men or by youths, and whether we look at scenes in which (money) bags are being offered or those without them, the story is the same. Courtship scenes are found from the earliest red-figure through to the early classic painters, that is, down to around 460 BC, but subsequently become rare. Popular, in particular, on cups down to 460, when they appear at all on later pots they have moved to other shapes.

It is not, of course, that scenes in which men or youths appear together, or appear with women, disappear from the imagery—very much the reverse; rather, the painters no longer choose to signal that there is a process of attraction and negotiation going on between the figures. Two cups, one from second and one from the third quarter of the fifth century will illustrate the iconography that comes to prevail in scenes of women with young men.

⁵⁵ Lezzi-Hafter (1976), 17.
⁵⁶ The only partial parallel is the solitary figure on the squat lekythos *ARV* 1210.67; Lezzi-Hafter (1976), S2.
⁵⁷ Eros: Lezzi-Hafter (1976), S4 (*ARV* 1208.34), cf. S52, S53, S61; lyre-players: S17, S48; Polyneikes S57; youth holding spit S62; youth by incense burner S71; youths flanking Eros S76.
⁵⁸ Lezzi-Hafter (1976), S42, S44, and S72 for the head, and 63 with reference to S10 and S19 for the pose.
⁵⁹ Lezzi-Hafter (1976), S2, S6, S10, S11, S12, S14, S17, S24, S25, S34, S44, S48, S50, S64, S82, S88, S90, S91, S95, S 97, S99.
⁶⁰ Lezzi-Hafter (1976), 63.

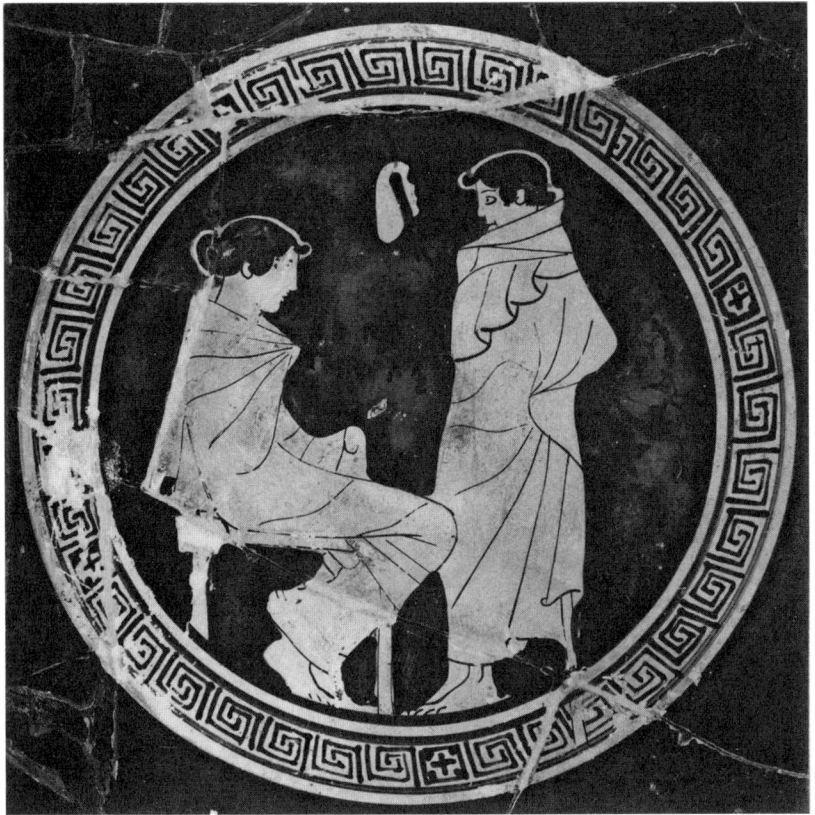

Figure 5.15–17. Red-figure cup, diameter 0.24 m, attributed to the Wedding Painter, acquired in Florence. *ARV* 922.10, Vienna Kunsthistorisches Museum ANSA IV 2150. © KHM-Museumverband.

A cup in Vienna (**5.15–17**), ascribed by Beazley to the hand of the Wedding Painter, shows on both exterior sides a woman between two youths, and on its interior a well-mantled woman seated on a stool with a well-mantled youth standing before her. The two figures on the interior seem to have made no eye contact, but between them hangs a (money) bag and an inscription "Heras is beautiful." On the exterior on one side the central woman, dressed in chiton and himation, is seated on a chair and, though it is hard to distinguish it, she appears to have a knee guard (*epinetron*) on her knee and to be working wool over it.[61] The woman stares down at her task, but in front of her stands a youth in a himation, resting his right armpit on a stick and holding out a large alabastron. Behind her another youth, similarly dressed and also with a stick, holds his hand up and gestures with his fingers. Above the woman are the remains of an inscription, perhaps reading "the boy is beautiful." On the other side the woman stands in the center, well-wrapped in a himation and holding out an empty hand. Facing her is a youth in a himation, again resting his armpit on a stick and gesturing with his right hand. Behind him on the wall are a

---

[61] Eichler (1951), 20, commentary on plate 21, gives a very helpful close description.

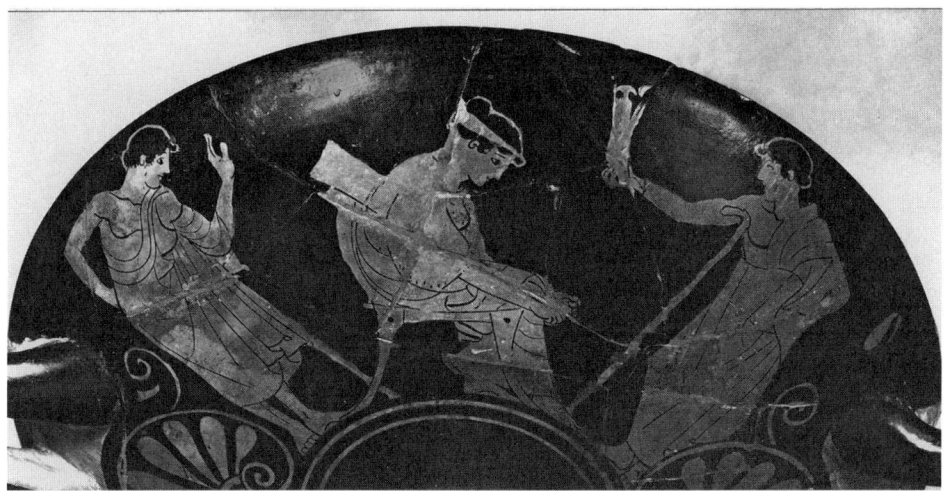

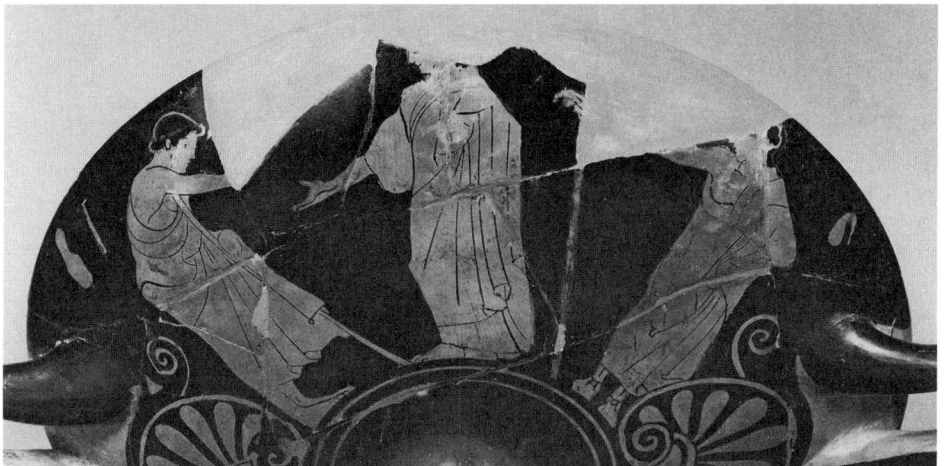

sandal and a straight object of uncertain identity. To the right is another himation-clad youth, his right arm extended and resting on a stick. Behind him is a (money) bag. There are lots of invitations here to speculation on what might be happening in this scene, but no privileging of any feature that would turn this into courtship.

From perhaps thirty years later is a cup in Boston that Beazley ascribed to the Calliope Painter (**5.18–20** and plate 24).[62] On the interior a youth in a himation and wearing a wreath holds an oval object over a block—perhaps a fruit or incense block over an altar. Behind him hangs a large bag. On one exterior side a similarly dressed youth holding out his himation in front of him "whether drawing the garment on or letting it down" stands facing a woman dressed in chiton and himation who looks him back in the eye. Behind him another woman in chiton and himation is engaged in wrapping her himation around herself—or perhaps unwrapping it. Between the figures hang two large bags and a large writing tablet fastened

[62] Caskey and Beazley (1963), 67–68 and plate 97.

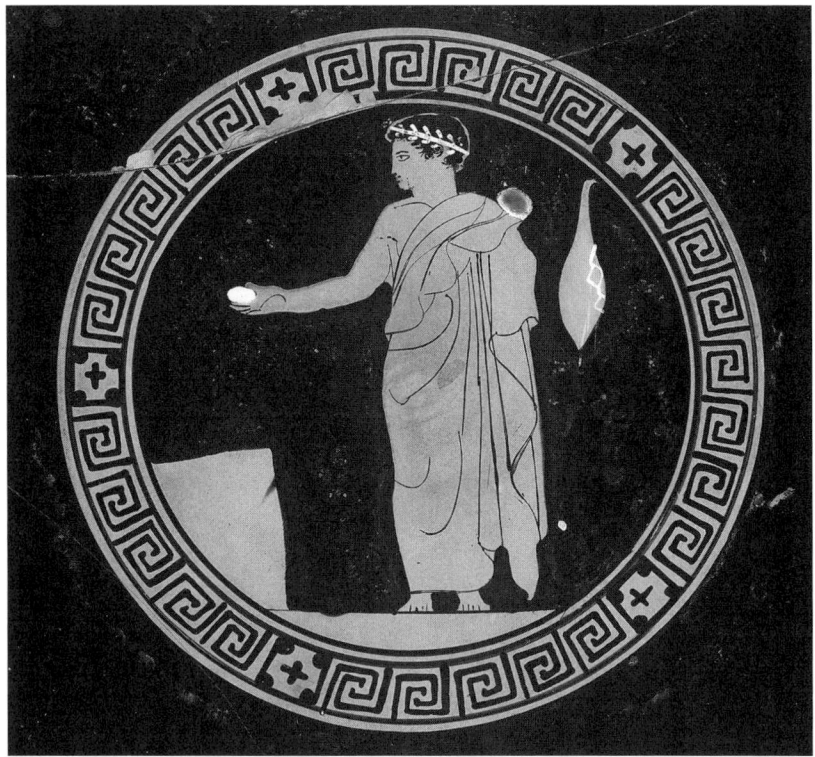

Figure 5.18–20. Red-figure cup, diameter 0.227 m, attributed to the Calliope Painter, said to be from Magna Graecia. *ARV* 1259.11, Boston Museum of Fine Arts 21.4. Photograph © 2017 Museum of Fine Arts, Boston.

with brown cords. On the other side a woman in chiton and himation holds out a wreath in two hands toward a youth in a himation who rests his right hand on a stick. Between them hang a pair of sandals. Behind the woman stands a youth in a himation seen from the back but with his head turned to look at the other figures and his arms held out in a shoulder-shrugging gesture. A sash hangs between him and the woman. In this cup too there is plenty of conversation-provoking detail, and all sorts of possible narratives, but again nothing that privileges a narrative that would highlight sexual relations.

To the story of various iconographies ceasing to attract red-figure artists' attention we have to add the story of scenes that come into red-figure painting for the first time only after 480. The most surprising of these is the wedding scene.[63] Wedding scenes had been repeatedly shown in black-figure, particularly in the form of showing the wedding procession with the bride and bridegroom in a chariot, and indeed black-figure versions of this scene continue into the fifth century. But early red-figure shows no interest at all in weddings, and when it does turn to them it does so very largely on vessels that have particular ritual functions at the wedding—the loutrophoros and the nuptial lebes (**5.21**). By contrast black-figure wed-

[63] Oakley and Sinos (1993), 43–47.

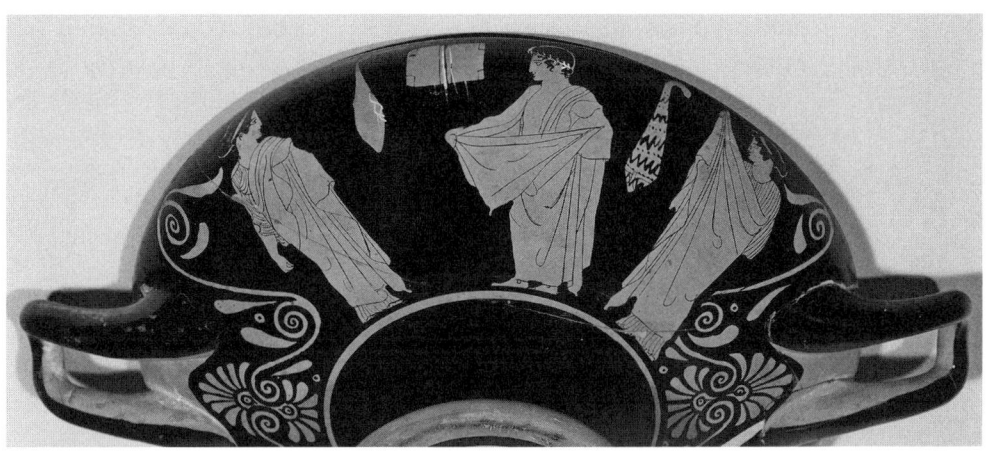

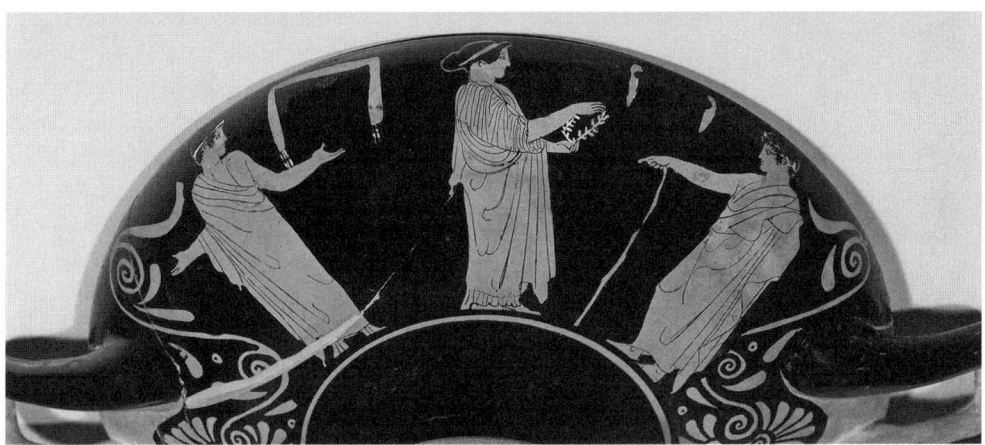

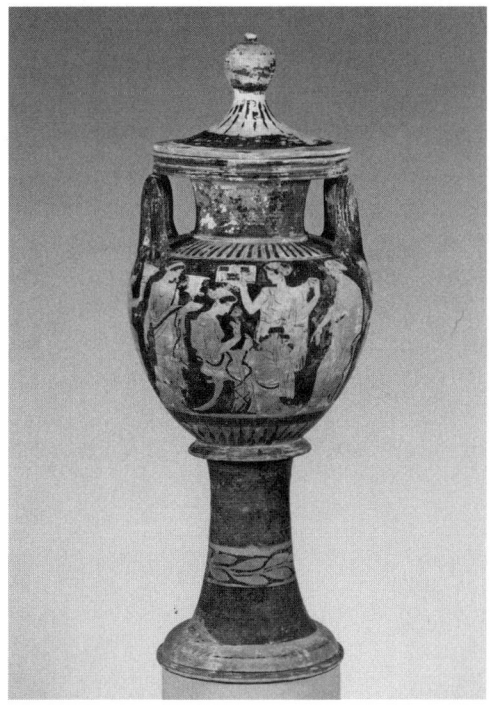

Figure 5.21. Red-figure nuptial lebes, height 0.422 m, attributed to the Painter of London 1923, from Greece, ca. 440–430. *ARV* 1103.5, New York Metropolitan Museum 06.1021.299. www.metmuseum.org.

COURTING CHANGE   145

ding scenes had appeared on amphoras, kraters, hydrias, and lekythoi. But if the shapes decorated with wedding scenes in red-figure is narrower, the range of scenes is wider. We see the wedding bath, the preparation for the bride, the wedding procession (most often without chariot), and dancing associated with weddings. Notable is what Oakley and Sinos have called the "more romantic mood" created in part by showing both bride and groom as flourishing young people.[64] This romantic mood is only enhanced when, shortly after the middle of the fifth century, Eros appears in some wedding scenes, followed shortly afterward by Aphrodite.

4. A Sexual Revolution?

The explicitness of the sexual imagery on black-figure and early red-figure pots is so striking to a modern viewer that changing iconography and the almost complete disappearance of such scenes from the pot-painter's repertoire have long been noted.[65] Given modern sensitivity to visual images of the erect penis or of masturbation, it is tempting to think that similar sensitivities were important in the ancient world. Scholars have suggested that the disappearance of sexually explicit scenes relates to changing social attitudes to sexual relations or to a changing market for Athenian pottery, with repeated suggestions that sexually explicit scenes were primarily made for the Etruscans.[66] Sutton, for example, suggested that "in the Archaic period, we find in the sexual scenes on cups and other symposium ware an emphasis on male self-expression, frequently in defiance of social norms, that encouraged aggressive individualism. These scenes provided both images to emulate and social catharsis for their male viewers and creators," whereas by the mid-fifth century "antisocial individual self-expression was no longer popular on vases, probably reflecting both a need for a more refined public self-image for the Athenian *dêmos* and changing markets for painted pottery."[67]

The relatively small number of sexually explicit images on Athenian pots at any period, the particular selection of pots on which they are shown—predominantly pots used at the symposium—and the restriction of some sexual practices wholly or largely to satyrs, all suggest that we are right to think that sexually explicit images explored the boundaries of what it was acceptable to display. At the same time, however, we have to acknowledge that on different occasions Athenians thought it appropriate to deposit pots with sexually explicit imagery into graves, including the grave of a child, and to dedicate on the Acropolis not only pots with sexually explicit scenes but

[64] Ibid., 44.
[65] Brendel (1970); Dover (1978), 7; Shapiro (1992); Sutton (1992), esp. 32–34 (cf. Sutton [2000]); Kilmer (1993); Lear and Cantarella (2008), 174–81.
[66] Stewart (1997), 156–71; Lewis (2002), 116–20, 129, 134, 212; La Genière (2009); Lynch (2009). See further Parker (2015), n. 22.
[67] Sutton (1992), 32 and 33. For attempts to explain changes in wedding iconography also in terms of changing views of the wedding itself, see Oakley and Sinos (1993), 46.

even a plaque specially painted with such a scene.[68] Whatever the sensitivities of the Athenians and those who acquired their pots, they do not map neatly onto the sensitivities of contemporary Western society.

When we see the changes in the way sexually explicit scenes and scenes of erotic relations between men or between men and women, including scenes of the wedding, are represented against the contemporary changes in the representation of quite different sorts of scenes, it becomes clear that explanations specific to these particular scenes are not appropriate.[69] The disappearance of various kinds of sexual activity from the pot-painter's—and in particular from the cup-painter's—iconographic repertoire parallels the disappearance of athletic activity and the disappearance of military activity. Just as Amazons continue to fight on pots after scenes that might represent wars between Greeks have disappeared, so gods continue to pursue mortals sexually and Eros to court young men and women with gifts after scenes or sexual pursuit by nonmythological figures have disappeared. Indeed, representations of Eros become distinctly more frequent. Red-figure painters down to and including Beazley's "late archaic" period show Eros on merely a dozen pots; Beazley's various "early classic" painters show Eros on more than eighty pots; his "classic" painters are responsible for another sixty.

Putting scenes that figure sexual relations into this wider context confirms Sutton's contention that "the evolution of erotic imagery on Attic pottery . . . marks a significant change in ideology," but it also makes clear that this ideological change needs to be understood not in terms specific to the erotic images themselves but as part of a much wider transformation in how the world is seen.[70] Just as in the case of athletes and soldiers we move from images that raise questions of achievement to images that focus on appearance, from a focus on performance and success to a focus on the person who will perform and might achieve the success, so with these images of sexual relations, the focus moves from the acts of courtship and sexual acts themselves to the circumstances in which a sexual relationship might be formed or be desirable.

Erotic images do not merely repeat again a story we can tell from other iconographies, however; they enable us better to understand that story. For

---

[68] La Genière (2009), 342–44; Parker (2015), 104–5; Athens, National Museum Akr. 1040 and A15418 and above n. 9. On pots with erotic subject matter found in Athenian burials, see Paleothodoros (2012) and Dipla and Paleothodoros (2012).

[69] Cf. Pfisterer-Haas (1991), 143, criticizing Peschel (1987): "Ein großes Problem der Arbeit is die isolierte Betrachtungsweise eines zugegebenermaßen großen Themenkreises. Daraus ergeben sich manche Fehl- oder Überinterpretationen der Verfasserin. So muß sich fragen, ob die Veränderungen in der Darsetllungsweise von Hetären beim Symposion und Komos jeweils auf eine veränderte Einstellung der Männer den Hetären gegenuber schließen läßt, ode rob es sich night vielmehr um Zeittendenzen handelt, die sich auch in anderen Themen niederschlagen (der Wandel von der Archaik zur Klassik geht am keinem Themen der griechischen Vasenmalerei spurlos vorbei)."

[70] Sutton (1992), 34. Cf. Stewart (1997), 162: "these black-figure pictures map Greek painting's generalized representational language of sexual domination and submission onto the sexual landscape." Parker (2015), 102, effectively makes a similar move when he suggests that: "What I think we are looking at in most of these objects is not our narrow concept of 'sex,' but a wider concept of 'The Good Things in Life,'" in which case it is not surprising that this selection of imagery should change as views of "the good things of life" changed.

in the case of images that explore the contours of desire, we can see the purchase of the aesthetic much more clearly than we can see it in those images that explore the human landscape of the battlefield or the gymnasium. Desire comes in through the eyes.[71] Appearances play a fundamental part in sexual relationships; while we find it perfectly understandable, and indeed appropriate, that people should deny that it matters what an athlete looks like, provided he or she is successful, and should emphasize the irrelevance of the appearance of a person to their fitness as a soldier, it would be strange indeed if a person denied that they had any interest in what their lover looked like.

But appearances are not given, they are created. The images on Athenian pots constantly stress this in all sorts of ways, from the armor taken by would-be hoplites through the strigils wielded by young men in the gymnasium to the mirrors that so frequently appear in scenes where men and women relate to each other. Creating a particular appearance indicates a whole attitude to life. What we see in the substitution of an imagery that focuses on attraction for an imagery that focuses on action is a transformation from an emphasis on achievement to an emphasis on attitude, from encouraging the revisiting of what has happened in the past to encouraging a focus on how to prepare for what might be achieved in the future.

Something of a parallel change can be observed in sculpture and in literature. The early classical statues known as the Riace Bronzes (10.15–16) expressed on their bodies the consequences of their past lives and what they had and had not done in them.[72] In a different way the subjects of Greek portraits will show off their past lives when portraiture makes its definitive appearance (the Themistokles bust from Ostia aside) in the middle of the fourth century.[73] By contrast, neither the sculptures of the Parthenon nor the grave reliefs that reappear in Athenian cemeteries around 430 represent bodies that offer a sight of past history.

When Aristophanes stages, as he does repeatedly, above all in *Wasps* and *Clouds*, the clash between generations, the older generation is identified not only as obsessed with the past (for example, *Wasps* 236–37, 1075–90, 1097–1100) but as brazen in its erotic and sympotic behavior (for example, *Wasps* 1351–63). The debate is most explicit in *Clouds* when in the debate between the Stronger and the Weaker Argument, the Stronger Argument champions "the education that bred the warriors at Marathon" (*Clouds* 986), an education that had boys go to school naked in all weathers and no boy anoint himself below the navel "so that their genitals sparkled with dew and down as on a quince" (978); then, boys spent time in the gymnasium, they looked gleaming and blooming and raced each other in the Academy (1002–6). This he contrasts with modern youth who wrap themselves up with cloaks and hide their genitals behind shields when dancing at the Panathenaia (987–89), who spend time chatting in the

---

[71] Frontisi-Ducroux (1996).
[72] Osborne (1998a), 161–62, (2010b). See below chapter 10, section 3.
[73] Dillon (2006), 61–98.

Agora or in petty disputes in the courts or in the bathhouse. Part of the contrast between past and present is that while Stronger Argument has "an obsession with boys' genitals," Weaker chooses adultery as the plausible offense of the young man of today (1079–80).[74] Aristophanes is certainly giving us no sort of considered history in these plays, but the contrast that he draws is one that we can broadly recognize in the changing interests of the images on Athenian pots—from an emphasis on actions and how they together form character and the body, to emphasis on interaction. The emphasis on actions is an emphasis on a life lived competitively and in public view; the emphasis on interaction is an emphasis on the right to privacy and to leaving scope for imagination.

Put like that, we can see in the contrasts Aristophanes offers between present and past something of the contrast Perikles draws between Spartan training and Athenian ability to take everything as it comes: "in education they go after manliness by means of laborious drill from the time when boys are very young, but we live in a relaxed manner and none the less face up to the same dangers" (Thuc. 2.39.1). Scholars have been shocked by this extreme "ideology of non-professionalism," so that Hornblower even wonders whether Thucydides has been "unconsciously influenced by the insouciant, oligarchic attitudes of the cavalry class."[75] Even in antiquity, Perikles's picture of Athenians turning their hands randomly to anything came under criticism.[76] But Perikles's sentiment should not be seen as "extreme insolence" and at odds with "l'idéal d'une république des hoplites," as Vidal-Naquet suggests, but rather to be part and parcel of a commitment to combining the right to a private life with universal participation, most explicitly expressed earlier in Perikles's funeral oration at 2.37.1–2, with no demands for some particular qualification or training preventing anyone doing their bit for the city, and equally no excuses for anyone to claim a "free ride," enjoying the benefits of being an Athenian without contributing to the city's civic life (so Perikles at Thuc. 2.40.2).[77]

Recent accounts of Greek history have rightly emphasized, notably in relation to the history of Sparta, the degree of "path dependency—the constraint of current choices by past decisions."[78] Just as the Athenians, by removing the qualifications required for participation in various civic offices, reduced the degree of path dependency in Athenian life, and just as Pericles promotes an ideology that makes a point of denying path dependency, so the changes in iconography on Athenian pottery, and more generally in classical Greek art, also avoid suggesting any particular path dependency. Rather than showing particular episodes and encouraging particular stories, classical Greek art selects scenes that offer minimal in-

[74] Obsession: Dover (1968), lxiv; Sommerstein (1982), on *Clouds* 966.
[75] Ideology of nonprofessionalism, Vidal-Naquet (1981), 133 = (1986), 89; Hornblower (1991), 304.
[76] For ancient critics, see, with Rusten (1990), 153, Plato *Republic* 561d.
[77] Vidal Naquet (1981), 133 = (1986), 90. Arguably, it is the very solidarity of the *demos* that this produces that draws the criticisms of [Xenophon] *Constitution of the Athenians*.
[78] Ober (2015), 194.

dication of any particular actions that might have been required to lead to the scene, and minimal indication of what particular actions might follow. Viewers are invited to contemplate the individuals and the situation and to imagine what a person who had every possible natural endowment might be able to do in those circumstances.

When we observe that the painters of Athenian pottery changed their selection of scenes of sexual relations, whether between (older and younger) men or between (older or younger) men and women, between the late archaic and the classical period, we should understand that change from explicit to implicit and from focusing on action to focusing on emotional bonds as part of a much wider change. But while it is true that sexual attraction has powerful political consequences and democratic ideology affects even the expression of sexuality, it is also the case that the visual signals of sexual attraction are not fixed but are conditioned by what a society looks for in individual behavior. Whether we talk in terms of democratization or reduction in path dependency or a sexual revolution, relating to the world differently is always a matter of seeing the world differently. But if relating to the world differently, then also relating differently to the gods.

6 ❧ Sacrificing Change

The gods loomed large in ancient Greek life. This was true in terms of the time and energy that were devoted to their worship and in terms of the degree to which human life could be thought to be determined by the gods. A very large amount of Greek poetry either concerned the gods or was produced for performance at festivals of the gods. Historians, even Thucydides, repeatedly concern themselves with the ways in which the human community related to the gods and the gods might intervene in human history. Philosophers debated the gods' nature and existence and the proper behavior that humans should adopt toward the gods. Public documents lay down in detail the rules for engagement between men and women and the gods in particular sanctuaries, and this is assumed to be a matter for the central political authorities, not simply for cultic personnel.

As with changing relations between men and women, however, so with changing relations between humans and gods, written texts provide only limited assistance. The survival of different genres of material from different periods is as much a problem in terms of attitudes to the gods as it is with attitudes of men to women. The surviving public documents, in the form of sacred laws, display different priorities at different times and in different places, but the relative contribution of time and place to these changes is not easy to fathom.[1] Scholars have suggested that the fifth century saw increasing questioning of the role of the gods in human life, and some historians have even talked of a crisis at the end of the century, but the basis of this lies with the space surviving texts happen to devote to religious incidents and critical theology, and it is not easy to be confident that we are doing more than constructing a picture from scattered pieces of a jigsaw puzzle that may turn out to have little connection with one another.[2]

There is no doubt that fifth-century Greeks engaged in questioning the nature and existence of the gods, something that comes out in philosophical debate about the nature of the gods and in tragic scrutiny of divine morality, but it is harder to be sure that such questioning was on the increase. There is no doubt too that there was ongoing intense interest in the divine; far from the gods and their behavior ceasing to be a matter of lively concern, the Athenians go on inventing new festivals and incorporating

---

[1] Cf. Osborne (2015a).
[2] Parker (1996), 199–217; Parker (1997); Price (1999), 76–88; cf. Eidinow (2007), 61–66.

the celebrations of new deities into the public calendar. The Athenians were proud of the amount of time, resources, and energy that they devoted to cultivating the gods in religious festivals.[3] There was a significant expansion of festival activity at the end of the sixth and start of the fifth century, and sanctuaries, as well as festivals, were massively elaborated in the course of the fifth century.[4] But how do these various currents in religious thought and behavior fit together? Precisely because the evidence is multifarious—literary, epigraphic, archaeological, art-historical—scholars have never taken a holistic view.

1. Libation

It has already become clear from earlier discussions that the changed way of seeing the world manifested in painted pottery in the fifth century did not simply change political relations and sexual relations, it changed relations with the gods. Something of the changed relations with the gods emerged in the discussion of scenes of soldiers. Scenes in which the liver of the sacrificial victim are examined in advance of military action ("hieroscopy" or "hepatoscopy") barely make it into red-figure painted pottery at all, and are never found later than the Persian Wars.[5] By contrast, as we have already seen, the departure of the hoplite, marked by the pouring of a libation, becomes an enormously popular scene in classical painted pottery. I count just half a dozen such scenes in Beazley's "early red-figure," some forty in his "late archaic," just over one hundred in Beazley's "early classic," and some 115 in his "classic" period.

Broadly speaking the distribution of hoplite departure scenes matches the distribution of other scenes of libation.[6] Here I count fewer than ten early red-figure scenes, forty late archaic, 125 early classic, and seventy-five classic scenes. This parallelism is worth noting since the personnel involved in hoplite departures and the personnel involved in other libation scenes are divergent in one important respect: throughout the history of libation scenes a high proportion of those scenes show libations being poured by gods.[7] The similar distribution of different sorts of libation scenes, and their presence on a wide range of different pot shapes at every period, suggests that the image of the act of pouring a libation, although not of any significant interest in the sixth century, was one that was thought increasingly good to think with as the middle of the fifth century approached.

[3] Thucydides 2. 38.1, [Xen.] *Ath. Pol.* 3.2.
[4] Osborne (1993); Fisher (2011); Parker (1996), 122–98.
[5] For catalogs, see Lissarrague (1989), 58; van Straten (1995), 238–43; Gebauer (2002), 341–48.
[6] The question of when a figure carrying a jug or holding a phiale becomes a figure making a libation is not one to which any definitive answer can be given, and so any statistics here have a strongly subjective element to them. My figures are for scenes I consider clearly to show libation, not just the holding of an offering bowl or jug.
[7] Simon's discussion of libation in *ThesCRA* (Simon, 2004) concerns itself almost exclusively with libations poured by gods. Cf. Simon (1953); Veyne (1990); Patton (2009), 3–180 and catalog 317–53.

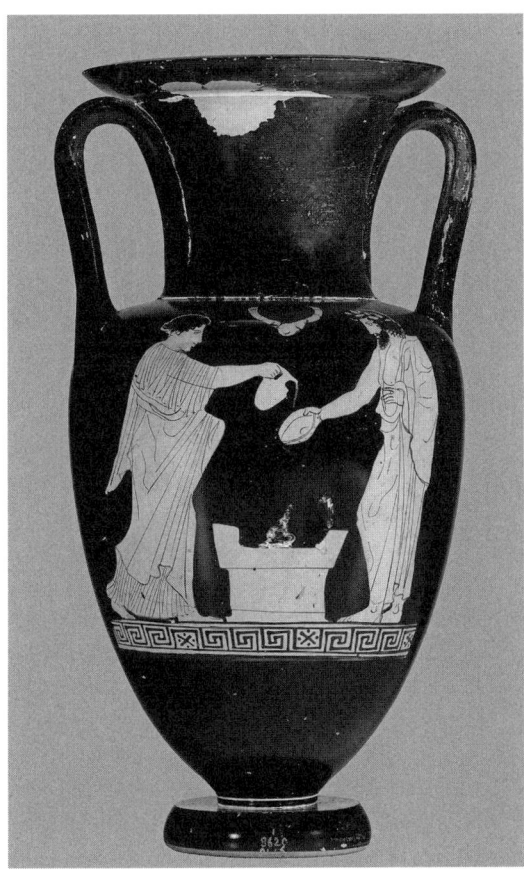

Figure 6.1. Red-figure Nolan amphora, height 0.332 m, attributed to the Phiale Painter, ca. 440, *ARV* 1016.36, Boston Museum of Fine Arts 01.16. Photograph © 2017 Museum of Fine Arts, Boston.

What were the attractions of the libation? Take the most basic of libation scenes, as shown on a Nolan amphora attributed to the Phiale Painter (**6.1**).[8] On the left a woman, dressed in chiton and himation and with a white cord wound round her hair, steps toward a smoking altar and holds out above it a jug from which she pours into a phiale held out in his right hand by a bearded man dressed in a himation and with a wreath on his head. The wine is shown pouring from jug to phiale and in drops from phiale to altar, and both participants fix their eyes upon it. Above the phiale and jug are a pair of horns or antlers, and brown paint on the altar may be meant to indicate blood. Although Oakley identifies the male figure as a king, there is no scepter or other sign of royal authority. This is an image much more of collaborative worship than of using religious ritual to reinforce social hierarchy: here we see cult activity in action—altar blazing, its sacrificial past emblazoned on it, and a man and a woman in the act of cooperating to acknowledge the gods. Whether the libation scenes show two people or one (**6.2** and plate 25) and whether or not an altar is present, scenes of libation show individuals who are caught at a very particular moment but for whom that moment is nevertheless not a moment of crisis but a moment that looks both forward and back—back to the gods' activ-

[8] Oakley (1990), no. 36.

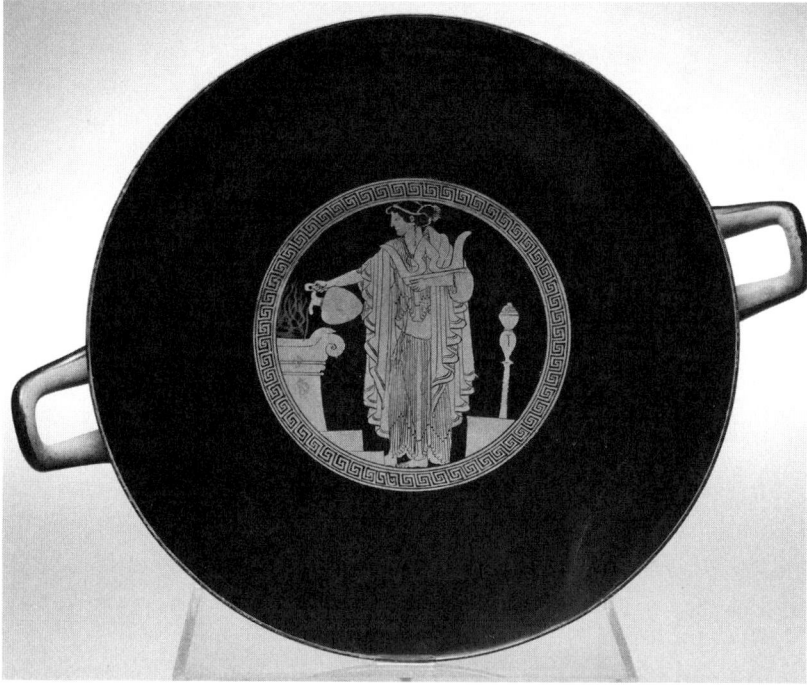

Figure 6.2. Interior of red-figure cup, diameter 0.287 m, attributed to Makron, ca. 480 (for the exterior see 5.7–8). Toledo Museum of Art, Toledo, Ohio, purchased with the funds from the Libbey Endowment, gift of Edward Drummond Libbey, 1972.55.

ity that has brought forth this manifestation of human piety, forward to the future that is the subject of the prayer implicit in the libation. This is a moment when the potential released by men collaborating with women and humans with gods is brought into focus.

2. Sacrifice

The attractions of this scene are best seen by looking at the changing popularity of other religious scenes. Scenes of sacrifice across the whole of archaic and classical Greek art have been analyzed by van Straten and those on pots by Gebauer.[9] Van Straten chose to organize his collection of material according to the stages of the sacrifice that were shown—prekill, the killing, postkill. These divisions according to the necessary actions of the sacrifice usefully reveal that even on pots the killing is only exceptionally shown, and that practically all votive reliefs concentrate on the bringing of

[9] Van Straten (1995), Gebauer (2002). Gebauer categorizes scenes slightly differently from van Straten, and has some material not in van Straten, but the broad chronological distribution of the scenes Gebauer considers is essentially similar; see further below nn. 10, 12. On the changing imagery of sacrifice, see also briefly Bažant (1985), 66; (1987), 35. Other studies of sacrificial imagery (e.g., Berthiaume [1982], Durand [1986], Peirce [1993]) have little interest in change over time.

the animal to sacrifice, not its subsequent killing and division.[10] Van Straten is also able to show that whereas pigs and sheep constitute over 80 percent of the victims shown on votive reliefs, and more than 90 percent of the victims listed in sacred calendars, on Athenian pottery more than 60 percent of the victims shown are cows—thus nicely highlighting the way in which the images on pots show the archetypal animal sacrifice rather than reflecting daily reality.[11]

To understand the changes in sacrificial imagery on pots over time, however, it is necessary to look more closely at which aspects of sacrificial activity the images concentrate upon. It is immediately apparent from van Straten's catalog that black-figure and red-figure attracted different sorts of scenes. Although prekill scenes are found throughout the sixth and fifth and into the fourth century, they were more popular in black-figure (fifty-seven examples) than in red (forty-four examples), and red-figure artists were least interested in these scenes while black-figure artists were still painting them; although more than 50 percent of the total antedate 475, two-thirds of the red-figure scenes postdate 475.[12] Postkill scenes were distinctly less popular in black-figure (only sixteen examples), but the red-figure scenes share the chronological distribution of red-figure prekill scenes: nearly three-quarters of the red-figure postkill scenes postdate 475. Among the postkill scenes those that show the cutting up of the body of the animal and those that show what van Straten calls, following a Homeric formula, "taratalla," "the other bits," and which are mostly scenes of young men carrying legs of meat, are shown only before 450, whereas scenes that show sacrificial equipment but no meat continue, and, in particular, scenes that show the entrails and tail on the altar and on spits prove most popular in the last quarter of the fifth century.[13]

Once more, the different attractions of these different scenes are best understood by looking at some examples. One of the earliest examples of a youth carrying a joint of meat comes in the tondo of a cup attributed to Oltos now in the British Museum (**6.3**) and to be dated a little before 500. A young man more or less fills the tondo, running to the right, his feet on the border of the painted zone, with a leg of meat extended in front of him in his left hand and a lyre in his right. On the outside of the cup are scenes

---

[10] Van Straten (1995), 186–88. Van Straten (1995) counts just seven Athenian pots with scenes of killing (catalog nos. V141–47). Gebauer (2002) similarly has seven pots in his category of "Schlachtung" (257–71).

[11] Van Straten (1995), 170–86. Sheep outnumber pigs in the sacred calendars; pigs outnumber sheep in votive reliefs—perhaps because while sacred calendars record community practice, votive reliefs frequently mark the offerings of individuals or families.

[12] For prekill and preparations at the altar, Van Straten's examples divide as follows: 600–551 3; 550–501 15; 500–476 37; 475–451 8; 450–426 17; 425–401 9; 400–351 11. For red-figure alone the numbers are: 550–501 4; 500–476 5; 475–451 6; 450–426 11; 425–401 9; 400–351 9. Similar Gebauer's "Pompe" scenes number 41 black-figure and 26 red-figure (2002), 25–118; cf. Gebauer (2002), 209: "In der ersten Hälfte des fünften Jahrhunderts tritt das Thema der Tieropferprozession in den Hintergrund."

[13] For "taratalla" as a phrase, see *Iliad* 1.465; *Odyssey* 3.462, 12.365. For various types of postkill scenes Van Straten's examples divide as follows:

of Herakles and Kyknos and of Dionysos and a giant. This anonymous youth is thus put into the company of gods and heroes, and his actions juxtaposed to their misdemeanors and heroic battles. But what is his action? Why the combination of lyre and meat? The viewer is challenged to come up with a narrative and complete the story. Has this youth stolen both lyre and meat from a sacrificial party? Has he received the meat for pleasing a would-be lover with his lyre playing? Only the wreath he wears offers a clue that he has been participating in some sort of celebration, but the youth's vigorous action encourages the thought that we are witnessing the consequences of a dramatic encounter.

Of similar date is a cup in Florence ascribed to the Winchester Painter (**6.4**). On the interior a wreathed youth with his garment wrapped around his waist crouches before an altar on which is the tail of the sacrificial beast and above which he holds meat on a spit. An inscription reads: "the boy is beautiful." On the outside of the cup are two athletes in identical postures, bent over with their arms stretched to the ground, in one case toward some jumping weights and on the other to a pick. The identical poses of the two naked youths in the gymnasium encourage the viewer to compare and contrast. All three of these youths share identical hairstyles as well as a propensity to crouch. It is tempting to see a little story here about the youth active in the gymnasium, on the one hand, and in the sanctuary on the other, and about following him from one sphere of action to the other. We enter into a day in the life of this particular young man.

An oinochoe dating to the third quarter of the fifth century shows three men engaged in animal sacrifice (**6.5–7**).[14] To the left of an altar we see a naked long-haired youth from back view. He holds out a spit over an altar. On the other side of the altar a bearded man with even longer hair and wearing a himation stands holding out a stemless cup over the altar in his

	cutting up carcass	tail, entrails, meat on spit	taratalla	basket etc. but no animal	Total
600–551	0	0	0	0 + 4 BF	4 BF 0 RF
550–501	0 + 1 BF	3 + 4 BF	8 + 1 BF	3 + 0 BF	6 BF 14 RF
500–476	0 + 1 BF	4 + 2 BF	8 + 1 BF	6 + 1 BF	5 BF 18 RF
475–451	2	7	8	19 + 1 BF	37
450–426	0	10	0	5	15
425–400	0	25	0	11	36
after 400	0	2	0	4	0

Van Straten's coverage of "taratalla" is incomplete: I count two additional examples from ca. 480, ascribed by Beazley to the Aigisthos Painter (*ARV* 504.5, 505.31) and one ascribed to Makron (Kunisch [1997], no. 47), additional examples from 475–451: *ARV* 822.22bis (*Para.* 421), 832.32, 887.145, 892.8, 906.109, and one or possibly two examples from 450–426: *ARV* 1114.3 and perhaps 1118.22. Gebauer's category "B" ("Darstellungen des Verbrennens des Götteranteiles und des Bratens der Splanchna"), which broadly overlaps with "tail, entrails, meat on spit" above, yields the following distribution: 3 black-figure scenes; among red-figure 5 before 500, 9 500–476, 9 475–451, 16 450–26, 28 425–401, 2 400–350. The fullest list of figures carrying or with joints of meat is provided by Tsoukala (2009), though this does not include all the examples above. Tsoukala's 54 examples are distributed as follows: 550–501: 6; 500–476: 10; 475–451: 37; 450–426: 1.

[14] This is one of just two pots, both once in the same collection and now in the Ashmolean Museum, that Beazley ascribed to an artist he named the Thomson Painter.

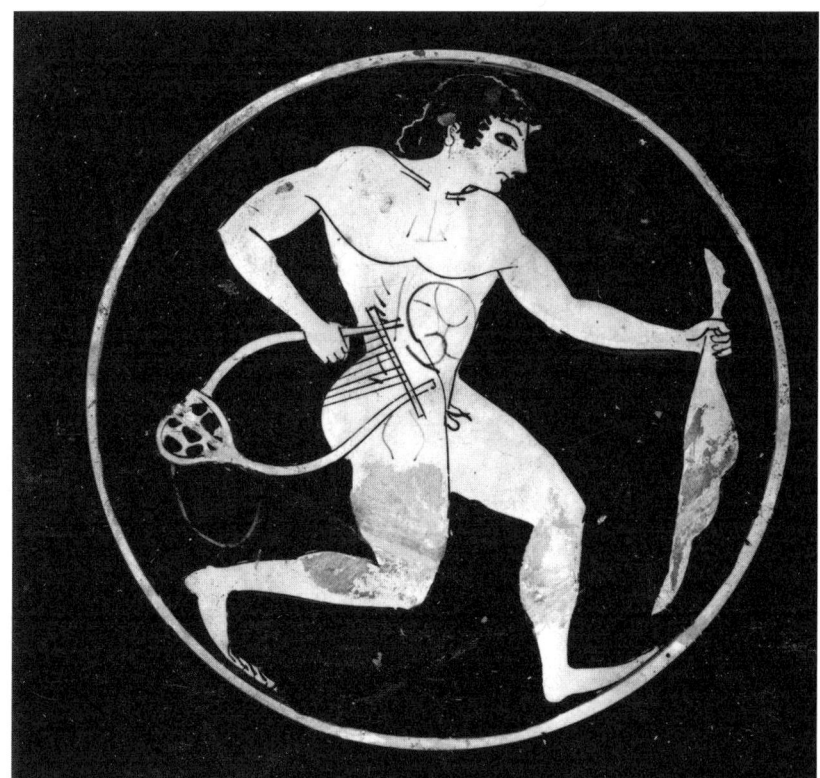

Figure 6.3. Interior of red-figure cup, diameter 0.33 m, attributed to Oltos, ca. 500. *ARV* 63.88, London, British Museum 1978,0411.10 (E8). © The Trustees of the British Museum.

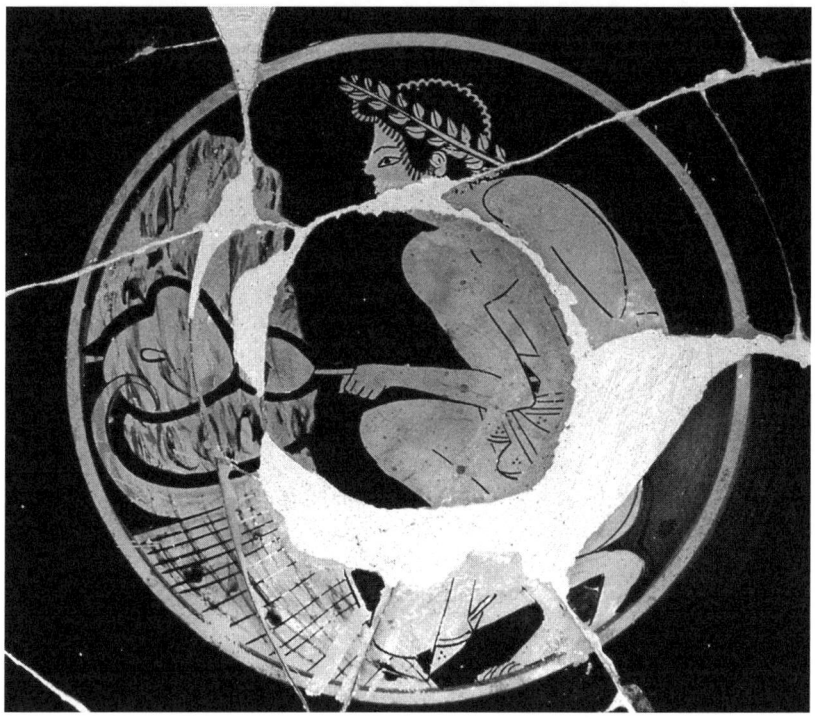

Figure 6.4. Interior of red-figure cup, diameter 0.44 m, attributed to the Winchester Painter, ca. 500. *ARV* 170.3, Florence 3930. Courtesy of the Soprintendenza ABAP Firenze.

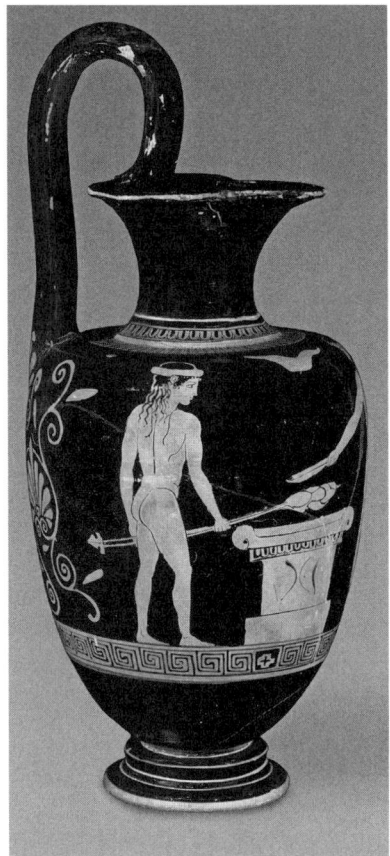 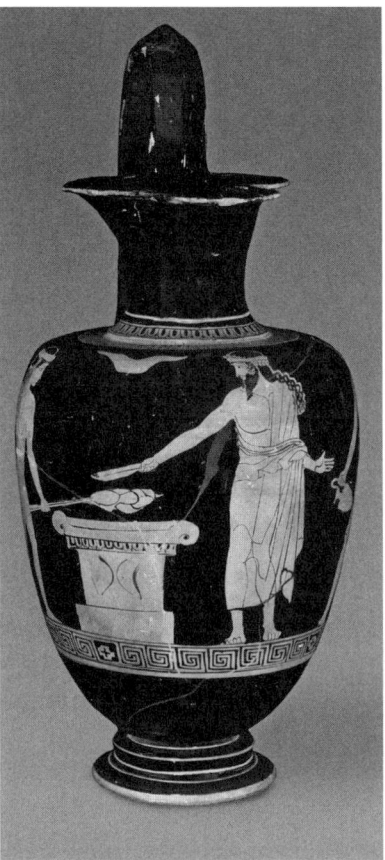 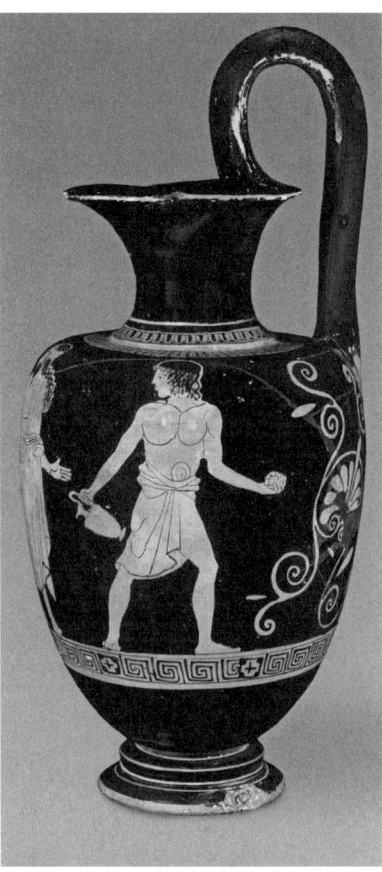

Figure 6.5–7. Red-figure oinochoe, height 0.233 m, attributed to the Thomson Painter, ca. 440. *ARV* 1069.2, Oxford Ashmolean Museum AN1931.9. Image © Ashmolean Museum, University of Oxford.

right hand and gesturing away from the altar with his left. Beyond him a youth, his himation tied round his waist, moves right, a jug in his right hand and some coals or pellets in his left. He looks back at the pair round the altar. Above the altar are the horns and skull of a sacrificed animal. This is a lively scene, and a narrative is easy to imagine in which the youth departing right has just been responsible for pouring the jug into the older man's cup for the performance of the libation. But nothing about this scene suggests any sort of story outside the context of the sacrificial scene itself. This is a picture that is about the performance of sacrifice, encouraging both memories of past sacrifices and plans for future sacrifices. Painted on a jug of just the shape that is held by the youth to the right of the altar, this scene even encourages the thought that this vessel itself might be used in pouring libations.

In moving from early red-figure representations of religious ritual to representations from the second half of the century we move from observing others engaged in these rituals, where the interest is in how those others take advantage of the opportunities that religious rituals afford, to being invited to join in the rituals that we observe as further participants. Where the youths portrayed by Oltos and by the Winchester Painter offer themselves to the viewer as young men setting about their lives with vigor, and perhaps a glint in the eye, the men on the Thomson Painter's jug, like those on the Phiale Painter's Nolan amphora, display little sense that theirs is a particular story. Rather, they are the ones who happen to be playing this role at this moment. But they could as well be doing something else, and you, the viewer, could as well be them.

Scenes of hieroscopy and scenes of young men carrying off legs of meat disappear from the iconography of sacrifice because in different ways both engage the viewer with a particular story. Whether we see the future of the hoplite through the lens of the omens disclosed at this moment, or the life of the youth given or giving a leg of meat through the interpersonal transaction managed by that exchange, these scenes invite us imaginatively to reconstruct another's story. The moment of examining the liver of the sacrificial victim and the moment of entering upon a particular gift exchange are moments when an individual risks consequences over which he has no control. The world might be about to go wrong. If this were a serial television drama, these images show moments of suspense at which the episode might end. Hardly so the Phiale Painter's image of libation or the Thomson Painter's image of sacrifice. These are routine activities, showing what the world does, the things that go on while individuals get on with their particular lives.

3. (In)Activity at an Altar

One of the most notable features of fifth-century red-figure iconography is the number of images that show a religious setting but no definitive action. A man, or more often a woman, stands or runs holding some item of potential religious significance in his or her hand (a phiale, or jug, or thurible, or torch, or garland, or basket, or whatever), perhaps in the vicinity of an altar, but the figure does not actually engage in any action. Such figures appear alone or in small groups. Such scenes appear occasionally from early in the fifth century and become increasingly popular.

An early example of a scene of this kind is provided by a lekythos (**6.8**), which Beazley reckoned a late product of the hand of the Berlin Painter (and so to be dated around 480). Here we see a young woman with long hair and a headband, dressed in a chiton and with her himation around her shoulders, running to the right with a torch in her right hand and a phiale in her left. No other figure appears on the lekythos but we seem to be witnessing some particular episode, as the keen glance and rapid movement of the woman attests to her intent to accomplish some definitive task.

Such scenes become very much more frequent in Beazley's "early classic" period. But by then their character has changed. A cup (**6.9** and plate 26),

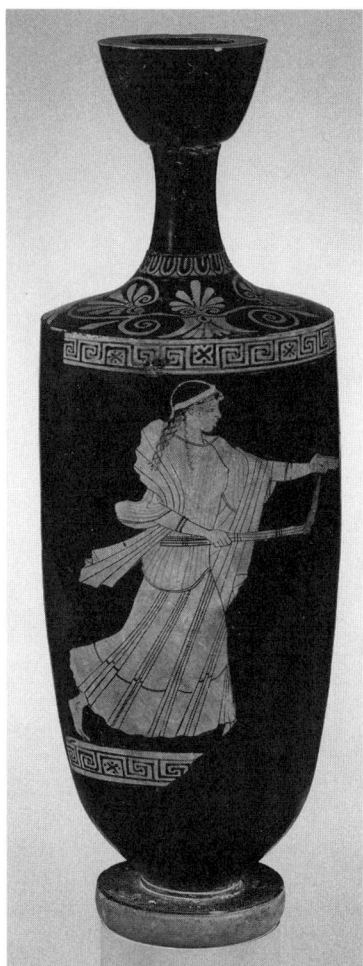
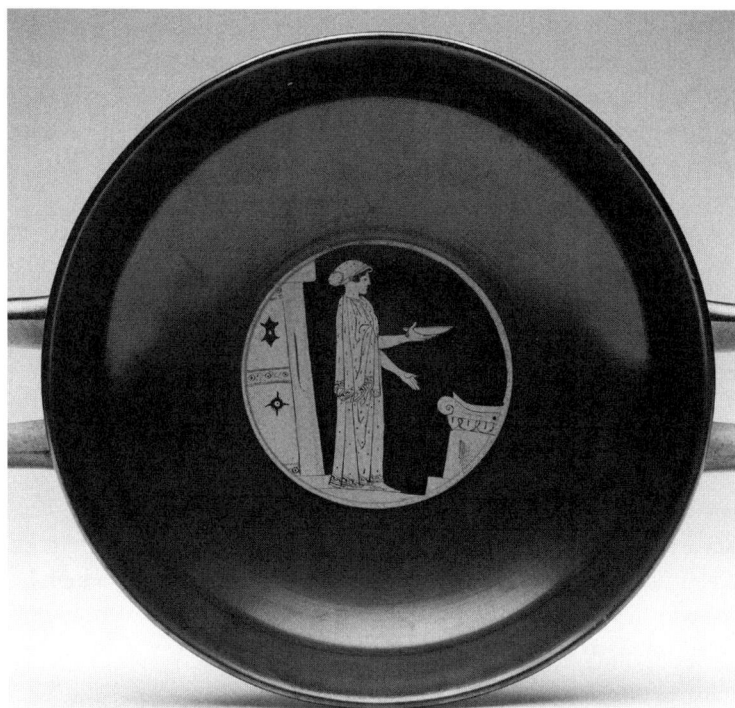

Figure 6.8. Red-figure lekythos, height 0.416 m, attributed to the Berlin Painter. *ARV* 211.203, New York Metropolitan Museum 21.88.163. www.metmuseum.org.

Figure 6.9. Interior of red-figure cup, diameter 0.19 m, in the manner of the Akestorides Painter (grouped by Beazley with the "Followers of Douris"), ca. 470. *ARV* 803.58, Harvard Art Museums / Arthur M. Sackler Museum, gift of E. P. Warren, Esquire 1927.155. Photo: Imaging Department © President and Fellows of Harvard College.

the exterior of which is plain black glaze and which Beazley grouped with the "Followers of Douris" but ascribed to no particular hand, shows a woman standing erect before an elaborate altar. She is wearing an elaborately decorated peplos with "running-dog" border decoration and a sakkos. She holds out a phiale in her left hand and with her right arm points to the altar. Behind her is a door with knocker and perhaps keyhole indicated. We are clearly being told that this is a posh woman in a posh environment, but that is all. For all her stiff formality, this woman stands more as a symbol of paradigmatic religious activity than as someone intently engaged in a particular ritual.

4. Images of the Gods

While some iconographies become rare or disappear altogether during the fifth century, this pattern where a broad iconographic scheme or general subject matter continues to be painted, but painted in ways that significantly change its force, is common. Take the representation of statues of the gods. The representation of statues of gods on pots is found throughout red-figure, particularly in connection with various mythical episodes, such as the rape of Cassandra, but it becomes much more common in the later fifth-century in Attic red-figure (and much more common too in the fourth century in south Italian pottery). The statue becomes a way of signifying that the space represented is a sanctuary, and it also gives scope for artists to explore their own art, juxtaposing figures of the gods with figures of statues of the gods.[15]

The images of herms on Athenian pots illustrate well the way in which the same elements were treated in a quite different way at the two ends of the fifth century. De Cesare lists fifty-three scenes in which Athenian red-figure painters show herms in clearly nonmythological contexts.[16] Of these, four date to the last quarter of the sixth century, eleven to the first quarter of the fifth, eighteen to the second quarter, ten to the third quarter, five to the last quarter, and five to the fourth century. Characteristic of Athenian scenes with herms down to shortly before the middle of the century are encounters of individuals with herms. Characteristic of the later fifth-century scenes is the appearance of herms as part of the background enriching the sense that the action is taking place in a sanctuary. Again two examples will illustrate this. A cup in Berlin attributed to the Triptolemos Painter, and painted around the end of the first quarter of the fifth century shows in its tondo a man carrying a large sack past a herm and an altar (**6.10**).[17] The man is naked and bearded, like the herm, and bent almost double under the weight of the sack, so that his head comes down to the level of the herm. The sack and the torso of the man are parallel to the line of the beard of the herm, and a straight line leads from the left foot of the man, through the erect phallus of the herm to the line of the lower arms of the man. The sack is stuffed full, like a sausage, and conspicuously tied at one end, giving it a phallus-like appearance.[18] There can be little doubt of the humor here—as if the burden of the man raises questions about what it might be to be burdened with the phallus of a herm. The exterior of the cup (7.14–15 and plate 31) shows a symposium scene with nine bearded men and one beardless aulos player. The symposiasts drink from, and play kottabos with, a variety of shapes of drinking vessel, and in a frieze below them a whole array of vessels are silhouetted, including a phallus-spouted skyphos and jug. This is a cup that explores encounter and the sexual undertones to every meeting of men. Despite the presence of the altar, this

---

[15] This is most famously the case with a fragment in the Allard Pierson Museum in Amsterdam showing Apollo next to a temple in which there is a statue of Apollo, which has become a favorite for book covers, Allard Pierson Museum 2579 (see de Cesare [1997], cat. nos. 9, 347, 483). For other explorations of encounter between gods in different ontologies, see de Cesare (1997), cat. 342–91.

[16] De Cesare (1997), cat. 239–312.

[17] De Cesare (1997), cat. 251, *LIMC* V 305 no. 162.

[18] Sacks are not frequent in red-figure painted pottery, but the particular features of this one come out clearly from comparison with that carried by the youth in the tondo of a cup attributed to Oltos, Berlin Staatliche Museen F 4220, *ARV* 61.76 (Beazley is wrong, I think, to describe this as a cushion).

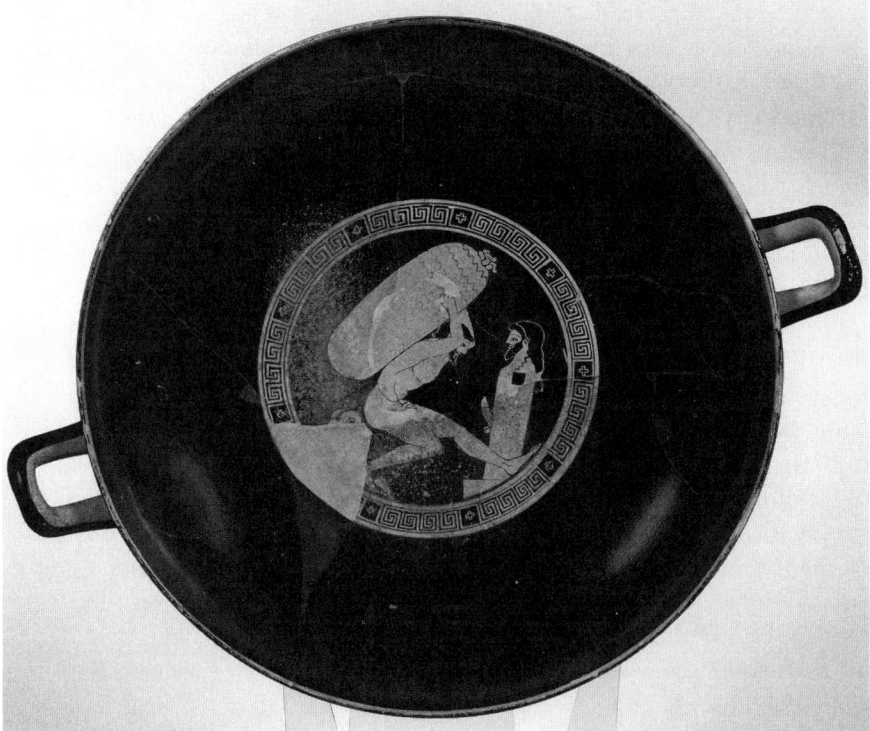

Figure 6.10. Interior of red-figure cup, diameter 0.315 m, attributed to the Triptolemos Painter, ca. 480 (for the exterior see 7.14–15). *ARV* 364.52, Berlin Staatliche Museen F 2298. © bpk / Antikensammlung, Staatliche Museen zu Berlin / Johannes Laurentius.

herm is not there to make sure that we recognize that the porter is moving through religious space; rather, the altar is there to point out that, despite what we might think, this sexually active space is also a sanctuary.

A bell-krater from the end of the fifth century makes a useful contrast (**6.11**).[19] Here again we have an encounter with a herm. But here the encounter is between the herm and an ox. The herm stands beside an altar facing a horned ox (not I think definitively a bull[20]), beside which stands a youth in a himation, behind whom a votive plaque with an image of a maenad is to be seen. This is not an image without humor, as the rhyme between the horn of the ox and the phallus of the herm indicates. But the humor comes not so much from any sexual undertones as from the juxtaposing of various ways of communicating with the gods. In their separate ways the herm, altar, votive plaque, and ox all signify human communication with the gods—but differently. Hermes's own infant escapade of stealing oxen lends a further quizzical touch to this scene.

In some ways the difference between these scenes is slight, but it is crucial. The Triptolemos Painter's cup shows a very particular moment, conjuring up an implausible episode in order to make a sexual joke—a joke that is in the end a joke not about herms but about sacks, showing that they, like pots, can be turned into sex organs. By contrast the bell-krater

[19] De Cesare (1997), cat. 299, *LIMC* V 301 no. 102bis.
[20] Contrast the very similar scene on a later Kabirion cup, where there is no doubt that a bull is shown: Kassel Staatliche Kunstsammlung T 424, *LIMC* V 301 no. 102.

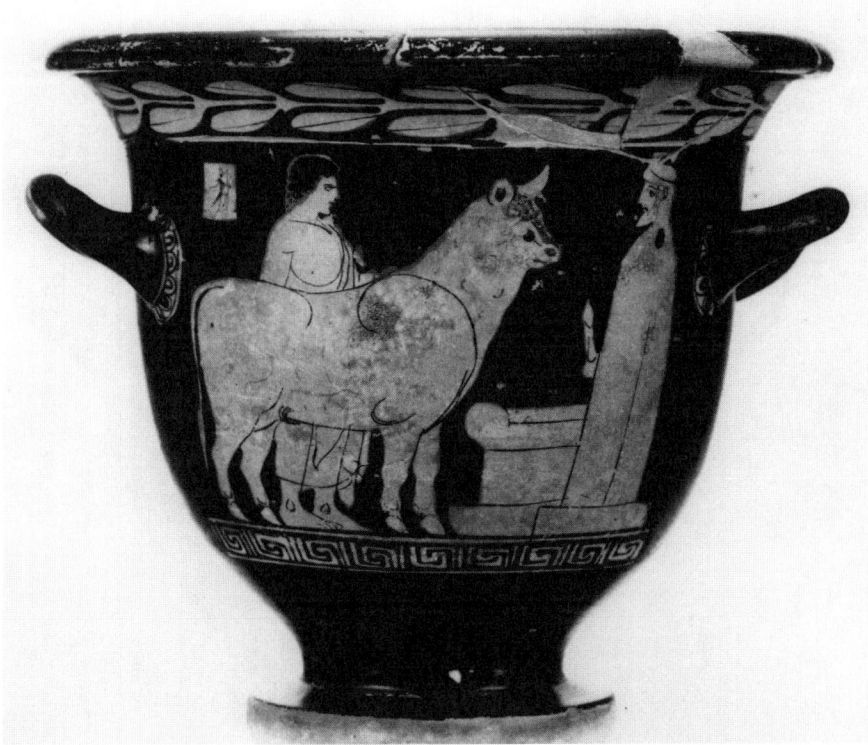

Figure 6.11. Exterior of bell-krater from Spina. ca. 410. *ARV* 1276.9bis, Ferrara Museo Archeologico Nazionale 42888.

from Spina reproduces what might be an everyday sanctuary scene, simply putting together the regular items of herm, altar, plaque, sacrificial animal, and token worshipper bringing the animal to sacrifice. Quizzical though it is, this is a pot that conjures up a moment that any viewer might themselves have enjoyed.

5. The Pyrrhic Dance

The most striking change of force in an imagery associated with cult is perhaps the change that occurs in images of the pyrrhic dance. The pyrrhic dance (that is, the dance in armor) at Athens was a feature of festivals both in Athens itself (notably the Panathenaia) and in the demes (for example, the Tauropolia at Halai Araphenides), and there is some reason to believe that armed dancing might also occur in funerary contexts.[21] Athenian pottery shows armed dancing on both black-figure and some red-figure pottery from the end of the sixth century. The scene almost invariably is made up of one or more men wearing at least the hoplite helmet and carrying shield and spear, along with a youth playing the double pipes. A fine early

---

[21] See generally Ceccarelli (1998), and on funerary armed dancing esp. 53–57, 230. The strongest pictorial support for the funerary use of armed dancing comes from an Athenian black-figure kantharos from the end of the sixth century showing pipe player, hoplites in step, and a corpse being carried to the tomb: Paris, Cabinet de Médailles 353, *ABV* 346.7.

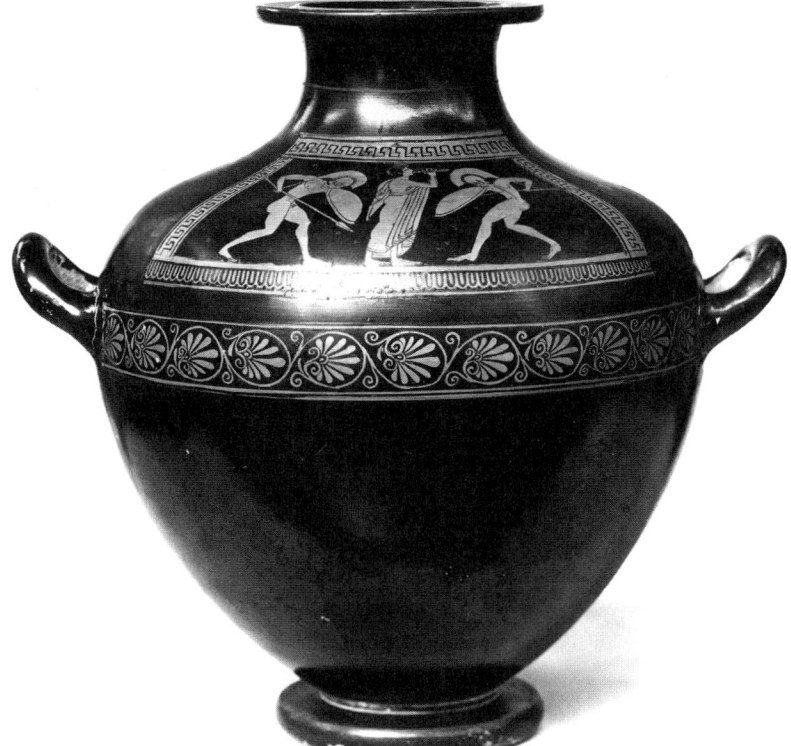

Figure 6.12. Red-figure hydria, height 0.38 m, attributed to the Pioneer Group, ca. 510. *ARV* 34.14, New York, Metropolitan Museum, Rogers Fund 1921, 21.88.2. © 2016. Image copyright The Metropolitan Museum of Art / Art Resource / Scala, Florence.

red-figure example is painted on a hydria belonging to the Pioneer Group (**6.12**). A youth wearing a himation with a fancy border stands in the center, head up, playing the aulos. On each side of him there are naked beardless men dancing, wearing hoplite helmets with large crests, and carrying shields held out before them and spears.

Shortly before the middle of the fifth century there is a striking change in iconography on Athenian pottery. Around 460 male armed dancers completely disappear (though one or two satyrs appear later), and shortly afterward female armed dancers appear. There is no overlap chronologically between the images of male and the images of female dancers.[22] Women armed dancers display a great deal of iconographic variety in how they are shown, but they frequently dance to music played by women and are often explicitly set either in a context in which only women appear or in the context of the symposium. Another hydria, from the end of the third quarter of the century, displays the change particularly clearly (**6.13** and plate 27). Here a naked dancer, with a breast-band, wearing a helmet with an elaborate plume and carrying shield and spear, stands with Eros in front of her with lyre in hand. In front of Eros is a well-dressed woman seated on a chair playing the double pipes, and in front of her a second long-haired

---

[22] This was demonstrated by Poursat (1968); see also Ceccarelli (1998), 230. From the fourth century, we have images of male armed dancers on monuments celebrating victory in the pyrrhic dance, most famously the Atarbos base (Athens Acr. 1338, *IG* ii² 3025; Shear 2003a).

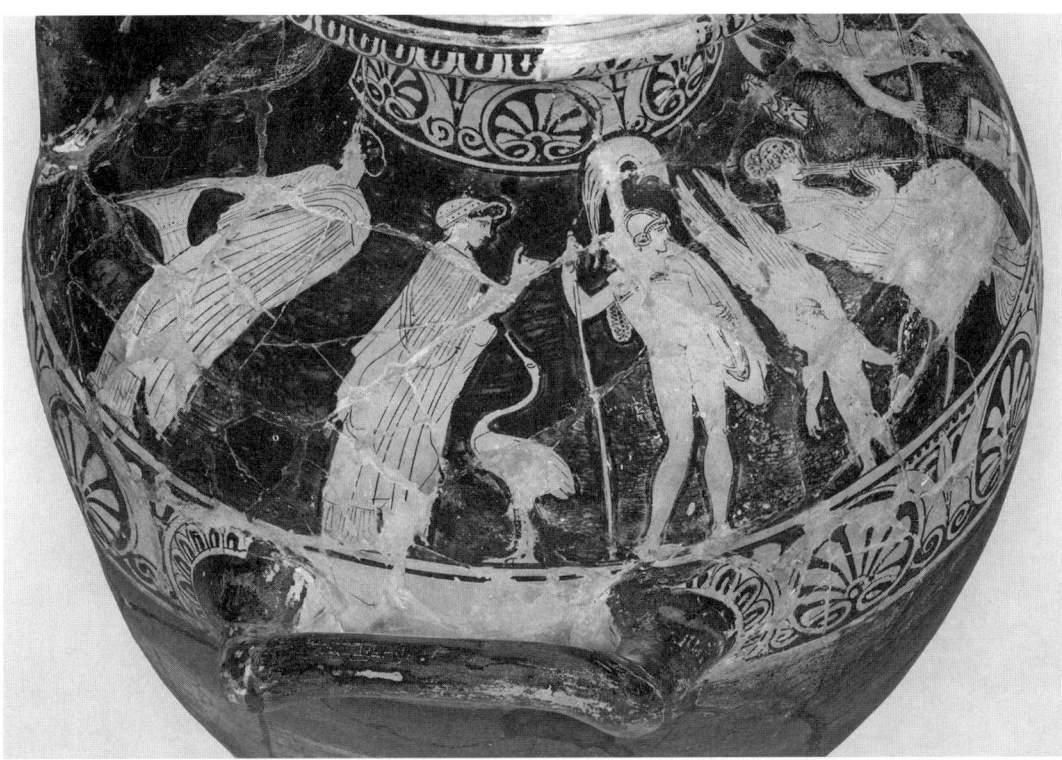
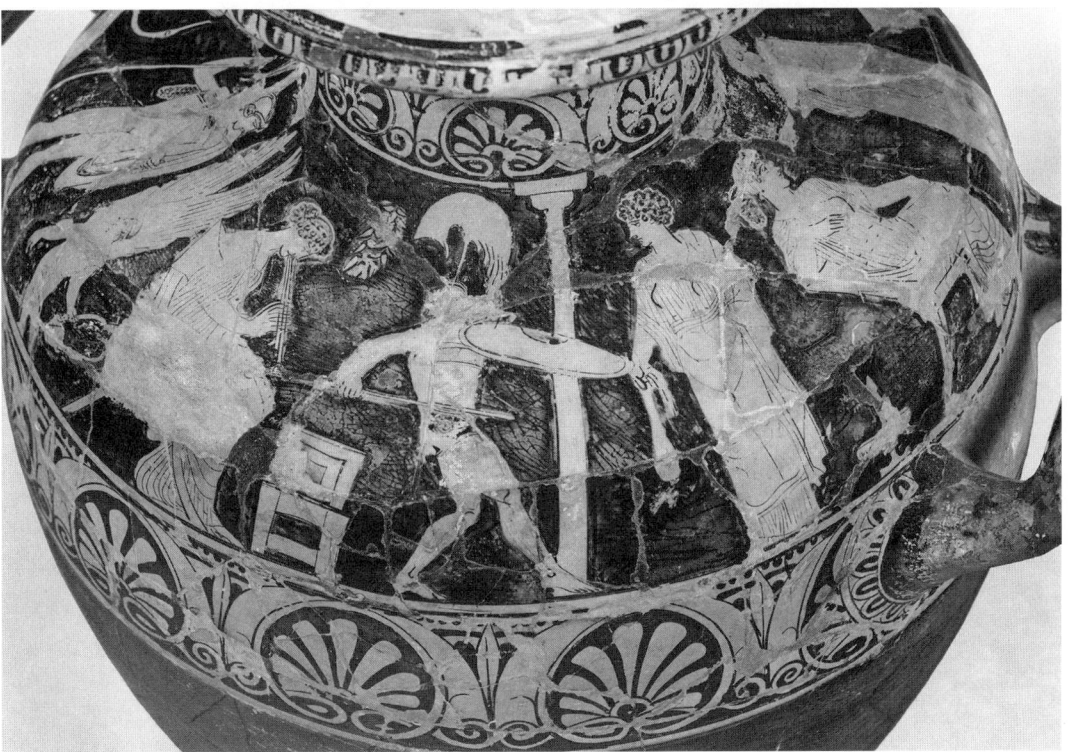

Figure 6.13. Red-figure hydria, height 0.40 m, unattributed, from Athens, ca. 430. Copenhagen National Museum 7359. CC-BY-SA, The National Museum of Denmark.

dancer dressed like the other, but shown dancing. The presence of Eros makes clear the eroticism of this image, but the erotic potential of the female dancer is shown here to be experienced and enjoyed in the first place by other women. Female armed dancing was not simply a fantasy of classical Athenian red-figure painters, as a reference to it by Xenophon (*Anabasis* 6.1.12) shows, but although we cannot trace the history of armed dancing in detail, and no doubt there was some change in practice during the fifth century, we know enough about the continuing practice of competitive armed dancing by young men to be sure that the change in the iconography does not reflect a change in the practice of armed dancing.

What does it reflect? Poursat suggests that classical painters simply preferred to represent women: "l'apparition de ce sujet, vers cette date, ne peut surprendre: cela correspond, avec la naissance du style classique, à un changement dans l'imagerie, qui préfère les representations féminines; cette seule explication peut suffire, peut-être à render compte de la disparition des scenes 'masculines.'"[23] Ceccarelli, although suggesting a link with the decline in the popularity of scenes of athletics on pots, notes also that the change coincides with a more general change in Athenian society and more particularly suggests that Athenian attitudes to young men's rites of passage have changed: "la fine, a epoca abbastanza alta, delle raffigurazioni di pirrica maschile è probabilmente indicative del fatto che il legame di questa danza con rituali di transizione è sentito in maniera sempre meno forte."[24]

Ceccarelli's second thought, that there must be some changing attitude to dances associated with rites of passage, comes from the temptation to think that changes in images that relate to life must relate in some more or less direct way to changes in the life to which they relate. We see this similarly with Patton's attempt to account for the appearance and disappearance of images of gods libating in terms of religious history: "It is possible that during this radical ideological shift that overturned archaic organizational units of power, a shift taking place over only a few decades, the highly conservative social institution of sacrifice was reinforced and upheld by images of sacrificing gods: Nothing more strongly reinscribes the significance of a ritual than the representation of a god's performing it.... The libating gods in vase-paintings mostly exit the iconographic stage around 450–440 B.C.E.... in other words at a time of Athenian self-confidence and religious stability, even optimism.... Perhaps it was no longer necessary to reinscribe foundational ritual piety so strongly, since the threat to those forms and practices had diminished."[25]

It has been one of the burdens of this book that the temptations of such arguments must be resisted. For all that Poursat's description of the changing imagery that comes with the classical style as characterized by a preference for the feminine is at best a very incomplete description, he is right to think that it is to the classical style that we must look for an explanation.

[23] Poursat (1968), 604.
[24] Ceccarelli (1998), 89, 230–31.
[25] Patton (2009), 178, 179.

The changing ways of seeing the world that I have been documenting were not simply changing ways of seeing the human world, they involved thinking about the relationship between the human and the supernatural world differently. In earlier imagery rituals are instrumental, they are resources to be exploited to further other aspects of one's life. In the later imagery, the ritual is not a means but an end in itself, it is participation in ritual that matters, not what the ritual might do for you.

Ceccarelli's first observation, that changes in the representation of pyrrhic dance relate directly to changes in the representation of athletes in general, was spot-on. As far as archaic red-figure painters were concerned, scenes of pyrrhic dancers are just another of those scenes of active competition that they loved to explore. Classical red-figure had no reason to identify specifically as pyrrhic dancers the young men standing about with their strigils in which it had so much interest—such images would be too specific and insufficiently inclusive. The story in which male pyrrhic dancers disappear and are replaced by female pyrrhic dancers is wonderfully neat, but is really made up of parts of two different stories—the story of the end of athletic competition, on the one hand, and the story of changing representations of the symposium on the other (7.19). It is the latter story that is the subject of the next chapter.

7 ❧ Drinking to and Reveling in Change

Containers for transporting wine and water (amphoras, hydrias), for mixing them (kraters, dinoi), for transferring the mixed wine and water to vessels from which it could be drunk (dippers, jugs), and drinking vessels themselves in a variety of shapes (bowls, cups, skyphoi)—all of these vessels were needed for a drinking party and all were at least sometimes made from pottery and might be decorated with figure scenes (**7.1**). Although, as we have seen already in this book, a great many scenes on pots used at drinking parties do not relate to drinking, thousands of images—like 7.1 that puts on display both young men reclining to drink and the various shapes of vessel that might be used in a sympotic context—show the drinking party itself or the reveling of those who have been at a drinking party (**7.2** and plate 28), and various images that do not themselves show drinking nevertheless explore the experience of intoxication at the drinking party.[1]

Over the last thirty or so years scholars have repeatedly emphasized the importance of the drinking party and of what went on there. What has caught scholarly attention has been the particular form of drinking party known as the symposium, an occasion at which relatively small numbers of men gathered in a small room and reclined on couches to drink and talk, their drinking and talking being regulated, after a fashion, by a master of ceremonies.[2] This form of drinking party is described in most detail in the dialogues titled *Symposium* by Xenophon and Plato, but lies more or less transparently behind much archaic poetry.

The question of what it took to create a symposium is still an open one. Scholars once thought that the symposium could not exist without the practice of reclining on couches, and that it was therefore an invention of the later seventh century when this practice was introduced from the Near East and is first shown on painted pottery.[3] But it is clear that drinking parties involving more or less intellectual games were already a feature of the eighth century, whether or not individuals reclined to drink at that time, and recent work has insisted that the symposium should be regarded

---

[1] Lissarrague (1987/1990) provides a rich description of the practices illustrated on painted pottery, many of which can be substantiated from material quoted by Athenaios in his third-century AD *Deipnosophistai*. For images exploring intoxication, see Osborne (2012).

[2] Davidson (1997), 43–49, offers a basic introduction.

[3] The crucial work here was Dentzer (1982); cf. also Fehr (1971). The history of work on the symposium and what it makes sense to believe about it are well reviewed by Corner (2015).

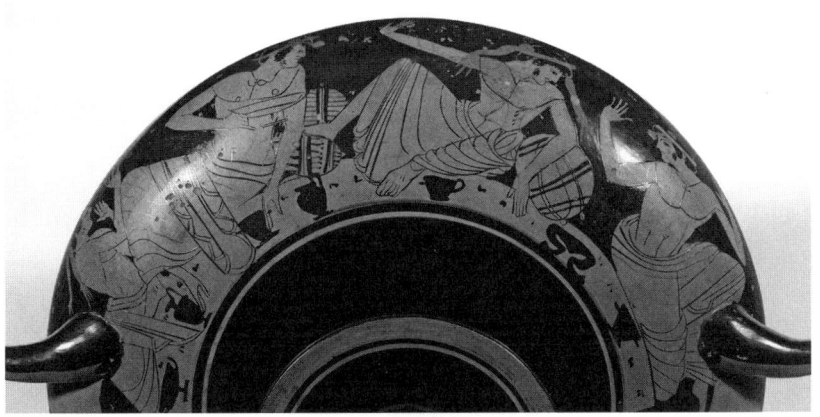

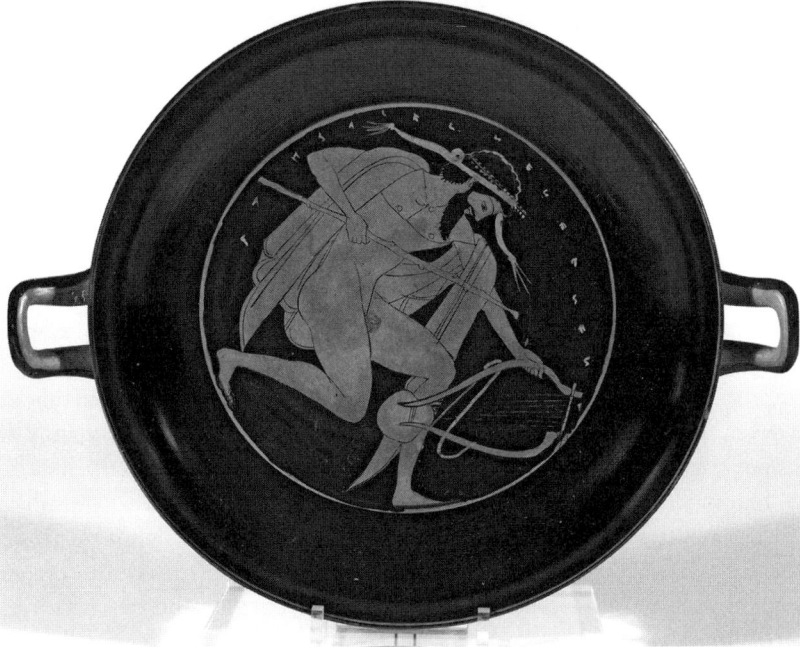

Figure 7.1–2. Interior and one exterior side of red-figure cup, diameter 0.273 m, attributed to the wider circle of the Nikosthenes Painter, ca. 500 (for the other side see 4.12). *ARV* 135.13, Cambridge, Fitzwilliam Museum GR 19.1937. © The Fitzwilliam Museum, Cambridge.

as already in existence in eighth-century Greece.[4] There is, in fact, no reason to restrict the name *symposion* to a particular form of drinking party.[5]

---

[4] The symposium lies behind such famous items as the "cup of Nestor" from Pithekoussai (ML 1) and the inscribed Dipylon jug (*IG* i³ 919), cf. Catoni (2010), 165–74. For a discussion of the early symposium, see Wecowski (2014).

[5] See Hobden (2013), 7–15, and note that Herodotos 2.78 happily uses the word to refer to Egyptians' parties at which a coffin is carried round to remind people of their mortality; Xenophon uses the term regularly in *Cyropaideia* for Persian parties that are in various respects distinctive, see esp. 8.8.10 and Gera (1993), 150; the writers of the Septuagint and Gospels are also happy to use the term (3 Maccabees 5.36, Mark 6:39) of occasions that obey very different commensal rules. See also Lynch (2015), 233–34.

Drinking accompanied by entertainment, which might be brought in or generated by the drinkers themselves, occurred in a very wide range of formats, some of them more refined, others distinctly coarse. It also happened in a variety of physical contexts, sometimes in rooms in houses that had been built and equipped for the purposes, sometimes in dining rooms in sanctuaries, similarly constructed; very often it must have happened in spaces that had many uses, and not infrequently, particularly perhaps in sanctuaries and after sacrifices as part of festivals, it happened in the open air with drinkers sitting on the ground.[6]

We are not in a strong position to discover how actual symposia changed over time. The nature of the evidence surviving from different periods is different: poetry for the symposium survives largely from the archaic period; full accounts of what happened at a symposium come from the early fourth century; snippets of data about drinking practices were collected by Athenaios of Naukratis in the early third century AD, who removed them from context so that we sometimes cannot date them. As a result, it is hard to judge whether the changing prominence of particular aspects of the symposium is simply a consequence of the changing evidential base.

We can however document quasi-sympotic activity in a public dining room in classical Athens as a result of the preservation of the contents of its pantry—contents that, as Susan Rotroff and John Oakley remark in publishing the material, evoke "*symposion* rather than *syssition*," that is, drinking rather than eating.[7] Not only did the pantry contain many kraters (fragments from fifty-three red-figure kraters were found), it also showed signs of pottery that had been bought in sympotic sets from particular workshops, and the abundant graffiti on the pots revealed an exchange of sexual abuse that would have been at home in the symposia attested by archaic poetry.[8] The adoption of sympotic habits in a context of public dining suggests that, if sympotic behavior was not previously spread across social classes, it came to be so spread in the course of the fifth century. That suggestion is reinforced by the evidence of old comedy and by further archaeological material from domestic contexts in the Agora, and this archaeological material suggests that any social spread was already occurring early in the century.[9]

The question about whether and in what ways the institution may have changed over time is even more difficult to answer for the activities surrounding the drinking party, which scholars refer to as the *komos*, or revel, than for the drinking party itself. It is clear, even from the literary evidence, that drinking parties might end up on the street with the participants engaging in various drunken activities, some of them noisy and violent.

---

[6] On all of this see Hobden (2013), 7–15. On Topper's view that sitting on the ground is a sign of reference to the legendary past, see above chapter 1, note 54, and cf. Yatromanolakis (2009); Lynch (2007), esp. 244–45.

[7] Rotroff and Oakley (1992), 46.

[8] Rotroff and Oakley (1992), 12–13 for sets; catalog nos. 26–78 for kraters; 27–28 for graffiti; see also Steiner (2002).

[9] Bowie (1995), 116; Lynch (2011), 169–75. See also more generally Fisher (2000).

Whether the sorts of intoxicated behavior that followed the symposium changed over time, our meager literary evidence does not allow us to see. Reveling is, however, variously represented on Athenian pottery from early in the sixth century through to the end of the fifth, with black-figure images emphasizing dancing and red-figure showing a much more varied set of scenes.[10]

1. Reveling

The changing iconographic preferences of red-figure painters can be seen particularly clearly in scenes of the *komos*. Revelers (*komasts*) attract a lot of attention from early red-figure painters, both as groups and as single figures. The famous group of twisting naked male figures, with which the "Pioneer" painter Euthymides shows off a skill "as never Euphronios" did, is a group marked out as consisting of *komasts* by the figure on the left carrying a kantharos (**7.3**). The attractions of the *komos* to those working out what was newly possible in red-figure emerge here as the variety of poses and body positions that could be deployed in exploring the loosened limbs and tongues of intoxicated revelers. A particular favorite of early red-figure cup painters is to show the single figure of the reveler, sometimes youthful, sometimes bearded, in the tondo of a cup (7.2), often one that is plain on the exterior. More than one hundred cups by those Beazley termed early red-figure cup painters show such a composition, so that drinkers who drained their cup found an image of what they might go on to do when they arose from their couch. The same group of painters only slightly less frequently show reveling on the exterior of their cups, this time with several figures involved, some bearded, some youthful, some clothed, some naked, frequently with musical instruments, sometimes with naked women among the company.

A cup attributed to the Epeleios Painter is typical of these *komast* and *komos* scenes, relatively unusual only in combining a *komast* on the interior with a *komos* on exterior (**7.4–6** and plate 29). The interior shows a single naked beardless youth seen from the back as he twists around, moving right but looking back to the left. He is marked out as a reveler by the *krotala* (castanets) in his hands. In the field is the acclamation "the boy is beautiful." Each side of the exterior of the cup shows six young men, naked or with a cloak draped over their shoulders, who variously hold out cups and skyphoi, manipulate a large amphora, dance, clap their hands, or wield *krotala*. In a more or less unique scene two of the youths waving cups in their hands ride piggyback on two youths who are bent over manhandling an amphora. The whole crowded composition gives a modern viewer a strong impression of good-humored larking about by these overexuberant

---

[10] For the black-figure material, the classic discussions are Greifenhagen (1929) and Ghiron-Bistagne (1976).

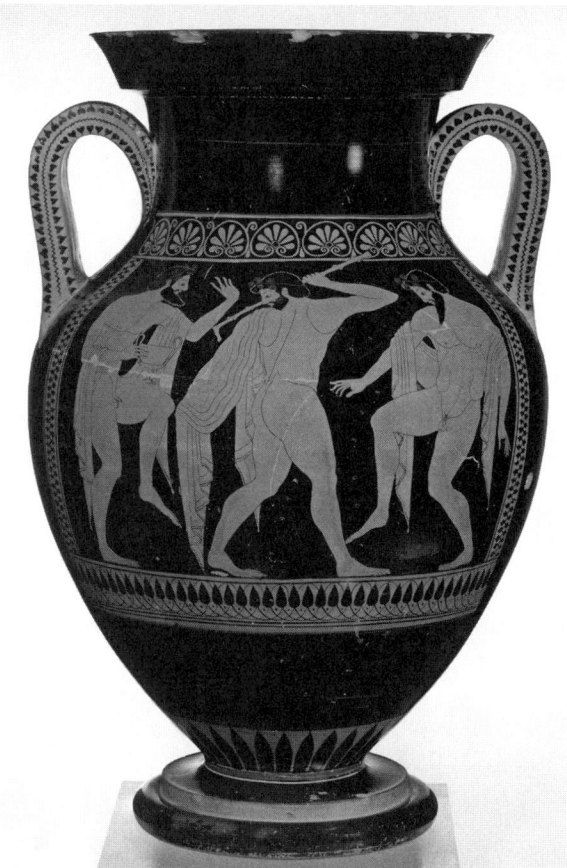

Figure 7.3. Red-figure amphora, height 0.60 m, signed by Euthymides son of Polios, from Vulci, ca. 510. *ARV* 26.1, Munich Staatliche Antikensammlungen 2307 (J 378). © Staatliche Antikensammlungen und Glyptothek München. Photograph by Renate Kühling.

young men—as if a snapshot has been taken of a party leaving a symposium as the revelers pass by on the street.

The Epeleios Painter's combination of *komast* on the interior and *komos* on the exterior becomes more common with the painters of late archaic cups. Eight of the Antiphon Painter's eleven cups with a *komos* on the exterior have a *komast* on the interior, and of his twenty cups with *komasts* on the interior, eight have a plain exterior, eight have a *komos* on the exterior, and only four have something different, in one case two scenes of Herakles. Similar patterns are found with other cup painters, such as the Dokimasia Painter, Douris, and Makron. But in the second quarter of the fifth century both the individual *komast* and *komos* scenes more generally fall out of favor. To the one hundred early red-figure single *komasts* can be added another 150 or so from late archaic red-figure, but from Beazley's early classic and classic periods the number is much closer to fifty. The decline in scenes of the *komos* is rather less abrupt—it is very popular with the Pan Painter and "early mannerists" (particularly the Leningrad Painter), but here too the roughly 250 *komos* scenes of early and late archaic red-figure compare with just over one hundred such scenes in Beazley's "early classic" period, and around eighty in his classic period.

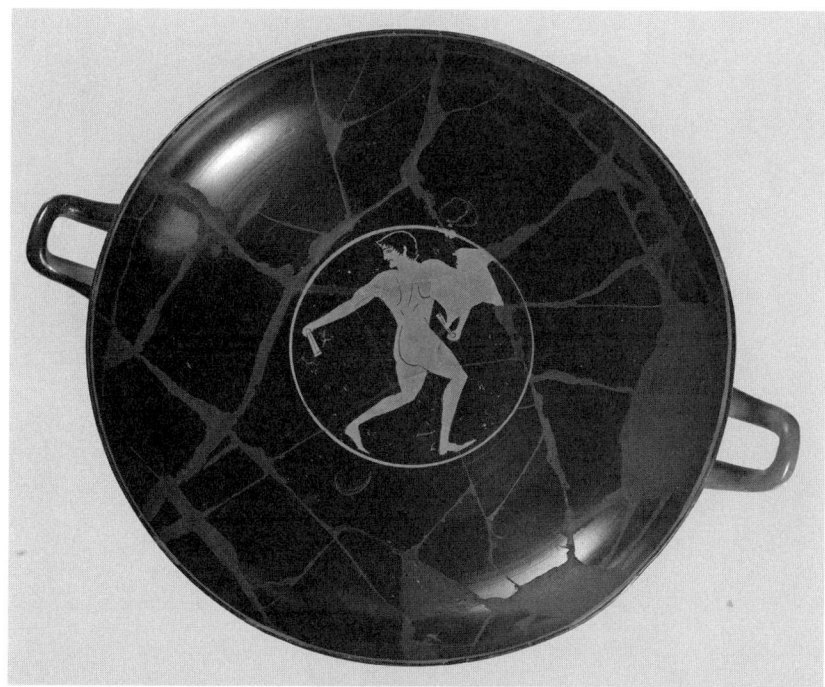
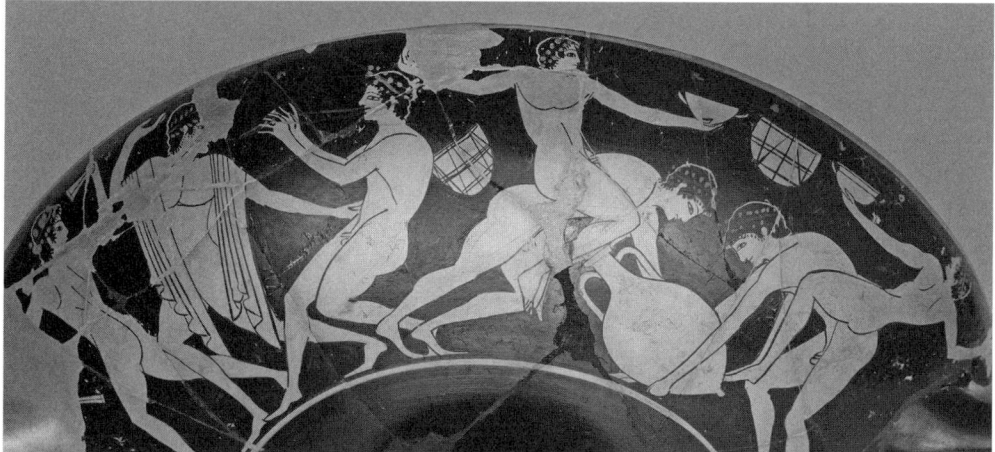
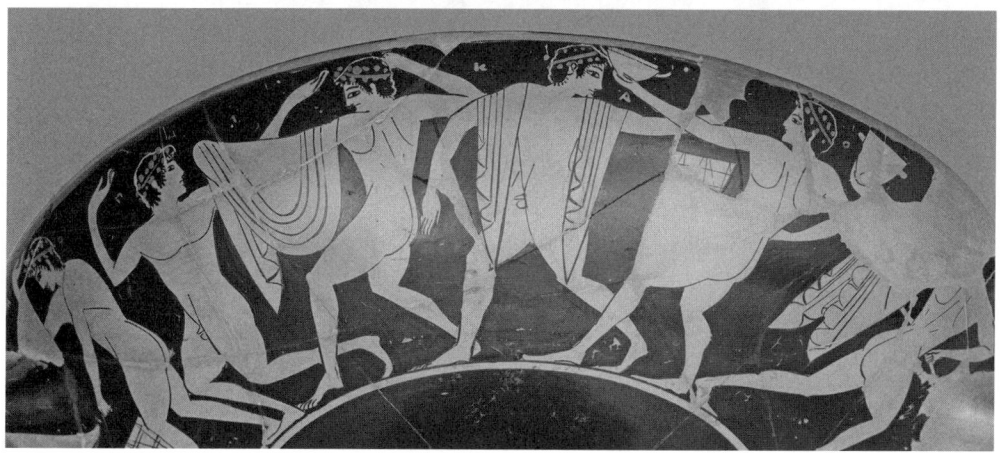

Figure 7.4–6. Red-figure cup, diameter 0.335 m, attributed to the Epeleios Painter, from Vulci, ca. 500. *ARV* 146.7, Brussels Musées Royaux A 3407. © RMAH.

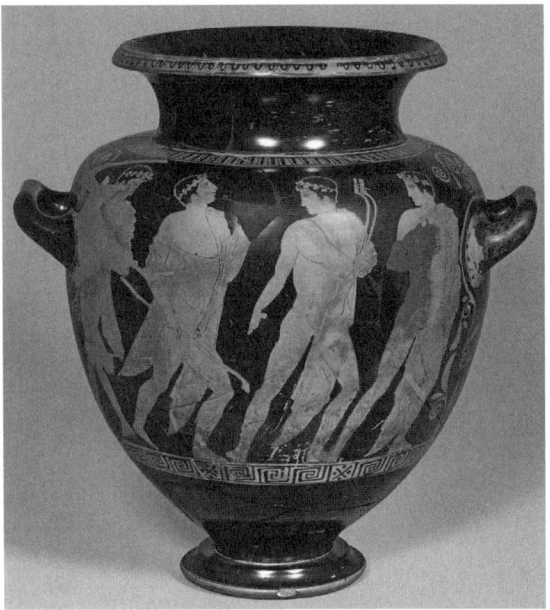 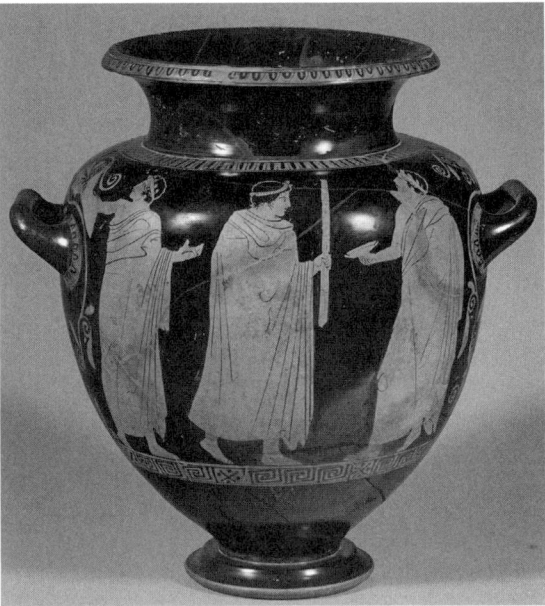

Figure 7.7–8. Red-figure stamnos, height 0.402 m, attributed to the Kleophon Painter, ca. 440. *ARV* 1144.9, Brussels Musées Royaux A 3091. © RMAH.

Once more what is at issue here is not simply the popularity of the scene but the manner of its depiction. A stamnos attributed to the Kleophon Painter offers a typical classical *komos* scene (**7.7–8** and plate 30).[11] On one side four young men are shown, effectively naked with their cloaks over their shoulders or arms. All are wreathed. Three move from left to right, but the figure farthest left moves left and looks back, perhaps executing a dance step. One figure, holding a stick in one hand and a cup or skyphos in the other, has his head thrown slightly back, and his mouth open, plausibly singing[12] to the music played on the curiously misdrawn lyre held by the youth next to him, the gesture of whose right hand holding a plectrum suggests that he has just struck a chord. On the reverse of the pot are three youths, all wearing himatia and headbands, two of them with wreaths too. The youth on the right holds a cup, the youth in the center a torch, flaming red. That we are seeing the aftermath of a drinking party there is no doubt, but there is no "larking about" here. Rather, we see rehearsed a number of standard activities of those reveling—carrying torches and drinking vessels, dancing, playing music and singing. The figures interact, but without any physical contact. The possibility of showing the twisting body in space attracts the Kleophon Painter as it had attracted Euthymides, but these twisting bodies are defying no one, and for all the waving about of drinking cups, very much under control. There is no individual character here, just as there is no leader.

[11] Matheson (1995), KL 10.
[12] For the thrown-back head of the singer, see Lissarrague (1987/1990), 131–32.

Other scenes of reveling by the Kleophon Painter have slightly more vigorous gestures, and busier activity, but the revelers still keep their arms close to their bodies and exist in self-contained spaces in a way that the earlier revelers did not.[13] Where the earlier revelers spoke through their gestures, these speak through their eyes. It is the relationship between the angle of the head and the position of the pupil in the eye that offers the viewer a clue as to how to understand the relationship between the figures and that insists that, for all the accoutrements of revelry, these are serious young men. Although the subject matter of these scenes is clearly the same as the subject matter of the Epeleios Painter's cup, both the tone of the drawing and the relationship between the scene and the viewer is quite different. This scene offers far less of a window onto the street, from which one watches others with amusement and sometimes raised eyebrows, and far more an invitation to join these revelers in their activities.

2. Booners

One further aspect of the changing iconography emerges from looking at one particular type of *komos* scene, scenes sometimes referred to as "Anacreontic" vases or "booners."[14] What marks out these scenes is the presence of bearded men wearing the chiton as well as the himation, a form of turban-like head covering, and sometimes earrings, and often carrying parasols (**7.9–10**). These figures appear both on their own, in the tondo of cups, and in groups along with women and occasionally of men who are more normally dressed. Beazley saw in these figures representations of the poet Anacreon, famous for his erotic poetry and known to have been a visitor to Athens in the late sixth century, along with his boon companions. Although there is one possible scene of this type from circa 540–530, figures of this sort begin to appear on a small number of pots, in black-figure and in red-figure, in the last two decades of the sixth century. Over the next forty years some forty pots carry scenes of this sort. Then after 460 the scene disappears, and booners are to be seen no more.

In comparison with other scenes of reveling, scenes showing booners are marked by the elegance of the actions and the importance of music. The booners themselves may carry the form of lyre known as the barbitos, associated with the performance of lyric and poetry (it is the instrument

---

[13] Seven other komos scenes are attributed to the Kleophon Painter, including a rare pair of stamnoi with near-identical scenes now in Saint Petersburg and Copenhagen (*ARV* 1144.7 and 8, Matheson [1995], KL 7 and 9), the latter from Orvieto, the former of unknown provenance.

[14] Kurtz and Boardman (1985), Frontisi-Ducroux and Lissarrague (1990), Price (1990). I adopt the term "booners" here since the basis for thinking that the costume or activity was strongly associated with Anacreon is weak (the presence of his name inscribed on a barbitos in a fragmentary scene attributed to the Kleophrades Painter, *ARV* 185.32; despite Price's claim, the presence of naked revelers on the lekythos by the Gales Painter, *ARV* 36.2, naming a lyre player in chiton and himation "Anakreon," precludes it from being considered part of the same series). Aristophanes's *Thesmophoriazousai* 163 suggests that dancing and wearing a sakkos, at least, was generally associated with Ionian poets. If we call these "Anakreontic" scenes we risk imagining that we are seeing them as Athenians saw them.

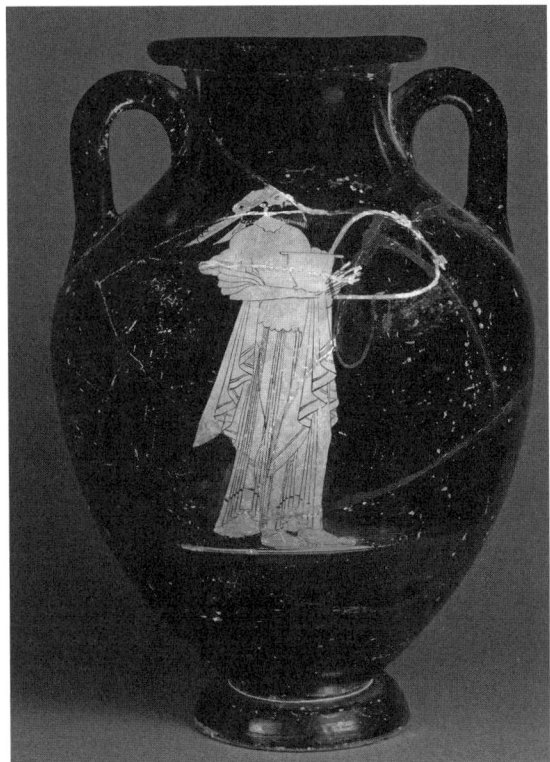 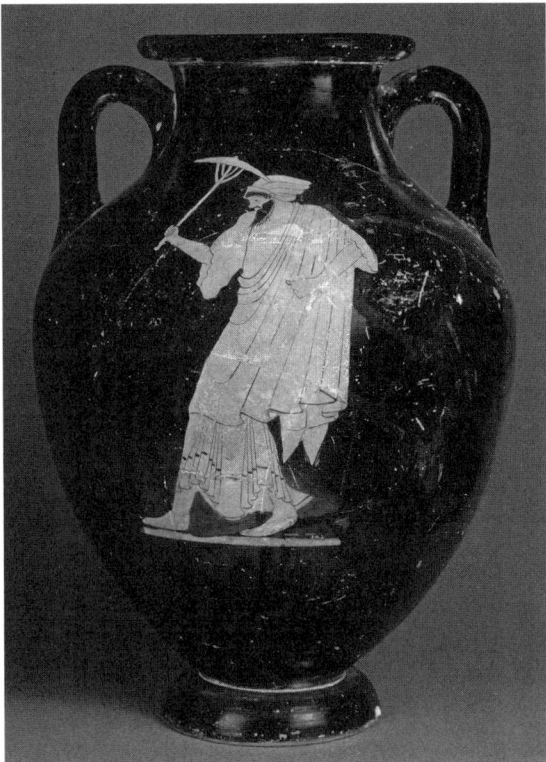

Figure 7.9–10. Red-figure amphora, height 0.40 m, attributed to the Flying Angel Painter, ca. 490. *ARV* 280.11, Paris, Louvre G220. Photo © RMN-Grand Palais (musée du Louvre)/ Hervé Lewandowski.

held by both Alkaios and Sappho on the Athenian pot that represents and names them both), and may be accompanied by women playing the double pipes.[15] Some booners throw back their heads in the gesture that is used to suggest singing. The booners themselves or their female companions may dance with *krotala*. The vessels associated with drinking and the symposium are regularly in evidence—booners carry cups or skyphoi, occasionally a krater is represented—but it is the dancing motions of the booners that draw the viewer's attention. The booners are indeed rather like the god Dionysos, who is regularly shown with his own particular cup, the kantharos, but whose enjoyment of music and dance is regularly more prominent than any signs of his intoxication. And Dionysos distinguishes himself from other gods, as the booners distinguish themselves from other men, by wearing the chiton as well as the himation.

More or less all the elements, except the barbitos, appear on a red-figure cup ascribed to the Briseis Painter (**7.11–12**). Circling clockwise from the garlanded krater under one of the handles, we have first a booner dressed in chiton, himation, and sakkos, with skyphos in one hand and knobbly stick in the other running in light-footedly and looking back. In front of him, another similarly dressed booner holds out his himation in an extrava-

---

[15] Representation of Alkaios and Sappho: red-figure "kalathoid vase with a spout," Munich 2416, *ARV* 385.228. See further Maas and Snyder (1989), 113–38; Bundrick (2005), 21–25.

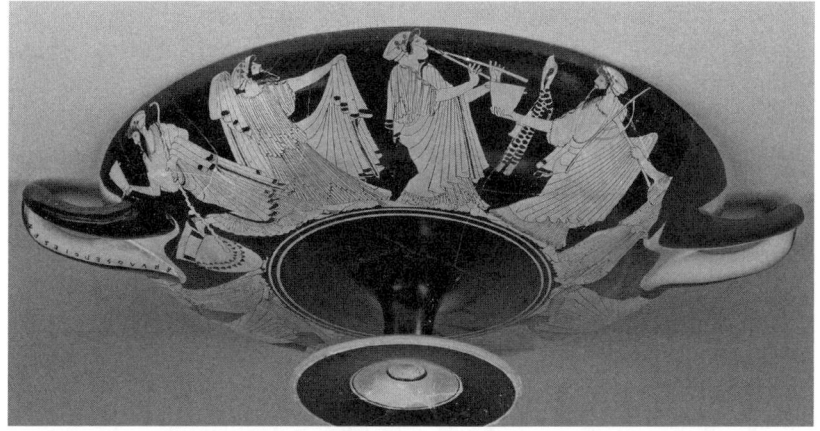

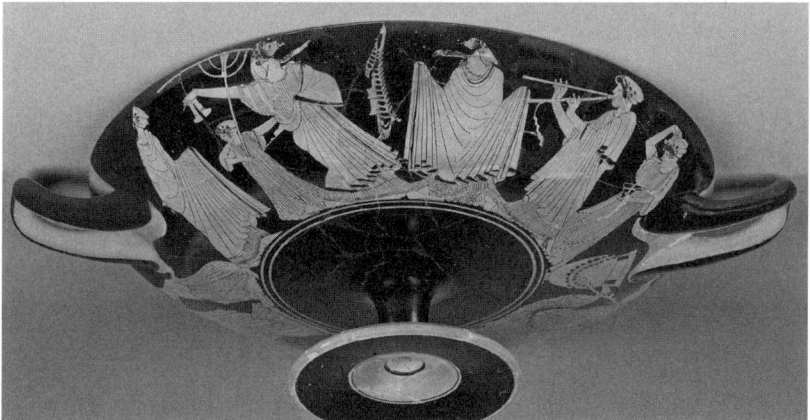

Figure 7.11–12. Exterior of red-figure cup, diameter 0.308 m, attributed to the Briseis Painter, ca. 480. *Para.* 372.8bis, J. Paul Getty Museum 86.AE.293. Digital image courtesy of the Getty's Open Content Program.

gant gesture while staring forward down his nose toward a woman in chiton, himation, and sakkos who plays the double aulos. She faces right to another booner, dressed in the same way, who himself moves right but looks back and stretches out a large skyphos in his right hand. In front of him is a figure in a chiton only, with a parasol. On the other side of the handles we see a booner in chiton, himation, and sakkos back view, and then a small figure in a chiton holding up a parasol for another booner who dances with the *krotala*. His head is thrown back, as is the head of the booner next to him who holds out his himation. They appear both to be singing to the music supplied by the woman in chiton and himation who plays the double pipes. Behind her, and next to the krater, a further woman, this time in chiton only, dances with *krotala*. This is a very sensuous scene. Not only do we have the music of the aulos and the singing of the booners, we have the rhythmic tapping of the *krotala* and are encouraged to feel the fabric of the booners' himatia as well as to appreciate the visual beauty of the way in which it swirls as they dance. The parasols here not only suggest that there is a delicacy to these dancers that needs to be protected from the sun but also something of the play of light and shade that their dancing provides. What the wine of the drinking party has enabled is a rich performance in which the booners approach to the condition of the god Dionysos himself.

Scholars have debated how we should understand these images. Are these sakkos-wearing figures with chitons under their himatia being celebrated, or ridiculed? Would Athenians have seen them as men dressed as women, or as men who had adopted dress that they associated with the East? Are these a product of painters' imaginations or a feature of Athenian life?[16] That these images evoke visually what Leslie Kurke has called the "cult of *habrosune*" is undoubtable, whether that cult of luxury was positively or negatively loaded.[17] These pots offered a view of the revel as a place of sensuous delight, and the truth is that different viewers, both in Athens and in the markets to which these pots were exported, would have found such revelers attractive, repellent, ridiculous, effeminate, or foreign. From the point of view of this investigation into the nature of and reasons for iconographic change, the notable feature of this iconography is its sudden death in the early classic period. Given the range of responses to which these images are open, it is striking that they should cease, and cease rather abruptly, to be images with which viewers wanted to engage.

What the scenes of booners offered was not just a glimpse of a particular, peculiar, sort of reveling, but a glimpse of a world that was other. Whether we take the challenge of the booners to be that they look foreign, female, or godlike, they offer a coherent but alien take on the experience of partying. They take the sensual aspects of the symposium, its music and song, its beautiful clothes, its delicate light, the bouquet of the wine and the scent of perfume, the dancing bodies of those providing entertainment, and they make those sensual aspects what is reperformed in the ongoing revel. They encourage those who view them to discover memories of what particular sympotic occasions have felt like, and to imagine particularly intense enjoyment of the sensual feast that drinking parties offered. And inevitably they challenge the viewer to face up to the poverty of those drinking parties, which leave as their trace merely a certain more or less boisterous parading through the streets, cup in hand.

Whether booners were a fact of history or a feat of the imagination, their world was not a world all could share. The refinements of their music, dress, and jewelry were refinements that picked out men of wealth and men of a certain taste. The images precisely aimed to bring out one extreme pole of the *komos* and to evoke one particular experience. The revels painted in the middle of the century were not interested in the extremes of experience, but in experiences that any viewer might have, or at least might have had when young. They focus on the regular and the ordinary, not the irregular and extraordinary. They encourage the viewer to find his own glance and his own experience among the glances exchanged by the revelers. Just as the single *komast* falls from favor, since the single *komast* is good for evoking particular experiences but poor at recreating the common sociality of

---

[16] Price (1990) sees here representations of actors imitating Anacreon and his companions and proposes that these performances became popular in Athens in the final decades of the sixth century. I see no signs in the imagery that a performance is being depicted, and no reason to think that the imagination of artists was so constrained by life.

[17] Kurke (1992), 97–104.

the group, so the booners had no place in the essentially sympathetic imagery of classical painted pottery.

3. The Symposium

Painters had never fallen in love with the solo symposiast as a subject for cup interiors to the degree that they had fallen in love with the solo reveler, nor did they choose the symposium as a whole as a subject nearly as frequently as the revel. But both are, nevertheless, well-represented in red-figure imagery (**7.13**). In the whole of red-figure I count around 120 solo symposiasts, mainly on cups and skyphoi, and around 300 scenes involving two or more people in a sympotic setting. No doubt part of the issue here was the more restricted possibilities offered by reclining figures, and particularly reclining figures on couches—indeed, painters frequently dispense with the couch. For single symposiasts—something of a contradiction in terms, but the image should be seen to encourage the drinker to reflect on his own place within the sympotic company—the history of the motif parallels the history of the representation of the solo *komast*: there are about twice as many images during the early and late archaic periods of red-figure as there are from the early classic period onward. The same history can be told of scenes of two figures (two men, two youths, less commonly a man and a youth or a man and a woman) reclining at a symposium.[18] But for scenes of the symposium as a whole, the history is different—I count around seventy-five many-figured symposia on pots painted in the early and late archaic periods, around 125 such scenes from the early classic period onward.

Two cups from the beginning of the fifth century well illustrate the characteristics of early red-figure sympotic scenes. The exterior of the cup in Berlin whose interior tondo was discussed above (6.10) shows on each side five wreathed males reclining on variously decorated cushions (**7.14–15** and plate 31). On one side all are bearded, on the other four are bearded but among them is a beardless youth playing the double pipes. To the left of the aulos player a bearded man holding a skyphos in his left hand, in front of whom a lyre hangs on the wall, throws his head back, supporting it with his right hand, and sings. Behind the aulos player is a group of three men, one twirling a cup around his finger in the game of kottabos (throwing dregs at a person or target) while looking the opposite way and gesticulating in the gesture of a man drinking from a cup, who is seen from the front, and a third man who looks back at him, holding up a cup in his left hand. On the other side two men, one cradling a bowl in his left hand, are engaged in a lively exchange in which the figure on the right is describing something with his right hand, which he holds expressively in the air.

---

[18] Scenes of a man and a youth are, however, in the majority among the nearly twenty such scenes from the hand of the painter known as the Marlay Painter, one of Beazley's "Classic cup painters," *ARV* 1278–80.

Figure 7.13. Interior of red-figure cup, diameter 0.34 m, attributed to the Nikosthenes Painter, ca. 510–500 (for the exterior see 1.3–4). *ARV* 124.3, Cambridge Fitzwilliam Museum GR 1.1927. © The Fitzwilliam Museum, Cambridge.

Figure 7.14–15. Exterior of red-figure cup, diameter 0.315 m, attributed to the Triptolemos Painter, ca. 480 (for the interior see 6.10). *ARV* 364.52, Berlin Staatliche Museen F 2298. © bpk / Antikensammlung, Staatliche Museen zu Berlin / Johannes Laurentius.

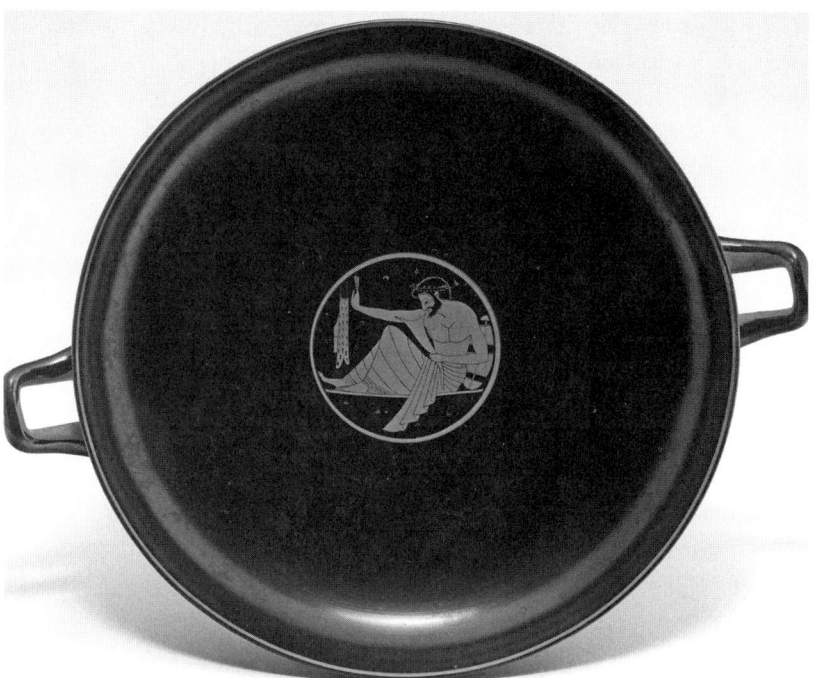

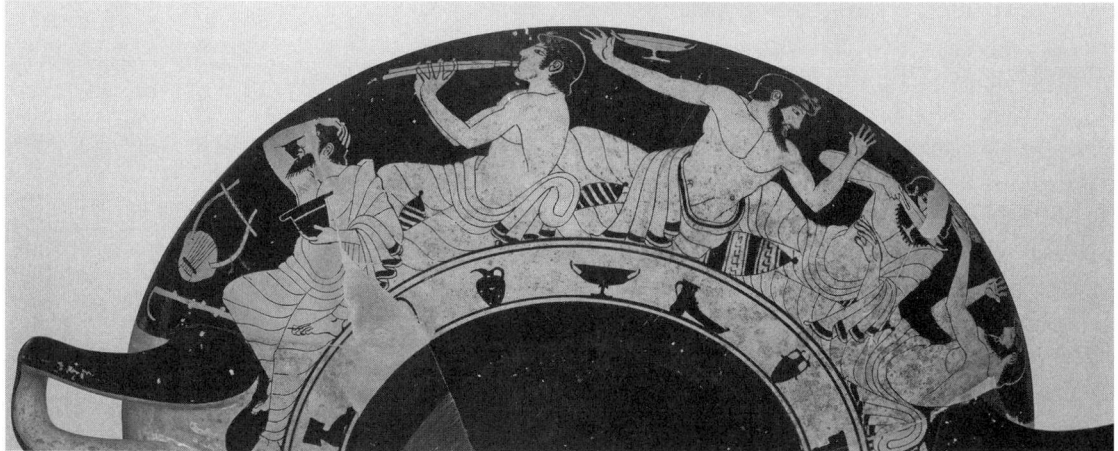

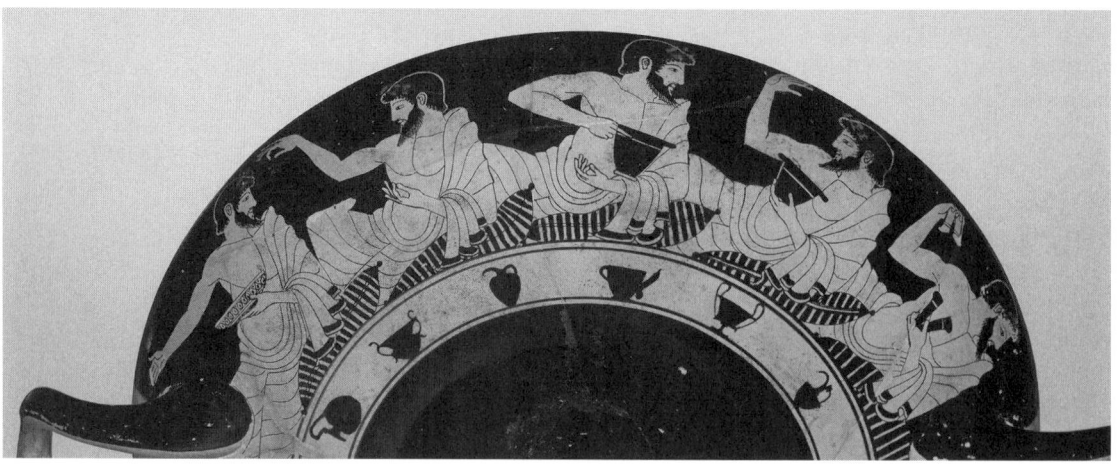

Behind them two other men, both holding skyphoi, are also in conversation, again conversation that causes one to hold his hand in the air with his fingers in a descriptive gesture. On the far right, and looking away to the handle behind him, is a man who plays the *krotala*. Just as the frieze below silhouettes a wide variety of shapes of pot, several of them sexually suggestive, so the symposiasts too parade the range of drinking and musical activities that go on at the symposium. Indeed, we might construe the side on which the aulos player is shown as signaling, with its variety of cushions, that this is a scene of different men engaging together, while the other side, with its repetition of the same striped cushion, might be read as showing, as if each figure were in a different frame of a film, the variety of action a single symposiast might engage in during the course of a symposium.

If the Triptolemos Painter here offers the array of standard sympotic behaviors, the Brygos Painter, on a cup in London, shows the breakdown of the symposium in behavior that can neither have been normal nor desired (**7.16–17** and plate 32).[19] Each side shows three figures including one playing the aulos. On one side a beardless youth reclines, with a wineskin as a cushion.[20] He gestures with his right hand while looking around and groping the back of a female aulos player, dressed in a chiton, who stands facing toward a man who is bent over horizontal, displaying his backside to the viewer and scratching his right buttock with his right arm. On the other side a naked youth kneels on a couch, swinging a wineskin back behind him ready to use it against another naked youth in the center who has his back to him and is aiming a kick at a youth in a himation playing the aulos—his cheeks inflated, and one of the pipes aimed at the kicking figure in evident defiance. The breaking up of the symposium in violence is rarely shown, but early and late archaic red-figure pot painters are not shy about showing the effects of excess (several scenes show symposiasts throwing up[21]), and this pot nicely indicates the limits of sympotic behavior that early red-figure images are happy to explore.

After 480 and in particular from around 460 onward the iconography of sympotic scenes becomes very much more regular, and the extremes of behavior are no longer explored.[22] Whether it is a cup or a krater or other closed shape that bears the scene, the norm is to show three or more figures reclining along with one figure standing, frequently a young woman playing the double pipes, but sometimes a youth bringing wine. The reclining figures variously sing, play the barbitos or the double aulos, drink, or play kottabos. Sometimes a drinker will look directly out at the viewer, sometimes the figures engage each other with their glances, but frequently each figure seems in his own world.

---

[19] The interior of the cup shows a young reveler, naked, with his fancy cloak over his shoulder, playing the pipes.
[20] *AA* 1964 294–99.
[21] *ARV* 402.12 (7.15), 427.2 (Rome Vatican 16561), *Para.* 372.11bis (= *ARV* 373.46), Karlsruhe 70/395.
[22] Cf. Schäfer (1997), 69–90, 108–9.

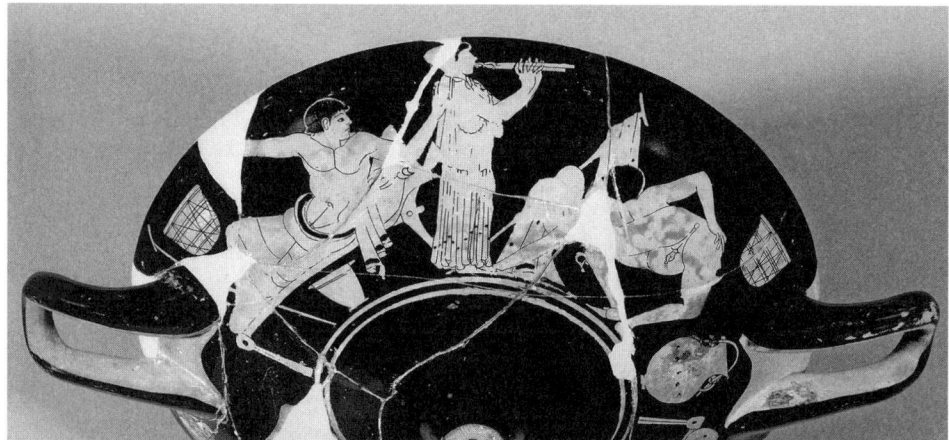

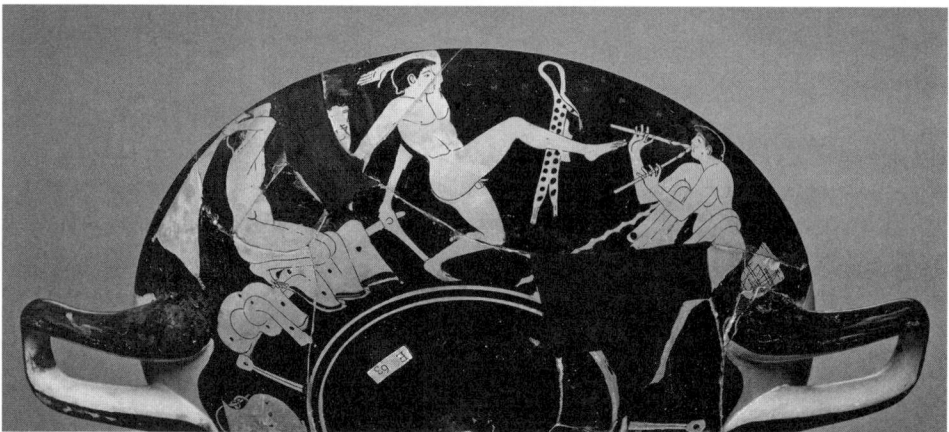

Figure 7.16–17. Exterior of red-figure cup, diameter 0.237 m, attributed to the Brygos Painter, ca. 480. *ARV* 372.29, London British Museum 1866.0805.4 (E 71). © The Trustees of the British Museum.

A relatively early example of what becomes the dominant composition is provided by a column krater attributed to the Florence Painter and probably to be dated to the decade before 450 (**7.18**). Two bearded men and a youth are shown reclining, their himatia over their shoulders, while a young woman, dressed in a chiton and with her himation over her left arm and around her waist, stands in front of their couches playing the double aulos, her cheeks puffed out. All are garlanded, one bearded man holds a phiale, the youth has a small black cup hanging from his right index finger, the other bearded man gestures with empty hand. The two bearded men look intently in the direction of the youth. A cup, two baskets, and an aulos case hang from the wall behind and two tables stand in front of the couches. There is nothing here that is not standard—we have an image of a scene that might be any symposium at which there was a girl playing the double aulos. It is almost as if the selling point of this pot is that it is absolutely standard. The drinker at the party for which wine is mixed in this krater can immediately place himself among these figures and join their party.

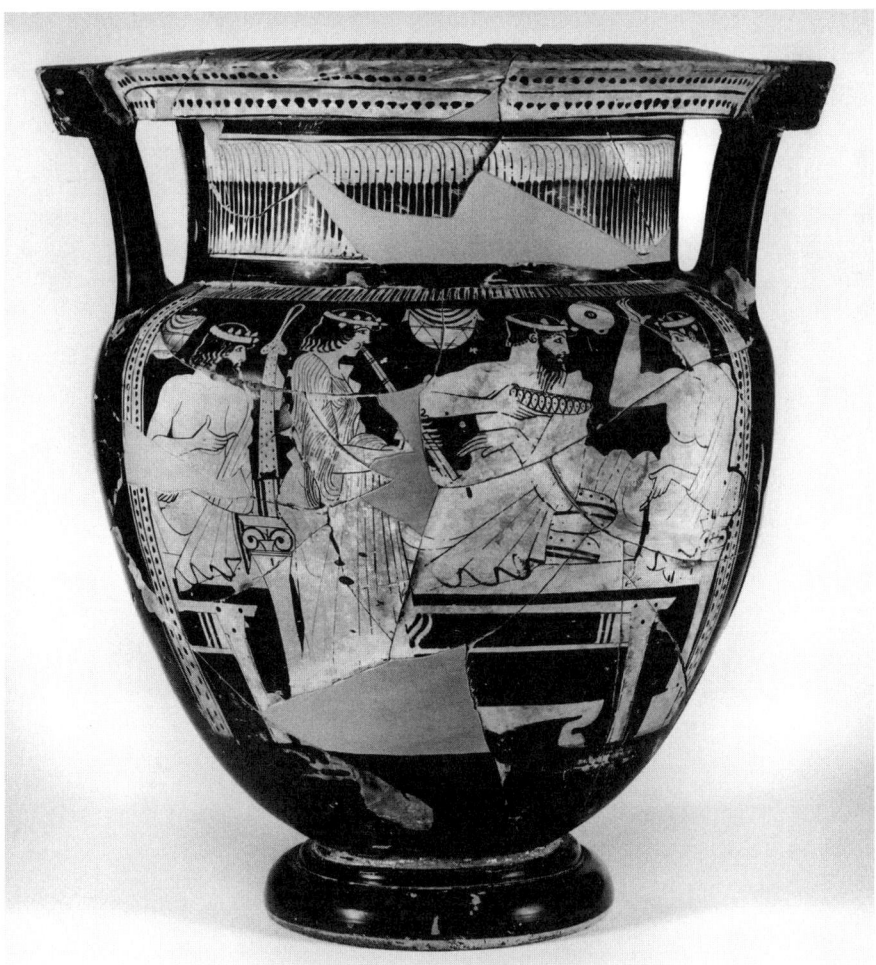

Figure 7.18. Exterior of column krater, height 0.482 m, attributed to the Florence Painter, ca. 450. *ARV* 543.36, Baltimore Walters Art Gallery 48.66. Courtesy of The Walters Art Museum.

4. Once More Pyrrhic Dancers

The link between this way of representing the symposium and the representation of women pyrrhic dancers is clear from a bell-krater dating to the middle of the fifth century attributed to the Lykaon Painter (**7.19**), which is one of two surviving pots on which a female pyrrhic dancer is explicitly placed at a symposium.[23] Here, picked out with white paint for her flesh, we see a young girl, wearing shorts and armed with shield and helmet, running past two couches on which are three youths and a bearded man. The bearded man is on the far left and is swinging a cup around a finger of his

---

[23] Poursat (1968), 599–600, no. 50; Matheson (1995), L 9. The other example is a Theban red-figure bell-krater, heavily influenced by Attic pots, Thebes 3830, see Poursat (1968), 602–3, no. 53.

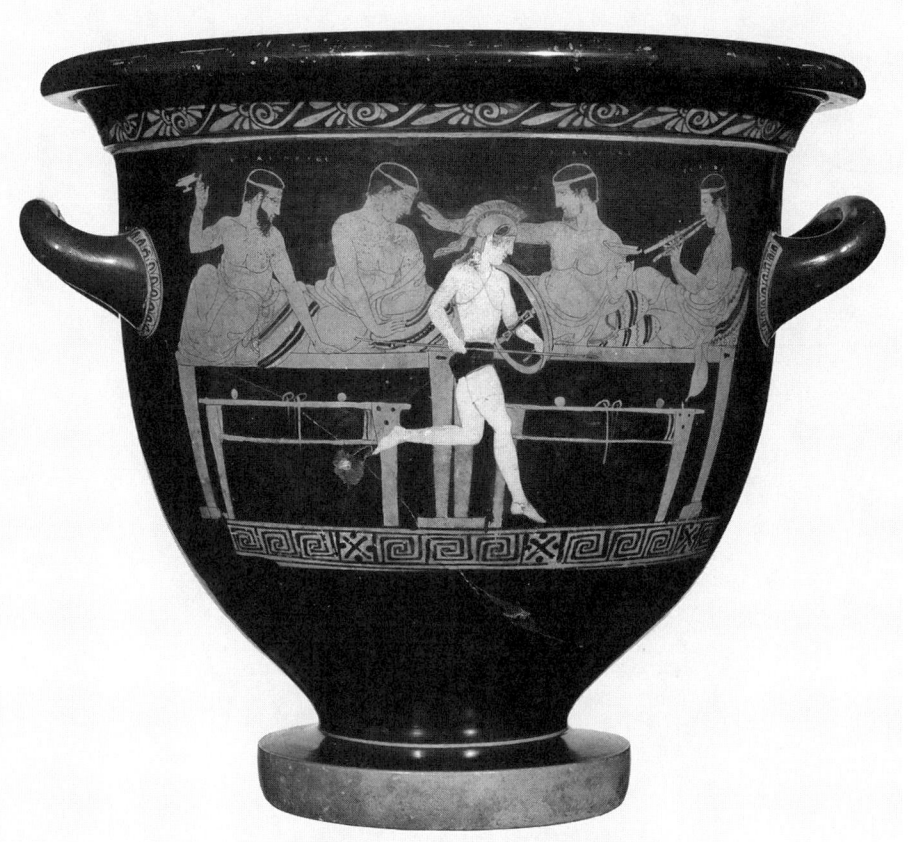

Figure 7.19. Exterior of bell-krater, height 0.39 m, attributed to the Lykaon Painter, ca. 450. *ARV* 1045.9, Naples Stg. 281. © Ministero dei Beni e delle Attività Culturali e del Turismo—Museo Archeologico Nazionale di Napoli.

right hand; we should perhaps think of him as targeting the dancer. The youth on the far right is playing the double aulos, and presumably providing the music for the girl's dancing. The two youths in the middle appear to have their eyes on each other rather than the dancer—the youth on the right holds out his right arm in a gesture that seems to be warning the youth on the left off doing something, perhaps off laying hands on the dancer, since his hand is wandering in that direction.

The wandering hand of the young man on this krater makes comparison with an earlier cup attributed to the Foundry Painter apt and enables us to revisit again the contrast between archaic and classical red-figure (**7.20–22** and plate 33). Here on one side of the exterior of a cup we see two couches on each of which recline two bearded men. On the left-hand couch one balding man holds up a cup in each hand and tips one to drink from it. Behind him a second balding man throws back his head and his right arm to sing, beating time with his left hand. The music to which he sings is provided by a naked female aulos player who stands behind him, her head and the top of her body turned in his direction while her left leg and lower body turn toward the other couch. Here a man whose himation has slipped

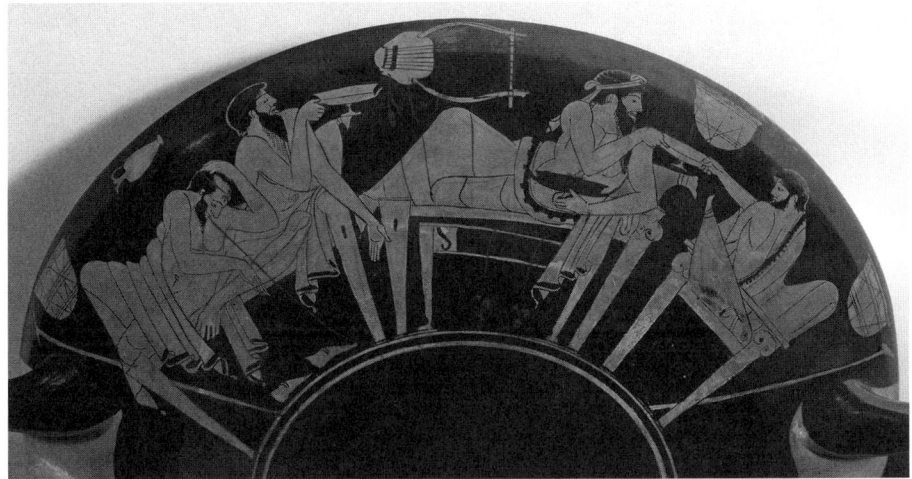

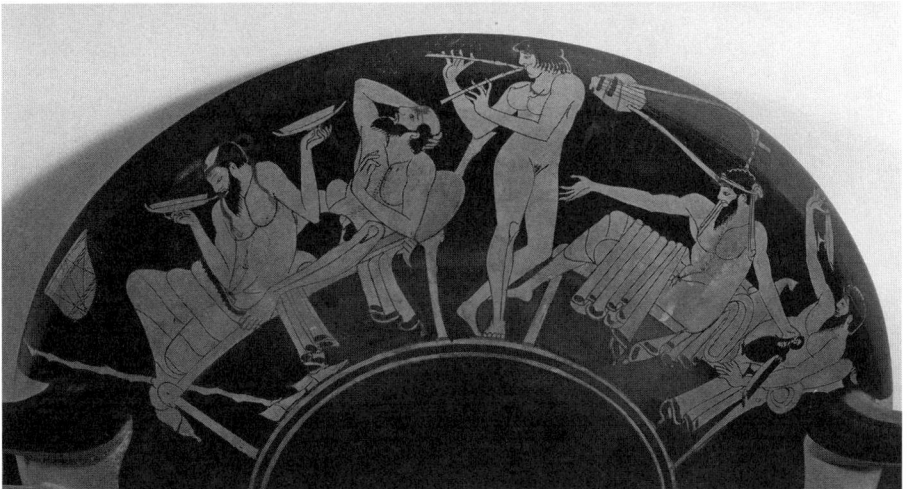

Figure 7.20–22. Exterior and interior of a red-figure cup, diameter 0.285 m, attributed to the Foundry Painter, ca. 480. *ARV* 402.12, Cambridge, Corpus Christi College (Fitzwilliam Museum Loan 103.18). © The Fitzwilliam Museum, Cambridge.

below his genitals spreads out his arms in an extravagant gesture, his left hand holding out a jug, his right feeling for the thigh of the aulos player. His companion on the couch behind him is twirling a cup in a game of kottabos, plausibly aiming at the aulos player. On the reverse we see four more bearded men reclining on three couches. On the right we see the end view of a couch on which is a symposiast who extends his right arm across his body to pass on or take a cup from the reclining figure who fills the central couch. That reclining figure holds a second cup in his left hand. On the left-hand couch the figure on the right holds out another cup toward the figure on the central couch, while behind him a balding symposiast holds his own head and turns it downward to vomit over a pair of shoes. On the interior a balding bearded man sits back on a couch playing the double pipes. Behind him hangs a barbitos, and in front a youth, with a spear but no elements of armor, performs a dance.

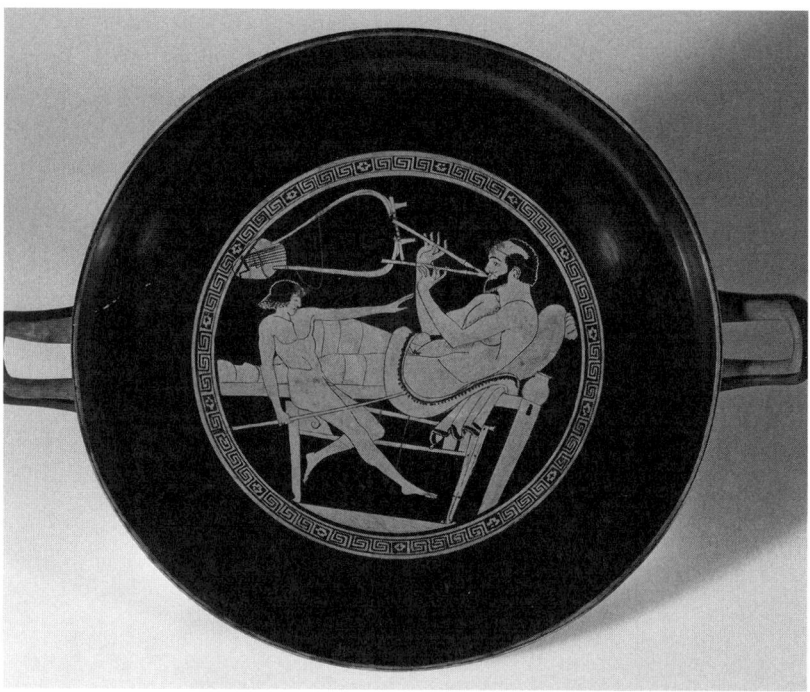

The scenes on this pot and the scene on the krater attributed to the Lykaon Painter share aulos music, armed dancing, playing kottabos, at least partial female nudity, and hints of groping. Yet the scenes have a quite different mood. To the gentle, and indeed rather disengaged, spectating of the krater the cup opposes vigorous action. The dancing here is more vigorous, the hand gestures of the symposiasts more demonstrative, the whole symposium much busier, and the signs of excess—whether vomiting or full-frontal female nudity—very much more emphatic. Everyone on the Foundry Painter's cup is performing, and the back view of one of the symposiasts signals to viewers that this is a party from which they are excluded and of which they can only be voyeurs. Rather than slotting oneself into the symposium, as the classic red-figure symposium scenes from later in the fifth century encourage one to do, the drinker who found himself in the company where this cup was used would be led to concentrate rather on discussing the excessive nature of the sympotic behavior depicted than on joining their evidently rather disparate discourse.

Although red-figure pots, which regularly show women dancing, rarely place their dancing women explicitly at the symposium, music and dancing went together, and there is no doubt that dancing might feature large on the sympotic agenda. Xenophon's *Symposium*, at which a whole sequence of dances is performed, provides good evidence for the potential importance of the dance as a focus for the drinking party and for the conversations that go on there.[24] Although only two pots place the woman pyrrhic

[24] Xenophon *Symposium* 2, 9.2–7; Wohl (2004); Hobden (2013), 213–28.

dancer at the symposium, the symposium is in fact the most plausible context for real-life performance of the pyrrhic dance by women. Most other scenes of women pyrrhic dancers show the dancer alone or in purely female company, where she contributes to the range of roles that women may have (cf. 6.12) and to the exploration of the variety of female erotic attractions.[25] Like the young woman, normally dressed in a chiton, playing the double aulos, who is so frequent in these scenes, or like the (often naked) youth serving wine, the young woman dancing the pyrrhic offers a more or less familiar figure from the sympotic landscape and puts before the viewer, as before the painted symposiasts, one of the frequent topics of sympotic discussion about physical beauty and sexual desire. The drinkers at a symposium where this krater is used find themselves drawn into a discourse not about the scene on this pot but about their own experience of the beauty and disarming power of dancing women.

[25] Ceccarelli (1998), 60–67.

8 ❧ The Changing City of Satyrs

There never were any satyrs. There were hardly even any stories about satyrs.¹ Yet satyrs uniquely populated a whole dramatic genre, the satyr play, and made their way onto thousands more Athenian pots than any other mythical figure. Their great advantage was that they were, as Hesiod already calls them, "of no account" (οὐτιδανοί, Hesiod *Catalogue of Women* fig. 123.2). With satyrs, what you see is what you get—although they bring expectations arising from the contexts in which they have previously been viewed and the actions they have previously been seen to perform, they carry no particular past history and no known future actions. In many respects just like men, they are nevertheless normally instantly recognizable as not men. Regular companions of Dionysos, they nevertheless had no counterpart in Dionysiac cult. Constant (sparring) partners of maenads, they contrast with maenads in having no real-life equivalents.² They appear anywhere, but belong precisely nowhere.

Satyrs constitute a test case for the thesis argued in this book. Since there were no real-life satyrs, except on the dramatic stage, there were no real-life activities of satyrs, except the activities of satyrs on stage, to be represented by painters, and so images of satyrs will never reflect changes in what satyrs did. Although satyrs' nonexistence does not stop them being imagined to populate a world parallel to or linked to the real world, their world will always be an imagined world, where the features represented appear because they are significant for the representation, rather than because they are the features of that world in reality. Images of satyrs never

---

¹ For what seems to me to be an unsuccessful attempt to argue for distinct bodies of myth about satyrs, see Hedreen (1992). Satyr plays are precisely not stories about satyrs any more than comedies or tragedies are stories about human actors, for satyr plays are stories in which episodes from known myths are played out in a world inhabited by satyrs.

² It is a consequence of this, but nevertheless a curiosity, that past studies more often limit themselves to satyrs or to maenads than study them together; cf. Bron (1987), Moraw (1998), Villanueva-Puig (2009), Lissarrague (2013). I have persisted in calling the women who appear with satyrs *maenads*, and not distinguishing between companions who operate in the mythical world from companions who operate in the ritual world, since painters themselves enjoy the fact that they do not have to distinguish these two ontological realms—as is nicely seen when the Villa Giulia Painter labels a female figure with a thyrsos who stands in front of a seated Hermes who holds the infant Dionysos *mainas*. For the contrary view, Hedreen (1994) and Carpenter (1997), 57–58. For Hedreen's denial of maenadic worship in classical Athens, see Osborne (1997a). For the absence of a division between the time of myth and the time of history, see Osborne (2002), 499. See further below.

show what the world is like, but they do show what the painters and purchasers of pots fantasized that a world unconstrained by social conventions might be like. Far more than images that are constrained by their link to reality, images of satyrs show the world of the imagination. Whereas we may sometimes be tempted by pictures of humans to believe that we are seeing pictures of the world as it is, and artists constantly play with that temptation, images of satyrs can never be thought to show the world as it is and must always be taken as a commentary on how the world is. The changing nature of that commentary wonderfully reveals the changing interests and attitudes of artists and their customers.

Taken as a whole, there is hardly any sort of activity that men performed in the Greek city that satyrs do not perform. Famous for their sexual activity (5.11) and their drinking, particularly in the revel but also at the symposium, satyrs play all sorts of musical instruments, dance, fight, engage in all sorts of religious—and irreligious—behavior, labor as servants and in craft activity, and act. In terms of the chapters of this book, only in the chapter on athletics would they have had virtually no place. But they were not equally imagined doing all of these things at every period. For the city of satyrs too undergoes a transformation.[3]

1. Satyrs and Dionysos

Satyrs make their first appearance in Greek art in the entourage of Dionysos in one of the friezes on the Athenian black-figure "François vase."[4] Labeled *silenoi* and already displaying their sexual excitement, as well as a horse's ears, tail, and legs, they take part in the scene of Hephaistos returning to Olympus, a scene in which they will be Dionysos's and Hephaistos's constant companions. The scene of Hephaistos's return becomes very popular in black-figure in the second half of the sixth century but is initially slow to catch on in red-figure, and when it returns to popularity in the early fifth century, the scenes show rather more interest in Hephaistos himself.[5] Hephaistos's return continues to be as popular on pots from the middle and second half of the fifth century as it was in those from the first half, and it provides a good introduction to how the world of the satyr becomes transformed.

Around 480 the same painter, who can be identified as Douris, painted two very similar scenes of the return of Hephaistos on two cups, both of which ended up at Vulci and both of which are now in the Cabinet de Médailles in Paris. They show the relatively novel iconography of Hephaistos on foot, rather than on a donkey, and in both he is being assisted by Dionysos, who clasps him by the wrist. In one case the pair of bearded gods

---

[3] The city of satyrs has been the subject of extensive commentary over many years by Lissarrague, brought together in Lissarrague (2013), the annexes of which offer a representative list of the range of activities in which satyrs are shown to be engaged.
[4] Florence, Museo Archeologico Nazionale 4209; Shapiro, Iozzo, and Lezzi-Hafter (2013).
[5] See Hermary, *LIMC* IV 653–54.

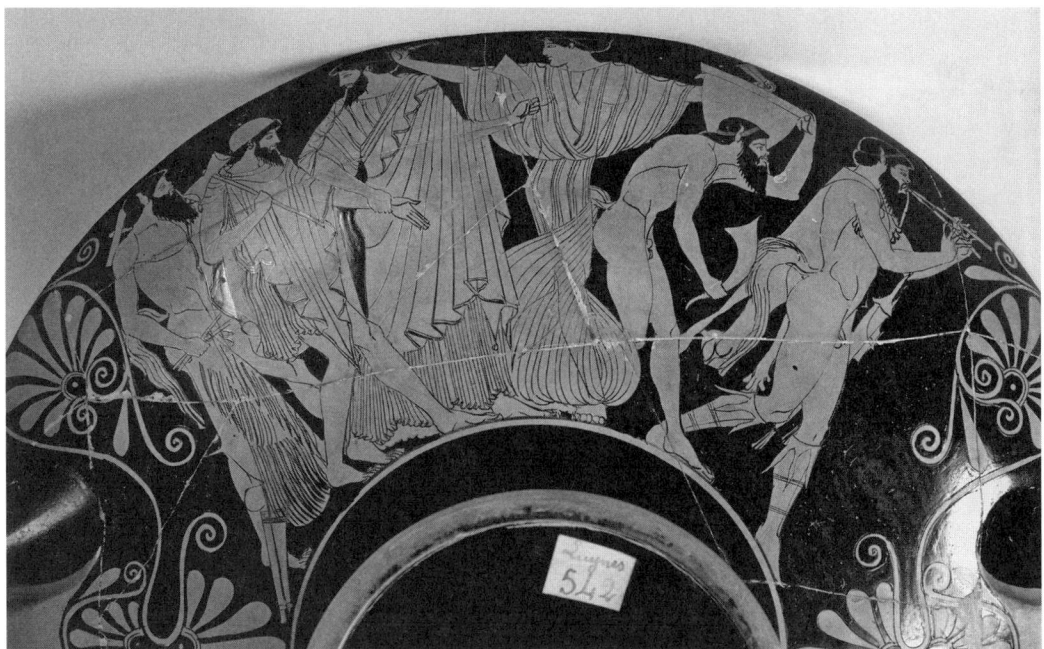

Figure 8.1. Exterior of a red-figure cup, diameter 0.317 m, attributed to Douris, from Vulci, ca. 480. *ARV* 438.133, Paris, Cabinet de Médailles 542. © Bibliothèque nationale de France.

is accompanied by four satyrs, in the other, shown here (**8.1**), by three satyrs and a maenad.[6] The leading satyr wears Thracian boots and a feline skin as a cloak, and plays the double aulos (the case for the pipes hangs from one arm). Behind him a satyr is bent under the weight of a krater, which he carries on his shoulder, and in his right hand he has a rhyton. Separating him from the pair of gods is a maenad, shown twirling around in a dance and looking back at the gods. The rear of the party is brought up by another satyr who carries Hephaistos's bag of tools.

Perhaps forty or fifty years later, a pelike attributed to the Kleophon Painter shows a similarly pedestrian Hephaistos, showing his blacksmith's trade by carrying both hammer and tongs containing a glowing coal, supported by a satyr (**8.2**). In front of this pair is Dionysos, with thyrsus and kantharos, who looks back at the pair, and in front of Dionysos a satyr and maenad dancing, with the maenad playing the tambourine, and the satyr, who again has a feline-skin cloak, making eyes at her.

In many ways similar, these two scenes nevertheless differ significantly in what they emphasize. On Douris's cup, the means by which Hephaistos was lured back to Olympus to release Hera is emphasized: the krater and the rhyton give no doubt at all of the role that intoxication plays in this. What is more, the whole iconography resembles that of a revel in which an aulos player leads a drunken party through the streets. The Kleophon Painter's pelike removes the emphasis from drunkenness, and Hephaistos becomes caught up instead in Dionysiac worship. His own downcast

[6] *ARV* 438.133 and 134, Paris, Cabinet de Médailles 542, 539.

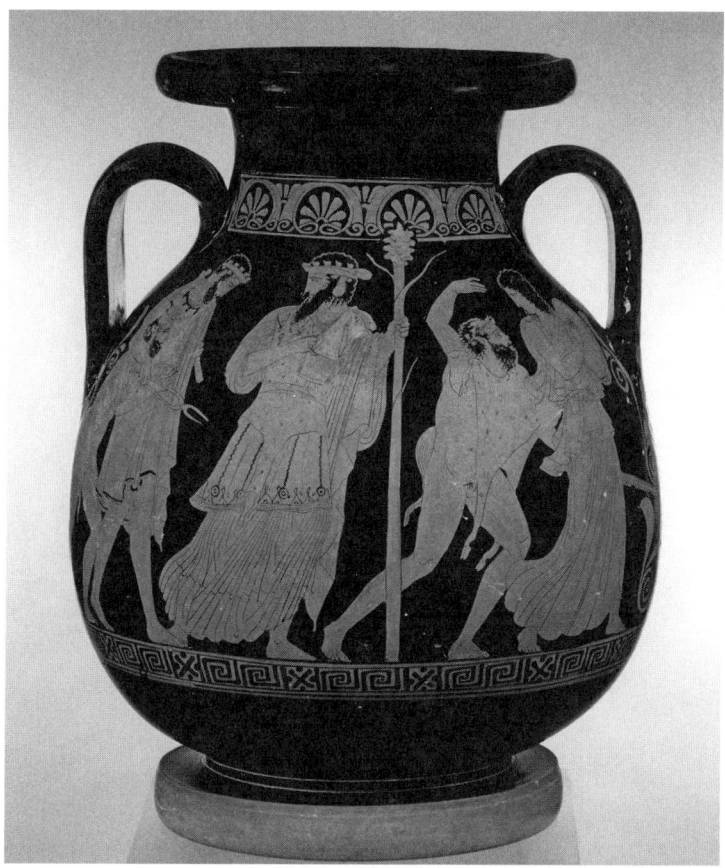

Figure 8.2. Exterior of a red-figure pelike, height 0.46 m, attributed to the Kleophon Painter, from Gela, ca. 440. *ARV* 1145.36, Munich, Staatliche Antikensammlungen 2361 (J.776). © Staatliche Antikensammlungen und Glyptothek München. Photograph by Renate Kühling.

glance encourages the viewer to speculate on what Hephaistos is thinking, just as the relationship between the dancing maenad and satyr encourages questions about the relationship between the other figures on the pot. The energy manifests in many earlier scenes, and at least latent in Douris's cup, is here dissipated as we move from the world of drunken parties and pranks to the world of divine worship.

Satyrs needed no mythical excuse to accompany Dionysos, and they are frequently shown with the god, providing him with wine or music. Scenes of a satyr with Dionysos are very much more common in archaic and early classic red-figure pots than later, and the same is true, if in a less marked way, of scenes with several satyrs and maenads and Dionysos. Once more, the ways in which the treatment changes are more remarkable than the change in frequency.

Comparison between a cup attributed to the Brygos Painter (of around 480) and a bell-krater attributed to the Lykaon Painter (around 440) shows up well the transformation that has occurred. The cup (**8.3–4** and plate 34), now in the Cabinet des Médailles, has a scene on its tondo of Dionysos, his head thrown back singing, accompanying himself on the barbitos while two small satyrs dance around him, playing the castanets; one of them brandishes a branch of a vine laden with grapes and the other

THE CHANGING CITY OF SATYRS   191

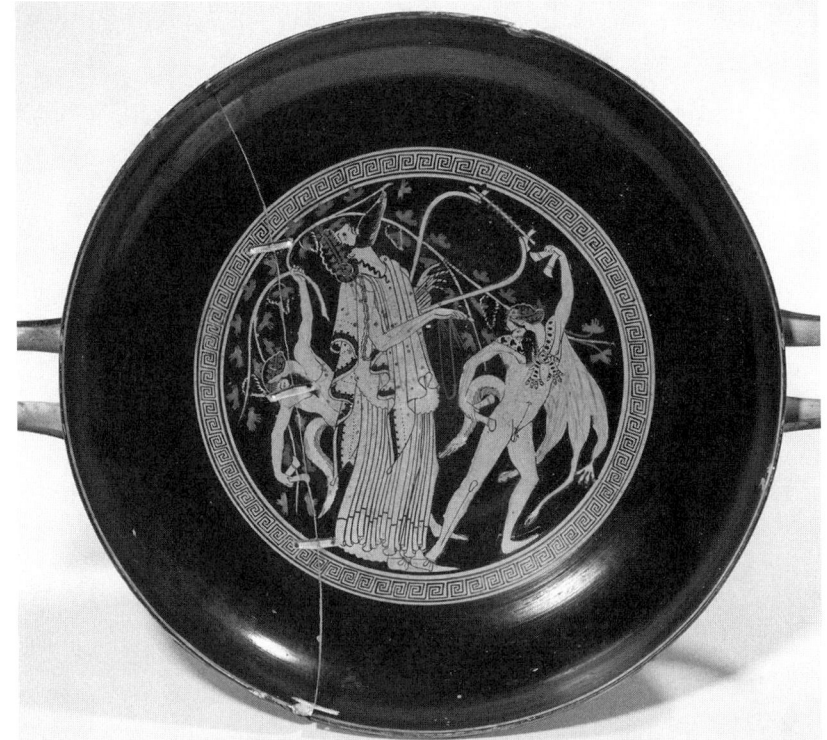

Figure 8.3–4. Interior and exterior of a red-figure cup, diameter 0.298 m, attributed to the Brygos Painter, ca. 480. *ARV* 371.14, Paris, Cabinet de Médailles 576. © Bibliothèque nationale de France.

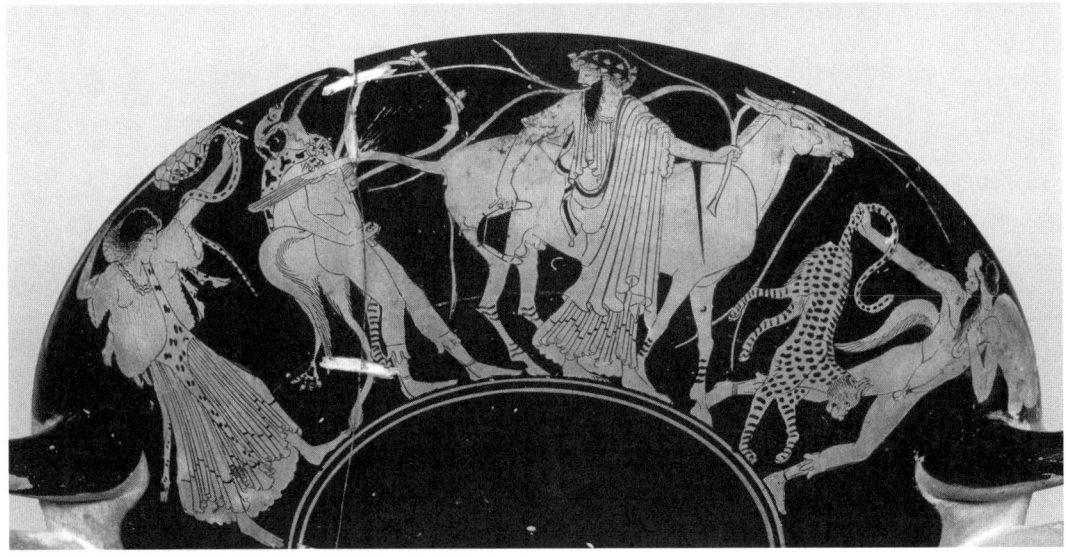

wears a feline-skin cloak, knotted around his neck. On the outside of the cup, it is the turn of a satyr to sing and play the barbitos. On one side Dionysos stands next to him in front of a donkey with kantharos and branch, and the pair are flanked by a maenad dancing with snake and thrysos and a satyr brandishing a spotted leopard by the tail. On the other side, the barbitos player is matched by another satyr playing the double aulos; they are separated by a maenad, who is amorously approached by a satyr, and

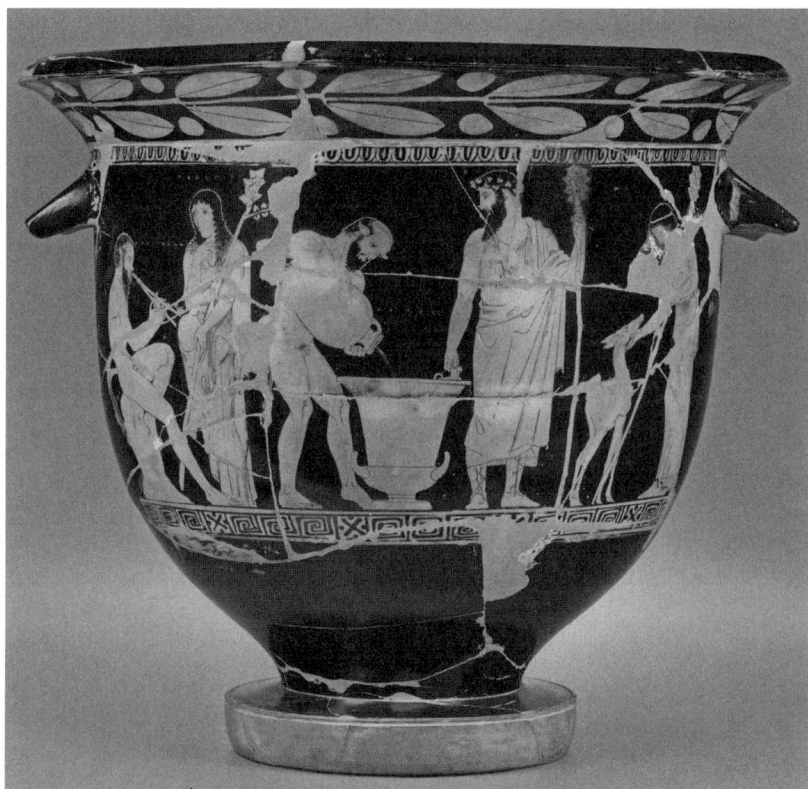

Figure 8.5. Exterior of red-figure bell-krater, height 0.416 m, attributed to the Lykaon Painter, ca. 440, reverse of 8.15. *ARV* 1045.6, Warsaw, National Museum 14235.

further maenads frame the scene, arms extended, dancing. All the maenads wear both chitons and feline skins, and one of the barbitos-playing satyrs also wears a feline skin. This is a scene of riotous Dionysiac excess, full of music, dancing, and the breaking down of inhibitions, whether with regard to sexual relations or with regard to relating to the animal world.[7]

The bell-krater attributed to the Lykaon Painter (**8.5**) also combines music, wine, and cult activity, but in a quite different way.[8] That is clearest of all from the maenad who stands on the far right of the scene, thyrsus in hand. She bends slightly to stroke a doe. Next comes Dionysos, his body presented frontally as he stands with thyrsus in one hand, dipping his kantharos down inside the krater next to him. He looks to his right at a satyr who pours from an amphora into the krater. Behind the satyr, a maenad with thyrsus gazes at a second satyr, who sits on a rock playing the pipes.

---

[7] Cf. on maenads, Moraw (1998), 253: "Die frührotfigurigen Vasenmaler entwickeln eine Reihe von Chiffren für die Darstellung mänadischer Ekstase, die hier ihren ersten Höhepunkt erreicht." Moraw seeks a historical explanation of the development: (255) "Die Intensität, der Grad, den die Monströsität der Mänade in diesen Darstellungen erreicht, kann wohl als Indikator gelten für die politischen und mentalen Erschütterungen der Zeit, den Ängsten, die in jener wandelnden Welt zwangsläufig auftraten."

[8] The satyrs and maenads on this pot are all named (itself a feature of later fifth-century maenad and satyr scenes); the satyrs are Mimas and Oinopion, the maenads Polynika and Mainas. See further Lissarrague (2013), 51–52.

By contrast to the exotic activity on the Brygos Painter's cup, this is a scene where all the activity is completely ordinary—an impression further reinforced by the scene on the other side, which I discuss below (8.15). The male figures here happen to be satyrs, and the women have the thyrsi of maenads, but the casual attitudes in which they sit and stand, and the normality of what they do, all make this as if Dionysos and his entourage are playing at being Athenians.[9] The satyrs and maenads whom the Brygos Painter showed to be quite other have here been normalized.

2. Satyrs and Maenads

Even more pots show maenads and satyrs together than show maenads and satyrs with Dionysos. Indeed, many cups are entirely decorated with various combinations of maenad and satyr, and in all of them issues of sexual relations are not far away. Maenads and satyrs interact in a variety of ways, sometimes dancing together happily, sometimes in some sort of conflict or potential conflict, where the maenad strikes the satyr with her thyrsus or the satyr pursues or grasps or otherwise accosts the maenad. Whereas black-figure scenes had almost always shown maenads who welcomed or at least tolerated the approaches made by satyrs, red-figure scenes, from at least the start of the fifth century onward, regularly raise the question of whether or not the maenad desires the attention directed to her.[10]

The limit case, in terms of the issue of whether maenads encourage or resist sexual approaches from satyrs, comes with the series of images of a satyr approaching a sleeping maenad with sexual intent. Although the earliest such image is on a black-figure amphora by the Amasis Painter, all other known versions of the scene date to the period of red-figure (though two are on black-figure lekythoi), but they spread from the end of the sixth to the beginning of the fourth century. Some painters seem to have been particularly attracted to the scene (more than one such scene is attributed to the Panaitios Painter, to the Pistoxenos Painter, and to the Mannheim Painter), but there is no obvious chronological pattern to the scene's popularity during the fifth century.[11] What is clear, however, is that the focus of interest in the scene changes.

A cup, reckoned to be among the early works of Makron, shows on its exterior two scenes that seem to be intended to be viewed as sequential (**8.6–7**).[12] On one side a maenad sleeps resting on a rock in front of a tree. Her right arm is thrown back beside her head in a posture that frequently

---

[9] So Moraw (1998), 258, writes of the red-figure images produced between 470 and 430: "Die Mänade erscheint auf dem größten Teil dieser Vasenbilder als das Idealbild einer bürgerlichen Athenerin."

[10] See Lissarrague (2013), 86–87, with reference to work by A. Lindblom, which nuances McNally (1978), on which see also Moraw (1998), 269.

[11] I have discussed these scenes in Osborne (1996a). The classic list of these scenes is by Beazley in Caskey and Beazley (1954), 96–98.

[12] Kunisch (1997), no. 2.

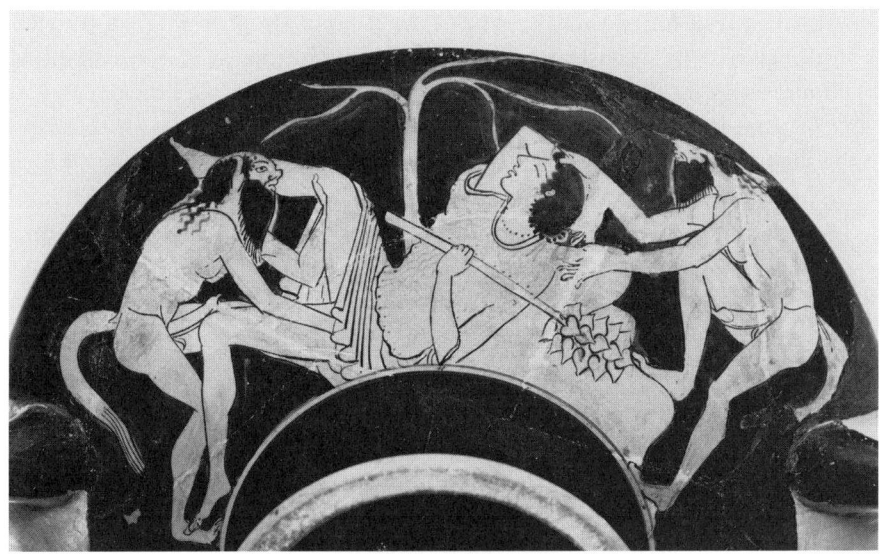

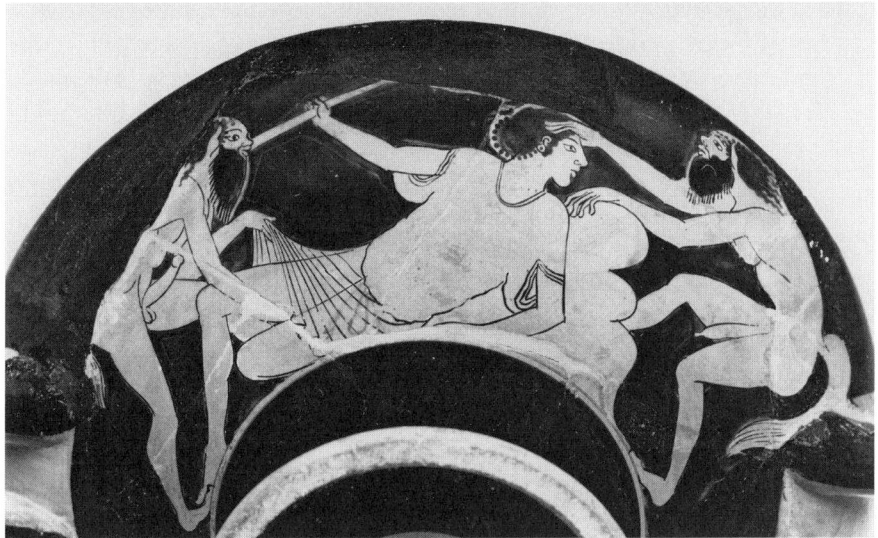

Figure 8.6–7. Exterior of red-figure cup, diameter 0.218 m, attributed to Makron, ca. 490. *ARV* 461.36, Boston Museum of Fine Arts 01.8072. Photograph © 2017 Museum of Fine Arts, Boston.

indicates sleep, and her left hand holds a thyrsus. A halfway sexually excited satyr, approaching from behind her, rests one foot and one hand on the rock and the other hand on her right arm and head. A second sexually excited satyr approaches from her feet, pushing her right leg aside with his left hand and with his right pushing up her chiton to the top of her thighs, while watching carefully to see whether she remains asleep. On the other side, we see a maenad lying, resting on a rock, but awake. She has turned her body toward the viewer and her head toward the satyr who approaches from behind and who still has one hand on her head. She brandishes the thyrsus in her right hand. The satyr at her feet holds the hem of her chiton with his left hand and has his right hand between her thighs, but the chiton is now pulled lower. Despite the apparent disappearance of the tree from the scene, it is hard not to read this as a narrative of a rape attempt that the maenad has foiled by waking up.[13] But it is not simply the satyrs who are foiled here, any viewer who enjoys the thought that the satyr is about to have sex with the sleeping maenad finds desire frustrated.

An oinochoe also in Boston, dating to around 420, shows nicely how the scene of a sleeping maenad approached by a satyr changes (**8.8**).[14] Once more, we have a sleeping maenad between two satyrs. The maenad is now naked and lies on a pillow, a long thyrsus in her left hand, while her right hand rests on her right thigh. The two satyrs are both in very animated postures, gesticulating in a dumb show that seems to carry on a debate as to whether or not this is an opportunity that should be taken. The satyr on the left shows partial sexual excitement, the satyr on the right none. Neither comes close to touching the maenad.[15] Rather than tempt the viewer to wonder exactly what sexual act the satyr will perform, or encourage the viewer to imagine himself running his hands along the thighs of the maenad, this pot foregrounds the ethical issue of whether or not sleeping maenads—indeed effectively whether naked young women—should be sexually exploited. We are offered here a female body that exposes to view far more erotic attractions than were on display in Makron's cup, where the line of the maenad's breasts is not indicated. But the hesitation of the satyrs raises the question of whether the female body, however beautiful, should be treated as merely a sex object—even the possibility that this body is too beautiful to disturb in any way. Rather than the pornographic attractions of vicariously raping a particular maenad, what this jug offers is a prompt to consider the pleasures that come from epiphany, from the vision and contemplation of the form of the female body.[16]

The same fundamental change from the presentation of a particular encounter between satyr and maenad to the use of the maenad and satyr to raise questions about male and female behavior in general can be seen across maenad and satyr scenes, even those of the most simple and basic type. An early red-figure cup attributed to the Chelis Painter shows on one side an encounter between a satyr and two maenads (**8.9**).[17] A sexually excited satyr leans forward and grasps hold of the hem of the chiton of a maenad. The maenad, who has a snake in her right hand, turns around and brandishes a thyrsus. From the right enters a second woman, identified as a maenad by her feline-skin cloak, gesturing to indicate that she has spotted what is happening and with a branch ready in her left hand.

---

[13] For a similarly constructed scene on a mid-fifth-century pot, see *ARV* 865.1 (Painter of Athens 1237), Oxford, Ashmolean 1924.2, where on one side a maenad is seated and sits stiffly still while satyrs dance around displaying their sexual excitement; on the other the maenad has sprung to her feet and waves a branch and pipes in the direction of satyrs who appear rather taken aback.

[14] Compare the oinochoe by the Eretria Painter (*ARV* 1258.1) where the naked maenad is named "Tragoidia" and the satyr dancing in front of her "Kissos" ("Ivy").

[15] Moraw (1998), 259, sees a more cooperative relationship between satyrs and maenads as a consequence of changes in the world of cult: "ist diese nauartige Kooperation von Mänaden und Satyrn auf den Vasenbildern wahrscheinlich eine Reaktion auf die Einführung neuer, sowohl Frauen also auch Männern offenstehender, dionysischer Kultvereine in Athen."

[16] For a modern painting playing with a similar trope, see Osborne (2007), 191–94.

[17] *ARV* 112.1, Munich 2589.

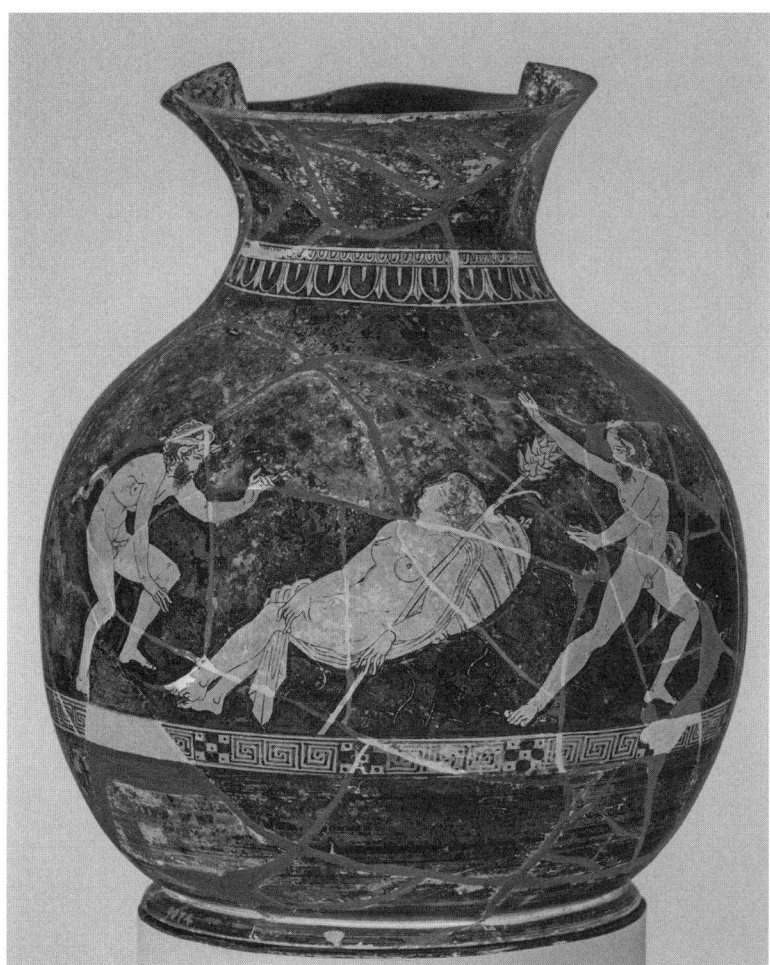

Figure 8.8. Red-figure oinochoe, height 0.216 m, unattributed, from Athens, ca. 420. Boston Museum of Fine Arts 01.8085. Photograph © 2017 Museum of Fine Arts, Boston.

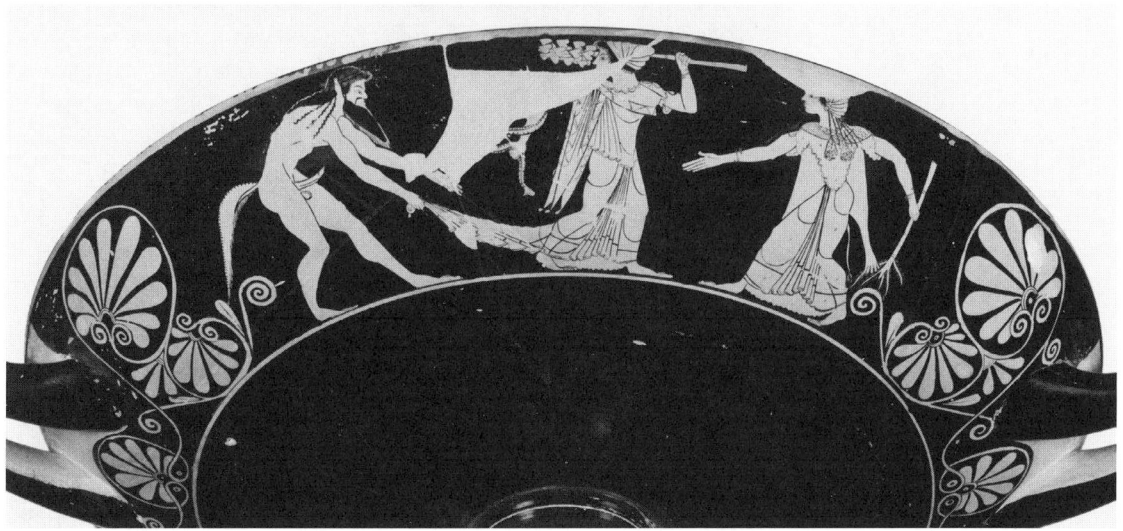

Figure 8.9. Exterior of red-figure cup, diameter 0.366 m, attributed to the Chelis Painter, from Vulci, ca. 500. *ARV* 112.1, Munich Staatliche Antikensammlungen 2589. © Staatliche Antikensammlungen und Glyptothek München. Photograph by Renate Kühling.

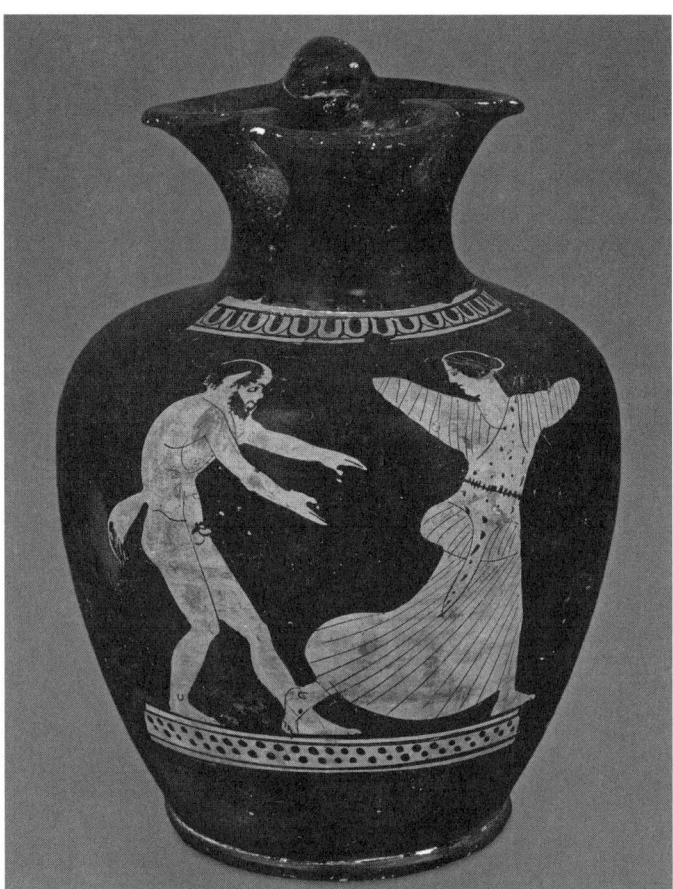

Figure 8.10. Red-figure oinochoe, height 0.180 m, attributed to the Clephan Painter, ca. 440. *ARV* 1215.1, Oxford AN1918.63. Image © Ashmolean Museum, University of Oxford.

Perhaps around 440 an artist known, after the former owner of this pot, as the Clephan Painter painted on an oinochoe a satyr pursuing a maenad (**8.10**). The satyr, who is not sexually excited, stares intently at the maenad while stretching out his arms toward her. She, dressed in chiton and animal pelt, is moving away in a large stride but turns back toward him, stretching out her arms. How are we to read this interaction? Are the satyr's arms extended ready for him to make one last plunge to grasp the maenad? His weight on his back foot does not suggest that. Or is he rather holding out his hands to offer to take her waist in his grasp, not as a threat but as a promise of intimacy? And is hers the backward glance of the desperate runner, afraid that they have been caught up with, or is it the glance of second thoughts, wondering whether flight is the appropriate action in this case?

Where the Chelis Painter's cup offers us a brief narrative, a glimpse of an amusing incident in which, yet again, a satyr gets his comeuppance for his impertinent action, the Clephan Painter's jug raises a question. How exactly should we construe the appropriate relations between satyrs and maenads? Do satyrs always only want sex, or might they be offering an affective bond marked by the full range of intimacies?

3. Satyrs and Men

The changes in satyr iconography are most obvious when we consider not satyrs' relations with Dionysos or with maenads, but their relations with ordinary men. Satyrs' relations with ordinary men come not from explicit encounters but from satyrs playing the part of men—as hoplite or more often peltast, as musician playing the barbitos or pipes, as hunter, as slave fetching and carrying, as craftsman, in relation to animals (donkeys, goats) as well as in relation to wine and sex. Two things particularly signal change: the arrival of satyr children and the acquisition of the himation.[18] The former normalizes the satyr by suggesting that this creature too has a domestic life. The latter turns all questions about the satyr's behavior into questions about human behavior. Whereas early red-figure had used the satyr to parade the limits of what is acceptable in human societies, classic red-figure uses the clothed satyr to ask whether there might not be a satyr under every ordinary man going about his ordinary daily business.

The range of activity that satyrs engage with from the middle of the fifth century onward becomes much more limited. We no longer find satyrs as peltasts or hoplites or hunters, we hardly find the satyr as solo aulos player. After the early classic period satyrs disappear from the symposium. None of this is, of course surprising—the symposium scenes painted in the second half of the fifth century do not explore the limits of sympotic behavior, and hoplites and peltasts in general disappear from the iconography. Satyrs continue to be found as *komasts*, though even here this is predominantly on the cups of a single painter, the Eretria Painter, and the changed *komos* gives us a glimpse of how the way in which satyrs relate to men has changed.

A cup attributed to Epiktetos (circa 500), though fragmented, gives an impression of how satyrs behave when reveling on early red-figure cups. On one side of a cup, seven satyrs are shown dancing and enjoying themselves with garlanded amphoras, which they have now evidently emptied (**8.11**). They roll about with them, tip them up to see whether there is anything left inside, and use the neck of the amphora as a sex aid. Most of the satyrs are sexually excited, but not all, emphasizing that even in satyrs this is not a fixed state and arousal is required. Both the numbers of amphoras that have been emptied—five are visible—and the use to which the amphoras are put, along with the display of sexual excitement, place the satyrs' behavior beyond the bounds of human revelry.

The *komos* scenes from two generations later attributed to the Eretria Painter are rather different. It is not that the Eretria Painter's satyrs lack energy or action. A cup, now in the Louvre, shows four satyrs on each side, all of them striking vivid poses, gesturing with their hands, casting piercing glances at one another, and giving a strong impression of lively interaction (**8.12–13**). But although two of the satyrs hold drinking horns, none of

---

[18] Cf. Lissarrague (2013), 63, for the former, 204 for the latter; Moraw (1998), 258, for both. The question of whether there could be a female satyr is neatly answered by the tondo of an early fourth-century cup attributed to the Q Painter, *ARV* 1519.13; see Osborne (1991), 259.

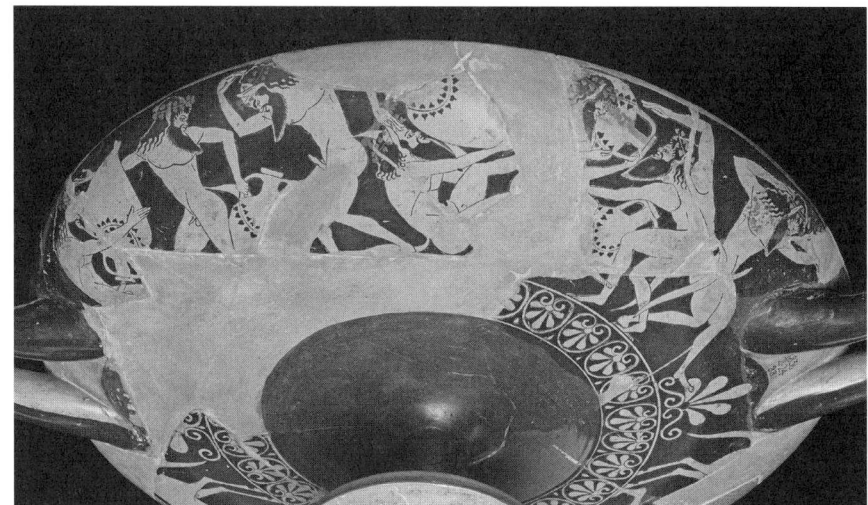

Figure 8.11. Red-figure cup, diameter 0.33 m, attributed to Epiktetos, from Vulci, ca. 500. *ARV* 74.38, London British Museum 1836,0224.88 (E 35). © The Trustees of the British Museum.

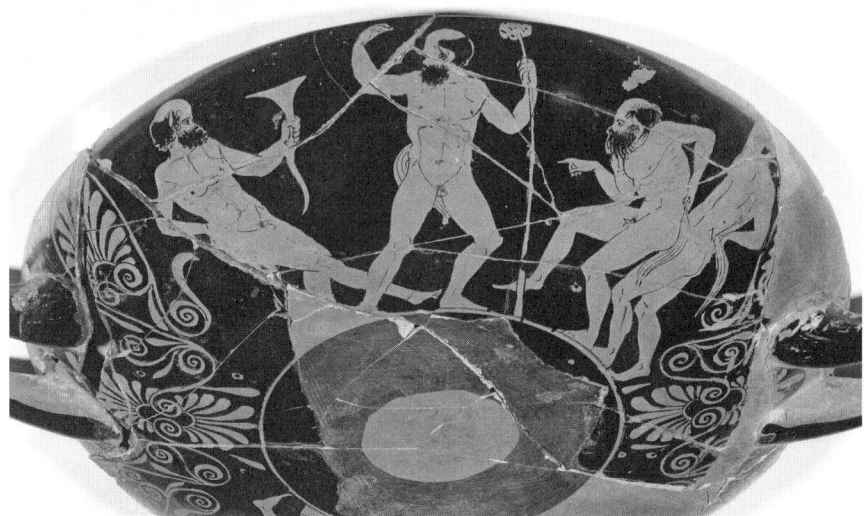

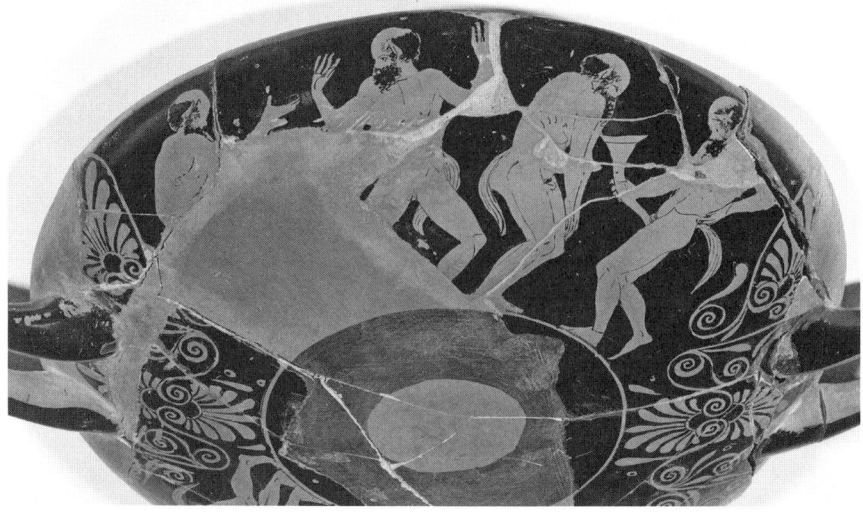

Figure 8.12–13. Red-figure cup, diameter 0.248 m, attributed to the Eretria Painter, ca. 430. *ARV* 1253.69, Paris, Louvre G450. Photo © RMN-Grand Palais (musée du Louvre)/ Patrick Lebaube.

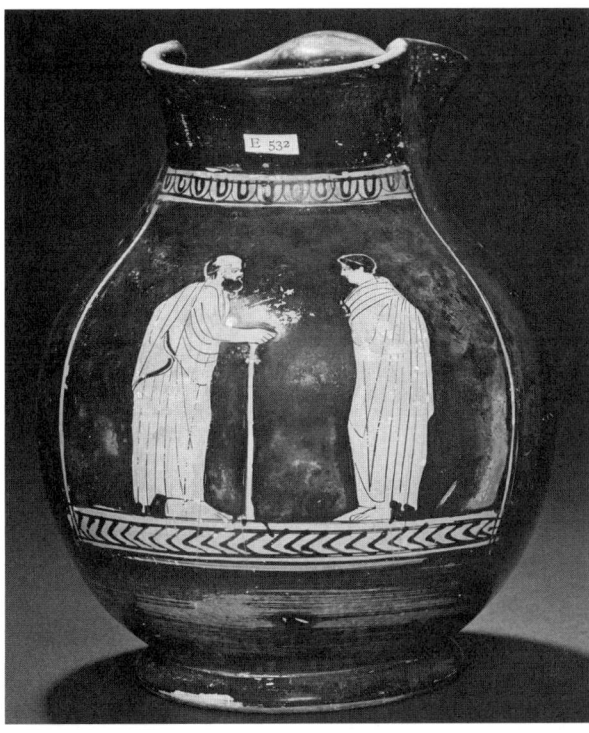

Figure 8.14. Red-figure oinochoe, height 0.229 m, unattributed, ca. 430. London, British Museum 1882,0225.1 (E 532). © The Trustees of the British Museum.

the normal equipment of the symposium is on display here—no cups, no skyphoi, no kraters, no amphoras. These satyrs may be lively, but there is no sense that they are out of control. And in one respect they are very much under control, for none of them is sexually excited. It is indeed not easy to know whether one should refer to this scene as a *komos* at all, since one of the satyrs carries a thyrsus, suggesting a religious occasion.[19] But in any case, the important feature of these scenes is that they encourage the viewer not so much to gaze on the action aghast but to see in these maneuvers, maneuvers with which he himself is familiar.

A scene on a jug, painted perhaps circa 430, provides a typical example of the way in which the satyr wearing the himation is used to produce just that sense of familiarity (**8.14**). On the left is a balding figure, clad in a himation, his hand resting on a stick. Only his ears, and perhaps the way in which his himation hangs behind him, mark him out as a satyr. On the right, facing him, is a young man, completely wrapped up in his himation. The two stare intently at each other. The viewer is left to construct whatever relationship occurs to him/her for this pair. Does this satyr have responsibility for this young man? Or is he courting him? or instructing him? What is at issue is how young men grow up; what relationship to wine and women will this young man acquire? Will this young man turn out to be a satyr himself?

[19] Similar questions arise with "komos" scenes on some of the Eretria Painter's rhyta, where presence of women who can be identified as maenads by their holding thyrsi or branches is combined with satyrs dancing around or with pointed amphoras: *ARV* 1251.36, 1251.37.

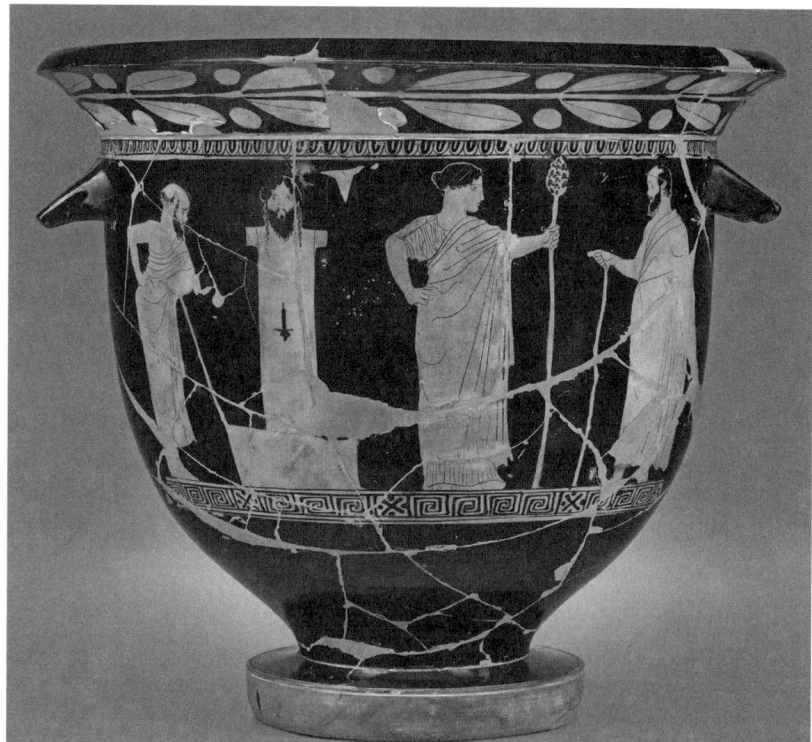

Figure 8.15. Exterior of red-figure bell-krater, height 0.416 m, attributed to the Lykaon Painter, ca. 440 (reverse of 8.5). *ARV* 1045.6, Warsaw, National Museum 14235.

The reverse side of the bell-krater ascribed to the Lykaon Painter, which I discussed earlier (8.5), uses the satyr to raise questions about how ordinary men react in cult situations that might be regarded as sexually provocative (**8.15**). Flanking the scene, looking inward, are two satyrs dressed in himatia. The satyr on the left leans on his stick and stares intently at a herm, which is shown frontally, its erect phallus picked out in black. The satyr on the right stands up straight, with his left hand resting on a stick in a stately manner. He stares at a maenad, who stands straight, dressed in chiton and himation and holding a vertical thyrsus, and returns his stare. The juxtaposition between the satyrs, here playing at being ordinary male residents of the city, and, on the one hand, a god who displays his sexual excitement as one might have expected the satyr to do, and on the other a maenad, by whom one might expect the satyr to be sexually provoked, raises questions not simply about what has happened to the satyrs, that they can stay so calm, but about whether the ordinary men who pay cult to herms or engage in Dionysiac worship are really satyrs, sharing their rarely controlled sexual urges, underneath.

In assimilating the satyr to the man in the street, Athenian painters do not stop using the satyr to explore areas of life different from those that they explore by showing ordinary men. This is strikingly the case when satyrs acquire children.[20] A calyx krater ascribed to the Niobid Painter and

[20] See briefly Shapiro (2003), 104–5.

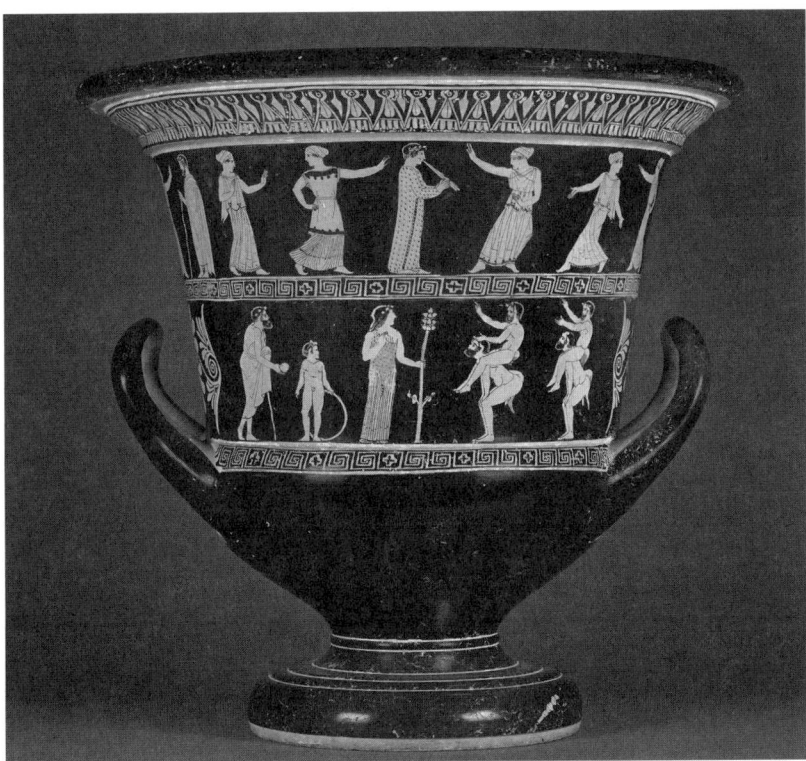

Figure 8.16. Red-figure calyx krater, height 0.49 m, attributed to the Niobid Painter, from Altamura, ca. 450. *ARV* 601.23, London, British Museum 1856,1213.1 (E 467). © The Trustees of the British Museum.

dated to shortly before the middle of the fifth century features two rows of figures. In the upper row is a scene of the birth/creation of Pandora and a chorus of women dancing to the music of an aulos player dressed in a highly decorated garment. In the lower row are two scenes. On one side, a chorus of Pans, figures with goats' feet, goats' horns and ears, but otherwise human bodies and wearing the shorts that are worn by chorus members in satyr plays. On the other side (**8.16**), we see at the left end of the scene a satyr dressed in a himation looking into the distance in front of him and holding out a ball in his right hand, as if deciding whether or not to throw it. In front of him is a child satyr, standing with his body frontal but holding a hoop in his left hand and looking sharply to his left. This sharp leftward gaze is shared with the maenad who stands next to the child satyr, holding a thyrsus in her left hand and clasping her right hand to her breast, which is clad in chiton and feline skin. Facing this satyr family on the right of the scene are two sets of satyrs playing piggyback—two naked satyrs are bent over, their large penises visible pointing vertically downward between their legs, carrying on their shoulders two other naked satyrs, who wave their arms in the direction of the family, as if encouraging the satyr-father to throw his ball. We seem to have an encounter here between a satyr family out to play with a hoop and ball, interrupted by a group of satyr-youths who come along wanting to join in the game.

This scene is very much in the spirit of the other mid- and late fifth-century pots we have examined in this book. Nothing here is shocking, nothing, apart from the very existence of the satyr, is "other." Although we have a ball here, no competitive game of piggy in the middle is being set up (contrast the ball player relief, 1.16). Although the satyr-child has a hoop, he is no Ganymede figure, setting himself up to be courted by powerful men. Although there are two satyrs giving piggyback rides, there is no sense that these two are in competition—they are set still, not in competitive motion. There is less a spectacle to watch here than a game to join in with. Except that these are satyrs. Or rather, because these are satyrs. As Shapiro observed, the normal family activities of games and outings and the normal family affection and discipline that satyrs are shown engaging in are in fact activities that ordinary men are not shown to engage in on Athenian pots. The very normality of this scene marks it as different. It is as if in order that the normal be noticed it has to be "staged" by satyrs. The closest parallel to these scenes of normal family life are in fact the scenes showing formal family rituals that can be found on some late fifth-century pots, and in particular on the choes that attract child-centered iconography.[21]

The scene of the satyr family on this pot has to be seen in the context of the other scenes. By showing the creation of Pandora, the painter emphasizes that woman is not born, but made, and that the sexual attraction that spectators find in women dancing to the aulos and that creates ordinary family life is itself a gift of the gods. By showing men dressed up not simply as satyrs but as Pans, the painter emphasizes the bestiality that men can put on in juxtaposition to the satyr family where the domestic side of the bestial, the man within every beast, is displayed. This is a pot about how for humans to be male, female, mothers, fathers, children, brothers they must perform roles rather than simply live lives. The krater encourages those who take wine from it at a symposium to reflect on the performance of their own sober life.

We observe something close to a complete revolution here. The satyrs who patrolled the boundaries of acceptable human behavior by doing, or at least attempting, things that ordinary men are never shown doing come to be represented doing things that ordinary men do all the time, but are never represented doing on contemporary pottery. It is as if satyrs represent the unrepresentable, but that the unrepresentable that is good to represent has changed. From representing the step too far, the action that a man is advised to think twice about before performing, satyrs come to represent the step that should already have been taken, the banal actions that men never talk about but need always to have done. The satyr's advantage, that he has no reputation to lose, was once what enabled him to do what was extraordinarily shameful; now it makes him unashamed to be ordinary, able to suggest that the exotic should be recognized in the ordinary.

[21] Shapiro (2003), 103–4; Hoorn (1951); Hamilton (1992). In my view, Hamilton takes his argument separating larger choes from the Anthesteria too far.

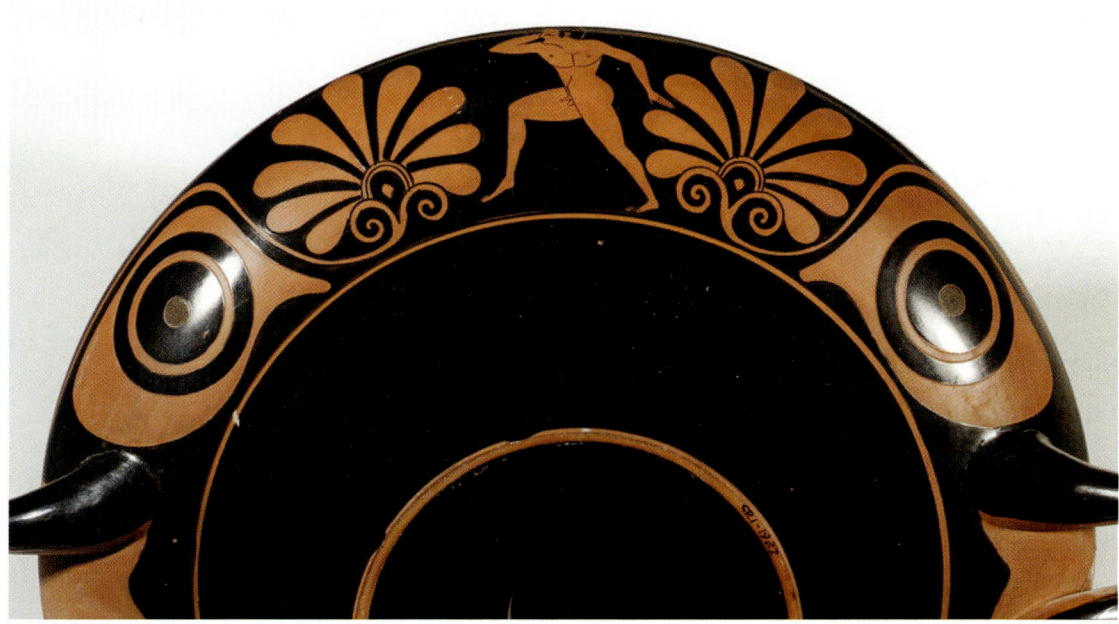

Plate 1 (fig. 1.4). Exterior of red-figure cup, diameter 0.34 m, attributed to the Nikosthenes Painter, ca. 510–500 (for the interior see 7.13). *ARV* 124.3 Cambridge Fitzwilliam Museum GR.1.1927. © The Fitzwilliam Museum, Cambridge.

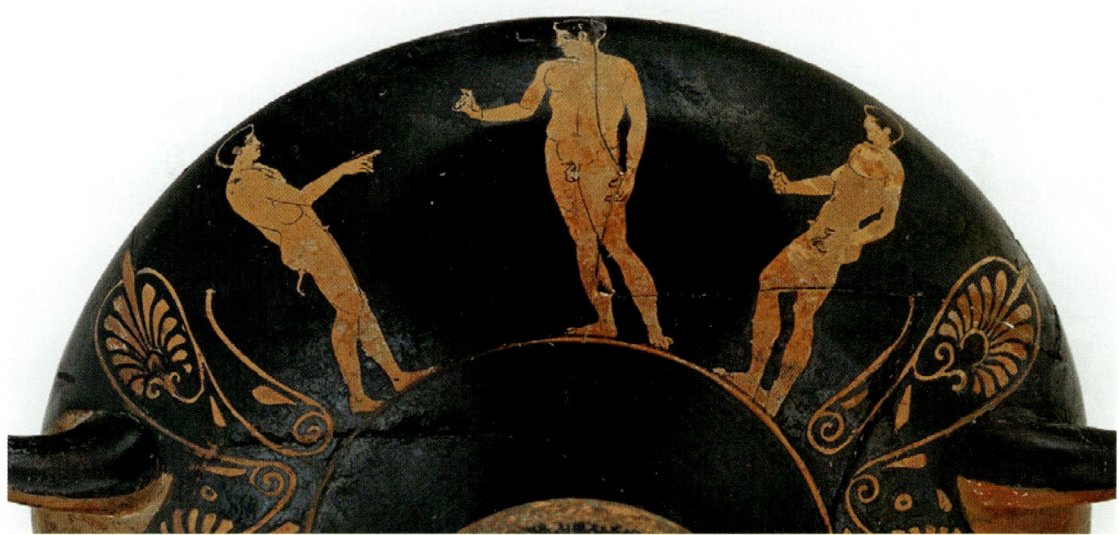

Plate 2 (fig. 1.6). Exterior of red-figure cup, diameter 0.215 m, name vase of the Painter of Cambridge 72 (close to the Codrus Painter), ca. 430 (for the interior see 11.2). *ARV* 1273.2. Cambridge Fitzwilliam Museum G72 = GR 50.1864. © The Fitzwilliam Museum, Cambridge.

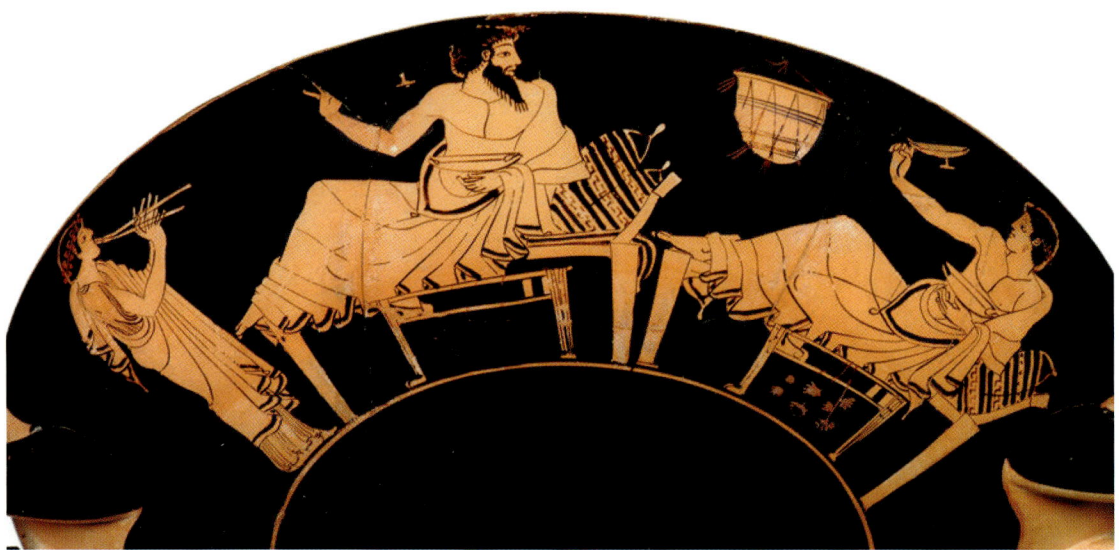

Plate 3 (fig. 2.3). Exterior of red-figure cup, diameter 0.287 m, attributed to Makron, from Vulci, ca. 490. *ARV* 467.126. Munich Staatliche Antikensammlungen 2643. © Staatliche Antikensammlungen und Glyptothek München. Photograph by Renate Kühling.

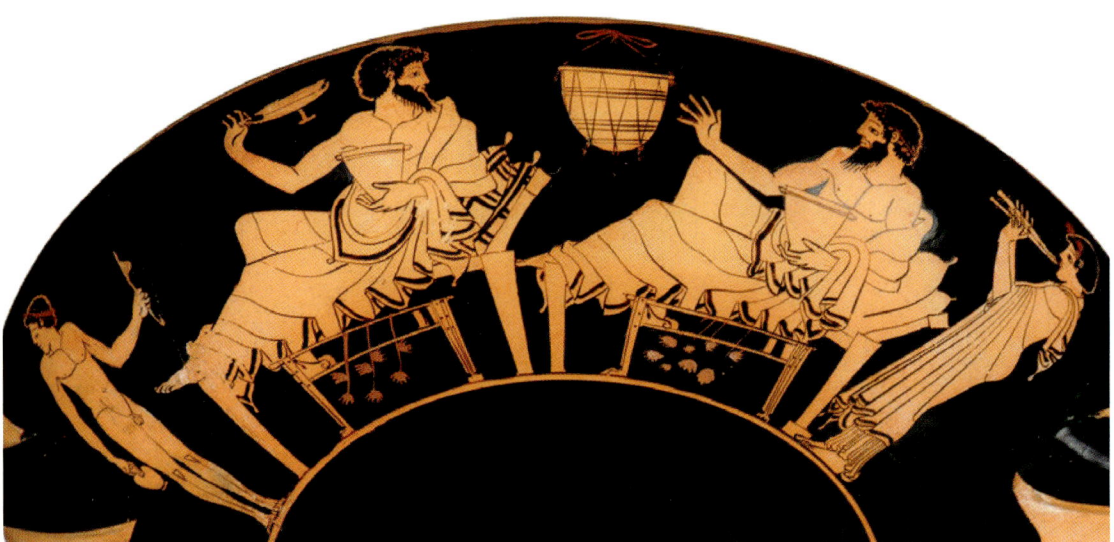

Plate 4 (fig. 2.4). Exterior of red-figure cup, diameter 0.287 m, attributed to Makron, from Vulci, ca. 490. *ARV* 467.126. Munich Staatliche Antikensammlungen 2643. © Staatliche Antikensammlungen und Glyptothek München. Photograph by Renate Kühling.

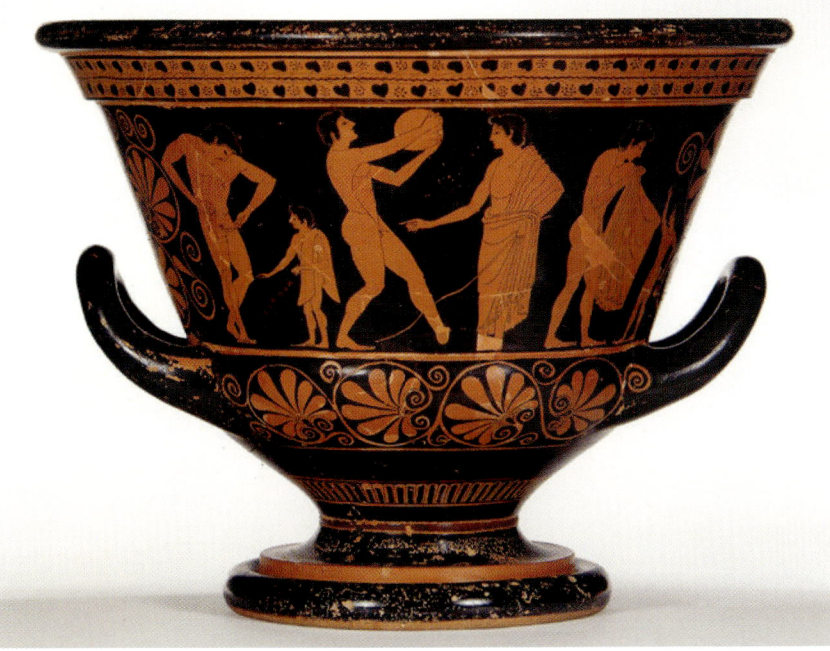

Plate 5 (fig. 3.6). Red-figure calyx krater, height 0.348 m, attributed to Euphronios, found at Capua, ca. 510 (for the reverse see 1.2). *ARV* 13.1. Berlin 2180. © bpk / Antikensammlung, Staatliche Museen zu Berlin / Johannes Laurentius.

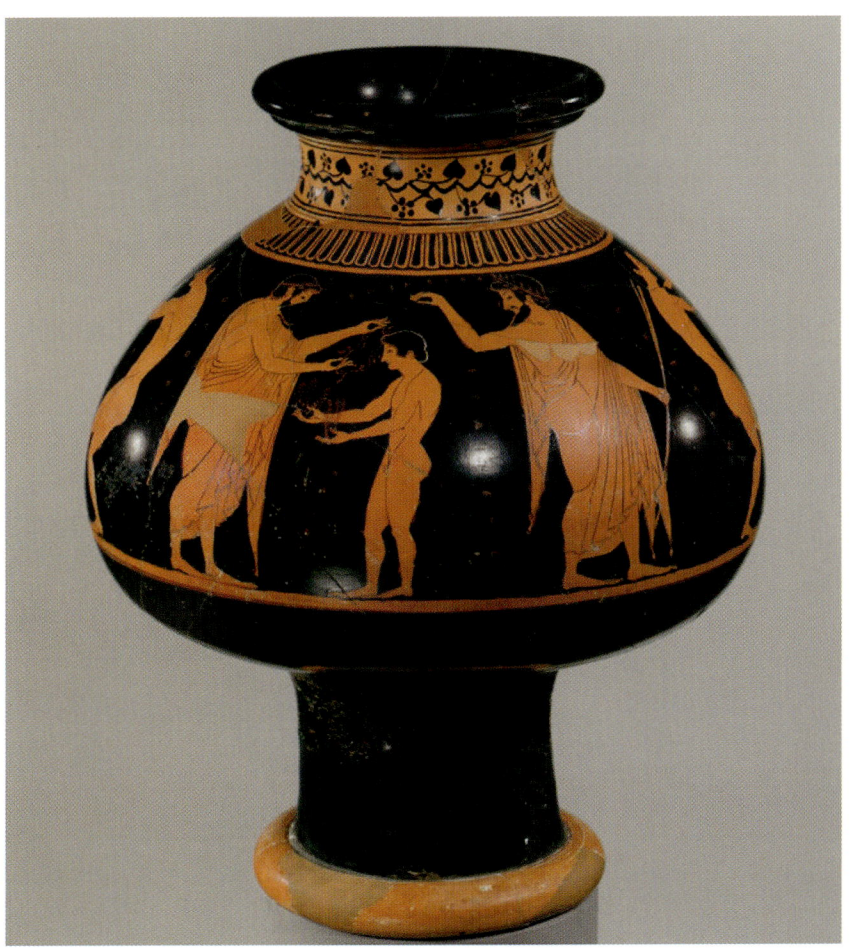

Plate 6 (fig. 3.8). Red-figure psykter, height 0.346 m, attributed to Oltos, found at Campagnano, ca. 500. *ARV* 54.7. New York Metropolitan Museum 10.210.18. www.metmuseum.org.

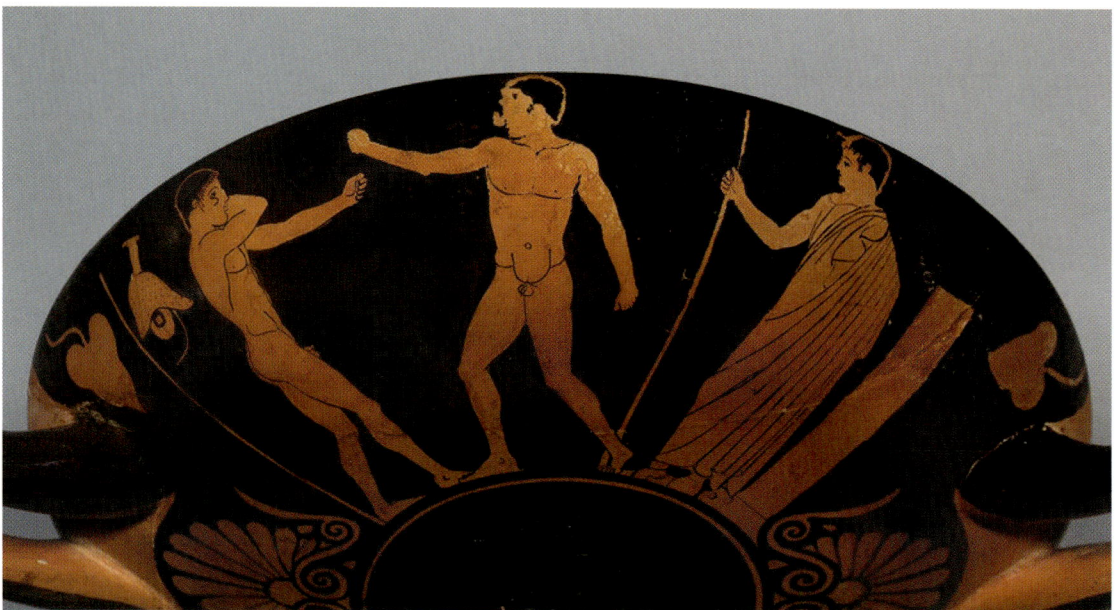

Plate 7 (fig. 3.16). Interior and exterior of red-figure cup, diameter 0.23 m, attributed to the Villa Giulia Painter, found at Tarquinia, ca. 460–450. *ARV* 625.101. Berlin 2522. © bpk / Antikensammlung, Staatliche Museen zu Berlin / Ingrid Geske.

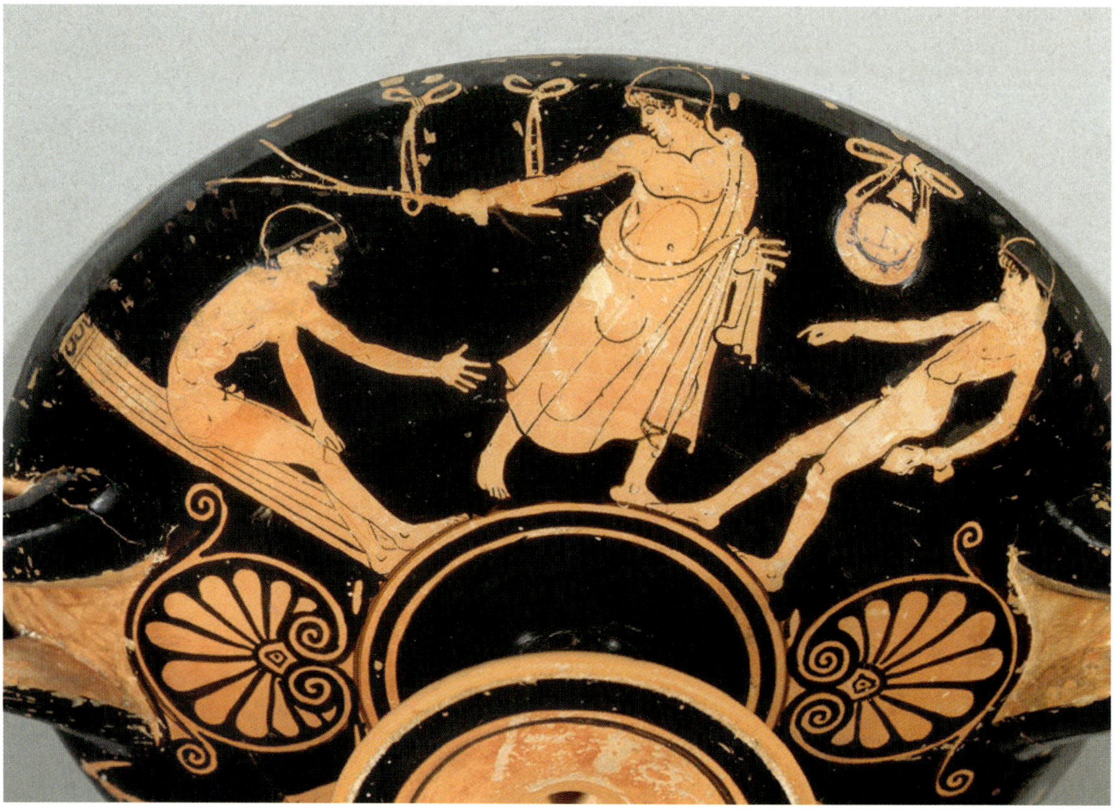

Plate 8 (fig. 3.18). Exterior of red-figure cup, diameter 0.238 m, attributed to the Penthesileia Painter, provenance unknown, ca. 460–450. *ARV* 882.36. Boston Museum of Fine Arts 28.48. Photograph © 2017 Museum of Fine Arts, Boston.

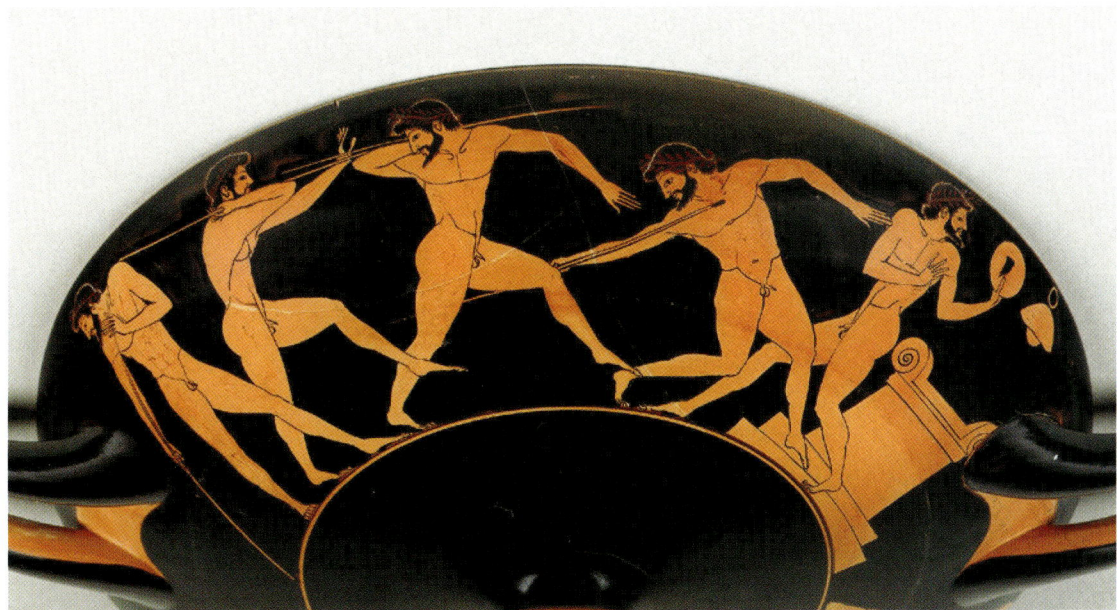

Plate 9 (fig. 3.20). Red-figure cup, diameter 0.305 m, attributed to the Carpenter Painter, provenance unknown, ca. 500. J. Paul Getty Museum, Malibu 85.AE.25. Digital image courtesy of the Getty's Open Content Program.

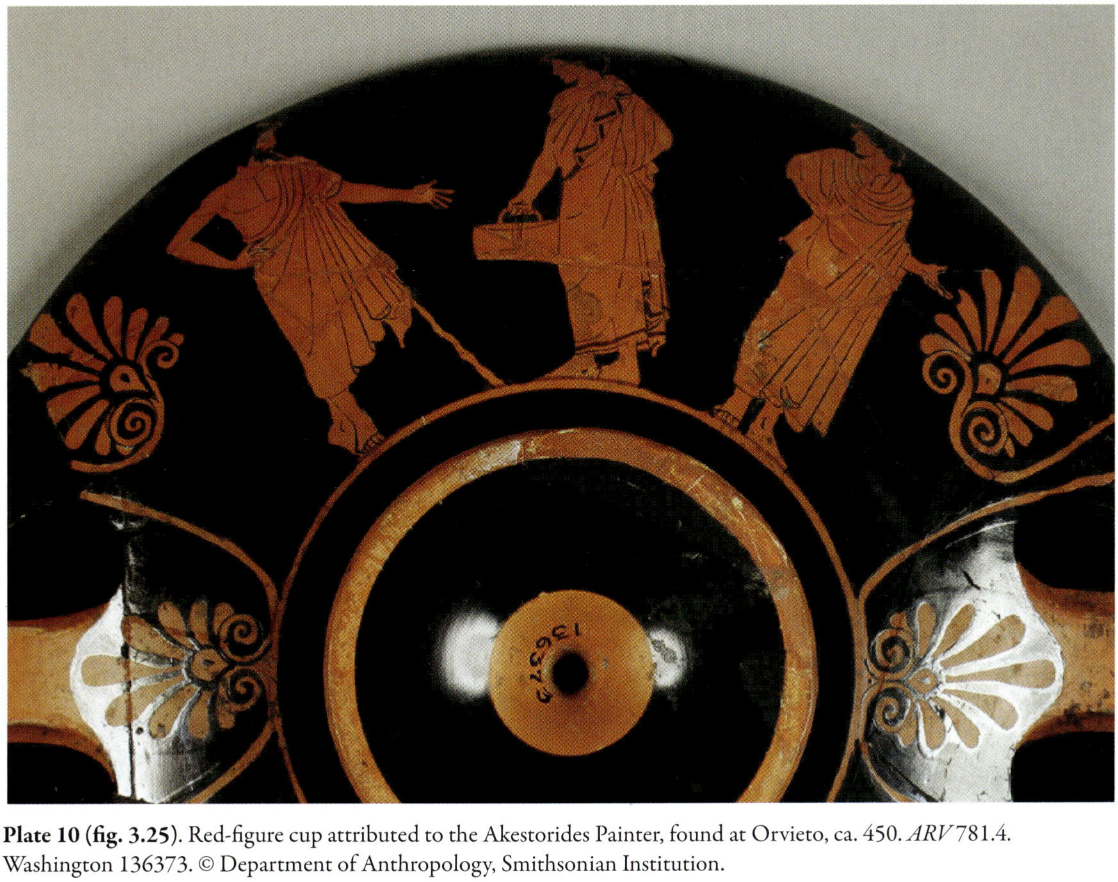

Plate 10 (fig. 3.25). Red-figure cup attributed to the Akestorides Painter, found at Orvieto, ca. 450. *ARV* 781.4. Washington 136373. © Department of Anthropology, Smithsonian Institution.

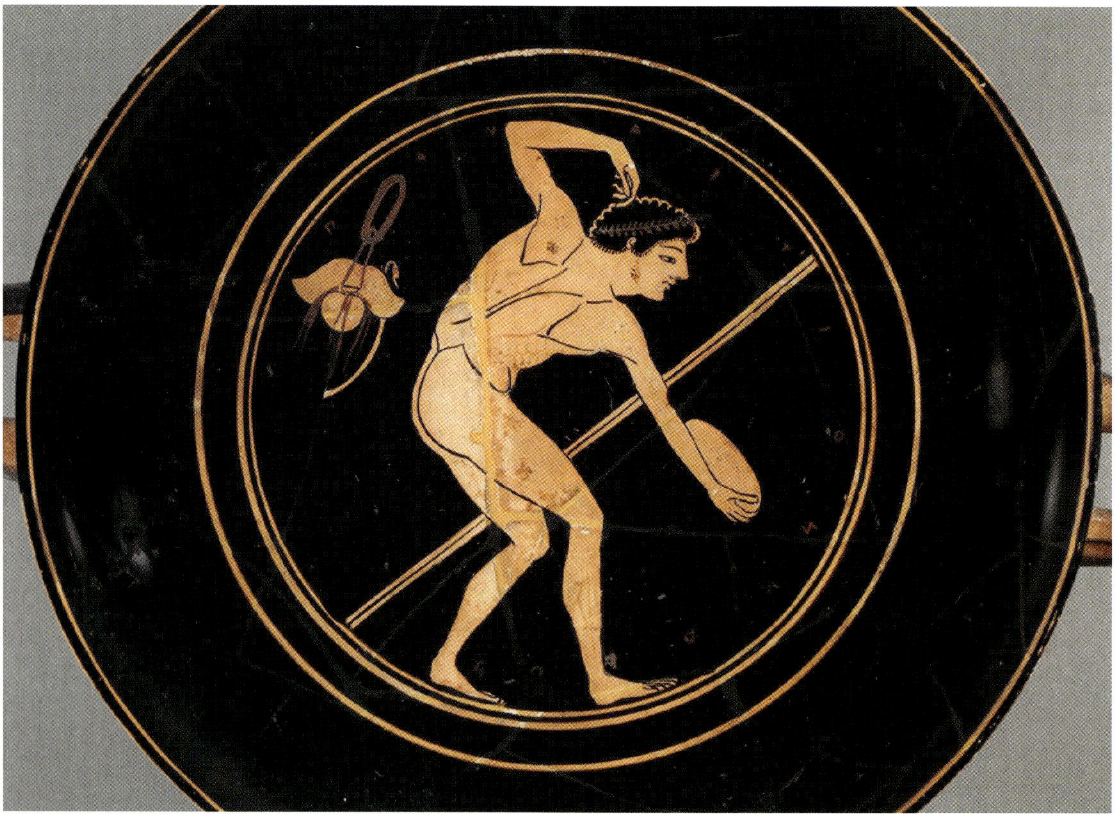

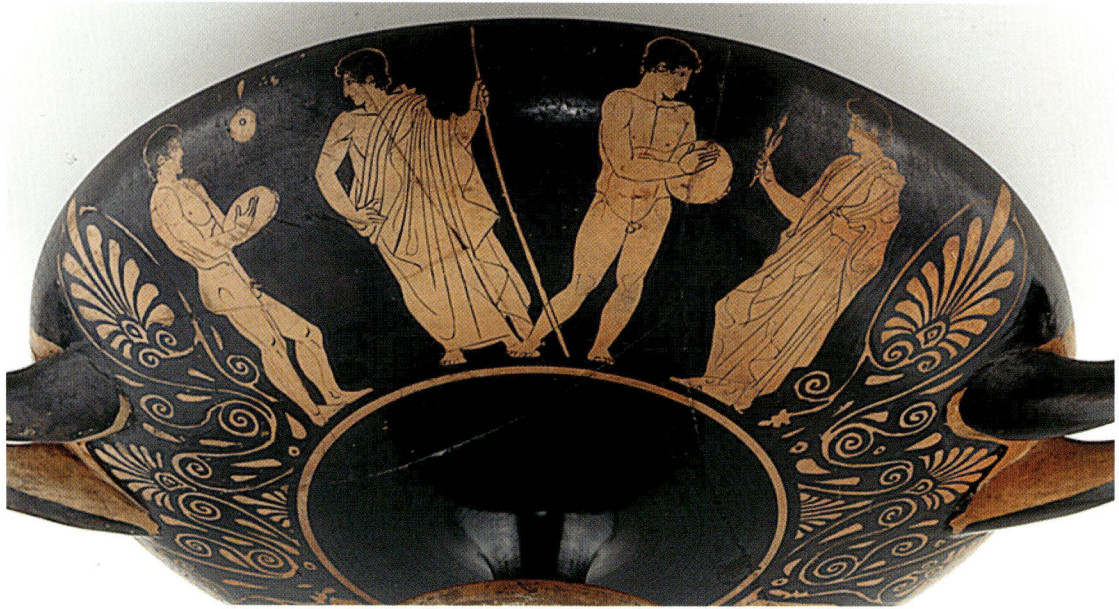

Plate 11 (fig. 3.26). Interior of red-figure cup, diameter 0.225 m, attributed to Onesimos, found at Orvieto, ca. 500. *ARV* 321.22. Boston Museum of Fine Arts 01.8020. Photograph © 2017 Museum of Fine Arts, Boston.

Plate 12 (fig. 3.27). Exterior of red-figure cup, diameter 0.26 m, attributed to the Eretria Painter, ca. 435. *ARV* 1254.73. Blanton Museum, Austin 1980.38. © Blanton Museum of Art, the University of Texas at Austin, Archer M. Huntington Museum Fund and the James R. Dougherty, Jr. Foundation 1980.

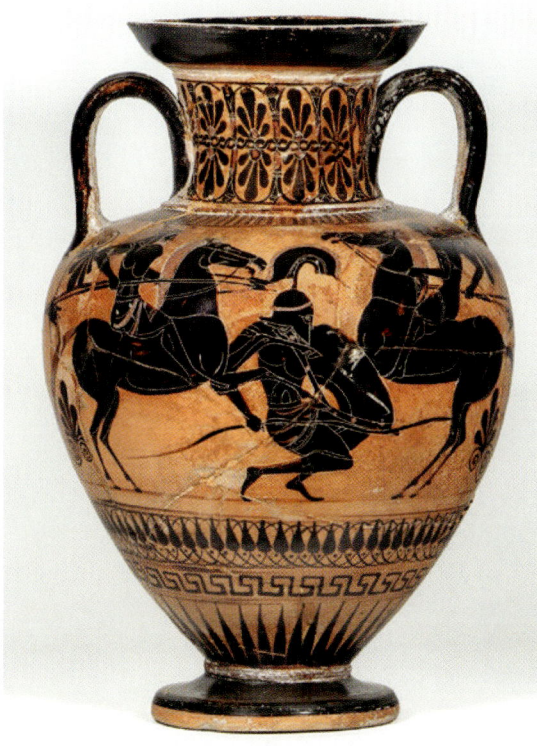

Plate 13 (fig. 4.2). Black-figure amphora, provenance unknown, 525–500. © Bonn Akademisches Kunstmuseum (Fontana collection, no. 40).

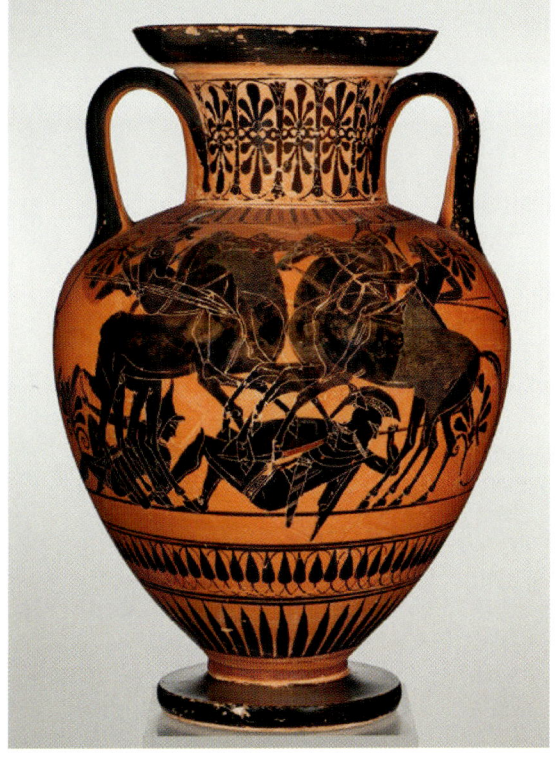

Plate 14 (fig. 4.4). Black-figure amphora, height 0.44 m, attributed to the group of Bologna 16, from Vulci, 525–500. *ABV* 285.1, Munich Staatliche Antikensammlungen 1509. © Staatliche Antikensammlungen und Glyptothek München. Photograph by Renate Kühling.

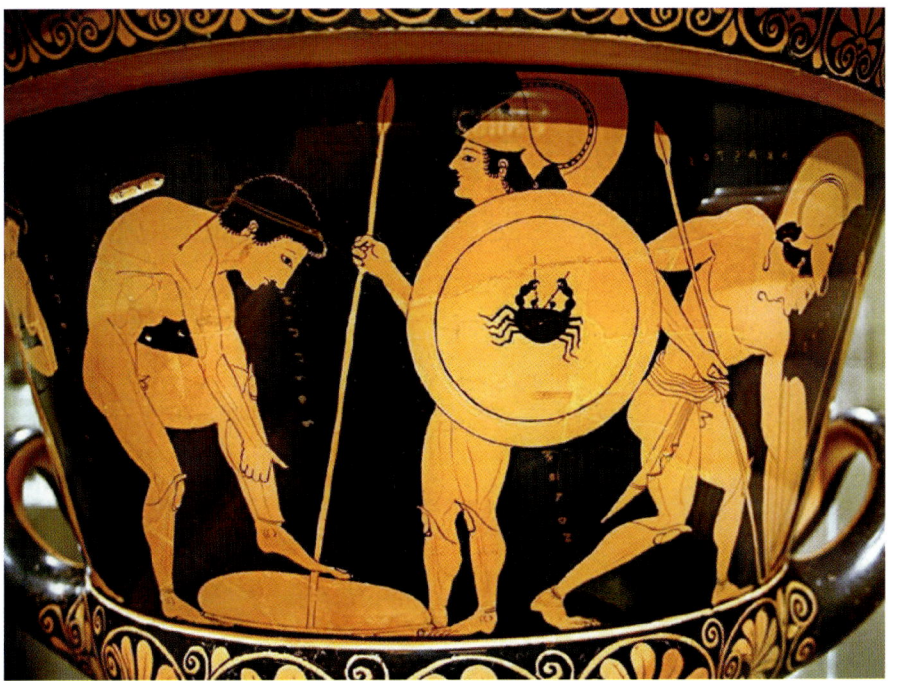

Plate 15 (fig. 4.7). Red-figure calyx krater, height 0.458 m, signed by Euphronios as painter and Euxitheos as potter. Provenance unknown. Beazley Addenda 404. Cerveteri, Museo Archaeologico. (ex N.Y. Met. 1972.11.10) CC BY-SA 3.0 Rolfmueller at the English language Wikipedia.

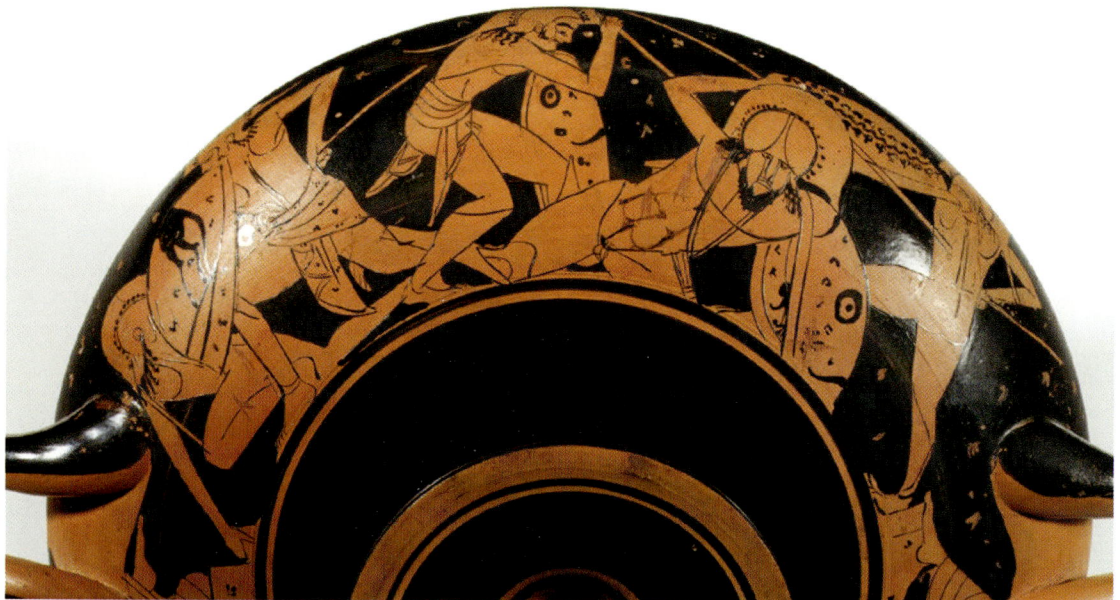

Plate 16 (fig. 4.12). Exterior of red-figure cup, diameter 0.273 m, attributed to the wider circle of the Nikosthenes Painter, ca. 500 (for the interior and other side see 7.1–2). *ARV* 135.13, Cambridge, Fitzwilliam Museum GR 19.1937. © The Fitzwilliam Museum, Cambridge.

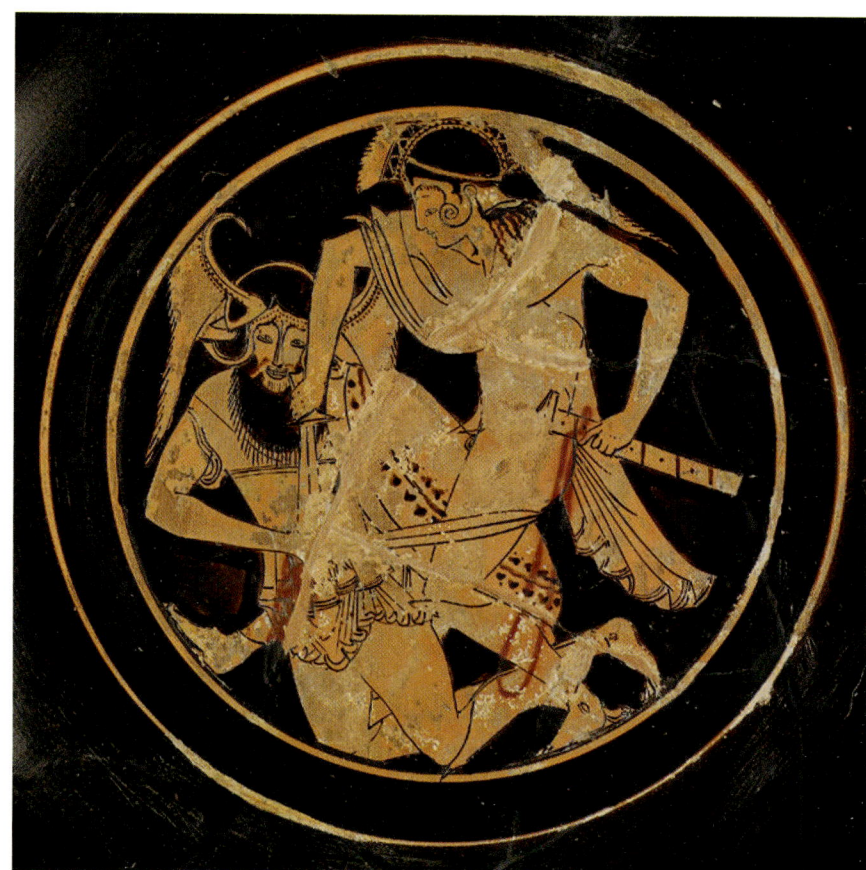

Plate 17 (fig. 4.13). Interior of red-figure cup, diameter 0.198 m, attributed to the Epidromos Painter / Apollodoros (the interior bears the inscription "Epidromos kalos"), from Chiusi, ca. 500. *ARV* 118.13, British Museum 1892,0718.6 (E43). © The Trustees of the British Museum.

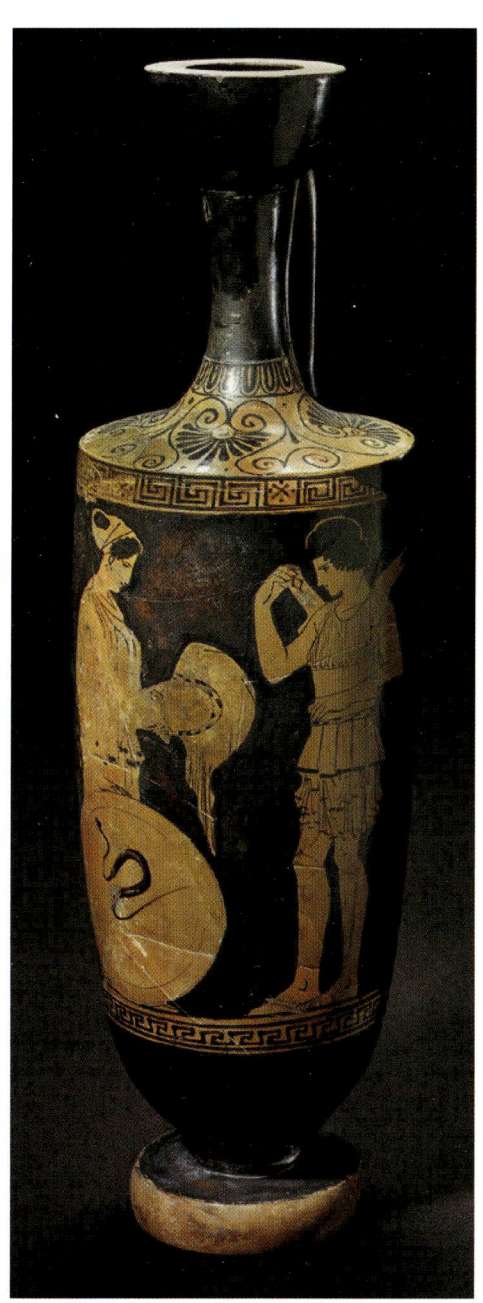
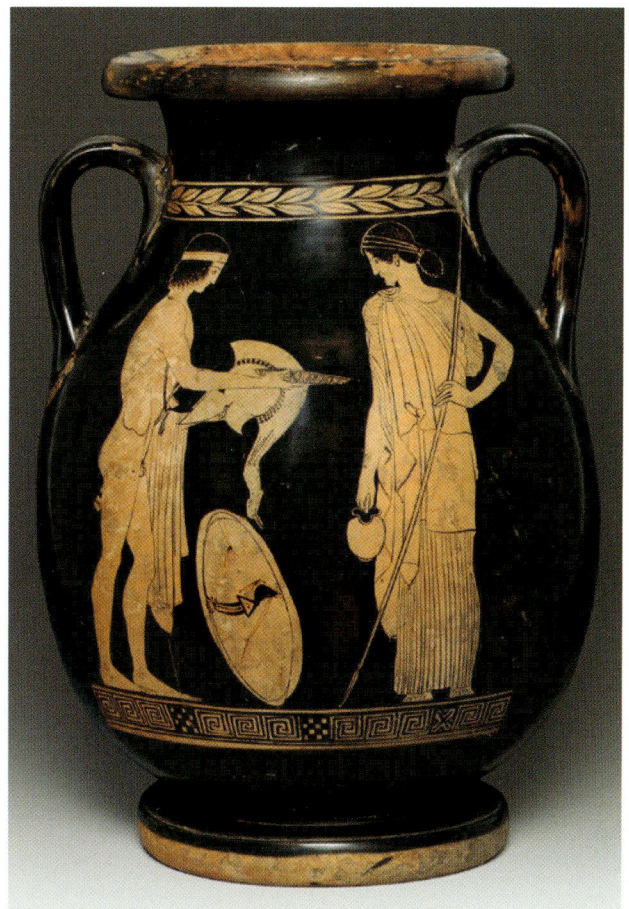

Plate 18 (fig. 4.19). Red-figure lekythos, height 0.343 m, attributed to the Phiale Painter, found in Sicily, ca. 430. *ARV* 1021.116. British Museum 1863,0728.440 (E 596). © The Trustees of the British Museum.

Plate 19 (fig. 4.22). Red-figure pelike, height 0.425 m, attributed to the Chicago Painter, found at Vulci, ca. 450 (for the reverse see 2.2). *ARV* 630.26. Paris, Cabinet de Médailles 394. © Bibliothèque nationale de France.

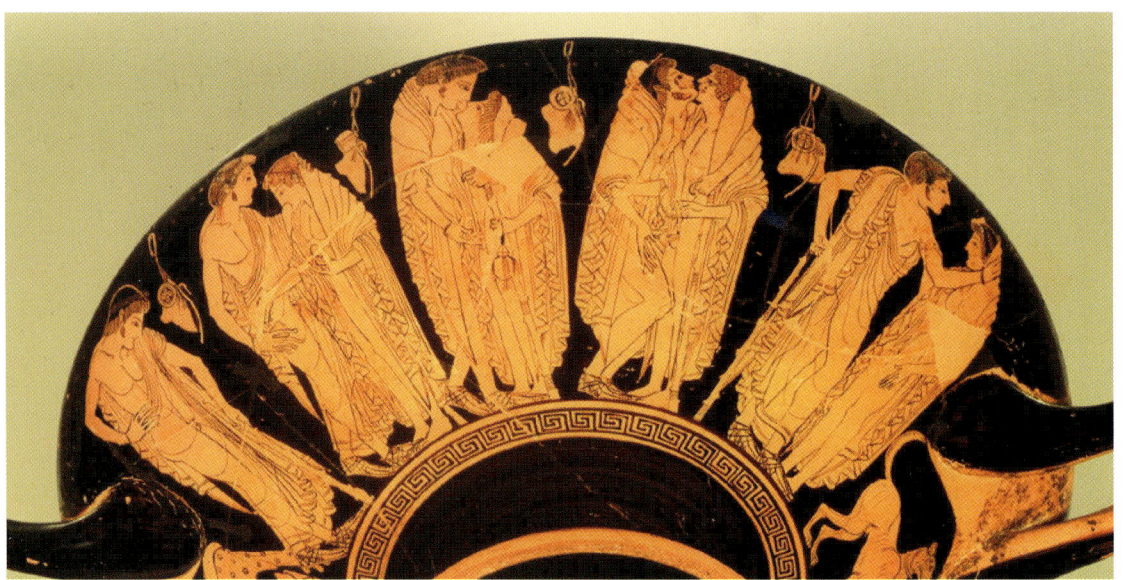

Plate 20 (fig. 5.4). Black-figure amphora, height 0.345 m, attributed to the Painter of Berlin 1686, from Vulci, ca. 540. *ARV* 297.16, British Museum 1865,1118.39 (W39). © The Trustees of the British Museum.

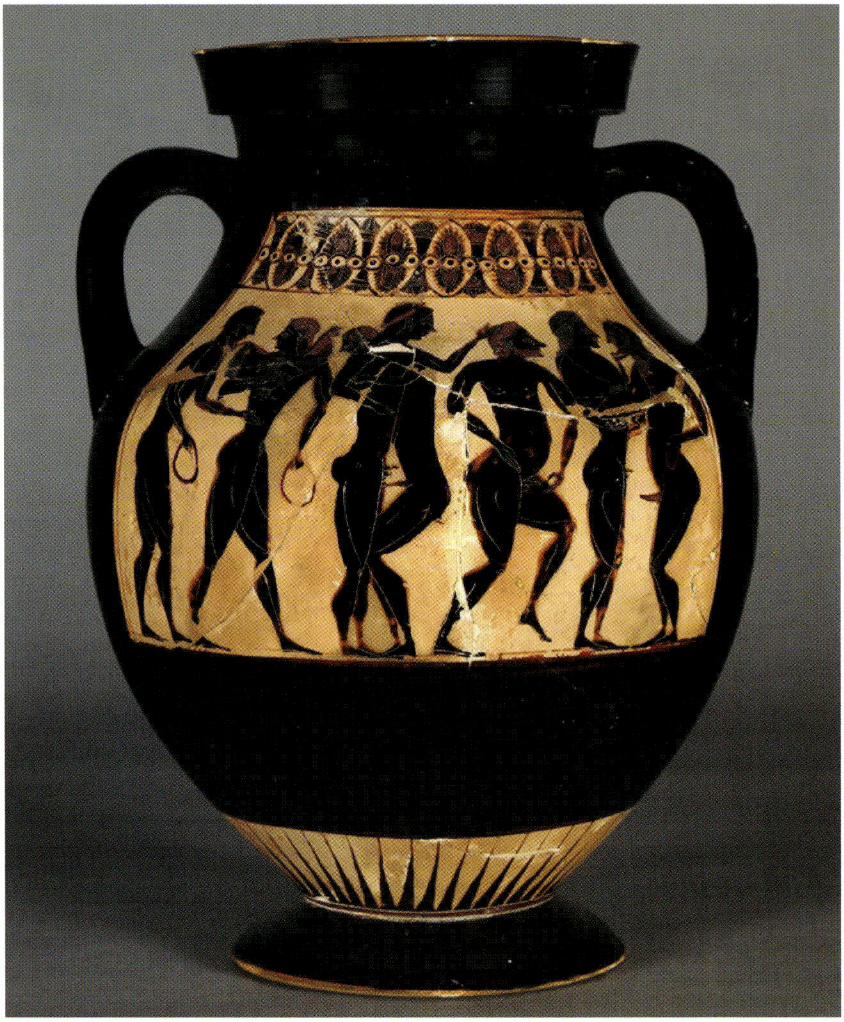

Plate 21 (fig. 5.6). Exterior of red-figure cup, diameter 0.34 m, signed by Peithinos as painter, from Vulci. ca. 500. *ARV* 115.2, Berlin Antikensammlung, Staatliche Museen F. 2279. © bpk / Antikensammlung, Staatliche Museen zu Berlin / Johannes Laurentius.

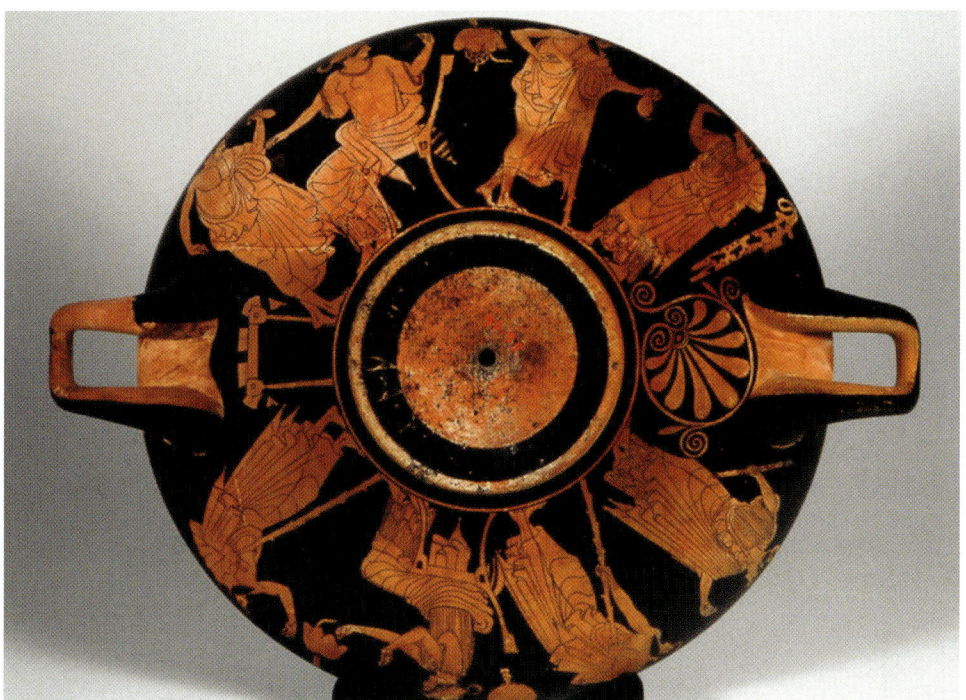

Plate 22 (fig. 5.8). Exterior of red-figure cup, diameter 0.287 m, attributed to Makron, ca. 480. Toledo Museum of Art, Toledo, Ohio, purchased with the funds from the Libbey Endowment, gift of Edward Drummond Libbey, 1972.55.

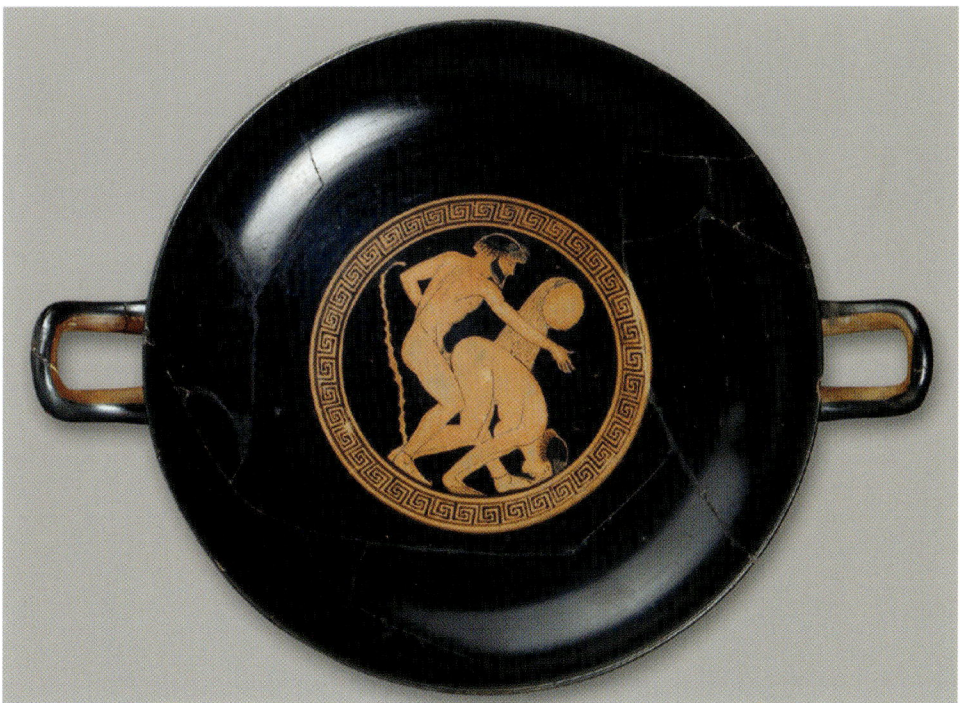

Plate 23 (fig. 5.10). Exterior of red-figure cup, diameter 0.237 m, attributed to the Briseis Painter, from Cervetri, ca.490. *ARV* 408.37, Oxford Ashmolean Museum AN1967.305. Image © Ashmolean Museum, University of Oxford.

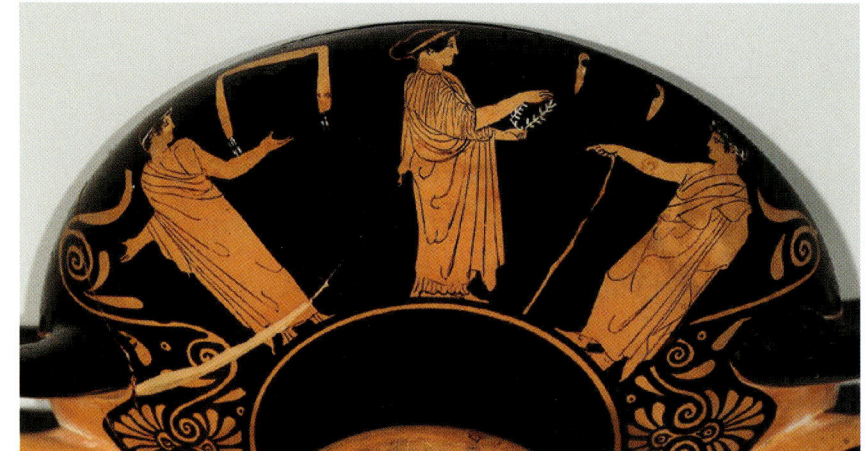

Plate 24 (fig. 5.20). Red-figure cup, diameter 0.227 m, attributed to the Calliope Painter, said to be from Magna Graecia. *ARV* 1259.11, Boston Museum of Fine Arts 21.4. Photograph © 2017 Museum of Fine Arts, Boston.

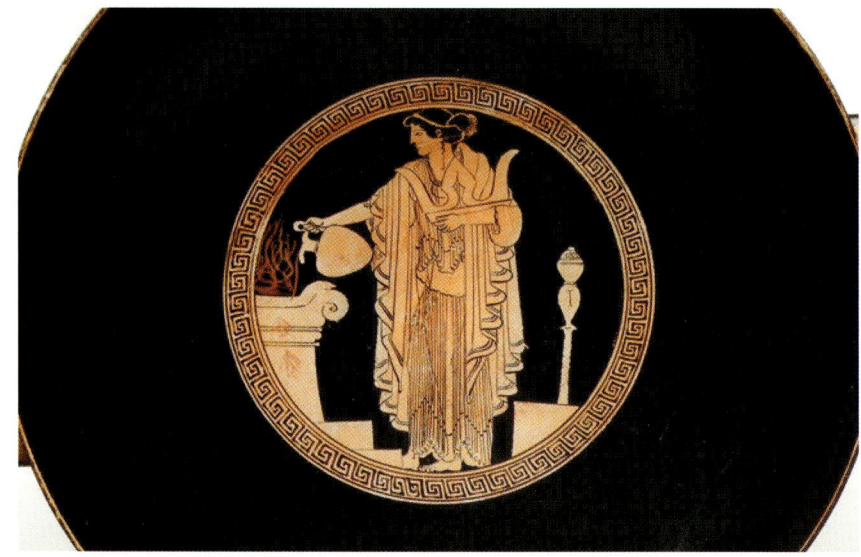

Plate 25 (fig. 6.2). Interior of red-figure cup, diameter 0.287 m, attributed to Makron, ca. 480 (for the exterior see 5.7–8). Toledo Museum of Art, Toledo, Ohio, purchased with the funds from the Libbey Endowment, gift of Edward Drummond Libbey, 1972.55.

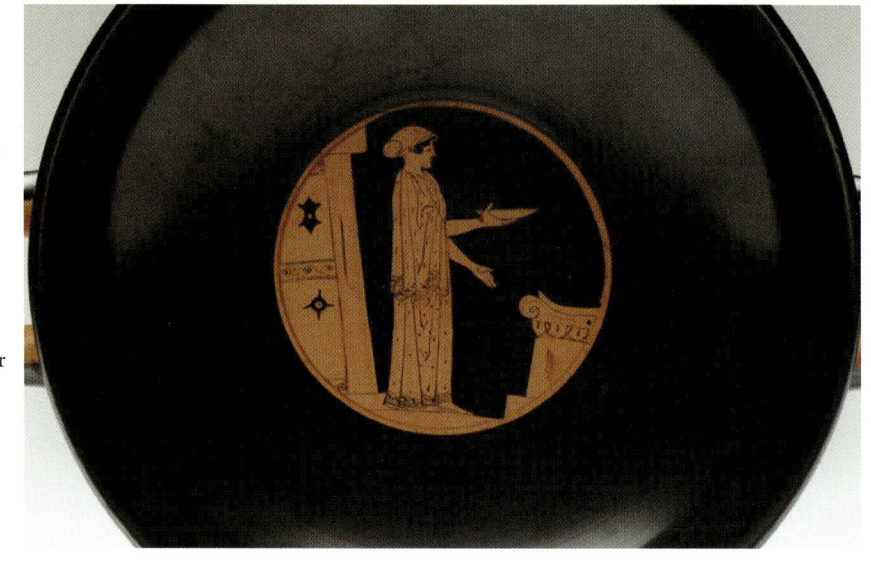

Plate 26 (fig. 6.9). Interior of red-figure cup, diameter 0.19 m, in the manner of the Akestorides Painter (grouped by Beazley with the "Followers of Douris"), ca. 470. *ARV* 803.58, Harvard Art Museums / Arthur M. Sackler Museum, gift of E. P. Warren, Esquire 1927.155. Photo: Imaging Department © President and Fellows of Harvard College.

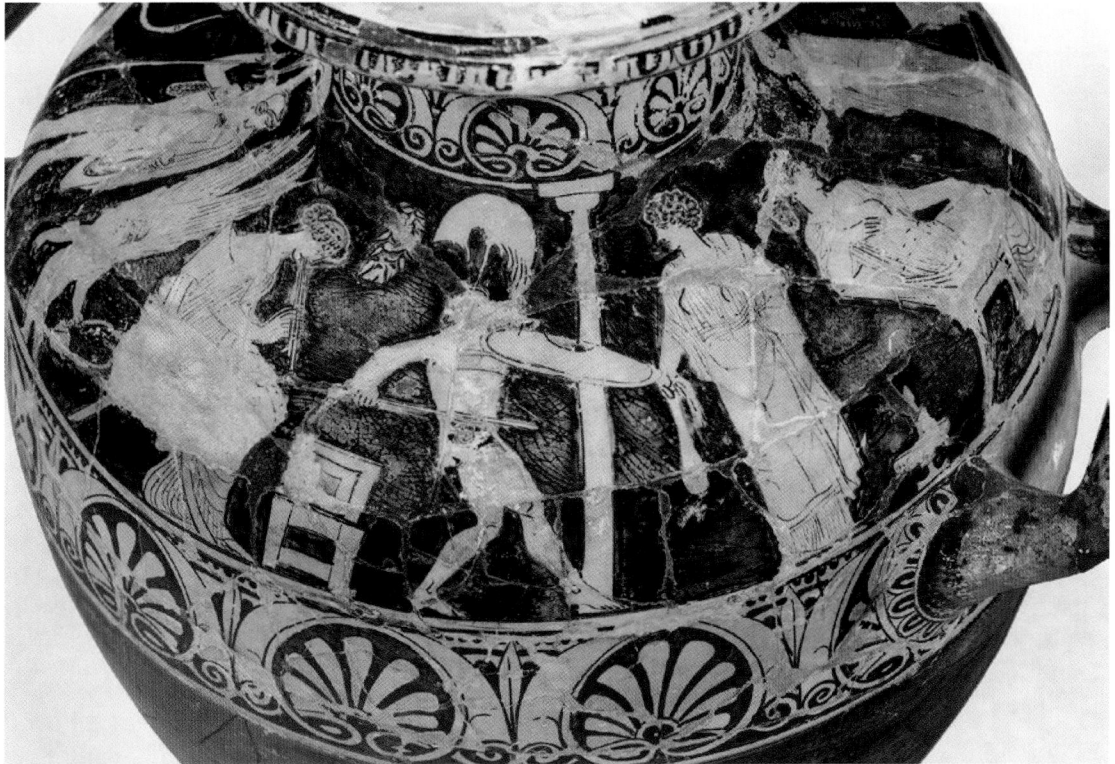

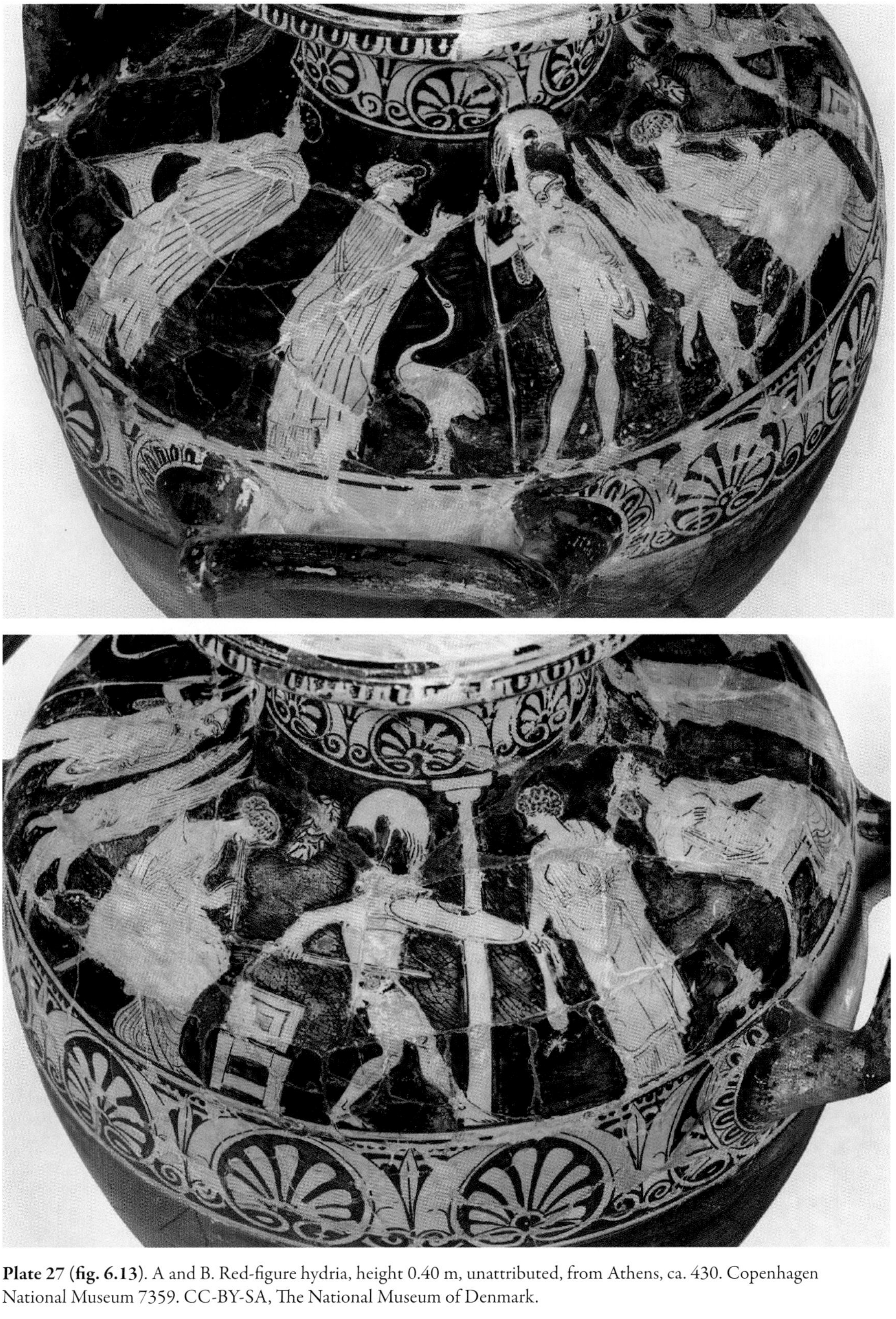

Plate 27 (fig. 6.13). A and B. Red-figure hydria, height 0.40 m, unattributed, from Athens, ca. 430. Copenhagen National Museum 7359. CC-BY-SA, The National Museum of Denmark.

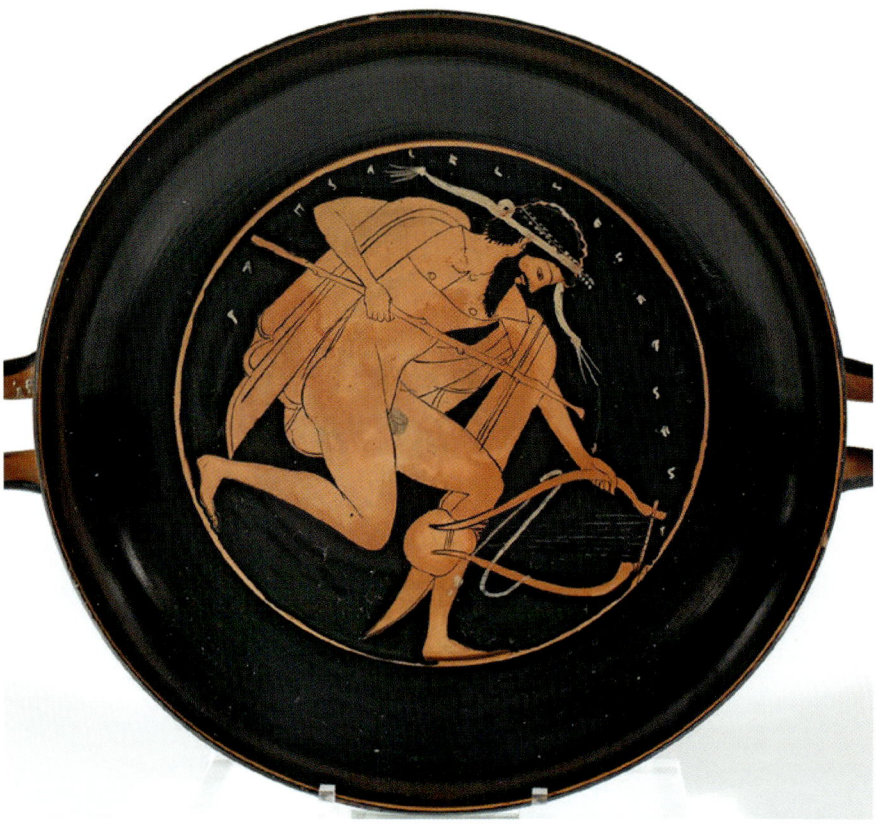

Plate 28 (fig. 7.2). Interior and one exterior side of red-figure cup, diameter 0.273 m, attributed to the wider circle of the Nikosthenes Painter, ca. 500 (for the other side see 4.12). *ARV* 135.13, Cambridge, Fitzwilliam Museum GR 19.1937. © The Fitzwilliam Museum, Cambridge.

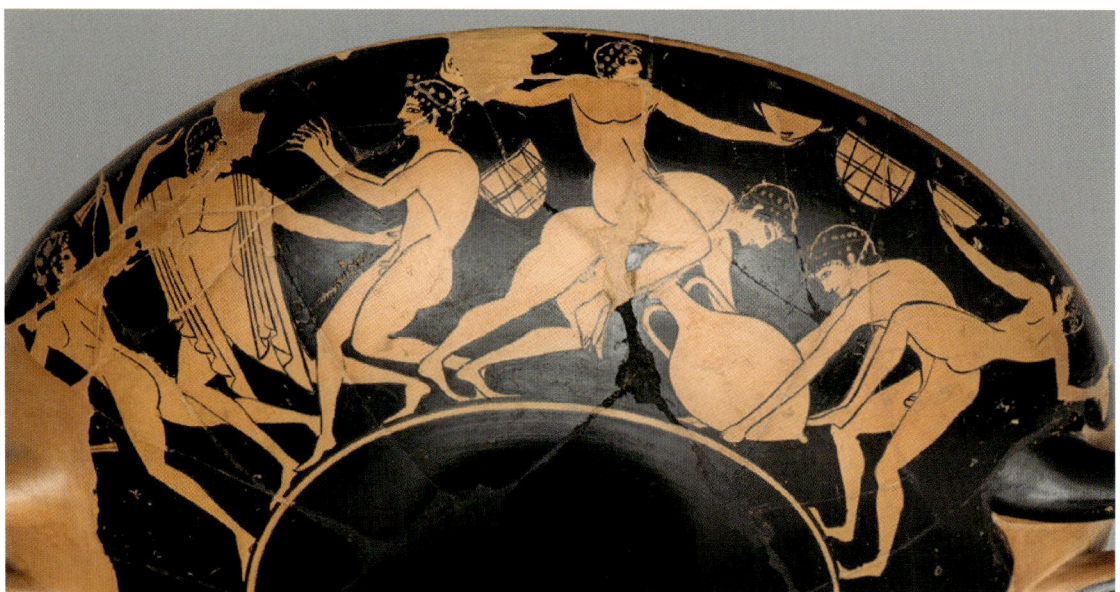

Plate 29 (fig. 7.5). Red-figure cup, diameter 0.335 m, attributed to the Epeleios Painter, from Vulci, ca. 500. *ARV* 146.7, Brussels Musées Royaux A 3407. © RMAH.

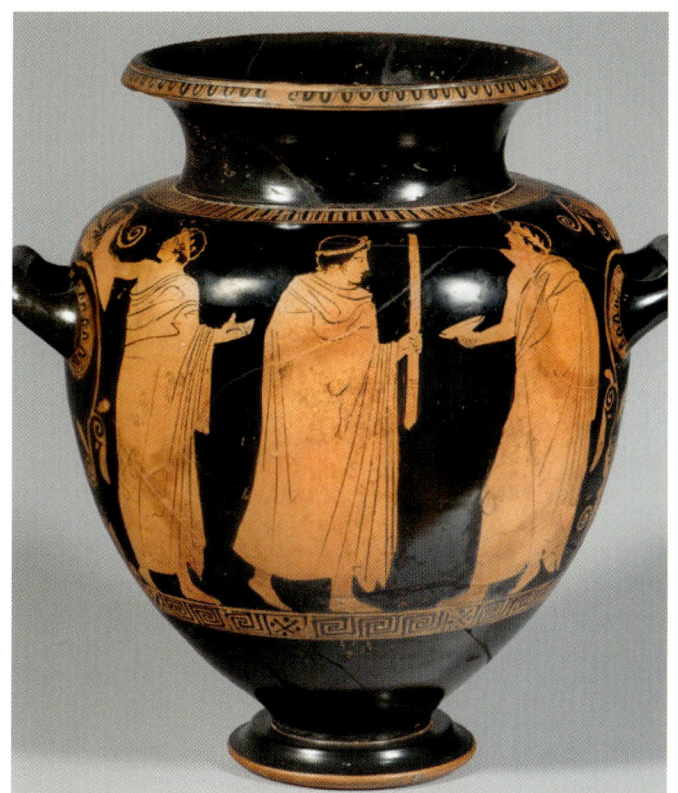

Plate 30 (fig. 7.8). Red-figure stamnos, height 0.402 m, attributed to the Kleophon Painter, ca. 440. *ARV* 1144.9, Brussels Musées Royaux A 3091. © RMAH.

Plate 31 (fig. 7.15). Exterior of red-figure cup, diameter 0.315 m, attributed to the Triptolemos painter, ca. 480 (for the interior see 6.10). *ARV* 364.52, Berlin Staatliche Museen F 2298. © bpk / Antikensammlung, Staatliche Museen zu Berlin / Johannes Laurentius.

Plate 32 (fig. 7.17). Exterior of red-figure cup, diameter 0.237 m, attributed to the Brygos Painter, ca. 480. *ARV* 372.29, London British Museum 1866.0805.4 (E 71). © The Trustees of the British Museum.

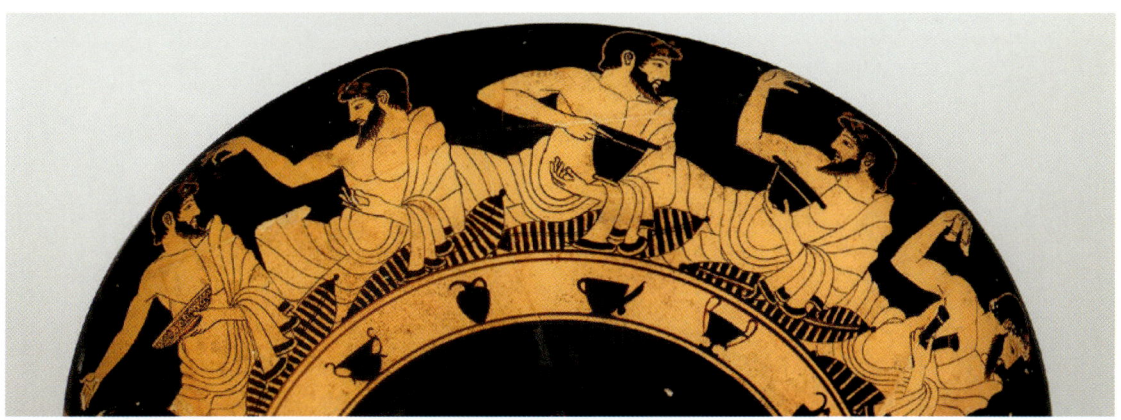

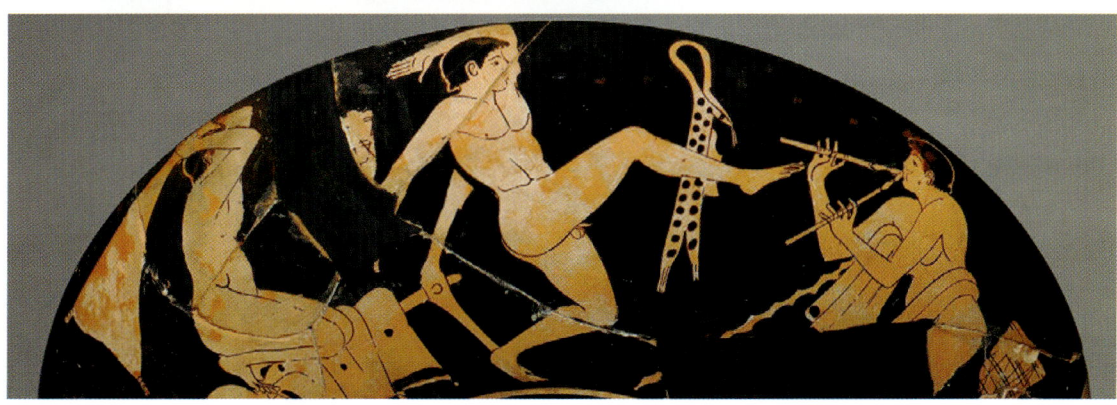

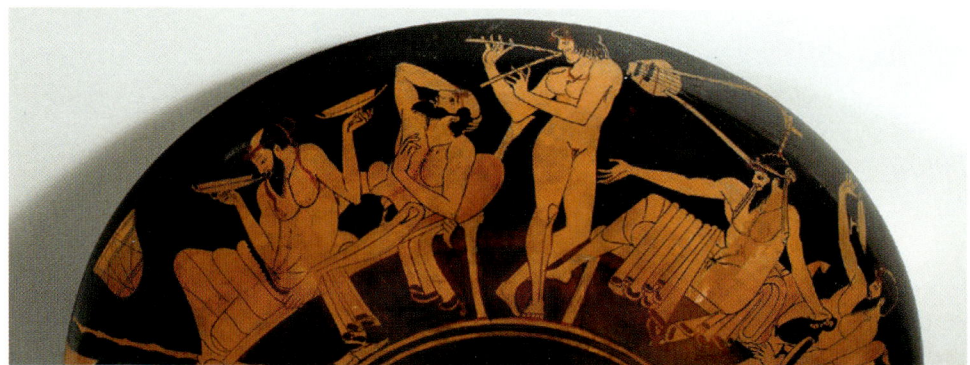

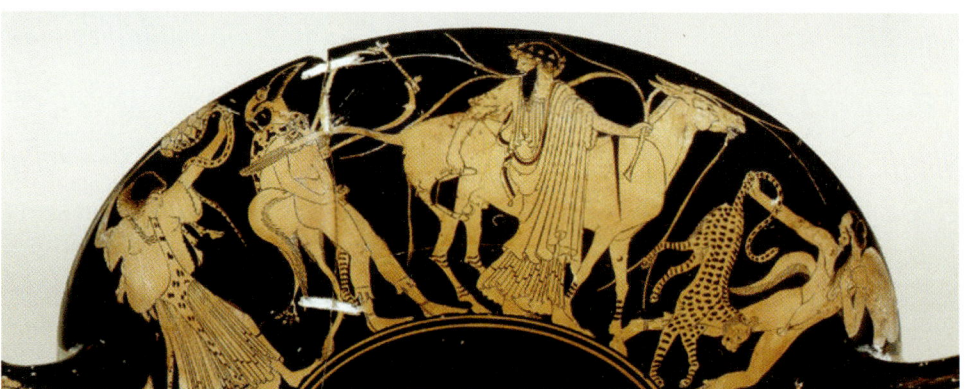

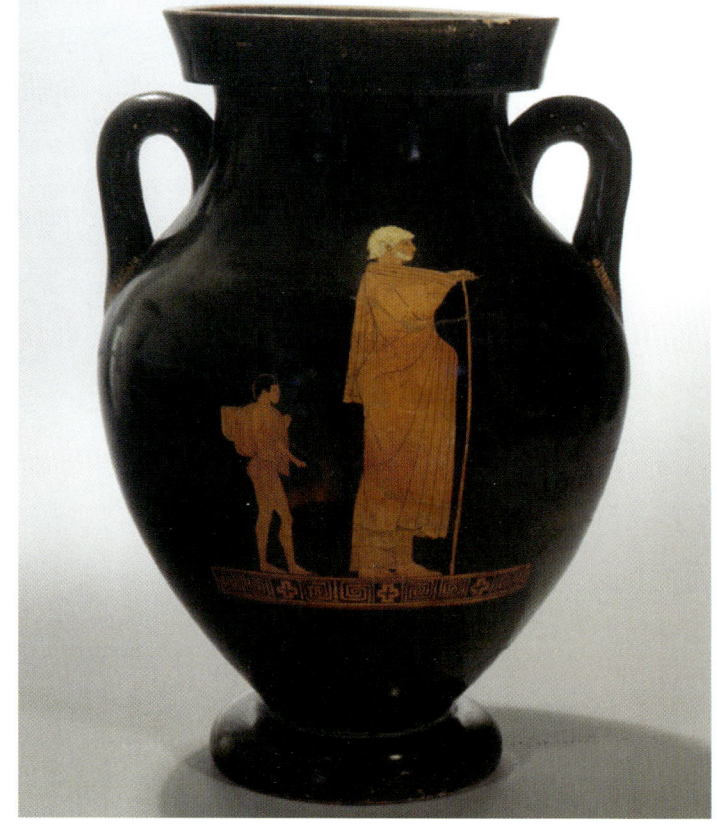

Plate 33 (fig. 7.21). Exterior and interior of a red-figure cup, diameter 0.285 m, attributed to the Foundry Painter, ca. 480. *ARV* 402.12, Cambridge, Corpus Christi College (Fitzwilliam Museum Loan 103.18). © The Fitzwilliam Museum, Cambridge.

Plate 34 (fig. 8.4). Exterior of a red-figure cup, diameter 0.298 m, attributed to the Brygos Painter, ca. 480. *ARV* 371.14, Paris, Cabinet de Médailles 576. © Bibliothèque nationale de France.

Plate 35 (fig. 10.4). Red-figure amphora, height 0.492 m, attributed to Syriskos / the Copenhagen Painter, from Vulci, ca. 470. *ARV* 256.1, Copenhagen 125. CC-BY-SA, The National Museum of Denmark.

ஃ III

9 ❧ Morality, Politics, and Aesthetics

It would be no small shock to discover that what was being done and made in a society at one moment was identical to what had been done and made there fifty years earlier. Change in itself needs no explanation. Human societies are made up of individuals, not of clones, and individuals learn something, at least, from their particular experiences. It is not change itself but patterns of change that demand explanation. Finding an explanation, however, requires that we understand what the question is, what the pattern of change is. Many explanations carry conviction while falling well short of proof, simply because they subsume a pattern of change in one area of life to a pattern of change in other areas of life. Explanations of this sort are particularly convincing if those other areas are areas that are plausibly dominant within that society or within that aspect of political, social, or cultural activity.

In chapter 1, I reviewed the sorts of patterns of change that scholars have distinguished in Greek sculpture and pot painting down to the fifth century, noting the sorts of pattern to which they have subsumed those changes to explain them and the sorts of pattern in which little or no interest has been taken. In chapter 2, I justified, and in the succeeding six chapters I pursued an exploration of changing patterns in the iconographic choices made by Athenian pot painters in relation to scenes with no definitive mythological content. For reasons that I have tried to explain, past interest in such changes in the choice of scene to paint has been limited, but I have tried to show that there are indeed very striking patterns of change in the choice of images of the gymnasium, of warfare, of sexual relations, of relations with the gods, of symposium and *komos*, and of scenes of satyrs, in the period from the introduction of the red-figure painting technique to the middle of the fifth century.

In the past six chapters I have variously compared the changes in the aspects of a particular activity shown on pots that are depicted with what we know of the history of that activity itself. I have done this in some detail with regard to those areas about which we are best informed by our texts, in particular military activity, and in rather less detail in the case of other activities, where the nature of the evidence itself changes over the period in question or is discontinuous. These explorations of textual material have become thinner in successive chapters partly because of the nature of the material available, but partly because the initial examples, of athletics and warfare, sufficiently indicated that the known history of the activity could not explain the changing iconographic choices, and because it became increasingly clear that the changing iconographic choices in the different areas were strongly correlated with each other, rather than peculiar to the activity in question.

In this chapter I explore further both how the changes in scenes of one type of activity relate to the changes in scenes of another, and how those changes relate to the much-discussed "Greek revolution," the dominant accounts of which I described in chapter 1. If we are looking not at various patterns of change but at a single pattern of change, is that pattern of change to be understood by seeing it as part of some wider pattern of change in social life or in political life, or should we account for it in more strictly art-historical terms?

1. Morality

It was a striking feature of the changes in the choice of imagery to do with warfare and athletics described in chapters 3 and 4 that they did not appear to relate to changes in warfare and athletics. We cannot construct any sort of history of relations between men and women, relations with the gods, or the symposium, independent of the images on pots, but we have variously seen the problems of relating changes in imagery to changes in how people behaved in those areas. Changes in the subject matter of the images on pottery appear not to correlate with changes in the subject matter from which the pots draw their images. While what artists choose to show when representing activities occurring in the world around them is clearly not independent of the visual features of those engaging in these activities, as the arrival of Persians into imagery of warfare demonstrates (4.15–16), what was to be seen nevertheless underdetermines what was shown. In particular, the major changes in what was shown were not determined by changes in what was to be seen.

If the changes that we have observed in scenes of warfare, scenes of the gymnasium, scenes in which men relate to women and men and women relate to the gods, and scenes of the symposium and of reveling, are not obviously related to changes in war, athletics, and so on, they *are* obviously related to one another. In all cases scenes of action become markedly less common or even disappear completely, and the performance of the core activity is no longer the prime focus of attention. Instead, attention is focused on the scenes that identify the actors but do not demand that those actors perform their defining action. The variety of different scenes shown shrinks, and even within the scenes that are shown the conventions as to how the scene is shown become much more restrictive. Although exact repetition continues to be shunned, innovation and originality cease to be at a premium.

One possible explanation for the changes can be ruled out. We are not dealing here simply with artists getting used to the possibilities of a new medium. It is true that the very earliest red-figure shows all sorts of fleeting iconographic experimentation, but the changes we have charted are primarily changes between what is shown by the second generation of red-figure painters, from the very end of the sixth century and start of the fifth, and what is shown by red-figure painters half a century later. What is more, although the much smaller quantity of sculpture that survives does not allow the same story to be documented in detail, it has become clear that a similar sculptural story can be told. The changes that I have described are most easily seen in red-figure pot painting, but they are not restricted to red-figure pot painting.

We have repeatedly seen that one way of describing the changes is in terms of changes in the way that the figures represented relate to one another on the pot—that is true in the case of athletes and soldiers, it is also true of sexual relations, of the symposium and *komos*, and of satyrs. The images of archaic red-figure are images of competition between individuals, whether in the gymnasium, on the field of battle, in the *komos*, or in sexual relations, and they are images of individuals getting on with it themselves. The figures may or may not be part of a group, but the focus of interest is not on how the figures relate to one another, but on the individual and on the question of how that individual measures up. The focus is on the individual performance (**9.1**). By contrast, the individual performance is more or less systematically excluded from the view offered in images of the middle of the fifth century. Athletes no longer compete, they are no longer seen to run, jump, throw discus or javelin, dance the pyrrhic dance, or whatever. Soldiers no longer fight except in the stylized warfare with Persians or in mythological combats. Booners disappear and the *komos* is tamed. Courtship ceases to be physically active. What we see is the athlete relaxing once the athletics is over, on his own or with others, the soldier within the domestic context, taking his helmet to go play his role in the army, the symposiast watching an entertainment, the bride preparing for her wedding, the satyr wearing a himation and playing with his family, individuals deep in thought, concentrating on what is to be done (**9.2**).

To describe the change in the choice of scenes in these terms is to describe a change in what social values are highlighted. Depending on where the emphasis is placed, this could be termed a shift from individualism to corporate values, or a shift from a world dominated by competitive values to a world prepared to embrace collaboration, or indeed a shift from a world of action to one of contemplation. Such descriptions are not unattractive—for one thing, they offer a way of relating the transformations to politics, for another, shifts of value in ancient Greek societies have been described by other scholars in very comparable terms.

During the 1990s Leslie Kurke and Ian Morris promoted a view of archaic Greek society where the elite were split between two warring ideologies, the elitist and the middling.[1] The elitist attitude, voiced most clearly in monodic lyric, embraces the oriental and the luxurious, along with ath-

---

[1] See particularly Kurke (1992; 1999); Morris (1996; 2000).

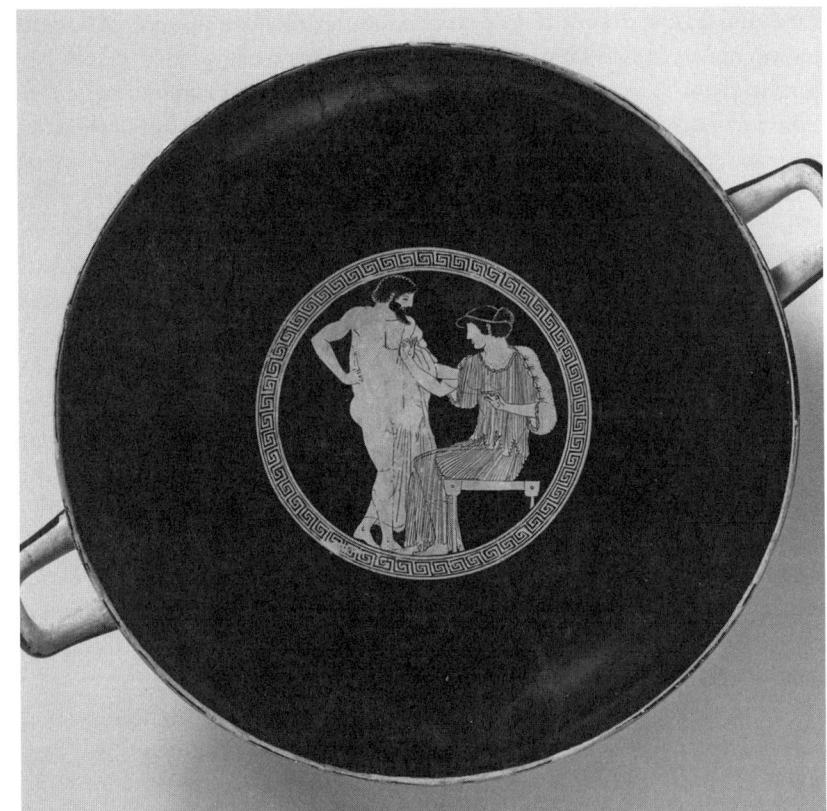

Figure 9.1. Interior of red-figure cup, diameter 0.333 m, signed by Hieron as potter and attributed to Makron as painter, from Vulci, ca. 490. *ARV* 468.146, New York, Metropolitan Museum of Art, Rogers Fund 1912, 12.231.1. www.metmuseum.org

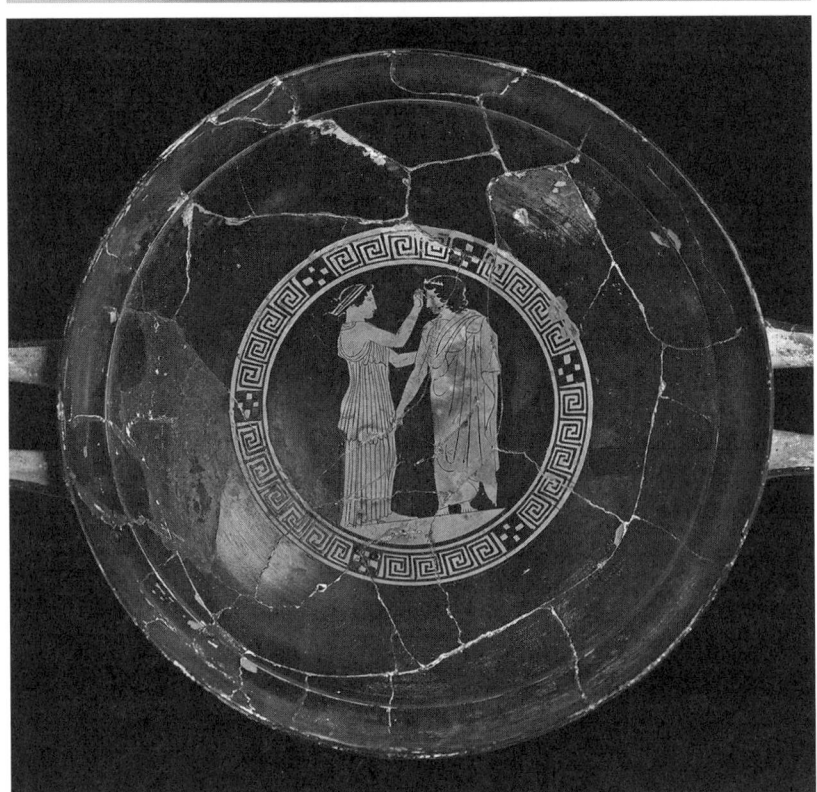

Figure 9.2. Interior of red-figure cup, diameter 0.241 m, attributed to the Calliope Painter, from Nola, ca. 430. *ARV* 1259.5, London, British Museum 1867,0508.1047 (E 93). © The Trustees of the British Museum.

letics and distinction. It represents a claim to superiority because the elite enjoy privileged links to a wider world and to the world of the gods. By contrast, the "middling" position stood for fair shares and the rule of law, it championed having enough rather than having as much as possible, and it was in favor of the transparent measuring involved in exchange of coinage rather than the obfuscation of quantity involved in the exchange of gifts.

The claims made by Kurke and Morris have been subjected to sustained criticism.[2] Although Kurke is insistent that her claims are about "discursive structures," those claims require that we are talking about something more than simply two positions that could be adopted for the sake of argument in particular circumstances. Morris wants to identify middling attitudes in real-life matters of egalitarianism, including dedicatory practices and urban planning, so that Kurke can summarize Morris's claim as being about "Panhellenic pressure towards egalitarian uniformity beginning in the eighth century."[3] Neither the discourse nor the reality, however, reveals any such well-defined opposition—orientalist motifs penetrate into quite humble artifacts, athletics elicits popular enthusiasm and polis support, and so on.

The criticisms of Kurke's and Morris's views notwithstanding, their formulations remain in some respects good to think with. We do not have to believe in clearly identifiable "middling" and "elitist" factions to accept that different people at different times (and indeed the same people at different times) wanted to advertise more or less elitist, more or less middling views. There were occasions for exchange of gifts, even for those most heavily involved in the monetary economy. As Kurke herself acknowledges, "in any given period, the available models of self are multiple, fluid, even contradictory," but because of this "it is worth considering what strategic use is made of different models by different ideologically interested positions."[4]

Something similar is true of an older model of change over time that has also been widely discredited. This is the model put forward by A.W.H. Adkins more than fifty years ago in his *Merit and Responsibility*, published in 1960. For Adkins the Homeric "system of values is . . . a system based on the competitive standard of *arête* . . . not involving the co-operative excellences at all."[5] For Adkins the explanation was straightforward: "Homeric society does value most highly the class it needs most: men who are well-armed, strong, fleet of foot and skilled in war, counsel and strategy. . . . In comparison with the competitive excellences, the quieter co-operative excellences must take an inferior position; for it is not evident at this time that the security of the group depends to any large extent upon these excellences."[6] The competitive virtues, in Adkins's view, dominated what it

---

[2] See particularly Hammer (2004), Kistler (2004), and, more generally on the archaic "aristocracy," Duplouy (2006).
[3] Kurke (1999), 23, for discursive structures, 21 for Morris's claims.
[4] Kurke (1999), 335.
[5] Adkins (1960), 46.
[6] Ibid., 36.

was to be an *agathos* until the fifth century when we begin to find, first, occasions when a man is termed *kakos* because of failures in cooperative virtues and then, in a fragment wrongly ascribed to Euripides's *Herakleidai*, *arête* defined entirely in terms of cooperative virtues: "There are three *aretai* which you must practice, my child. Honour the gods, your parents and the common laws of Greece, and in so doing you will have for ever an excellent, *kallistos*, garland of *eukleia*, fair fame."[7] Adkins suggested that "it might not be coincidental" that this new emphasis "appeared at a time when Athens, now mistress of an empire, could look forward to more material prosperity than any Greek state had ever known, and could hence afford to give more prominence to the quieter virtues."[8]

The methodological problems with Adkins's approach and the inadequacy of his conclusions are serious. He simply overlooked virtues that were not described in simple evaluative language (by the use of the term *agathos*)—such as the virtue of wise counsel.[9] And his opposition between competitive and collaborative virtues ignored the way in which it is fundamental to the Homeric epics, as to life, that competitive success (above all, winning the Trojan War) depends on collaboration.[10] But if Adkins was wrong to think that there was a fundamental change in moral compass, that does not mean that there was no change of emphasis. The fact that Adkins's very restricted lens detected a marked change in the usage of *agathos* is itself significant, even if not as significant as Adkins himself thought. In the literary evidence, as in the images on painted pottery, there is a change in the social values that are highlighted.[11]

2. Politics

Adkins had no doubt why it was that different social values came to be emphasized in the writings of Athenians of the fifth century. For him the difference was a "difference between the values of tyranny and oligarchy and those of democracy; and it is a difference not based on sentiment but on practical realities."[12] He went on to explain: "Since both poor and rich now participate both in defence and deliberation, *agathos* must surely cease to be a term denoting and commending a social class and instead denote men of all classes with certain specific attributes which make them valuable to the state; and if the co-operative excellences prove to be among these attributes, they will be enrolled forthwith among the *aretai*."[13]

---

[7] Euripides fr. 853N (quoted by Stobaeus 3.1.80), as translated in Adkins (1960), 176.
[8] Adkins (1960), 179.
[9] See Schofield (1986).
[10] Williams (1993), 195n17; Long (1970), 122–26.
[11] Cf. Bažant (1985), 77: "Voilà, la raison principale de la disparition de notre 'magnifique Athénien' de l'imagerie du 5ᵉ siècle. S'il n'était plus possible de le représenter en tant que héros épique, il préfère quitter l'imagerie définitivement: il peut se moquer de lui-même mais il ne tolérait pas qu'on rie de lui. Et les peintres devaient le respecter."
[12] Adkins (1960), 197.
[13] Ibid., 197–98.

Adkins's picture of Athenian democracy is in many ways an odd one. Athenian democracy continued to be highly competitive (consider only ostracism). Indeed, Adkins's own method of detecting the change relies upon continued competitiveness, since what he does is to identify who it is that lays claim to being *agathos*, and who is recognized as *agathos*. Such claims are not claims to have reached a certain standard of proficiency that all might meet, they are competitive claims to excel. Nor is it plausible to think that the terms of the competition have been transformed—it is not obvious, for instance, that it was cooperative excellences that won an individual election to the generalship (the role of nonmilitary skills in the general's job is still treated as a matter that needs demonstrating by Xenophon *Memorabilia* 3.4). Skills in fighting still mattered. If the change in the value system is related to democracy, then we need a subtler account of democracy.

It has long been recognized that Athenian democracy was not born fully formed out of the head of Kleisthenes in 508. The debate about whether Athenian democracy should be thought to begin with Kleisthenes, to have already begun with Solon in the early sixth century, or only to begin with the Ephialtic reforms of 462 has crucially depended upon what democracy is taken to be.[14] Scholars with different views of what constitutes democracy in the modern world are keen to assert the democratic credentials of whatever Athenian arrangements offer best justification for their preferred modern constitution. But the contemporary political factors that determine where individual scholars place *the* democratic revolution should not hide the fact that the Athenian constitution changed over time because the formal constitutional arrangements changed and because Athenian attitudes to political participation changed.

It is unlikely that the slogan under which Kleisthenes gathered support for his reform program was *demokratia*. The terms used both in the near-contemporary texts that (falsely) celebrated the contribution of the "tyrant-slayers," Harmodios and Aristogeiton, to political revolution and in Herodotos's later description of what Kleisthenes did, are *isegoria* and *isonomia*—equality of speech and equality before the law. It was not placing power (*kratos*) in the hands of the people (*demos*) that was advertised by these terms, but the end of distinctions among the citizen body when it came either to political participation or legal rights. Whether or not these were the slogans bandied about in 508, and some modern scholars have been skeptical,[15] Athenians will have supported Kleisthenes on the basis of his substantive proposals, and it is these that offer the best gloss on why the Athenians backed Kleisthenes and passed the reforms to the political system that he proposed.

Kleisthenes's system of new tribes, trittyes, and demes, was distinctly complex. All three units were new. The demes mapped onto existing communities, but not all existing communities will have become politically

---

[14] See Osborne (2006).
[15] Ober (1989), 72–74, is skeptical; see the discussion of Raaflaub (1996), 143–45.

recognized as demes (some were too small to justify a representative on the council). There had been trittyes and tribes previously, but the new units of those names cut across the old ones. One advantage that may have sold the new system to the Athenians, as we have seen earlier, was the possibility of deploying it to produce a more efficient and effective army. But some political advantages must also have been perceived.

One political advantage may have been the simple advantage of change. If Athenians were worried by the fact that the old political arrangements, to which Athens seems to have reverted once Hippias was expelled, were proving once more divisive, raising the specter of another coup, then Kleisthenes could at least promise that his proposals meant change. But change for its own sake can hardly have been enough: these changes ought to have something particular to recommend them. The way in which the new tribes and trittyes cut across the old ones promised routes to power independent of any previous networks. The use of the lot to select members of the council from the new demes, and the existence of quotas for each deme, pointed to an equality at the level of the individual and at the level of the group. But this was an equality of opportunity to participate. No one can have been under any illusion but that within the random group thrown up by the lot, competition for influence would still go on—a body of five hundred was simply too big to carry out discussions by going around the room asking everybody for their opinion. Kleisthenes opened up the system so that everyone could compete, but the system he created made no promises that everyone would play an equal part. Whether there was a property qualification for the new council we do not know, but property qualifications certainly remained for other offices.[16] Kleisthenes's promises must have been about opportunity, not about equal achievements.

It is highly relevant to the imagery on Athenian painted pottery that Kleisthenic encouragement of competition showed itself in two particular areas—in warfare and in competitive festivals. The close link between Kleisthenes's constitutional change and military success at Athens was already emphasized by Herodotos, in his comments on the defeat of the Boiotians and Chalkidians (5.78) and in the implications of his story of how much easier it was for Aristagoras to persuade the Athenians to support the Ionian Revolt than to persuade the Spartans (5.97.2). But there was an equally intimate link between Kleisthenes's constitutional changes and the enhancement of the competitive element at Athenian festivals. The new Kleisthenic tribes were repeatedly deployed as the basis for new festival competitions, and the festival calendar was expanded with new celebrations accompanied by competitive events.[17]

But if the Kleisthenic constitution rejoiced in competition, the political pressures to remove barriers to taking part ended up by undermining that competition. The story of post-Kleisthenic constitutional reforms at Athens is the story of the progressive removal of barriers to participation. The

---

[16] Rhodes (1972), 2, thinks that thetes were excluded from membership of the council, but that, as with the archonship later, the exclusion was not actively enforced.

[17] Osborne (1993), Fisher (2011).

decision to choose archons by lot from a preelected group, rather than by direct election, taken in 487/486, randomized the opportunity to serve in the highest magistracy.[18] The further decision to open the archonship beyond the top two property classes to the *zeugitai* in 457/456 significantly enlarged the eligible body.[19] The decision, at more or less the same date, to pay those serving on the popular juries, together with the extension effected by the Ephialtic reforms of the range of cases heard by popular juries, reduced, if it did not remove, the practical bar to taking an active part in the judicial system (where membership of a particular jury was allocated by lot).[20]

These constitutional changes need to be seen alongside a series of interventions in the ordering of Athenian religious life. Apart from the earliest of all Athenian decrees (*IG* i³ 1), which concerns the sending of settlers to Salamis, every surviving inscribed record of an Athenian decision that can be more or less firmly dated to the period down to 460 concerns religious matters—as do all but one of the earliest decisions that we know to have been made by Athenian demes. Although many of these inscriptions are fragmentary and the precise force of their provisions uncertain, they include detailed specification of who can hold particular religious offices and what they are to do, specification for particular rituals, detailed regulation of the Eleusinian Mysteries, and adjudication of where the responsibilities of one particular *genos* (family with traditional religious responsibilities) lay.[21] What can be said with some certainty is that these various interventions show the Athenians keen to assert that controlling access to the gods was a matter for the community as a whole. Already in the regulation of a festival of Herakles in the years before the Persian Wars the organization is put in the hands of thirty men over the age of thirty, chosen three from each of the ten tribes.

These changes to political and religious access were intimately linked, and their importance cannot be overestimated. Politics and religion were not separate spheres—the city community took responsibility for relations with the gods, just as it took responsibility for relations with other Greek cities or foreign powers (another early decree relates to relations with the

---

[18] [Aristotle] *Constitution of the Athenians* 22.5. [Aristotle] says that the preselected group numbered five hundred. This has been doubted by some scholars (see Rhodes [1981], 273–74) on the grounds that later, when the final allotment was on the basis of preallotment, rather than preelection, only one hundred were preallotted ([Aristotle] *Constitution of the Athenians* 8.1) and that hardly more than five hundred will have been eligible. But there is no reason why preallotment and preelection should involve bodies of the same size, and inclusion of almost all those eligible may have been precisely the point.

[19] [Aristotle] *Constitution of the Athenians* 26.2.

[20] [Aristotle] *Constitution of the Athenians* 27.3 (cf. Plutarch *Perikles* 9.2–3); Plato *Gorgias* 515e2–7; Aristotle *Politics* 1274a8–9.

[21] *IG* i³ 3 (laying down what sort of person should be appointed to run games of Herakles); i³ 4B, regulating what officials can do and what the sanctions are on their behavior; i³ 5 (= OR 106) detailing an Eleusinian sacrifice; i³ 6 extensive regulations for the Eleusinian Mysteries; i³ 7 (= OR 108) regulation of the role of the Praxiergidai in rituals of Athena; i³ 8 regulation of cult activity at Sounion; i³ 230–34 highly fragmentary sacred laws dating between 510 and 460; i³ 243 fragmentary decree of deme of Melite on religious matters; i³ 244 (= OR 107) decree of Skambonidai on deme sacrifices.

city of Phaselis²²). The interventions over the organization of religious cult removed one of the bases on which political superiority might be claimed. In important ways the opening up of religious and political responsibility made possible a new attitude to Athenian citizenship. In effect Athens was being changed by degrees from a city where most, if not all, citizens had theoretical opportunity to become one of the political elite (for example, by putting their name forward for allotment to the council of 500) to a city where the citizen body *was* the political elite. If being able to attend the assembly and put oneself forward for service on the council or as a juror in the courts constituted being part of the political elite, then after Pericles's citizenship law of 451/450 masculine gender and birth from two Athenian parents was enough. At this point it becomes reasonable to think of a "citizen club," as it has sometimes been called, of which adult Athenians simply *were* part without any need to demonstrate that they were worthy of club membership.²³

One place where the effect of this change becomes apparent is in the creation of the notion of the "good Athenian citizen," the creation of distinctively "democratic" virtues. These virtues are shown off most particularly in the funeral oration that Thucydides puts in the mouth of Perikles at the conclusion of the first year of the Peloponnesian War. Whatever the relationship between the words that Thucydides gives to Perikles and the words that Perikles spoke on that occasion, the coincidence of themes between this speech and other later funeral orations effectively guarantees that this speech reflects the persistent sentiments paraded in these annual speeches.²⁴

Perikles's emphasis is on the laws offering equal justice to all, on poverty not barring the way to contributions to public life, and on military achievement that is a product of a relaxed approach to individual freedom that relies on natural courage, not on forcing courage by painful discipline.²⁵ Perikles makes a strong division between private and public life, where a liberal attitude toward what others do in private combines with obedience to those holding public office and to the laws (2.37.2–3), and where abundant public provision of recreation exists alongside private elegance (2.38.1). Private wealth provides opportunities for doing things, rather than the basis of boasting difference (2.40.1). Participation in politics is not an opportunity but a duty: "we regard those who take no part in public matters not as unambitious but as useless" (2.40.2). The universal ability of all Athenians to come to a view is extolled, rather than the less widely shared skill in originating ideas. Athenians are willing to die, risking their

---

²²*IG* i³ 10 (OR 120).

²³Bažant (1985), 79: "ces images sont étroitement liées avec une société hétérogène de citoyens égaux, c'est à dire avec la société libre', going on to observe that 'Ces images évoquent la liberté de la pensée et de l'action, c'est vrai. Mais par ce fait meme ells peuvent aussi masque l'absence de cette liberté, ells peuvent faire penser à elle là où elle n'est nullement."

²⁴So particularly Loraux (1981), 222 = (1986) 220, cf. Balot (2014), 14.

²⁵On the distinctive notion of democratic courage, see Balot (2014), particularly chap. 2. I am, however, not convinced by Balot that the ridicule to which Persian courage is subjected in Aeschylus's *Persai* constitutes evidence that a distinctive idea of democratic courage had been formulated by 472.

lives because of the importance they attach to the provision that the Athenian state makes for all (2.43.1). Inevitably, Perikles treats the deaths as an offering that was made in common; notoriously, the thought that any citizen can take the place of any other leads him to summon those not past child bearing to beget further sons to replace those who have died (2.44.3).

A speech commemorating all the war dead is constrained by the occasion. Stress on the achievements of particular individuals would be inappropriate and invidious. Nevertheless, the ways and the terms in which the common contribution of all to the city is stressed are notable. This is an image of what democracy means that is very different from Kleisthenes's provision of opportunities for all to compete. Participation has become itself the glory, and the institutions of the city what all are fighting to maintain (2.43.1–2). That different individuals have different skills is alluded to, but every effort is made to avoid ranking those skills. Getting on, "advancement in public life," is made dependent not on individual efforts but on the verdict of the community, it "falls to reputation for capacity" (2.37.1).

There is, then, good reason to believe that what Athenian democracy was and had been for some time by 431 was different from what Athenian democracy was in 508. Athenian values had changed, if not from elitist to middling or from competitive to cooperative then certainly from more individualist to more corporate, from democracy giving everyone opportunity for distinction to democracy conferring distinction on all. Kleisthenes attracted support by offering a theater in which any individual could perform. Perikles offers a vision where Athenians as a whole perform for the rest of the Greek world.

Behind the changed constitutional rules and the imagination of a changed citizen body lay a background of changed Athenian roles in real life. If Athenians of the sixth century were obliged to watch the same political conflicts being played out again and again, no longer was that true. The democracy that ran the Athenian empire was much more in need of ciphers than of leaders—men who would take on and reliably perform the offices required to maintain Athens's control over her allies, rather than men who saw political office as a route to personal power. The bureaucracy of empire created a large number of similar jobs that needed to be similarly performed—quite apart from the uniformity upon which military success, whether on land or at sea, depended. The numbers of Athenian citizens had probably doubled (at least) between 507 and 450, and the practicality of playing a major role in political initiative, rather than decision, had become quite distant.[26] Athenian belief in their difference was basic to their imperialism, but that difference was now construed as wholesale difference between Athenians and others.

Outside the assembly, it was at festivals and when mustering for war that the Athenian citizen body most showed itself off. Little wonder then if scenes that relate to warfare and athletics show the impact of a changing

---

[26] Patterson (1981), Watson (2010).

conception of the Athenian citizen body and what distinguished it. In both areas, we move from images that put the emphasis on the variety of those taking part and the prizes that are out there to win to images in which the prizes are taken for granted and the participants notable for their uniformity, not their difference. The new emphasis is on bodies that cannot be told apart, performing actions that do not open themselves up to judgments as to whether they are well or badly done. What has changed is not what people do but the aspects of behavior that are kept foremost in mind. Participation has become the name of the classical democratic game; Kleisthenic competition and individual stories of success or failure are out.

3. Aesthetics

That there should be a correlation between the world imagined in the funeral oration and the world imagined on pottery painted in Athens will hardly cause surprise, particularly to those who "have been profoundly affected by Michel Foucault's claim that everything is political: that language and knowledge, like everything else in culture, are not separate, disinterested spheres exempt from the play of differential power relations, but are discourses generated and structured by those relations."[27] Power relations undoubtedly played out differently in the middle of the fifth century from the way in which they had played out at the end of the sixth century. The changes in differential power relations will have generated discourses that were different and differently structured by comparison to those of half a century earlier, but that had much in common across different areas of culture. But if we stress only the way in which power relations generate and structure discourses, we make the continual "bottom-up" adjustments and innovations in ways or seeing and representing the world impossible to understand and we reduce politics to a top-down question of who has dominance.[28]

Foucault himself saw that the relationship between knowledge and power was two-way—it is not simply that discourses are generated and structured by differential power relations but that differential power relations are generated and structured by discourses. Power is not the only thing that affects discourse. When individuals and groups discourse, they do so to help organize their experiences, to understand the natural, the social, and indeed the supernatural world in which they live—an understanding that, even if aimed at eventual dominance, cannot be reduced to a simple assertion of power. As we saw in chapter 1, we need to ask not simply how politics—that is, in this context, not simply the way members

---

[27] So Dougherty and Kurke (1993), 5, citing Foucault (1977), 27: "there is no power relation without the correlative constitution of a field of knowledge, nor any knowledge that does not presuppose and constitute at the same time power relations."

[28] Hammer (2004), 506; my formulations in this and the next paragraph owe much to Hammer's work.

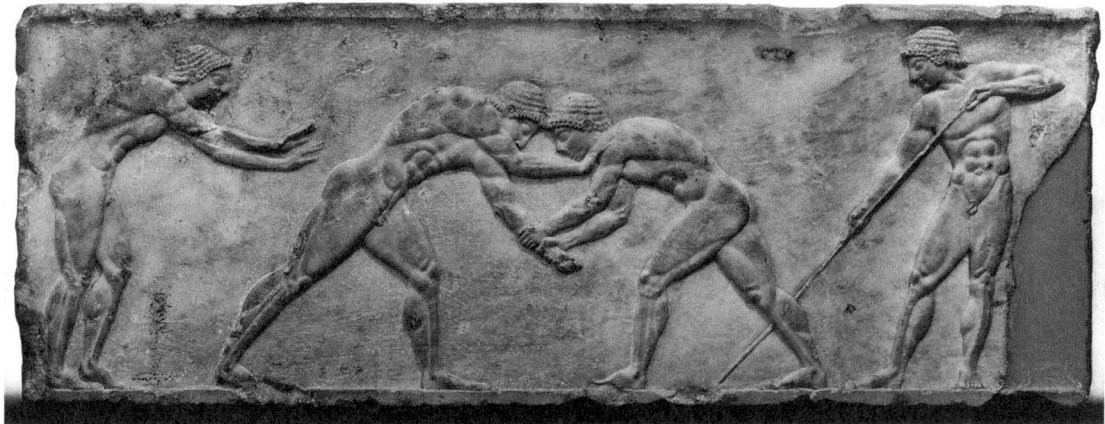

Figure 9.3. One side of a base for a *kouros*, found in the Themistoklean wall (for another side see 1.16). Athens National Archaeological Museum 3476. © Hirmer Fotoarchiv Munich.

of a community relate to each other, and that the community relates to other communities, but also the way the community relates to its gods—affects art but how art affects politics.

We have already seen enough of what happens to Greek art between circa 520 and 440 to see that explaining the changes to the selection of images in political terms is not only theoretically inadequate, it is also inadequate in terms of the actual evidence. For although I have predominantly traced the changes in imagery through analysis of what was painted on Athenian pottery, the changes in the images on Athenian pottery are closely paralleled by changes in the imagery in Greek art more generally, and in particular in Greek sculpture. The focus on athletic action and competition found in archaic red-figure is paralleled by the focus on athletic action in the reliefs on the base for an Athenian *kouros* from the late sixth century (**9.3** cf. 1.16). The depiction of the athlete as a figure in a gymnasium holding a strigil or otherwise engaged in pre- or postgym activity found in classical red-figure pottery is paralleled in late fifth-century Attic grave stelai such as that of Eupheros (3.2), but also in Polykleitos's Diadoumenos (3.28) and the Westmacott athlete (10.1).

Polykleitos is a crucial figure here because he was not an Athenian; he is referred to as an Argive by Plato (*Protagoras* 311c) and Pausanias (6.6.2), as from Sikyon by Pliny (*N.H.* 34.55).[29] There is no reason to believe that the originals of either the Diadoumenos or the Westmacott athlete were set up in Athens, even if we reject the identification of the Westmacott athlete with Polykleitos's bronze statue of the boy boxer Kyniskos of Mantineia, which Pausanias (6.4.11) saw at Olympia and whose base survives with cuttings for feet that correspond to the foot position of the statue (*IvO* 149).[30] To explain what happens to the imagery on pottery and in

---

[29] Sikyon was ruled by an oligarchy throughout the fifth century; Argos became democratic in the second quarter of the fifth century. For an argument that Polykleitos's Doryphoros personified the Argive demos, see Vollmer (2014/2015).

[30] For discussion, see Borbein (1996), 78: the argument turns on the belief that the Olympia

sculpture in terms of Athenian politics would require us to think that changes effected by changed power relations in Athens were replicated across the Greek world, even in cities where there was no similar change in power relations.

The archaic *kouros* base does not simply show a different aspect of athletics from Polykleitos's statues, it shows it in a different sculptural style. As we have seen in chapter 1, the stylistic revolution that transforms the late archaic athlete into Polykleitos's classical body has regularly been explained either as a consequence of an internal evolution in artistic style or as a consequence of outside events, and in particular of the Persian Wars. My demonstration that the change in representational practice is not a matter of style alone but also of the subject matter depicted has offered a supplement to traditional descriptions of the "Greek revolution," not a replacement for them. It is time to ask how these considerations about subject matter affect the possibilities for "imaginative reconstruction" of the world, to revert to Gombrich's phrase, or, in the terms recently championed by Jeremy Tanner, what part they play in the changing "way in which a set of generative codes conditions the possibilities of affective communication."[31]

One way of thinking about the difference between these late archaic and classical images is in terms of their temporality.[32] It has been tempting for scholars to think that what is to be seen in early red-figure images has a direct relationship to what was to be seen in late archaic life because late archaic red-figure paintings and late archaic reliefs seem to catch a particular moment—the ball has just been thrown (1.16), the runner is just about to start (9.3), the soldiers are caught at just *this* moment of putting on their arms and armor (4.17–18), and so on. Even among *kouroi*, late figures such as Aristodikos, whose hands break away from his thighs, altering his whole poise and balance, seem to be captured at a particular instance; there is something uneasy about this figure, who has acquired a momentary quality. Pose plays a part here, but so does the hardness of contour: these are bodies under some stress. Archaic sculptures are sometimes referred to as static,[33] but to talk about them in this way is to mistake what is particular about them; it is not that they are static but that they are tense, they show bodies under stress, bodies that are not relaxed—just look at the clenched fists of the *kouros*. This stress, and this sense of moment, becomes still more heightened in work of the so-called severe style, where a certain theatricality, the striking of a pose, which Pollitt associated with the term *rhythmos*,

---

inscription could not be later than 450 and that the Westmacott athlete must belong between the Doryphoros and Diadoumenos and cannot date before 430. The only work of Polykleitos that can be independently dated is the replacement cult statue for the Argive Heraion that had been burned down in 423.

[31] Tanner (2006), 70–71, for this phraseology. In the language of archaeologists influenced by J. J. Gibson, my question is about the affordances of the new iconographic and stylistic preferences. See Gibson (1977; 1979).

[32] Compare Barthes (1980) on the "punctum."

[33] Cf., e.g., Neer (2010), 4.

dominates groups like the Tyrannicides (10.2), or Myron's Athena and Marsyas, and gives an elastic power to Myron's Discobolos.[34]

In the classical figures, by contrast, whether it is on pots or as freestanding or relief sculptures, the sense of moment is gone. For a viewer interested in incident there is nothing to take home from a glance at these images. These figures demand not a glance but a gaze.[35] This is not a matter of whether figures are still or in motion, but whether they are or are not caught at a moment. The horsemen of the Parthenon frieze are in motion, but they are not caught at a moment. The insistent detail of archaic red-figure painted pottery draws attention to a particularity that is momentary. The generic features of the classical figures insist that they transcend the moment. If we are to see anything we have to stop and gaze—a movement the Parthenon frieze compels by making the viewer see the continuous run of figures only in chunks viewed through the outer colonnade of the temple.[36]

This contention could be illustrated from many of the pots discussed in this book, but I offer one particular example. A stamnos signed by Smikros and to be dated to around 510 shows a symposium in full swing (**9.4–5**).[37] To the right of one handle we see a young man, his garment tied round his waist, bent over under the weight of an amphora that he is carrying toward a large dinos on a stand, next to which are two jugs on the ground. He gesticulates toward a bearded man who is about to lift another amphora to empty into the dinos. On the other side from these preparations we see the symposiasts themselves, two young men reclining, one of them in the company of a female aulos player, and with his head thrown back singing, who is labeled as "Smikros," and one with a cup cradled in his left hand reaching out with his right hand toward a young woman wearing bracelets and earrings, dressed in chiton and himation but with her himation down around her waist, who is untying a sash from around her head. Whether we concentrate here on this young woman or on the young man about to empty the amphora we have a strong sense of the momentary. We have caught a glimpse of social relations as they happen—the young servant signaling to the older, the young woman deciding that this is the moment at which the next stage of intimacy should begin.

Juxtapose this to one more scene of a hoplite departing. Another stamnos, ascribed to the Kleophon Painter and dated to around 430, shows a woman with a jug and a hoplite with a phiale in the company of an old man with a stick and another woman (**9.6**).[38] The drawing is extremely detailed and sensitive, with a very vivid eye gazing at the viewer from the shield, but

---

[34] Pollitt (1972), 56–60. For theatricality, and its polar opposite, absorption, see Fried (1980).

[35] On the opposition between the gaze and the glance, see Bryson (1983), 87–131. For what is at issue with classical sculpture being a reconfiguration of the relation of image to beholder, see Neer (2010), 4, though I see the change differently from Neer (contrast, for example, his use of theatrical on p. 6 and my uses of theatrical).

[36] Osborne (1987).

[37] The "self-portrait" here is discussed at length by Hedreen (2016), who argues that "Smikros" is actually a fiction and that the pots signed by him were painted by Euphronios.

[38] Matheson (1995), KL 2. The Kleophon Painter produced several hoplite departure scenes of

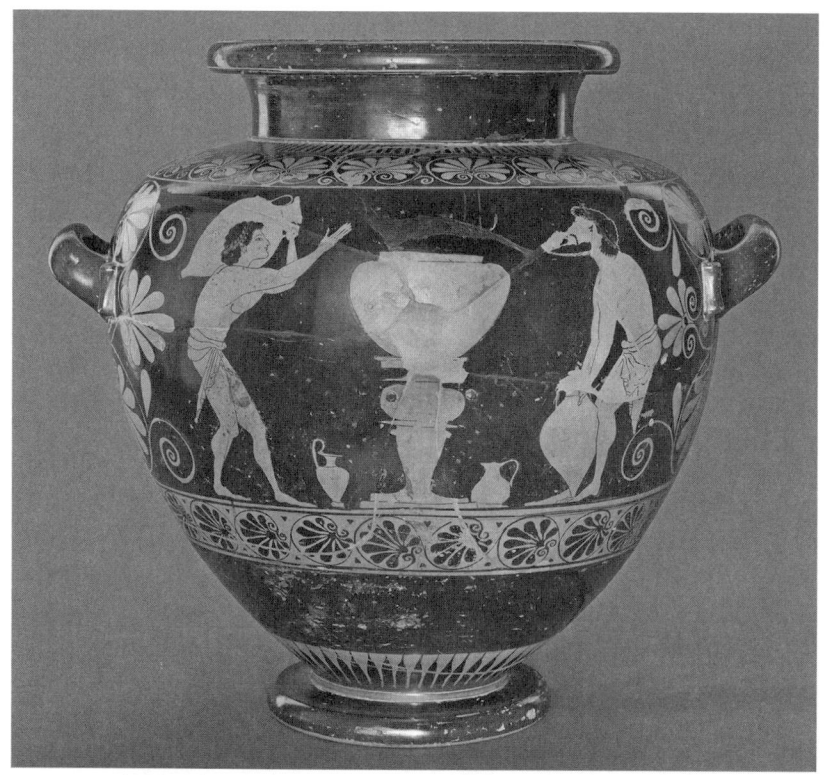

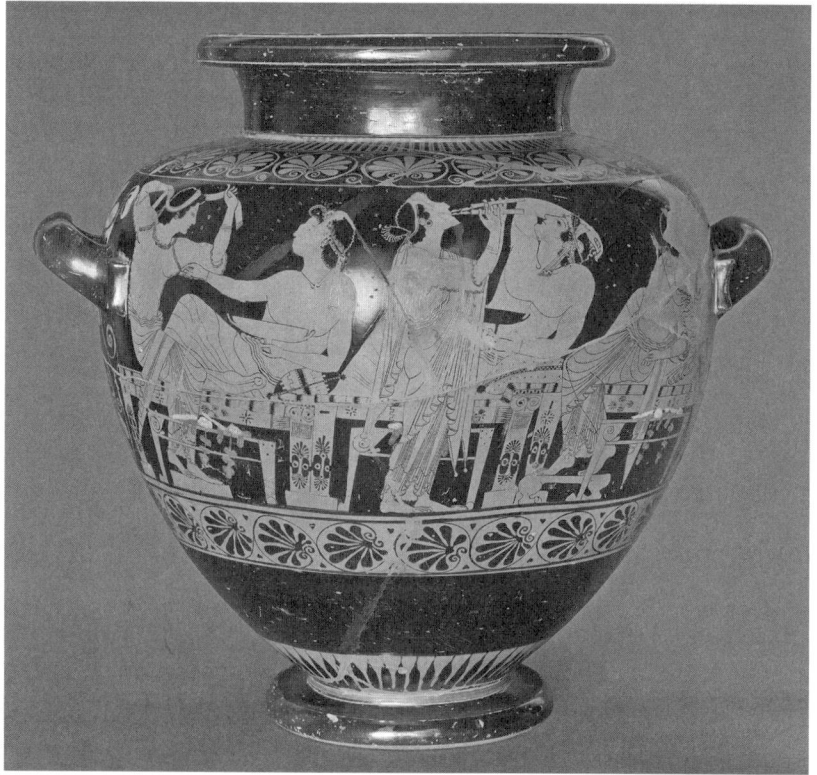

Figure 9.4–5. Red-figure stamnos, height 0.385 m, signed by Smikros as painter, ca. 510. *ARV* 20.1, Brussels Musées Royaux A717. © RMAH.

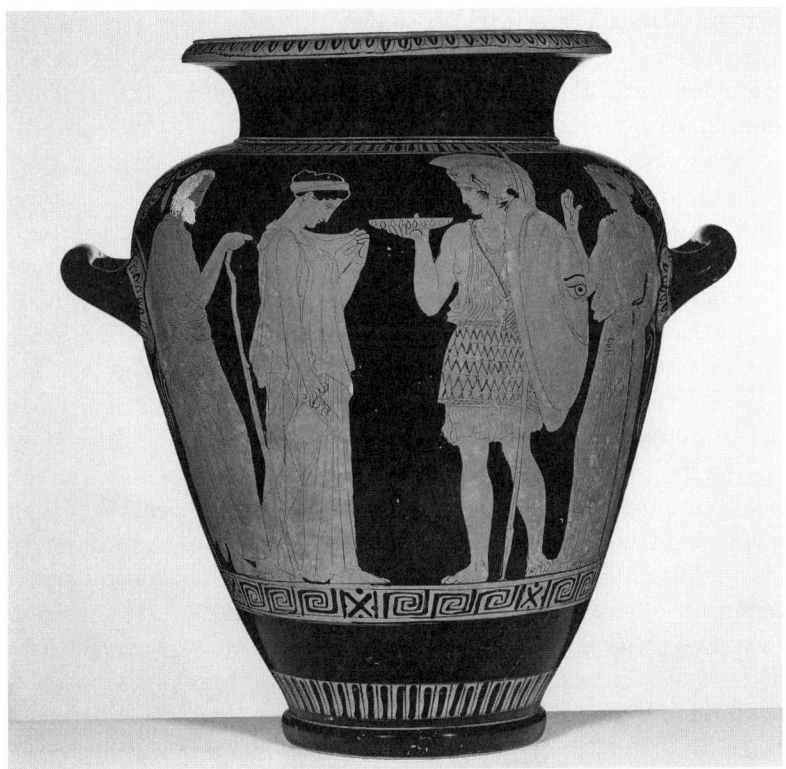

Figure 9.6. Red-figure stamnos, height 0.44 m, attributed to the Kleophon Painter, from Vulci, ca. 440. *ARV* 1143.2, Munich Staatliche Antikensammlung en 2415. © Staatliche Antikensammlung en und Glyptothek München. Photograph by Renate Kühling.

there is no sense that we have caught a particular moment in the interaction. This despite the fact that the woman who flanks the composition on the right raises her hand in what looks to be a sudden emotive reaction. Here what that reaction contributes is not a sense that this is a special moment, but rather an indication of the heightened emotions that attend all warrior departures. Cued in by the eye on the shield, and directed by her gesture, we see his seeing and her averted gaze and we feel their emotion. These figures stand in for every warrior, his wife and his parents, offering not the view of the harrowing experience of a particular family but of the emotions structured in to military service. We are invited not to enjoy a particular chance glimpse of people who are at an unusually revealing moment in a developing relationship but to gaze in contemplation at one example of the hundreds of families where this scene is repeated every time the assembly votes for another military campaign.

The invitation to gaze is an invitation to step outside time, to enter the frozen time of the figure represented, to match and mimic the absorption of that figure. By refusing to give the viewer more than a minimal external narrative—"young hoplite leaves those with whom he shares domestic re-

---

similar composition, with another in Saint Petersburg State Hermitage Museum being particularly close to this (*ARV* 1143.3).

ligious rituals and has strong affective bonds to go off to fight"—the painter invites the viewer to construct an internal narrative, a narrative that will account not simply for what the figure does but for who the figure is and so understand what motivates him.

In his discussion of the gaze, Bryson insists that the gaze dematerializes the viewer, writing of Vermeer's *The Artist in His Studio* that it "dissolves the bodily address of Albertian space in the computative space of a notional point outside duration and extension. Unique, discontinuous, discarnate bodies, move in spatial apartness, under the gaze of the Other."[39] But however true that is of the viewer's gaze at a Vermeer, it is not true of the gaze invited by classical painted pottery or sculpture. The classical body is not the machine for doing things that is the body of late archaic art, which invited the viewer only to note that it was doing things; the classical body has become the habitation of a person, the expression of what it is to be a human in this or that situation. The focus has shifted from what the action is to what the action means to the actor. But therefore also to the observer. To gaze upon the soldier taking his helmet, or upon the athlete standing at easy ready to deploy the strigil but not urgent to do so, is to enter into the sensuous materiality of the young man in this circumstance. The hard flesh of the late archaic figure has become soft, the muscles have relaxed, the bodies move gently in a space rather than balance uneasily on a podium or stage. The viewer no longer assesses what will happen from the action alone, for the figures relate and react to one another, as the viewer reacts to them.[40]

Subject matter and style are bound up together in this revolution. As the case of scenes of hoplites arming or departing shows, it is not that there is nothing in common between the world registered in late archaic painted pottery and the world presented in classical painted pottery. But the focus has changed, from a sharp focus upon incident to a soft focus upon actors. Except that *actors* has become the wrong word, not just because there is so much less action, but because we are no longer in the world of acting, whether that means of doing things or of showing off the doing of things—as the bearded javelin thrower shows off his skills on the Carpenter Painter's cup (3.20–22 and plate 9). The classical scenes offer us not actors doing things but humans in the course of being, at the same time corporeal and thinking and feeling beings (**9.7**).[41]

This aesthetic revolution carries a heavy burden. It is a revolution in what demands attention and in what is valued.[42] The changed style in which the figures are presented strongly reinforces the changed vision of the relationship between individual and group that we had already de-

---

[39] Bryson (1983), 117.

[40] Although theorized and described in rather different ways, there is much in common between what I seek to describe here and what Fehr has variously described. See, e.g., Fehr (2009).

[41] Bažant (1985) writes of the pots painted in the fifth century: "C'était donc sur ces vases céramiques que les peintres prenaient, pour la première fois dans l'histoire de l'art, le chemin du réalisme dans la représentation de la vie."

[42] For the involvement of beauty with attention and value, see Scarry (1999), 66, and Porter (2012), 351–52 and n. 10.

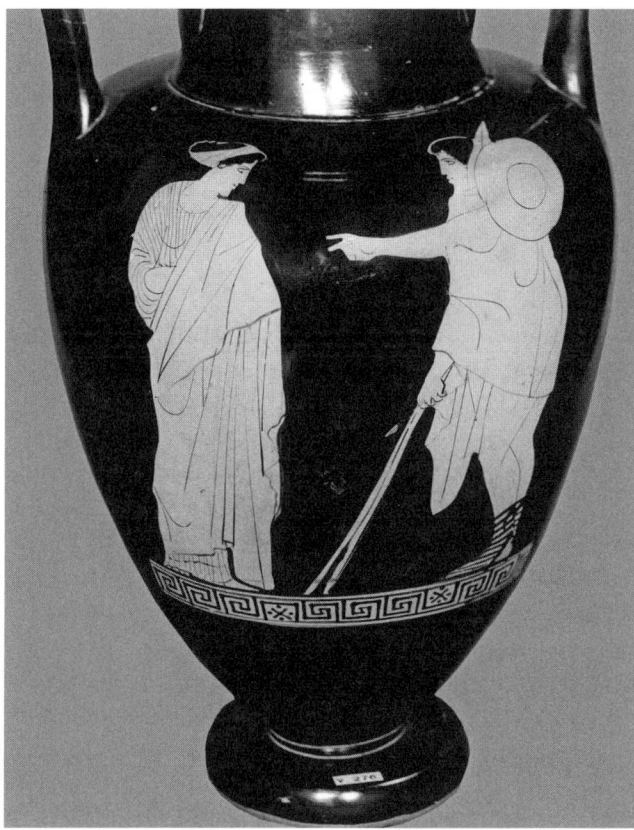

Figure 9.7. Red-figure Nolan amphora, height 0.33 m, attributed to the Phiale Painter, from Nola, ca. 450. *ARV* 1016.28, Oxford, Ashmolean Museum EF C.106 (V 276) = ANFortnum C.106. Image © Ashmolean Museum, University of Oxford.

tected in the changed choice of preferred subject. The way in which the figures are presented ensures that the viewer, as well as the figure represented, is absorbed within the group, is made to see him or herself as part of a group—the group of all who go to war, the group of all who exercise in the gymnasium. It is not hard to see that the absorption of the classical figures would be incompatible with the busyness, if not outright theatricality, of the late archaic scenes; but so too the hard-edged late archaic style would leave the figures standing about in the gym or departing for war oddly isolated, disappointed of opportunities for action.

What is at issue in the new classical aesthetics is how one sees the world.[43] Does one see other people as individual actors in their own drama, competitors existing in some parallel world, or does one see them as extensions of oneself, figures less to be admired, or criticized objectively, for what they do than allowed their own subjectivity and sympathized with? To see the world as putting on a series of shows that one observes is to see the world as other. That is how one sees the world of Herakles's labors—extraordinary achievements of figures who cannot be measured on a normal human scale—precisely the sorts of scenes and figures to which early ath-

[43] Cf. Bažant (1985), 74: "Ce qu'on veut représenter ici, ce n'est pas cette situation-ci ou cette situation-là car la vie n'est pas une série de situations absolument incohérentes et purement fortuites. Le but de la représentation de la vie sociale est toujours un ensemble de situations."

letic scenes are juxtaposed and early arming figures assimilated. To see the world sympathetically and empathetically one must see the world as like, inhabited by people with a subjectivity of their own. But to see a world that is other as a world that is like is to show oneself blind—whether the blindness stems from delusion, arrogance, or ignorance. How we see the world has moral, political, and indeed theological, implications.[44]

As Richard Neer has rightly insisted, "the effect of a given work of sculpture," and the same applies to works of painting, "—its solicitation and retention of a beholder's attention, its specific modes of appeal, gratification, frustration—is not an incidental or trivial fact about it."[45] But neither sculpture nor painting achieves its effects automatically. Effects are dependent both on the artist and the beholder—different beholders respond differently to the solicitations of different works of art. Artists may lead the way to new effects, but only if beholders follow will those new effects become general, come to constitute a new "style." The art produced in any period is always a consequence of an ongoing, if often silent, exchange between sculptors and painters and the people who buy their images about what images they want to produce and the images they want to consume.

Neither in the case of sculpture nor in the case of painted pottery was this an exchange that went on within the confines of a single polis. Although all the pots we are looking at were produced in Athens, the great majority of those I have illustrated were found in Etruria. We do not know for certain where all the sculptures to which I have referred were displayed or where they were found—several are known only from Roman copies—but as well as their having been created by non-Athenians there can be little doubt that comparable pieces were on display at Olympia, Delphi, and other major sanctuaries. The revolution in the way of seeing the world that is embodied in the sculptures and on the painted pottery was a way of seeing that came to be widely appreciated.[46]

If we think of interpersonal relations as entirely a matter of power relations we might reckon that the widespread adoption of a way of seeing forged in Athens was a matter of emulation of the values of the city with the greatest economic and political power. But this is an implausible view. What would it be for wealthy individuals who were in the very act of showing off to emulate a style that moved them off their elitist pedestal and encouraged ordinary sanctuary visitors to think themselves into their place? The more we think that choosing this selection of scenes and this style of representation carries moral and political baggage, the more we need to appreciate also its independent attractions.

---

[44] I do not explore the theological implications here, but they are important and flow directly from the way in which the classical style requires that the figure is seen as like, not other. I have discussed this in a slightly different context in Osborne (2011); cf. Tanner (2006), chap. 2.

[45] Neer (2010), 1. This is in the second paragraph of his introduction, which he titles "An Apology for Style."

[46] It would later be a way of seeing deliberately reactivated in the Roman world by Augustus, as Zanker (1988) demonstrated.

Following Vernant's work on archaic images, Neer has recently insisted that we need to account for classical sculpture too in terms of wonder (the Greek term *thauma*).[47] He suggests that classical sculpture evoked wonder by its ability to conjure up the existence of bodies under clothing, muscles and sinews under skin, a mind within the body. This is a valuable reminder that part of the attractions of images is always technical expertise, the way in which very different physical means—stone, bronze, painted line—are made to conjure up not just any human figure but a particular human figure in a particular disposition. The capacity of sculpture and painting to be breathtaking cannot be over emphasized.

In chapter 1, I drew attention to T. J. Clark's insistence that "when a painting recasts or restructures its own procedures—of visualizing, resemblance, address to the viewer, scale, touch, good drawing and modeling, articulate composition— . . . it puts pressure not just on social detail but social structure."[48] There are, I think, good reasons for reckoning that in fifth-century Greece—and not just Athens, though it is in Athens that we can trace what happens in greatest detail—we see a clear case where precisely the recasting of the ways in which painting and sculpture visualized, dealt with resemblance, addressed the viewer, drew, modeled and articulated composition (including what elements they did and did not include in their compositions) puts pressure on social structure. That recasting did not take place in a vacuum, the sculptors and painters who pioneered the new ways of seeing and of representing were members of moral and political communities, and engaged in other discourses than the discourse of art. But any account that reduces what they did to reflecting changes in other discourses, or fails to account for the power of images upon other discourses, misses something vital about what was changing in fifth-century Greece, and why.

---

[47] Neer (2010a), index s.v. wonder. Neer further discusses the art-historical importance of Vernant's work in Neer (2010b).

[48] Clark (1999), xxiv (preface to the rev. ed.). I have myself recast Clark's statement, which he gives in the form "it is only when . . . that it puts."

10 ❦ The Road Not Taken

The account that I gave in chapters 3 to 8 of the changing imagery of war, athletics, sexual relations, relations with the gods, drinking parties and reveling, and of satyrs was a broad-brush account. I was concerned to reveal a massive change in what is shown on pots that has gone largely unremarked. In chapter 9, I put the changes in the representation of these two particular areas of life into a wider context, but focused again on the two poles, late archaic and mid-fifth-century pot painting and sculpture, in order to assess what was at stake in the change and how we might account for it. In this chapter I contextualize the changes within the history of art between 500 and 440 by paying attention not simply to works that represent scenes with a close relation to "daily life" but also to works that relate to myth. In particular, I examine some of the visual experiments that are to be found in the quarter century or so after the Persian Wars, experiments that give some sense of the ways in which the tensions between archaic theatricality and the classical absorption were played out, and of alternative routes tried and not taken. It is important to understand why these routes are not taken in order to understand that the emergence of the classical style in Greek art was not a gradual matter but a result of a conversation between artists and the society of which they were part, in which the various ways in which art might make the world, and the wonderful things that art could do, were put on display and variously encouraged or rejected.[1]

1. The Kritios Boy versus the Tyrannicides

The "poster boy" of the Greek revolution, the Kritios Boy (1.15), might seem to show the radical change that I have outlined in the last chapter to have been accomplished already by shortly after 480.[2] Here is a youth who, like the *kouros*, is engaged in no particular activity, but who engages not the viewer but the wider world with his gaze so that, rather than inviting the viewer to become self-absorbed, as the *kouros* does, the Kritios Boy

---

[1] This chapter is in dialogue with Neer (2010a), a work that seems to me to harness wonderful observations to a mistaken thesis.

[2] For the circumstances of the discovery of this statue, insofar as they can be reconstructed, see Hurwit (1989).

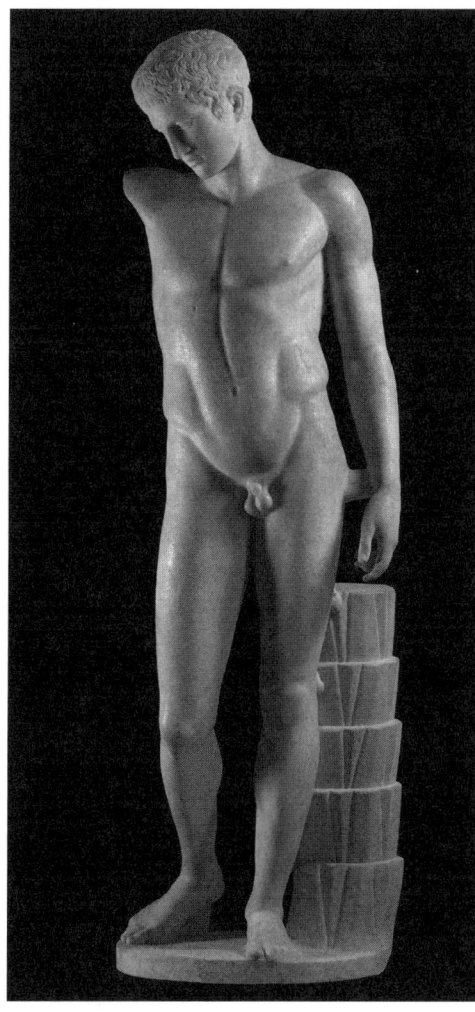

Figure 10.1. The Westmacott athlete, height 1.49 m, British Museum 1754. © The Trustees of the British Museum.

invites the viewer to enter his head. For all that the serious facial expression, rounded chin, and stiff hair set him apart from the classical, this soft, relaxed, and youthful body seems a near relative of such classical icons as the Westmacott athlete (**10.1**).

But the figure from which the Kritios Boy derives his attribution, because of his facial similarity, the tyrannicide Harmodios from the group produced by Kritios and Nesiotes and now known only from Roman copies (**10.2**), is a very different figure.[3] Harmodios is theatrical rather than absorbed, engaged in a definitive activity rather than in no definite activity at all. By contrast to the ambivalent movement common to both *kouroi* and classical figures like Polykleitos's Diadoumenos (3.28), there is no doubting the forward motion of these tyrannicides.[4] For all that "no earlier work so convincingly unites the depiction of subdermal musculature

---

[3] On the tyrannicides and their history, see Brunnsåker (1971), Azoulay (2014).

[4] For the ambivalence of movement common to *kouroi* and to classical statues, see Himmelmann (1998), 166.

THE ROAD NOT TAKEN 229

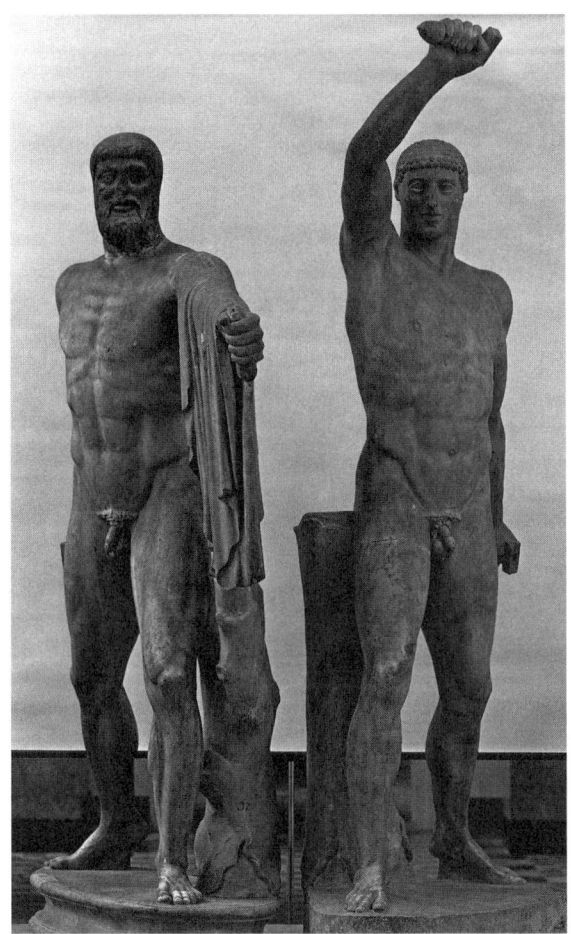

Figure 10.2. The Tyrannicides, height 1.85 m. Museo Nazionale Naples G103–4. © Hirmer Fotoarchiv Munich.

with that of vigorous movement," it would be hard on the basis of this group alone to be confident that there had been a "decisive break with the Archaic style."[5] But in contrast to such earlier action figures as Theseus carrying off Antiope from the Eretria pediment, Kritios and Nesiotes's wonder-inducing innovations in sculptural skill are utilized to intensify the impression that we are seeing here a particular action performed by particular men. Had Harmodios and Aristogeiton not been these *particular* men, the sculptural detail seems to imply, with these particular bodies that were sexually attracted to each other, the murder of Hipparchos would never have occurred.

If we accept the attribution of the Kritios Boy and these tyrannicides to the same sculptors, and imagine that the originals of the Naples versions of the tyrannicides are based displayed something of the sensitivity to bodies of different ages on display in the Kritios Boy, we can see how Kritios and Nesiotes were exploiting the potential of their sculptural innovations in two contrasting ways. On the one hand they used them to make both

---

[5] Quotations from Neer (2010a), 78. Neer himself, despite proclaiming the decisive break, also acknowledges that "the result is, in effect, a kouros in motion."

vivid and comprehensible in human terms a historic action that had come to be freighted with quasi-mythical significance. On the other, they used them to endue an anonymous youth with an inner life, encouraging those who came to worship Athena on the Athenian Acropolis to cast in their minds what manner of life might open up before a young man in their times.[6]

2. The History of Myth from the Mannerists to the Temple of Zeus at Olympia

The tyrannicides not only represent a definitive action, an act of killing, they also represent a particular historical event, the killing of Hipparchos. Specific historical events are rarely shown in either Greek sculpture or Athenian painted pottery, but the killing of Hipparchos was one of the few historical episodes that also attracted a pot painter. A stamnos attributed to the Copenhagen Painter/Syriskos, which has plausibly been influenced by, but does not simply show, the Kritios and Nesiotes group, represents Hipparchos being accosted and stabbed (**10.3**).[7] This painter liked active and even violent scenes—he twice paints the death of Aigisthos, shows the stabbing of the Minotaur and other deeds of Theseus and Herakles, and so on.[8] But if he has a liking for the theatrical and specific, he also has a liking for the absorbed and nonspecific.

We see this interest in absorption very clearly on the pot that gave him the name "Copenhagen Painter" (**10.4–5** and plate 35), an amphora that shows on one side a white-haired but apparently youthful man standing, well-mantled in a himation he wears over a chiton and with one hand firmly on a stick;[9] behind him is a tiny naked figure, with cloak folded over his left shoulder, a basket on his back, and enough of a snub nose to suggest that he is intended to be identified as African (and a slave). On the other side of the amphora there is a young man, wearing a himation and carrying a stick in his right hand, with a money bag in his left, standing looking down toward an amphora on the ground in front of him. There is no interaction between the figures, all of whom stand entirely still. It is not clear whether we should construct any narrative link between the two sides, or, if we do, whether we should tell a story of the white-haired man going to purchase an amphora, or of the white-haired man having just sold the amphora to the youth with the money bag. As Robertson writes, "the effect

---

[6] We do not know what the base on which the Kritios Boy stood said, and whether it identified the boy as a particular mythical figure, but the provision of some mythical name would alter the way the viewer thought about the statue only insofar as myth would provide a life story that the viewer might think through. For a suggestion about mythological identification, see Hurwit (1989), 77 with n. 148.

[7] The provenance is not known. On the question of the identity of the painter, see Robertson (1992), 135–40.

[8] *ARV* 257.6 and 7 show death of Aigisthos, 257.9 shows Theseus and Procrustes and Theseus and the Bull, 257.11 shows Theseus and the Minotaur, 257.15 shows Herakles and Antaios.

[9] On the white-haired man, see Scheibler (1987), 75.

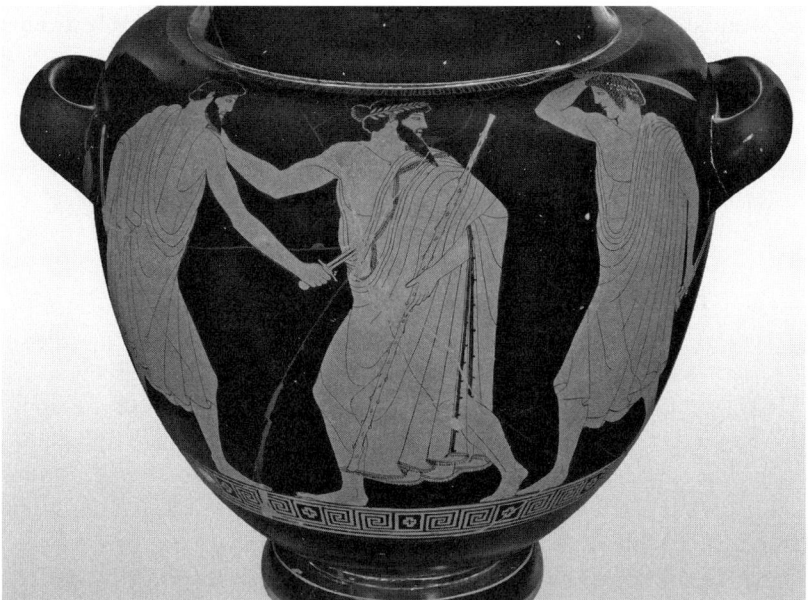

Figure 10.3. Red-figure stamnos, height 0.342 m, attributed to Syriskos / the Copenhagen Painter, ca. 470. *ARV* 256.5, Würzburg 515. © Martin von Wagner Museum der Universität Würzburg, Foto: P. Neckermann.

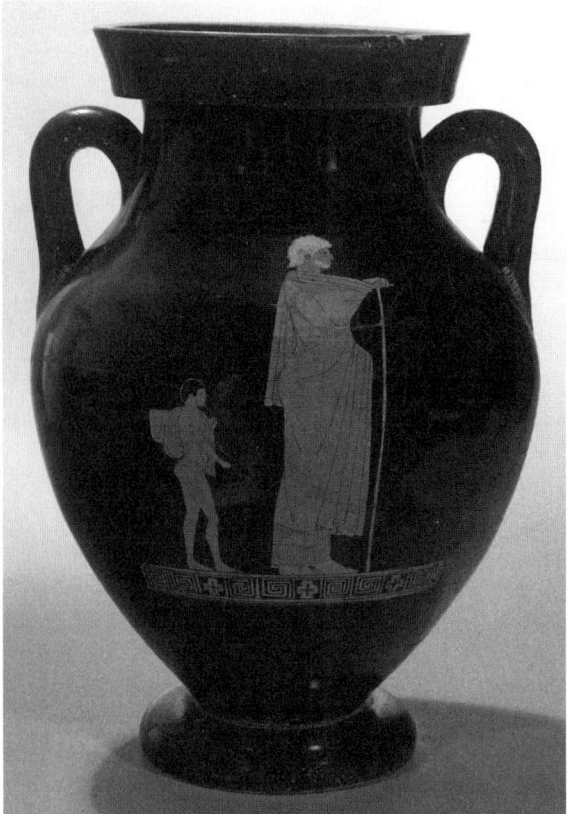
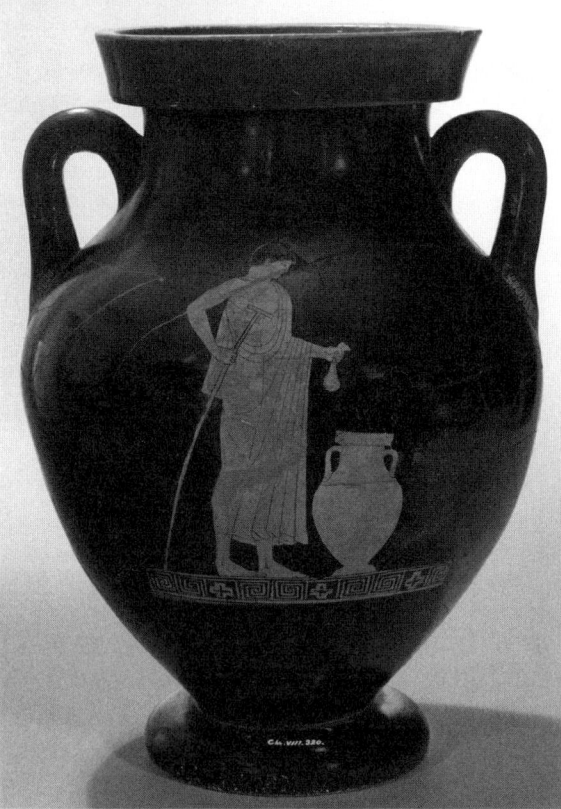

Figure 10.4–5. Red-figure amphora, height 0.492 m, attributed to Syriskos / the Copenhagen Painter, from Vulci, ca. 470. *ARV* 256.1, Copenhagen 125. CC-BY-SA, The National Museum of Denmark.

is plain, quiet, rather austere; and this is one frequent manifestation of the new, classical spirit which is taking over"; there are here "shades of feeling which were hardly within an archaic artist's grasp."[10]

The tension between theatricality and absorption, and the tension between the specific and the nonspecific, that is visible even on individual pots by the Copenhagen Painter/Syriskos,[11] is replicated across much pot painting in the quarter century after the Persian Wars. The pots painted by the so-called Mannerists, for instance, are full of colorful incident and theatrical poses—whether they show scenes from mythology or quirky aspects of life (which are the only aspects of life in which they show much interest). The focus here is on the particularity of what is happening, on the situation, the gesture. One might, for example, take the pelike attributed to the Pan Painter showing Herakles and the Egyptians.[12] This is a scene full of action and gesticulation where the foreignness of the Egyptians' shaven heads and circumcised genitals reinforces the foreignness of the foiled attempt at human sacrifice and justifies the barbarity of Herakles's use of an Egyptian as a human hammer.[13]

Amid all the narrative busyness of these "Mannerist" images, however, there are also early classical figures absorbed in their own worlds. We find these moments of absorption in the case of isolated figures, sometimes in very specific circumstances (the soldier who stands beside the pile of armor he is about to put on and cuts a lock of hair, on a lekythos attributed to the Oionokles Painter, for example [**10.6**]) and sometimes with no particular circumstance alluded to (so notably in two cases of a goddess standing on the interior of a white-ground cup).[14] But we also find these moments of absorption invading the most theatrical of action scenes: it is because, on the bell-krater from which the Pan Painter takes his name, we find Artemis absorbed in taking aim at Aktaion (**10.7**), shown while she could still change her mind (but we know she won't), that we find this scene so powerful and so theologically compelling.[15] The theatricality mocks the absorption, the absorption undermines the theatrical: we are not simply seeing a tableau here, life is at stake.

In these "Mannerist" pots there is a general correlation between the theatrical and the specific—we see figures who can be more or less clearly identified as other, engaged in particular adventures—the absorbed and the nonspecific. For all that he is bearded and shown in great detail, the Oionokles Painter's warrior cutting a lock of his own hair is identifiable

---

[10] Robertson (1992), 139.

[11] As Robertson (1992), 139–40, notes, a fine example is a stamnos in a Swiss private collection with the killing of the minotaur on one side and standing contemplative figures on the other (*ARV* 257.11/1640, Philippaki [1967] plate 33).

[12] *ARV* 554.82, Athens NM 9683, from Boeotia. On representations of this scene generally, see Miller (2000).

[13] This is an example of a particular subject matter being encouraged by the particular shape of the field offered by this shape of pot. See Osborne (2015a), 253–58.

[14] Hera is shown on the interior of a cup from Vulci by the Sabouroff Painter *ARV* 837.6; a goddess on the interior of a cup by the Villa Giulia Painter, N.Y. Met. 1979.11.15 (Robertson [1992], fig. 178).

[15] Cf. Osborne (1998b), 28–30.

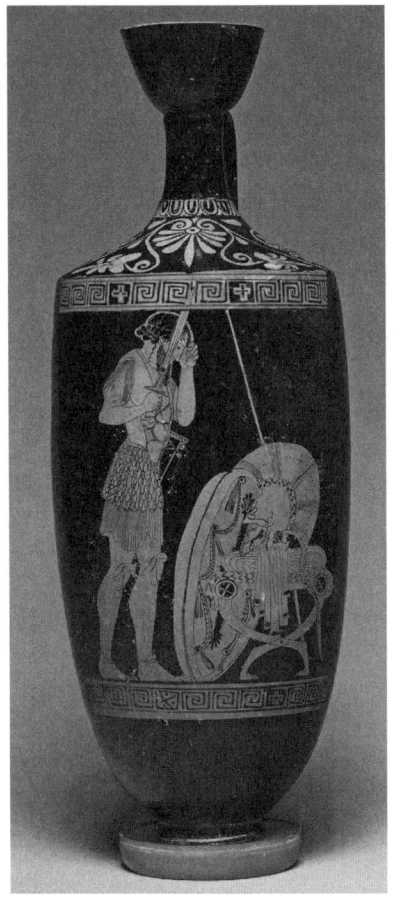
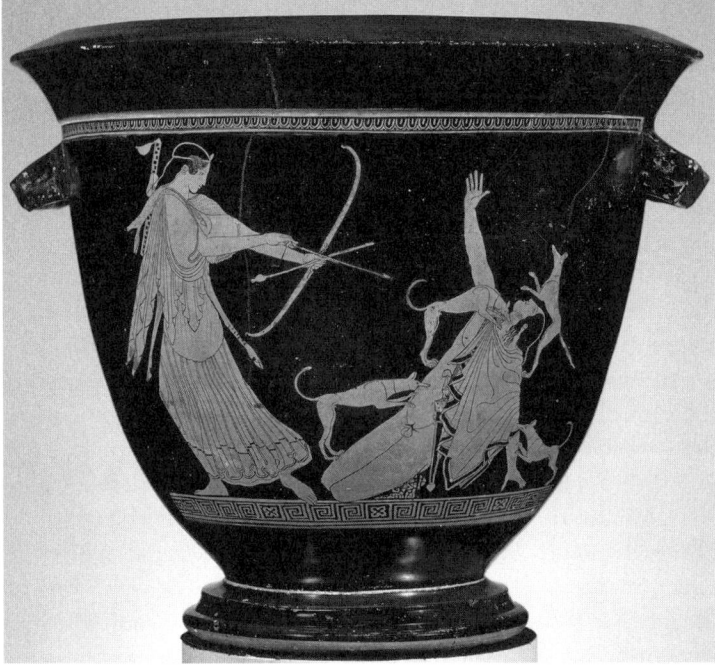

Figure 10.6. Red-figure lekythos (oil pitcher), attributed to Oionokles Painter, ca. 480–470. *ARV* 648.37, from Italy. Red-figure terra-cotta; overall: 43.50 x 16.50 cm (17 1/8 x 6 7/16 inches). The Cleveland Museum of Art, The Charles W. Harkness Endowment Fund 1928.660.

Figure 10.7. Red-figure bell-krater, height 0.37 m, attributed to the Pan Painter (name vase), from Cumae, ca. 460. *ARV* 550.1, Boston Museum of Fine Arts 10.185. Photograph © 2017 Museum of Fine Arts, Boston.

only, by his beard, as an older man. But, as the Pan Painter's Artemis and Aktaion shows, there is a sense in which moments of absorption are always threatening to take over even the most specific scenes. That takeover was probably visible on a large scale in the wall paintings of Polygnotos at Delphi to judge from the description by Pausanias.[16] It is certainly visible in the works of the pot painter who has been held to have been most influenced by wall painting, the Niobid Painter.[17] Not only does his name vase, in its scene of the slaughter of the Niobids by Artemis and Apollo, repeat the trick of the Pan Painter by having Apollo's arrow still on the string and Artemis taking an arrow from the quiver so as to cast the emphasis back onto the thoughts of the gods, but in the scene on the reverse of that krater

---

[16] Pausanias 10.25–31, Pollitt (1990), 127–40.

[17] For the Niobid Painter and the impact of wall painting on pot painting, see Barron (1972); Pollitt (1972), 43–45.

the action is supplied entirely by the viewer, who has to map onto the absorbed mythical characters their lives to come.[18]

The takeover of scenes of mythology by the absorbed figure is well seen at Olympia. At first sight, the pediments at Olympia seem to offer a theatrical battle between nonspecific lapiths and centaurs at the west, and the total absorption of the specific parties waiting to be in the chariot race between Pelops and Oinomaos at the east. But in both cases the situation is more complex.

It matters that the tussling lapiths and centaurs of the west pediment at Olympia are seen under the gaze of Apollo (**10.8**). At the center of this struggle stands the god, his arm and his gaze signaling his engagement with what is going on around him. For all the vivid portrayal of figures in combat, the subject of this pediment is not the brawl itself but the relationship of the human struggle to order the world to the justice meted out by the gods. The sculptors turned the figures at the angles of the pediment into beholders, absorbed in the spectacle of the struggle, and in doing so further emphasized the theatrical nature of the fighting parties (**10.9**). But even as they strike a pose, the very reticence of the facial expressions of both male and female lapiths, and indeed of some centaurs, encourages the viewer to ask about their thoughts too. What do they think is at stake?

By contrast to the west pediment, where applying the name "Theseus" or "Peirothoos" to one of the lapith figures makes no significant difference to the viewer's understanding of what is going on, in the east pediment names matter. They matter because it is important that the figures awaiting the race with their chariots are deadly combatants. We need to know the story of this particular race, and its background, in a way that we do not need to know any particular story about Peirothoos's wedding. But the power of the east pediment does not belong with Pelops and Oinomaos, but with a set of figures whose roles alone matter—the stable boy, the charioteer, and above all the seer (10.20). The viewer's consciousness of the varying degrees of ignorance, innocence, implication, and enlightenment of these variously absorbed figures is basic to the theological force of the pediment.

The metopes mixed scenes in which Herakles is seen performing his labors (as with the beheading of the Lernaean hydra, the tethering of the Cretan bull, the clubbing of the Kerynian hind, the battling to the ground of the Amazon, the taking of the mares of Diomedes, the defeat of Geryon, and the capture of Kerberos) with scenes in which the labor is complete and Herakles brings the trophy to Athena (the Nemean lion, the Stymphalian birds, the apples of the Hesperides, the cleansed stables) or, in the case of the Erymanthian boar, to a frightened Eurystheus. In these latter scenes there is room for reflection (**10.10**): what does Athena think of all this? Is she amazed at Herakles's feat, or does she wonder at the futility of some of these tasks? Both the theatricality of the scenes of action and the absorption of the scenes when labor is complete have a theological point: Hera-

---

[18] *ARV* 601.22, Louvre G 341 from Orvieto.

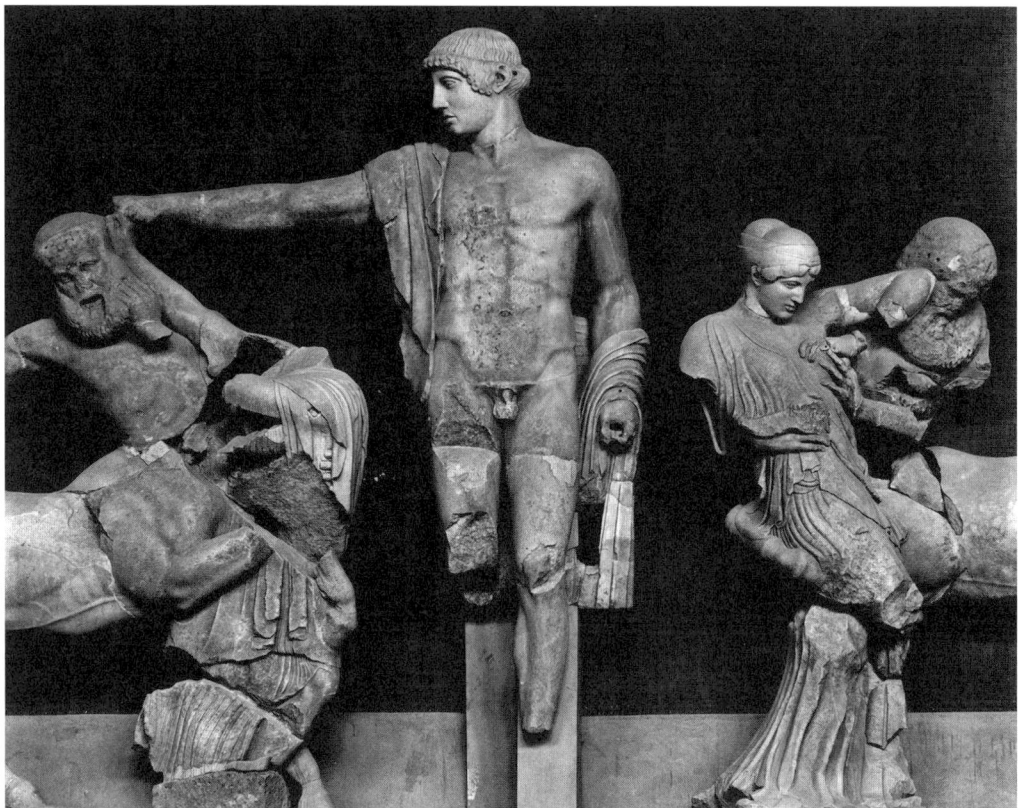

Figure 10.8. Apollo from the west pediment of the temple of Zeus at Olympia, ca. 460. © Hirmer Fotoarchiv Munich.

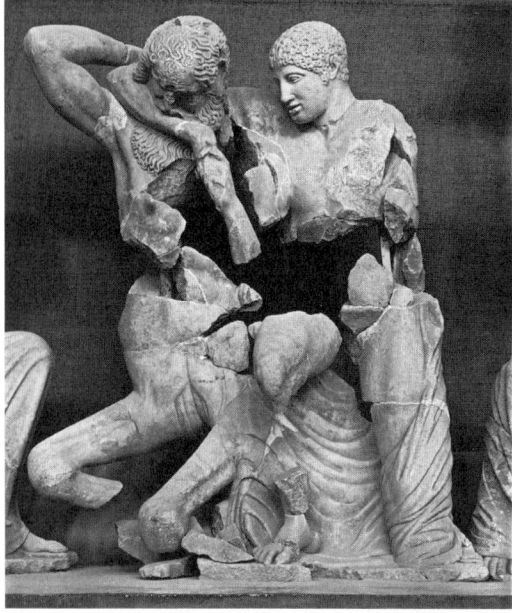

Figure 10.9. Centaur and lapith from the west pediment of the temple of Zeus at Olympia, ca. 460. © Hirmer Fotoarchiv Munich.

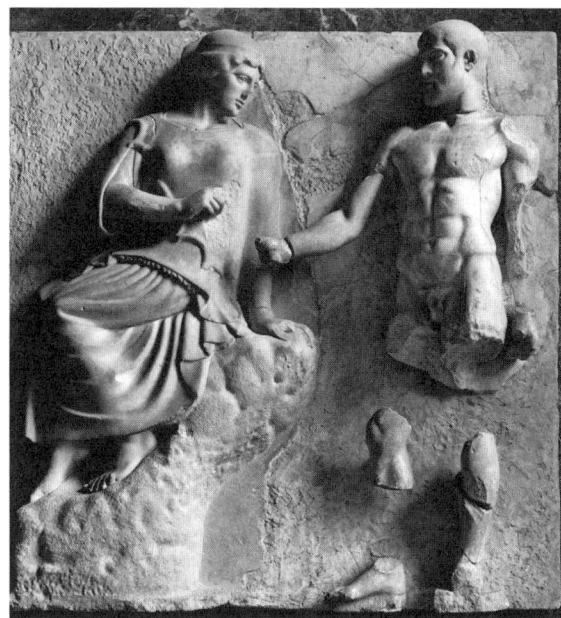

Figure 10.10. Metope from west frieze of temple of Zeus at Olympia: Athena receives the Stymphalian birds from Herakles. © Hirmer Fotoarchiv Munich.

kles's labors themselves must remain other, tasks no mortal could manage, but the presentation of the results of labor to the gods, that is the responsibility of all. Even if we accept that the gods' power is theodical, that they intervene to see justice done, we must nevertheless face up to the fact that in many situations what is just is not apparent, and humans must take thought for their own actions, and those of others, and cannot disengage from responsibility.

3. The Rise and Fall of the Individual

Myth offered a framework in which absorption and theatricality might be combined. The viewer's knowledge of at least the broad outlines of the "story to come" meant that the artist was never working with a blank canvas. What was going to happen was pre-scripted, and so to refrain from showing the action was not to leave what was going to happen open but to refrain from presenting the action in a particular way. Sculptors took over from the painters of black-figure pottery the awareness that one way of provoking the viewer to contemplate the theatrical action they were staging was to introduce spectators.[19] Temple pediments lent themselves to this—the Parthenon would repeat that trope—but other sculptures could be set up in a similar way. One nice example, whose south-Italian origin emphasizes that this is a very widespread phenomenon, is the Ludovisi throne, where the theatrical raising of Aphrodite from the water on the face is flanked by the structurally opposed naked and clothed absorbed figures on the ends (**10.11–13**).[20] What do the sex-worker and the religious servant see when they conjure up the scene of Aphrodite's birth? Which of these visions do we share?

Individual freestanding sculptures presented different sorts of issues and different possibilities. All the work had to be done by a single statue, which limited both the possibilities for theatricality and the possibilities of providing within the sculpture an internal absorbed viewer. Nevertheless, the way in which absorption takes over here is again striking.

The bronze Zeus from Artemision (**10.14**) is in one sense an obviously theatrical figure.[21] But the balance of the figure and its refusal to commit itself to lunging forward, question what the action is. Will Zeus throw the

---

[19] For spectators in black-figure pottery, see Stansbury-O'Donnell (2006).

[20] On the Ludovisi throne, see Neer (2010a), 125–29; Osborne (2010c). Although its genuineness has sometimes been doubted, none of the arguments that show the Boston throne to be fake apply to it, and a very plausible origin has been identified.

[21] Because this statue was found in the sea, we do not know the context in which it was displayed or intended to be displayed. Had the person or thing at which Zeus throws his thunderbolt been shown, a different scenario would have been played out from the one I describe here. But the vast majority of statues of Zeus showed Zeus alone—of the more than sixty images of Zeus to which Pausanias refers, only five put him in the context of other figures (Pausanias 2.17.3, 3.18.10, 3.19.3, 7.20.3, 8.47.3). At 5.22.5 Pausanias records a (seated) Zeus with thunderbolt, at 5.22.7 a separate Zeus with thunderbolt appears to be standing, at 5.24.9 a Zeus has a thunderbolt in each hand: in none of these cases was any would-be victim depicted. The chances are very high that the Artemisium Zeus never was, and was intended to be, accompanied by the object of his wrath.

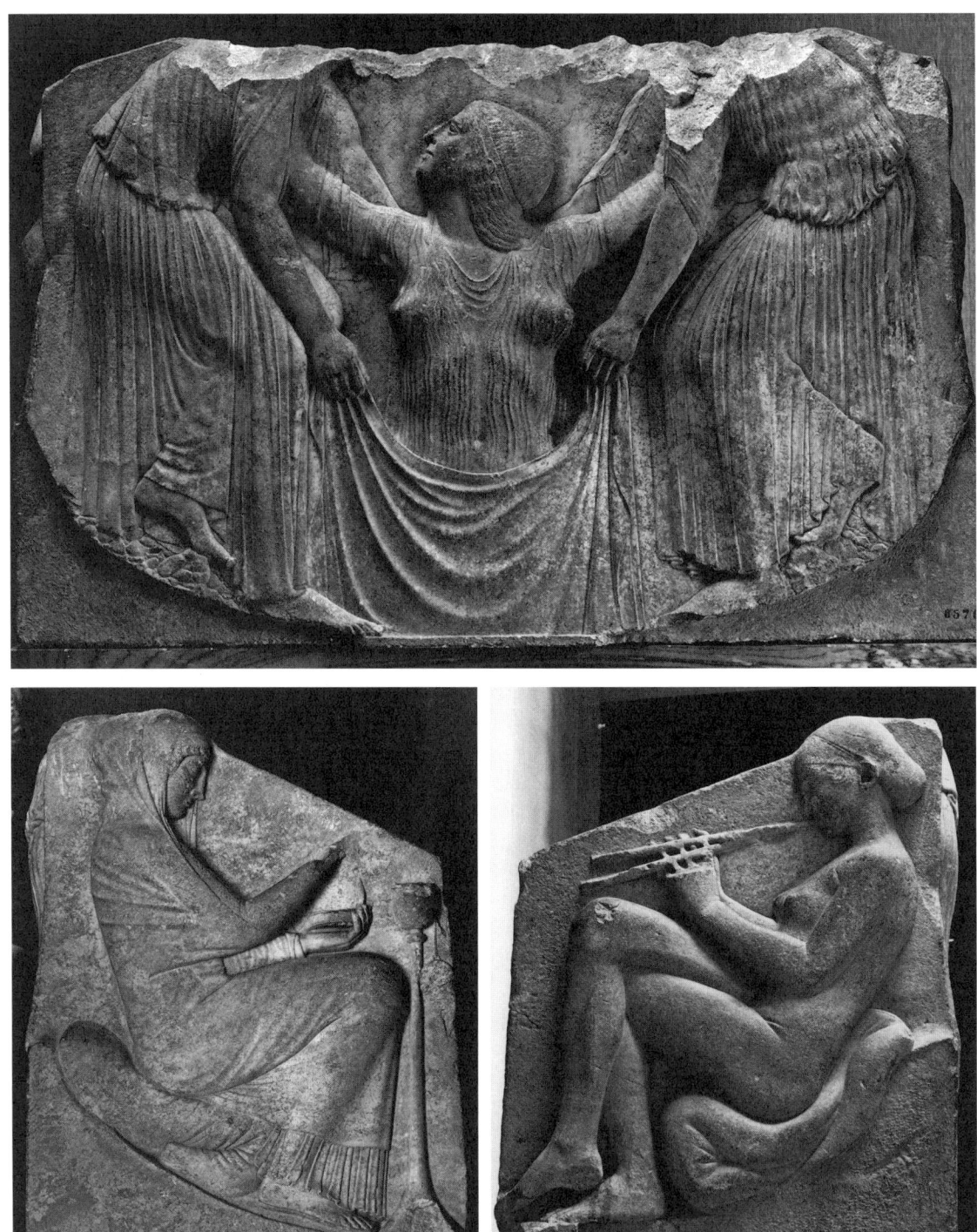

Figure 10.11–13. Front and sides of the so-called Ludovisi Throne, maximum height 0.9 m, Museo Nazionale Romano, Palazzo Altemps, 85702. © Hirmer Fotoarchiv Munich.

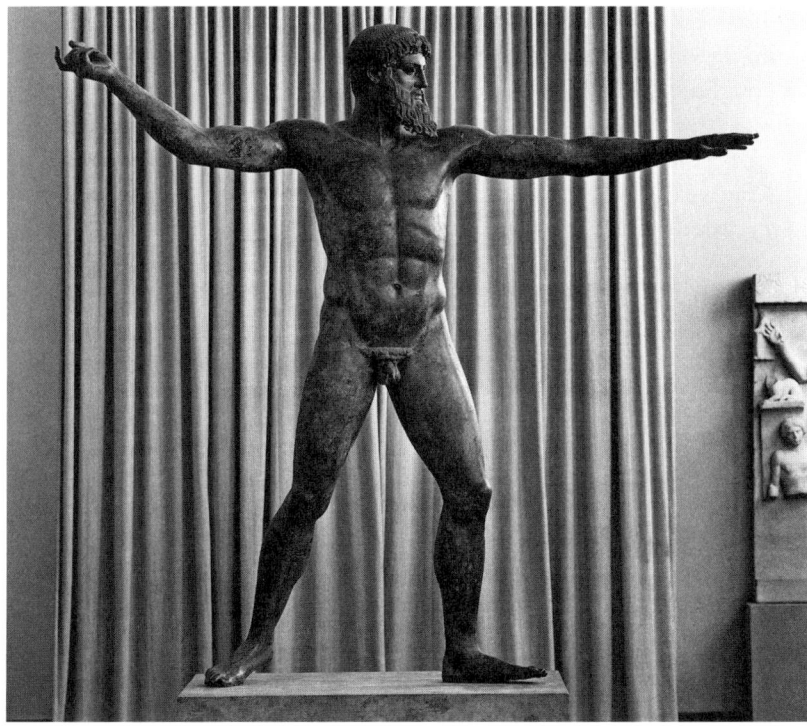

Figure 10.14. Bronze statue of Zeus, height 2.09 m, recovered from the sea off Cape Artemision. Athens National Museum Br. 15161. © Hirmer Fotoarchiv Munich.

thunderbolt, or will he change his mind and desist? The inscrutable face offers no clue—and the glass eyes that have been lost are more likely to have sharpened that question than to have answered it. This theatrical figure turns out rather to be a figure absorbed, a figure inviting the viewer not to dodge the thunderbolt, as the viewer of the tyrannicides dodges their spear thrusts, but to contemplate when and why Zeus might wield this weapon. The absence of a definite narrative here—there is no single myth of Zeus punishing a mortal with a thunderbolt—allows the god to become absorbed, and has viewers ransack their mythological knowledge for moments when Zeus put his weaponry into action. When might Zeus have looked like this? Is this reticent face compatible with every occasion on which Zeus has deployed his thunderbolt, or is it unthinkable that he could have looked like this when . . . ?

The ambivalence that is theological when it concerns the actions of a god becomes political when no gods are involved but only men. There is no doubt about the theatricality of the pose of Myron's Diskobolos; whether or not any actual discus thrower ever looked like this, this athlete is giving a demonstration. But even if the original commemorated a particular athletic victor, nothing about the body visible in the Roman copies individualizes, and the often-observed absence of torsion in the torso, together with the relaxed facial expression (should not a serious discus thrower be mentally as well as physically wound up at this moment?), questions whether viewers are being invited to contemplate a particular and decisive moment in an athlete's successful career, the moment before the big throw, or are rather being invited to think what it might be to be a (winning) athlete, themselves to become, with the discus thrower himself, absorbed in these actions. Is to put oneself in the position of this athlete to put oneself in a position of effortless superiority? What would it be to make *this* the image by which one was known?

Were we to have Myron's original statue we might discover ourselves in a very different relationship. This has been clear since the discovery of the two bronze statues found in the sea off Riace Marina in southern Italy (**10.15**, **10.16**). These bronzes have shown for the first time the capacity of some classical sculptors working in bronze, at least, to capture the specifics of the body to an extraordinary degree. The two figures are the same size and adopt very nearly the same pose. Yet they seem to be unrelated individuals—the relationship of skin to muscle to bone is quite different in the two cases. Beholders find themselves constructing contrasting life histories for these two bodies, life histories based on no evidence other than the evidence of the sculpted body itself. What the Riace warriors both share is that they are absorbed by the action around them, but because they are so particularized they invite not generic reflections on the life of the warrior but specific reflections on what it might be to be a warrior if you were the person who had got yourself a body like *that*. If these statues were, as has been suggested, part of a monument that originally included several more figures, whether as part of a commemoration of the Persian Wars or part of a mythological group, the effect of discrimination between the bodies would have been even more powerful.

These statues simultaneously insist that they are like the beholder, so that the beholder can imagine what it was to be them, and insist on their otherness, their particularity. If these statues represented historic figures these are historic figures who have yet to join Harmodios and Aristogeiton as types, they remain fiercely historical, refusing to become figures of myth. The combination of absence of a theatrical tableau, to stand proxy here for some particular achievement, and presence of insistent individualism brings the viewer face to face with an other life, a life that is larger than life and to which the viewer can never attain. These are figures who have been put onto a pedestal to show off their own very particular capacities: these individuals have very different affordances from those of the beholder.

Whether there were other early classical bronzes comparable to the Riace Warriors is unknown. What is clear is that the classical sculpture that survives not only does not achieve the subtle particularism of the Riace Warriors, it does not seek to achieve it. This is true not merely of sculptures representing identifiable divine or mythical figures, like the pedimental sculptures of the Parthenon, or reliefs that set out to show a whole social group where most or all individuals are anonymous, as in votive reliefs or the Parthenon frieze (**10.17**), but also of funerary reliefs that commemorate Athenian residents (3.2, 10.18). In all these cases, although the situation of the figures may be shown in great variety, the facial and bodily features refuse any allusion to individuality—even to the extent that varia-

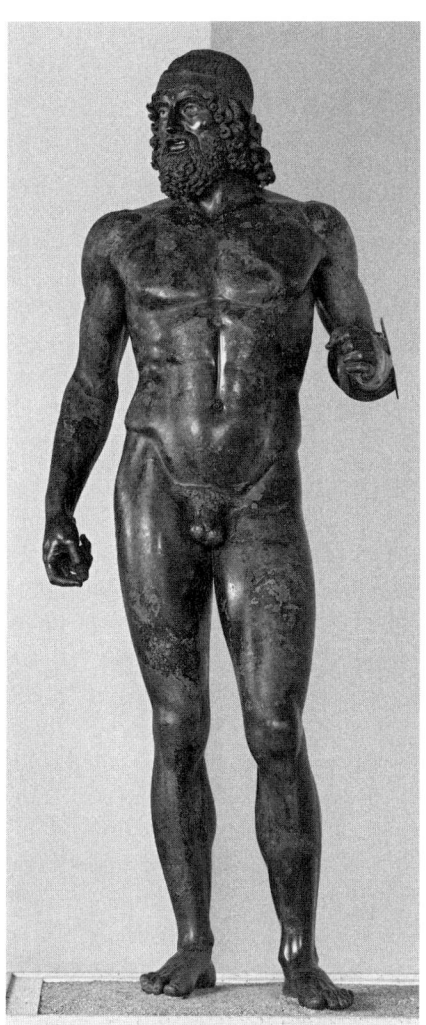
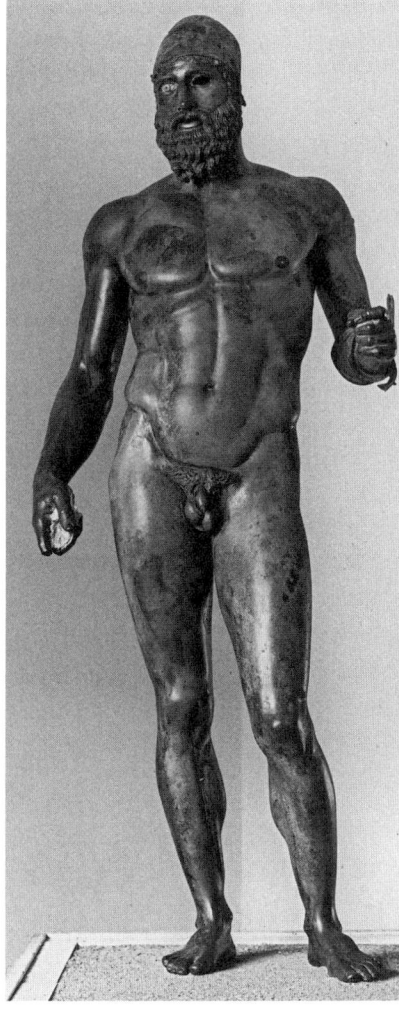

Figure 10.15. Bronze statue of a warrior, "Warrior A," height 2.03 m, recovered from the sea off Riace Marina. Museo Nazionale, Reggio Calabria. © Hirmer Fotoarchiv Munich.

Figure 10.16. Bronze statue of a warrior, "Warrior B," height 1.965 m, recovered from the sea off Riace Marina. Museo Nazionale, Reggio Calabria. © Hirmer Fotoarchiv Munich.

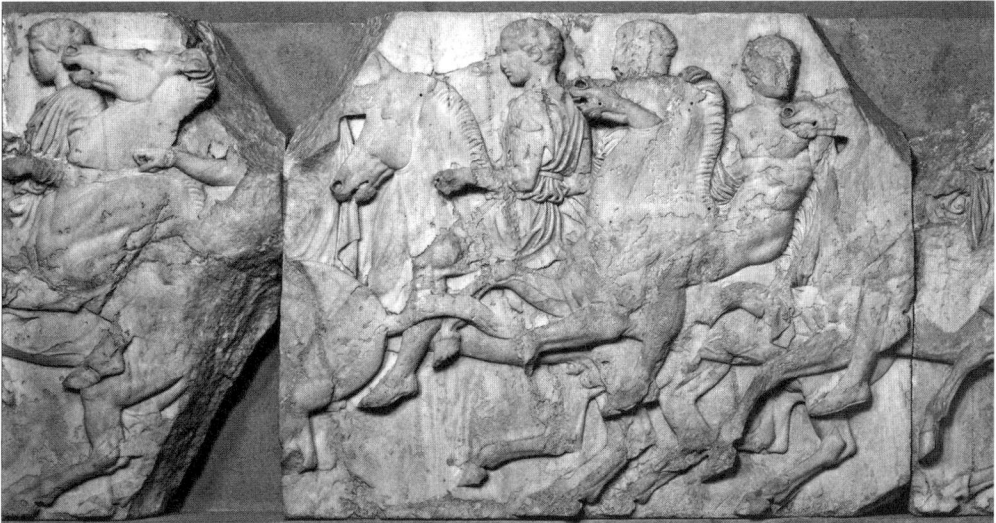

Figure 10.17. Frieze of the Parthenon, Athens; North XXXVIII. British Museum. © The Trustees of the British Museum.

tion over time is insufficient to produce any scholarly consensus on the dating of many of these monuments.[22]

4. Promises of Happiness?

Athens went in for masked drama, and there are times when classical sculpture seems to be a masked drama.[23] As our ability to recognize individuals by their faces demonstrates, the world around us displays an inexhaustible variety of facial appearance; the faces worn by classical sculptures, by contrast, belong essentially to a small number of types. This applies particularly to faces representing the inhabitants of the classical world, as witnessed by the endlessly similar faces on classical grave stelai. Grave stelai (**10.18**) offer differentiation of more and less mature individuals, with some increasing differentiation in the later part of the fourth century, but the strong sense is of meeting the same cast of characters again and again, with only their hairstyles changing.[24] More surprisingly, the restricted physiognomic range also applies to the faces of creatures of fantasy. The highly varied and often richly expressive faces of the centaurs on the metopes of the Parthenon are succeeded by the centaurs on the Bassai frieze who play, at most, slight variations upon a theme.

The restricted range of faces is matched by a restricted range of bodies.[25] Bodies, or at least clothing, differentiate mortal from divine—at least insofar as the female body revealed beneath diaphanous drapery is restricted to divinities and other nonmortal figures, and likewise the naked male body is allowed for bearded figures only if they are gods.[26] Among mortal men and women there are relatively few choices of clothing and a very restricted range of body types. Youth and maturity are distinguished in the male body, as is maturity from old age, but even the variation in male costume that is constituted by the wearing of the chiton under the himation, as famously in the portrait sculpture of Aischines, is very rarely present in funerary sculpture.[27] The youthful riders on the Parthenon frieze (10.17)

---

[22] Dohrn (1957).

[23] Wiles (2000), 148: "Tragic masks of the classical period are characterized by a lack of expression. Pale skin colour signifies a woman, and dark a man; but no indication is given of character or feeling."

[24] On the facial types in Greek grave stelai, see Bergemann (1997), 97–105; Dillon (2006), 67–73, who summarizes the position (72) as: "There were two main categories of representation [of adult males]: the mature male in the prime of life and the male well-advanced in age. There was one main head type used for the mature male, ... There was a wider range of head types—approximately five different formulations—used to represent males well advanced in age." Cf. also Dillon (2010), 108–9.

[25] Bergemann (1997), 76–86.

[26] On the conventions about the naked male body in sculpture, see Osborne (1995).

[27] Clairmont records just three cases where a man wears a short-sleeved chiton under his himation (his nos. 2.711, 3.374c, and 4.190) along with four cases where a man wears the chiton alone. The latter seems, often at least, to be one mark of being a priest. Clairmont has just one case of a young man wearing just a chlamys (2.268), though in two cases he notes that naked youths have over their shoulder a piece of cloth of substantial size, which should perhaps be taken to be a chlamys (1.364, 1.866), and to them Dillon (2006), 109, would add Chairedemos (Clairmont in his discussion of this, his 2.156, identifies "a mantle (rather than a chlamys)."

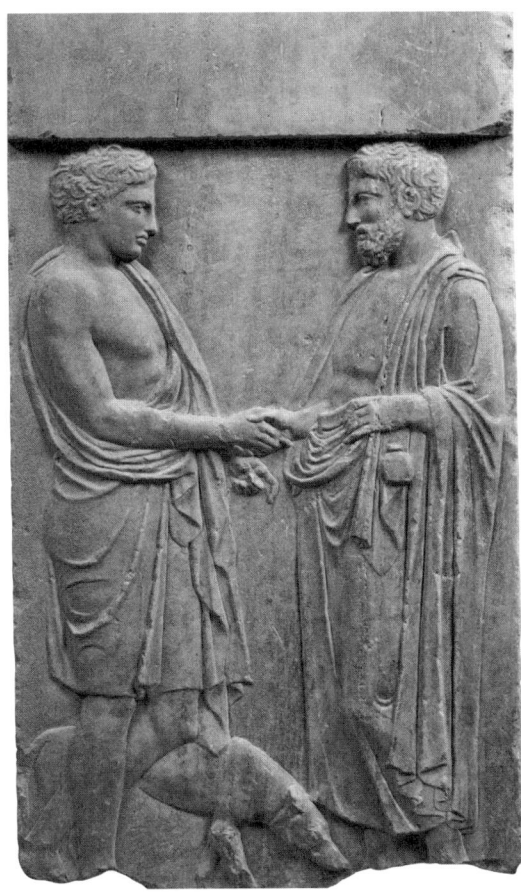

Figure 10.18. Grave stele, height 1.03 m, from Athens, Athens National Museum 2894.

appear to be positively anarchic in the variety of their costume by comparison with subsequent classical Athenian relief sculpture.[28]

The fact of restriction is remarkable. The *korai* from the Athenian Acropolis and from cemeteries in Attica, with their characterful range of facial features and clothing (cf. 1.12), show that in archaic Athens there was no such template, either for faces or for dress. But it is also important to take note of what the features are that are chosen to represent the types of young men and women, mature men and women, and old men. Whether they appear in sculpture or in painted pottery, these are faces with clean and simple lines. The profile could not be more straightforward: the line of the flat forehead continues, with no more than the slightest bend, down the nose, the lips purse slightly, and the chin is marked by a smooth concave line to produce a shadow that underlines the seriousness of expression. No cheekbones are visible, and the relatively narrow slits of the eyes are completely protected by the overarching brow and heavy eyelids. Just occasionally, folds of flesh run down from the corners of the mouth or nose, giving a more complex contour to the cheeks. The faces offer no hint of emotion, neither curling into a smile nor knitting into a frown. The eyes offer intense

[28] Neils (2001), 135–36.

engagement, but no reaction. The mouths are full and expressive, but give expression to nothing particular.

Yet these faces are powerful. For two reasons. One is that they are full of potential. Their very refusal to tell any story, to give any reason to the viewer to posit a particular life history that has led to this look, leaves them open to any future. Their equanimity denies arrogance, even when they are shown at the height of achievement. Nothing that is humanly possible for a person of that general age could not be done by these individuals, but whatever they do will not alter their equipoise. But the second reason is that these faces and bodies are beautiful—not with the beauty that comes from sharp-edged and vivacious mobile features that send the message that we are observing a person who has thought of and tried everything and come out on top, but with a soft-edged beauty that advertises both innocence and empathy while also hinting at unlimited capacity. The freshness of bloom on the youthful faces makes this beauty elegiac in the context of the funerary relief, bursting with promise among the young horsemen of the Parthenon frieze. The viewer comes not so much to want to protect these creatures, for they show no vulnerability, but to share something of their ability to be involved in the world but unmarked by it. These are aspirational images. They promise happiness.[29]

5. What's Not to Like?

One of the effects of theatrical masks was to put emphasis on gesture. It was pointless for the audience to fixate on trying to see the facial expressions of the actors, so they had to concentrate instead on their actions.[30] The very featurelessness of the faces offered by masks enhanced the theatricality. But it did so not to make the masked figure's character irrelevant but to draw attention back to the mental processes behind the action. Indeed, scholars have claimed that "emotion is most powerful when it is created and placed on the mask by the spectator's imagination."[31]

So too with classical Greek art. Even at the most theatrical moments, like those in the frieze of the temple of Apollo at Bassai, or in some public and private grave reliefs, such as the Albani relief and the stele of Dexileos (**10.19**), the dramatic gestures nevertheless serve only to frame the heads, which draw the viewer's attention.[32] The action merely defines the field within which the viewer's imagination is set to work. Sculptors can indeed discard any regard for naturalism in their dramatic settings, as the extraordinary drapery not just at Bassai but in both Albani relief and the relief of Dexileos demonstrates, since the viewer reads everything as framing device.

[29] See chapter 11.
[30] Compare Taplin (1978), 14–15; Wiles (2000), 148.
[31] Wiles (2000), 149.
[32] See chapter 9, section 3 on the effect of the expressive gesture of the framing figure in Kleophon's scene of a warrior's departure (9.6).

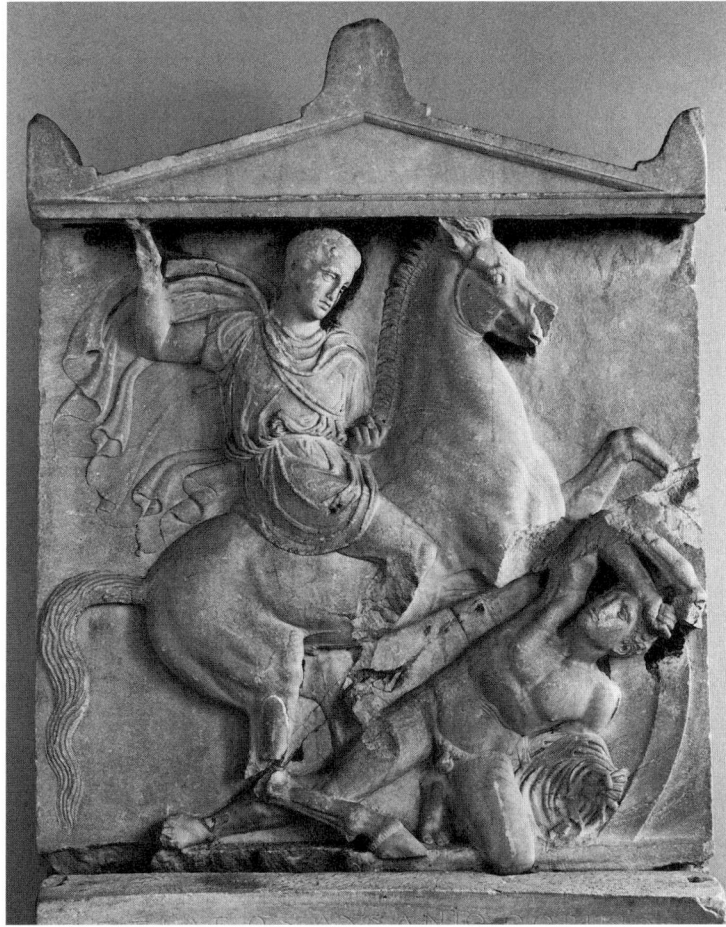

Figure 10.19. Stele of Dexileos, 394/3. © Hirmer Fotoarchiv Munich.

The threat that the conventions of classical art fend off is the threat of too much information. The uniformity of clothing in grave stelai is one way of achieving this. The restricted range of scenarios is another. The unreality of the swirls of drapery in the Bassai frieze, which can acquire no significance from the viewer's experience of clothing in real life, similarly combine with the known stories to restrict the information that the viewer either needs or is given. To some extent there is a payoff between visual simplicity and complexity of subject. The Parthenon frieze gets away with its variety of dress for the horsemen because they are held within the framework of a procession, and indeed, as Ian Jenkins has shown, ordered into groups of ten to subsume the individuals into members of a tribe.[33]

By contrast, the Riace bronzes offered too much information. Not in the sense that the action in which they were involved was too complex, for although we do not know what that action was, or even whether it was historical or mythical, we can be confident from their poses that the viewer

[33] Jenkins (2005).

was being asked to reflect on participation in some great and surely readily identifiable event with a relatively straightforward story. The sense in which the Riace warriors offered too much information is the sense in which they offer us two very different individuals, individuals who, unlike the horsemen of the Parthenon frieze or the figures on Athenian votive or grave reliefs, have their own history and have it written on their bodies. The heads of these warriors are not masks onto which the viewer can place the emotions he or she has imagined; these are the heads of passionate men, men who are differently passionate but in neither case obviously compassionate. These are men who have been shaped, even scarred, by their past, and who know what they intend to achieve in the future. Whether we think that the sculptor has wonderfully captured the actual dispositions of historic figures in insightful portraits or has vividly imagined for himself what it must have been like to be this or that mythical character, he has done the viewer's imagining for him or her, and presented the viewer with a fait accompli—and in more senses than one. These have become the inhabitants of nightmares or of fantasies—in principle as well as in fact.[34]

The east pediment at Olympia might also be thought to offer too much information, if in a rather different way. By comparison to the west pediment and the metopes, with their immediately accessible stories, the east pediment has a story that requires piecing together from clues—and primarily from the clue provided by the highly expressive face of the seer (**10.20**). It is his information-rich aged body that unmasks the events that are to come and reveals the mix of innocence and plotting that lies behind the other expressionless faces. This is a story where the different actors involved know either too little or too much for there to be room for imaginative exploration by the viewer.

When an action is generic (as in throwing the discus, or going to war, or indeed killing an enemy in war), showing the moment immediately before the action opens a field for the viewer's imagination to roam over without determining what exactly the viewer imagines. But when the action that is about to happen is pre-scripted in detail, the effect of showing the moment before the action is to constrain the viewer. Our admiration for the sculptors of the east pediment at Olympia comes from the skill with which they have captured what it "would have been like" to be the seer who foresaw at that moment the race to come, just as our admiration for the sculptors of the Riace warriors comes from the sense that they have captured what particular historical figures "must have been like" or particular mythical figures "would have been like." Our sense is that particular historical actors or mythical moments have been captured for us. We are being shown what they were like, but we are not being invited ourselves to come to understand what it would have been like for us to stand in their place.

Building on the work of Gibson, the anthropologist Webb Keane has recently coined the term "ethical affordances," which he defines as follows:

[34] Taplin (1989), 88–89.

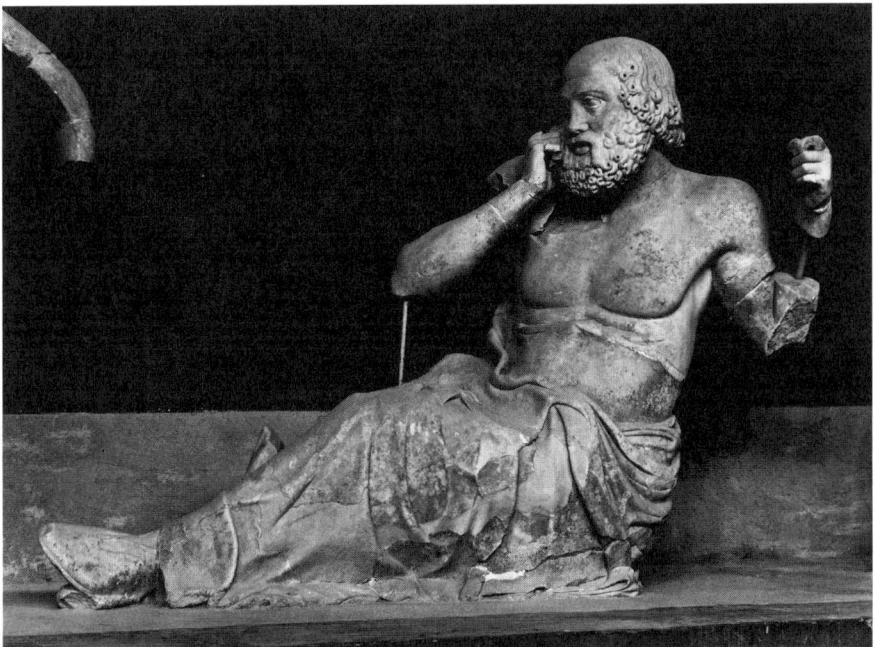

Figure 10.20. The seer from the west pediment at Olympia. © Hirmer Fotoarchiv Munich.

Ethical affordances are those features of the world, as people experience it, that can be construed in ethical terms. By "ethics," I refer to people's ability to evaluate acts as good or evil, people as virtuous or vicious, lives as worthy or worthless, and to their awareness of being themselves evaluated in turn. Typically these evaluations arise in interactions with other people, but they may involve any entity at all (such as divine beings) whose actions can be judged in these terms and so can be held responsible for purposeful harm or benefit.[35]

The east pediment at Olympia and the monument to which the Riace bronzes originally belonged offered the viewer no ethical affordances, that is, no opportunities to evaluate people and acts as good and virtuous *and to be aware of being themselves evaluated in turn*. The race for the hand of Hippodameia is something that happened to other people, long ago and far away and is not an event the viewer could imagine himself taking part in. The two Riace warriors are so individualized as to insist that they are not like the viewer. In both cases the viewer is turned into a spectator rather than given the chance to write him or herself into the story. By contrast the viewers of the Parthenon frieze or of a classical Attic grave stelai not only can write themselves into the story, they are challenged to do so by the refusal of the figures represented to individuate and so distance themselves.

There is no doubting the wonder that the sculptural skill responsible for the Olympia seer or the Riace warriors evokes, to return to the terms in which Richard Neer has written about the emergence of the classical style

[35] Keane (2014), S316.

in Greek sculpture.[36] The technology here is utterly enchanting.[37] But the Riace warriors have no successors, not because classical bronze statues have been melted down but because wonder and enchantment were not everything in sculpture. The changed emphasis between archaic and classical Greek art when it comes to rendering anatomy, to the relationship between clothing and bodies, to the placement of the body in space do not sit *alongside* the classical concern to have the viewer inhabit the mind of the sculpted subject, they are in service to that concern.

The various early classical experiments reviewed in this chapter show that classical artists had the technical means to achieve a whole array of mimetic effects that they decided to eschew. The story of the emergence of classical art is not a story of cumulative development or gradual change, it is the story of the end determining the means. That end was, and here I agree with Neer, a particular relationship between image and beholder. But we understand that relationship only if we cast our attention not simply to style alone, as Neer would have us do,[38] but to the choices made as to what was and was not to be represented, choices that, as chapters 3 to 8 have sought to show, are most easily appreciated if we look not at sculpture but at painted pottery. For what was at stake was not merely how art works, but the ethical relationship between individuals. Artists did not gradually discover a different way of seeing the world, or of having those who viewed their art see the world; they came to see their own task differently because they came to live in a world that, partly but not entirely because of the artists' own contribution, saw itself differently, where the values had changed. Classical art offered a means by which to visualize the world of changed values, and in doing so came to reinforce those values, but the processes that led to the conventions of classical art cannot be understood merely by looking at style alone.

---

[36] What I say in this paragraph is in conversation with Neer (2010a), esp. 4–5.
[37] For the language of enchantment, see Gell (1992).
[38] Cf. Neer (2010a), 1–19, "Introduction: An Apology for Style."

11 ❧ The Transformation of Art

This book has tried to substantiate two claims, one in relation to art history and one in relation to Greek history. The big claim in relation to art history is that style and subject matter cannot be treated separately. What artists observe and record and how they observe and record are intimately linked. In particular, to tell and explain the story of what happens to Greek art between the end of the sixth and the middle of the fifth century, the story of what has become known as "the Greek revolution," in terms only of increasing naturalism, is to miss half the story. What happens in those years is not just a revolution in style, though it is certainly that, it is a revolution in the subject matter of art. The artists of classical Greece saw and represented things differently from the artists of late archaic Greece, but that was part of their seeing different things. We are never going to understand "the emergence of the classical style" unless we understand that the emergence of this style was bound up with the emergence of a new content, a different subject for art.

The big claim in relation to Greek history is that the "Greek revolution" in art was also a historical revolution. The changed way of seeing was the result of a changed way of looking, and that way of looking was a matter of choice.[1] The revolution in art was not a phenomenon limited to art or to artists, but the vision of the world upon which it depended crucially flourished because it was shared and disseminated by artists and by those who consumed art. This way of seeing rejected the conception of the world as a place where distinctive individuals competed for limited goods and where every individual was challenged to enter the competition. Instead, it saw the world as a place inhabited by people who were essentially similar, and were engaged in essentially similar lives facing similar situations. This world was not one the viewer was challenged to enter, for this was the world in which the viewer already lived. Rather than an invitation to enter another world and perform differently, the new vision offered an assurance that the world out there was the same as the world in which the viewer lived, and that the viewer could seamlessly slip into that world.

Jaś Elsner has suggested that we should see the change effected by the Greek revolution as a change "in which the viewer moved from being a direct participant to being an outside observer, from being actively inter-

---

[1] Cf. Berger (1972), 8.

rogated by works of art to being a voyeur of a process of discussion taking place in an imaginary world."[2] But this is to mistake the nature of the change. The claim made by classical art is not that it shows an imaginary world, but that it shows the world as it is. The endlessly repeated claims that classical art is "naturalistic"—claims that will not bear a moment's scrutiny if "naturalistic" is understood to mean "reproduces all the visual features of nature"—attest to the success of the visual rhetoric of classical art in pushing this claim. Classical art is keen always to tell us that the world that the artist imagines is a world that is already familiar—we are not looking through a keyhole but into a mirror. It is archaic art, by contrast, where the invitation to the viewer to enter and join in is, not infrequently, an invitation to become a voyeur.

But to talk in these terms is to return to the art-historical story. The story here, as far as Greek history is concerned, is a story about the demystification of the world. It is indeed the story about the "creation of mythology," about how the extraordinary came to be consigned to a distinct world of myth as part of insisting that the past operated on the same rules as the present—the fundamental claim that Thucydides foregrounds in his "Archaeology."[3] This is a moment marked in painted pottery by the disappearance of the vaguely mythical scenes of warfare that nevertheless never identify themselves as any of the particular mythical wars that were so popular in black-figure;[4] the painters of classic red-figure frequently turn to mythology for their subjects, but, satyrs and maenads apart, it is to specific, identifiable, myths that they turn. Creating mythology as a distinct category was a necessary part of asserting the possibility of controlling the world, the denial that there were any bounds to what could be conquered by reason.[5] But what is at stake here is not simply whether some humans in general, and some Greeks in particular, might be able to comprehend what has happened, is happening, and will happen in the world, but whether that is something that all Greeks can do. As Protagoras sees, in Plato's dialogue named for him, the defense of democratic government rests on a claim that people as a whole are capable, if not of working out what has happened and is happening, at least of judging whether others' accounts of what is happening are or are not correct.[6] It is the possibility that anyone can aspire to any role that painters of pottery and sculptors equally embrace in the middle of the fifth century.[7]

To describe in these terms the change in the way of seeing the world is to make clear the parallels between what is manifested in Greek painted pottery and sculpture and what can be observed in other areas of Greek intellectual endeavor. Ways of seeing, in the literal sense, are necessarily

---

[2] Elsner (2006), 91.
[3] Classic, and still unsurpassed, on the creation of mythology is Detienne (1986).
[4] And which gave Lissarrague his subject in *L'autre guerrier* (1989).
[5] Cf. Buxton (1999), Fowler (2011).
[6] See particularly Farrar (1988).
[7] To leave to one side the politics of this, embraced in Thucydides's version of Perikles's funeral oration; see chapter 9, section 2.

part of, and inseparable from, ways of cognition more generally. That there was a distinct change in the cognitive grip on the world displayed by those we have retrospectively named the "pre-Socratic philosophers" has been long known and investigated.[8] Crucial to changing philosophical views of the world was the development of methods of argument and rules for debate—developments in which what was happening in civic life, in terms of political and judicial decision making, was part and parcel of what was happening in speculations about the nature of the world.

But this book has tried to do more than simply offer a better account of the changes that occurred in Greek history and in the history of Greek art between the end of the sixth and the middle of the fifth century. It has tried to show how those changes manifested themselves in Greek, and most particularly in Athenian, life, and it has tried to reveal something of the causal nexus underlying the changes.

We register only a tiny fraction of the visual stimuli that our eyes and brain receive. What we picture in our brains, let alone what artists picture in the images they draw or paint or sculpt, is very far from a complete record of the world in which we live. But because what we picture is what we see, and what we see affects, just as it is also affected by, what we think and what we do, and because what artists picture affects what we see and picture, the view of the world that we can acquire from Athenian artists' pictures, the "city of images" that Athenian artists offer us, bears a strong similarity to the view of the world, to the city, that Athenians saw. Athenian artists shared the social conditioning of other Athenians, or at least of other Athenians of their class, such that they were disposed to view the world as other Athenians viewed it. But the drawings and sculptures that they produced, because they were distributed widely across the Mediterranean world, themselves contributed to the social conditioning of other Athenians and of Greeks over a much wider geographical space than simply Athens and Attica, and also of some non-Greek peoples, particularly the Etruscans. When painters working at Athens see the world differently, they encourage others to see the world differently, and given that the world that they see differently is the world of Athens, their different view of the world encourages not simply seeing differently but seeing in an Athenian way.[9]

Why did Athenians, and Athenian artists, come to see the world as one where the salient fact was that very similar individuals were facing up to the actions expected of them, rather than to see the world as one where quite distinct individuals and personalities took the opportunities that they happened upon? Traditionally, as we saw in chapter 1, the explanation offered for the artistic revolution that occurred early in the fifth century BC has been either that the invention of democracy at Athens encouraged the ideological view that everyone was essentially the same, or that Greek success in the Persian Wars led to a new confidence in what any Greek

---

[8] Classic is Lloyd (1979).

[9] For an attempt to describe that world on the basis of largely literary sources, see Osborne (2008)—a revision of a team effort of 1984.

could achieve. There is no doubt some truth in both of these explanations, but it must be noted that the spread of classical art across the Greek world, as manifested above all in sculpture, comes in the face of ongoing critiques of the very principles of democracy and of suspicion of Athens, and that the legacy of the Persian Wars was as much in recriminations over who had and had not taken part in resistance to the Persian invasion as it was in celebration of some general "Greek" achievement.[10]

What we have seen, in tracing the transformation through painted pottery, is that the changes in social and moral attitudes were also a matter of aesthetics. The changes in the activities that painters choose to represent go together with changes in the way they represent those performing the activities. The attractions of late archaic individuality are clear—it provides a vivid sense of a particular individual performing a particular action and reacting to a particular situation. These attractions come across even in images that initially look rather uniform, like the great set of late archaic *korai* from the Acropolis that combine a single pose with an endless variety of ways of dressing. Individuality is fun to behold, whether to mock or to admire. But what were the attractions of classical conformity? Both the specifically artistic commitment to what has often blandly been termed "classical idealism" and the theoretical underpinnings of that notion are important here.

What classical artists did was both debated and explicitly theorized. The sculptor Polykleitos produced a famous treatise, the *Kanon*, which is now lost but was much commented on in antiquity. In this he laid down how a statue ought to be constructed, insisting that the key lay in proportions. He illustrated this theoretical work with a statue of his own, and that statue was almost certainly what we know as the Doryphoros. However Polykleitos himself described what he was aiming for in his work, later writers and thinkers certainly took him to be aiming to produce "bodily forms which are as beautiful as possible (*speciosissima*)," and that what this involved was, in Galen's phrase, "looking for the mean."[11] Several classical authors similarly tell the story of the painter Zeuxis creating a picture of Helen, and in order "that his mute image would contain within itself the preeminent beauty of the female form" basing his image on different features drawn from five different young women of Kroton "for he did not think all the things he looked for in beauty (*quae quaeret ad venustatem*) could be found in one body."[12] The basic idea here is already contained in Xenophon's story of a discussion between Socrates and the painter Parrhasios. Socrates here

---

[10] For Greek disunity and recriminations, see Osborne (1996b/2009), 339–43/321–25. Arguably, we owe to the general atmosphere of recrimination Herodotos's decision to write his history "in order that human actions might not be rubbed out by the passage of time and that the great and wonderful achievements, both of the Greeks and of the barbarians, might not lose their glory," in the words of his proem.

[11] Quintilian *Institutio Oratoria* 5.12.21 stresses beauty, Galen *de Temperamentis* 1.9, stresses "the mean" (and how hard it is to achieve).

[12] The story is related most extensively in Cicero *De Inventione* 2.1.1–3 (the quotation is from 2.1.3); cf. also Dionysios of Halikarnassos *de Imitatione* 6, Pliny *Natural History* 35.64. Note also the parody in Lucian *Eikones* 3–7.

offers Parrhasios an account of his practice that involves "combining the most beautiful details of several people and so making the whole figure look beautiful."[13]

What Polykleitos is doing in producing a statue as an example of what a beautiful body ought to be like, what Zeuxis is doing in combining features from a number of different models, and what Socrates has Parrhasios agree to be his practice, is undertaking a process exactly parallel to Socrates's famous philosophical practice. Socrates searched for the meaning of a concept not by looking at a particular example embodying the concept but at what different examples have in common. It is in this sense that classical art is "idealist," presupposing that behind any particular example of a concept or object lies a perfect exemplification of that concept or object, and, importantly, that it is the perfect exemplification of the concept or object that one ought to be seeking after.

In the hands of Plato, the point of seeking the perfect example of a concept or thing is epistemological. Only if one knows what courage or piety or virtue is "really" like can one reliably identify courage or piety or virtue in the world around one. Despite Plato's own dismissal in *Republic* 10 of the visual arts, on the basis that they can only ever imitate the particular objects that the artist sees, the point of idealism in art can be seen to be similar: only if one knows what a really beautiful man or woman might look like can one see beauty in the men and women one encounters. But whereas Plato's next move is to conclude that only those who have managed to perceive courage, piety, and virtue as they really are should be trusted to make judgments about courage, piety, and virtue in the world around them, the works of classical artists effectively claim that the particular and the ideal reflect on each other in an ongoing process.

The feedback loop between the observed world and the world of art is vitally important. Artists' observations of beautiful people and objects enable them to offer an embodiment of ideal beauty that in turn offers a template against which to observe facets of beauty in the world around. It is here that we find the payoff of seeing the world differently: the viewer of classical art learns to view beauty in the world. Plato thinks that writers and artists are bad educators because they have seen only particulars; writers and artists themselves claim to be good educators because they have been able to use the particular features of the world they observe to create images that transcend that observed world, and that enable those who read their works, see their plays, or gaze upon their sculptures and paintings to transcend that world also. Whereas late archaic art has encouraged the viewer to perceive what life might be like in another world, a world always competitively distinguishing itself from this world, classical art encourages the viewer to perceive what life might be like in this world, entices the viewer into a world in which they can be collaborators. Socrates goes on, in Xenophon's story of the encounter with Parrhasios, to insist that in depicting the external features of a person—the eyes, the facial expression,

---

[13] Xenophon *Memorabilia* 3.10.2.

the postures—the artist also reveals the internal features of a person, the person's character.[14]

For Kant, classical Greek sculptures could not be beautiful, or at least could not be models of what he terms "free beauty," because they carried with them too much baggage—precisely as a result of their role as models in subsequent Western culture.[15] This future burden was not an issue for fifth-century Greeks, but nevertheless the figures in the sorts of scenes that I have been analyzing would remain for Kant dependent, because they were so heavily implicated in a particular set of actions. By contrast to such works as Hippolyte Flandrin's *Study (Young Male Nude Seated beside the Sea)* (**11.1**), of which Théophile Gautier remarked that it offered no precise meaning and communicated "the dreams of the painter beyond the trammels of subject-matter," the scenes of hoplites departing (4.22 and plate 19, 4.23), or athletes standing in the gymnasium (**11.2**, 1.5–6 and plate 2, 3.23–5), or a young couple embarking on a sexual adventure (5.14) foreground those "trammels of subject-matter" in their very clear references to observed behavior.[16] But, as French nineteenth-century critics, and particularly Baudelaire, recognized, the Kantian tradition set the bar unrealistically high: "Beauty is made up of an eternal, invariable element, whose quantity it is excessively difficult to determine, and of a relative, circumstantial element, which will be, if you like, whether severally or all at once, the age, its fashions, its morals, its emotions. Without this second element, which might be described as the amusing, enticing, appetizing icing on the divine cake, the first element would be beyond our powers of digestion or appreciation, neither adapted nor suitable to human nature."[17]

Although in the twentieth century beauty came to be defined in purely formalist terms, and hence at best politically irrelevant and at worst a distraction from the real life of politics, the beauty that is explored in fifth-century Greek sculpture and painted pottery is not a formalist beauty but closer to the beauty that Baudelaire perceived in the dress coat and the frock coat, when he wrote that "the dress-coat and the frock-coat not only possess their political beauty, which is an expression of universal equality, but also their poetic beauty, which is an expression of the public soul—an immense cortège of undertaker's mutes (mutes in love, political mutes, bourgeois mutes . . .). We are each of us celebrating some funeral."[18] Just as the beauty of the frock coat makes the viewer see in humble figures a cer-

---

[14] Xenophon *Memorabilia* 3.10.3–5. Porter (2010), 171, bizarrely claims that Socrates here is "denying the power of painting to capture the invisible"—the very reverse of the truth: Socrates is insisting that art cannot avoid conveying the invisible.

[15] Prettejohn (2005), 54.

[16] Gautier (1855–56), 286–87, quoted in Prettejohn (2005), 67.

[17] Baudelaire (1964), 3. Baudelaire goes on to remark that "Stendhal . . . approached the truth more closely than many another when he said that 'Beauty is nothing else but a promise of happiness,'" citing chap. 17 of Stendhal's *De l'amour* and chap. 110 of his *Histoire de la Peinture en Italie* where he writes, "La beauté est l'expression d'une certaine manière habituelle de chercher le bonheur." Cf. Prettejohn (2005), 102.

[18] Baudelaire (1965), 118. This passage is preceded by a passage very similar to that quoted above about all forms of beauty containing an element of the transitory and an element of the eternal. Cf. Prettejohn (2005), 108–9.

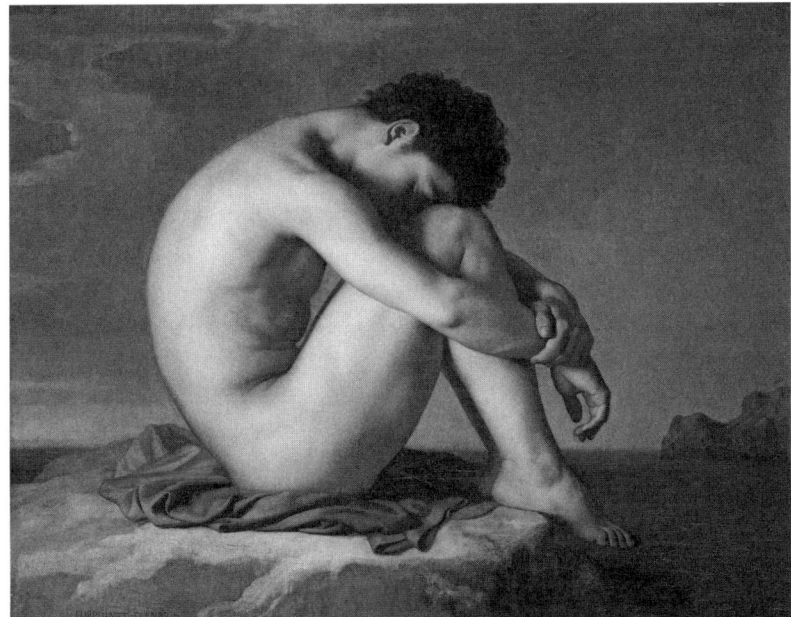

Figure 11.1. Hippolyte Flandrin, *Study (Young Male Nude Seated beside the Sea)* 1835–36. Paris, Louvre. Photo © RMN-Grand Palais (musée du Louvre)/ Michel Urtado.

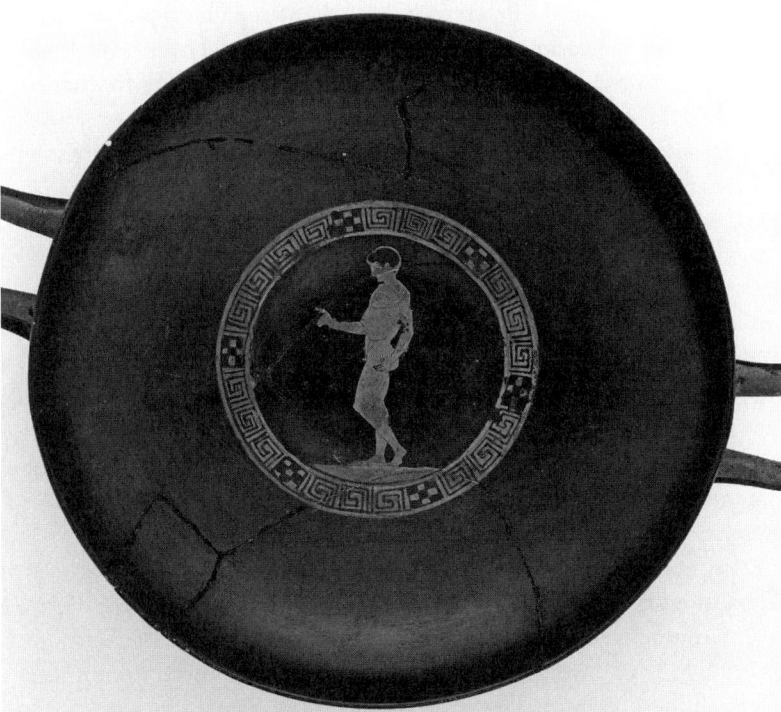

Figure 11.2. Interior of red-figure cup, diameter 0.215 m, name vase of the Painter of Cambridge 72, close to the Codrus Painter (for the exterior see 1.5–6), ca. 430. *ARV* 1273.2. Cambridge Fitzwilliam Museum G72 = GR 50.1864. © The Fitzwilliam Museum, Cambridge.

tain majesty, so the beauty of the departing soldier or the young man in the gymnasium or the woman pouring a libation from a jug (6.1) or dancing the pyrrhic (6.12, 7.19) is both a political and a poetic beauty, making the viewer see in those humble figures, and so in themselves as individuals who might take on one or the other of those roles, a certain majesty. Neither poetic nor political beauty can be said to be on display in Euphronios's scenes of the gymnasium (1.2, 3.6 and plate 5) or the Brygos Painter's scenes of arming (4.17–18) or Peithinos's scene of courtship (5.5–6 and plate 21). For all the attractiveness of some of the figures, their focus is upon their actions, upon doing, not being, and their characters are defined by the tasks they perform.

The way in which classical artists saw the world, and saw beauty in the world, was not simply a feature of the history of art; it was a feature of Greek history. For all that, in Elsner's words, classical art offers "a performative model whereby the viewer observes an imaginary world that is insulated within its own context and to which he or she must relate by identification or some form of wish-fulfilment fantasy," the fantasy that it requires involves adopting a particular attitude to the world.[19] The view of the world as other, as it is presented for instance in Aeschylus's *Persians* in 472, is replaced by the view of the world as made up of people who, however exotic their situation, are like us, as it is presented in Sophocles's *Philoktetes* in 409.

The "city of images" offered to us by Athenian painted pottery is not a record of how the various aspects of civic life changed over time. Painters do not document how armor developed or the changing frequency of light-armed troops;[20] they do not show us which athletic events became more popular and which less; nor do they show us how behavior changed at the symposium, or document increasing or decreasing violence toward women. What the city of images, when examined diachronically, shows us is how Athenians came to see the world differently. It shows us not what was happening but how painters working in Athens saw what was happening—what they noticed, what they brought to each other's notice. The similarity between what they saw and what sculptors working in Athens and working elsewhere saw, gives us reason to think that the city of images is neither exclusively Athenian nor narrowly the viewpoint of the sort of men who ended up painting pottery. The distribution of Athenian pottery guarantees that the painters' way of seeing the city was, in any case, widely spread.

Historians are inclined to think that what matters is what happened. Archaeologists often have little choice but to think that the changing material environment that they excavate was the changing material environment in which history unfolded. What Athenian painted pottery reminds us is that both these assumptions are mistaken. What matters is not what happens, but what is perceived to be happening. The environment in which

---

[19] Elsner (2006), 89.

[20] Despite the claims that Boardman has made that the presence of naked soldiers on pots corresponded to soldiers going to war naked (e.g., Boardman [2004], 49).

history unfolds is constituted by those aspects of the world around them that historical actors register. For most of history we are relatively poorly informed about what the majority of people registered about their world, but for archaic and classical Greece we have the good fortune that cheap and widely consumed pottery carried images that offer us glimpses—albeit partial glimpses—of the world that was seen.

The glimpses of the world that was seen by Athenian pot painters between circa 520 and circa 440 that I have examined in this book have proved to be not random but coordinated. Not only do different painters working at the same time make similar observations, but different painters working at different times make different observations. Between the end of the sixth century and the middle of the fifth century, Athens was redrawn. More than that, parallels with the rather less numerous monuments left by Greek sculptors allow us some confidence that Greece as a whole was remodeled.

The redrawing of classical Greece was not a trivial matter. It involved a radical transformation in how people regarded each other and how they regarded themselves. That transformation is unlikely to have been independent of the major trauma that was constituted by the Persian Wars. It is certainly not independent of the political revolution that led to a massive opening up of political involvement, especially but not only in Athens. But it was also a transformation in which artists themselves played a part as they revealed the attractions of a world seen differently. There needs to be a place not just in the history of Greek art but in the history of classical Greece for what happens when artists begin to see and show classical beauty in the world.

Bibliography

Adam, S. K. 1966. *The Technique of Greek Sculpture in the Archaic and Classical Periods.* London.

Adkins, A.W.H. 1960. *Merit and Responsibility: A Study in Greek Values.* Oxford.

Alcock, S. E., and R. G. Osborne, eds. 2007. *Classical Archaeology.* 2nd expanded ed. 2011. Blackwell Studies in Global Archaeology. Oxford.

Armstrong, J. I. 1958. "The Arming Motif in the *Iliad.*" *American Journal of Philology* 79: 337–54.

Arrington, N. 2014. *Ashes, Images, and Memories: The Presence of the War Dead in Athens.* Oxford.

Azoulay, V. 2014. *Les Tyrannicides d'Athènes: Vie et mort de deux statues.* Paris.

Bäbler, B. 1998. *Fleissige Thrakerinnen und wehrhafte Skythen.* Stuttgart.

Badian, E. 2000. "Back to Kleisthenic Chronology." In *Polis and Politics: Studies in Ancient Greek History Presented to Mogen Herman Hansen on His Sixtieth Birthday, August 20, 2000,* edited by P. Flensted-Jensen, T. H. Nielsen, and L. Rubenstein, 447–64. Copenhagen.

Balot, R. 2014. *Courage in the Democratic Polis: Ideology and Critique in Classical Athens.* Oxford.

Barrett, A., and M. J. Vickers. 1978. "The Oxford Brygos Cup Reconsidered." *Journal of Hellenic Studies* 98: 17–24.

Barron, J. P. 1972. "New Light on Old Walls: The Murals of the Theseion." *Journal of Hellenic Studies* 92: 20–45.

Barthes, R. 1980. *La chambre Claire: Note sur la photographie.* Paris. English trans., *Camera Lucida: Reflections on Photography.* New York, 1981.

Baudelaire, C. 1964. *The Painter of Modern Life and Other Essays.* Translated by J. Mayne. London.

———. 1965. *Art in Paris, 1845–1862.* Translated by J. Mayne. London.

Baxandall, M. 1972. *Painting and Experience in Fifteenth-Century Italy.* 2nd ed., 1988. Oxford.

———. 1981. "L'oeil du quattrocento." *Actes de la recherché en sciences sociales* 4: 10–49.

Bažant, J. 1984. "Les vases athéniens et les réformes démocratiques." In *Images et société en Grèce ancienne: L'iconographie comme method d'analyse,* edited by C. Bérard, C. Bron, and A. Pomari, 33–40. Lausanne.

———. 1985. *Les citoyens sur les vases athéniens du 6ᵉ au 4ᵉ siècle av. J.-C.* Prague.

Beard, M. 1985. "Reflections on 'Reflections on the Greek Revolution.'" *Archaeological Review from Cambridge* 4: 207–13; reprinted in *Journal of Art Historiography* 2 (2010).

———. 1991. "Adopting an Approach II." In *Looking at Greek Vases,* edited by T. Rasmussen and N. J. Spivey, 12–35. Cambridge.

Beazley, J. D. 1911. "The Master of the Berlin Amphora." *Journal of Hellenic Studies* 31: 276–95.

———. 1918. *Attic Red-Figured Vases in American Museums.* Cambridge, MA.

———. 1922. "Citharoedus." *Journal of Hellenic Studies* 42: 70–98.

Beazley, J. D. 1947. "Some Attic Vases in the Cyprus Museum." *Proceedings of the British Academy* 1947: 195–247.

———. 1948. "Hymn to Hermes." *American Journal of Archaeology* 52: 336–40.

———. 1951. *The Development of Attic Black-Figure*. Berkeley, CA; 2nd ed., 1986.

———. 1989. *Greek Vases: Lectures*. Edited by D. C. Kurtz. Oxford.

Benson, J. 1988. "Symptom and Story in Geometric Art." *BABesch* 63: 69–76.

Bentz, M. 1998. *Panathenäische Preisamphoren: Eine athenische Vasengattung und ihre Funktion vom 6.-4. Jahrhundert v. Chr.* Basel.

Bentz, M., and E. Böhr. 2002. "Zu den Maßen attischer Feinkeramik." In *Vasenforschung und Corpus Vasorum Antiquorum—Standortbestimmung und Perspektiven*, edited by M. Bentz, 73–80. Munich.

Bentz, M., and N. Eschbach, eds. 2001. *Panathenaïka: Symposion zu den Panathenäischen Preisamphoren*. Mainz.

Bérard, C., et al. 1984/1988 *La cité des images: Religion et société en Grèce antique*. Paris. English trans., *A City of Images: Iconography and Society in Ancient Greece*. Princeton, NJ, 1988.

Bergemann, J. 1997. *Demos und Thanatos: Untersuchungen zum Wertsystem der Polis im Spiegel der attischen Grabreliefs des 4 Jahrhunderts v. Chr. und zur Funktion der gleichzeitigen Grabbauten*. Munich.

Berger, J. 1972. *Ways of Seeing*. London.

Berthiaume, G. 1982. *Les rôles du mágeiros: Étude sur la boucherie, la cuisine et le sacrifice dans la Grèce ancienne*. Leiden.

Blanckenhagen, P. von. 1976. "Puerilia." In *In Memoriam Otto J. Brendel: Essays in Archaeology and the Humanities*, edited by L. Bonfante and H. von Heintze, 37–41. Mainz.

Bloesch, H. 1940. *Formen Attischer Schalen*. Bern.

Boardman, J. 1972. "Herakles, Peisistratos, and Sons." *Revue archéologique* 7: 57–72.

———. 1974. *Athenian Black Figure Vases: A Handbook*. London.

———. 1975a. *Athenian Red Figure Vases: The Archaic Period; A Handbook*. London.

———. 1975b. "Herakles, Peisistratos, and Eleusis." *Journal of Hellenic Studies* 95: 1–12.

———. 1989. *Athenian Red Figure Vases: The Classical Period; A Handbook*. London.

———. 1998. *Early Greek Vase Painting, 11th–6th Centuries BC: A Handbook*. London.

———. 2002. *The Archaeology of Nostalgia: How the Greeks Re-created Their Mythical Past*. London

———. 2004. "Nudity in Art." In *Reception of Classical Art: An Introduction*, edited by D. C. Kurtz, 47–54. Oxford.

Borbein, A. H. 1996. "Polykleitos." In *Personal Styles in Greek Sculpture*, edited by O. Palagia and J. J. Pollitt, 66–90. Cambridge.

Boulter, C., and K. Luckner. 1976. *Corpus Vasorum Antiquorum Toledo Fasc. 1, U.S.A. Fasc. 17*. Toledo, OH.

Bourdieu, P. 1967. "Postface." In *Architecture gothique et pensée scholastique*, edited by E. Panofsky, 135–67. Translated into French by P. Bourdieu. Paris.

Bourdieu, P., and Y. Desault. 1981. "Pour une sociologie de la perception." *Actes de la recherché en sciences sociales* 4: 3–9.

Bovon, A. 1963. "La représentation des guerriers perses et la notion de barbare dans la première moitié de Ve siècle." *Bulletin de Correspondance Hellénique* 87: 579–602.

Bowie, E. L. 1995. "Wine in Old Comedy." In *In Vino Veritas*, edited by O. Murray and M. Tecusan, 113–25. London.

Brendel, O. 1970. "The Scope and Temperament of Erotic Art in the Graeco-Roman World." In *Studies in Erotic Art*, edited by T. Bowie and C. Christenson, 3–108. New York.

Bresson, A. 2015. *The Making of the Ancient Greek Economy: Institutions, Markets, and Growth in the City-States*. Princeton, NJ.

Bresson, A., and F. de Callataÿ. 2013. "Introduction: The Greek Vase Trade; Some Reflections about Scale, Value, and Market." In *Pottery Markets in the Ancient Greek World (8th–1st Centuries B.C.)*, edited by A. Tsingarida and D. Viviers, 21–24. Brussels.

Brijder, H.A.G. 1983. *Siana Cups I and Komast Cups*. 2 vols. Amsterdam.

———. 1991. *Siana Cups II: The Heidelberg Painter*. 2 vols. Amsterdam.

———. 2000. *Siana Cups III: The Red-Black Painter, Griffin-Bird Painter, and Siana Cups Resembling Lip-Cups*. 2 vols. Amsterdam.

Bron, C. 1987. "Porteurs de thyrses ou bacchantes." In *Images et société en Grèce ancienne: L'iconographie comme method d'analyse*, edited by C. Bérard, C. Bron, and A. Pomari, 145–53. Lausanne.

Brunnsåker, S. 1971. *The Tyrant-Slayers of Kritios and Nesiotes: A Critical Study of the Sources and Restorations*. 2nd ed. Stockholm.

Bryson, N. 1983. *Vision and Painting: The Logic of the Gaze*. Cambridge.

Bugh, G. R. 1988. *The Horsemen of Athens*. Princeton, NJ.

Buitron-Oliver, D. 1995. *Douris: A Master-Painter of Athenian Red-Figure Vases*. Mainz.

Bundrick, S. 2005. *Music and Image in Classical Athens*. Cambridge.

———. 2015. "Eye-Cups in Context." *AJA* 119: 295–341.

Burn, L. M. 1985. "Honey Pots: Three White-Ground Cups by the Sotades Painter." *Antike Kunst* 28: 93–105.

Buxton, R.G.A., ed. 1999. *From Myth to Reason? Studies in the Development of Greek Thought*. Oxford.

Cairns, D. L. 1993. *Aidôs: The Psychology and Ethics of Honour and Shame in Ancient Greek Literature*. Oxford.

Cantarella, E., and A. Lear. 2008. *Images of Ancient Greek Pederasty: Boys Were Their Gods*. London.

Carey, C. 2007. "Pindar, Place, and Performance." In *Pindar's Poetry, Patrons, and Festivals: From Archaic Greece to the Roman Empire*, edited by S. Hornblower and C. Morgan, 199–210. Oxford.

Carpenter, T. H. 1986. *Dionysian Imagery in Archaic Greek Art*. Oxford.

———. 1997. *Dionysian Imagery in Fifth-Century Athens*. Oxford.

Carter, J. B., and L. J. Steinberg. 2010. "*Kouroi* and Statistics." *American Journal of Archaeology* 114: 103–28.

Caskey, L., and J. D. Beazley. 1954. *Attic Vase Paintings in the Museum of Fine Arts, Boston*. Part 2. Oxford.

———. 1963. *Attic Vase Paintings in the Museum of Fine Arts, Boston*. Part 3. Oxford.

Catoni, M. L. 2010. *Bere Vino Puro: Immagini del Simposio*. Milan.

Ceccarelli, P. 1998. *La Pirrica nell' Antichità Greco Romana: Studi sulla Danza Armata*. Pisa.

Chankowski, V. 2013. "La céramique sur le marché: L'objet, sa valeur et son prix; Problèmes d'interprétation et de confrontation des sources". In *Pottery Markets in the Ancient Greek World (8th–1st Centuries B.C.)*, edited by A. Tsingarida and D. Viviers, 25–38. Brussels.

Clairmont, C. W. 1983. *Patrios Nomos: Public Burial in Athens during the Fifth and Fourth Centuries B.C.; The Archaeological, Epigraphic-Literary, and Historical Evidence*. Oxford.

———. 1993–95. *Classical Attic Tombstones*. 6 vols. Kilchberg.

Clark, T. J. 1973a. *The Absolute Bourgeois: Artists and Politics in France, 1848–51*. London.

———. 1973b. *Image of the People: Gustave Courbet and the 1848 Revolution*. London.

———. 1999. *The Painting of Modern Life: Paris in the Art of Manet and His Followers*. Rev. ed. London. 1st ed., 1984.

———. 2013. *Picasso and Truth: From Cubism to Guernica*. Princeton, NJ.

Cloché, P. 1931. *Les Classes, les métiers, le traffic*. Paris.

Cohen, B. 2006. *The Colors of Clay: Special Techniques in Athenian Vases*. Malibu, CA.

Connor, W. R. 1988. "Early Greek Warfare as Symbolic Expression." *Past and Present* 119: 3–29.

Cook, R. M. 1959. "Die Bedeutung der bemalten Keramik für den griechischen Handel." *Jahrbuch des deutschen archäologischen Instituts* 74: 114–23.

Cook, R. M. 1987a. "'Artful Crafts': A Commentary." *Journal of Hellenic Studies* 107: 169–71.

———. 1987b. "Pots and Pisistratan Propaganda." *Journal of Hellenic Studies* 107: 167–69.

Corner, S. 2015. "Symposium." In *A Companion to Food in the Ancient World*, edited by J. Wilkins and R. Nadeau, 234–42. Chichester.

D'Agostino, B. 1990. "Military Organization and Social Structure in Archaic Etruria." In *The Greek City from Homer to Alexander*, edited by O. Murray and S. Price, 59–82. Oxford.

Davidson, J. 1997. *Courtesans and Fishcakes: The Consuming Passions of Classical Athens*. London.

Davies, J. K. 1971. *Athenian Propertied Families, 600–300 B.C.* Oxford.

De Cesare, M. 1997. *Le Statue in Immagine: Studi sulle Raffigurazioni di Statue nella Pittura Vascolare Greca*. Rome.

Dentzer, J.-M. 1982. *Le motif du banquet couché dans le proche-orient et le monde grec du VIIe au IVe siècle avant J.-C.* Rome.

De Ste. Croix, G.E.M. 2004. *Athenian Democratic Origins and Other Essays*. Edited by D. Harvey and R. Parker. Oxford.

Detienne, M. 1986. *The Creation of Mythology*. Translated by M. Cook. Chicago.

Dillon, S. 2006. *Ancient Greek Portrait Sculpture: Contexts, Subjects, and Styles*. Cambridge.

———. 2010. *The Female Portrait Statue in the Greek World*. Cambridge.

Dipla, A., and D. Paleothodoros. 2012. "Selected for the Dead: Erotic Themes on Grave Vases from Attic Cemeteries." In *Encountering Imagery: Materialities, Perceptions, Relations*, edited by I.-M. Back Danielsson, F. Fahlander, and Y. Sjöstrand, 209–33. Stockholm.

Dohrn, T. 1957. *Attische Plastik vom Tode des Phidias bis zum Wirken der Grossen Meister des IV Jahrhunderts v Chr.* Krefeld.

D'Onofrio, A.-M. 1982. "Korai e kouroi funerary attici." *AION Archeologia e Storia Antica* 4: 135–70.

Donohue, A. A. 2005. *Greek Sculpture and the Problem of Description*. Cambridge.

Dougherty C., and L. Kurke L., eds. 1993. *Cultural Poetics in Archaic Greece*. Cambridge.

Dover, K. J. 1968. *Aristophanes: Clouds*. Edited with introduction and commentary. Oxford.

———. 1978. *Greek Homosexuality*. London.

Ducat, J. (1971) *Les Kouroi du Ptoion: Le Sanctuaire d'Apollon Ptoieus à l'Époque Archaïque*. Paris

Duplouy, A. 2006. *Le Prestige des élites: Recherches sur les modes de reconnaissance sociale en Grèce entre les Xe et Ve siècles avant J.-C.* Paris.

Durand, J.-L. 1986. *Sacrifice et labour en Grèce ancienne*. Paris.

Effenterre, H. van. 1976. "Clisthène et les mesures de mobilisation." *Revue des Etudes Grecques* 89: 1–17.

Eichler, F. 1951. *Corpus Vasorum Antiquorum Österreich 1. Wien Kunsthistorisches Museum 1.* Vienna.

Eidinow, E. 2007. "Why the Athenians Began to Curse." In *Debating the Athenian Cultural Revolution*, edited by R. Osborne, 44–71. Cambridge.

Elsner, J. R. 1990. "Significant Details: Systems, Certainties, and the Art-Historian as Detective." *Antiquity* 64: 650–52.

———. 2006. "Reflections on the 'Greek Revolution' in Art." In *Rethinking Revolutions through Classical Greece*, edited by S. Goldhill and R. Osborne, 68–95. Cambridge.

Eschbach, N. 2014. "Athenian Vases for Whom? A New Workshop of the Late 4th Century in the Athenian Kerameikos." *Mètis* 12 (2014): 99–118.

Farrar, C. 1988. *The Origins of Democratic Thinking: The Invention of Politics in Classical Athens*. Cambridge.

Fehr, B. 1971. *Orientalische und griechische Gelage*. Bonn.

———. 1996. "Kouroi e korai: Formule e tipi dell'arte arcaica come expression di valori." In *I Greci 2.1*, edited by S. Settis, 785–846. Turin.

———. 2009. "*Ponos* and the Pleasures of Rest: Some Thoughts on Body Language in Ancient Greek Art and Life." In *The Archaeology of Representations: Ancient Greek Vase-Painting and Contemporary Methodologies*, edited by D. Yatromanolakis, 128–58. Athens.

Ferrari, G. 2002. *Figures of Speech: Men and Maidens in Ancient Greece*. Chicago.

———. 2003. "Myth and Genre on Athenian Vases." *Classical Antiquity* 22: 37–54.

Fisher, N.R.E. 1992. *Hybris: A Study in the Values of Honour and Shame in Ancient Greece*. Warminster.

———. 2000. "Symposiasts, Fish-Eaters and Flatterers: Social Mobility and Moral Concerns." In *The Rivals of Aristophanes: Studies in Athenian Old Comedy*, edited by D. Harvey and J. Wilkins, 355–96. London.

———. 2011. "Competitive Delights: The Social Effects of the Expanded Programme of Contests in Post-Kleisthenic Athens." In *Competition in the Ancient World*, edited by N. Fisher and H. van Wees. Swansea.

Fisher, N.R.E., and H. van Wees. 1998. *Archaic Greece: New Approaches and New Evidence*. London.

Foucault, M. 1977. *Discipline and Punish: The Birth of the Prison*. Translated by Alan Sheridan. London.

Fowler, R. L. 2011. "Mythos and Logos." *Journal of Hellenic Studies* 131: 45–66.

Foxhall, L. 1997. "A View from the Top: Evaluating the Solonian Property Classes," In *The Development of the* Polis *in Archaic Greece*, edited by L. G. Mitchell and P. J. Rhodes, 113–36. London.

Frel, J. 1983. "Euphronios and His Fellows." In *Ancient Greek Art and Iconography*, edited by W. Moon, 147–58. Madison, WI.

———. 1984. *The Death of a Hero*. Malibu, CA.

Fried, M. 1980. *Absorption and Theatricality: Painting and the Beholder in the Age of Diderot*. Berkeley, CA.

Frontisi-Ducroux, F. 1996. "Eros, Desire, and the Gaze." In *Sexuality in Ancient Art*, edited by N. Kampen, 81–100. Cambridge.

Frontisi-Ducrous, F., and F. Lissarrague. 1990. "From Ambiguity to Ambivalence: A Dionysiac Excursion through the 'Anacreontic' Vases." In *Before Sexuality: The Construction of Erotic Experience in the Ancient Greek World*, edited by D. Halperin, J. J. Winkler, and F. I. Zeitlin, 211–56. Princeton, NJ.

Frost, F. 1984. "The Athenian Military before Cleisthenes." *Historia* 33: 283–94.

Gaifman, M. 2012. *Aniconism in Greek Antiquity*. Oxford.

Gardiner, E. N. 1930. *Athletics of the Ancient World*. Oxford.

Gautier, T. 1855–56. *Les Beaux-Arts en Europe: 1855*. Paris.

Gebauer, J. 2002. *Pompe und Thysia: Attische Tieropferdarstellungen auf schwarz- und rotfigurigen Vasen*. Münster.

Gell, A. 1992. "The Technology of Enchantment and the Enchantment of Technology." In *Anthropology, Art, and Aesthetics*, edited by J. Coote and A. Shelton, 40–67. Oxford.

Gera, D. L. 1993. *Xenophon's* Cyropaedia: *Style, Genre, and Literary Technique*. Oxford.

Ghiron-Bistagne, P. 1976. *Recherches sur les acteurs dans la Grèce antique*. Paris.

Gibson, J. J. 1977. "The Theory of Affordances." In *Perceiving, Acting, and Knowing*, edited by Robert Shaw and John Bransford, 127–43. Hoboken, NJ.

———. 1979. *The Ecological Approach to Visual Perception*. Boston.

Gill, D.W.J. 1991. "Pots and Trade: Spacefillers or Objets d'art?" *Journal of Hellenic Studies* 111: 29–47.

Giuliani, L. 2003. *Bild und Mythos: Geschichte der bilderzählung in der Griechischen kunst*. Munich. US translation by J. O'Donnell, *Image and Myth: A History of Pictorial Narration in Greek Art*, Chicago, 2013.

Golden, M. 1998. *Sport and Society in Ancient Greece*. Cambridge.

Goldhill, S. 1998. "The Seductions of the Gaze: Socrates and His Girlfriends." In *Kosmos:*

Essays in Order, Conflict, and Community in Classical Athens, edited by P. Cartledge, P. Millett, and S. von Reden, 105–24. Cambridge.

Gombrich, E. 1960. *Art and Illusion: A Study in the Psychology of Pictorial Representation.* London.

Gomme, A. W. 1925. "The Position of Women in Athens in the Fifth and Fourth Centuries." *Classical Philology* 20: 1–25.

———. 1937. *Essays in Greek History and Literature.* Oxford.

———. 1956. *A Historical Commentary on Thucydides.* Vol. 2, *The Ten Years' War.* Books II–III. Oxford.

Goulaki-Voutira, A. 1994. "Nike auf musikalischen Darstellungen der klassischen Zeit." *Hamburger Jahrbuch für Musikwissenschaft* 12: 83–101.

Graef, B., and E. Langlotz. 1925–33. *Die antiken Vasen von der Akropolis zu Athen.* 2 vols. Berlin.

Greenhalgh P.A.L. 1973. *Early Greek Warfare: Horsemen and Chariots in the Homeric and Archaic Ages.* Cambridge.

Greifenhagen, A. 1929. *Eine attische schwarzfigurige Vasengattung und die Darstellung des Komos im VI. Jahrhundert.* Königsberg.

———. 1935. "Attische schwarzfigurige Vasen im Akademischen Kunstmuseum au Bonn." *Archäologischer Anzeiger*: 407–93.

Gulaki, A. 1981. *Klassische und klassizistische Nikedarstellung.* Bonn.

Gunter, A. 2009. *Greek Art and the Orient.* Cambridge.

Hall, J. M. 2007. *A History of the Archaic Greek World, c. 1200–479 BCE.* Malden, MA.

Hamilton, R. 1992. *Choes and Anthesteria: Athenian Iconography and Ritual.* Ann Arbor, MI.

Hamilton, R. 1996. "Panathenaic Amphoras: The Other Side." In *Worshipping Athena: Panathenaia and Parthenon,* edited by J. Neils, 137–62. Madison, WI.

Hammer, D. 2004. "Ideology, the Symposium, and Archaic Politics." *American Journal of Philology* 125: 479–512.

Hartog, F. 1980. *Le Miroir d'Hérodote: Essai sur la représentation de l'autre.* Paris.

Haskell, F. 1987. *Past and Present in Art and Taste: Selected Essays.* New Haven, CT.

Hedreen, G. M. 1992. *Silens in Attic Black-Figure Vase-Painting: Myth and Performance.* Ann Arbor, MI.

———. 1994. "Silens, Nymphs, and Maenads." *Journal of Hellenic Studies* 114: 47–69.

———. 2001. *Capturing Troy: The Narrative Functions of Landscape in Archaic and Early Classical Greek Art.* Ann Arbor, MI.

———. 2016. *The Image of the Artist in Archaic and Classical Greece: Art, Poetry, and Subjectivity.* Cambridge.

Henle, J. 1973. *Greek Myths: A Vase Painter's Notebook.* Bloomington, IN.

Himmelmann, N. 1998. *Reading Greek Art. Essays by Nikolaus Himmelmann.* Princeton, NJ.

Hindley, C. 1999. "Xenophon on Male Love." *Classical Quarterly* 49: 74–99.

Hobden, F. 2013. *The Symposion in Ancient Greek Society and Thought.* Cambridge.

Hoffmann, H. 1977. *Sexual and Asexual Pursuit.* London.

———. 1997. *Sotades: Symbols of Immortality on Greek Vases.* Oxford.

Hölscher, T. 1973. *Griechische Historienbilder des 5. un 4. Jahrhunderts v. Chr.* Würzburg.

Hollein, H-G. 1988. *Bürgerbild und Bildwelt der attischen Demokratie auf den rotfigurigen Vasen des 6.–4. Jahrhunderts v. Chr.* Frankfurt.

Hoorn, G. van. 1951. *Choes and Anthesteria.* Leiden.

Hornblower, S. 1991. *A Commentary on Thucydides.* I. Books I–III. Oxford.

———. 2000. "The *Old Oligarch* (Pseudo-Xenophon's *Athenaion Politeia*) and Thucydides. A Fourth-Century Date for the *Old Oligarch?*" In *Polis and Politics: Studies in Ancient Greek History Presented to Mogens Herman Hansen on His Sixtieth Birthday, August 20, 2000,* edited by P. Flensted-Jensen et al., 363–84. Copenhagen.

Hurwit, J. 1989. "The Kritios Boy: Discovery, Reconstruction, and Date." *American Journal of Archaeology* 93: 41–80.

———. 2015. *Artists and Signatures in Ancient Greece*. Cambridge.
Immerwahr, H. R. 1990. *Attic Script: A Survey*. Oxford.
Isler-Kerenyi, C. 1969. *Nike: Der Typus der laufenden Flügelfrau in archaischer Zeit*. Erlenbach.
———. 1987. "Dal ginnasio al simposio." *Numismatica e antichità classiche* 16: 47–85.
Ivanchik, A. 2005. "Who Were the 'Scythian' Archers on Archaic Attic Vases?" In *Scythians and Greeks: Cultural Interactions in Scythia, Athens, and the Early Roman Empire (Sixth Century BC–First Century AD)*, edited by D. Braund, 100–113. Exeter.
Jacoby, F. 1944. "Patrios Nomos." *Journal of Hellenic Studies* 64: 37–66.
Jenkins, I. 2005. "The Parthenon Frieze and Perikles' Cavalry of a Thousand." In *Periklean Athens and Its Legacy*, edited by J. Barringer and J. Hurwit, 147–61. Austin, TX.
Jenkins, R.J.H. 1936. *Dedalica: A Study of Dorian Plastic Art in the Seventh Century B.C.* Cambridge.
Johnston, A. W. 1987. "*IG* II^2 2311 and the Number of Panathenaic Amphorae." *Annual of the British School at Athens* 82: 125–29.
Juncker, K. 2003. "Namen auf dem Pronomoskrater." *Athenische Mitteilungen* 118: 208–27.
Kaempf-Dimitriadou, S. 1979. *Die Liebe der Götter in der attischen Kunst des 5. Jahrhunderts v. Chr.* Bern.
Karakasi, K. 2003. *Archaic Korai*. Los Angeles.
Keane, W. 2014. "Rotting Bodies: The Clash of Stances toward Materiality and Its Ethical Affordances." *Current Anthropology* 55, no. S10, *The Anthropology of Christianity: Unity, Diversity, New Directions*, S312–21.
Keesling, C. 2003. *The Votive Statues of the Athenian Acropolis*. Cambridge.
Kephalidou, E. 1996. *ΝΙΚΗΤΗΣ: Ειχονογραφιχή μελέτη του αρχαίου Ελληνίχου αϑλητισμόυ*. Thessaloniki.
Kilmer, M. 1993. *Greek Erotica on Attic Red-Figure Vases*. London.
Kistler, E. 2004. "'Kampf der Mentalitäten': Ian Morris' 'Elitist' versus 'Middling-Ideology'?" In *Griechische Archaik: Interne Entwicklungen—Externe Impulse*, edited by R. Rollinger and C. Ulf, 145–75. Berlin.
Kitto, H.D.F. 1951. *The Greeks*. Harmondsworth.
Kluiver, J. 1992. "The 'Tyrrhenian' Group, Its Origin and the Neck-Amphorae in the Netherlands and Belgium." *BABesch* 67: 73–109.
Kunisch, N. 1997. *Makron*. 2 vols. Mainz.
Kunze-Götte, E. 2002. "Ornamentik und Werkstatt." In *Vasenforschung und Corpus Vasorum Antiquorum—Standortbestimmung und Perspektiven*, edited by M. Bentz, 97–110. Munich.
Kurke, L. 1992. "The Politics of ἁβροσύνη in Archaic Greece." *Classical Antiquity* 11: 91–120.
———. 1993. "The Economy of *kudos*." In *Cultural Poetics in Archaic Greece*, edited by C. Dougherty, and L. Kurke, 131–63. Cambridge.
———. 1999. *Coins, Bodies, Games, and Gold: The Politics of Meaning in Archaic Greece*. Princeton, NJ.
Kurtz, D. C. 1983. *The Berlin Painter*. Oxford.
Kurtz, D. C., and J. Boardman. 1971. *Greek Burial Customs*. London.
———. 1986. "Booners." *Greek Vases in the J. Paul Getty Museum* 3: 35–70. Malibu, CA.
Kyle, D. G. 1984. "Solon and Athletics." *Ancient World* 9: 91–105.
———. 1987. *Athletics in Ancient Athens*. Leiden.
La Genière, J. de. 1987. "Vases des Lénéennes?" *Mélanges de l'École Française de Rome—Antiquité* 99: 43–61.
———. 2006. "Clients, potiers et peintres." In *Les clients de la céramique grecque: Cahiers du Corpus Vasorum Antiquorum France no. 1*, 9–15. Paris.
———. 2009. "Les amateurs des scenes érotiques de l'archaïsme récent." In *Shapes and Uses of Greek Vases (7th–4th Centuries B.C.)*, edited by A. Tsingarida, 337–46. Brussels.
Langdale, A. 1999. "Aspects of the Critical Reception and Intellectual History of Baxan-

dall's Concept of the Period Eye." In *About Michael Baxandall*, edited by A. Rifkin. Oxford (= *Art History* 21: 479–97).

Langdon, S. 2008. *Art and Identity in Dark Age Greece, 1100–700 B.C.E.* Cambridge.

Langridge-Noti, E. 2013. "Consuming Iconographies." In *Pottery Markets in the Ancient Greek World (8th–1st Centuries B.C.)*, edited by A. Tsingarida and D. Viviers, 61–72. Brussels.

Lear, A., and E. Cantarella. 2008. *Images of Ancient Greek Pederasty*. London.

Lesky, M. 2009. "Das Beispiel 'Perizomagruppe': Attische Kunsthandwerker und ihre etruskischen Kunden—zum Handel und Kulturaustausch in spätarchaischer Zeit." *Hephaistos* 25: 69–84.

Lezzi-Hafter, A. 1976. *Der Schuwalow-Maler: Eine Kannenwerkstatt der Parthenonzeit*. Mainz.

———. 1988. *Der Eretria-Maler: Werke und Weggefährten*. Mainz.

———. 1997. "Offerings Made to Measure: Two Special Commissions by the Eretria Painter for Apollonia Pontica." In *Athenian Potters and Painters*, edited by J. Oakley, W. Coulson, and O. Palagia, 353–69. Oxford.

Lissarrague, F. 1985. "La libation: Essai de mise au point." *Image et rituel en Grèce ancienne*, Recherches et Documents du Centre Thomas More, 48: 3–16.

———. 1987. "Voyages d'images: Iconographie et aires culturelles." *Revue des Études Anciennes* 89: 261–67.

———. 1987/1990. *Un Flot d'Images*. Paris. English trans., *The Aesthetics of the Greek Banquet: Images of Wine and Ritual*. Princeton, NJ, 1990.

———. 1989. *L'autre Guerrier: Archers, peltastes, cavaliers dans l'imagerie attique*. Paris.

———. 2013. *La cité des satyres: Une anthropologie ludique (Athènes VIᵉ–Vᵉ siècle avant J.-C.)*. Paris.

Lloyd, G.E.R. 1979. *Magic, Reason, and Experience: Studies in the Origin and Development of Greek Science*. Cambridge.

Long, A. A. 1970. "Morals and Values in Homer." *Journal of Hellenic Studies* 90: 121–39.

Loraux, N. 1981. *L'invention d'Athènes: Histoire de l'oraison funèbre dans la "cité classique."* Paris. English trans., *The Invention of Athens: The Funeral Oration in the Classical City*. Cambridge MA, 1986.

Lynch, K. 2007. "More Thoughts on the Space of the Symposium." In *Building Communities: House, Settlement, and Society in the Aegean and Beyond*, edited by R. Westgate, N. Fisher, and J. Whitley, 243–49. British School at Athens Studies. London.

———. 2009. "Erotic Images on Attic Vases: Markets and Meanings." In *Athenian Potters and Painters II*, edited by J. H. Oakley and O. Palagia, 159–65. Oxford.

———. 2011. *The Symposium in Context: Pottery from a Late Archaic House Near the Athenian Agora*. Hesperia Supplement 46. Princeton, NJ.

———. 2015. "Drinking Cups and the Symposium at Athens in the Archaic and Classical Periods." In *Cities Called Athens*, edited by K. Daly and L. Riccardi, 231–71. Lewisburg, PA.

Lyons, C. 2009. "Nikosthenic pyxides between Etruria and Greece." In *Athenian Potters and Painters II*, edited by J. H. Oakley and O. Palagia, 166–80, Oxford.

Maas, M., and J. M. Snyder. 1989. *Stringed Instruments of Ancient Greece*. New Haven, CT.

Malagardis, N. 1997. " 'Attic Vases, Etruscan Stories': Les échanges et les homes; Origine, vie brève et mort d'une forme de vase attique archaïque." In *Athenian Potters and Painters*, edited by J. H. Oakley, W. Coulson, and O. Palagia, 35–53. Oxford.

Marconi, C. 2004. *Greek Vases: Images, Contexts, and Controversies*. Boston.

———. 2007. *Temple Decoration and Cultural Identity in the Archaic Greek World: The Metopes of Selinus*. Cambridge.

Marr, J. L., and P. J. Rhodes, eds. 2008. *The "Old Oligarch": The Constitution of the Athenians Attributed to Xenophon*. Oxford.

Matheson, S. 1995. *Polygnotos and Vase Painting in Classical Athens*. Madison, WI.

———. 2005. "A Farewell with Arms: Departing Warriors on Athenian Vases." In *Periklean*

Athens and Its Legacy: Problems and Perspectives, edited by J. Barringer and J. Hurwit. 23–35. Austin, TX.

———. 2009. "Beardless, Armed, and Barefoot: Ephebes, Warriors, and Ritual on Athenian Vases." In *An Archaeology of Representations: Ancient Greek Vase-Painting and Contemporary Methodologies*, edited by D. Yatromanolakis, 373–413. Athens.

McNally, S. 1978. "The Maenad in Early Greek Art." *Arethusa* 11: 101–35.

McNiven, T. J. 1995. "The Unheroic Penis: Otherness Exposed." *Source: Notes in the History of Art* 15: 10–16.

Meyer, M. 1988. "Männer mit Geld: Zu einer rotfigurigen Vase mit 'Alltagsszene.'" *Jahrbuch des deutschen archäologischen Instituts* 103: 87–125.

Miller, M. C. 1997. *Athens and Persia in the Fifth-Century B.C.: A Study in Cultural Receptivity*. Cambridge.

———. 2000. "The Myth of Bousiris: Ethnicity and Art." In *Not the Classical Ideal: Athens and the Construction of the Other in Greek Art*, edited by B. Cohen, 413–42. Leiden.

———. 2010. "I Am Eurymedon: Tensions and Ambiguities in Athenian War Imagery." In *War, Democracy, and Culture in Classical Athens*, edited by D. Pritchard, 304–37. Cambridge.

Mingazzini, P. 1971. *Catalogo dei Vasi della Collezione Augusto Castellani*. Rome.

Mitchell, A. G. 2009. *Greek Vase-Painting and the Origins of Visual Humour*. Cambridge.

Monaco, M. C. 2000. *Ergasteria: Impianti Artigianali Ceramici ad Atene ed in Attica dal Protogeometrico all Soglie dell' Ellenismo*. Rome.

Moon, W. G., ed. 1983. *Ancient Greek Art and Iconography*. Madison, WI.

Moraw, S. 1998. *Die Mänade in der attischen Vasenmalerei des 6. und 5. Jahrhunders v. Chr. Rezeptionsästhetische Analyse eines antiken Weiblighkeitsentwurfs*. Mainz.

Morelli, G. 1892–93. *Italian Painters: Critical Studies of Their Works*. 2 vols. London.

Morgan, C. A. 1990. *Athletes and Oracles: The Transformation of Olympia and Delphi in the Eighth Century B.C.* Cambridge.

Morris, I. 1996. "The Strong Principle of Equality and the Archaic Origins of Greek Democracy." In *Demokratia: A Conversation on Democracies, Ancient and Modern*, edited by J. Ober and C. Hedrick, 19–48. Princeton, NJ.

———. 2000. *Archaeology as Cultural History: Words and Things in Iron Age Greece*. Oxford.

Morris, S. P. 1992. *Daidalos and the Origins of Greek Art*. Princeton, NJ.

Morrison, J., and R. Williams. 1968. *Greek Oared Ships, 900–322 B.C.* Cambridge.

Muth, S. 2008. *Gewalt im Bild: Das Phänomen der medialen Gewalt im Athen des 6. und 5. Jahrhunderts v. Chr.* Berlin.

Neer, R. T. 1997. "Beazley and the Language of Connoisseurship." *Hephaistos* 15: 7–30.

———. 2002. *Style and Politics in Athenian Vase-Painting: The Craft of Democracy, ca. 530–460 B.C.E.* Cambridge.

———. 2009. "Connoisseurship: From Ethics to Evidence." In *An Archaeology of Representations: Ancient Greek Vase-Painting and Contemporary Methodologies*, edited by D. Yatromanolakis, 25–49. Athens.

———. 2010a. *The Emergence of the Classical Style in Greek Sculpture*. Chicago.

———. 2010b. "Jean-Pierre Vernant and the History of the Image." *Arethusa* 43 (2): 181–96.

———. 2012. *Art and Archaeology of the Greek World c. 2500–c. 150 BCE*. London.

Neils, J. ed. 1992a. *Goddess and Polis: The Panathenaic Festival in Ancient Athens*. Princeton, NJ.

———. 1992b. "Panathenaic Amphoras: Their Meaning, Makers, and Markets." In Neils (1992a), 29–51, 195–99.

———. 1994. "The Panathenaia and Kleisthenic Ideology." In *The Archaeology of Athens and Attica under the Democracy*, edited by W. Coulson, O. Palagia, T. L. Shear, H. A. Shapiro, and F. J. Frost, 151–60. Oxford.

———. 2001. *The Parthenon Frieze*. Cambridge.

Neils, J, ed. 1996. *Worshipping Athena: Panathenaia and Parthenon*. Madison, WI.
Noble, J. V. 1966. *The Techniques of Attic Painted Pottery*. London. Rev. ed., London, 1988.
———. 1968. "Some Trick Greek Vases." *Proceedings of the American Philosophical Society* 112: 371–78.
Oakley, J. H. 1990. *The Phiale Painter*. Mainz.
———. 2004. *Picturing Death in Classical Athens: The Evidence of the White Lekythoi*. Cambridge.
Oakley, J. H., ed. 2014. *Athenian Potters and Painters III*. Oxford.
Oakley, J. H., W. Coulson, and O. Palagia, eds. 1997. *Athenian Potters and Painters*. Oxford.
Oakley, J. H., and O. Palagia, eds. 2009. *Athenian Potters and Painters II*. Oxford.
Oakley, J. H., and R. Sinos. 1993. *The Wedding in Classical Athens*. Madison, WI.
Ober, J. 2003. "Tyrant-Killing as Therapeutic Conflict: A Political Debate between Images and Texts." In *Popular Tyranny: Sovereignty and Its Discontents in Ancient Greece*, edited by K. Morgan, 215–50. Austin, TX. Reprinted in J. Ober, *Athenian Legacies: Essays on the Politics of Going On Together*. Princeton, NJ, 2005, 212–47.
———. 2015. *The Rise and Fall of Classical Greece*. Princeton, NJ.
Osborne, M. J., and S. G. Byrne. 1994. *A Lexicon of Greek Personal Names II: Attica*. Oxford.
Osborne, R. 1985. "The Erection and Mutilation of the Hermai." *Proceedings of the Cambridge Philological Society*, n.s., 31: 47–73. Reprinted with endnote in Osborne (2010), 341–67.
———. 1987. "The Viewing and Obscuring of the Parthenon Frieze." *Journal of Hellenic Studies* 107: 98–105. Reprinted with endnote in Osborne (2010), 291–305.
———. 1988. "Death Revisited, Death Revised: The Death of the Artist in Archaic and Classical Greek Art." *Art History* 11: 1–16.
———. 1991. "Whose Image and Superscription Is This?" (Review article on *A City of Images.*) *Arion,* 3rd ser., 1 (2): 255–75.
———. 1993. "Competitive Festivals and the Polis: A Context for Dramatic Festivals at Athens." In *Tragedy, Comedy, and the Polis*, edited by A. Sommerstein, S. Halliwell, J. Henderson, and B. Zimmermann, 21–38, Bari. Reprinted with endnote in Osborne (2010), 325–40.
———. 1994. "Archaeology, the Salaminioi, and the Politics of Sacred Space in Archaic Attica." In *Placing the Gods: Sanctuaries and Sacred Space in Ancient Greece*, edited by S. Alcock and R. Osborne, 143–60. Oxford.
———. 1996a. "Desiring Women on Athenian Pottery." iIn *Sexuality in Ancient Art*, edited by N. B. Kampen, 65–80. Cambridge. 65–80.
———. 1996b. *Greece in the Making, 1200–479B.C.* London. 2nd ed., 2009.
———. 1997a. "The Ecstasy and the Tragedy: Varieties of Religious Experience in Art, Drama, and Society." In *Greek Tragedy and the Historian*, edited by C.B.R. Pelling, 187–211. Oxford. Reprinted with endnote in Osborne (2010), 368–404.
———. 1997b. "Men without Clothes: Heroic Nakedness and Greek Art." *Gender and History* 9 (3): 504–28.
———. 1998a. *Archaic and Classical Greek Art*. Oxford.
———. 1998b. "Inter-personal Relations on Athenian Pots: Putting Others in Their Place." In *Kosmos: Essays in Order, Conflict, and Community in Classical Athens*, edited by P. Cartledge, P. Millett, and S. von Reden, 13–36. Cambridge.
———. 2001. "Why Did Athenian Pots Appeal to the Etruscans?" *World Archaeology* 33 (2): 277–95.
———. 2002. "Archaic Greek History." In *Brill's Companion to Herodotus*, edited by E. Bakker, I. de Jong, and H. van Wees, 497–520. Leiden.
———. 2004a. "Images of a Warrior: On a Group of Athenian Vases and Their Public." In *Greek Vases, Images, and Controversies*, edited by C. Marconi, 41–54. Boston.
———. 2004b. *The Old Oligarch: Ps.-Xenophon's* Constitution of the Athenians. LACTOR 2. London.

———. 2004c. "Workshops and the Iconography and Distribution of Athenian Red-Figure Pottery: A Case Study." In *Greek Art in View: Essays in Honour of Brian Sparkes*, edited by S. Keay and S. Moser, 78–94. Oxford.

———. 2006. "When Was the Athenian Democratic Revolution." In *Rethinking Revolutions through Ancient Greece*, edited by S. Goldhill and R. Osborne, 10–28. Cambridge.

———. 2007. "Sex, Agency, and History: The Case of Athenian Painted Pottery." In *Art's Agency and Art History*, edited by R. Osborne and J. Tanner, 179–98. London.

———. 2009. "The Narratology and Theology of Architectural Sculpture; or, What You Can Do with a Chariot but Can't Do with a Satyr on a Greek Temple." In *Structure, Image, Ornament: Architectural Sculpture in the Greek World*, edited by P. Schultz and R. von den Hoff, 2–212. Oxford.

———. 2010a. "The Art of Signing in Ancient Greece." *Arethusa* 43 (2): 231–51.

———. 2010b. *Athens and Athenian Democracy*. Cambridge.

———. 2010c. "Beauty from the Sea." In *What Makes a Masterpiece? Encounters with Great Works of Art*, edited by C. Dell, 34–37. London.

———. 2010d. "Negotiating Citizen Roles in Attic Funerary Sculpture: Ideology and Event." In *War, Democracy, and Culture in Classical Athens*, edited by D. Pritchard, 245–65. Cambridge.

———. 2010e. "Who's Who on the Pronomos Vase." In *The Pronomos Vase*, edited by O. Taplin and R. Wyles, 149–58. Oxford.

———. 2011. *The History Written on the Classical Greek Body*. Cambridge.

———. 2012. "Polysemy and Its Limits in Classical Vase Painting." In *Vasenbilder im Kulturtransfer: Zirkulation und Rezeption griechischer Keramik im Mittelmeerraum*, edited by S. Schmidt and A. Stähli, 177–86. Munich.

———. 2014. "Intoxication and Sociality: The Symposium in the Ancient Greek World." In *Cultures of Intoxication*, edited by A. McShane and P. Withington, 34–60. Past and Present Supplement 9. Oxford.

———. 2015a. "Decontextualising and Recontextualising: Why Mediterranean Archaeology Needs to Get Out of the Trench and Back into the Museum." *Journal of Mediterranean Archaeology* 28: 241–61.

———. 2015b. "Unity vs. Diversity." In *The Oxford Handbook of Ancient Greek Religion*, edited by E. Eidinow and J. Kindt, 11–20. Oxford.

———. 2018. "Greek Pederasty: An Illustrated History." In *How to Do Things with History*, edited by D. Allen, P. Christesen, and P. Millett. Oxford.

———. Forthcoming. "Stuff and Godsense." In *The Stuff of the Gods*, edited by M. Haysom and J. Wallenstein. Stockholm.

Osborne, R., ed. 2008. *The World of Athens: An Introduction to Classical Athenian Culture*. Cambridge.

Paleothodoros, D. 2012. "Sex and the Athenian Woman: A Contextual Analysis of Erotic Vase-Paintings from Attic Graves of the 5th Century BC." In *The Contexts of Painted Pottery in the Ancient Mediterranean World (Seventh–Fourth Centuries BCE)*, edited by D. Paleothodoros, 21–40. Oxford.

Papakonstantinou, Z. 2003. "Alcibiades in Olympia: Olympic Ideology, Sport, and Social Conflict in Classical Athens." *Journal of Sport History* 30: 173–82.

Parlama, L., and N. Stampolidis. 2000. *Athens: The City beneath the City*. Athens.

Parker, H. N. 2015. "Vaseworld: Depiction and Description of Sex at Athens." In *Ancient Sex: New Essays*, edited by R. Blondell and K. Ormand, 23–142. Columbus, OH.

Parker, R.C.T. 1983. *Miasma: Pollution and Purification in Early Greek Religion*. Oxford.

———. 1996. *Athenian Religion: A History*. Oxford.

———. 1997. "Gods Cruel and Kind: Tragic and Civic Theology." In *Greek Tragedy and the Historian*, edited by C.B.R. Pelling, 143–60. Oxford.

Pasquier A., and M. Denoyelle. 1990. *Euphronios peintre à Athènes au viè siècle avant J.-C*. Paris.

Patterson, C. 1981. *Pericles' Citizenship Law of 451–50 B.C*. New York.

Patton, K. C. 2009. *Religion of the Gods: Ritual, Paradox, and Reflexivity*. Oxford.

Peirce, S. 1993. "Death, Revelry, and *thysia*." *Classical Antiquity* 12: 219–66.

Perry, B. 1952. *Aesopica: A Series of Texts Relating to Aesop or Ascribed to Him or Closely Connected with the Literary Tradition That Bears His Name*. Urbana, IL.

Peschel, I. 1987. *Die Hetäre bei Symposion und Komos in der attisch-rotfigurigen Vasenmalerei des 6.–4. Jh. v. Chr.* Frankfurt.

Pfisterer-Haas, S. 1991. Review of Peschel (1987). *Hephaistos* 10: 139–45.

Philippaki, B. 1973. *The Attic Stamnos*. Oxford.

Pinney, G. F. See also s.v. G. Ferrari. 1983. "Achilles Lord of Scythia." In *Ancient Greek Art and Iconography*, edited by W. Moon, 127–47. Madison, WI.

———. See also s.v. G. Ferrari. 1984. "For the Heroes Are at Hand." *Journal of Hellenic Studies* 104: 181–83.

Pollitt, J. J. 1972. *Art and Experience in Classical Greece*. Cambridge.

———. 1990. *The Art of Greece: Sources and Documents*. Cambridge.

Porter, J. I. 2010. *The Origins of Aesthetic Thought in Ancient Greece: Matter, Sensation, and Experience*. Cambridge.

———. 2012. "The Value of Aesthetic Value." In *The Construction of Value in the Ancient World*, edited by J. K. Papadopoulos and G. Urton, 336–53. Los Angeles.

Poursat, J.-C. 1968. "Les representations de danse armée dans la céramique attique." *Bulletin de Correspondance Hellénique* 92: 550–615.

Prettejohn, E. 2005. *Beauty and Art*. Oxford.

Price, S. D. 1990. "Anacreontic Vases Reconsidered." *Greek, Roman, and Byzantine Studies* 31: 133–75.

Price, S.R.F. 1999. *Religions of the Ancient Greeks*. Cambridge.

Pritchard, D. M. 1999. "Fool's Gold and Silver: Reflections on the Evidentiary Status of Finely Painted Attic Pottery." *Antichthon* 33: 1–27.

———. 2003. "Athletics, Education, and Participation in Classical Athens." In *Sport and Festival in the Ancient Greek World*, edited by D. Phillips and D. Pritchard, 293–350. Swansea.

———. 2013. *Sport, Democracy, and War in Classical Athens*. Cambridge.

Puritani, L. 2009. *Die Oinochoe des Typus VII: Produktion und Rezeption im Spannungsfeld zwischen Attika und Etrurien*. Frankfurt.

Raaflaub, K. A. 1996. "Equalities and Inequalities in Athenian Democracy." In *Demokratia: A Conversation on Democracies, Ancient and Modern*, edited by J. Ober and C. Hedrick, 139–74. Princeton, NJ.

———. 1997. "Soldiers, Citizens, and the Evolution of the Early Greek *polis*." In *The Development of the Polis in Archaic Greece*, edited by L. G. Mitchell and P. J. Rhodes, 49–59. London.

Raeck, W. 1981. *Zum Barbarenbild in der Kunst Athens im 6. und 5. Jahrhundert v. Chr.* Bonn.

Rasmussen, T., and N. Spivey, eds. 1991. *Looking at Greek Vases*. Cambridge.

Reden S. von. 1995. *Exchange in Ancient Greece*. London.

Reusser, C. 2002. *Vasen für Etrurien: Verbreitung und Funktionen attischer Keramik im Etrurien des 6. und 5. Jahrhunderts vor Christus*. Zurich.

Rhodes, P. J. 1972. *The Athenian Boule*. Oxford.

———. 1981. *A Commentary on the Aristotelian* Athenaion Politeia. Oxford.

Richter, G.M.A. 1961. *The Archaic Gravestones of Attica*. London.

———. 1968. *Korai: Archaic Greek Maidens; A Study of the Development of the Kore Type in Greek Sculpture*. London.

———. 1970. *Kouroi: Archaic Greek Youths; A Study of the Development of the Kouros Type in Greek Sculpture*. 3rd ed. London.

Ridgway, B. S. 1970. *The Severe Style in Greek Sculpture*. Princeton, NJ.

———. 1977. *The Archaic Style in Greek Sculpture*. Princeton, NJ. 2nd ed., Chicago, 1993.

———. 1981. *Fifth-Century Styles in Greek Sculpture*. Princeton, NJ.

———. 1997. *Fourth-Century Styles in Greek Sculpture*. Madison, WI.

Robert, C. 1881. *Bild und Lied: Archäologische Beiträge zur Geschichte der griechischen Heldensage*. Berlin.

Robertson, C. M. 1950. "Origins of the Berlin Painter." *Journal of Hellenic Studies* 70: 23–34.

———. 1982. "Beazley's Use of Terms." In *Beazley Addenda*, edited by L. Burn and R. Glynn, xi–xviii. Oxford.

———. 1992. *The Art of Vase Painting in Classical Athens*. Cambridge.

Robson, J. 2009. *Aristophanes: An Introduction*. London.

Rotroff, S. 2009. "Early Red-Figure in Context." In *Athenian Potters and Painters II*, edited by J. H. Oakley and O. Palagia, 250–60. Oxford.

Rotroff, S., and J. H. Oakley. 1992. *Debris from a Public Dining Place in the Athenian Agora*. Hesperia Supplement 25. Princeton, NJ.

Rouet, P. 2001. *Approaches to the Study of Attic Vases: Beazley and Pottier*. Oxford.

Ruffell, I. A. 2011. *Politics and Anti-Realism in Athenian Old Comedy: The Art of the Impossible*. Oxford.

Rusten, J. 1990. *Thucydides: The Peloponnesian War Book II*. Cambridge.

Sapirstein, P. 2013. "Painters, Potters, and the Scale of the Attic Vase-Painting Industry." *American Journal of Archaeology* 117: 493–510.

———. 2014. "Demographics and Productivity in the Ancient Athenian Pottery Industry." In *Athenian Potters and Painters III*, edited by J. H. Oakley, 175–86. Oxford.

Scarry, E. 1999. *On Beauty and Being Just*. Princeton, NJ.

Schäfer, A. 1997. *Unterhaltung beim griechischen Symposion: Darbietungen, Spiele und Wettkämpfe von homerischer bis in spätklassische Zeit*. Mainz.

Schauenberg, K. 1975. "ΕΥΡΥΜΕΔΩΝ ΕΙΜΙ." *Athenische Mitteilungen* 90: 97–121.

Scheibler, I. 1983. *Griechische Töpferkunst: Herstellung, Handel und Gebrauch der antiken Tongefäße*. Munich.

———. 1987. "Bild und Gefäss: Zur Ikonographischen und funkionalen Bedeutung des attischen Bildfeldamphoren." *Jahrbuch des Deutschen Archäologischen Instituts* 102: 57–118.

Schnapp, A. 1997. *Le chasseur et la cité: Chasse et érotique en Grèce ancienne*. Paris.

Schofield, M. 1986. "*Euboulia* in the *Iliad*." *Classical Quarterly* 36: 6–31.

Schreiber, T. 1999. *Athenian Vase Construction*. Malibu, CA.

Seki, T. 1985. *Untersuchungen zum Verhältnis von Gefässform und Malerei attischer Schalen*. Berlin.

Shapiro, H. A. 1981. "Courtship Scenes in Attic Vase-Painting." *American Journal of Archaeology* 85: 133–43.

———. 1990. "Old and New Heroes: Narrative, Composition, and Subject in Attic Black-Figure." *Classical Antiquity* 9: 114–48.

———. 1992. "Eros in Love: Pederasty and Pornography in Greece." In *Pornography and Representation in Greece and Rome*, edited by A. Richlin, 53–72. Oxford.

———. 2000. "Modest Athletes and Liberated Women: Etruscans on Attic Black-Figure Vases." In *Not the Classical Ideal: Athens and the Construction of the Other in Greek Art*, edited by B. Cohen, 315–37. Leiden.

———. 2003. "Fathers and Sons, Men and Boys." In *Coming of Age in Ancient Greece: Images of Childhood from the Classical Past*, edited by J. Neils and J. Oakley, 85–111. New Haven, CT.

———. 2004. "Leagros the Satyr." In *Greek Vases: Images, Contexts, and Controversies*, edited by C. Marconi, 1–11. Leiden.

Shapiro, H. A., M. Iozzo, and A. Lezzi-Hafter. 2013. *The François Vase: New Perspectives*. Kilchberg.

Shear, J. L. 2003a. "'Atarbos' Base and the Panathenaia." *Journal of Hellenic Studies* 123: 164–80.

———. 2003b. "Prizes from Athens: The List of Panathenaic Prizes and the Sacred Oil." *Zeitschift für Papyrologie und Epigraphik* 142: 87–105.

Shear, T. L. 1993. "The Persian Destruction of Athens: Evidence from Agora Deposits." *Hesperia* 62: 383–482.

Siewert, P. 1982. *Die Trittyen Attikas und die Heeres reform des Kleisthenes*. Munich.

Simon, E. 1953. *Opfernde Götter*. Heidelberg.

———. 2004. "Libation." *ThesCRA* I. 2b. Los Angeles. 237–53.

Singor, H. W. 2000. "The Military Side of the Peisistratean Tyranny." In *Peisistratos and the Tyranny: A Reappraisal of the Evidence*, edited by H. Sancisi-Weerdenburg. Amsterdam.

Smith, A. C. 1999. "Eurymedon and the Evolution of Political Personifications in the Early Classical Period." *Journal of Hellenic Studies* 119: 128–41.

———. 2006. "The Evolution of the Pan Painter's Artistic Style." *Hesperia* 75: 434–51.

Smith, R.R.R. 2002. "The Use of Images: Visual History and Ancient History." In *Classics in Progress: Essays on Ancient Greece and Rome*, edited by T. P. Wiseman, 59–102. Oxford.

Sommerstain, A. 1982. *Aristophanes* Clouds Edited with an Introduction, Translation, and Notes. Warminster.

Sourvinou-Inwood, C. 1975. "Who Was the Teacher of the Pan Painter?" *Journal of Hellenic Studies* 95: 107–21.

Sparkes, B. A. 1996. *The Red and the Black: Studies in Greek Pottery*. London.

Spence, I. G. 1993. *The Cavalry of Classical Greece: A Social and Military History*. Oxford.

Spiess, A. B. 1992. *Der Kriegerabschied auf attischen Vasen der archaischen Zeit*. Berlin.

Spivey, N. J. 1991. "Greek Vases in Etruria." In *Looking at Greek Vases*, edited by T. Rasmussen and N. Spivey, 131–50. Cambridge.

———. 2005. *How Art Made the World*. London.

Stallabrass, J. 2004. *Art Incorporated*. Oxford. Reissued as *Contemporary Art: A Very Short Introduction*, Oxford, 2006.

Stansbury-O'Donnell, M. 2006. *Vase Painting, Gender, and Social Identity in Archaic Athens*. Cambridge.

Stansbury-O'Donnell, M. 2009. "Structural Differentiation of Pursuit Scenes." In *The Archaeology of Representations: Ancient Greek Vase-Painting and Contemporary Methodologies*, edited by D. Yatromanolakis, 341–72. Athens.

Steiner, A. 2002. "Private and Public: Links between *Symposion* and *Syssition* in Fifth-Century Athens." *Classical Antiquity* 21: 347–80.

———. 2007. *Reading Greek Vases*. Cambridge.

Stewart, A. 1990. *Greek Sculpture: An Exploration*. New Haven, CT.

———. 1997. *Art, Desire, and the Body in Ancient Greece*. Cambridge.

———. 2008a. *Classical Greece and the Birth of Western Art*. Cambridge.

———. 2008b. "The Persian and Carthaginian Invasions of 480 B.C.E. and the Beginning of the Classical Style: Part 2, the Finds from Other Sites in Athens, Attica, Elsewhere in Greece, and on Sicily; Part 3, the Severe Style: Motivations and Meaning." *American Journal of Archaeology* 112: 581–615.

Stieber, M. 2004. *The Poetics of Appearance in the Attic Korai*. Austin, TX.

Stissi, V. 2009. "Why Did They End Up There? The Role of Iconography in the Distribution, Purchase, and Use of Siana Cups." In *Shapes and Images: Studies on Attic Black Figure and Related Topics in Honour of Herman A. G. Brijder*, edited by E. M. Moorman and V. V. Stissi, 21–35. Leuven.

Sutton, R. F. 1992. "Pornography and Persuasion on Attic Pottery." In *Pornography and Representation in Greece and Rome*, edited by A. Richlin, 3–35. Oxford.

———. 2000. "The Good, the Base, and the Ugly: The Drunken Orgy in Attic Vase-Painting and the Athenian Self." In *Not the Classical Ideal: Athens and the Construction of the Other in Greek Art*, edited by B. Cohen, 180–202. Leiden.

———. 2009a. "The Invention of the Female Nude: Zeuxis, Vase-Painting, and the Kneeling Bather." In *Athenian Potters and Painters II*, edited by J. Oakley and O. Palagia, 270–79. Oxford.

———. 2009b. "Lovemaking on Attic Black-Figure Pottery: Corpus with Some Conclusions." In *Hermeneutik der Bilder—Beiträge zu Ikonographie und Interpretation griechischer Vasenmalerei*, edited by S. Schmidt and J. H. Oakley. Munich.

Svenbro, J. 1988. *Phrasikleia: anthropologie de la lecture en Grèce ancienne*. Paris. English trans., Ithaca, NY, 1993.

Tanner, J. 2006. *The Invention of Art History in Ancient Greece: Religion, Society, and Artistic Rationalisation*. Cambridge.

Taplin, O. 1978. *Greek Tragedy in Action*. London.

———. 1989. *Greek Fire*. London.

———. 1992. *Comic Angels and Other Approaches to Greek Drama through Vase-Paintings*. Oxford.

———. 2007. *Pots and Plays: Interactions between Tragedy and Greek Vase-Painting of the Fourth Century B.C.* Los Angeles.

Taplin, O., and R. Wyles, eds. 2010. *The Pronomos Vase and Its Context*. Oxford.

Taylor, M. C. 1997. *Salamis and the Salaminioi: The History of an Unofficial Athenian Demos*. Amsterdam.

Topper, K. 2012. *The Imagery of the Athenian Symposium*. Cambridge.

Tosto, V. 1999. *The Black-Figure Pottery Signed ΝΙΚΟΣΘΕΝΕΣΕΠΟΙΕΣΕΝ*. Amsterdam.

Traill, J. S. 1986. *Demos and Trittys: Epigraphical and Topographical Studies in the Organisation of Attica*. Toronto.

Trendall, A. D., and T.B.L. Webster. 1971. *Illustrations of Greek Drama*. London.

True, M. 2006. "Athenian Potters and the Production of Plastic Vases." In *The Colors of Clay: Special Techniques in Athenian Vases*, edited by B. Cohen, 240–49. Malibu, CA.

Trümpf-Lyritzaki, M. 1969. *Griechische Figurenvasen des reichen Stils und der späten Klassik*. Bonn.

Tsingarida, A. 2008. "Nikosthenes Looking East? Phialai in Six's and Polychrome Six's Technique." In *Essays in Classical Archaeology for Eleni Hatzivasiliou (1977–2007)*, edited by D. C. Kurtz et al., 105–14. Oxford.

———. 2009. "Vases for Gods and Heroes: Early Red-Figure Parade Cups and Large-Scaled Phialai." In *Shapes and Uses of Greek Vases (7th–4th Centuries B.C.)*, edited by A. Tsingarida, 185–201. Brussels.

Tuna-Nörling, Y. 1997. "Attic Black-Figure Export to the East: The 'Tyrrhenian Group' in Ionia." In *Athenian Potters and Painters*, edited by J. H. Oakley, W. Coulson, and O. Palagia, 435–46. Oxford.

Turnure, J. 1981. "Again 'Dirty Trick' Vases." *American Journal of Archaeology* 85: 175–77.

Van Straten, F. 1995. *Hierà Kalá: Images of Animal Sacrifice in Archaic and Classical Greece*. Leiden.

Veness, R. 2002. "Investing the Barbarian? The Dress of Amazons in Athenian Art." In *Women's Dress in the Ancient Greek World*, edited by L. Llewellyn-Jones, 95–110. London.

Veyne, P. 1990. "Images des divinités tenant une phiale ou patère: La libation comme rite de passage et non pas offrande." *Métis* 5: 17–30.

Vickers, M. 1975. "A Dirty Trick Vase." *American Journal of Archaeology* 79: 282.

———. 1980. "Another Dirty Trick Vase." *American Journal of Archaeology* 84: 183–84.

———. 1985. "Artful Crafts: The Influence of Metalwork on Athenian Painted Pottery." *Journal of Hellenic Studies* 105: 108–28.

———. 1987. "Value and Simplicity: Eighteenth-Century Taste and the Study of Greek Vases." *Past and Present* 116: 98–137.

Vickers M., and D. Gill. 1994. *Artful Crafts: Ancient Greek Silverware and Pottery*. Oxford.

Vidal-Naquet, P. 1981. *Le chasseur noir: Formes de pensée et forms de société dans le monde grec*. Paris. Translated as *The Black Hunter: Forms of Thought and Forms of Society in the Greek World*, Baltimore, 1986.

Villanueva-Puig, M. C. 2009. *Ménades: Recherches sur la genèse iconographique du thiase féminine de Dionysos, des origins à la fin de la période archaïque*. Paris.

Visa-Ondarçuhu, V. 1999. *L'image de l'athlète d'Homère à la fin du Ve siècle avant J.-C*. Paris.

Viviers, D. 2006. "Signer une oeuvre en Grèce ancienne: Pourquoi? pour qui?" In *Les clients de la céramique grecque: Cahiers du Corpus Vasorum Antiquorum France no. 1*, edited by J. de la Genière, 141–54. Paris.

Vollmer, C. 2014/15. "Eine Allegorie der Demokratie? Zur Benennung des polykletischen Doryphoros." *Athenische Mitteilungen* 129/130: 125–46.

Von Bothmer, D. 1976. "Der Euphronioskrater in New York." *Archäologischer Anzeiger*: 485–512.

———. 1985. *The Amasis Painter and His World: Vase-Painting in Sixth-Century BC Athens*. Malibu, CA.

———. 1986. "An Archaic Red-Figured Kylix." *J. Paul Getty Museum Journal* 14: 5–20.

Vos, M. F. 1963. *Scythian Archers in Archaic Attic Vase Painting*. Groningen.

Vout, C. 2013. *Sex on Show: Seeing the Erotic in Greece and Rome*. London.

———. 2014. "The End of the 'Greek Revolution'?" *Perspective: Actualité en histoire de l'art*: 246–52.

Waddell, G. 1991. "The Greek Pentathlon." *Greek Vases in the J. Paul Getty Museum* 5: 99–106.

Wagner, C. 1999. "The Potters and Athens: Dedications on the Athenian Acropolis." In *Periplous: Papers on Classical Art and Archaeology Presented to Sir John Boardman*, edited by G. Tsetskhladze, J. Prag, and A. M. Snodgrass, 383–87. London.

———. 2001. "The Worship of Athena on the Athenian Acropolis: Dedications of Plaques and Plates." In *Athena in the Classical World*, edited by S. Deacy and A. Villing, 95–104. Leiden.

Wallinga, H. T. 1993. *Ships and Sea-Power before the Great Persian War: The Ancestry of the Ancient Trireme*. Leiden.

Watson, J. 2010. "The Origin of the Metic Status at Athens." *Cambridge Classical Journal* 56: 259–78.

Webster, T.B.L. 1935. *Der Niobidenmaler*. Leipzig.

———. 1972. *Potter and Patron in Classical Athens*. London.

Wecowski, M. 2014. *The Rise of the Greek Aristocratic Banquet*. Oxford.

Wees, H. van. 1998. "Greeks Bearing Arms: The State, the Leisure Class, and the Display of Weapons in Archaic Greece." In *Archaic Greece: New Approaches and New Evidence*, edited by N.R.E. Fisher and H. van Wees, 333–78. London.

———. 2004. *Greek Warfare: Myths and Realities*. London.

———. 2006. "Mass and Elite in Solon's Athens: The Property Classes Revisited." In *Solon of Athens: New Historical and Philological Approaches*, edited by J. Blok and A. Lardinois, 351–89. Leiden.

———. 2013. *Ships and Silver, Taxes and Tribute: A Fiscal History of Archaic Athens*. London.

Welch, E. 1997. *Art and Society in Italy, 1350–1500*. Oxford.

Whitehead, D. W. 1981. "The Archaic Athenian *Zeugitai*." *Classical Quarterly* 31: 282–86.

Whitley, A. J. 1997. "Beazley as Theorist." *Antiquity* 71: 40–47.

Wiles, D. 2000. *Greek Theatre Performance: An Introduction*. Cambridge.

Williams, B.A.O. 1993. *Shame and Necessity*. Berkeley, CA.

Williams, D. 1991. "The Invention of the Red-Figure Technique and the Race between Vase-Painting and Free Painting." In *Looking at Greek Vases*, edited by T. Rasmussen, and N. Spivey, 103–118. Cambridge.

———. 1996. "Refiguring Attic Red-Figure: A Review Article." *Revue Archéologique*, n.s., 2: 227–52.

———. 2008. "Some Thoughts on the Potters and Painters of Plastic Vases before Sotades." In *Papers on Special Techniques in Athenian Vases*, edited by K. Lapatin, 161–72. Los Angeles.

———. 2013. "Greek Potters and Painters: Marketing and Movement." In *Pottery Markets in the Ancient Greek World (8th–1st Centuries B.C.)*, edited by A. Tsingarida and D. Viviers, 39–60. Brussels.

Wilson, P. J. 1999. "The *aulos* in Athens." In *Performance Culture and Athenian Democracy*, edited by S. Goldhill and R. Osborne, 58–95. Cambridge.

———. 2000. *The Athenian Institution of the* Khoregia. Cambridge.

Wohl, V. 2004. "Dirty Dancing: Xenophon's *Symposium*." In *Music and the Muses: The Culture of "Mousikē" in the Classical Athenian City*, edited by P. Murray and P. Wilson, 337–63. Oxford.

Woodford, S. 2003. *Images of Myths in Classical Antiquity*. Cambridge.

Yatromanolakis, D. 2009. "*Symposia*, Noses, Πρόσωπα: A *kylix* in the Company of Banqueters on the Ground." In *The Archaeology of Representations: Ancient Greek Vase-Painting and Contemporary Methodologies*, edited by D. Yatromanolakis, 414–64. Athens.

Zanker, P. 1988. *The Power of Images in the Age of Augustus*. Ann Arbor, MI.

Zeitlin, F. I. 1981. "Travesties of Gender and Genre in Aristophanes' *Themophoriazousae*." In *Reflections of Women in Antiquity*, edited by H. P. Foley, 169–217. London. Reprinted in F. I. Zeitlin, *Playing the Other: Gender and Society in Classical Greek Literature*. Chicago, 1996, 375–416.

Ziomecki, J. 1975. *Les représentations d'artisans sur les vases attiques*. Wrocław.

❧ Index

absorption (as opposed to theatricality), a feature of classical style, 221n34, 223, 225, 228, 231, 233, 235, 237–39, 240, 244 . *See also* contemplation

Achilles, dicing, 93, 94; on cup with Herakles and an athlete, 72; named on pot, 94; and Penthesileia, 107; on Siphnian treasury, 20

Achilles Painter, 119

Acropolis, Athenian, *korai* from, 19, 252; Peisistratos and, 35; Persian *akinakai* dedicated on, 108; pottery from, 42, 48, 124, 146–47; sculpture on, 24n54, 231; victory in athletics commemorated on, 57; victory in war commemorated on, 90

Adkins, Arthur W. H., 211–12

Aeschylus, *Persai*, 109, 256

Aesop, 32

aesthetic values, changes in, xvii, xviii, xix, 13, 19, 84–85, 148, 166–67, 218–27, 249–57

affordances, 220n31, 240, 246–47

age, distinctions of in classical sculpture, 242; distinctions of in painted pottery, 64, 68–69, 126, 129. *See also* bearded men

Agora, Athenian, pottery from, 48, 124; Painted Stoa in, 92; public dining room in, 170

Aias, shown with Achilles, 93, 94

Aigina, Athenian war with, 92; pottery from, 124

Aigisthos, 231

Aineias, representation of and the Etruscans, 48

Aischines, on athletics, 60

Akestorides Painter, 81–83, 84, 160

akinakes, Persian sword, 108–9

Akraiphnion, sanctuary at, 17

Aktaion, 233–34

Alkaios, 176

Alkibiades, 54n7, 56, 57

Altamura, Athenian pottery from, 203

altar, in religious scenes, 132, 143–44, 153, 156–57, 158, 161–63; in scene of athlete, 74, 79

Amasis Painter, 49, 94, 124–25, 194

Amazons, 94, 100, 109, 147; relation to Persians, 107–8

Anakreon, erotic poetry of, 128, 175; in painted pottery, 175, 178n16

Anakreontic vases. *See* booners

Anaphe, *kouros* from, 17

Andokides Painter, 62, 64, 66, 67, 71, 84

Andokides, orator, gymnasiarch, 57, 100n56

Anthesteria, 55, 138, 204n21

Antiope, 137, 230

Antiphon Painter, 64, 172

Aphrodite, representation of, 146, 237–38

Apollo, representation of, 15, 62–63, 64, 101n59, 141, 161n15, 234, 235; temple/sanctuary of, 15, 17; "Strangford Apollo," 17

Apollodoros, orator, *Against Neaira*, 123, 133n29

Apollodoros, painter, 105

archers, representation of on Athenian pottery, 72n71, 93, 94–100, 106–7, 110, 112; presence of in Peisistratean Athens, 97. *See also* Scythians

arete, changing nature of, 211–12

Aristophanes, on athletics, 60, 82n86; on clash of generations, 148–49; on Scythians, 100n56; on wearing sakkos, 175n14; and women, 122

arming, scenes of on Athenian pottery, 93, 94, 98, 109–16, 118–20, 220, 226, 233, 256. *See also* departure

army, Athenian, nature of, 87–93, 117

art history, nature of, xvii, xviii, 3, 5–7, 23, 25, 218–27, 248–49

art, classical, history of, xvii, 3–5, 7, 9–22, 25, 219–48

Artemis, representation of, 15, 63, 64, 101n59, 233–34

artists, reactions to society of, 5–7; role in driving art's history, 9, 30, 31

aryballos, as mark of athlete, 58, 66, 71, 78, 129

Athena, and Herakles, 235; on Panathenaic amphoras, 53; and Peisistratos, 35; and struggle for tripod, 63; worship of, 231

Athenaios, on athletes, 58; on symposium, 168n1, 170

❧ 277

Athens, painted pottery from, xvii, 3, 7; pots found at, 11, 14, 40, 197; army of, 87–93; athletics at, 53–60, 214
athletes, treated as benefactors, 55, 84, 211; used as ambassadors, 56; on grave reliefs, 58; representations of solo athletes, 72–74; sexual activity of, 134. *See also* gymnasium
athletics, at Athens, 53–60, 214; popularity of, 56, 211; representation of, xviii, 7, 20, 24, 25, 46, 53–86, 118, 120, 147–48, 156, 166–67, 207, 208, 209, 217–18, 219, 220, 224, 228, 254, 256
attribution, of pottery to particular painters, 28–29
aulos players, and athletes, 66–69, 79; and dancing, 203, 204; and drama, 43–45; satyr as, 14, 192, 193, 199; in *komos*, 138, 176, 177; for armed dancing, 163, 164, 184; in courtship scene, 131–33; at symposium, 161, 179, 181, 182, 184, 185, 186, 187, 221

Bacchylides, 56
ball games, representation of, 20–21, 58, 203–4, 220
barbitos, 138, 175, 176, 181, 185, 191–93, 199
Bassai, temple of Apollo, sculpture from, 242, 244, 245
bathing, scenes of, 36n50
Batrakhos, as Athenian name, 68
Baudelaire, Charles, 254
Baxandall, Michael, 5–6, 7
Bažant, J., 7n10, 25n57, 34n41, 60n41, 93n33, 212n11, 216n23, 224n41, 225n43
bearded men, and athletics, 62, 64, 69n61, 70, 71, 75, 78, 79, 80, 81, 224; in classical sculpture, 242; and hoplite warfare, 104, 110, 111, 233–34; in *komos*, 171, 175–79; and sexual intercourse, 124–27, 128; at symposium, 179, 182, 183–84, 185
beauty, classical discussion of, 252–54; of classical faces, 244; displayed in dancing, 177, 187; displayed in gymnasium, 66–67; discussed in symposium, 187; of Greek pottery, 13; and Polykleitos, 252; role of, xviii, 224n42, 252–57
Beazley Archive, in Oxford, xix, 31, 49
Beazley, Sir John, on Anakreontic vases, 175; on black-figure pottery, 12–13; distinguishing artists' hands, 27–28, 31, 32, 34, 42, 49; on iconography, 33; methods of, 3
Berlin Painter, 49, 78, 137, 159–60
black servants, on Athenian pots, 95, 231
Boardman, Sir John, 9, 10–12, 31, 35, 98n49, 256n20
boat race, 55, 57
body, and athletics, 58–60, 61, 63, 64, 66, 70, 74, 80, 81, 84, 220; contrast between archaic and classical, 224, 247; depiction of, 5, 6, 84; in early classical sculpture, 229–30, 240, 245–46; sexual attractions of in male youths, 126, 129
Boiotia, *kouros* from, 17
Boiotian shields, symbolism of, 94, 95
booners, 175–79, 209
Boreas, pursuing Oreithuia, 138
boundary stone (*horos*), of gymnasium, 74, 75, 78
Bourdieu, Pierre, 5n3
boxer/boxing, 53, 60, 61, 66n49, 68, 72, 74, 75; on grave relief, 58
Briseis Painter, 78n79, 79, 133, 134–35, 176–77
Brygos Painter, 107, 111, 133, 181, 182, 191–94, 256
Brygos, potter, 107
Bryson, Norman, 18n42, 221n35, 224
bucchero, Etruscan, imitation of in Athens, 46
burial, armed dancing at, 163; in Etruria, 24, 26, 40–41, 42n65; in Sicily, 42n66; pots and, 9, 23, 40–43, 124. *See also* cemeteries

Calliope Painter, 143–45, 210
Campagnano, Athenian pottery from, 67
cap of victor, 70
Capua, Athenian pottery from, 4, 64, 65, 139
Carpenter Painter, 79–81, 224
Cassandra, rape of, 161
cavalry, at Athens, 88–89, 149; on Athenian pottery, 93, 94–100, 106
Ceccarelli, Paola, 166–67
cemeteries, pots from, 40–41, 124, 128n19, 138, 146; sculpture from, 15–16, 19. *See also* burial
census classes, at Athens, 88–89, 215
centauromachies, representation of, 109, 235–36
Cervetri, Athenian pottery from, 27, 107, 101, 114, 135; pots of Penthesileia workshop from, 37n52
chariots, in painted pottery, 9, 23, 93, 98, 110, 144; races of, 53, 54, 56, 69n61; in victory monument, 92
Chelis Painter, 196–97, 198
Chicago Painter, 28, 29, 108, 113–15
Chiusi, Athenian pottery from, 46n47, 105
Cicero, Marcus Tullius, buying sculpture, 31n25
Cité des Images, 34
citizenship, at Athens, 55, 59, 70, 74, 78, 82, 84, 87, 89, 213, 216–18
Clairmont, C. W., 58
Clark, T. J., 6–7, 227
classical style, in sculpture, 20, 219–27, 228, 229, 242–48, 252–54. *See also* art: classical, history of
Clephan Painter, 198
Cloché, Paul, 33
clothes, language of, 130. *See also* dress
cock-fighting, representation of, 20

cock, as love-gift, 124–25, 126, 130, 132
Codrus Painter, 8, 255
coinage, ideology of, 211
color palette, choice of, 3, 5, 6
comedy, Athenian, and warfare, 120, 122; women in, 122. *See also* Aristophanes
commissioning of pottery 33, 41–45
competition, representation of in early red-figure, 69, 74, 75, 78, 82, 84, 120–21, 149, 166, 167, 204, 209, 219, 253; ideology of, 211–15, 217–18, 225, 249
composition, artistic, 3, 28; related to graphic technique, 36
Connor, W. Robert, 89
contemplation, images encouraging, 74, 78, 84, 125, 150, 196, 209 . *See also* absorption
Cook, Robert M., 39–40
Copenhagen Painter/Syriskos, 231–33
Corinth, painted pottery of, exported for its contents, 47; influence on Athenian pottery, 10–12; showing arming scenes, 110
council of 500, at Athens, 91, 214–16
courtship, representation of, xviii, 70–71, 124–33, 136–37, 138, 141, 147, 209, 256; of men contrasted with courtship of women, 129–31
cow. *See* ox
Crete, sculpture from, 15
crown games, 53, 55n16, 56
Cumae, Athenian pottery from, 234

D'Hancarville, Baron, 32–33
Daedalic style, in sculpture, 15
dancing, 186; armed/Pyrrhic, competition in 54–55, 57, 68, 148, 163–67, 209; Dionysiac, 189–93, 194, 199; after parties, 171; at symposia, 178, 183–87; by women, 102, 164–67, 183–87, 256. *See also* maenads
death, depictions of, 9, 18, 23, 95, 97, 116, 231
Delos, sculpture from, 15
Delphi, display of sculpture at, 226; Polygnotos' painting at, 234; Pythian games at, 53, 61; Siphnian treasury at, 17, 20; war memorials at, 92
demes, Athenian, 68n56, 91, 213–15; festivals in, 44, 163; theater of, 44
democracy, Athenian, impact of, 48, 55, 56, 59, 89, 150, 212–18, 251–52, 257
Demosthenes, as *khoregos*, 57
departure scene, of hoplite, 95, 109–16, 221–24, 246, 254, 256. *See also* arming
Dexileos, 35, 244–45
dicing, scenes of, 93, 94
Dinos Painter, 138–39, 140
Diodoros, on early Greek sculpture, 15
Dionysia, at Athens, and Pronomos vase, 43; expense of, 55n9, 57
Dionysos, representation of, 102, 156, 176; emulated by booners, 177; and satyrs, 188–94, 202

discus-throwing, 53, 60, 64, 68, 69, 72, 74, 79, 239–40, 246; discus as attribute, 75, 78, 84
Diskobolos, of Myron, 239–40
dogs, in hoplite departure scenes, 95; in hoplite arming scenes, 110
Dokimasia Painter, 47, 133, 172
door, use of in imagery, 138–39, 160
Douris, 29n13, 66, 70–71, 106, 111n82, 133, 134–36, 172, 189–91
Dreros, sculpture from, 15
dress, in classical sculpture, 242–43, 245, 247; of satyrs, 199, 201, 202, 203, 209; styles of, 19, 24n56, 252; wearing of animal pelt, 104, 190, 192–93, 196, 198, 203; wearing of mantle, 69, 71, 75, 142, 148. *See also* clothes
drinking party. *See* symposium
duplication, absence of in Greek art, 22, 36–40, 41, 208

earrings, men in, 175; women in, 131, 221
East, influence of, on booners, 178; on Greek art, 10, 15; on symposium, 168
economics, and images, 5, 7, 33
education, scene of on pots, 81–82
egalitarianism, 211, 213–14, 216–18
Egypt, influence of on Greek sculpture, 15; people of caricatured, 233
Eleusis, Mysteries at, 215
Elsner, Jaś, 19–20, 23, 249–50, 256
Eos, sexual pursuit by, 137–38
Epeleios Painter, 104–5, 171–73, 175
Ephialtes, reforms of, 213, 215
Epidromos Painter, 104–5
Epiktetos, 103, 133n33, 199–200
equestrian competitions, at Panathenaia, 53–54
Eretria, archaic pedimental sculpture from, 230; Athenian white-ground lekythoi from, 41
Eretria Painter, 84–85, 196n14, 199–200
Eros, and courtship, 138, 147; popularity of, 147; in scene of armed dancing, 164–66; and weddings, 146; on work by Shuvalov Painter, 141
Etruscans, use of Athenian pottery by, 24, 26, 33, 40, 42, 46–48, 124, 146, 226, 251
Euaichme Painter, 111
Euandria, 71n67
Euergides Painter, 72–73, 104
Eupheros, grave stele of, 59, 219
Euphronios, 3–4, 64–67, 100–1, 110, 171, 221n37, 256
Eupolis, on athletes, 58–59
Euripides, 56n20, 58, 134
Eurymedon, oinochoe featuring, 106
Euthymides son of Polios, 101, 110n79, 171, 172
Euxitheos, potter, 101
Exekias, 49, 93, 94
experience, shaped by images, 5–7, 10; without influence on images, 9, 117. *See also* life
eye-cup, 8, 46n73, 72

facial types, in Greek sculpture, 239, 242–44, 253. *See also* frontality
Fat Boy Painter, 31
Flandrin, Hippolyte, 254–55
Florence Painter, 182–83
flowers, in painted pottery, 62–63, 70, 71, 124–25, 130, 131, 132–33; in sculpture, 16
Flying Angel Painter, 176
Foucault, Michel, 218
Foundry Painter, 28, 133, 134–35, 184–86
François vase, 189
frontality, in sculpture, 5, 19, 20, 23
funeral games, for Amphidamas, 53; at Athens, 93; for Patroklos, 53; funeral oration, 149, 216

Galen, on Polykleitos, 252
Ganymede, 138, 204
garlands, worn/carried by athletes, 60, 66, 69, 79–80; worn/carried in courtship scenes, 126, 131, 133; worn/carried in *komos* scenes, 174; worn/carried in religious scenes, 153, 156, 159; worn at symposium, 178, 182; worn/carried in other scenes, 143–44
Gautier, Théophile, 254
gaze, as opposed to glance, 83, 193, 221–24, 228–29
Gebauer, Jörg, 154
Gela, Athenian pottery from, 41, 108, 191
geometric pottery, Athenian, 9–11, 18; distinguishing gender, 123
Gibson, J. J., 220n31, 246
gigantomachies, representation of, 109
gods, relations with, civic responsibility for, 215–16; justice of, 237; pouring libations, 152; representation of, xviii, 150, 151–63, 207, 208, 228; in sexual pursuit scenes, 137; statues of, 161–63
Goluchow Painter, 14
Gombrich, Sir Ernst, on development of Greek sculpture, 18, 20, 22, 220
graffiti, on pots, 169n4, 170. *See also* writing
grave stelai, 58–59, 148, 240, 242–43, 244–45, 246, 247
"Greek revolution", nature of, 5, 208, 220, 249
gymnasium, as place of education, 81–82; general scenes of, 61–67, 74–84; as meeting place, 60, 66, 69–70, 75, 79–83, 225; wealth of those at, 59–60, 84. *See also* athletics

hairstyle, as dating criterion, 15, 17
Hamilton, Sir William, 33
hare, as love-gift, 70–71, 127, 128n20, 130, 131, 132
Hasselmann Painter, 139
Hector, named in hoplite scene, 101, 110n79
Helen, in scenes of sexual pursuit, 137; Zeuxis's painting of, 252
Hephaistos, 189
Herakles, and centaurs, 102; combined with scenes of hoplite, 102, 113, 226; combined with scenes of *komos*, 172; festival of, 215; and Egyptians, 233; and Geryon, 72, 235; and Kerberos, 94n40, 235; and Kerkopes, 20; and Kyknos, 68, 101, 102, 156; labors of, 225, 231, 235–37; and Nessos, 23, 123; and Nemean lion, 72, 102, 235; and politics, 35; struggles for tripod, 62–63, 94n35, 136n44
Hermes, pursuing boy, 138; stealing oxen, 162
herms, mutilation of, 54n7; representation of, 35, 161–63, 202
Herodotos, on Athenian army, 87, 90, 214; on democracy at Athens, 87, 90, 214; on Ionian revolt, 92, 214; on Kimon, 56, 89; on marriage of Agariste, 53; motivation of, 252n10; on Peisistratos, 35, 56; on Persian royal gifts, 108; on Scythians, 100; on Spartan invasion of Attica, 90
Hesiod, and funeral games of Amphidamas, 53; on satyrs, 188
Hieron, potter, 38–39, 210
hieroscopy (inspection of liver of sacrificial victim), 98, 112, 152, 159
Hipparchos, named on Athenian pot, 35, 64, 231
Hippias, 87, 90, 214
Hischylos, potter, 99
historians, Greek, motivations of, xviii, 252n10
historical events, representation of, 18, 23, 34–35, 106, 229–32
history, nature of, xvii, xviii, 7, 25, 249, 256
Homeric epic, and geometric art, 10; and Athenian pottery, 22, 81–82
homoeroticism, of gymnasium, 66–67, 70–71, 74, 78, 80–84, 125; of hunting, 125
homosexual relations, representation of, 124–31, 136, 138–39, 230. *See also* courtship
hoplite armour, dancing in (*see* dancing); running in, 53, 60, 72, 74. *See also* arming
hoplites, shown on pots with athletes, 72–74; place in Athenian army, 88–93; representation of on Athenian pottery, 93–121. *See also* departure
Hornblower, Simon, 149
horses, representation of, on pots, 72, 93, 94, 95, 98, 102, 109; racing, 46n74, 69n61; in statuettes, 15. *See also* cavalry; chariots
humor, in painted pottery, 30, 106, 161–62
hunting, representation of, 34, 115–16, 120n98; and homoeroticism, 125–27; and satyrs, 199

iconography, changes in on Athenian pottery, xvii, xviii–xix, 6, 7–9, 13, 22, 23, 34, 36, 47–50; 60–86, 87–88, 93–121, 123–47, 150, 152, 155–67, 171–87, 189–204, 207, 219, 220, 228, 248, 256–57; of Greek sculpture, 15, 20, 22; and the market, 31, 33, 40–42, 45, 47, 226; study of, 13, 32–34
idealism, of classical art, 252–53

280 INDEX

ideology, displayed in pot painting, 142, 147; elitist and middling, 209–11, 217
Iliad, arming scenes in, 110; games in, 53; phraseology from used on pot, 81n83; on sacrifice, 155n13
Individualism, 23, 56, 58, 85, 116, 120–21, 146, 150, 153, 159, 161, 174, 209, 217–18, 240, 251–52
Ionian revolt, 92

javelin, as attribute, 74, 75, 78, 120; thrown, 53, 60, 61, 64, 68, 72, 74, 79, 224
Jenkins, Ian, 245
jewelry, of *korai*, 19. *See also* earrings
jumping, 53, 60, 61, 68, 72, 74, 79, 156; jumping weight as attribute, 81

kalos names, 45, 64, 66, 71; other *kalos* inscriptions, 142, 156, 171. *See also* writing, on Athenian pots
Kamiros, pottery from, 125
Kant, Immanuel, on beauty, 254
Keane, Webb, 246–47
khoregia, 55n9, 57
Kimon, son of Stesagoras, 56, 89
Kleisthenes of Athens, constitutional reforms of, 87, 90–91, 213–15, 217. *See also* democracy
Kleisthenes of Sikyon, 53
Kleophon Painter, 174–75, 190–91, 221–23
Kleophrades Painter, 49
Kleophrades, potter, 38
knowledge, and power, 82, 218
komos representation of, xviii, 66, 72, 74, 101n58, 102, 138, 168, 170–78, 190, 207, 208, 209, 228; satyrs in, 189, 199–201
korai, 3, 15–22, 243, 252
kottabos, 161, 179, 181, 183–84, 185, 186
kouroi, 3, 5, 15–22, 219, 220, 228
krater, volute, uses of, 43
Kritios, Greek sculptor, 20–21, 22, 57, 228–31
Kurke, Leslie, 55n16, 178, 209–11, 218n27
Kylon, attempted coup by, 56, 57
Kyniskos of Mantineia, 219

Langdon, Susan, 9–10
Leach, Bernard, 32
Leagros, greeted as *kalos*, 64, 66, 67n51
lekythoi, iconography of, 41, 42, 60, 61, 106, 112, 124, 141n56, 146, 159, 233
Lenaia, festival of, 57; pots with scenes perhaps related to, 46
Leningrad Painter, 172
Leto, representation of, 15, 64, 101n59
libation, representation of, xviii, 152–54, 158, 166, 256; in hoplite departure scenes, 110n77, 112–13, 115, 132, 152
life, relationship to images, 7, 9, 24–25, 49, 61, 117–18, 166–67, 178, 189, 207–27, 228, 251, 253, 256. *See also* experience

ligaturing, of penis, 64, 66
light-armed soldiers, in Peisistratean Athens, 97; representation of on Athenian pots, 94–100, 256
Lissarrague, François, 24n56, 47n77, 93n33, 94, 98n52, 168n1, 174n12, 189n3, 194n10
Little Master Cups, sex scenes on, 124, 133
Locri, Athenian pottery from, 140
love gifts, 71, 125, 126, 127, 130–33, 137, 138, 147
Ludovisi throne, 237–38
luxury, attitudes to, 178
Lykaon Painter, 183–84, 186, 191, 193–94, 202
Lysias, orator, *Against Eratosthenes*, (1) 123; *On a charge of accepting bribes*, (21) 55n12, 57

maenads, representation of, 38n53, 72, 102, 113, 124, 136–37, 188, 190–91, 192–98, 250; sleeping, 194–97, 198, 202, 203
Makron, 28, 37, 38n53, 39, 131–33, 172, 194–95, 196, 210
"Mannerist" Painters of pots, 233–35
Mannheim Painter, 194
Marathon, battle of, 90, 92, 148; tomb of war-dead at, 48
market, for pottery in antiquity, xviii, 31, 32, 33, 40–41, 226; discerning about quality, 31; relatively undiscerning about iconography, 42, 45, 47; for sculpture in antiquity, 31n25; desire for identified artists in modern, 30
marriage, link of *korai* to, 16, 18; of Peleus and Thetis, 123. *See also* wedding
masks, theatrical, 242, 244, 246
masturbation, representation of, 128, 133, 134, 136, 146; female, 136
meat, gifts of, 130, 131, 155–56, 159; on spit, 156
Menelaos, 137
Miltiades, 92, 100; named on an Athenian pot, 35
Minotaur, 231, 233n21
mirror, representation of, 132, 148
money-bag, 71, 130, 131–33, 141, 142, 143, 231
moral attitudes, changes in, xvii, xviii, xix, 5, 25, 121, 147, 209–12, 216–18, 224–25, 226, 246–48, 249, 252
Morelli, Giovanni, 28nn9, 11
Morris, Ian, 209–11
musicians, representation of, 14, 15, 43, 60, 66, 81, 102, 132–33, 138, 163–64, 203; competing, 54, 77; in *komos*, 171, 174, 175–79; satyrs as, 191, 192, 199; at symposium, 179, 181, 221. *See also* aulos
Myron, sculptor, 239–40
mythology, and black-figure technique, 49, 61, 250; creation of, 250; and death, 23, 41n64; identification of, 33, 123; influencing artists, 9, 10, 18, 250; shown together with athletes,

mythology (*cont.*)
  62–64, 66, 72, 82; shown together with hoplites, 93–94, 100–1, 102, 113, 250; used to explore gender relations, 123–24; wars of, popularity of, 108–9, 117, 209; world of continuous with the present, 24n56, 250

narrative, art and, 18, 20, 144, 156, 158, 195, 198, 223, 231, 233, 239
naturalism, as explanation of sculptural development, 15–22, 244, 249, 250
Naukratis, pottery from, 124; Athenaios from, 170
navy, Athenian, 57, 87, 91–93
Neer, Richard T., 10, 20n48, 226, 227, 247–48
Nesiotes, Greek sculptor, 20, 229–31
Nessos Painter, 23
Nestor, on painted pottery, 111, 112n84; cup of, 169n4
Nikandre, *kore*, 16
Nike (Victory), represented on pots, 69, 77–79, 83; in hoplite departure scene, 113, 116n90, 118–19; on monument, 92
Nikosthenes Painter, 8, 104, 136, 169, 180
Nikosthenic workshop, imitating Etruscan bucchero, 46; distribution of products of, 46, 48
Niobid Painter, 33, 202–3, 234–35
Nola, Athenian pottery from, 38, 99, 139, 210
nudity, of athletes, 63, 64–66, 74, 75, 81; in black-figure pottery, 61; in Cretan statues, 15; and Etruscans, 46; in hunting scenes, 116n91; in *komos*, 171, 174; of *kouroi*, 16–17; in religious scenes, 156–58, 161, 164, 237; in sex scenes, 124, 127, 130, 138; of soldiers, 98, 102–6, 108–9, 113–14, 116, 256n20; at symposium, 181, 184

Oakley, John H., 170
Odyssey, games in, 53; sacrifice in, 155n13
Oinomaos, 235
Oionokles Painter, 233
Oltos, 28, 67–68, 69, 72, 101–2, 104, 155–57, 159, 161n18
Olympia, display of sculpture at, 219, 226; sculpture of temple of Zeus at, 235–37, 246–48
Olympic games, importance of, 53, 55, 56
Onesimos, painter, 84–85
oratory, forensic, evidence of, 122–23
orientalism, 10, 15, 211
Orvieto, Athenian pottery from, 46n74, 82–83, 85, 94
ox, at altar, 162–63; as prize in Panathenaia, 54; preferred sacrificial victim on painted pottery, 155

Paidikos alabastra, 128
Painter of Athens 1237, 196n13
Painter of London 1923, 145
Painter of the Louvre Centauromachy, 99
Painter of the Oxford Brygos, 107
painters, of pots, individuality of, xvii, 28–32, 48, 49; responsibility for iconography, 42
palaistra, 59, 60, 63, 67, 75
Pamphaios, 26, 102n60, 103, 113–14, 116
Pan Painter, 28, 172, 233–34
Pan, representation of, 203, 204
Panaitios, 194
Panathenaia, carrying arms at, 89–90; competitions at, 53–55, 57, 61, 62, 148, 162; prize amphoras from, 39, 53–55, 60, 62, 68
Pandora, birth of, 203
Pankration, 56, 57, 58, 68
Panofsky, Erwin, 5n3
parasol, carried by booners, 175–77
Parrhasios, 252–54
Parthenon, sculptures of, 148, 221, 237, 240–41, 242, 244, 245–46, 247; Amazons on, 107
participation, practice and ideology of at Athens, 60n40, 121, 141, 149, 156, 167, 212–18
Pater, Walter, 28n12
Patton, Kimberley, 166
Pausanias, on monuments on the Athenian Acropolis, 24n54, 57, 90n16; on Athenian public burial of war dead, 93; on Polygnotos' painting, 234; on Polykleitos, 219; on statues of Zeus, 237n21
Peisistratos, 35, 56, 87, 88, 89, 117
Peithinos, 128n20, 129–30, 256
Peleus, and Thetis, 68, 123, 128, 131
Pelops, 235
peltasts, representation of on Athenian pottery. *See* light-armed troops
Penthesileia Painter, 75, 77
Penthesileia workshop, 36
Perikles, funeral oration of, 149, 216–17
"period eye," 5–6
Perizoma group, 46
Persian War, 87, 122, 220, 228, 233, 240; influence of, 20, 22, 49, 106, 108, 119, 251–52, 257; sack of Athens in, 48
Persians, on Athenian pottery, 106–9, 208, 209
Pezzino group, 67–68, 69–70
Pheidippos, painter, 99
Phiale Painter, 38, 153, 159
Phintias, 3–4, 64–65, 66, 67
Phrasikleia, *kore*, 16, 19
Phyllobolia, 69, 77, 78
pigs, sacrifice of, 155
Pindar, 56
"pioneers" of red-figure painting, 36, 45n70, 64, 67n51, 100, 164, 171
Pistoxenos Painter, 194
Pithos Painter, 31n24
"plastic vases," 32
Plato, on democracy, 250; epistemology of, 253; on erotic relations, 128; on gymnasium, 60;

on symposium, 168; on Polykleitos, 219; on visual arts, 253
Pliny, on Polykleitos, 219; on Zeuxis, 252n12
poets, influence on artists, 9
politics, of images, xvii, xviii, 6, 7, 10, 19–20, 23, 25, 35–36, 218–19, 226, 239–42, 250; and moral values, 212, 216–18, 226
Pollitt, J. J., 7, 220–21
Polygnotos, mural painter, 234
Polygnotos, pot painter, 138
Polykleitos, 219–20; *Diadoumenos* of, 84, 86, 219, 229; *Doryphoros* of, 252–53; *Kanon* of, 252
potters, Athenian, study of, 26–27, 32; specialising in particular shapes, 38–39
pottery, Athenian, bilingual, 13, 61, 72, 102; commercial value of, xviii, 30; dating of, 24, 28, 34, 48; history of, 9–14, 47, 207; relation between shape and subject of, 36, 40, 42; relation between shape and use, 24, 26–27, 31, 32, 42, 45–46; size of production of, 39–40; study of, 26–36; use of, 40–41
pottery, Athenian black-figure, development of, 10–13, 22, 23; iconography of, 11–12, 13–14, 36, 87–88, 93–97, 120, 124–28, 133, 134, 155, 175, 189, 237, 250; techniques of, 10, 13–14, 26, 49, 61; use for Panathenaic amphoras, 54
pottery, Athenian red-figure, characteristics of, xvii, xviii, 7, 13, 26, 36–43, 209; techniques of, 26, 49, 61. *See also* iconography
pottery, Corinthian, 10–12
pottery, Etruscan, 26
Poursat, J.-C., 166
power, anatomy of, 82, 213, 214, 217, 218, 220, 226, 227
pre-Socratic philosophers, 251
prizes, at festival competitions, 53–55
Pronomos vase, 43–45
prostitutes, identification of in painted pottery, 132–33, 141; in sculpture, 237
Protagoras, on democracy according to Plato, 250
proto-Attic pottery, 10–11, 123
pyrrhic dance. *See* dancing: armed
Python, potter, 38

Q Painter, 199n18

rape, of Cassandra, 161; of Deianeira by Nessos, 123; of maenad by satyr, 136, 195–96
reading, scenes of on pots, 81–82
regional styles, in pottery, 10–12; in sculpture, 15, 16
religion, Greek, history of, 151–52
religious rituals, Greek, representation of, 121, 152–67. *See also* libation; sacrifice
revel. See *komos*
Rhodes, pottery from, 124
Riace Bronzes, 148, 240–41, 245–46, 247–48

Richter, Gisela M. A., on *kouroi* and *korai*, 3
Ridgway, Brunhilde S., history of sculpture, 5
Riegl, Alois, 5n3
Robertson, C. Martin, 13–14, 31
Rotroff, Susan, 170
Ruvo, Athenian pottery found in, 43–44

sacks, in red-figure pottery, 161, 162
sacrifice, representation of, xviii, 24, 25, 34, 154–59; before battle, 98. *See also* meat
sakkos, 130, 131, 160, 175n14, 176–78,
Salamis, 88, 91, 215; battle of, 92
sanctuaries, herms as signal of, 161; pots from, 40, 42; sculpture from, 14–15, 17, 23, 226
sandals, 144; erotic significance of, 130, 134, 138
Sappho, 176
satyr-plays, 188, 203; criticising athletes, 58; representation of, 43–45
satyrs, representation of, xviii, 14, 24n56, 34, 38n53, 45, 62, 66, 72, 102, 113, 114, 116, 188–204, 207, 209, 228, 250; children of, 199, 202–4; female, 199n18; and Hephaistos, 189–91; as hoplite, 199; and men, 199–204; as peltasts, 98, 100, 199; sexuality of, 124, 134, 136–37, 138, 146, 189, 194–98, 199, 202
Schnapp, Alain, 13n28, 34, 116n91, 125n11, 126n16
sculpture, Greek, architectural, 20, 24; history of, xviii, 3, 5, 9, 148, 207, 209, 219–21, 226, 228–31, 235–48; influence of on painted pottery, 13
Scythians, on Athenian pots, 35, 94n39, 95–100, 110; relation to Persians, 106–7
sexual abuse, in graffiti on pots, 170
sexual excitement, male display of, 126–27, 133, 138, 146; of satyrs, 189, 194, 196, 198, 199. *See also* herms
sexual pursuit, 137, 198; homosexual pursuit, 138
sexual relations, representation of, xviii, 7, 24, 25, 46, 122–50, 207, 208, 209, 228, 254; of armed dancer, 164–66; ; heterosexual intercourse, 48–49, 124, 133–34, 138–41, 147; of satyrs and maenads, 190–91, 193, 194–98; sexual control, shown by ligature, 66; sexual attraction, in gymnasium, 66–67, 70–71; sources for, 122. *See also* courtship
Shapiro, H. Alan, 204
sheep, as sacrificial victims, 155
ships, on Athenian black-figure pottery, 93; in Athenian red-figure pottery, 97n48
Shuvalov Painter, 140–41
Sickert, Walter, 3
signatures, of potters and painters, 5, 12, 26, 27, 28, 39, 62–63, 71, 99, 101, 102n60, 103, 107, 113–14, 129, 210, 221–22
singing, by Dionysos, 191; in *komos*, 174, 177; at symposium, 179, 184, 221

Siphnian treasury, at Delphi, 17, 20
slaves, representation of, 64, 66, 231; satyrs as, 199
Smikros, 26, 221–22
social history, and art history, 5–7, 13, 19–20, 23, 25, 34, 146–50, 151–52, 168–71, 207–12, 249–57
Socrates, and athletics, 56; and beauty, 252–54
sodomy, scenes of, 124, 136
soldiers. *See* warfare
Solon, 12, 55, 58, 213
Sophilos, 12
Sophocles, *Philoktetes*, 256
Sotades, potter, 38
Sparta, military intervention of in Athens, 90; path-dependency in, 149
spectators, in scenes on painted pottery, 14, 36, 63, 75, 112, 134, 138, 237. *See also* voyeurism
Spina, Athenian pottery from, 163
sponge bag, of athlete, 71, 78, 130, 131, 132
Stansbury-O'Donnell, M., 14, 36n48, 137n47, 237n19
statuettes, of animals, 14–15
status, visibility of at Athens, xvii, 60n40, 133, 134. *See also* slaves
Stendhal (Marie-Henri Beyle), 254
Stewart, Andrew F., 20
strigil, as mark of athlete, 58, 74, 75, 84, 120, 148
style, of individual artist, xvii, xviii, 3, 5; of period, 5, 9–10, 12–13, 15, 22, 36; of individual pot painters, 3, 5, 26, 27–30; development of in sculpture, 15–22, 228–31, 235–48, 249. *See also* regional styles
subject matter, of art. *See* iconography: choice of
symposium, changes in, 118–19, 168–71, 208; nature of, 168–71; pots made for, 27, 38, 42–43, 60, 74, 84, 118, 134, 146, 170, 204; representation of, xviii, 24, 25, 102, 138, 161, 164, 167, 179–87, 207, 208, 209, 221–22, 228, 256; sex at, 134
Syracuse Painter, 106
Syria, influence from on geometric art, 10; on Cretan statues, 15
Syriskos/Copenhagen Painter, 231–33

Tanner, Jeremy, 5n1, 27n52, 220, 226n44
Tarquinia, Athenian pottery from, 76, 134
team competitions, at Panathenaia, 54–55
technology, enchantments of, 9, 10, 248
temporality, of images, 220–24
textiles, influence on Athenian pottery, 13
texts, literary, and painted pottery, 33
theatre, activities at shown on pottery, 43–44; influence on sculpture, 19
Themistokles, 92; bust of, 148
theology, of artistic choices, 19n45, 226, 233, 235, 239

Theseus, 72, 137, 230, 231, 235
Thespiai, athletic victor listed among war dead at, 55n16
Thessaly, cavalry of, 90
Thomson Painter, 156n14, 158, 159
Thracians, cavalry shown as on Athenian pottery, 98; clothing of worn by satyrs, 190; peltasts shown as on Athenian pottery, 98
Thucydides, on Alkibiades' chariot racing, 56; "Archaeology" of, 250; on casualties in Egypt and Sicily, 119; on human relations with gods, 151, 152n3; Perikles's funeral speech in, 149, 216–7; on public burial of war dead, 93; on tyrannicides, 89
Tityos, 64
torch race, 55, 57, 59
tragedy, Athenian, treatment of gods in, 151; of war in, 117–8, 122; of women in, 122
trainer, represented on pots, 60n40, 62–63, 64, 68, 75
tribes, Athenian, 213–14; and army, 87, 90–91, 245; and festival competitions, 54–55, 72n67, 215
"trick vases," 27
tripod, Herakles and, 62–63, 94n35, 136n44; as sign of victory, 69, 78
Triptolemos Painter, 66n49, 133, 134, 161–62, 180–81
trittys, Athenian, role of, 91, 213–14
tyrannicides, Athenian, 89, 213; representation of, 35, 229–31, 240
Tyrrhenian amphoras, sex scenes on, 124, 133
Tyrtaios, on athletes, 58

van Straten, Folker, 154–55
Vermeer, Jan, 224
Vernant, Jean-Pierre, 227
victor, athletic, representation of, 58, 60, 67–71, 74, 77–78, 131
victory monuments, Athenian, 90, 92–93
Vidal-Naquet, Pierre, 149
Villa Giulia Painter, 75–76
voyeurism, in archaic art, 250; in courtship scenes, 128; in scenes of satyrs, 196; in sex scenes, 134, 138; at symposium, 186
Vuillard, Edouard, 3
Vulci, Athenian pottery from, 4, 29, 37, 39, 46, 62, 64, 65, 70, 79, 96, 99, 111, 115, 124, 127, 129, 172, 173, 189, 190, 197, 200, 210, 232

war-dead, commemoration of, 93, 117, 119, 216–17; depiction of, 94, 95, 98, 114, 116
warfare, in Athens, 87–93, 214, 216; athletes given special place in, 55; widespread concern with, 122, 225; representation of, in geometric pottery, 9, 23; in statuettes, 15; in black-figure pottery, 46n74, 61, 87–88, 93–98, 117, 250; in red-figure pottery, xviii,

7, 9, 24, 25, 34, 86, 88, 97–121, 147–48, 207, 208, 209, 217–18, 220, 228
Webster, T.B.L., 33, 45n70
Wedding Painter, 142–43
wedding, representation of, 144–46, 147, 209, 235
Westmacott athlete, 219, 229
Winchester Painter, 156–57, 159
Woman Painter, 31
women, representation of, 34, 36n50, 46n74, 123–25, 128–48; as armed dancers, 102, 164–67, 183–84, 186–87; as dancers, 186, 203, 204; in hoplite arming/departure scenes, 95, 110, 113–15, 116, 120, 121, 221–24; combined with hoplite scenes, 102; in *komos*, 171, 175–77; in religious scenes, 153–54, 159–60; as sexually desiring, 137–38; at symposium, 181, 182, 184, 221. *See also* Amazons; sexual relations
wonder, importance of, 227, 230, 247, 248
wool-working, 142
workshops, of potters, 26, 27n6, 36, 46–47; stylistic distinctions between, 5, 11, 28; and training of painters, 22, 28, 29
wreath. *See* garland
wrestling, 53, 56, 60, 61, 62–63, 68
writing tablet, 81–82, 143
writing, on Athenian pots, 26, 45, 64, 66–67, 68, 71, 142, 156, 193n8, 221; of nonsense, 68. *See also* graffiti; signatures

Xenophanes, on athletes, 58
Xenophon, on athletic competition, 56; on beauty, 252–54; on female armed dancers, 166; on generalship, 213; on homosexual relations, 126, 128; on symposium, 168, 169n5, 186; on Theodote, 133
[Xenophon] on festivals, 152n3; on popular attitude to athletics, 59; on solidarity of *demos*, 149n77

Zeus, from Artemision, 237–39; and Ganymede, 138; statues of, 237n21
Zeuxis, 252